I0824320

The Great AMERICAN RETRO ROAD TRIP

A CELEBRATION OF ROADSIDE AMERICANA

ROLANDO PUJOL

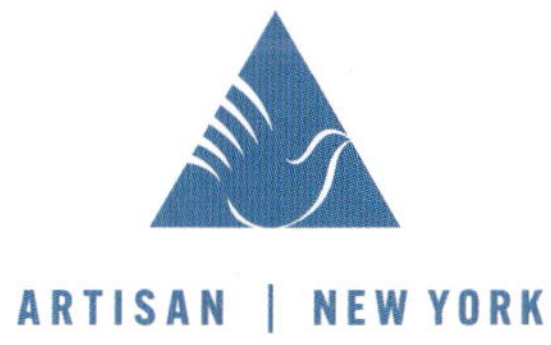

ARTISAN | NEW YORK

Copyright © 2025 by Rolando Pujol

Hachette Book Group supports the right to free expression and the value of copyright. The purpose of copyright is to encourage writers and artists to produce the creative works that enrich our culture.

The scanning, uploading, and distribution of this book without permission is a theft of the author's intellectual property. If you would like permission to use material from the book (other than for review purposes), please contact permissions@hbgusa.com. Thank you for your support of the author's rights.

Library of Congress Cataloging-in-Publication Data

Names: Pujol, Rolando, author.
Title: The great American retro road trip : a celebration of roadside Americana / Rolando Pujol.
Other titles: Celebration of roadside Americana
Description: New York : Artisan, [2025] | Includes index.
Identifiers: LCCN 2024050845 | ISBN 9781648293719 (hardback)
Subjects: LCSH: United States—Guidebooks. | Roadside architecture—United States—Guidebooks. | Roadside architecture—United States—Pictorial works. | Curiosities and wonders—United States—Guidebooks. | Curiosities and wonders—United States—Pictorial works. | Automobile travel—United States—Guidebooks.
Classification: LCC E158 .P98 2025 | DDC 917.304—dc23/eng/20241218
LC record available at https://lccn.loc.gov/2024050845

Design by Jack Dunnington
Endpapers by Trutta/Shutterstock.com
Map on pages 6–7 by Jack Dunnington

Artisan books may be purchased in bulk for business, educational, or promotional use. For information, please contact your local bookseller or the Hachette Book Group Special Markets Department at special.markets@hbgusa.com.

The publisher is not responsible for websites (or their content) that are not owned by the publisher.

The Hachette Speakers Bureau provides a wide range of authors for speaking events. To find out more, go to hachettespeakersbureau.com or email HachetteSpeakers@hbgusa.com.

Published by Artisan,
an imprint of Workman Publishing,
a division of Hachette Book Group, Inc.
1290 Avenue of the Americas
New York, NY 10104
artisanbooks.com

The Artisan name and logo are registered trademarks of Hachette Book Group, Inc.

Printed in China (APO) on responsibly sourced paper

First printing, April 2025

10 9 8 7 6 5 4 3 2 1

Apex Automotive and this roadside gem can be found in Fromberg, Montana.

For my parents, Rolando and Pura Pujol

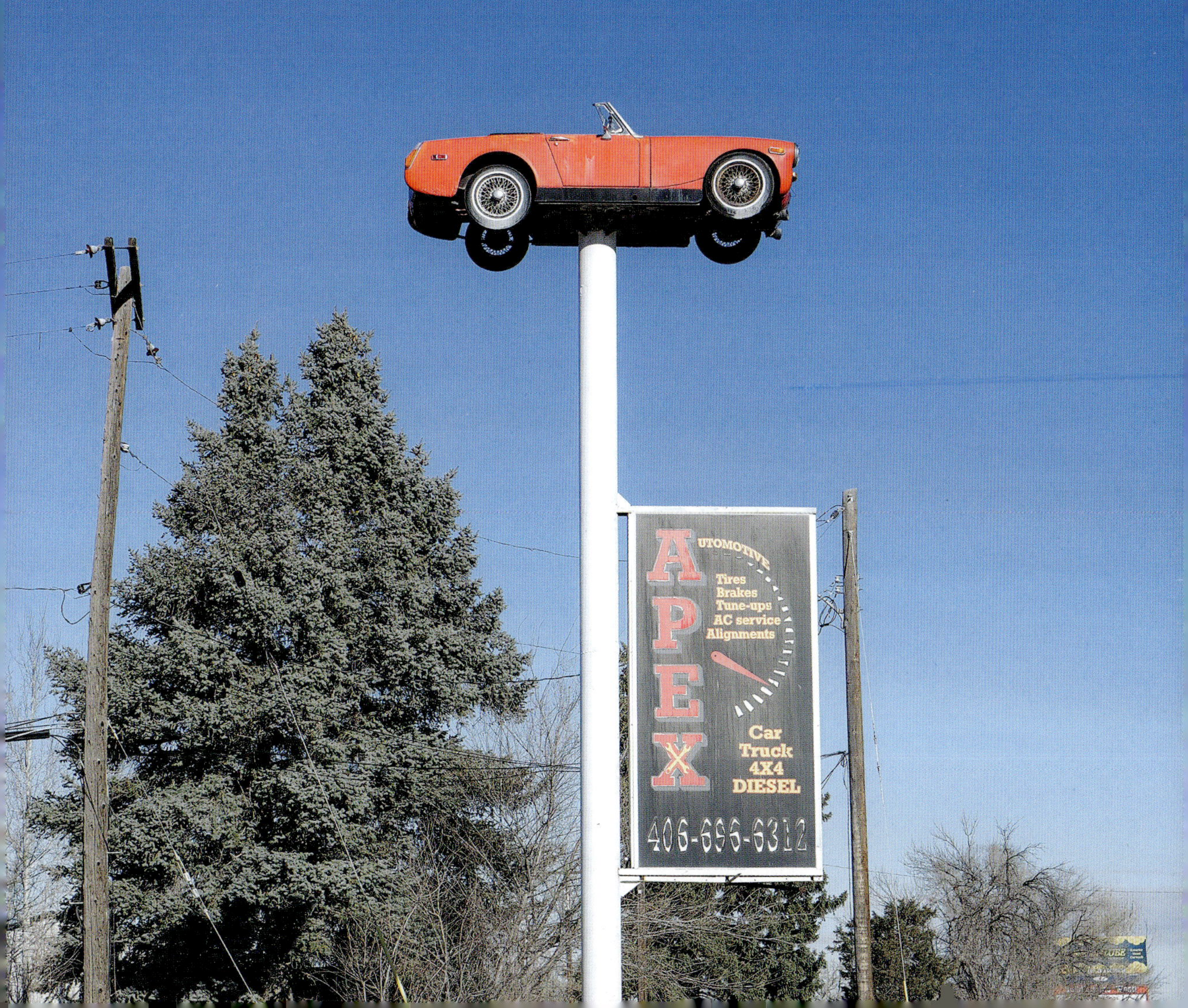

INTRODUCTION

I've been on the great American retro road trip my whole life, even when I didn't quite realize it. As a young boy, I adored those orange roofs of Howard Johnson's, the Holiday Inn "Great Signs," the McDonald's PlayPlaces, the Muffler Men, the shiny diners, the mysterious bars with jaunty cocktail glass illustrations, and so much more eye candy that kept me transfixed in the back seat of the family station wagon as this nostalgic parade passed me by.

When those signposts of my youth began to fall, a tiny part of my childhood went with them. I began to appreciate how significant these places were, how almost criminally *underappreciated* they were by much of society. And so began my determined journey to document them, first in the pages of newspapers and later on news websites, social media, and a Substack newsletter. And now, it is such an honor to do so in the book you are holding.

I treasure the places we're about to visit. I wrote this book as an act of love for these businesses and the people who keep them alive. Mom-and-pops are not easy to run, and even the many chain establishments here—the supposed enemies of the local business—are often operated by your neighbors trying to make an honest living of their own. The two can and do coexist.

These pages teem with layers of history—you can approach each stop from a design perspective or culinary or cultural ones. You can look for clues about the time in which it was founded. That makes these selections so intriguing—each is a world unto itself.

The book is divided into regions to help us grasp it all: the Northeast, New England, the Mid-Atlantic, the Southeast, South Central, the Midwest, the Heartland, the Desert Southwest, the Mountain West, the Pacific Northwest, and California, the latter so vast and complex that it gets its own chapter.

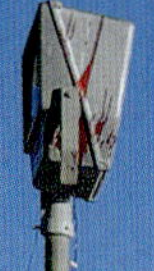

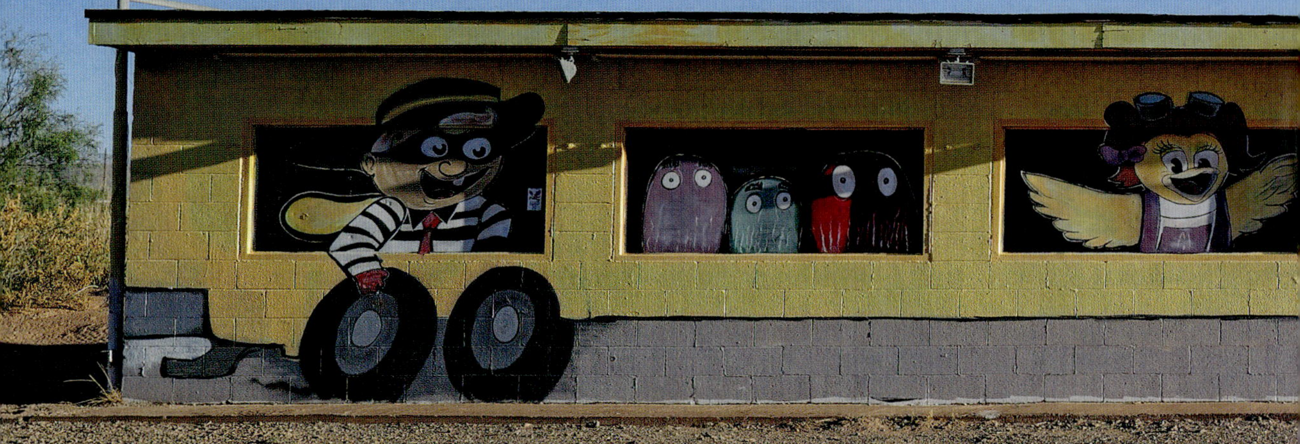

Within each chapter, I've broken down our stops by category: Roadside Quirks (like Muffler Men, a Smiling Peanut, and the World's Largest Popcorn Ball), Roadside Eats (classic burger shops, hot dog stands, and the like), Mainstays of Main Street (places you'll find in a typical American downtown or strip mall), On with the Show (theaters and stops related to entertainment or broadcasting, like radio station buildings), The Inn Crowd (places to spend the night), Sweet Stops (candy stores and ice-cream stands), and Cheers! (bars, taverns, and liquor stores). Plus, I've sprinkled sidebars throughout, including profiles of chain restaurants and dives into unique places like Wildwood, New Jersey.

You'll find that great roadside stops are everywhere when you begin to look for them, but we take them for granted at our own risk. As I worked on this book, almost weekly came heartbreaking news of the closure of some place I had visited not long ago, or of the loss of a classic sign. I've noted where that's happened, pointing it out to underscore how vulnerable these places are and why you should visit sooner rather than later. I hope this book compels you to support these landmarks, to share your photos of them on social media, and to do your part to keep them around for more of us to enjoy. A lot of people doing a little goes a long way.

Thank you for coming along as my vicarious travel buddy. I hope many great American retro road trips of your own await you. Please drop me a postcard from the road—I'd love to hear from you.

Rolando Pujol
New York, New York
November 24, 2024

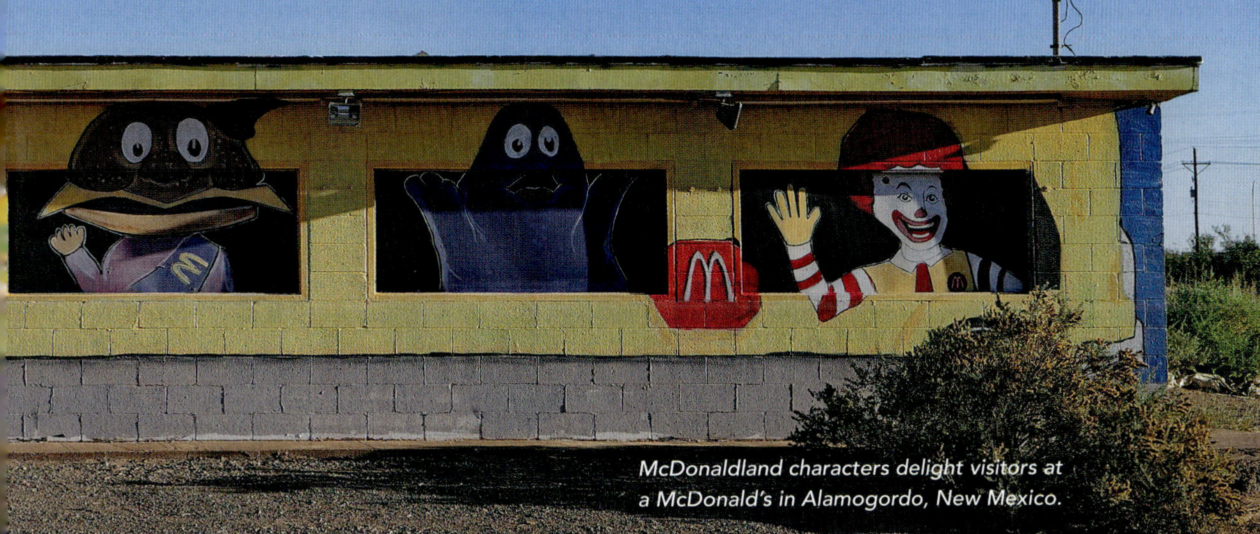

McDonaldland characters delight visitors at a McDonald's in Alamogordo, New Mexico.

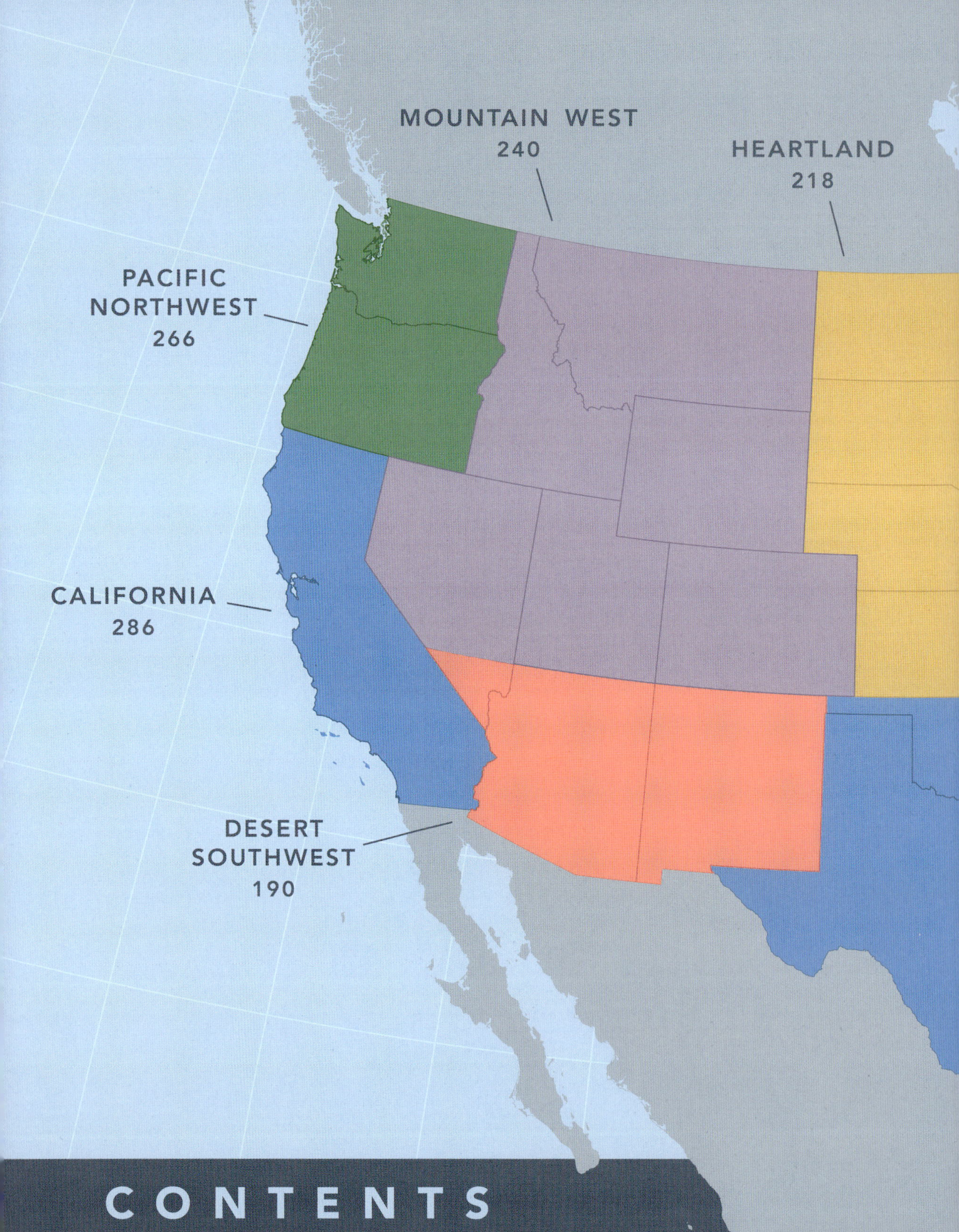
MOUNTAIN WEST
240
HEARTLAND
218
PACIFIC
NORTHWEST
266
CALIFORNIA
286
DESERT
SOUTHWEST
190
CONTENTS

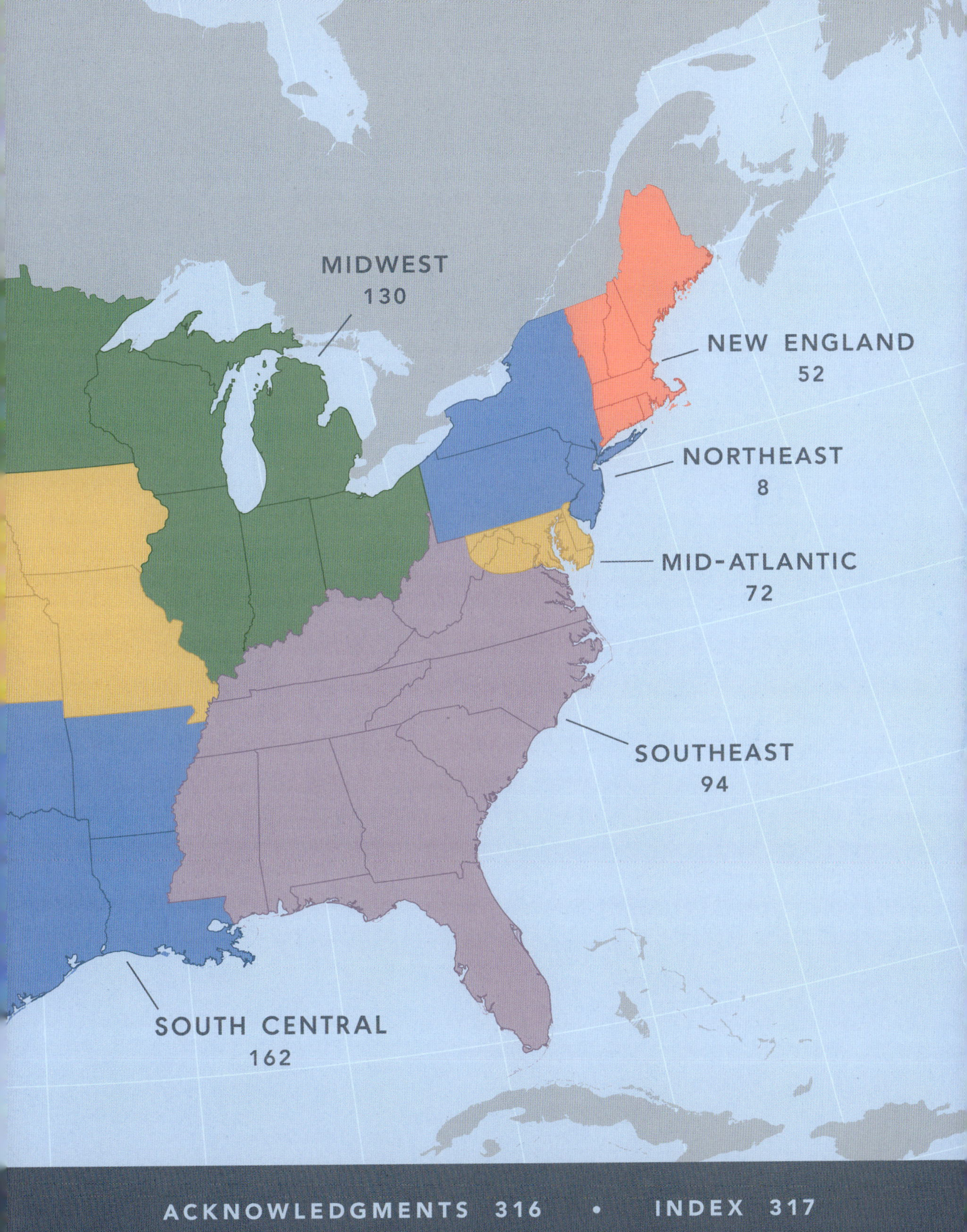
MIDWEST
130
NEW ENGLAND
52
NORTHEAST
8
MID-ATLANTIC
72
SOUTHEAST
94
SOUTH CENTRAL
162

NORTHEAST

NEW YORK · NEW JERSEY · PENNSYLVANIA

For me, the Northeast is home, and a natural place to begin our adventure. We'll be covering a big chunk of it in this chapter: New York, New Jersey, and Pennsylvania. The rest of the region is covered in the New England chapter (starting on page 52). Let's begin where, for me anyway, it all started.

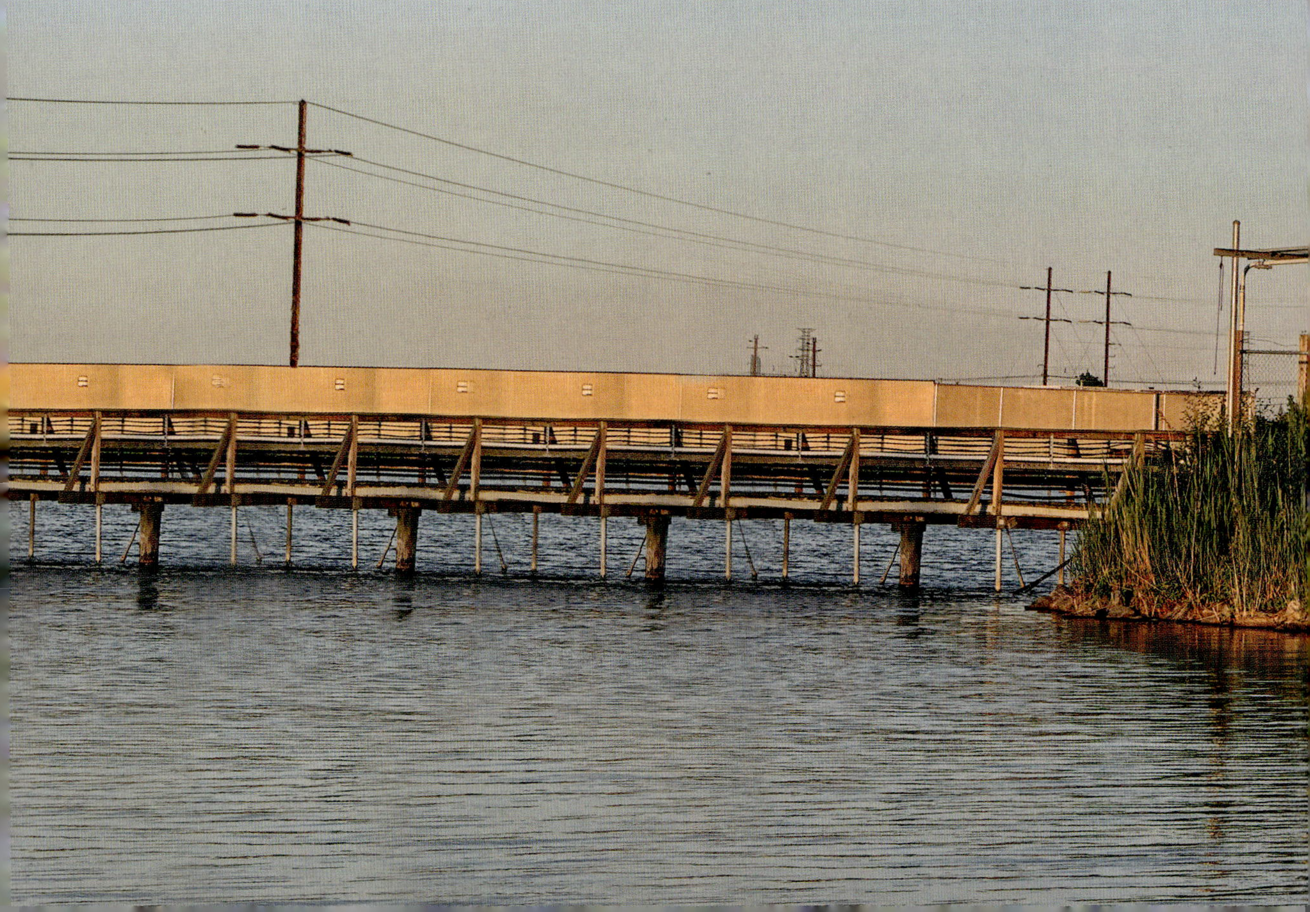

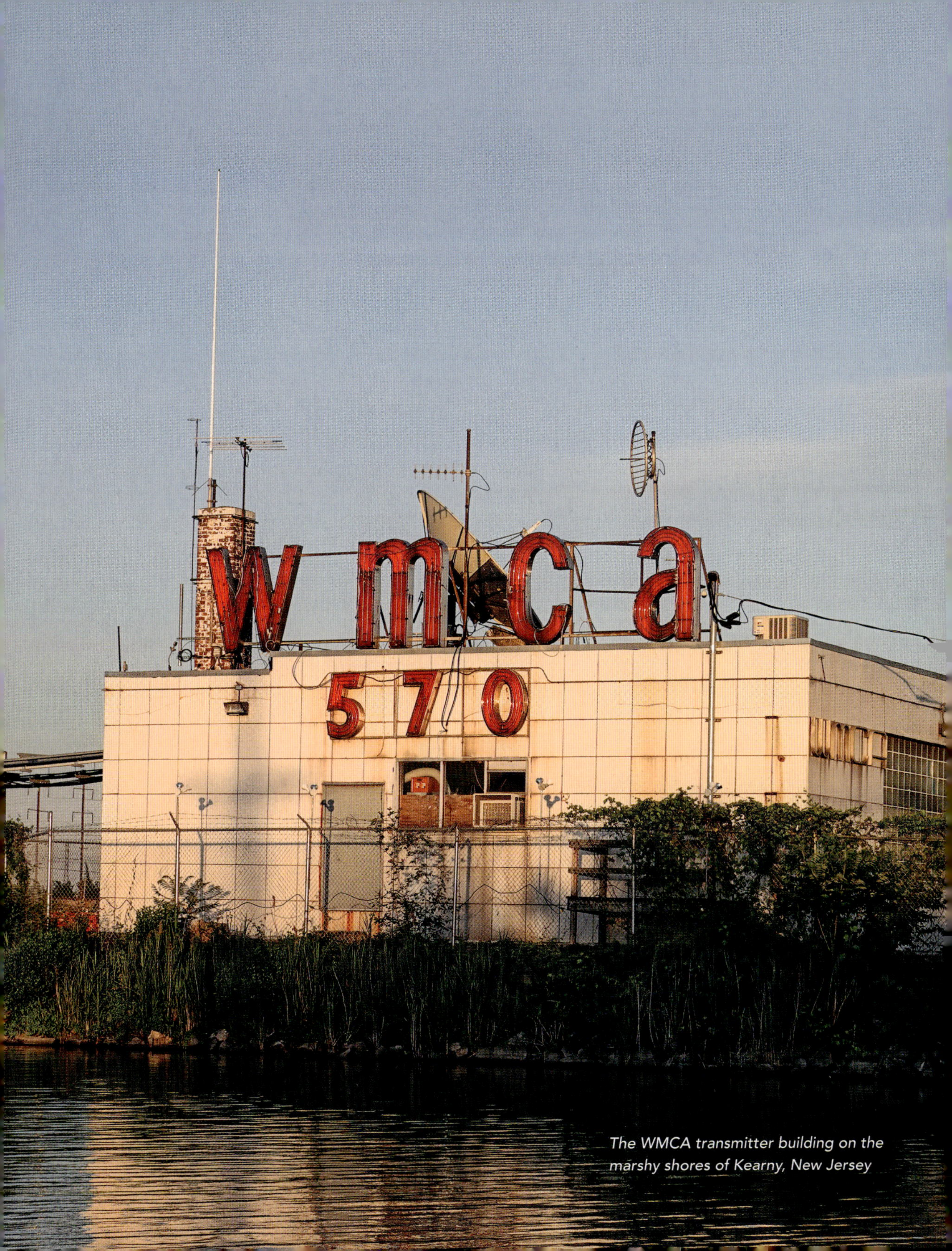

The WMCA transmitter building on the marshy shores of Kearny, New Jersey

ROADSIDE QUIRKS

Some of the very places we are visiting in this chapter inspired my love for roadside Americana. Without them, I never would have written this book.

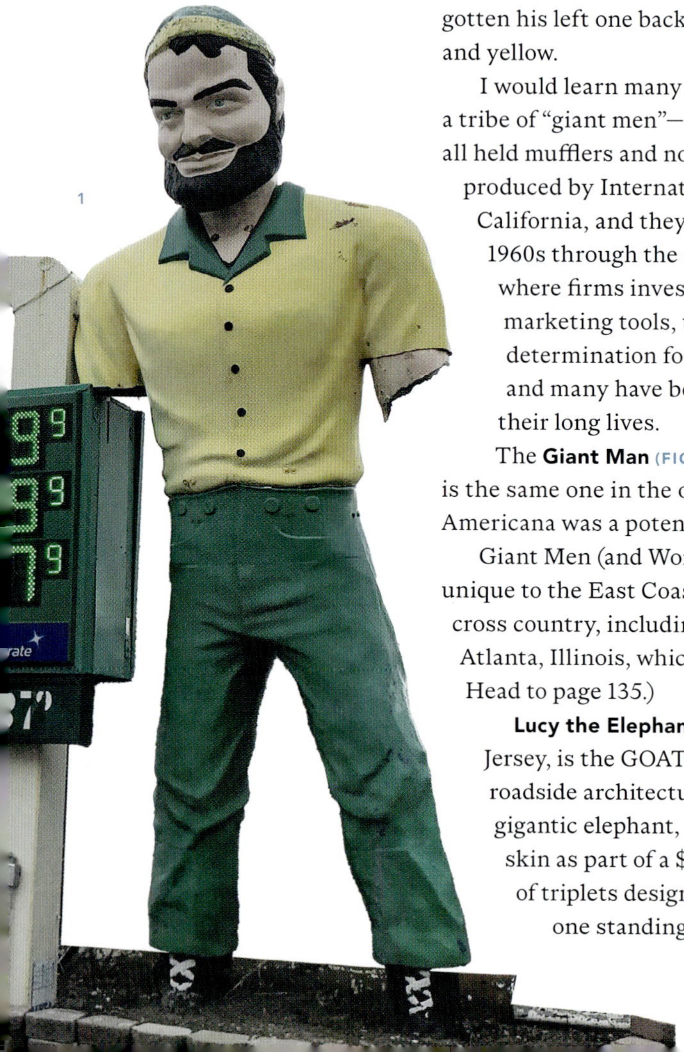

ROADSIDE GIANTS

The Amoco station (FIG. 1) in Elmsford, New York, a northern suburb of New York City, was home to "the giant," or "el gigante," as I used to tell my parents in Spanish. Little me thought he was unique, and with his missing arms, one of which was lost to a truck, he is. (He's since gotten his left one back!) He is now dressed in the BP colors of green and yellow.

I would learn many years later that he was actually part of a tribe of "giant men"—also called "Muffler Men," although not all held mufflers and not all were men. The roadside giants were produced by International Fiberglass, which was based in Venice, California, and they marched across the nation from the early 1960s through the mid-1970s, when the company folded. In an era where firms invested in signage and roadside attractions as key marketing tools, the Giant Men toiled with steely, lantern-jawed determination for a diverse number of businesses and brands, and many have been repurposed multiple times in the course of their long lives.

The **Giant Man** (FIG. 4) holding a roll of carpet in Jersey City is the same one in the opening credits of *The Sopranos*. Roadside Americana was a potent backdrop on the HBO series.

Giant Men (and Women) dot the Northeast but they are hardly unique to the East Coast and will crop up as our journey takes us cross country, including a stop at the American Giants Museum in Atlanta, Illinois, which celebrates their lot. (Want to go there now? Head to page 135.)

Lucy the Elephant (FIG. 2), a treasure of Margate City, New Jersey, is the GOAT of road-trip attractions, billed as the oldest roadside architectural novelty in America. Dating to 1881, the gigantic elephant, 6 stories tall, recently received a new metal skin as part of a $2.3 million renovation. She was part of a set of triplets designed by James V. Lafferty, but she's the only one standing because a committee of Lucy lovers rescued

1

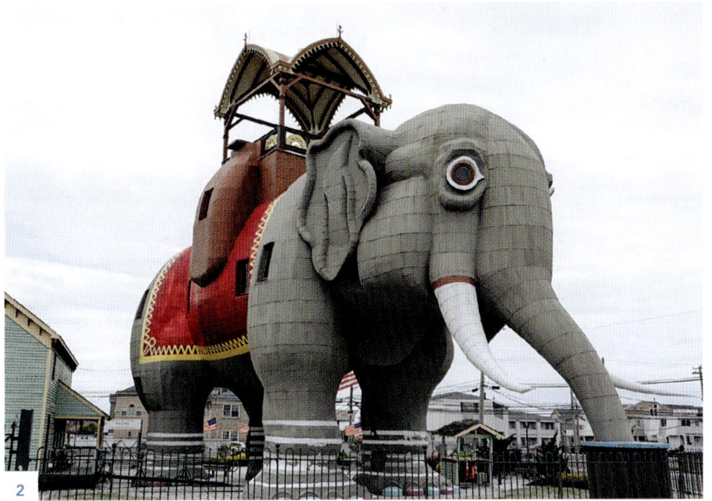
2

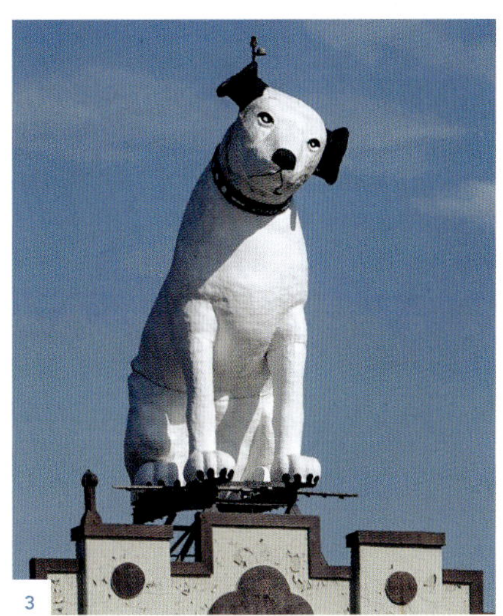
3

her in 1970 just as she was on her last legs. She's such an icon that none other than Fred Rogers visited her in 1986 for an episode of *Mister Rogers' Neighborhood.* And if that doesn't make her a national landmark, rest assured she is an officially designated one.

What a good boy! And what a big boy! Meet **Nipper** (FIG. 3), the beloved RCA mascot who's kept a watchful eye over Albany, New York, since 1958. These statues were once a fixture in record and appliance stores, but Albany's Nipper is said to be the largest of its kind, standing 28 feet tall and weighing 4 tons. He was placed here by Harold Gabrilove, who owned a company called RTA that distributed RCA electronics from this warehouse. Architect Harry Sanders brought Nipper to life. The pooch was built in Chicago and brought to Albany by rail in five parts, a 10-story crane hoisting him into place.

Missing is the windup cylinder phonograph to which other large Nipper statues are usually raptly paying attention. Albany's Nipper may not be listening to a phonograph, but his right ear has an aircraft beacon to alert low-flying planes.

The Big Duck (FIG. 5) of Flanders, New York, is such a big deal that it has come to symbolize this particular style of form-follows-function architecture. While on a Depression-era road trip, duck farmer Martin Maurer and his wife, Jeule, fortified themselves with a cup of java inside a building shaped like a big coffeepot. They reasoned, "If the world can have a big coffeepot, then why can't it have a big duck?" And so, they built one, in a time when duck farms were common out this way. Today, actual ducks have been swapped out for rubber duckies in the Big Duck's belly-turned-gift-shop.

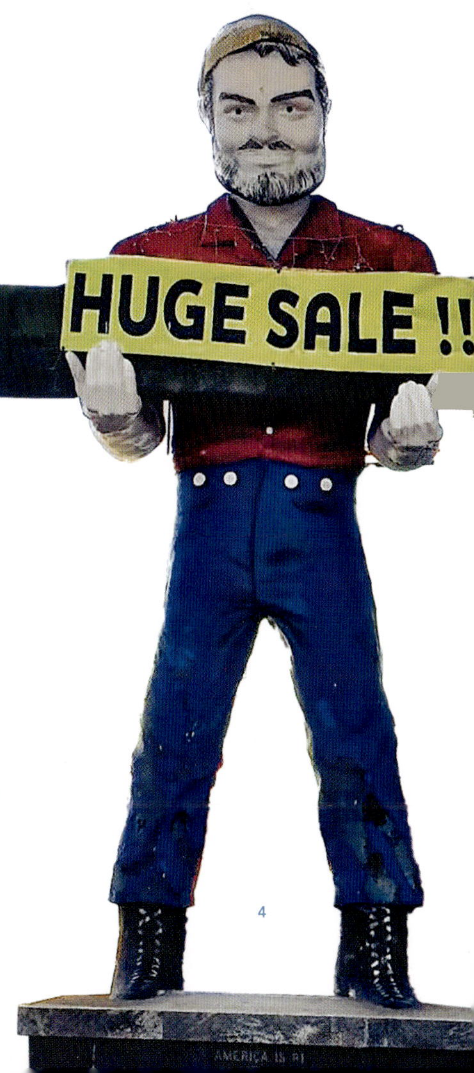

4

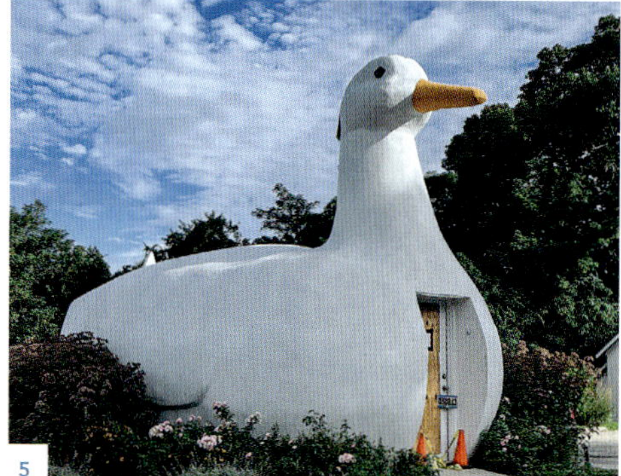
5

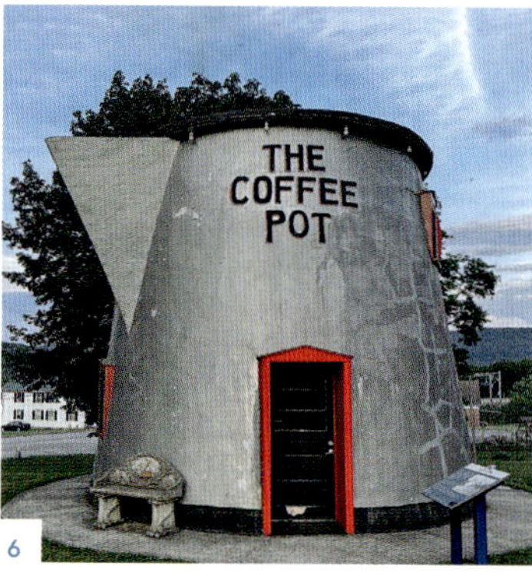

6

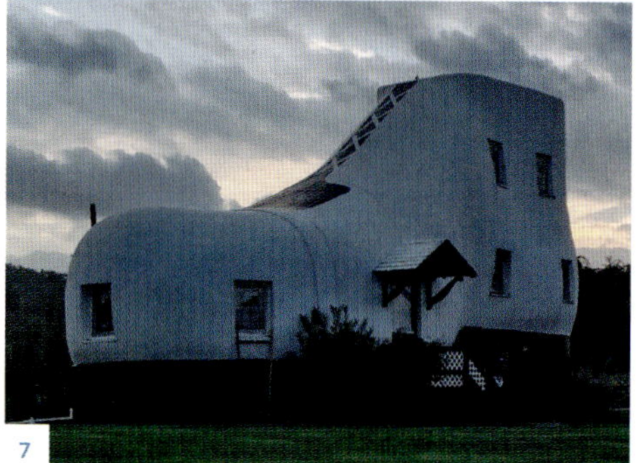
7

One has to wonder if it was **The Coffee Pot** (FIG. 6) in Bedford, Pennsylvania, that inspired the Big Duck's creators. An aptly named example of programmatic architecture, The Coffee Pot opened in 1927 along the Lincoln Highway as a service-station luncheonette designed to compel drivers to pull over and fuel up their cars, their bodies, and maybe even their souls. In an era when the road trip was a novelty and shops wanted to pocket those tourist dollars, architecture needed to be novel as well. The Coffee Pot eventually served its last cup, and preservationists saved it from demolition and moved it to its present location.

Also along the Lincoln Highway, about two hours to the east, is the **Haines Shoe House** (FIG. 7), in York, Pennsylvania. The stucco-sheathed wooden structure was built in 1948 at the order of "Shoe Wizard" Mahlon Haines, who sought to create a giant shoe to promote his chain of shoe stores, the design based on one of his work boots. The house has charming stained-glass windows, and Haines himself is featured.

In every guidebook to the Lincoln Highway, **Dunkle's Gulf Service** (FIG. 8) in Bedford (home of The Coffee Pot) makes the cut. And how could it not? It's an art deco masterpiece, a wonder of polychrome terra-cotta tile, the last of its kind that was still operating as a Gulf station until 2023, when owner Jack Dunkle died. He had continued to run the business that his father, Dick, had opened in 1933. Here, you would be reminded why they used to call gas stations "service stations." The Dunkles would make sure your car was good to go before you hit the road again.

8

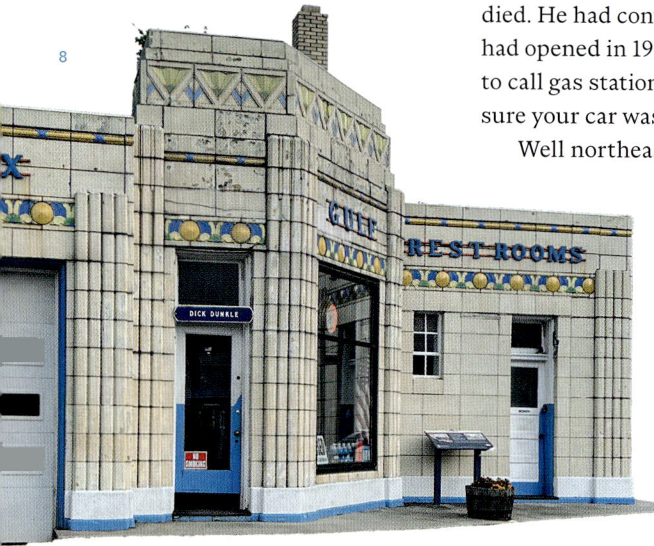

Well northeast of Dunkle's, in the village of Millerton, New York, you can tempt your car with the kind of service it could get only back in the day. You and your vehicle can admire the re-created **Mobil gas station** (FIG. 9). This was indeed a Mobil station in 1957, the year of inspiration, and last pumped gas under the Getty brand in the second decade of the twenty-first century.

Rob Cooper, a local resident, bought the station and turned it back into a gleaming,

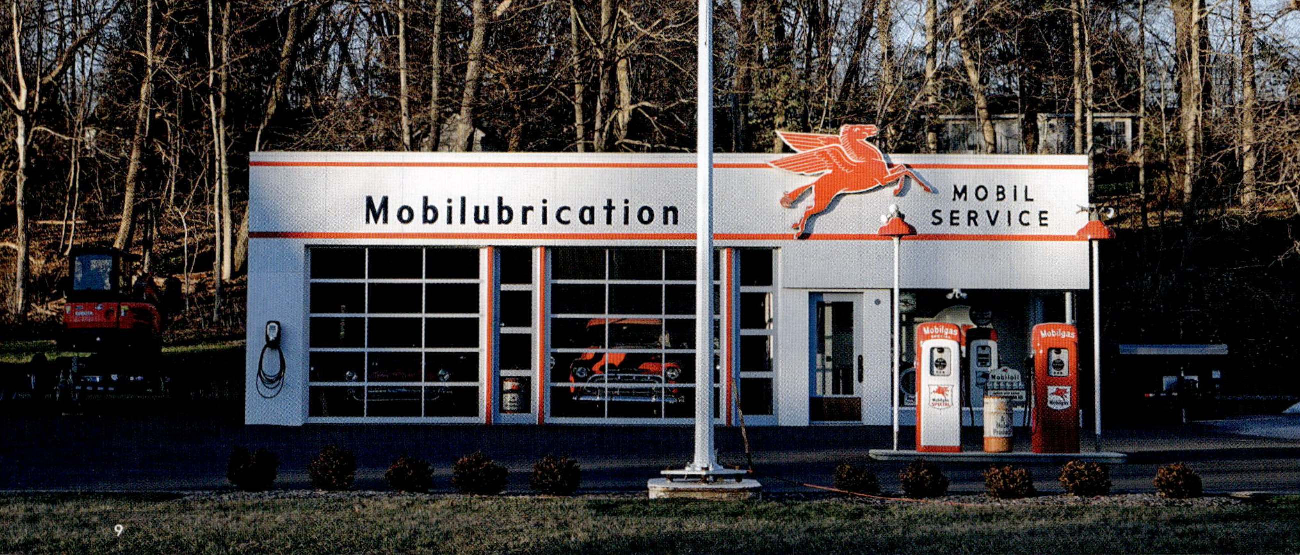

9

pristine 1950s "Mobilgas" station. The pumps are disconnected, and, regrettably, an earnest young man, responding to the chimes set off by a wheel-crushed rubber hose, won't run out to top off your oil and spot clean your windshield. But that's all beside the point—this is now one of the best stops in the nation.

From car fuel to nightmare fuel: In New Jersey, one of the most iconic roadside attractions is **Calico, the Evil Clown of Middletown** (FIG. 10), which stands outside the former Food Circus supermarket. The gigantic clown has woven itself into the nightmares of residents, including New Jersey director and producer Kevin Smith, whose films the clown has haunted. Menacing though it may be, the clown is a symbol of the area, and so beloved that campaigns to save it spring up whenever there is a threat to develop his shopping center, where he has stood since the mid-1950s.

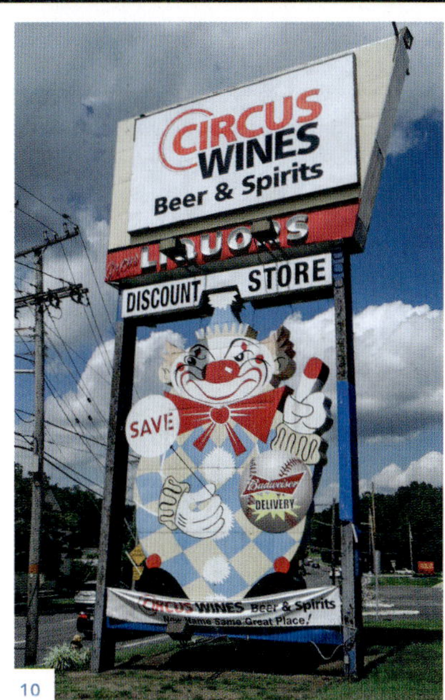

10

Calico's closest relative is farther down the shore, in Asbury Park, where a replica of Tillie, the dementedly smiling boardwalk symbol of this seaside oasis, has materialized outside the **Wonder Bar** (FIG. 11). Calico and Tillie were designed by Leslie Worth Thomas. The original Tillie, captured toward the end of its life in a *Sopranos* episode, was placed in storage along with a twin, and they have yet to see the light of day at this writing. But his visage is everywhere here on the Jersey Shore.

11

SPOTLIGHT:
WILDWOOD

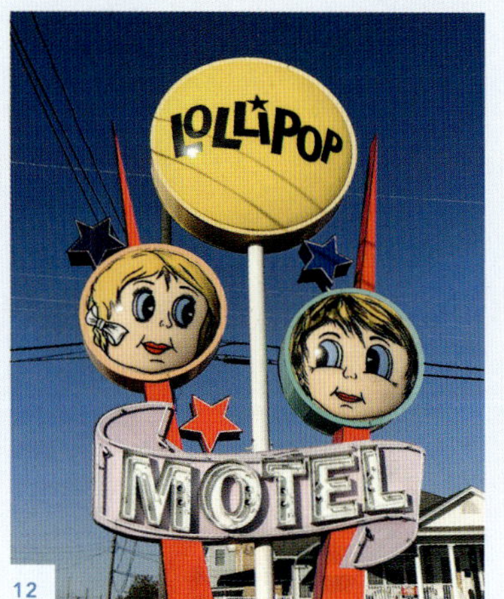

12

Just saying the word "Wildwood" makes me swoon and has since my first visit as a child. In 1980, my family skipped Miami Beach and headed for the Jersey Shore. Known for its 1950s–60s "Doo Wop" style motels, the seaside resort area comprises three communities—Wildwood, Wildwood Crest, and North Wildwood—but they coexist in the public mind under the rubric of Wildwood. Despite rampant motel demolitions starting in the 1990s, Wildwood still dazzles, thanks to the crucial Doo Wop Preservation League and growing national awareness that protected dozens of these motels. The motels feature shared design elements, including striking signage, usually on a pole, thrilling shapes and colors working together to catch the eye, inviting pools, and plastic palm trees. The style's West Coast equivalent is Googie (see page 297), and the name comes from the association with Wildwood's glory days of vacation development in the late 1950s and the rise of the doo wop style of music. My very favorite, the **Lollipop Motel** **(FIG. 12)** in North Wildwood, has been my avatar for almost a decade on Instagram.

Wildwood is an open museum, but there are stops that can enhance the experience. The **Doo Wop Museum** is a feast for the eyes. Here, dozens of vintage signs from demolished properties have found their forever home. And the **Wildwood Historical Society** is teeming with fascinating artifacts and archives you can explore. There is no such thing as a quick visit here—almost everything captures my attention.

Admire the motels, vintage businesses, and boardwalk amusements.

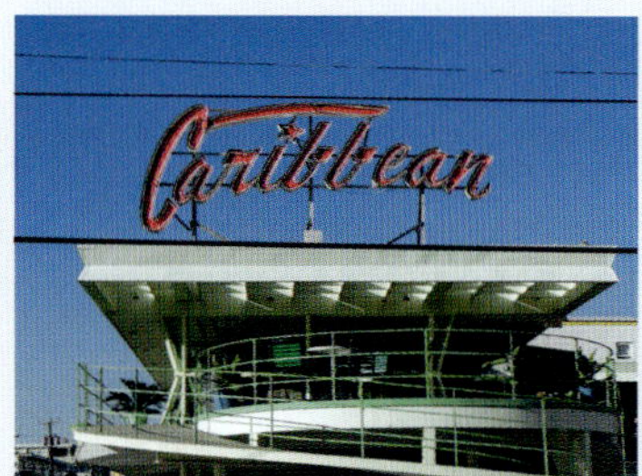

The Caribbean

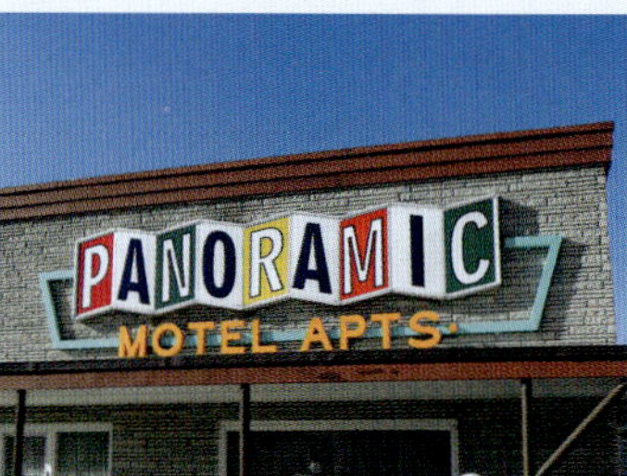

The Panoramic

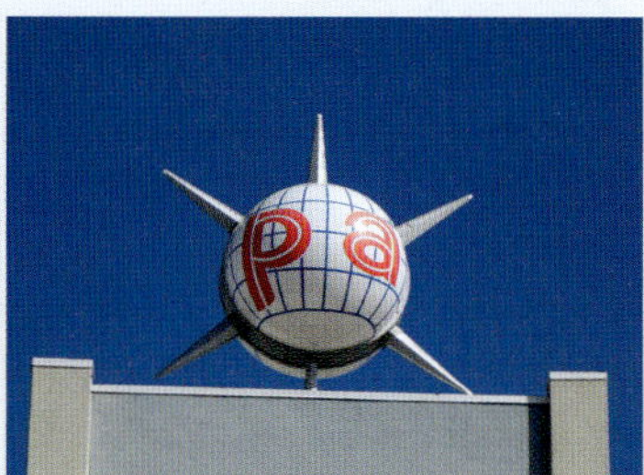

The Pan American

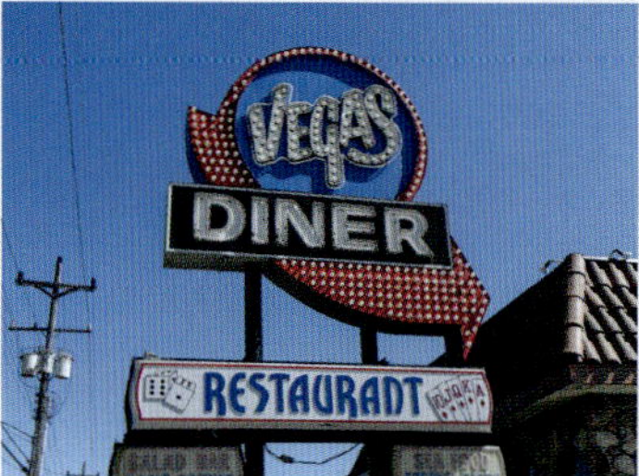

Vegas Diner

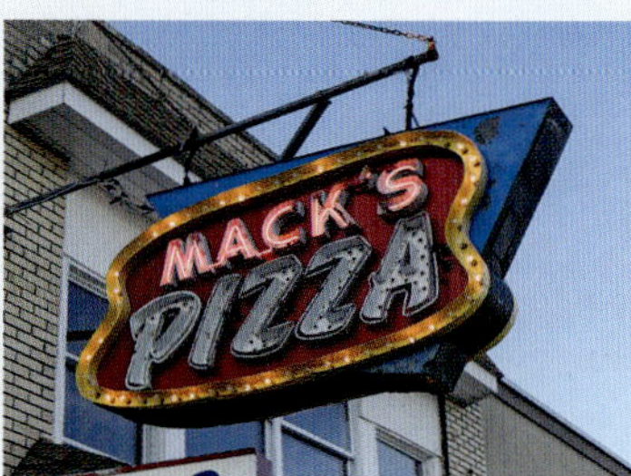

Mack's Pizza

From unforgettable faces to places that are out of this world, New Jersey has it all. **The Futuro Houses** (FIG. 13)—prefabricated modernist concept homes—recall a popular conception of a UFO. One remains at the center of a park in Willingboro, New Jersey.

Want more UFOs? Head to **Grovers Mill**, New Jersey, to see the country town where Orson Welles set his alien invasion in *War of the Worlds*, complete with a stop at the Grovers Mill coffee shop with a beautiful mural depicting the faux radio alien invasion of Halloween Eve 1938.

For UFOs in New York, head to **Pine Bush**, which features a cleverly curated museum devoted to alleged alien sightings, strange lights in the night sky, and folkloric mysteries of the Hudson Valley.

If you're Pennsylvania bound, put **Kecksburg** (FIG. 14) on your list, home of a giant acorn with pseudohieroglyphics (a leftover prop from the filming of an *Unsolved Mysteries* episode). The alien craft that supposedly landed here resembled a giant acorn—and vanished under a government cover-up, or so say some.

Fairy Tale Forest (FIG. 15) in Oak Ridge, New Jersey, is a 1950s family attraction that was shuttered for decades. But like a realized wish from a generous fairy princess, the park was reopened in 2024 after a long limbo. The brainchild of German immigrant Paul Woehle Sr., the park grew more elaborate over the decades, allowing visitors a portal into the magical world of the Brothers Grimm. The place was a particular delight at Christmas, so much so that part of Mariah Carey's video for her ever-popular "All I Want for Christmas Is You" earworm was shot here. If your Christmas wish was for Fairy Tale Forest to return one day, Woehle's granddaughter, Christine Vander Ploeg, delivered.

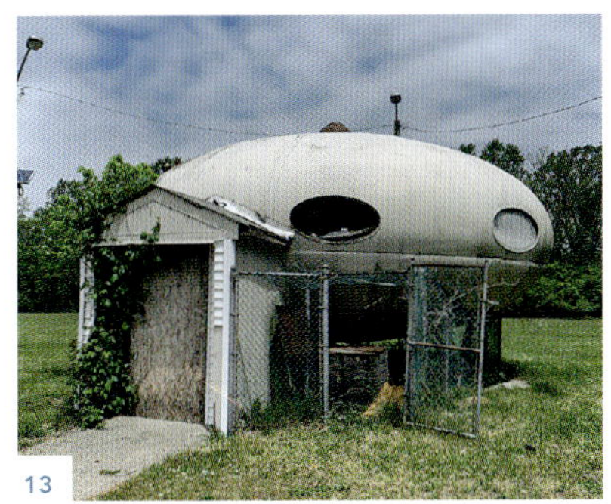
13

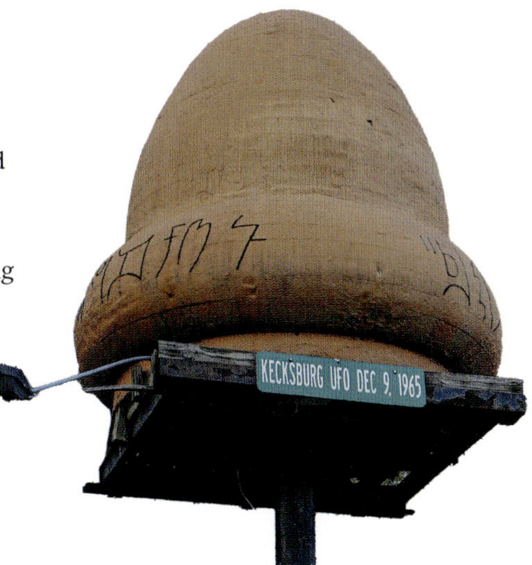

14

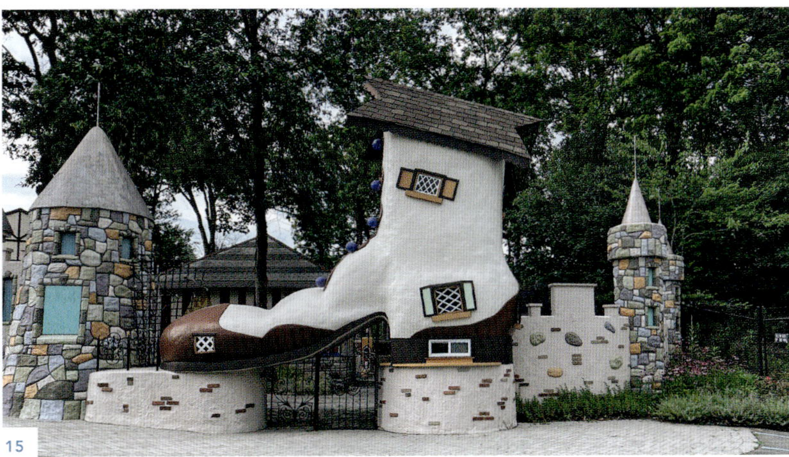
15

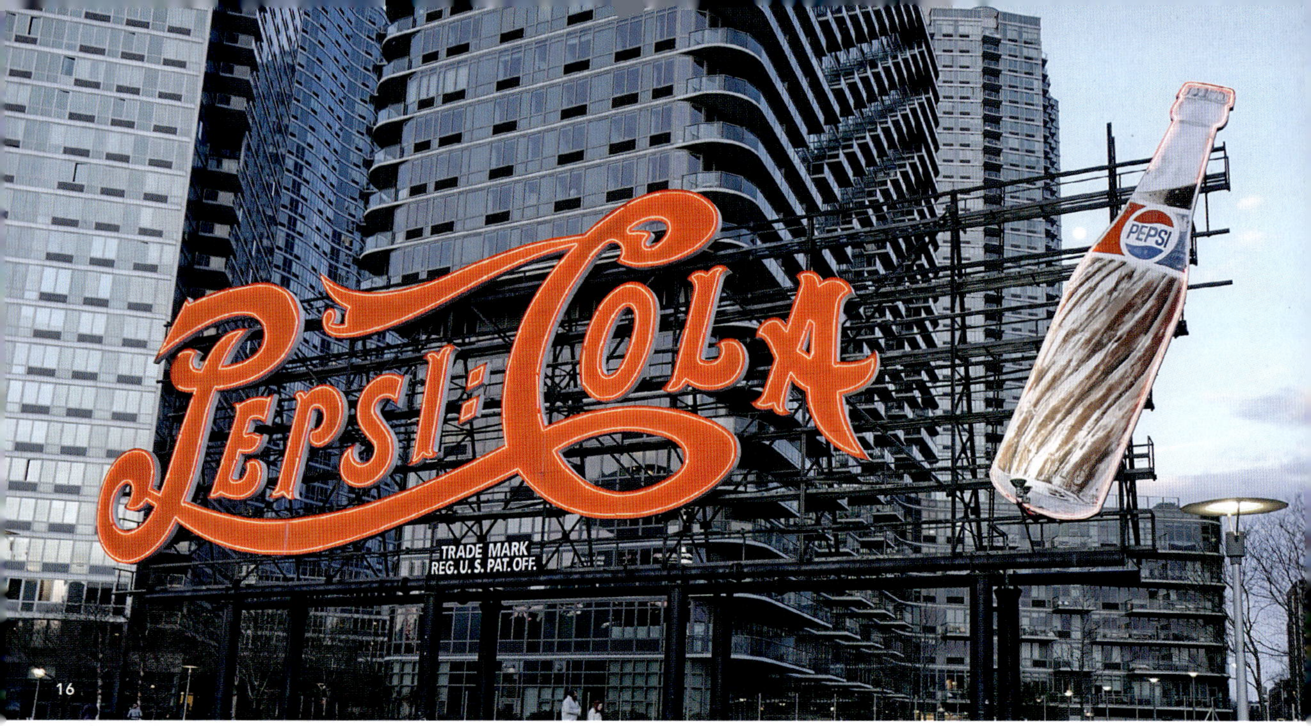

16

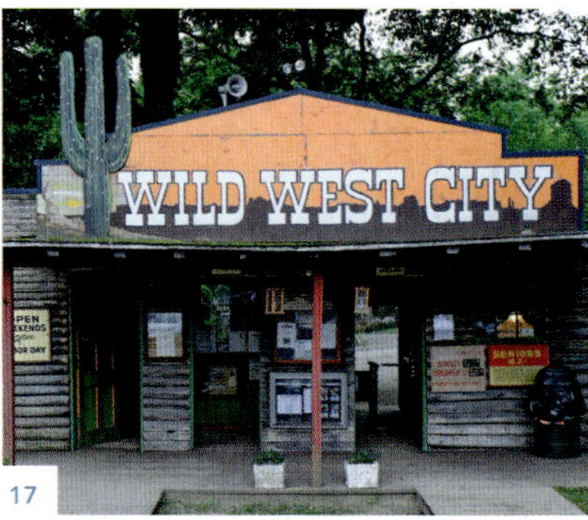

17

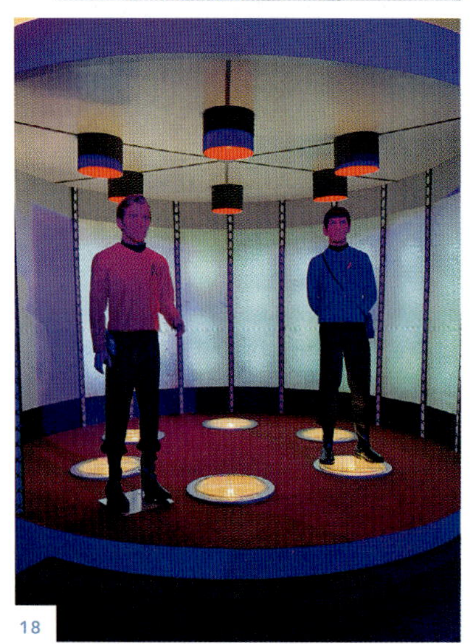

18

Since we're on this tour of North Jersey gems, why not stop at the **Wild West City** (FIG. 17) theme park in Stanhope, New Jersey. When I visited in June 2019, I met actor Larry Storch, a star of the 1960s sitcom *F Troop*, who has a saloon named after him here. The passage of decades and evolving cultural sensitivities haven't laid a glove on this place, where you can still witness *High Noon*–style mock showdowns that make you think Westerns are still in primetime and kids are going around wearing Davy Crockett hats.

In Ticonderoga, New York, *Star Trek* fans can experience an out-of-this-world wonder, the **Star Trek Original Series Set Tour** (FIG. 18), an immersive and stunningly faithful re-creation of the set of the original series. William "Captain Kirk" Shatner has made pilgrimages here, adding to the trippy nature of this attraction. (Check out the neon signage for **Circle Court and Stone House motels** while in town.)

One of the greatest signs in existence is the **Pepsi sign in Long Island City, Queens** (FIG. 16). This massive sign is a holdover of the now-posh area's industrial waterfront past. The original version was installed in 1940, reflecting the era when the script logo featured a double hyphen rather than a dash and an extended fancy flourish on the top of the letter *C*. An earlier version had the word "DRINK" in that flourish.

Artkraft Strauss reconstructed the sign itself in the 1990s. (A version of the 1970s bottle had replaced an earlier one.) Pepsi's plant closed here in 2003, but the sign would find a new home at Gantry Plaza State Park nearby.

Pepsi signs at bottling factories can be grand, like the **giant bottle cap** (FIG. 19) at the facility in St. Marys, Pennsylvania. Typical Pepsi signs and especially privilege signs—those provided to stores for free in exchange for perpetual promotion—are common across the country, but the older they are, the scarcer they become.

Pepsi was founded in New Bern, North Carolina, by pharmacist Caleb Bradham, and was originally called Brad's Drink. While Bradham lost control of his company, his contributions to our soft-drink culture are not forgotten. His simple gravestone at **Cedar Grove Cemetery** in the town where he invented his concoction is emblazoned with the Pepsi-Cola logo.

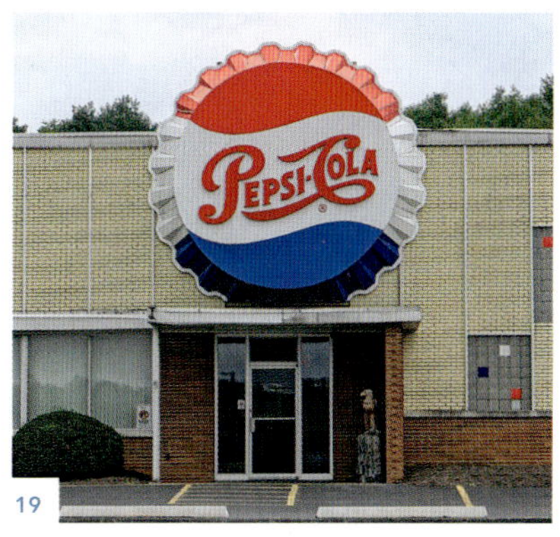

19

ROADSIDE EATS

LET'S EAT! That's one of the most exciting signs you'll see on any road trip, and if it's neon-lit, all the better. In this section, we'll explore cherished spots that I adore, and I hope you will, too.

Let's start our restaurant tour at the spot where Coney Island meets the boardwalk, the beach, and the Atlantic Ocean: **Nathan's Famous** (FIG. 20). There are few places in New York that have been in business for more than a hundred years—and in the very same spot. Nathan's and its hot dogs have survived the development pressures that have stripped much of the area of its carny character. Nathan's, which opened in 1916, had never once closed before the apocalyptic wrath of Superstorm Sandy came along in 2012. And then came COVID-19, and still it stands. Every Fourth of July, it hosts its Hot Dog Eating Contest, which on a slow news day fills up airtime and column inches.

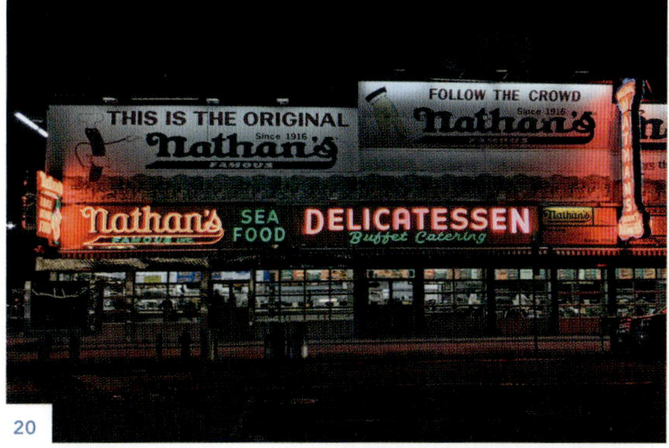

20

In that elite club of restaurants that are well into their second century stands, since 1888, the most iconic of New York Jewish delis, **Katz's Delicatessen** (FIG. 21), on East Houston Street in Manhattan. It was the place to "Send a Salami to Your Boy in the Army" and was the site of Sally's fake orgasm in the 1989 rom-com *When Harry Met Sally*, prompting the oft-quoted line, "I'll have what she's having." (The spot where the scene was filmed is marked by a sign.)

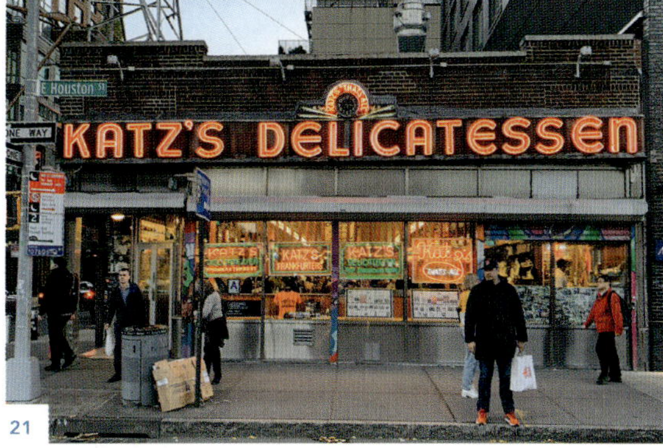

21

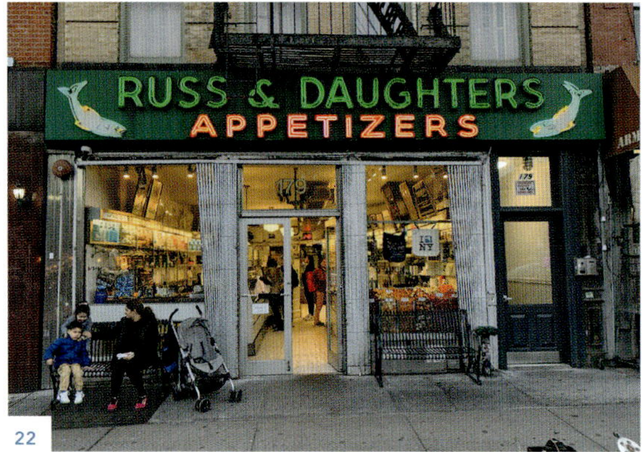

22

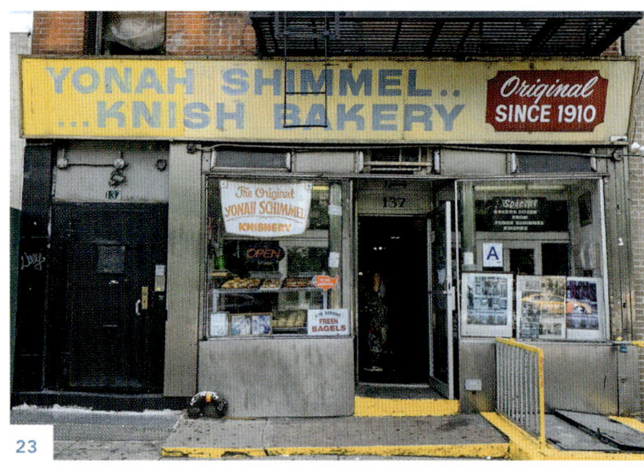

23

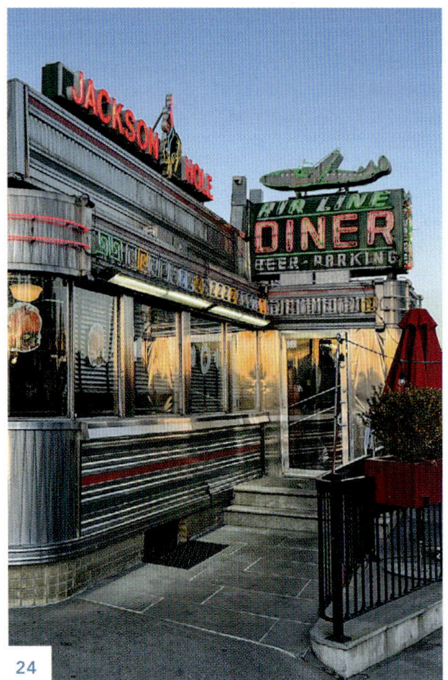

24

A block west from Katz's is **Russ & Daughters** (FIG. 22). You could be forgiven for thinking "appetizing" shops were simply extolling how tasty their food is. But in this use, appetizing means foods like lox and spreads that go with a bagel.

Joel Russ started it all, a Polish immigrant who had a barrel of herring and a dream. Yes, his business started out of a barrel on the street on the Lower East Side after he arrived in 1907. By 1920, it moved here, its second physical location after years of selling from a pushcart and later a horse-drawn wagon. His daughters were brought into the business as kids—the shop says it was the first business to use the phrase "and daughters" in America, and it's still in the family.

Our final stop on our Houston Street century-club tour is **Yonah Schimmel Knish Bakery** (FIG. 23). Like Russ & Daughters, Yonah Schimmel's began as a pushcart business, originally down in Coney Island. A knish (the *k* is pronounced) is traditionally a baked dough delicacy stuffed with potatoes that can be flavored with savory or sweet ingredients. The storefront has been here since 1910, and it's impossible to think of anything else occupying this plot of earth.

Cross the East River to Queens, to the environs of LaGuardia Airport and the **Jackson Hole** (FIG. 24), née the Air Line Diner. The Air Line in East Elmhurst landed here in 1952. Its high-traffic location has served it well. Unlike other diners of the 1950s that have changed hands, opened and closed multiple times, and broken hearts along the way, the Air Line has been immune to that kind of tragedy. Before it was absorbed into the Jackson Hole hamburger chain, the diner was conferred cinematic immortality in *Goodfellas*, in an iconic scene with Ray Liotta and Joe Pesci.

The folks at Jackson Hole knew to leave well enough alone when they took over. They added their own neon signage, complementary to the original though confusing to the casual

▸▸▸ Pull Over!

New York once had many diners, and today, we still have treasures throughout the five boroughs, like the **Lindenwood Diner** in Brooklyn and the **Empire Diner** in Manhattan. That said, take them for granted at your own risk. Development pressure puts them all, to some extent, on endangered lists.

passerby who must process that the diner appears to have two names. That has hardly hurt business.

As vital as diners are, a related species of New York eatery venue feeds off nostalgic appetites, and that is the luncheonette. When you visit the **Lexington Candy Shop** (FIG. 25) on Manhattan's Upper East Side, the past is present—and you can taste it, one egg cream at a time. The Lexington Candy Shop opened in 1925 and last had a major overhaul in 1948. That's when they doubled down on the lunch side of the business and gave up making the sweets. But they kept the sweet Lexington Candy Shop name.

Owner John Philis grew up at the candy shop, working as soon as he was old enough to take the subway from Queens. His granddad, a Greek immigrant, founded it. Philis officially went into the family business in 1980 to help his pop and figured it would be a fun gig for a couple of years. The years turned into decades.

Robert Redford sidles up to this counter in the 1975 spy thriller *Three Days of the Condor*, in which a young Philis can be heard yelling "Chicken platter!" It's hardly changed since that day.

Manhattan icons run the gamut from your humble lunch place to your swanky red-sauce joint. **Patsy's Italian Restaurant** (FIG. 26) on West 56th Street in Manhattan was the cherished turf of Frank Sinatra, where he was always the chairman of the board. Pasquale "Patsy" Scognamillo opened the restaurant in an adjacent building in 1944. A decade later, he moved it to its current location, and it's hard to think of anything else here.

A different nightlife world was born on October 14, 1980, when **The Odeon** (FIG. 27) opened and, one can argue, the 1980s truly began in Manhattan. Back then, Tribeca was in a liminal moment, caught between its industrial past—all workaday warehouses by day and dark, empty streets by night—and a sophisticated future with chic lofts, shops, and trendy people living the good life in the shadow of the glittering Twin Towers, still the new kids on the skyline.

The Odeon was an instant success—in a blip it was declared restaurant of the year—and a mere month after its opening, the *Daily News* described it as overrun with intriguing people willing to wait hours to dine in a beautiful space. The Odeon became a late-night haunt of the gorgeous, the talented, the rich.

The neon—and much of the interior—is a brilliant example of adaptive reuse. This is the site of the 1930s Towers cafeteria, which by 1979 was languishing. The cafeteria was an intact art deco design when it was revitalized in 1980. The "cafeteria" neon on the left side was preserved, and "The Odeon" was added to the facade.

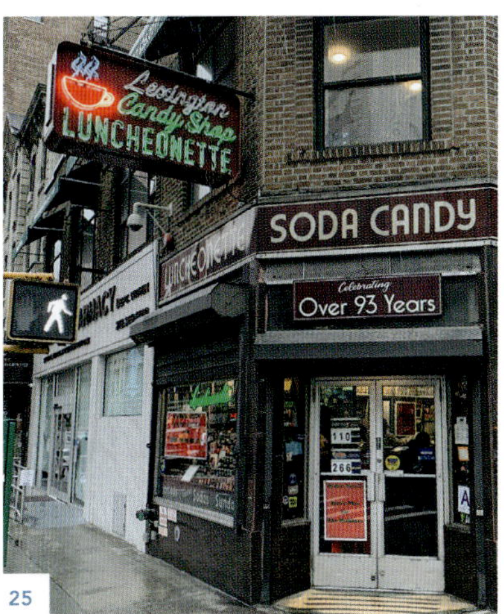

25

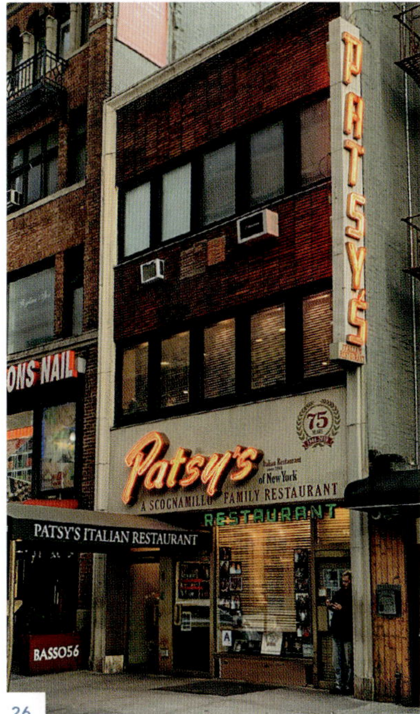

26

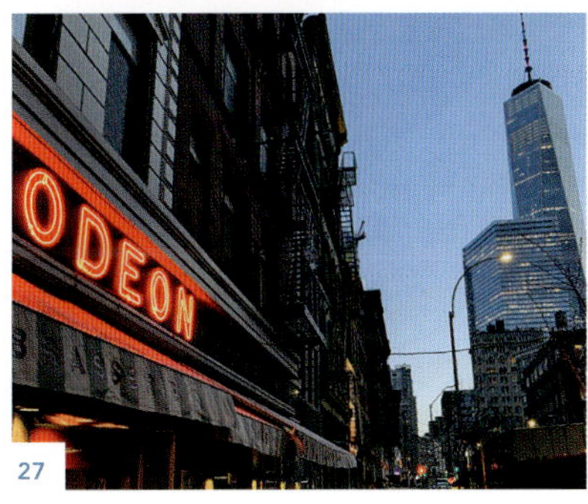

27

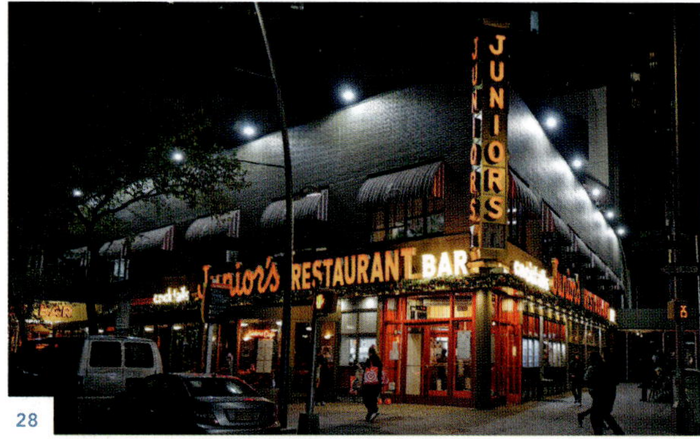

28

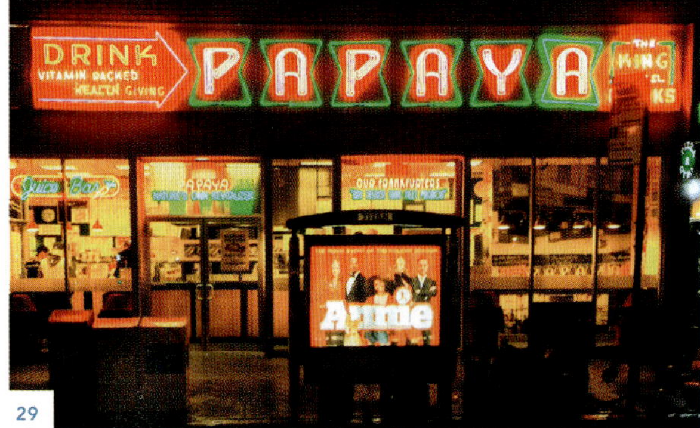

29

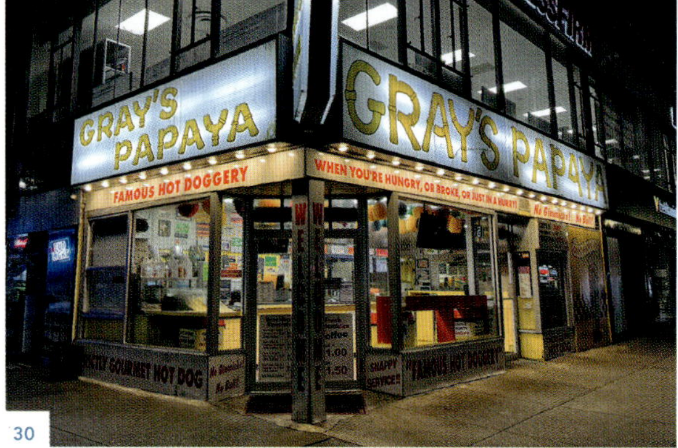

30

Brooklyn's most famous restaurant perhaps is **Junior's** (FIG. 28), its epic neon-and-light-bulb-bedecked signage a signature of life in Brooklyn since 1950. Opened by Harry Rosen at the site of an earlier cafe the family ran since 1929, Junior's refers to Harry's two sons, Walter and Marvin, who themselves would become the restaurant's proprietors. People come here for the cheesecake; a round of press in 1973 spilled the secrets of Junior's to the wider world, and a 1981 fire that shuttered the restaurant for almost a year prompted sidewalk pleas to "save the cheesecake"—or so goes the story. Beyond the baked goods and the mouthwatering Jewish delicatessen staples, there's something else that's special here, something you can't put a price on. In 2014, Alan Rosen, a grandson of the founder, walked away from a $45 million offer to sell the property, saying that Junior's as we know it would have disappeared. Since then, its renown has only spread, with a spectacular second annex in Times Square (the first there opened in 2006) that has the architectural spirit of the original—you'd think it's been there since 1950, too.

Behold **Papaya King** (FIG. 29). For the outsider, it is a quirky combination: tropical drinks and hot dogs. It only makes sense if you think of the history of Yorkville, the neighborhood where Papaya King opened in 1932, and survived for ninety years. Founder Constantine "Gus" Poulos, fresh from a visit to Cuba, was keen on selling tropical drinks. The residents in heavily German Yorkville hungered for heartier fare. So Poulos began serving hot dogs, and a New York institution was born.

Papaya King spawned imitators, including the iconic **Gray's Papaya** (FIG. 30), hunkered down at West Seventy-Second Street and Broadway since 1973 and famed for its recession specials. Papaya King, to their credit, always thought big, trying their hand at franchising and opening new locations. In the 2010s, they had two additional stores in New York that played off the vibe of the neon at the original store. Those closed, and alas, the original, ousted by a landlord, finally did, too, in its ninetieth year. Papaya King has since moved across the street, unfortunately without its great signage.

We've spent a lot of time in New York City in this chapter, but places with a Gotham vibe don't obey boundaries on a map. In Nassau County lies what I have often called The Most Beautiful Storefront in America. That's **Hildebrandt's** (FIG. 31) in Williston Park, New York.

As the 1920s roared, Henry Hildebrandt opened this luncheonette and ice-cream parlor. It was a time when stores like Hildebrandt's were the heartbeats of American downtowns. But by the early twenty-first century, Hildebrandt's was among the last of its kind.

Under inspired new ownership after a brush with death, Hildebrandt's is thriving as its hundredth birthday looms. Owners Randy Sarf and Spencer Singer have committed to revitalizing Hildebrandt's by highlighting its historical character while making tweaks to the menu but still preserving the classic dishes customers crave. And they are making sure the culinary crown jewel here gets the shine and spotlight it deserves—the ice cream. It's made on the premises and comes in more than a dozen flavors.

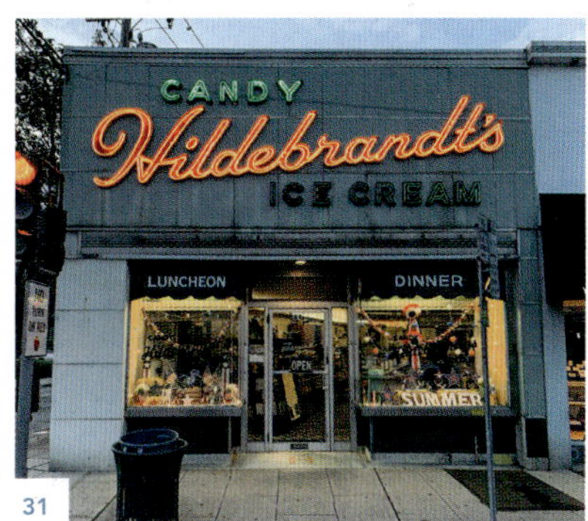

31

Let's head east to the **Northport Sweet Shop** (FIG. 32), a Great Gatsby–era luncheonette that's still going strong. Stepping inside is like entering the world of the history books of yesterday's downtowns. You'll find a luncheonette serving up treats like homemade ice cream, glass candy-display cases teeming with chocolates made in the shop's kitchen, and cozy booths to enjoy it all with family and friends. Year-round, this is a magical place, but it is especially so at Easter. It's worth a stop to enjoy the chocolate bunnies and other sweet goodies made by owner Pete Panarites himself.

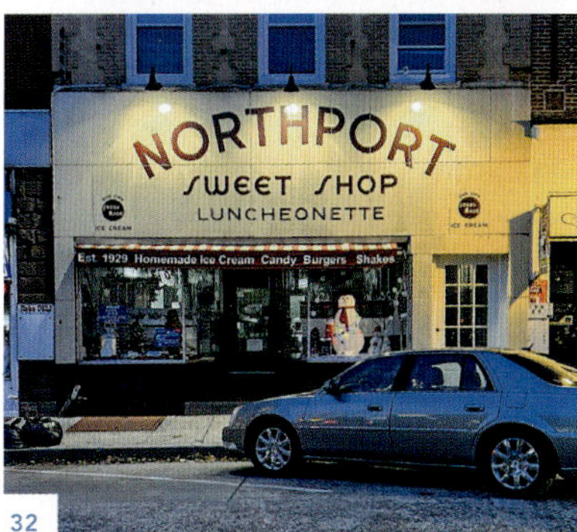

32

At the **All-American Hamburger Drive-In** (FIG. 33) in Massapequa, New York, on Long Island, the sizzle of the neon is the appetizer to the sizzle of the griddle, where juicy quarter pounders keep customers waiting patiently for their first bite—and keep them coming back, year after year, as they have since 1963.

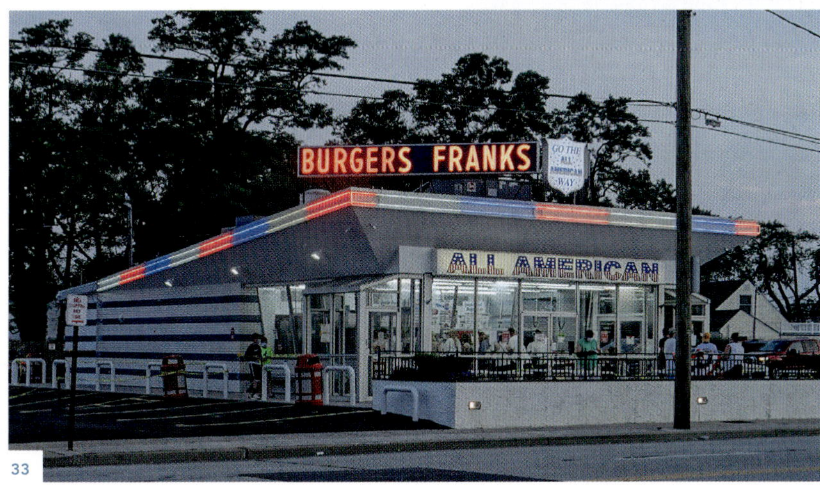

33

Long Island grew up during the postwar years, and before the invasion of the chains it was places like the All-American Hamburger Drive-In that

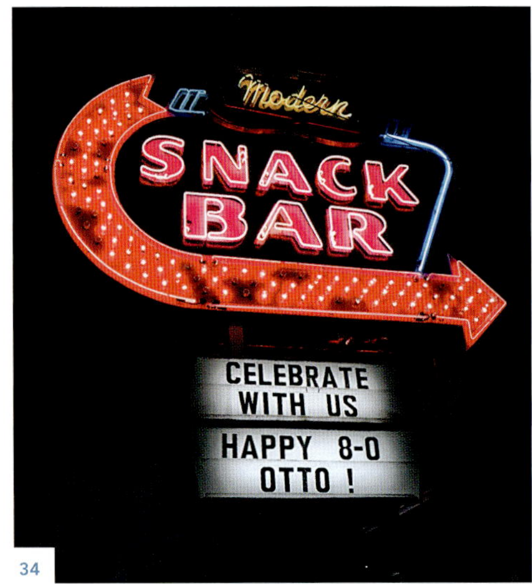

34

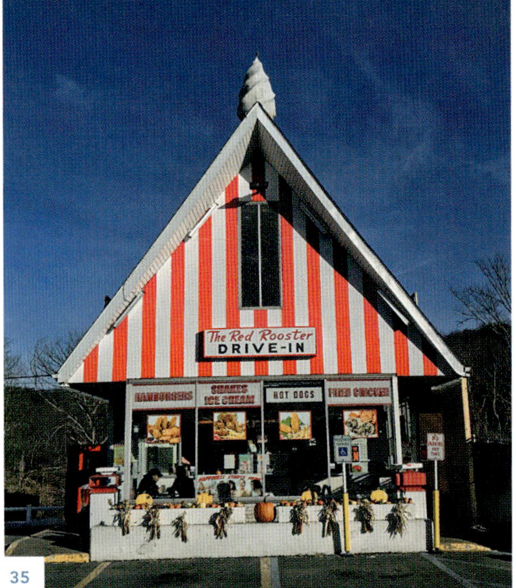

35

gave the island its roadside character. It has withstood chains like the regional Wetson's and national ones like Jack in the Box, which once had a presence in New York. It has more than held its own against McDonald's, Burger King, and all the rest.

The sign for the **Modern Snack Bar** (FIG. 34) in Aquebogue, New York, is an icon of the American road. It looks, well, as modern as it did back in 1956, the year it was installed.

Folks in Putnam County know they have a treasure as well in **The Red Rooster** (FIG. 35) in Brewster, New York, an all-American retro roadside attraction that serves up a mean hamburger—and ample portions of midcentury ambience. The A-frame old-school standby on Route 22 teems with character: the candy-stripe design, the classic signage, the ice-cream-cone cupola. A low-slung extension for indoor dining built in 2019 retains the 1963 architectural flavor of the original barn.

Let's make a detour to Pennsylvania, and consider a bite at one of the two remaining locations of the **Dutch Pantry** (FIG. 36) restaurant chain. Dutch Pantry began in 1945 near Selinsgrove, Pennsylvania, and the once-family-owned chain would spread its country kitchens as far south as Florida. The one shown here dates to 1974. The look of the restaurants pays homage to Pennsylvania Dutch culture, which springs from the community of German pioneers who settled in the Keystone State. "Dutch" is a corruption of the word "Deutsch," or "German." The word's use here has nothing to do with the Netherlands. The stores recall a Pennsylvania Dutch barn, complete with hex signs.

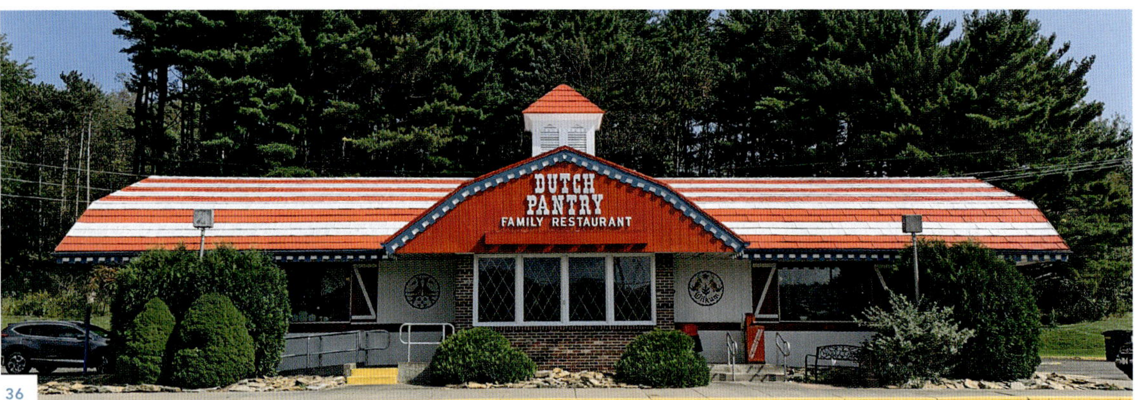

36

TEMPLES OF THE SLIDER

Each of these local restaurants is unique, offering twists in decor, hours, menus, you name it. They also all share a certain road-food pedigree. The "white" refers to cleanliness, the "system" perhaps to the efficient and orderly process of getting that savory slider to your plate and keeping the joint spotless. They all take a page from the legacy of White Castle.

New Jersey has a thing for sliders and diners. There's the **White Manna** (FIG. 37) in Hackensack. This tiny art deco temple to the humble slider is truly manna from heaven. The White Manna has been on the banks of the Hackensack River since 1946, moving to its present location in 1969. It often ends up on lists for best burgers in America, had the imprimatur of Anthony Bourdain, and enjoyed the *Diners, Drive-Ins and Dives* treatment.

The White Manna is not to be confused with Jersey City's **White Mana** (FIG. 38)—yep, one *n*, thanks to a long-ago sign snafu. Its oval counter makes for a unique dining experience. It landed here in 1946.

This state also has a thing for hot dogs, Taylor ham sandwiches, and other greasy-spoon favorites. All these things come together beautifully at **White Rose Diner** (FIG. 39) in Linden, New Jersey.

The White Rose, housed in a Kullman Diner, was once part of a small chain of diner-based slider shops, first opened in the 1950s and run for decades by the Hemmings family of North Carolina. Other White Roses survive on their own, in Roselle and Highland Park. In Clark, you can visit the **White Diamond** (FIG. 40). Up in Albany, New York, a beautiful **White Tower** (FIG. 41) building survives.

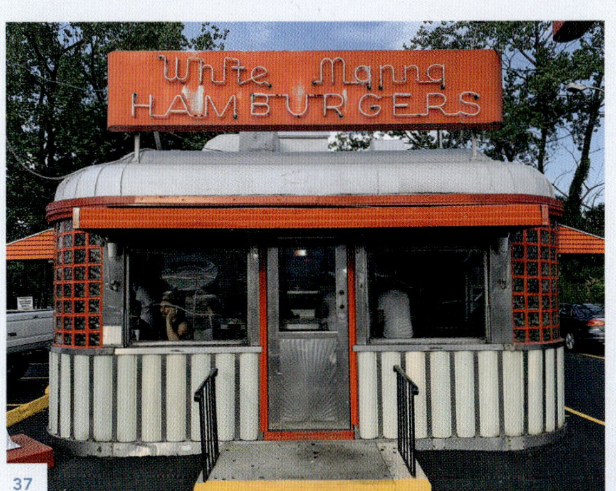

37

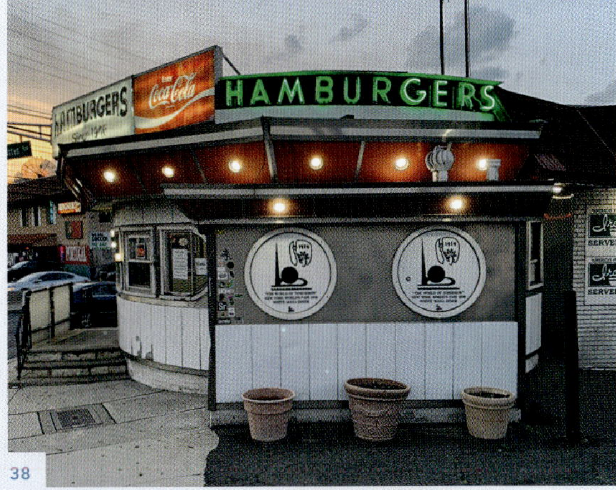

38

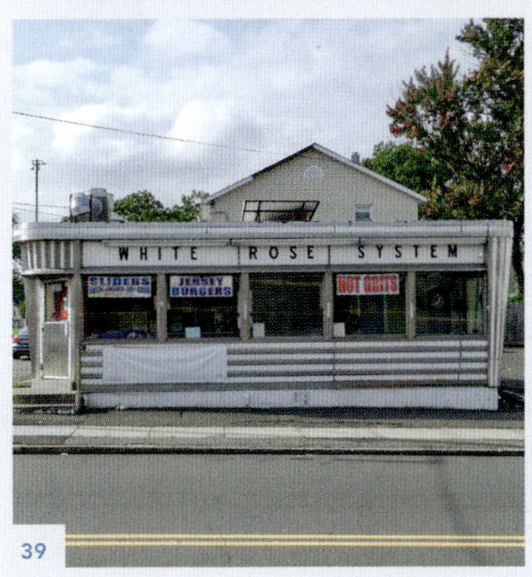

39

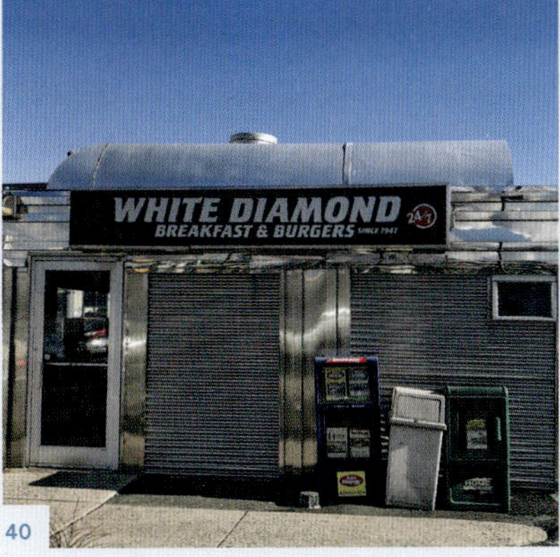

40

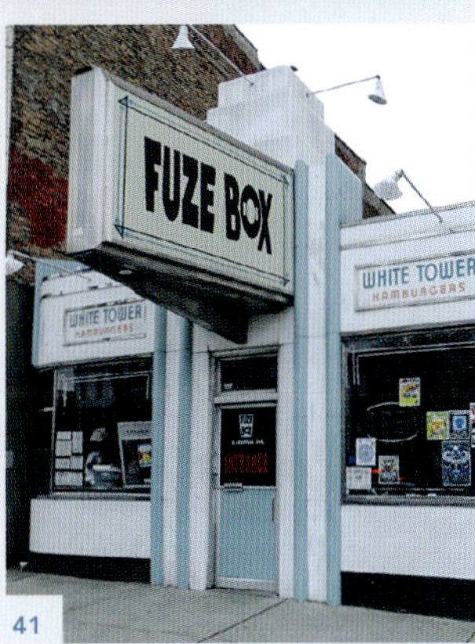

41

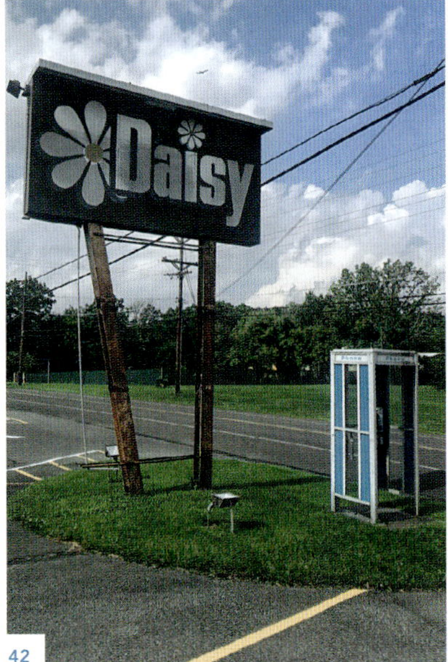

42

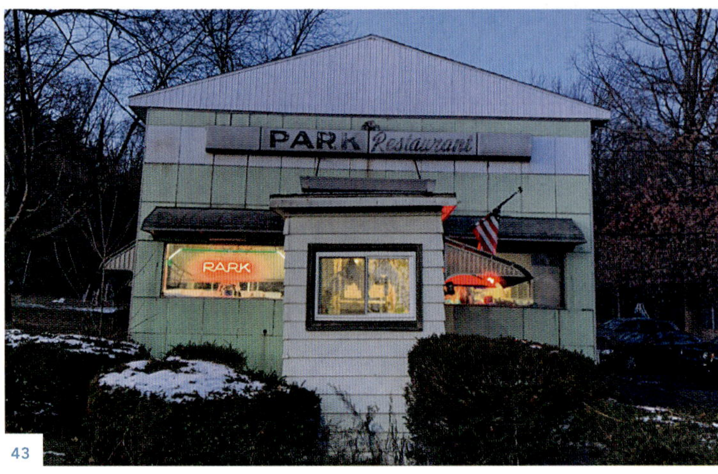

43

The **Daisy Family Restaurant** (FIG. 42) in Wind Gap, Pennsylvania, is the stuff of midcentury-summer dreams. How can you not pull over when you see a telephone booth standing next to this adorable sign? The Daisy began as a seasonal drive-in and has since become a year-round restaurant offering comfort food in a cozy environment.

Park Restaurant (FIG. 43) in the anthracite coal country of Pennsylvania, which is indeed in a park, began as a gaming room where folks could enjoy ice cream. In the 1950s—give or take, the dates are fuzzy—this Shenandoah restaurant evolved into the place you see today. Very little has changed inside since. There's a little cash-register shrine to Mother Teresa, beloved in these parts. She visited nearby Mahanoy City in 1995.

Vanessa Brown is working her own daily miracles at the counter of **Mickey's Restaurant** (FIG. 44) in Berwick, Pennsylvania, dishing out homemade comfort food and coffee at the unbeatable price of 25 cents a cup. Vanessa's great-grandfather was Mickey Zajac, the restaurant's namesake, who founded the place in 1939. His name survives on the vintage Pepsi-branded sign outside, and inside, his photo greets you at the door. His family has curated a wall featuring newspaper clippings, old advertisements, and photos of Mickey, his wife, Lydia, as well as friends, family, and co-workers from over the many years.

Also in Berwick, the **White Horse Grill** (FIG. 45) is one of the most beautifully preserved art deco–era restaurants in existence. Today, it's a breakfast joint, but back in the day, it was a place to enjoy a drink, dance, and have a good time. The White Horse was the local watering hole for workers from the nearby American Car and Foundry (ACF) plant, where tankers were manufactured for World War II.

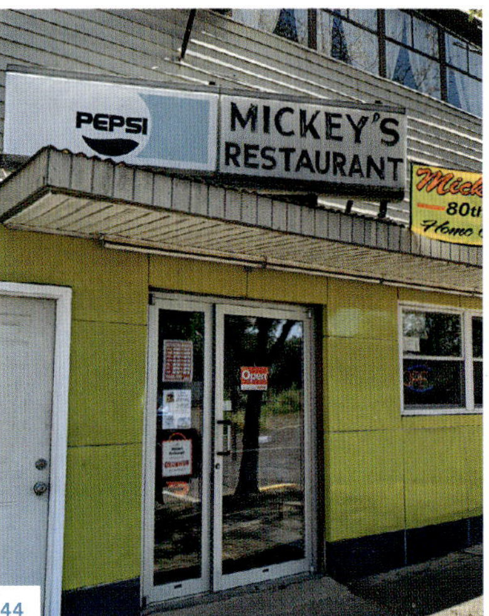

44

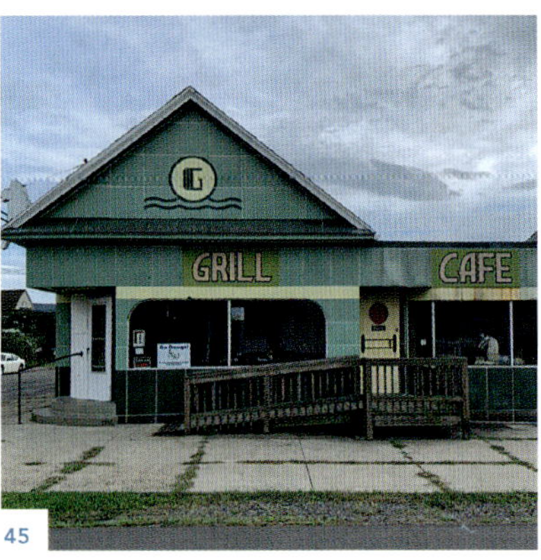

45

Another gem of Pennsylvania comfort is **Tony's Lunch** in Girardville. Tony's opened in the 1940s and has been under its present ownership since 1975. It's a greasy spoon famous for its Screamer hamburger slathered with hot chili sauce, as well as its Fluff Burger, in which good-old Marshmallow Fluff is added to the Screamer.

From burgers to hot dogs, and some of the best you can get in Pennsylvania, **The Squeeze-In** (FIG. 46) is a must-stop. Opened in 1945, the legendary business is tucked into a slim alley in Sunbury, Pennsylvania, and features minimal accommodations such as a vintage orange counter and stools.

And **The Very Best** luncheonette in Pottstown, Pennsylvania, is beloved for their signature hot dogs, along with all the greasy and yummy comfort foods you hanker for.

Davy's Hot Dogs and Grill is an outpost of Switzerland in New Jersey. This restaurant in Mount Arlington began when namesake David Ferrara graduated from high school in 1982. He asked his parents for a pushcart as a gift, and he got right to work. He went to college but kept at the pushcart hustle during the summers, and eventually, the pushcart begat a Winnebago. By the mid-1990s, the Winnebago begat a Swiss chalet. Ferrara's dad had served in World War II and had been so impressed with the Swiss chalets he saw in Europe that he resolved to build himself one stateside someday. His son would pay tribute to his pop's dream house by building his restaurant in the same style. But to remind us of those humble beginnings, that old pushcart is still out front.

Now Southeastern Pennsylvania is proud of its cheesesteaks, and the greats include **Pat's King of Steaks** in Philadelphia—its sign features a big crown for a reason. But an hour north on the Pennsylvania Turnpike is **Zandy's**. The interior is frozen in amber, but this amber is bubblegum pink. Zandy's has always been in the Zandarski family, with the third generation now running this show.

Just outside Philadelphia, **Weber's Drive-In** (FIG. 47) in Pennsauken, New Jersey, draws you in with its fantastical motorized sign. Once you're settled in under Weber's carport, simply flash your lights, and a friendly carhop takes your order and delivers it within minutes on a metal tray that's adroitly hooked onto your window.

White House Subs is the stuff of legends. The Atlantic City institution has been making submarine sandwiches at the corner of Arctic and North Mississippi since 1946. Frank Sinatra, Oprah Winfrey, Rocky Marciano, Joe DiMaggio, and the Beatles are said to have partaken of the goods here.

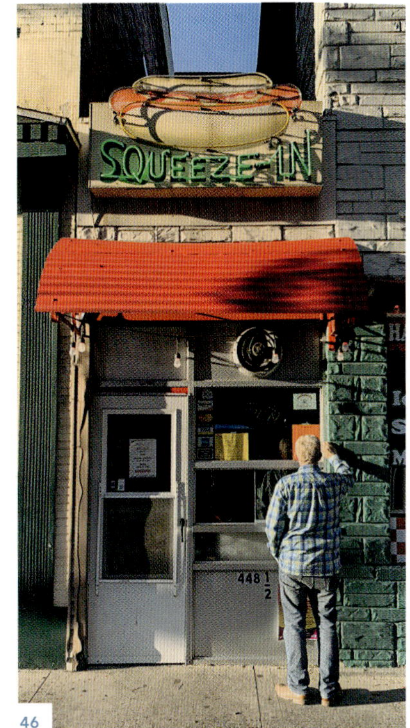

46

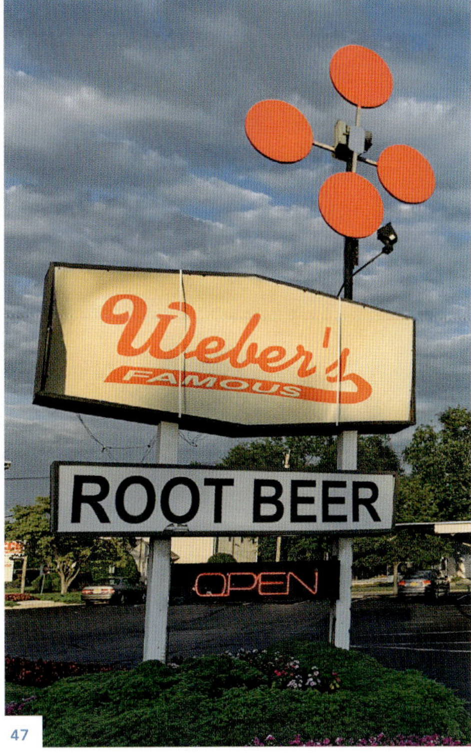

47

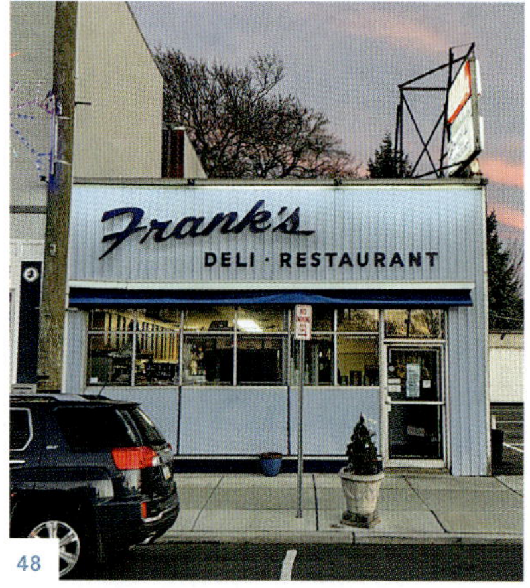

48

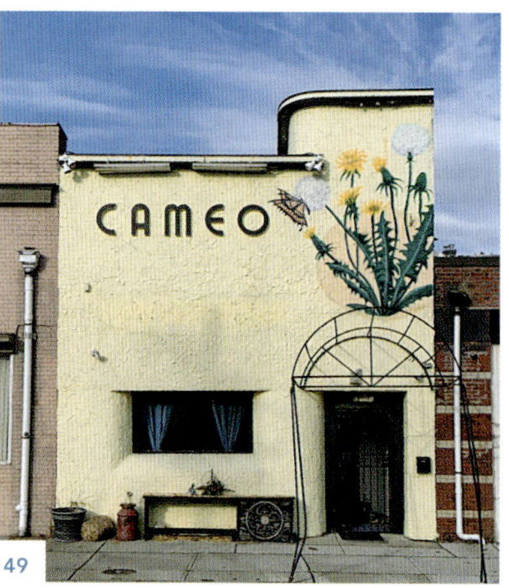

49

And no less an authority than the James Beard Foundation named the place an "American classic."

Next, let's visit **Frank's Deli** (FIG. 48) in Bruce Springsteen's Asbury Park, where he made his mark at The Stone Pony. Frank Maggio had served in the Army in World War II, studied aeronautical engineering, and gone into the family bakery business before he sensed an opportunity at 1406 Main Street.

He bought an existing shop in 1960 and quickly built a foundation for a business that's still going strong. In 2015, Leonia, New Jersey, native Anthony Bourdain visited as part of a tour of Garden State mom-and-pop eateries, which solidified the shop as an icon.

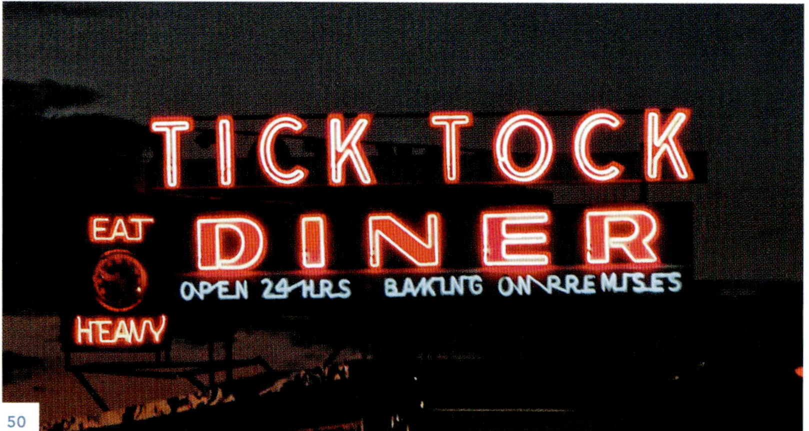

50

Down the street is the **Cameo Love Market** (FIG. 49), a beautiful bistro and coffee bar with various past lives, dating back to the 1930s. It's a fantasy in art deco curves inside and out, shown here in an earlier incarnation.

The diner is deeply associated with Garden State life, and there are many to highlight, including this cinematic crowd-pleaser, the **Tick Tock Diner** (FIG. 50) on Route 3 in Clifton. It's so successful that it has spawned an eponymous spinoff in Manhattan, right by Penn Station, so Garden State commuters can enjoy a taste of home just 12 miles away, but really in another world. The diner was founded in 1948 and descended from a Greek immigrant's lunch cart. The sign's motto is truth in advertising—"Eat Heavy."

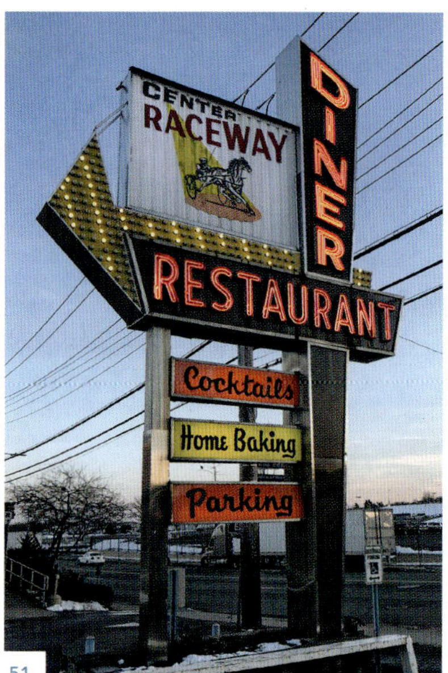

51

We're galloping past many Garden State diners to the **Raceway Diner** (FIG. 51) in Yonkers, New York, which has one of the most spectacular signs anywhere. The sign dazzles in all its electromechanical exuberance, a wonder of neon, incandescence, 1960s typeface, and, well, 1960s imagination and boldness.

Owner Louis Katsihtis arrived in America from Greece with big dreams and a small wallet. He worked his way up with determination, learning the trade in the kitchens of Manhattan restaurants and later in country clubs. He bought the Raceway Diner in 1959, and by May 17, 1966, seventeen years after arriving in America, he had rebuilt the diner in a $200,000 overhaul, tripling the number of seats.

CHAINS OF FOOD

Howard Johnson's

Howard Deering Johnson founded something that was quite common in America in 1925: a pharmacy with a soda fountain that dispensed homemade ice cream. But then he did something uncommon with it. Johnson grew the HoJo's chain to more than a thousand restaurants at their peak, many attached to his motor lodges, which started to pop up in 1954. A HoJo's down the road with its pitched orange roof, Simple Simon and the Pieman weathervane atop a turquoise cupola, was a dependable place to dine with your family. Tendersweet clams, HoJo's ice cream, and other treats tempted tummies.

The restaurants dwindled down to one, with the last restaurant closing in 2021, in Lake George, New York, and so ended a legendary American brand. Today this location (right) is one of countless HoJo's relics that dot the country.

Pizza Hut Classics

Stepping into a Pizza Hut Classic is the closest thing to chain-restaurant time travel. In 2019, Pizza Hut brought back its 1974 logo, banking on its nostalgic appeal. There were no announced plans to bring the logo back into stores, much less redesign the restaurants to look like old Pizza Huts from the chain's heyday. But then, something great happened. With no fanfare whatsoever, Pizza Hut has been taking legacy stores and converting them into "Classics," emulating the look and feel of the restaurants during their peak.

There are now dozens of these Classics around the country. The one you see here is in Bryson City, North Carolina. The first one I spotted was on U.S. 6 in Tunkhannock, Pennsylvania. Of the almost seventy I have counted, I've been to just a handful, and once you've seen one, you've seen them all—yet I still want to see them all!

▸▸▸ Pull Over!

You don't have to dine at the Tick Tock to eat heavy, rest assured. Some of the most cinematic eateries in New Jersey include the **Arlington Diner** in North Arlington, the **Salem Oak Diner** in Salem, the **Summit Diner** in Summit, and the **Bendix Diner** in Hasbrouck Heights.

Let's take a moment to talk about the Bendix, not so much because of the signage, the chrome sheen, or the leather booths, though each of those is great, but because of its owner. John Diakakis, who is blind, can be described in many ways: a joy, a blessing, and a great deal of fun, and you need to visit to experience this beautiful diner—and his bright, bantering presence.

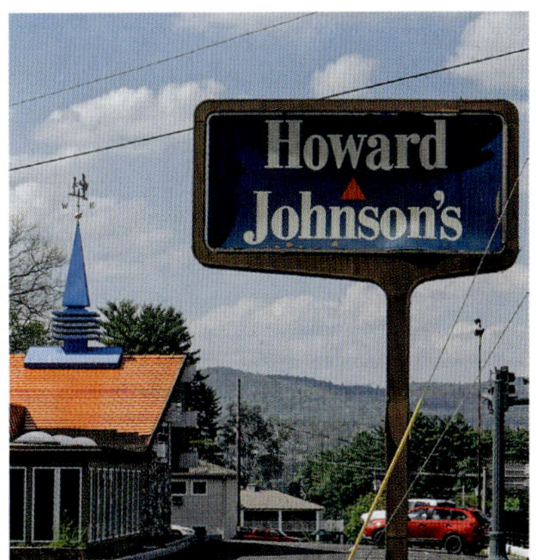

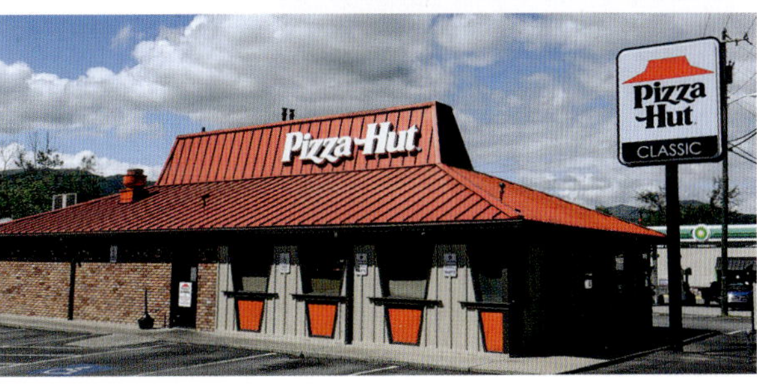

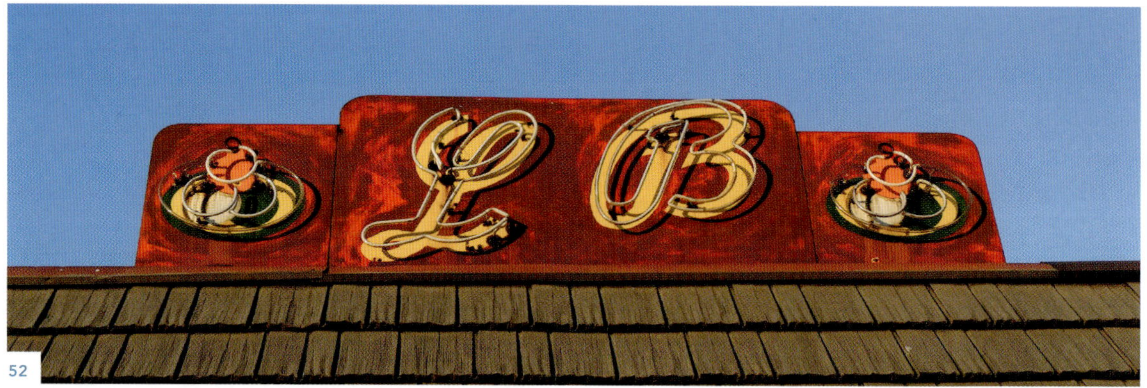

52

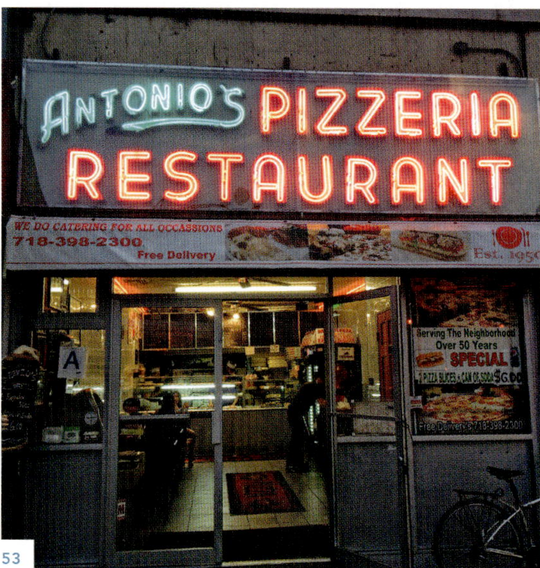

53

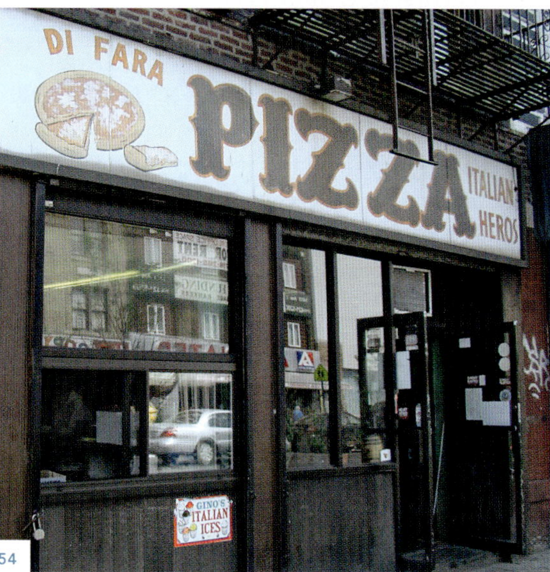

54

PIZZA PIZZA!

If it's pizza you want—architecture selling it and pizzaiolos serving it—the Northeast is a treasure trove. Here's a taste:

Brother's Pizzeria was long a source of inspiration—I'd catch glimpses of the storefront from the Long Island Expressway, where I was usually in a rush to get somewhere, or, often enough, in a crush of cars not getting anywhere. The place in Fresh Meadows is a vintage gem inside and out, dating to 1963. The sign has since been redone, with some of the flair of the old. Give it a few decades and it'll have some patina.

In Brooklyn, which takes pride in its pizza like few other places on earth, the choices are legion. **L&B Spumoni Gardens** (FIG. 52) in Bensonhurst is a trek worth taking for its pizza, pasta, and spumoni for dessert.

On the Park Slope/Prospect Heights border, **Antonio's** (FIG. 53) is a delight and its neon is some of Brooklyn's finest.

And of course, one cannot do a survey of vintage Brooklyn pizzerias without a tip of the hat to **Di Fara's** (FIG. 54), a Midwood institution since 1965. With a little help from glowing reviews and word of mouth, the mastery of maven Dom DeMarco, who died in 2022, elevated Di Fara's to a standout among the countless slice joints in a city where it's hard to find bad pizza.

Not all Gotham slice joints need to be old to be retrologist-worthy, nor do they need to be New York style. **Ace's Pizza** (FIG. 55) in Williamsburg specializes in Detroit-style pizza, in a cozy 1980s-style environment that is relatable to nostalgics and "anemoics" alike, those who hanker for a time they never experienced. The storefront design is the work of Noble Signs, a Brooklyn-based sign company using classic techniques to restore vintage-inspired vitality to New York's streets. (And they've started a sign museum, to boot, with signage around NYC they've saved from ending up in the landfill. I'm proud to say I helped save one of them!)

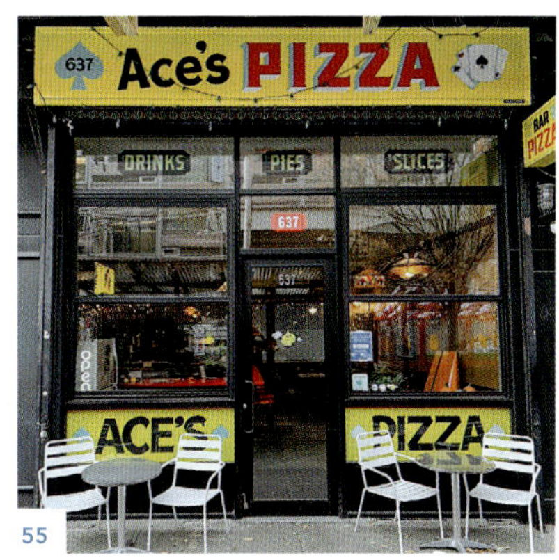

55

SPOTLIGHT: RAY'S PIZZA

There was a time in New York City when you could torture a New York Telephone operator by asking for the phone number of Ray's Pizza, the reason being that there were dozens and dozens of Ray's pizzerias in various permutations and combinations, including but not limited to: Original Ray's, World Famous Original Ray's Pizza, Ray Bari Pizza, Not Ray's Pizza, Ray's Original Pizza, and the one you see here, **The Famous Ray's Pizza**. It opened in 1973 at the corner of Sixth Avenue and West Eleventh Street. When its original owner, Mario DiRienzo, hung up his apron in the 1980s, others kept operating the shop until it closed in 2011. DiRienzo himself took command of the corner in 2012, proclaiming that New York needed him and renamed it Famous Roio's Pizza to honor his native Italian village, Roio del Sangro. Sadly, he died shortly thereafter, and pizza is no longer served from this iconic corner.

Since 1959, there have been a dizzying number of naming variations, lawsuits, false claims, braggadocio, references on *Seinfeld*, and God knows what else in the endless saga of Ray's. It's enough to have you reaching for the Pepto. If you'd like to see a Ray's storefront with some vintage character, behold Famous Original Ray's Pizza, on Manhattan's Upper West Side.

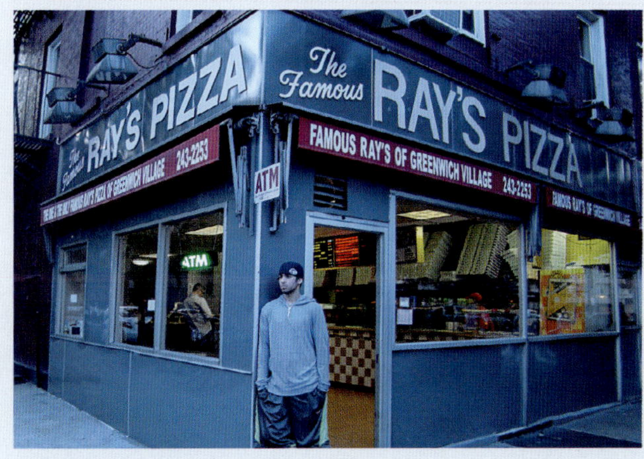

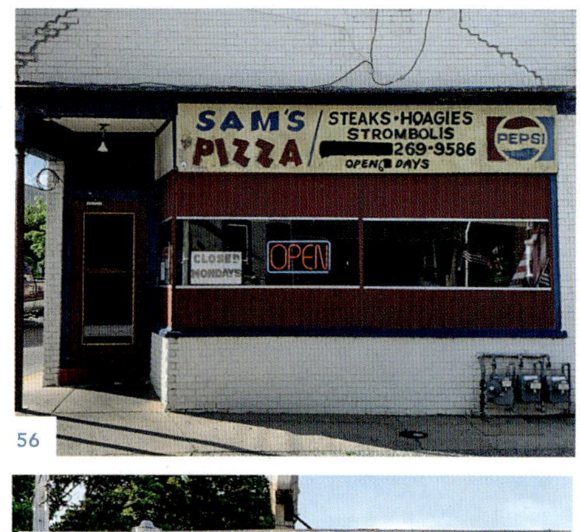

56

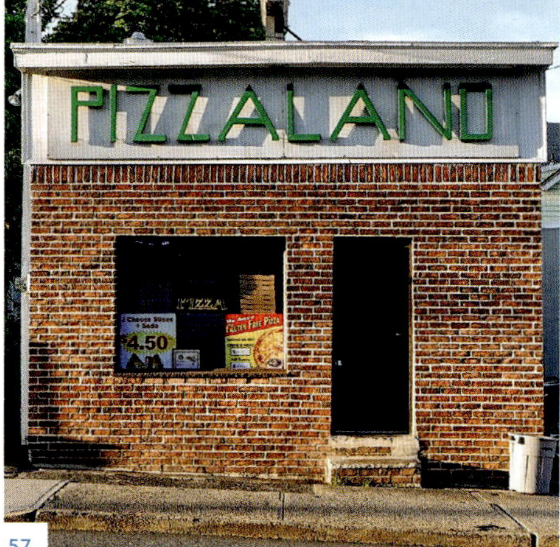

57

Up in north Jersey is the splendid **Pizza Town, U.S.A.** (FIG. 58), with Uncle Sam serving as mascot. Bruce Tomo, with his sister Michelle, long carried on the traditions started by their father, Ray, when he founded Pizza Town in 1958, slathering it in patriotic regalia to demonstrate his bona fides as a veteran—and address prejudice against these newly arrived Italians from Brooklyn.

Raymond Tomo was in the wholesale produce trade in Brooklyn and was transporting watermelons when he spotted this well-positioned Elmwood Park parcel on Route 46 near the Garden State Parkway, and he knew it would be an ideal place for a pizza joint, Bruce told me. In 1958, pizza was still a novelty, and *The Paterson Morning Call* wrote on July 25 of that year that pizza was supplanting the frankfurter in American popular taste, but finding a good slice still took some doing. Gentle readers were told that their search had ended at Pizza Town. Slices were fifteen cents and pies were a buck or a buck fifty. Today, Pizza Town is in new hands, hands that understand what they've been entrusted with.

Pulling ourselves from Gotham's gravitational pizzeria pull, **Sam's** (FIG. 56) in Downingtown, Pennsylvania, is a slice of old-school pizza heaven. It has the classic look of the pizza parlors of yore, a gem from 1977 teeming with locals who love it.

Pizza Land (FIG. 57) in North Arlington, New Jersey, makes a mean slice and drips with old-school character. Its inclusion in the opening credits of *The Sopranos* gave it pop-culture immortality.

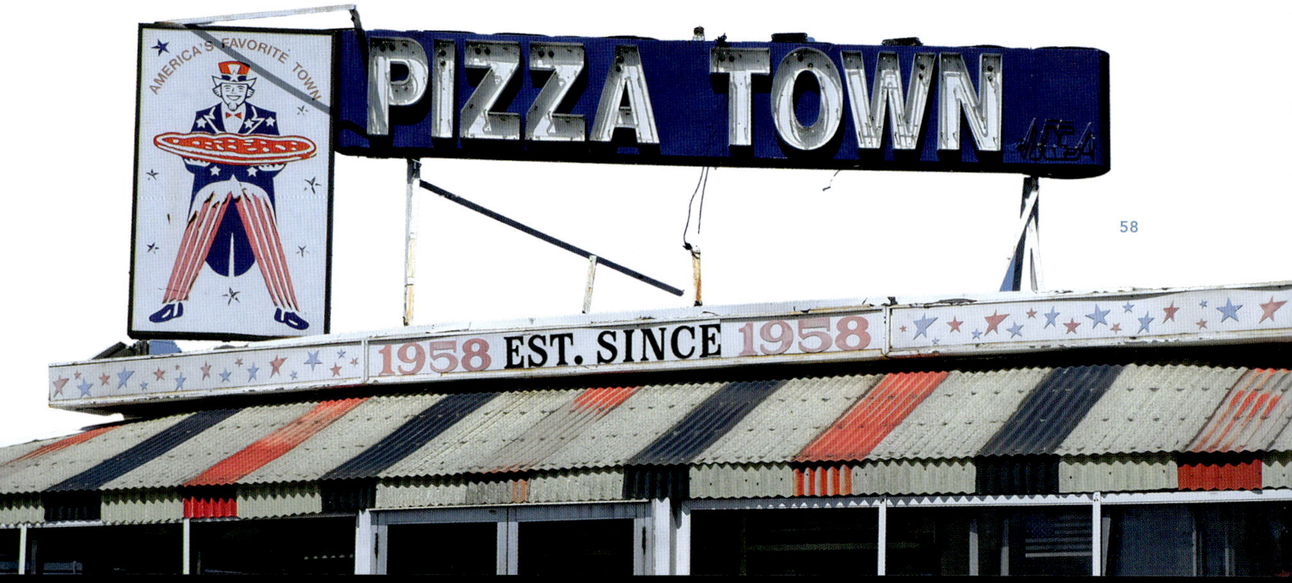

58

MAINSTAYS OF MAIN STREET

There are places that every town—or city's downtown—had or once had. They are the mainstays of Main Street, and in this section, I'll explore some of my favorite places that give (or gave, alas) their communities their special character.

Block Drugs (FIG. 59) is one of the most beautiful storefronts in New York City. Starting in 1885, the druggists at this corner of the East Village have been healing the sick or keeping the healthy away from the doctor. It wasn't until sixty years after opening, in 1945, that this store joined the now-defunct Block Drug chain.

Block Drugs has been in the caring hands of the Palermo family since 1962. They've been such good custodians—and neighbors—that they received an award from the Greenwich Village Society for Historic Preservation.

As somebody who decades ago visited Philadelphia almost every weekend, I've long had a soft spot for the **Bambi Cleaners** (FIG. 60) sign on Broad Street. It's a beloved Philadelphia icon and even inspired a work of art that briefly hung outside an art gallery in Manhattan—the work of Alex Da Corte, a native of the Philadelphia area, who saw Bambi as a reflection of his roots there.

Town & Country (FIG. 61) in Liberty, New York, a *Dirty Dancing*–era treasure of the Catskills, is now an antiques store, and the most valuable antique is the building itself and its stunning storefront designed in the 1950s, back when the existing building was converted into a clothing store for men and boys. Town & Country exudes Mondrian vibes—and, to the 1970s TV kid in me, a little *Partridge Family* bus and *Brady Bunch* staircase! But what I most appreciate here is the wonderful optimism of this facade.

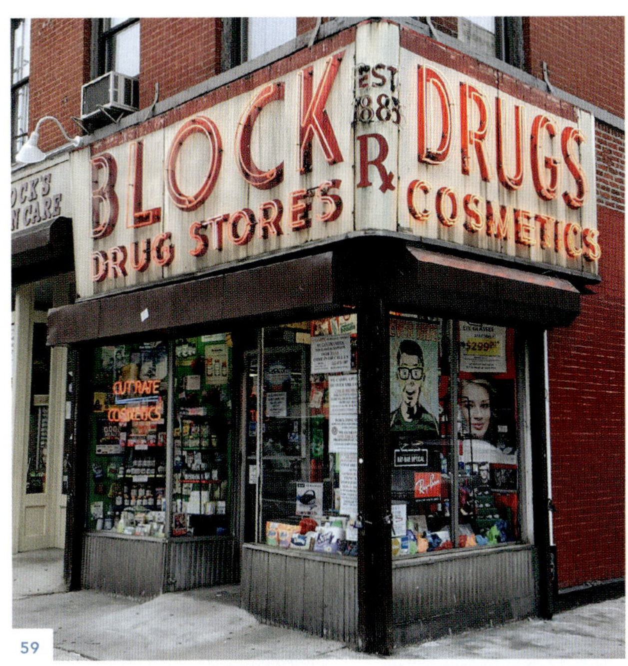

59

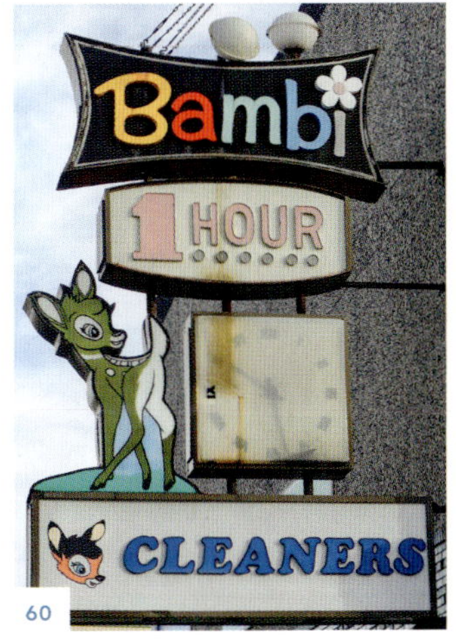

60

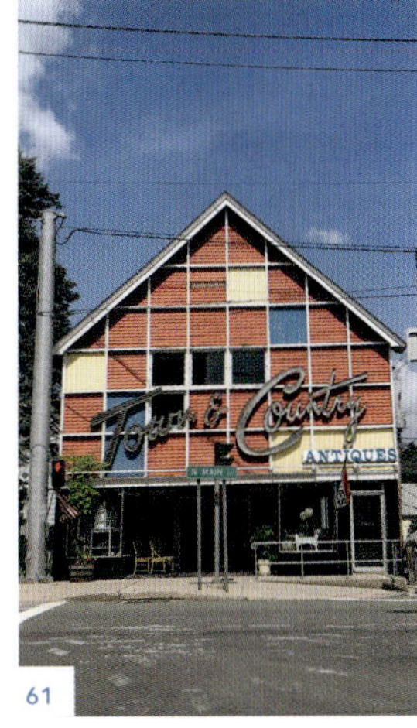

61

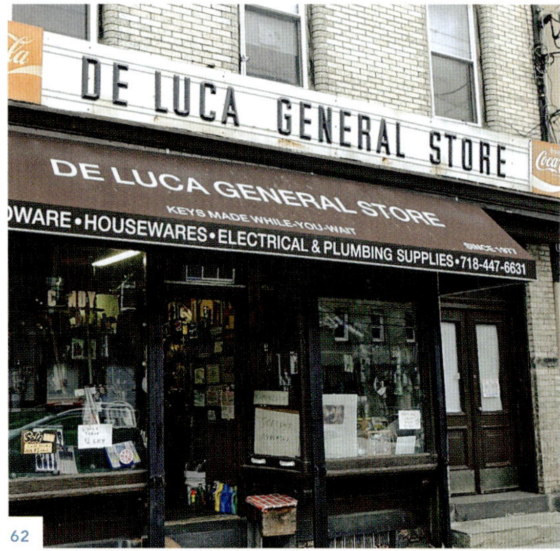

62

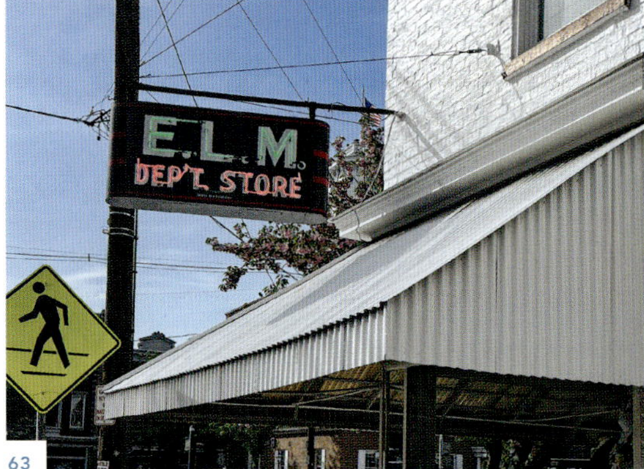

63

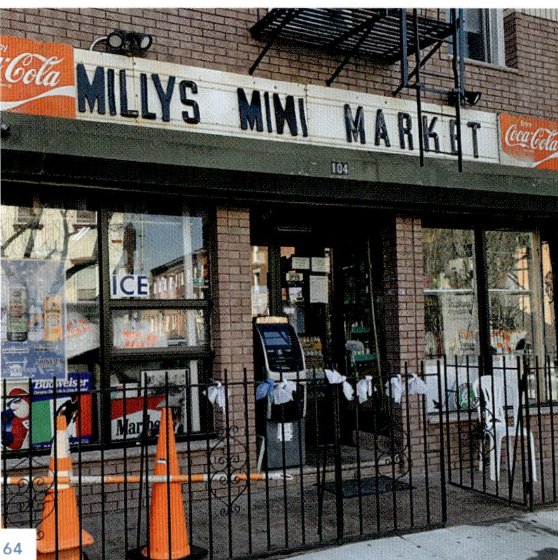

64

In the early days of the pandemic, I stopped in the Staten Island neighborhood of Rosebank to pay my respects to **De Luca General Store** (FIG. 62). Its beloved proprietor, John De Luca, died in April 2020 at age ninety, and the *Daily News* had listed the shop as one of many New York City businesses that did not survive the horrors of 2020. Frankly, I was just hoping the sign was still up. Instead, I was greeted by Enzio and Salvatore De Luca, Mr. De Luca's sons.

The brothers reopened their father's store in July 2021. The Coca-Cola privilege sign was still there, and the shelves were as packed as ever. You can even buy a Coke if you're thirsting for one—the old sign is still accurate. Indeed, this shop, which opened in 1977, is more than a hardware store. It doubles as an art gallery featuring the work of a Staten Island folk artist of Sicilian roots—their dad, John De Luca. He kept a workbench in the back where he'd bring to life all kinds of things—planes, model space shuttles, lamps—out of discarded soda and coffee cans and other daily detritus.

At the front door, you are met with a model of the Verrazzano-Narrows Bridge, made by De Luca, complete with the upper and lower levels and colorful little cars. De Luca's sons have other jobs, but they're keeping the lights on here. This place meant so much to their dad, and their dad meant so much to them, so it lives on.

Goodness do I ever love finding a classic mom-and-pop department store, especially if it's still open and serving the public. One of the nicest examples in the Northeast (just barely) is **Elm Department Store** (FIG. 63) in Greencastle, Pennsylvania, just above the Mason-Dixon Line. It's been family owned since the 1940s and still features a beautiful neon sign. Inside, it's full of cozy reminders of shopping from another time.

In South Williamsburg, Brooklyn, **Milly's Mini Mart** (FIG. 64) still exists because of the most powerful force in the world—a mother's love. In the early 1980s, Paula Lopez came to the United States from her native Peru but had to leave her daughter, Milly, behind. She found work in New York and scrimped and saved, but convincing skeptical immigration officials to let her bring Milly to New York was another matter. Her inspired solution was a dilapidated building everyone thought she was crazy to buy—104 South Second Street, a former Polish bodega with two uninhabitable floors above, gutted in a fire.

She ignored the well-meaning naysayers and renovated it herself. She even learned how to patch a roof with layers of newspaper, which held for decades. And best of all, she finally brought Milly to her new home in America and affixed her name onto the old Coca-Cola privilege sign.

Fading away, too, and at this writing, at risk of demolition, is the **Brand Park Memorial Pool** (FIG. 65) in Elmira, New York. The final summer of splashing happened here in 2005, and the toll the years of dereliction have taken on the pool is both painful and haunting. But the building's art deco curves, its elegance, beauty, and dignity, are still very much there.

65

The original pool in Brand Park opened in 1927 but was destroyed in the great flood of 1946. The city decided to rebuild, and today's pool was dedicated on July 23, 1949. It sprang from the drawing board of architect Wesley Bintz, who designed around a hundred aboveground pools in his career. The pool was a summer favorite for decades. In 1952, for instance, almost sixty-four thousand people swam here.

George's Song Shop (FIG. 66) in Johnstown, Pennsylvania, founded in 1932, has been at its current home since the late 1970s, and the charming counter by the front door proves that disco-era vintage. Crammed within the shop are millions of albums, a staggering collection of music, along with what I call patina and possibilities.

I strongly recommend, if you collect vinyl, as I do, to come armed with your wish list and time to spare because chances are, the object of your desire is in here, somewhere. Owner John George is the most expert of guides.

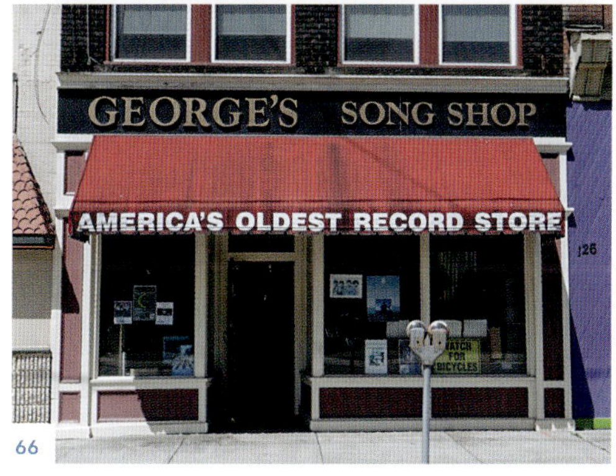

66

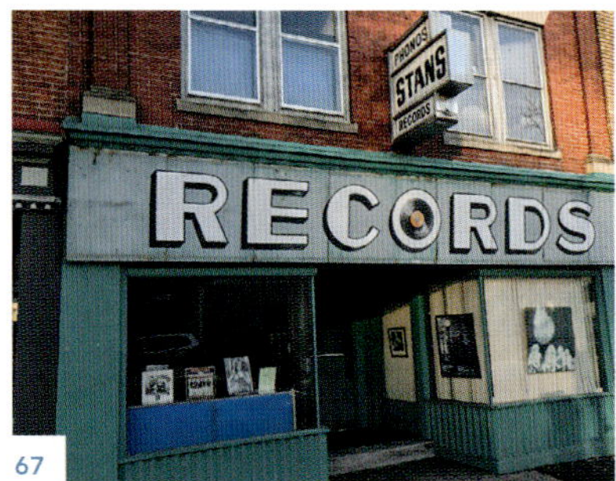

67

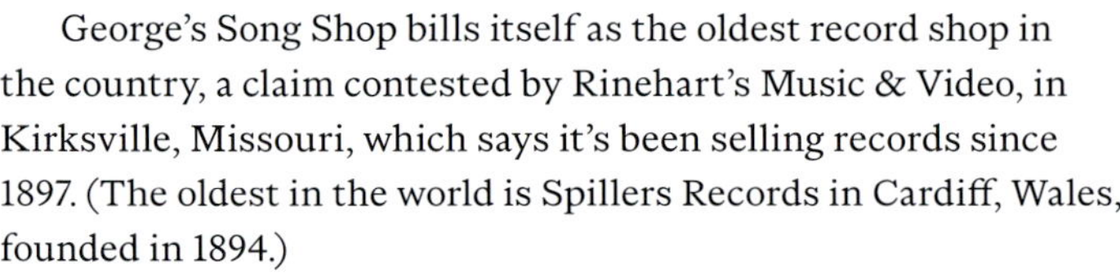

George's Song Shop bills itself as the oldest record shop in the country, a claim contested by Rinehart's Music & Video, in Kirksville, Missouri, which says it's been selling records since 1897. (The oldest in the world is Spillers Records in Cardiff, Wales, founded in 1894.)

Stan's Record Bar (FIG. 67) in Lancaster, Pennsylvania, is a good place to supplement your collection or start it from scratch. Stan's has been here since the dawn of the rock 'n' roll era—and it's still spinning. I love this storefront, complete with an album filling in for the letter *o* in "records." The plastic signage up above promotes "phonos" as well.

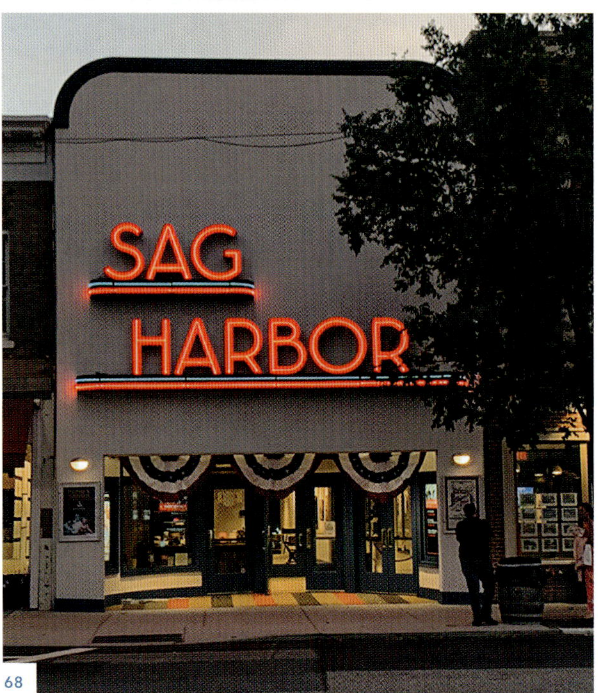

68

When **WMCA-AM** (see photo on pages 8–9) was building its stunning art deco transmission facility in 1940 in a New Jersey salt marsh, construction workers dug up petrified tree stumps. The discovery of the "prehistoric relics" was reported by the *Daily News*, and the fossils were dispatched to the American Museum of Natural History for examination. To know this wild slice of shoreline in Kearny is to believe that this is exactly the sort of place where you might dig up ancient traces of life on Earth.

This building, glimpsed from the New Jersey Turnpike, has fascinated me since I was a kid. WMCA was a New York–radio powerhouse, a pioneering AM station that embraced Top 40 and talk formats before most others. The station dates to 1925, its call letters a nod to its first home—the Hotel McAlpin (note the first three letters) in Herald Square. In 1940, AM 570 began beaming its 5,000 watts toward NYC, where it was a top station in the 1960s and brought Beatlemania to the masses. By 1970, with FM ascendant and archnemesis WABC ever stronger, WMCA went all talk. By 1989, WMCA switched to religious programming.

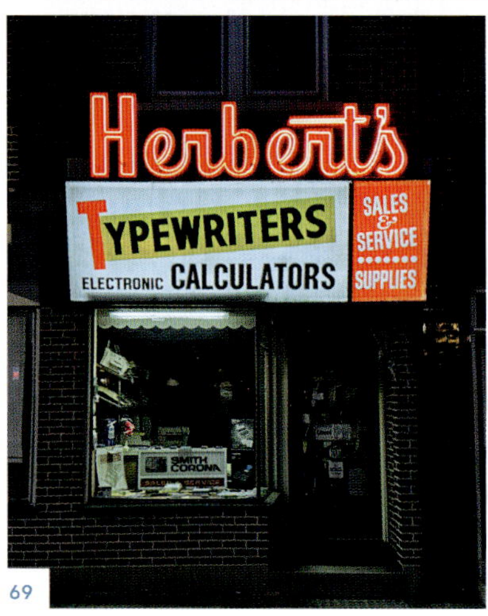

69

But its 1960s heyday under the DJs known as the "Good Guys" still captivates. All those memories emanated from this gorgeous hut, itself now a fossil from the early days of broadcasting in America.

From the radio we go to the movies, first inside: On December 16, 2016, the **Sag Harbor Cinema** (FIG. 68) as it exists today was only a dream, a dream that had gone up in smoke. A fire devastated this historic building—with roots in the vaudeville era—on Long Island's East End. Silent films gave way to talkies here, and twentieth-century-Hollywood magic dazzled locals in what was once a simple fishing village that the writer John Steinbeck called home.

But all was not lost for the cinema. The neon sign was saved, as was the main auditorium inside. Also not lost was the grit and determination of a group of volunteers. They stuck to the vision of transforming the creaky art-house theater into a vital community hub for the arts. The longtime owner sold them the charred husk of the cinema, and they got to work. "Got to work" glosses over just how much effort went into raising money and realizing their dream. But less than five years later, Main Street in this charming village was whole again. The facade is restored. The sign glows anew. The theater inside is a crisp, sophisticated affair featuring three screening rooms, a top-floor bar with wonderful sunset views, a chic cafe and shop, and much more.

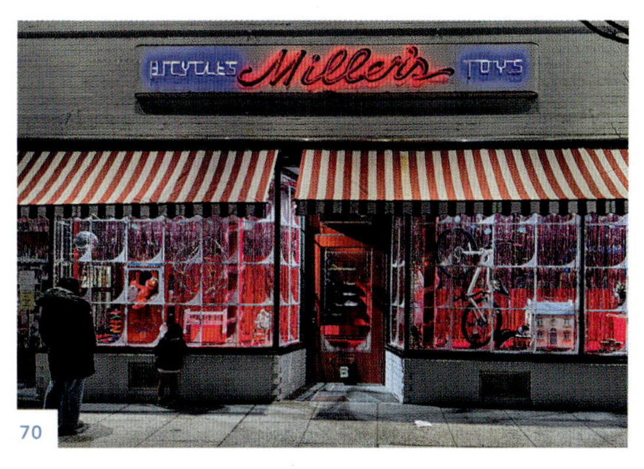

70

Malta Drive-In (FIG. 71) in Malta, New York, puts on a show at first glance, with its majestic Googie sign.

In Pennsylvania, the **Mahoning Drive-In Theater** almost became another sad statistic in the slow purge that has claimed 92 percent of America's drive-in theaters, which peaked around four thousand in 1958. The costly transition to digital projection should have killed this theater, but instead, they opted to go retro, showing only classic 35-millimeter prints of films.

Herbert's Typewriters (FIG. 69) in Bethlehem, Pennsylvania, opened in 1928 and picked up its fantastic signage decades later. The last time the signage was updated, calculators were the hot new thing. I hope to drop off my precious typewriter (an Olivetti Valentine) here someday for some TLC.

In 1908, Joseph Miller founded **Miller's** (FIG. 70), a bike and baby carriage shop in the Harlem neighborhood of New York City. His son moved the business to Mamaroneck, New York, in Westchester County, in 1948, and settled into this storefront about a decade later. Miller's is still in the family, still sells bikes and offers a carefully selected collection of toys. It is the mom-and-pop toy store of your imagination, perhaps your dreams.

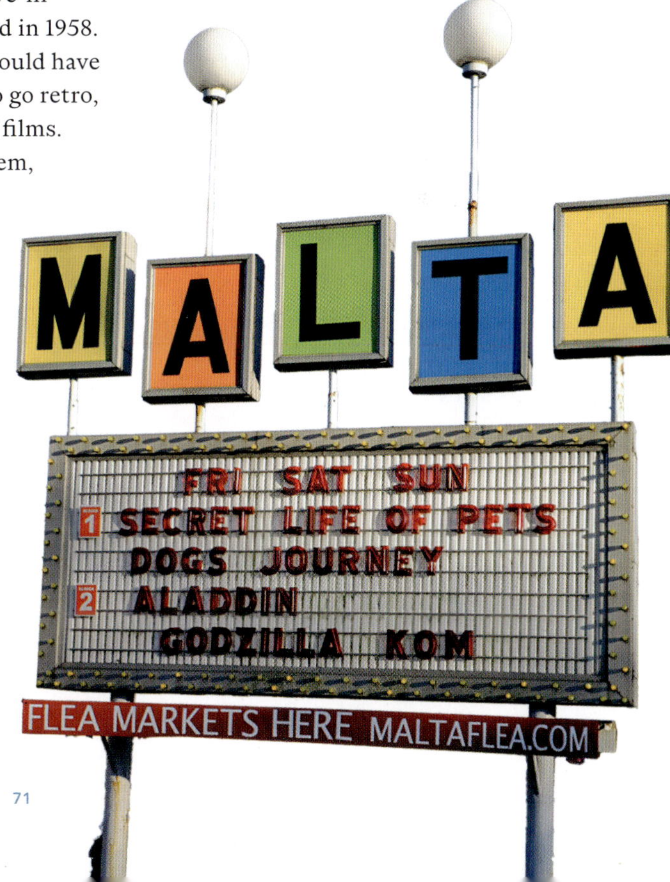

71

HERITAGE BRANDS

I have a soft spot for advertising and the use of symbols and characters in signs and storefronts across the nation. In this section, we'll explore how Madison Avenue is never far from Main Street.

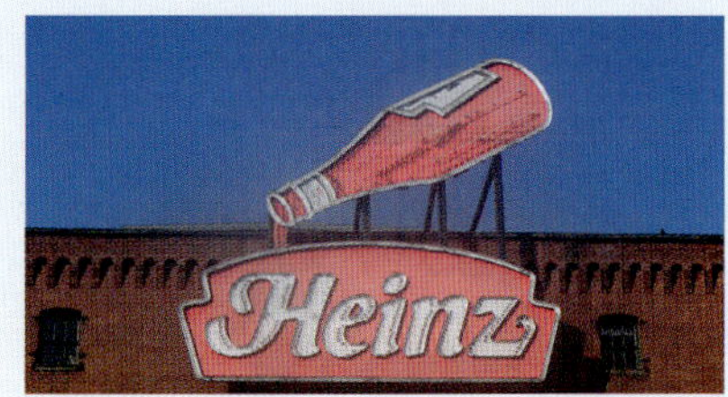

The epic **Heinz ketchup sign** in Pittsburgh makes me think of the old "Anticipation" TV commercials for Heinz featuring the Carly Simon tune. In those late-1970s ads, you'd wait for that ketchup to ooze out of the bottle and onto a hamburger, or in the tribute here, to empty into the Heinz logo.

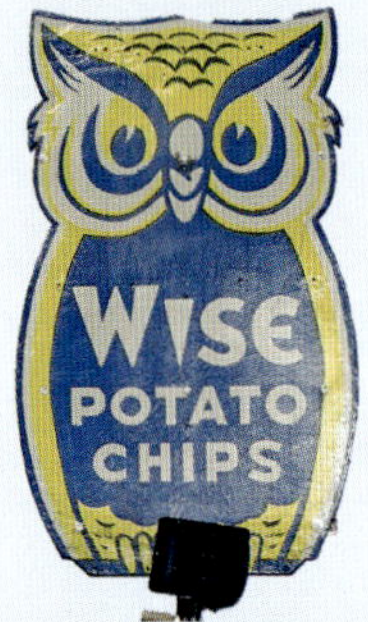

Growing up just north of New York City, **Wise Potato Chips** was my go-to bag. The company traces its roots to a smart fellow named Earl Wise, a Berwick, Pennsylvania, grocer who in 1921 began to cook chips from his excess potatoes in his mom's copper kettle. He'd put them in brown paper bags and sell them at his deli. His chips business took off, growing rapidly and surviving a calamitous factory fire in 1944. His last name, Wise, led to the owl logo, of course. After Wise's death in 1963, he was heralded as "a living testimony to the verity of the legend of American enterprise" in the *Danville News*.

Fortunately for admirers of the New York area's industrial heritage, a replica of the classic **Domino Sugar Co.** sign in Williamsburg, Brooklyn, was reinstalled in 2023 at the site of the long-shuttered factory. The original sign was removed in 2014, so this promised return was a long time coming.

There are significant differences between the old and new signs, chiefly that LED technology has replaced the neon, though this new sign is brighter. It's made of aluminum, in contrast with the Artkraft Strauss original, which was made of stainless steel and porcelain.

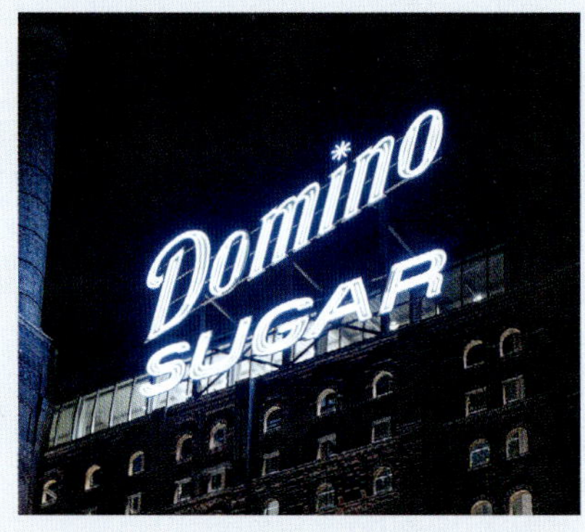

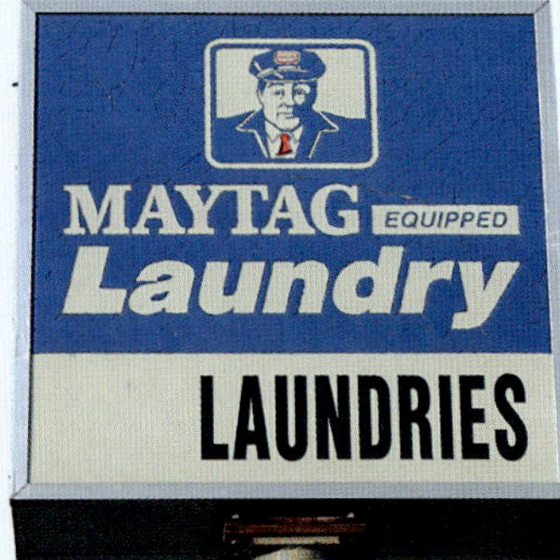

They call him Ol' Lonely, and he looks extra lonely outside this laundromat in Wilmington, Delaware. Ol' Lonely is, of course, the **Maytag Repairman**, an iconic advertising character.

The Maytag Repairman first hit the airwaves in 1967 and was played by actor Jesse White. The conceit was that the Maytag Repairman was lonely because his company's products were so reliable that they never needed fixing, and so Ol' Lonely waited and waited for his dusty telephone to ring.

Ol' Lonely eventually got a basset hound for company and, starting in 1989, he was depicted by a different actor, Gordon Jump, best known for playing Mr. Carlson on the sitcom *WKRP in Cincinnati*.

The **Sullivan Dairy** (FIG. 72) in Hurleyville, New York, and **Krauss Photo** (FIG. 74) in Port Jervis, New York, feature storefronts with beautiful porcelain enamel and art deco vibes. Sullivan Dairy no longer dispenses fresh milk and cream. When I visited a few years ago, they were dispensing fresh haircuts. This building is a vivid link to the area's days as a dairy-farming bastion.

Gus Krauss operated Krauss Photo for much of the twentieth century. After his death in 1977, he was praised for his pivotal role in chronicling this upstate city and for the collection of postcards and photographic equipment he amassed. The facade is a masterpiece of retail beauty, and the Kodak sign was once a familiar sight in downtowns across the land.

How about this for a generational family business: When I visited **Battley's Barber Shop** (FIG. 73) in 2020, Jimmy Battley was ninety-five years young. He's been cutting hair at Battley's Barber Shop, the family business, in Hazleton, Pennsylvania, since 1935. A quick calculation will tell you that he was just a kid when he began to learn the trade and, indeed, he needed to jump on a crate to give his first haircuts.

Just fifteen years later, Jimmy was named head barber after his father was injured in a coal-mining accident. And seventy years later, he was still giving haircuts like the boss that he is. He showed off the sharp cut he was giving a gentleman visiting from Harrisburg. The customer seemed as excited as I was to be there, where the chairs date to the Kennedy Administration and have ashtrays built into the armrests.

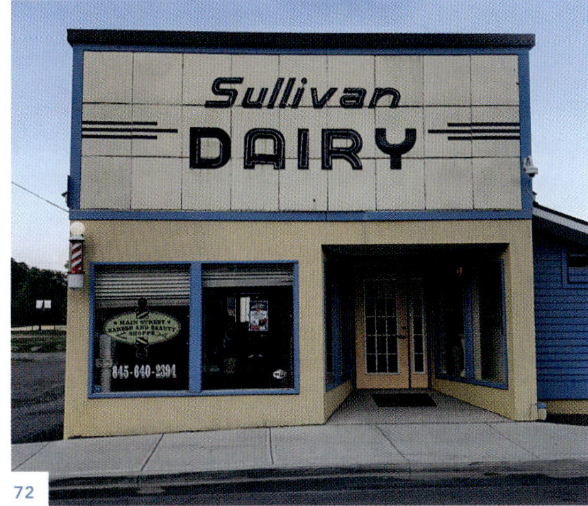

72

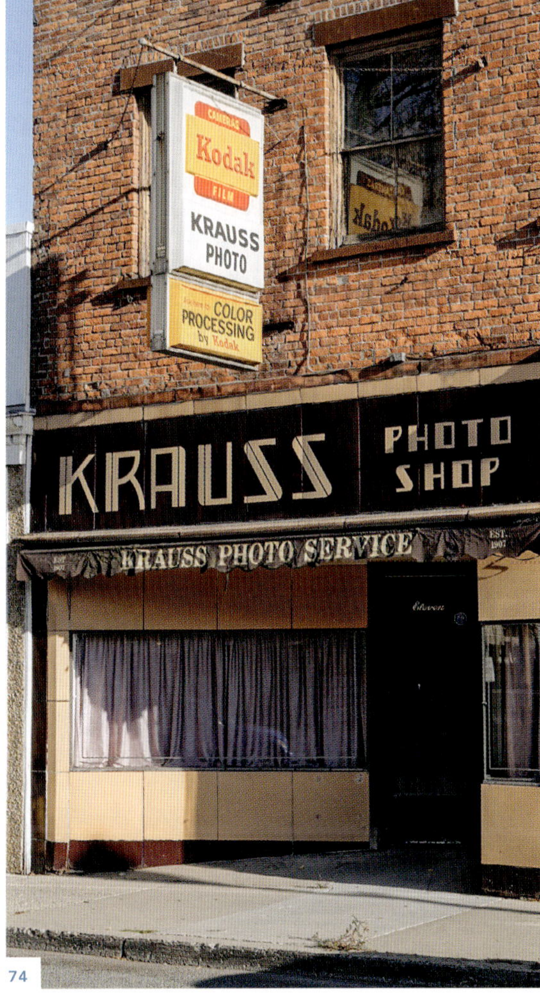

74

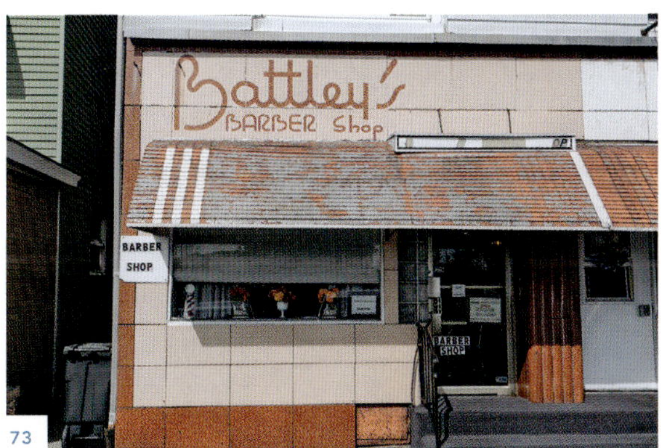

73

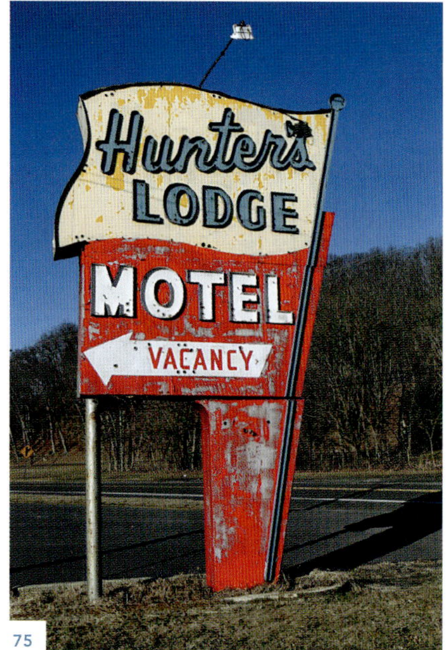

75

THE INN CROWD

After all this driving so far from home, here are some spots to get some rest—or at least memorable photos.

The Hunter's Lodge (FIG. 75) was a final stop on one of my long and winding drives along beautiful Route 46 in New Jersey, taking you from the George Washington Bridge to the Pennsylvania border. Along the way are charming Victorian towns, creeks, scenic hills, sun-kissed chrome diners, and Sinclair gas stations with statues. Hunter's Lodge is the special gift that awaits near the end of the highway. Everything about it is grand: the colors, the fonts, the shape, even the shadow the sign casts on Route 46 from the low winter sun. Put this sign on your bucket list, too—along with a drive along underappreciated Route 46.

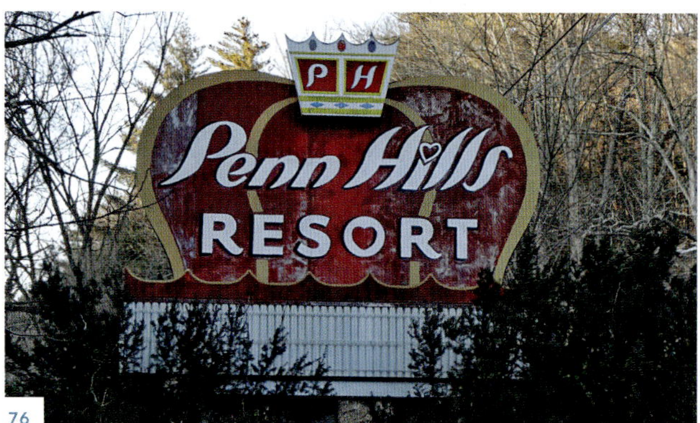

76

Penn Hills Resort (FIG. 76) in the Poconos, not far from Hunter's Lodge, has been abandoned for many years. The sprawling complex has deteriorated dramatically since closing shortly after its 102-year-old cofounder died in 2009. The sign, made famous in ads that ran continuously on local TV in the 1970s and '80s, was still standing in 2018, but last I heard had been defaced.

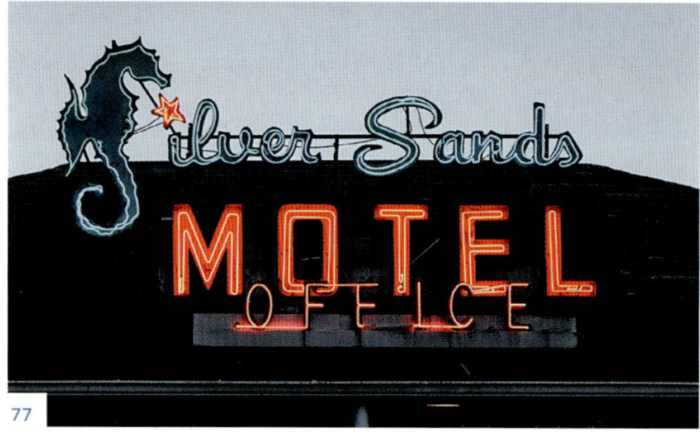

77

Down on the eastern end of Long Island is a reminder that the world needs more neon seahorses. When you take one look at the sign for the **Silver Sands Motel** (FIG. 77) in Greenport, New York, it's easy to see why. This motel has been sitting on a slice of heaven on Long Island's North Fork since 1957. The Silver Sands has its own private beach, Peconic Bay at your feet, and Shelter Island is a short ferry ride away. After a recent renovation, the motel remains a midcentury gem freshened up for today, an escape by the sea hidden by acres of woods from Route 25.

On Long Island's South Fork, the **Memory Motel** (FIG. 78) is an easy place to make good memories. More than forty years ago, the story goes, this same motel inspired the Rolling Stones' song "Memory Motel," released in 1976 on the group's *Black and Blue* album. The ballad, a collaboration between Mick Jagger and Keith Richards, is said to have come to life during an extended visit the band made to Andy Warhol's nearby estate.

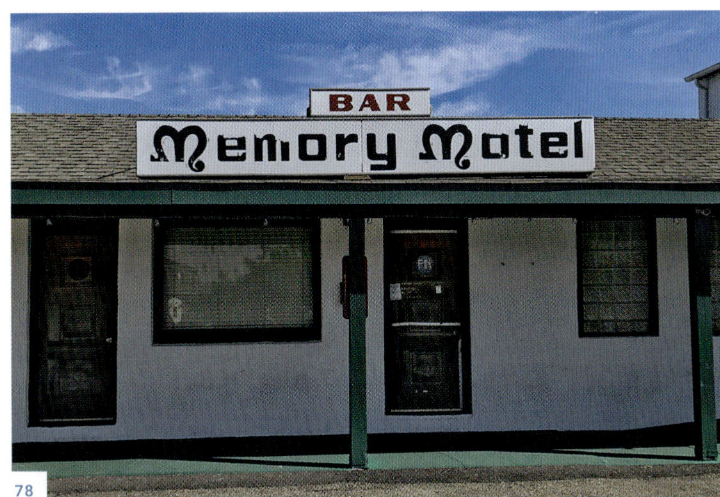

78

A few hours upstate, Alix Umen was starstruck when she drove by the **Starlite Motel** (FIG. 79) in Kerhonkson, New York, a hamlet tucked into the lovely Shawangunk Mountains region of Ulster County. Alix is a former Brooklyn resident who has worked in fashion and design for thirty years and had moved up this way. One day while driving, she pulled over and struck up a conversation with Hildegard Simcik, who'd been running the motel alone since her husband, Walter, died in 2003. Hildegard was in her eighties and had few customers, and was ready to call it quits, Alix told me in an email interview in 2020.

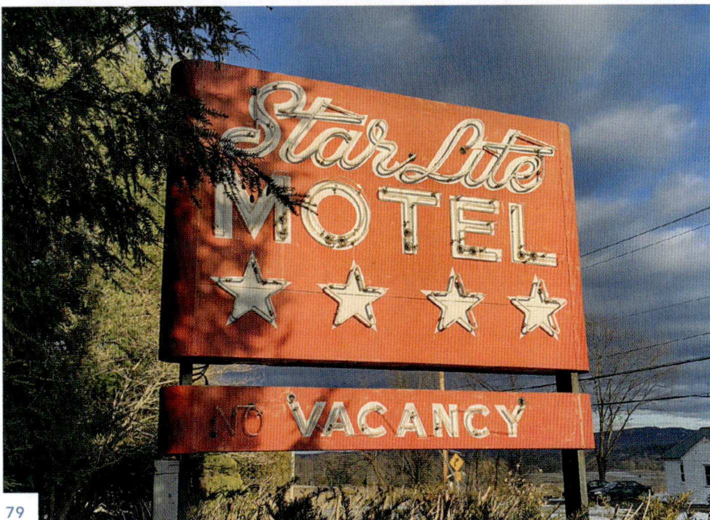

79

Alix bought the motel in 2018, and with her partner, the artist Adriana Farmiga, set about, over the course of a year, renovating the place—through a fabulous filter that blends the aesthetic of filmmaker Wes Anderson with Scandinavian and midcentury design.

The motel reopened in December 2019. Alix and Adriana have really captured the soul of the place. To wit, the blue/teal color they selected for the doors turned out to be remarkably similar to the choice the original owners, the Simpson family, made in the 1960s. In its heyday, the motel had an ice-cream shop and was even featured in the 1985 cult horror movie *The Stuff*, in which the neon sign gets a well-deserved close-up. Today, there is an on-site canteen, a gift shop, and even a collection of postcards featuring different Starlite motels around the country.

STORES OF YORE

Across the Northeast are ghosts of chains that are no more, like Ames, and stores that are almost no more, like Kmart and Sears, and stores that are no more but are now back for more, like Toys "R" Us. Then there are the former mighty chains that somehow persist as a loosely connected agglomeration of stores—really mom-and-pops with a shared corporate heritage—such as Ben Franklin. The retrologist mindset is that of an urban archaeologist. It's about looking for traces of what was, often hiding in plain sight. One of the finest examples of this can be found in the hunt for defunct chains. Here are handful of examples in the Northeast.

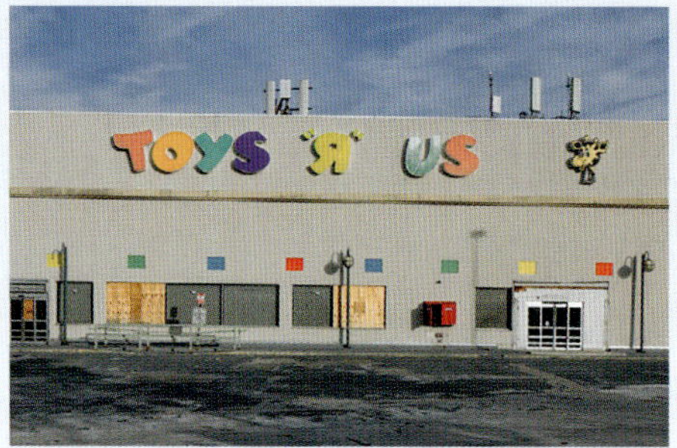

I'll always be a Toys "R" Us kid, and until the spring of 2018, the United States was home to hundreds of **Toys "R" Us** stores, a handful still sporting their iconic 1970s–80s brown mansard roofs and candy-striped fascia.

The chain thrives in Canada. In the United States, the intellectual property was scooped up and the brand, launched as Children's Bargain Town by Charles Lazarus in 1948, is being revived. But we have lost the unique vibe—or distinctive olfactory experience—of the old-school Toys "R" Us shops in the United States.

Another toy-store ghost haunts an **Ollie's Bargain Outlet** in Lancaster, Pennsylvania. This is a well-preserved example of the defunct **Child World/Children's Palace** toy-store chain, which went bankrupt in 1992. Child World was founded in Quincy, Massachusetts, in 1962, and when it acquired another chain called Children's Palace, they had assembled enough stores to become number two only to Toys "R" Us.

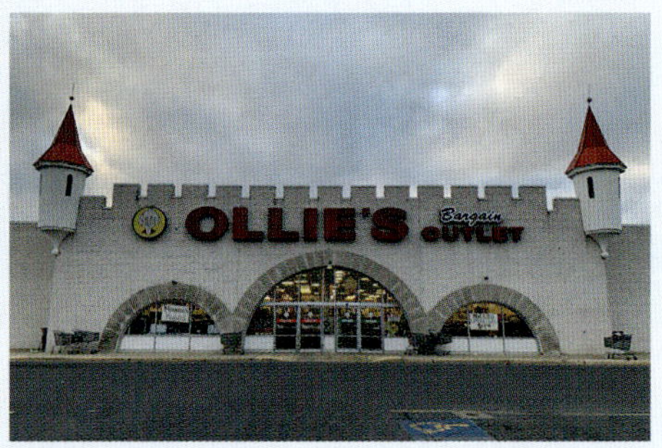

Child World embraced the architecture of Children's Palace, which involved turning the toy warehouse into a massive castle on the outside, with turrets, battlements, and arches galore. Child World held its own during the 1970s and '80s, when mascot Peter Panda hawked toys in TV commercials.

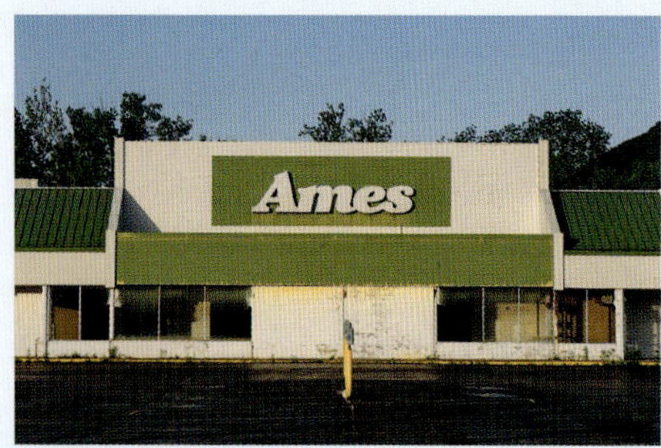

It's been more than twenty years since anyone has shopped at an **Ames** department store. But at its peak, Ames was in twenty states and boasted seven hundred stores, with more than $2 billion a year in sales, and was up there with the Kmarts of the world as a go-to place for savings. Stores were clustered mainly in the Northeast, but they also extended into the Midwest and Southeast, including Florida. The discount chain, saddled by a heap of debt and a lack of customers, finally closed after forty-four years in August 2002.

However, in the Southern Tier section of New York State, you'll find perhaps the best-preserved remnant of Ames in the village of Horseheads (seen here), and while a little worse for the wear, it was still holding on in 2022, when I visited.

Its roots may have been in Boston, but **Ben Franklin** is associated not with big cities but with small towns. Ben Franklin was one of the great five-and-dime chains of the twentieth century, once numbering around twenty-five hundred locations. A number of them are still hanging on, but not really part of a chain anymore. Behold this beauty on the Jersey Shore in Lavallette.

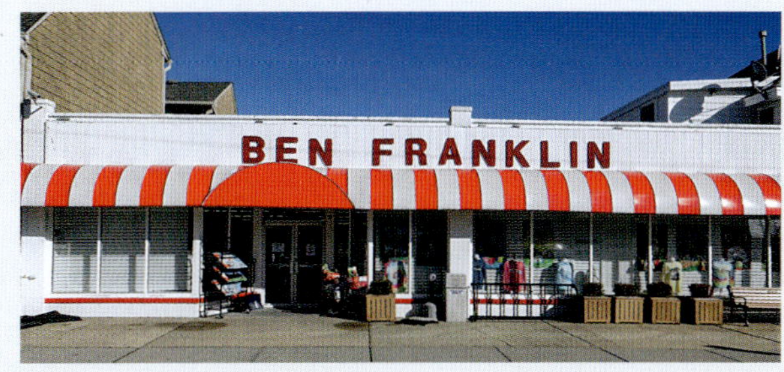

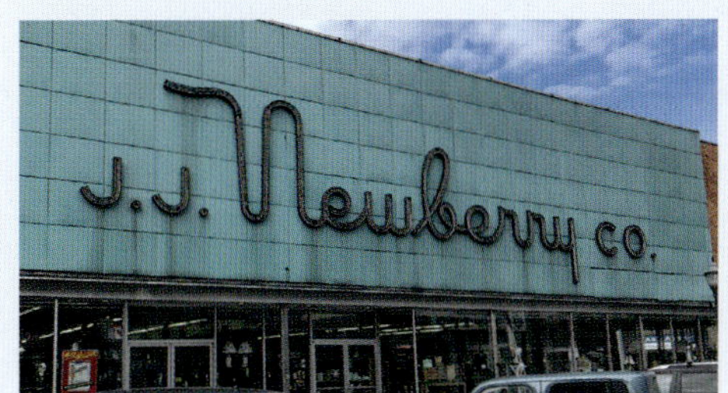

The last of the **J.J. Newberry** stores closed in 2001 after a ninety-year run, but many downtowns across America still bear traces of the vanished five-and-dime. A truly gorgeous example survives upstate in Owego, New York. The store opened in 1958 and looks much the same today. The turquoise tiles and sweeping neon script draw you in, and what awaits you inside is an antiques mall that preserves much of the DNA of the old store.

Perhaps the greatest of supermarket chains was the Great Atlantic & Pacific Tea Company, known to you and me as **A&P**. The chain went bust in 2015. One of the finest surviving traces of A&P remained until recently in Clinton, New Jersey, and what a joy it was, the 1970s logo standing here until the very end.

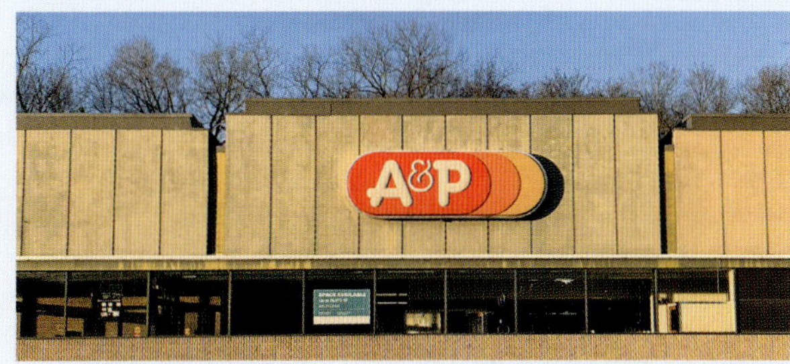

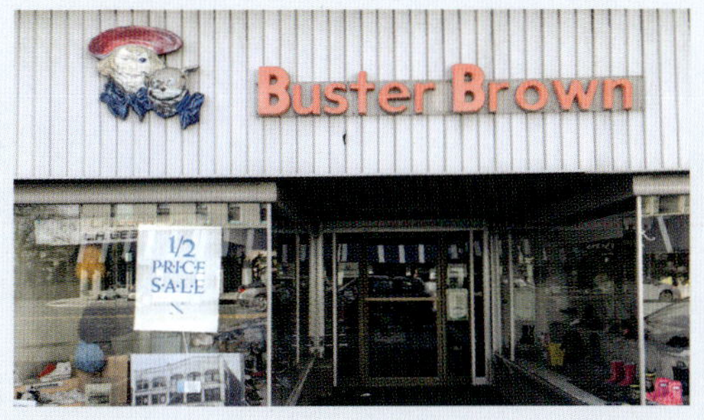

Back in 2019, a dear friend, knowing me too well, texted me a photo of something I never thought I'd see again: a **Buster Brown** shoe sign "in the wild." This was on the facade of now-closed Jim's House of Shoes in Pittsfield, Massachusetts.

Over the years I had photographed two long-gone Buster Brown facades, in Jackson Heights and Forest Hills, both neighborhoods in Queens, New York. And I have fond memories of being fitted with these shoes at the Buster Brown on Broadway in Tarrytown, New York.

In Pottstown, Pennsylvania, is the stunning facade of the **New York Store**. Repurposed as New York Plaza after the shop closed in the 1980s, it still makes a mighty impression in the heart of downtown.

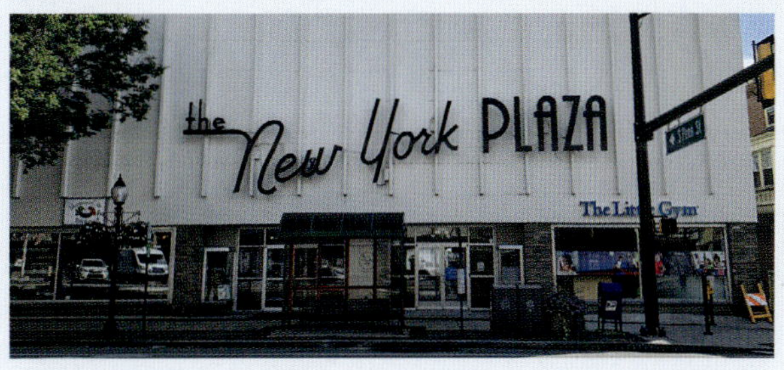

SWEET STOPS

From ice cream to candy to rugelach—if it's sweet and it's historical, it has a home here.

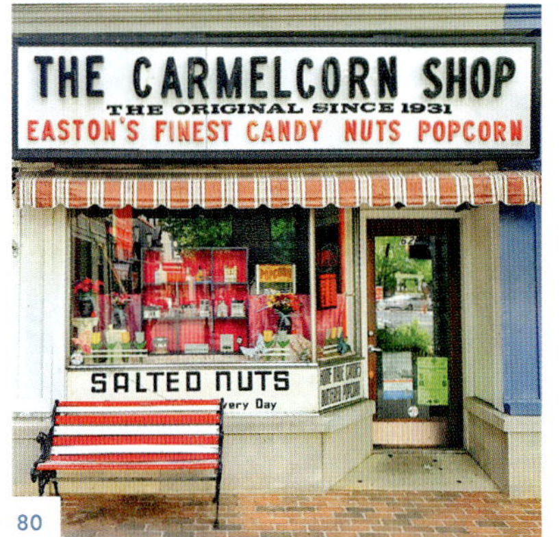

80

The **Carmelcorn Shop** (FIG. 80) in Easton, Pennsylvania, is a sweet tooth's paradise—or downfall. The business traces back to 1931 and is just what a candy store should look like. Everything from homemade caramel popcorn and fudge to nuts and old-time candies is purveyed. I love that a candy shop that opened in the Great Depression and survived a fire in 2006 is still going strong.

Parkside Candy (FIGS. 81, 82) must be seen to be believed. And its chocolates, ice cream, and famous sponge candy (a western New York thing) must be tasted to be believed. The beloved Buffalo, New York, confectioners first opened in the Parkside neighborhood in 1917, acquiring the name it would retain when it moved to this prominent corner of University Heights in 1927.

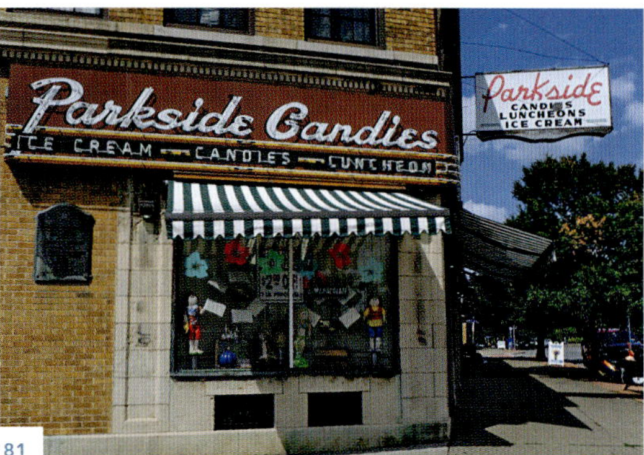

81

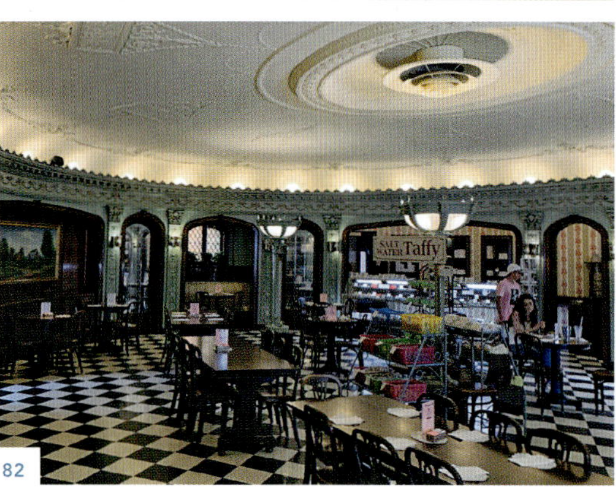

82

The business was founded and run by the Kaiser family until Philip Buffamonte took over in 1981, and he has been a caring custodian of the business, recently completing a $250,000 renovation that left the place looking better than ever. Oh, and I'll leave it to Parkside itself to get to the heart of what sponge candy is: "Our rich milk chocolate Sponge Candy is crunchy on the inside with a molasses taste. It will melt in your mouth with smooth rich creamy chocolate on the outside. Parkside Candy is famous for this chocolate classic treat." In other words, it's good!

Old Monmouth Candies (FIG. 83) in Freehold, New Jersey, is a delight at all times of year, but the Big Easter Candy Show is as sweet a time as any to go. It's an annual tradition at Old Monmouth, which started in the kitchen of a long-vanished diner down the street in 1939. During the downtimes, one of the owners, Lou Dey, put his German candy-making skills to use, and they soon found that the candy was more popular than the sandwiches.

Old Monmouth Candies moved here in 1948, the property expanding over the years as demand for their sweets grew—in particular the peanut brittle, a dangerously addictive recipe dating to 1910.

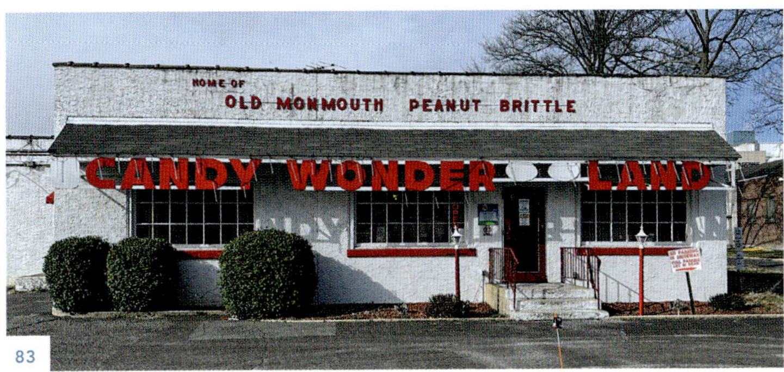

83

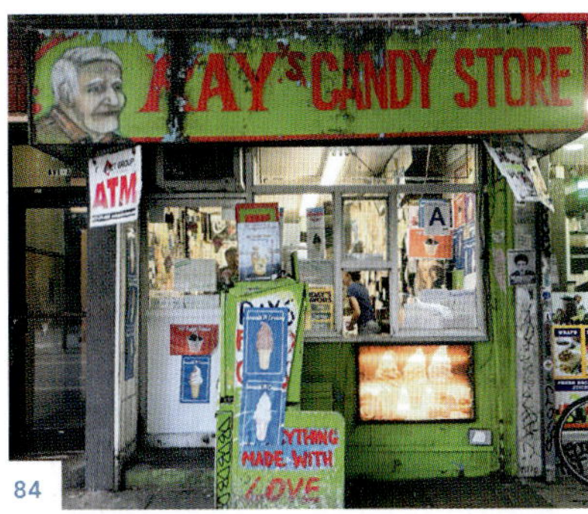

84

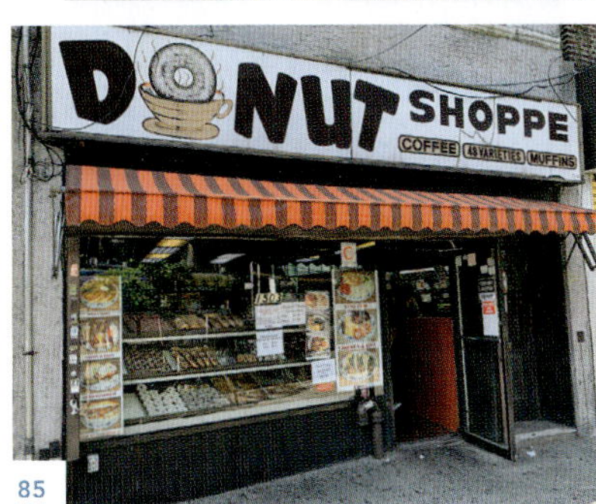

85

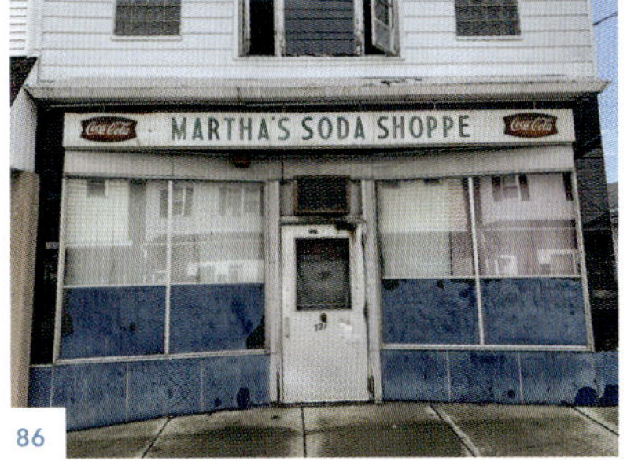

86

New Jersey sure has a sweet tooth, which is satisfyingly indulged at the **Caramel Shop** on Route 35 in Ocean Township. Back in 1933, the year the store opened, peanut brittle was 19 cents a pound and pure cream caramel set you back 20 cents more. Today, a pound of assorted chocolates goes for between $24 and $48. Times change, but not demand for tasty, homemade candy.

Ray's Candy Store (FIG. 84) in New York's East Village, and its delightful, eponymous nonagenarian shopkeeper, is still thriving, offering egg creams to wash down the savory deli offerings.

Now we'll go from sweets to donuts—an easy enough transition. Remaining in New York, we head over to south Brooklyn and the **Donut Shoppe** (FIG. 85). Although it has a new name, the sixty-plus-year-old business still proudly embraces its baking heritage in the signage—and on the racks inside as well. That's all thanks to Shaikh Kalam, who first worked here in 1983, bought the business in 1994, renamed the place after himself but respected its heritage enough to leave that wonderful sign alone. If you google "Donut Shoppe," you'll see Shaikh's Place come up. The names are used interchangeably.

A showpiece of downtown Avoca, Pennsylvania, is **Martha's Soda Shoppe** (FIG. 86), which is closed and brimming with mystery. A ramble through decades of newspaper clippings puts together a story of a very special place, where Andrew and Martha Coffee (their real names) created a home away from home for neighborhood kids, as Mr. Coffee's 2010 obituary reported. The old shoppe had a counter, a pool table and snacks, and soda, of course. It was a simple place that had already been around for almost a quarter century when Andrew's wife died, way back in 1979. He carried on.

We've seen lots of sweet stories in this section, but **Sweetheart Corner** (FIG. 87) in Syracuse, New York, wins the prize. Here we play the third wheel to an amorous couple admiring each other on the store's signage. The market is long gone, but the sign lives on outside a Rite Aid.

87

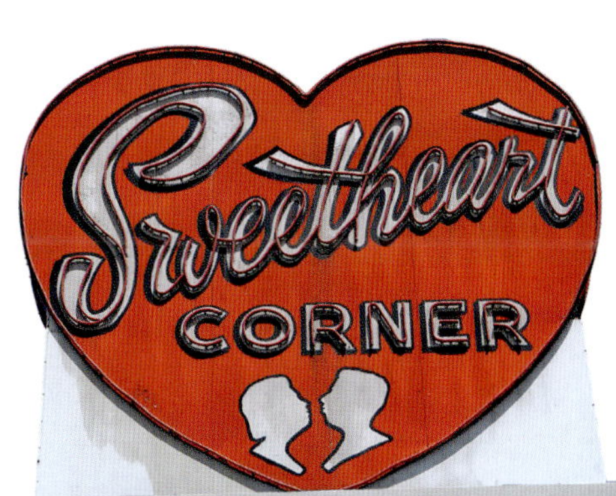

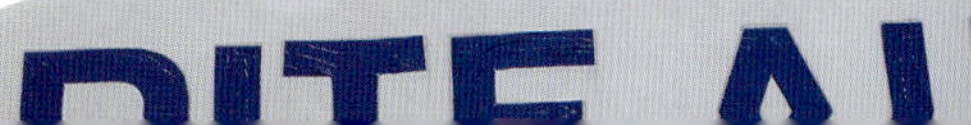

SOFT SERVE EMPIRE: CARVEL

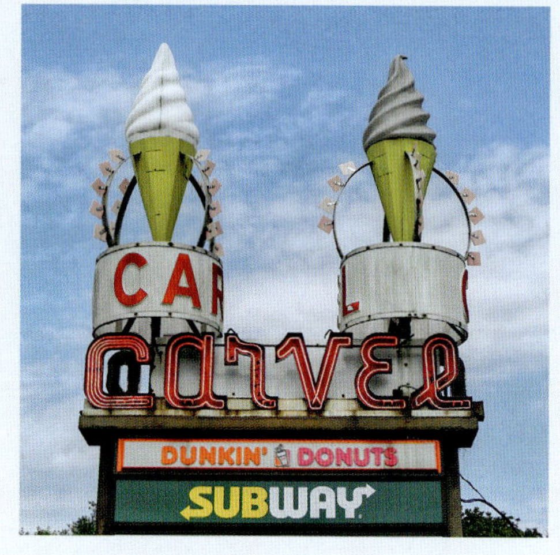

On Memorial Day weekend in 1934, Thomas Carvelas was twenty-eight years old but had already racked up a lifetime of living. At the age of four, he'd emigrated from Greece to Manhattan's Lower East Side, his big family among the legions trying to find their way in America. The young Carvelas had already tried out a few careers, among them Dixieland band drummer and auto mechanic in New York City. He had a head for machinery, too, which would come in handy later.

His life took a fateful turn in 1932, when a doctor told him he had tuberculosis. Carvelas figured he'd be wise to get out of the city. Westchester County, just to the north, beckoned, promising a restorative elixir of fresh air and nature. Turned out, Carvelas did not have TB, but no matter, he'd find his life's calling in Westchester: iconic ice-cream man with an Anglicized last name, Carvel.

There were no Carvel stores in the early days—just a truck he'd bought with a $15 loan from his wife, Agnes, which he would joke that he never repaid. That truck broke down on Memorial Day weekend 1934, a flat tire marooning him across from a pottery store at 95 South Central Avenue in Hartsdale, New York. He made a sale before he could figure out what to do. Customers didn't mind the melty ice cream, and they kept coming. He stayed put for the weekend, hooking up his truck to a power outlet at the pottery shop, and cleared $100—a pretty good haul in the middle of the Great Depression. Soft ice cream, huh? Okay, soft ice cream it is. Fate had served him with a big idea. Carvel, the lore goes, turned what could have been a ruinous experience into a recipe for building a business that would lead to hundreds of stores and wealth so vast he owned three homes, along with his own golf course.

Carvel retired in 1989, selling the company he and his wife owned for more than $80 million. (We can assume she got back her $15 at this point.) Tom Carvel did not get to enjoy that retirement for very long. The next year, after a day of golfing, Carvel died in his sleep at the age of eighty-four.

Carvel the brand is alive and well, and several legacy stores from Tom Carvel's time survive, many in a form he would recognize. Alas, the original location in Hartsdale was demolished after closing in late 2008. But a plaque in the grass just outside the building—now a hibachi restaurant—honors Carvel's legacy.

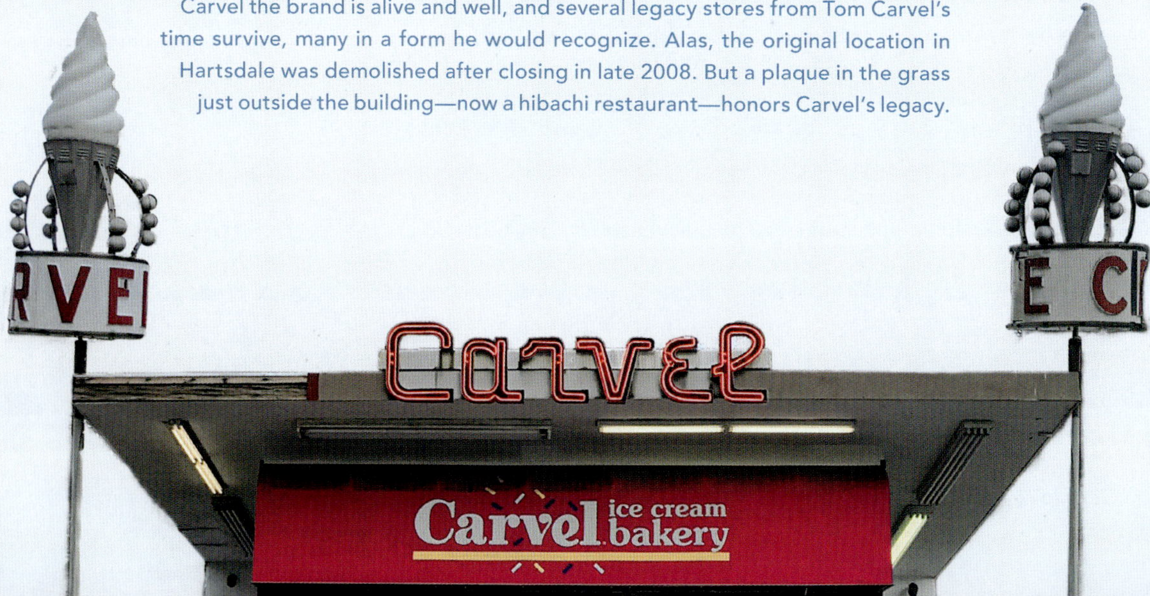

One of America's most beautiful roadside eateries, **Schell's** (FIG. 88) has been serving up comfort food in Temple, Pennsylvania, since 1952. The complex features a restaurant and ice-cream bar, the **Dairy Swirl**, right next door. Together, they make quite an impression.

In 1933, King Kong scaled the Empire State Building in the film starring Fay Wray, and forty years later, he was back, tackling a much more manageable target: the **King Kone** (FIG. 89) ice-cream stand in Elmira, New York. In 1973, Ulisse Spaziani and his wife, Nellie, opened King Kone. The emphasis was on soft serve. No hard serve, in part because scooping it could be hell on the arms after a while, Mrs. Spaziani told the *Star-Gazette* in 2004.

The gorilla cutout is a local landmark, with King Kone here trading his beloved Ann Darrow for a vanilla ice-cream cone. In the 1933 movie, gunfire from pesky planes leads to Kong's downfall. On April 7, 1986, it was a malevolent gust of wind that knocked King Kone to the ground. Replacing it wasn't high on Mr. Spaziani's priority list at first, but customers were bereft without their cherished 7-foot-tall plywood cutout, and a rebuilt Kong soon scaled the shop's heights anew.

The Adirondacks is a preserve of memory-making ice-cream stands. I first visited **Custard's Last Stand** (FIG. 90) in the summer of 2019, and it was quickly evident to me that this classic ice-cream shop in Long Lake, New York, was popular. Custard's is now under new ownership, partnered with another old-school ice-cream stand, Jones Humdinger of Binghamton.

Whitebrook Dairy Bar (FIG. 91) is another Adirondack gem, the very picture of an idyllic country ice-cream stand. It's in Wilmington, New York, a charming town that features mini golf, an A&W root beer stand, and a Santa theme, as it's home to a hamlet—and fun family attraction—named North Pole! Just the perfect place, in other words, for an ice-cream stand.

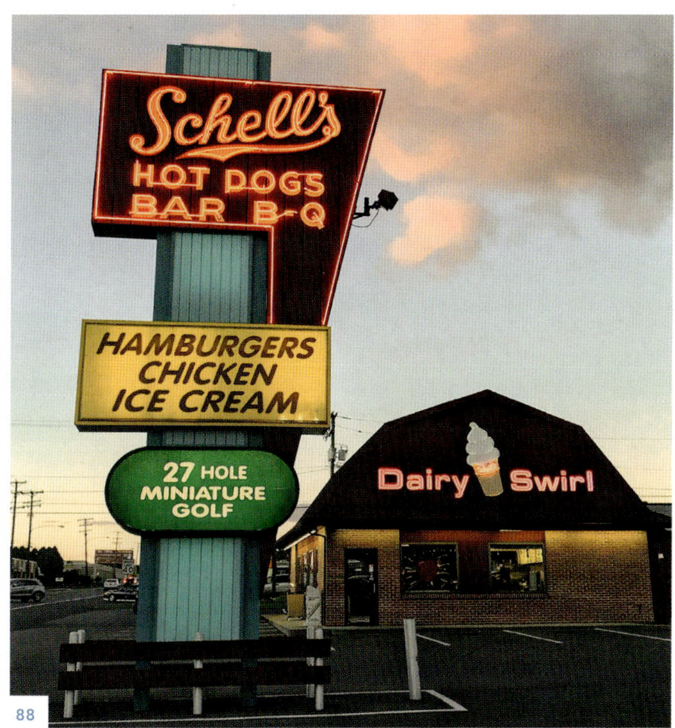

88

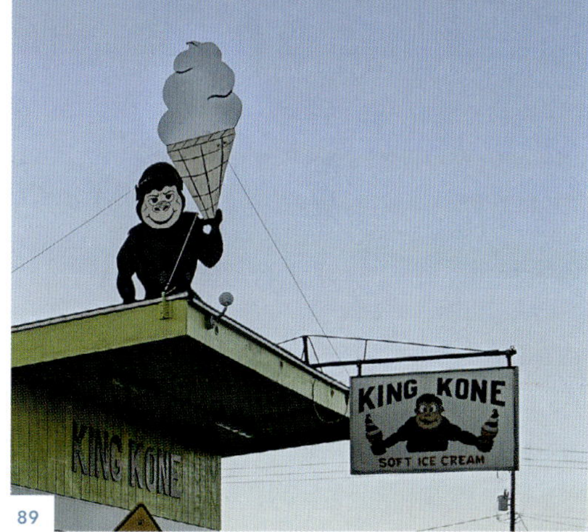

89

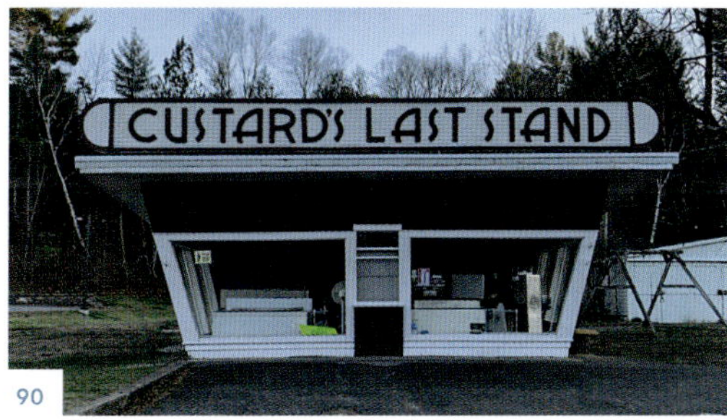

90

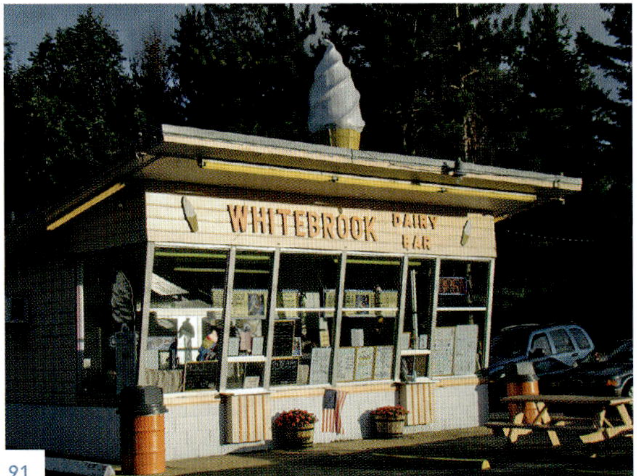

91

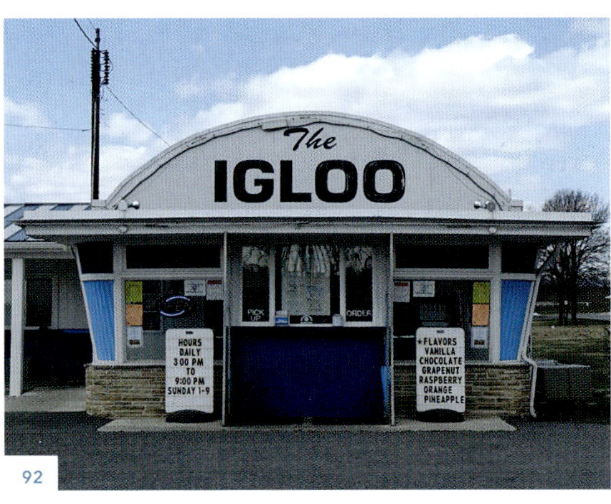

92

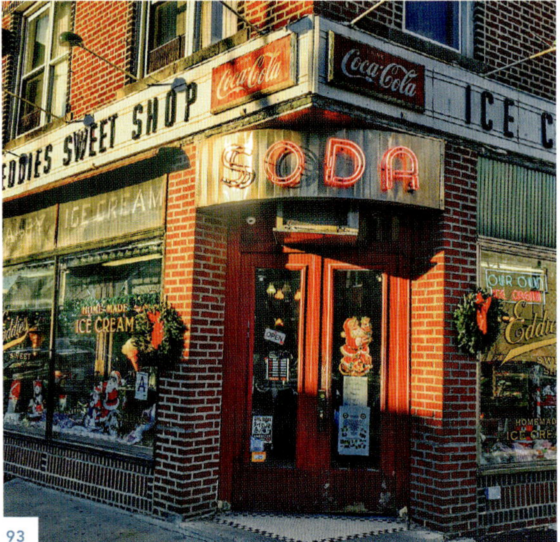

93

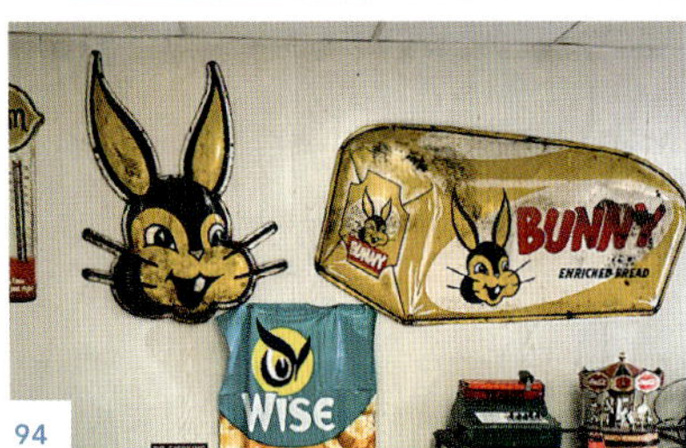

94

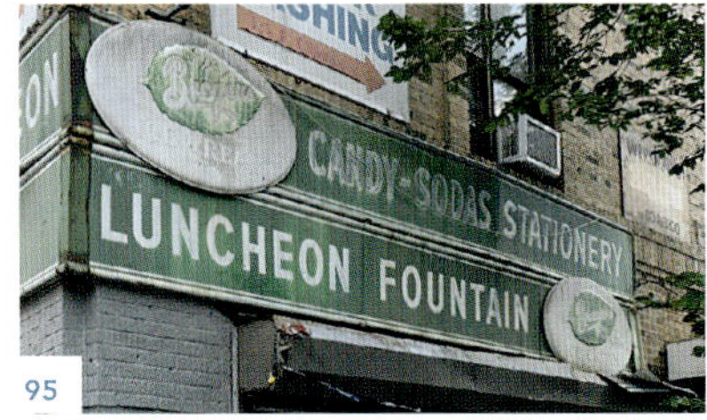

95

The Igloo (FIG. 92) would be right at home in Wilmington, but it's far away, on Route 11 in Chambersburg, Pennsylvania, where it's stood since April 1950. Its original owner, John Robertson, ran this oasis of dairy deliciousness for thirty-nine years. Subsequent owners, inspired by Mr. Robertson's example, have kept everything pretty much the same. That includes keeping the Grapenut ice cream on the menu. I'm told you can't go wrong with it.

Eddie's Sweet Shop (FIG. 93) in Forest Hills, Queens, has been serving up homemade ice cream since 1909—the toppings and whipped cream are even made on the premises. Inside, the soda-fountain stools with worn leather seats, the tin ceiling, the chandeliers, and the glass display cases make you question whether you've been here before, in some unknowable past. It feels . . . like home.

At **Weaver's** (FIG. 94) in Allenwood, Pennsylvania, you can satisfy your sweet and savory teeth while surrounded by a veritable museum of iconic American brands. My favorite vintage signs here include the ones for Bunny Bread and the Wise Potato Chips Owl just outside.

Another iconic ice-cream brand, **Breyer's**, can still be found in the wild here and there, like at this bodega (FIG. 95) on 233rd Street in the Bronx, or at **Lucille's Country Kitchen** in Barnegat Township, New Jersey. (Look for the wooden Jersey Devil outside!)

CHEERS!

These are places where everybody knows your name—wonderful taverns, bars, and dives, along with some liquor stores, that know how to put on an architectural show.

The Dublin House (FIG. 96) on Manhattan's Upper West Side recently celebrated its centennial, which it rang in with a fabulous restoration by Let There Be Neon, the revered Manhattan sign shop. This glorious neon harp is perhaps the grandest of them all in NYC. The sign was such a big deal in 1934 that *Signs of the Times* magazine wrote a small article about it. New York neon historian Tom Rinaldi calls signs of this vintage "so ephemeral, so improbable."

The same can be said for the saga of the **Subway Inn** (FIG. 97) and its sign. Like a train on the move—a very slow-moving one—the Subway Inn is now on its third stop on a journey that began in 1937. It sat for decades across from Bloomingdale's on East Sixtieth, survived there until 2014, until it finally settled in its latest home, not too far away on Second Avenue. The iconic neon sign came along for the ride. But the third time was not the charm—the inn announced it was closing in December 2024.

A subway ride away in Brooklyn, **The Long Island Bar** (FIG. 98) opened in 1951, back when the Brooklyn waterfront around Atlantic Avenue was the province of longshoremen and the bars that catered to them. After closing for many years, the bar was magnificently restored and reopened in 2013, though there no longer are longshoremen left to sip cocktails—perhaps a few of their grandkids have picked up the tab. Those working-class patrons of yore would surely recognize the architecture and the grand neon.

On Atlantic Avenue in Brooklyn Heights, the waterfront a short walk away, is the magical **Montero Bar & Grill** (FIG. 99), a nautical-themed bar where the ghosts of those long-ago old salts still mingle in the glow of the neon. That sidewalk light turned author Frank McCourt's front room

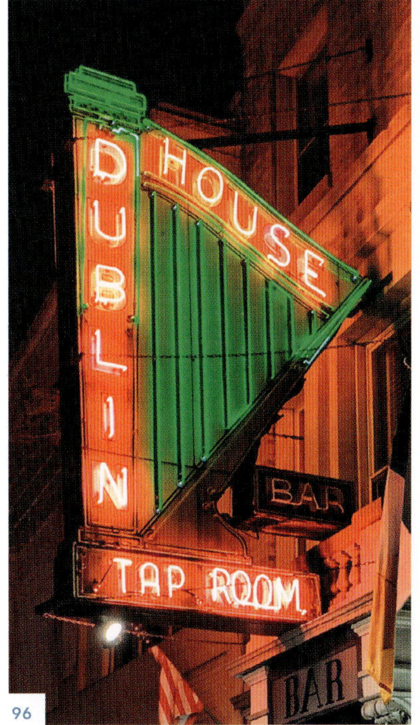

96

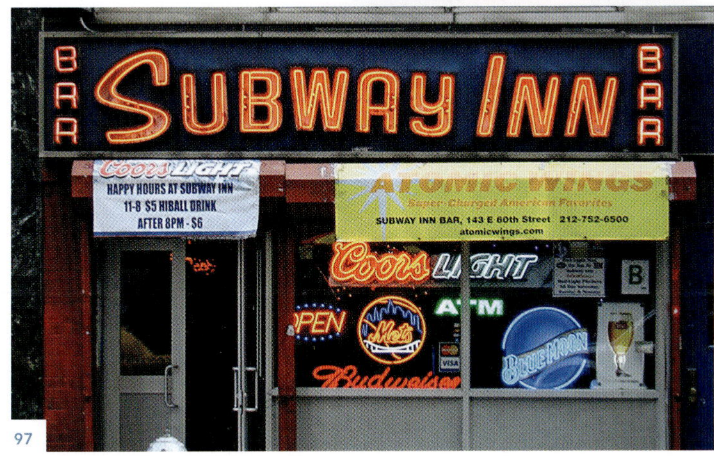

97

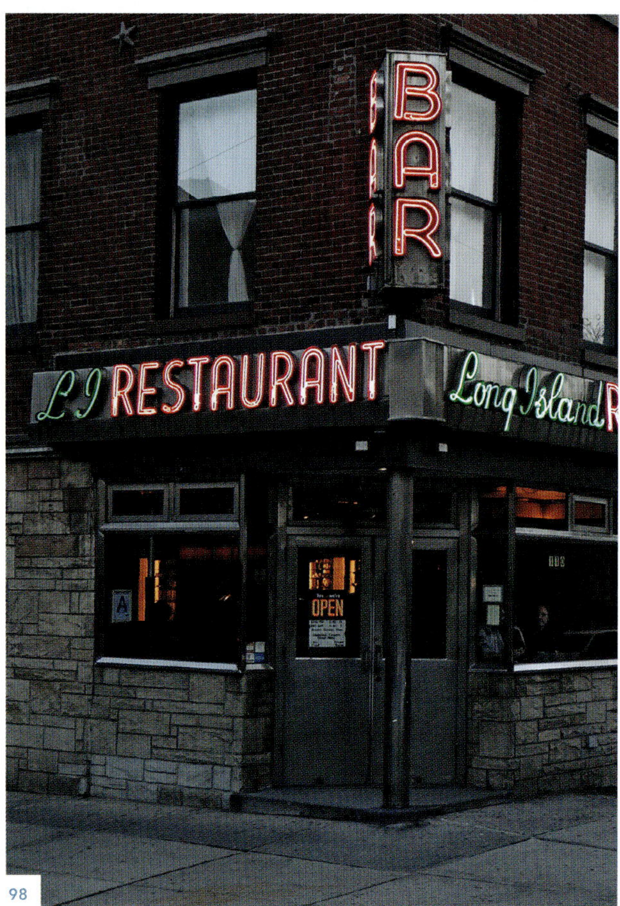

98

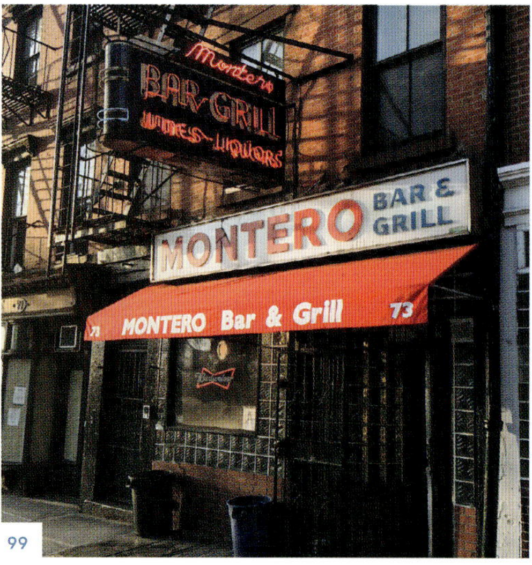

99

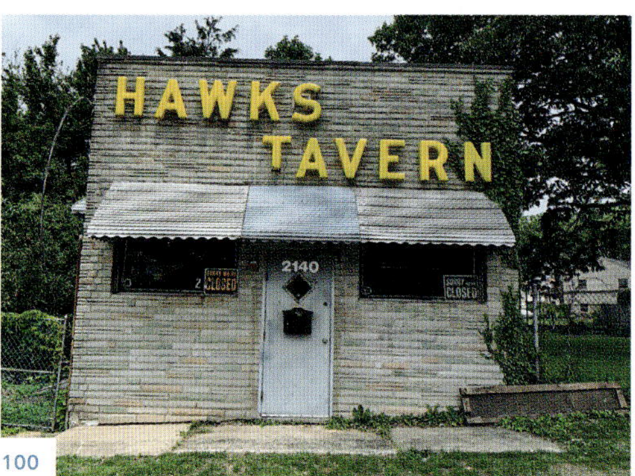

100

from “scarlet to black to scarlet,” he wrote in *Teacher Man* about his days living above the bar. In a visit to Montero’s in 2002, I saw the owner, Pilar Montero, holding court at the bar, and was awed. Her husband, Joseph, with whom she’d founded the bar in 1945, had died in 1999. They’d kept it a sailor’s bar—even as that era sailed away. It was, then and now, a revelation. Her 2012 *New York Times* obituary explained that she bridged old Brooklyn—the longshoremen—and new Brooklyn, the young folks enamored of the borough who sift its storefronts for authenticity. Here, they struck gold.

Neon is easy on the eyes. But for some humble watering holes, it may have been a bit too uptown—places like **Hawks Tavern** (FIG. 100) in the Vauxhall section of Union Township, New Jersey, which had been closed for several years when I photographed it in 2019.

Hundreds of miles away in McKeesport, Pennsylvania, is the **Theatre Bar** (FIG. 101). It is one of the most beautiful art deco storefronts in America. Presently closed except for special

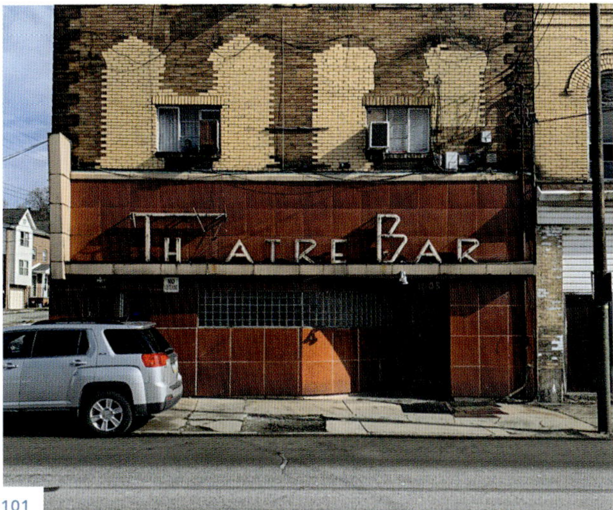

101

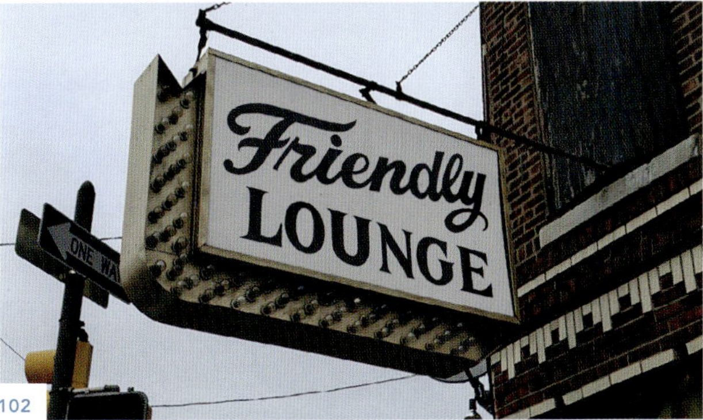

102

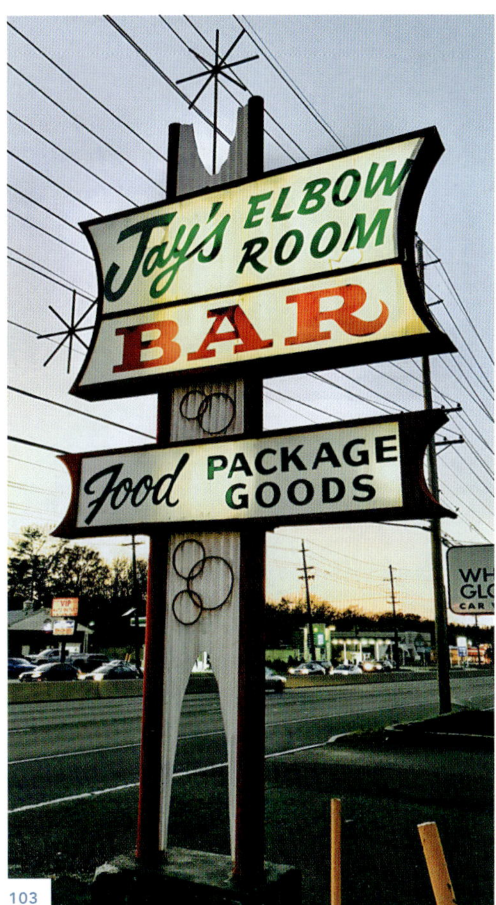

103

occasions, the bar has been under the same ownership for more than fifty years.

It's easy to cast admiring glances at **The Friendly Lounge** (FIG. 102), which has long been a secret of sorts among dive-bar connoisseurs in South Philadelphia. It's the kind of dimly lit joint that you stop in for a bottle of domestic beer or something harder and friendly conversation with your barstool companions. The TV set blares traditional fare like Channel 6's *Action News*, as more than one reviewer has pointed out—in other words, this place is as Philly as Philly gets, or better, as Philly as a slice of Philly once was.

You'll find more friends in Pennsylvania at **Jimmie Kramer's Peanut Bar** in Reading, Pennsylvania, which opened on Penn Street back in the early 1930s. The peanut theme and the shell-covered floors became a tradition around 1935.

Just outside Philadelphia, in Maple Shade Township, New Jersey, is **Jay's Elbow Room** (FIG. 103), voted New Jersey's best dive bar by readers of NJ.com a few years ago.

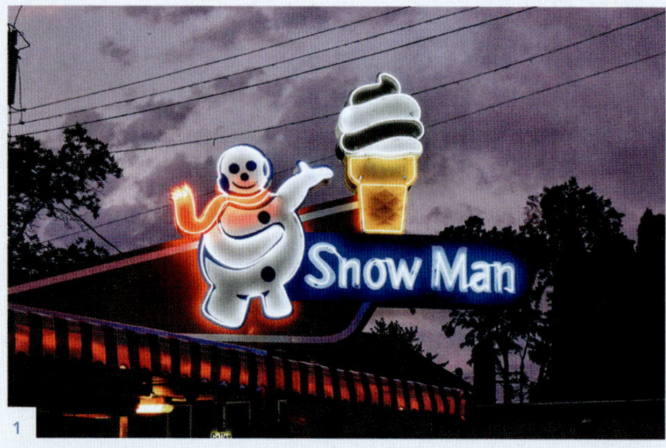

1

2

SENSATIONAL SIGNS

Each of these beauties has become for someone, maybe you, a part of the family, a part of life. That's what makes these signs represent so much more than a business or a brand.

1. Snow Man, Troy, New York
2. Moon Motel, Howell, New Jersey
3. Blue Comet Diner, Hazleton, Pennsylvania
4. Drift-In, DeRuyter, New York
5. Coney Island Lunch, Shamokin, Pennsylvania
6. Dolly Madison Ice Cream, Ridgefield Park, New Jersey
7. Anthony's Pizza Town, Bordentown, New Jersey
8. Dutch Haven, Ronks, Pennsylvania
9. Talking McDonald's Apple Tree, Nesquehoning, Pennsylvania
10. Media Theatre, Media, Pennsylvania
11. Big Mac Museum, Irwin, Pennsylvania

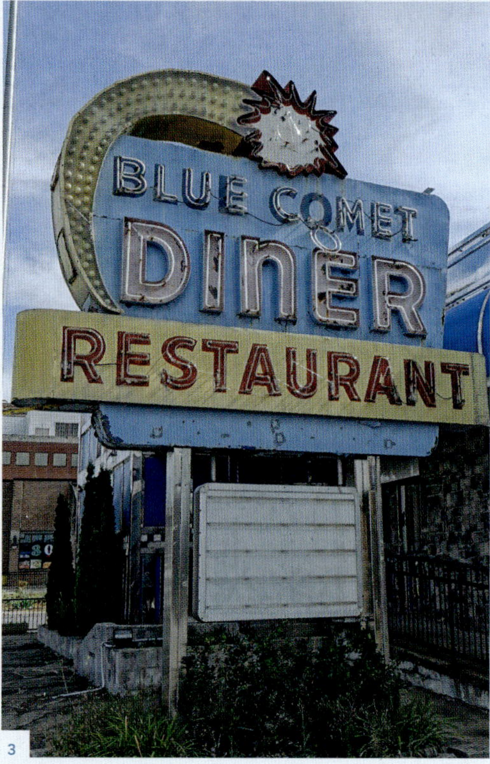

3

DRIFT-IN

4

CONEY ISLAND
LUNCH

5

SODAS
DOLLY MADISON
ICE CREAM

6

Anthony's
PIZZA TOWN
Italian Cantina
STEAK HOAGIES
Cold BEER

7

THE PLACE THAT MADE SHOO FLY PIE FAMOUS
DUTCH HAVEN
SHOO-FLY PIE BAKERY
SHOO-FLY PIES
DUTCH HAVEN
AMISH STUFF
Amish Crafted
GIFTS-FURNITURE
SHOOFLY PIES
ARE BACK
ROOT BEER
PECAN PIES

8

9

MEDIA
LIVE ON STAGE
THE SOUND OF MUSIC
NOW TO JAN 8
GIFT CARDS MAKE
GREAT GIFTS
THE HILLS ARE ALIVE WITH
THE SOUND OF MUSIC
NOW TO JAN 8

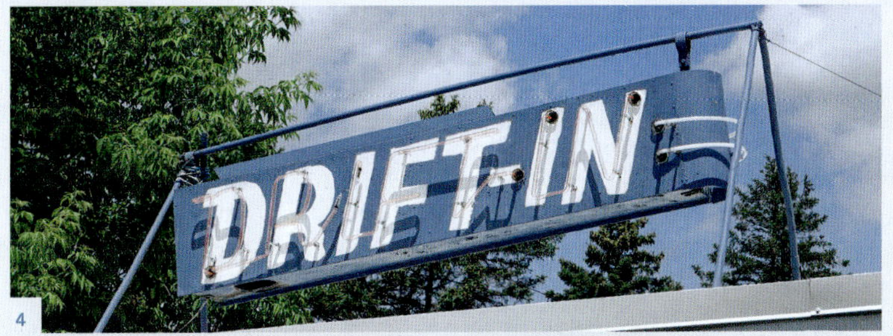

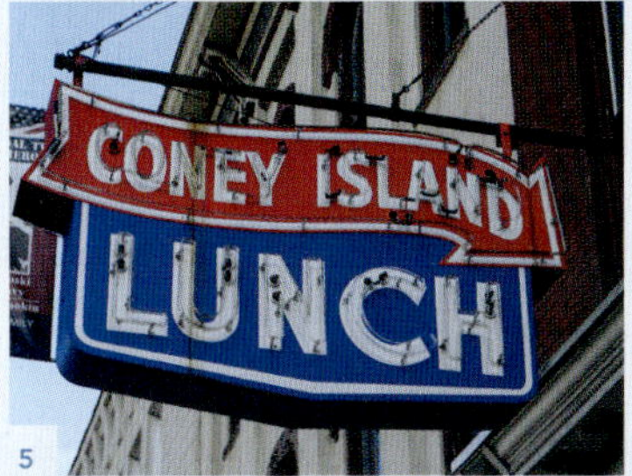

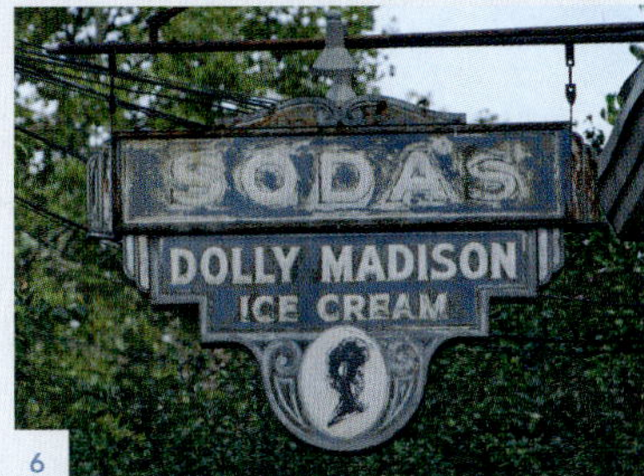

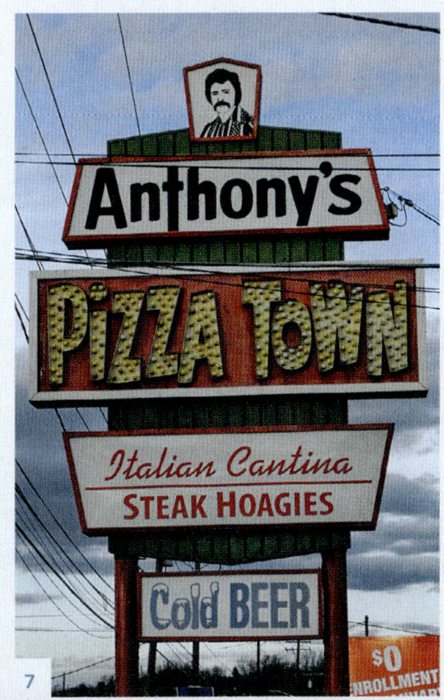

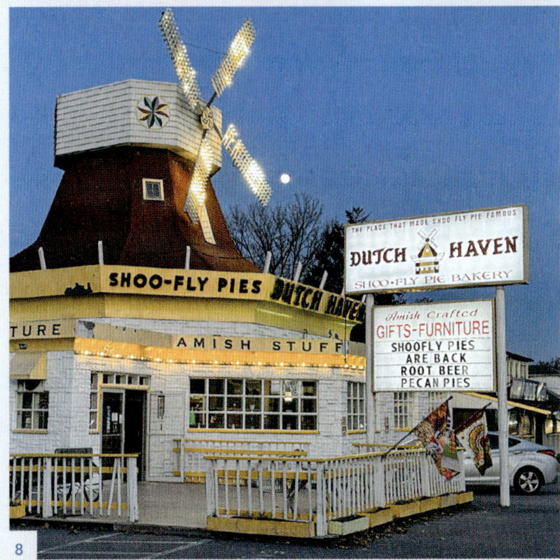

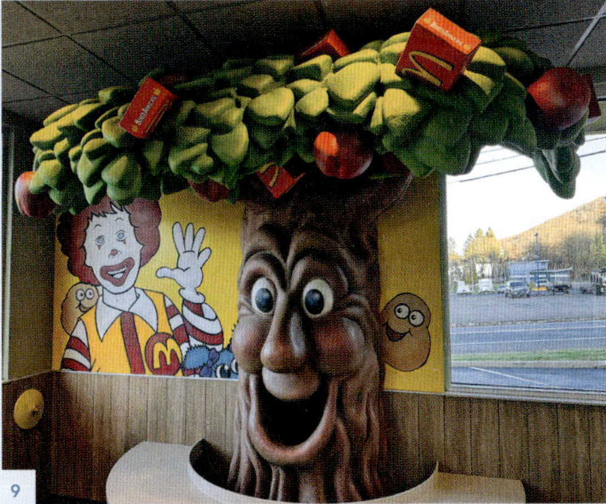

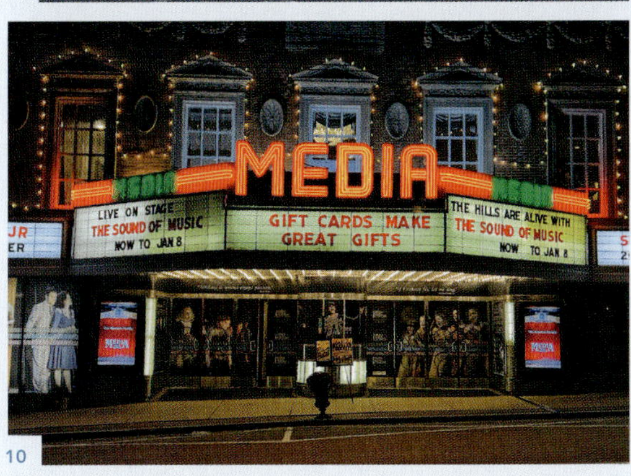

10

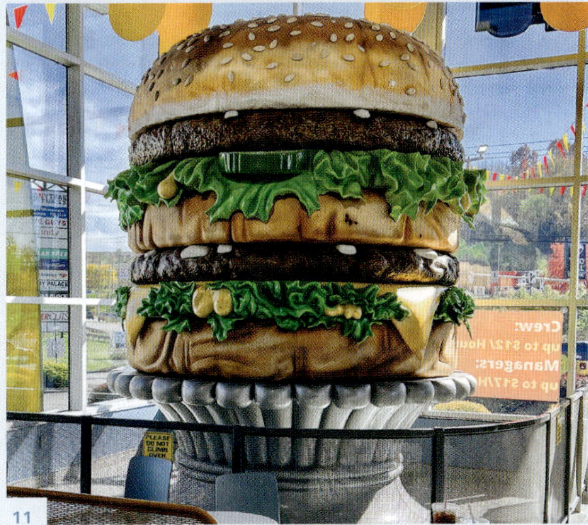

11

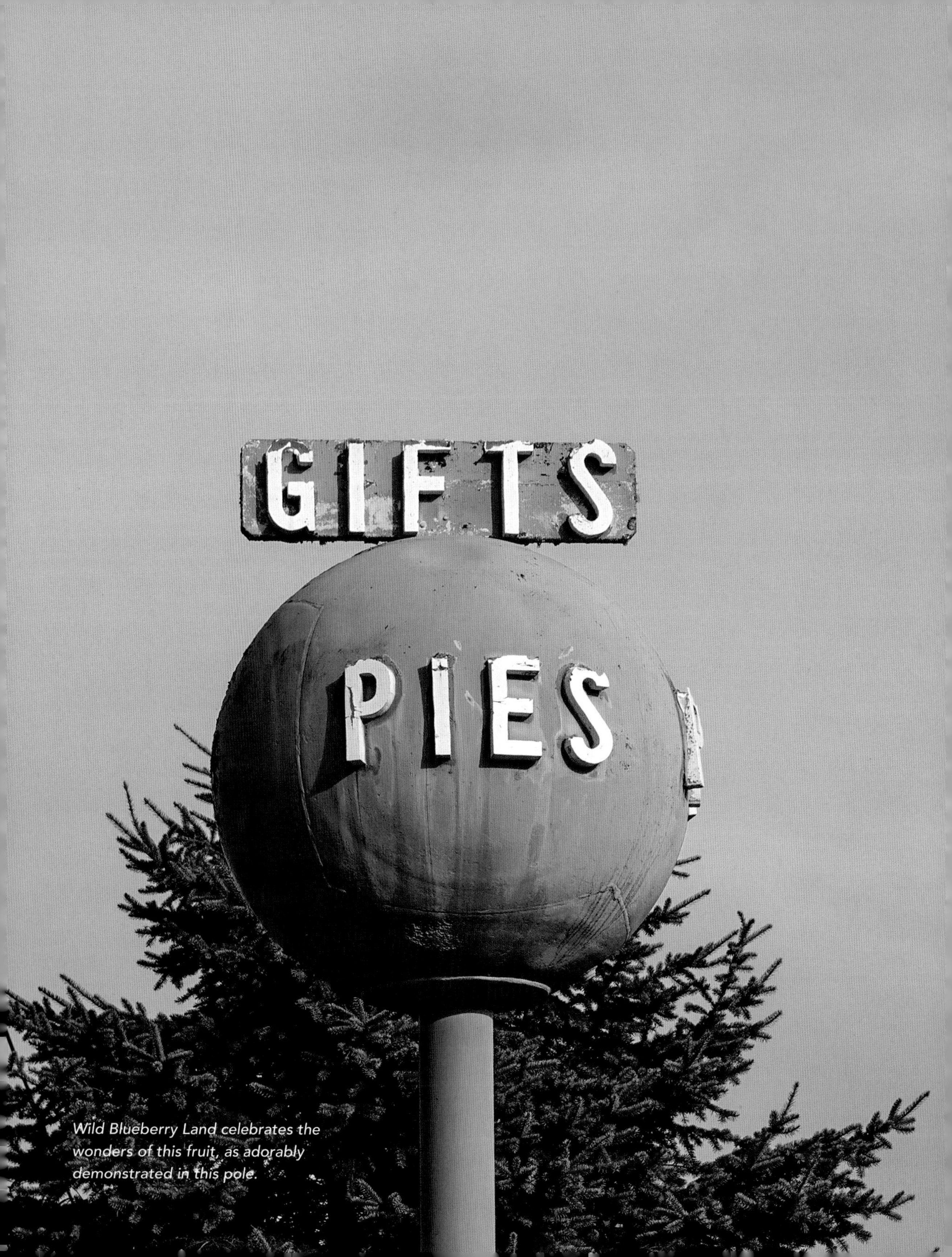

Wild Blueberry Land celebrates the wonders of this fruit, as adorably demonstrated in this pole.

NEW ENGLAND

**MASSACHUSETTS · RHODE ISLAND
NEW HAMPSHIRE · VERMONT
MAINE · CONNECTICUT**

The wonders of New England are many and varied. Our journey will take us from the sea to the mountains and, along the way, celebrate all that makes the region rich turf for the admirer of roadside Americana.

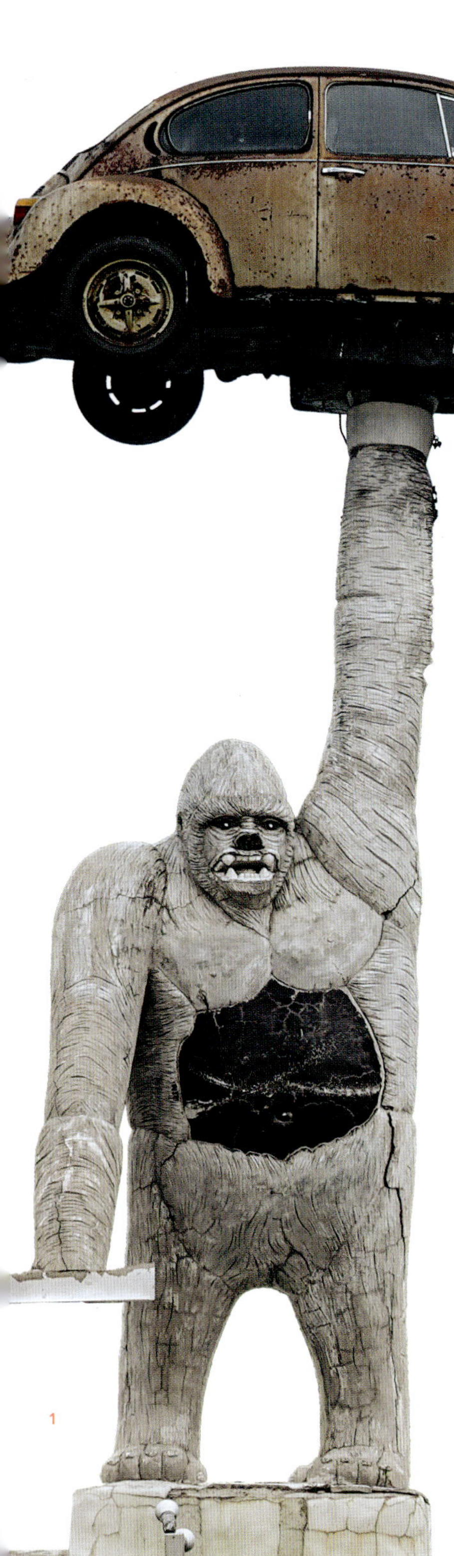

1

ROADSIDE QUIRKS

New England's proud colonial spirit and its history of billboard banning (Vermont and Maine) might suggest a paucity of twentieth-century roadside Americana, but these spots will prove otherwise.

All hail **Queen Connie** (FIG. 1)! In 1987, Joan Cameron O'Neil, the owner of Pioneer Auto Sales in Leicester, Vermont, teamed up with Florida-based sculptor and artist T.J. Neil and asked him to create a sculpture involving a car, to stay on brand. Neil had the idea of building a giant gorilla, and O'Neil wanted a car on top, so, to wit, the world was given a gorilla holding a Volkswagen Beetle, then a still-common car on the roads. The work was a sensation. After all these years, the 20-foot-tall steel-and-concrete structure is still the queen of her roadside realm.

You might say **Big Jim** (FIG. 2) is the king of Downeast Maine. He's imposing in a Potemkin Village kind of way, a towering but simple cutout metal figure. He's ready for the worst weather the Maine coast can unleash, protected by a matching sou'wester and raincoat that would fill the Gorton's Fisherman with envy.

Big Jim was constructed in 1959 by the Maine Sardine Council at a time when Maine's sardine industry was thriving. His first gig was to hold a giant sardine can that read "Maine Sardines Welcome You to Vacationland & Sardineland" in

Kittery, at the border with New Hampshire. Jim became Maine's unofficial greeter. By the end of the twentieth century, with the sardine business in decline, Big Jim was moved to Prospect Harbor, at the Stinson Seafood plant, and held a can of their sardines. But then Bumble Bee, the tuna people who bought the sardine cannery, decided to cut bait on Stinson in 2010. Big Jim was almost out of a job until the operation converted to lobster packing, and since 2012, he has been holding today's catch.

Big Jim, in his new role as lobsterman, might be overwhelmed by the challenge posed by the so-called **World's Largest Inflatable Lobster** (FIG. 5) that sits atop the Taste of Maine in Woolwich. Larry the Lobster is a cute photo op, and at seven hundred pounds, a heavy one! Larry joined the family in 2018 to mark the restaurant's fortieth anniversary and his imposing presence may inspire you to take on the "World's Largest Lobster Roll" inside.

If a gigantic lobster stops you in your tire tracks, then keep on driving until you're in Freeport, Maine, the home of the **L.L.Bean Flagship Store** (FIG. 3). The giant Bean Boot here is too big for even Big Jim, coming in at size 410. The boot is complemented by the Bootmobile that makes the rounds around the country. The big boot is a favorite photo op at all hours of the day, literally—the store never closes.

While you may associate Maine with lobsters and duck boots, you may not realize the cultivation of blueberries is a point of pride here, and in 2001, the fruit was honored by its very own wonderland in Columbia Falls—**Wild Blueberry Land** (FIG. 4), housed in a gigantic blue geodesic dome. Outside, you'll find playful bollards painted in blue; inside, you can explore many things to eat with everyone's favorite antioxidant-rich berry. Packed into this place are historical exhibits with a midcentury-diorama charm. Wild Blueberry Land is the brainchild of Dell and Marie Emerson, farmer and baker respectively, who feel the world needs to know about the restorative virtues of the wild blueberry, smaller than the ones you'll see at the supermarket but, unlike many of those, native to America.

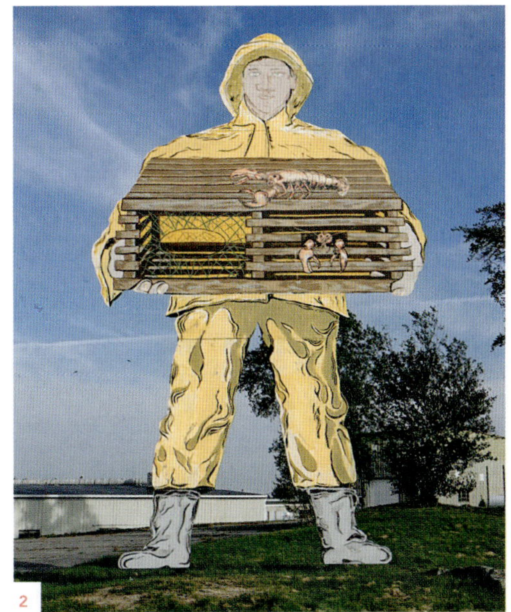
2

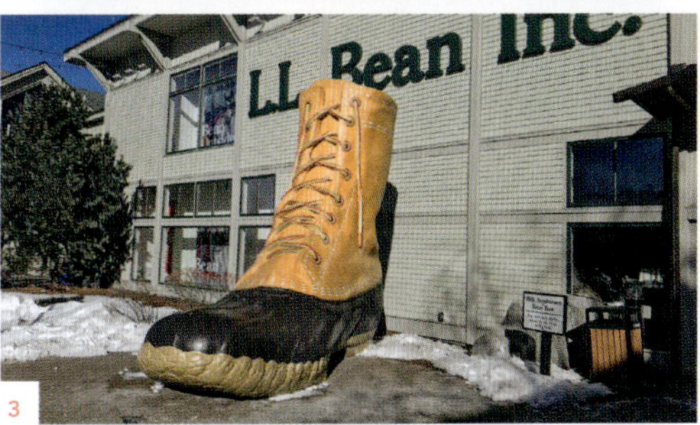

3

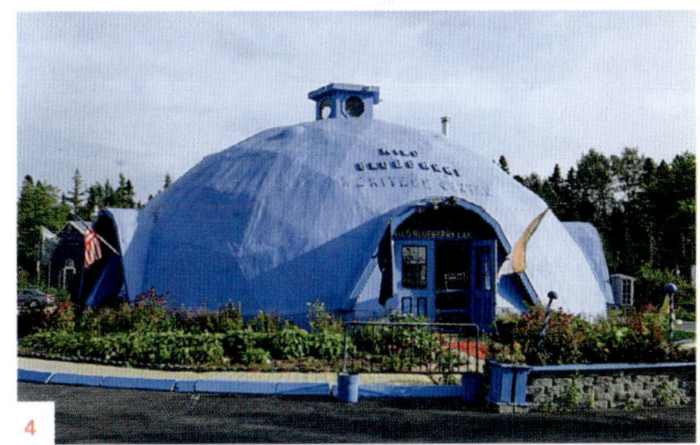
4

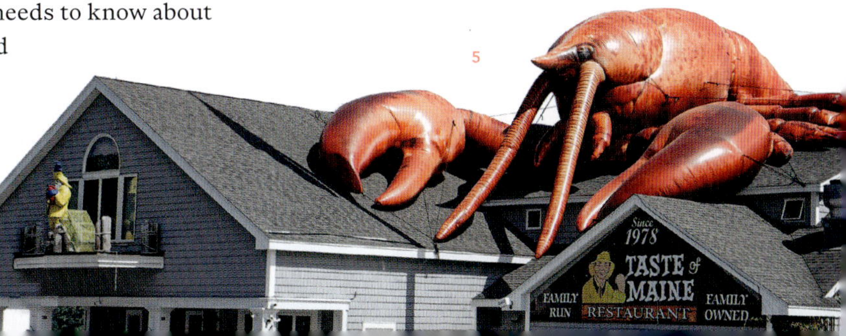

5

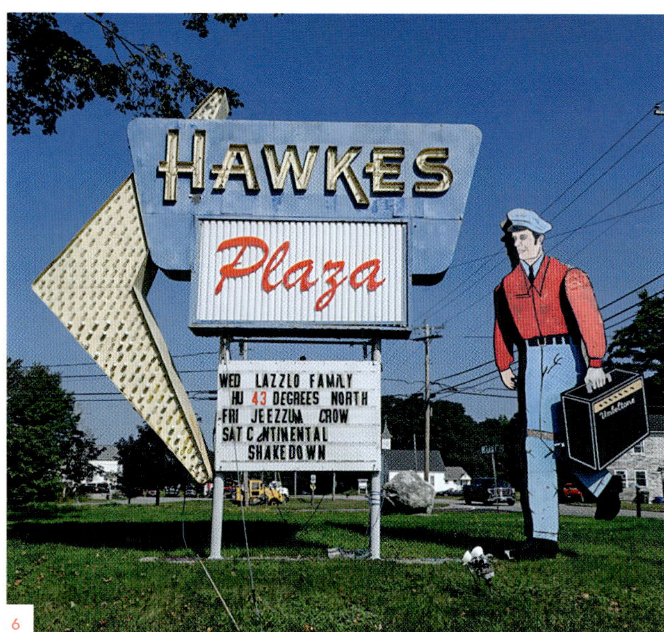

6

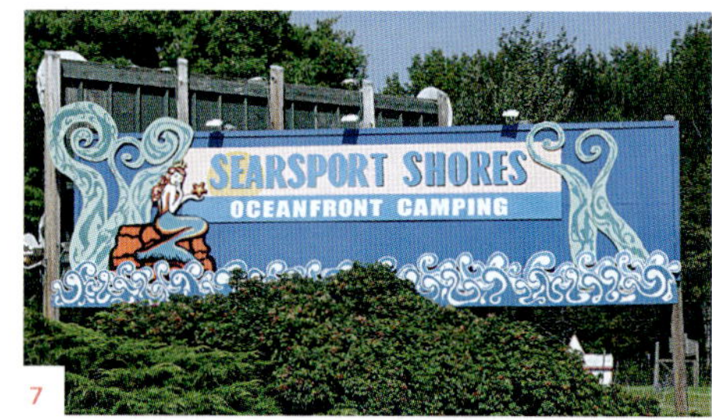

7

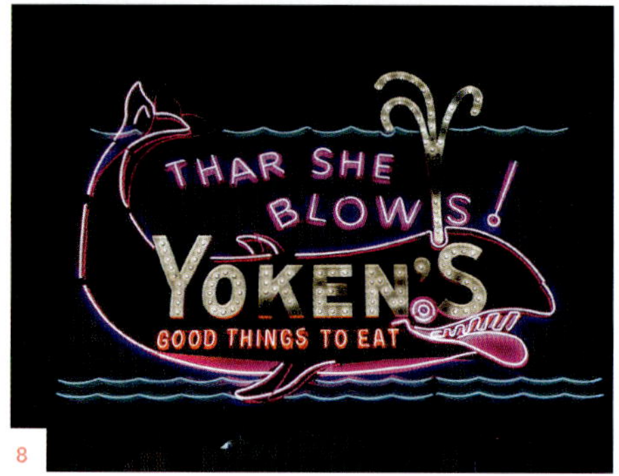

8

Heading down toward Boston, one is obligated to meander through Saugus, Massachusetts, a treasure trove of roadside quirk. You might spot, for instance, an **Orange Dinosaur** (FIG. 9) perched high on a hill, there for no apparent reason except perhaps to delight us and prompt a detour. This grinning T-rex was part of a mini-golf complex that was cleared for residential development in 2016, but the developer retained the services of our prehistoric pal, to the relief of many.

Lenny's at Hawkes Plaza (FIG. 6) is a live-music venue with a tall sign of neon and incandescent lighting featuring a television repairman, captured in mid-stride with toolkit in hand. The TV repair shop in Westbrook, Maine, is long gone, but the sign, built in 1962, remains as a much-beloved roadside symbol of Maine.

With Maine's proud seaside heritage, it should come as no shock that we're due for a mermaid sighting. The billboard for Maine's **Searsport Shores** (FIG. 7) campground is a beguiling throwback and incredibly rare, as Maine has outlawed billboards since January 1, 1978. Mermaids rightfully get a pass while about three thousand other billboards didn't.

The **"Thar She Blows" neon sign** (FIG. 8) has also gotten a pass from the sad fate of so many other neon signs. The happy whale, which once represented the long-defunct Yoken's Seafood restaurant in Portsmouth, New Hampshire, is a beautifully restored bright spot of New England midcentury Americana.

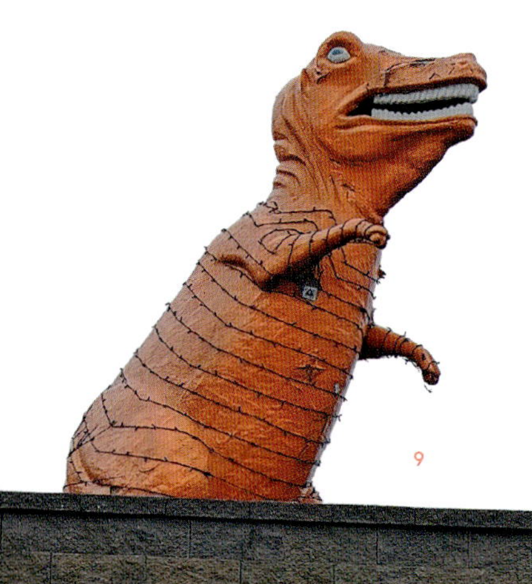
9

The shopping center's developers went on a bit of a fishing expedition, but they managed to navigate the political and economic complexities of saving the whale. It took $60,000 dollars to get this sign back into spoutin' form in 2015, when the last owner of the restaurant was given the honors of flipping on the neon. Yes, it's a seafood-restaurant sign without a seafood restaurant.

The Boston area loves its roadside quirks, and the spectacular **Shell sign** (FIG. 10) in Cambridge, Massachusetts, has been to hell and back. I mean, really to *HELL*. When the 1933 neon sign was designated a historical landmark in 1996, some in the community decried the celebration of a commercial symbol, which, an opponent pointed out, would sometimes spell out the world "HELL" during malfunctions. In 2011, an LED replica replaced the battered original, and suddenly, the Boston area had one of its beloved symbols glowing anew.

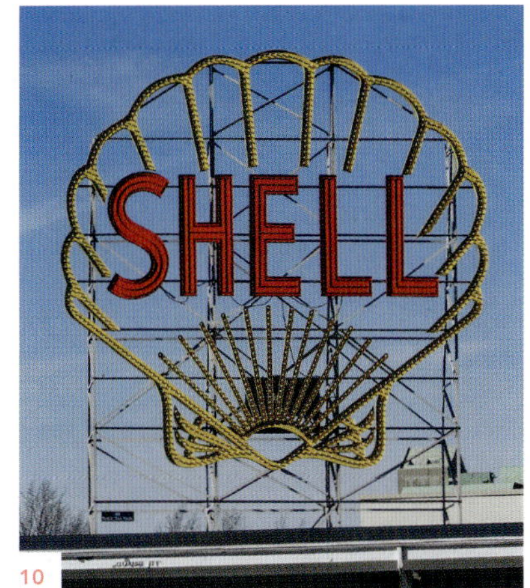

10

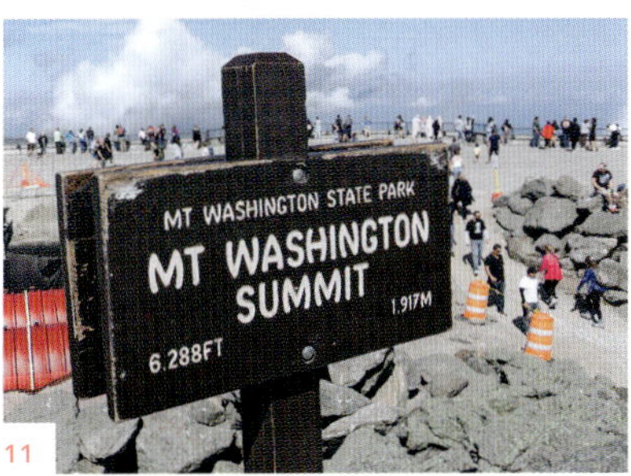

11

The **Schrafft's** (FIG. 12) neon sign—atop a former candy factory at what is now called Schrafft's City Center, an office complex—is another Boston skyline favorite, a reminder of the legendary purveyor of sweet goods. Schrafft's often gets the credit for inventing the jelly bean, marketing them as treats to be sent to soldiers on the Civil War battlefront. The company developed a popular restaurant chain, concentrated in New York City, and stayed in the candy business until the factory here in Boston closed in 1984. The Schrafft's name may make a sweet comeback—an effort is afoot to revive the restaurant brand, and a pop-up Schrafft's stirred nostalgic optimists at a Fifth Avenue street fair in 2023, right outside Tiffany's where, in the film *Breakfast at Tiffany's*, Holly Golightly (Audrey Hepburn) indulges in a Danish and cup of coffee from Schrafft's.

Most of the recommendations in this book lean into wonders that were built to compel motorists to pull over, but here, I present a natural wonder you should (carefully!) drive up and down. The journey up the **Mount Washington Auto Road** (FIG. 11) in New Hampshire is stirring—just don't let your eyes wander so much that you run off the road—and once you reach the summit, food and souvenirs can be found at the Sherman Adams Visitors Center. Take your picture at the alpine summit, 6,288 feet in the sky. I must confess that I did the drive to get my hands on that iconic bumper sticker, which they hand out when your car makes it to the top, that says "This Car Climbed Mt. Washington."

12

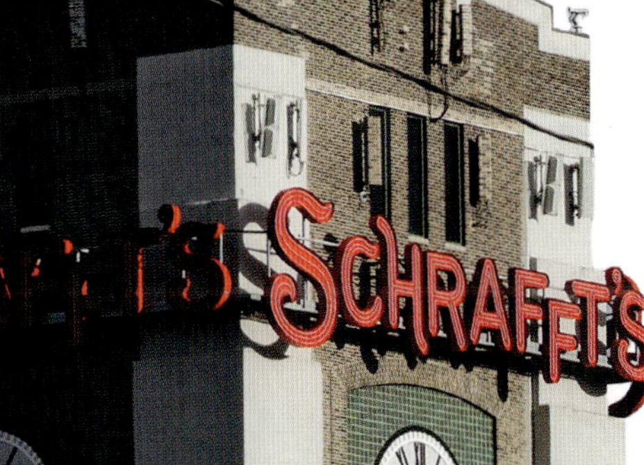

ROADSIDE EATS

New England is the birthplace of the humble diner, and we'll see plenty of these on our trip. But I've tasted some of the best pizza anywhere here—as well as regional delights at places like lobster shacks and snack bars. Here's a sampling!

The Olympia Diner (FIG. 13) in Newington, Connecticut, is a transcendent experience in any weather, but on a rainy night, with the reflection of the neon on the wet parking lot pavement, it's proof heaven can be found on earth, along the Berlin Turnpike, to be exact. The Olympia has sat here since 1955 and has been run by the Gavrilis family since 1974, a hospitable bunch if there ever was one. At this writing, the diner has been sold and the structure's future is uncertain.

The great **Frank Pepe's** (FIG. 14) has been on Wooster Street in New Haven, Connecticut, since 1925 and is the dean of the legendary local pizza scene, with scrumptious thin-crust pizza pies made in coal-fired brick ovens. My go-to is the classic tomato pie, downed with some Foxton birch beer. Sure, there's a wait in line, but it wouldn't be Pepe's without a taste of delayed gratification.

Down the street is **Sally's Apizza** (FIG. 15), another great exemplar of the New Haven thin-crust pizza scene, purchased by Filomena Consiglio, sister of Frank Pepe, in 1938, and run by her son Sal for decades. Sally's has its own lore and devotees. Sally's is still run (though no longer owned) by the Consiglio family and has additional locations.

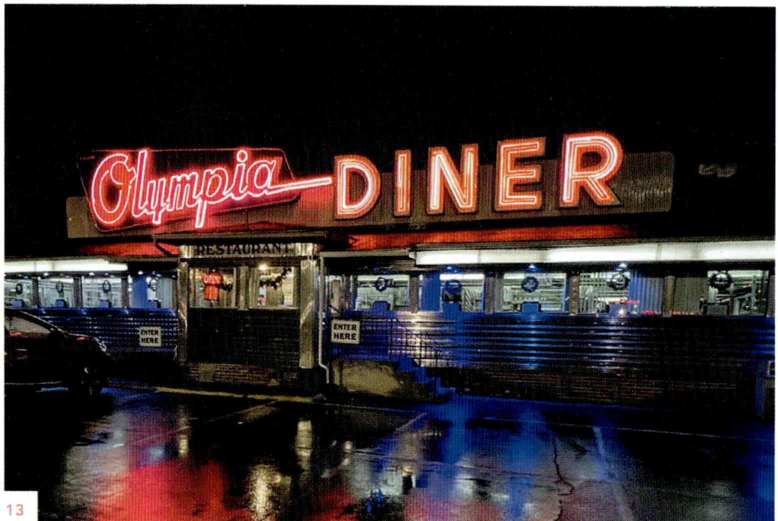

13

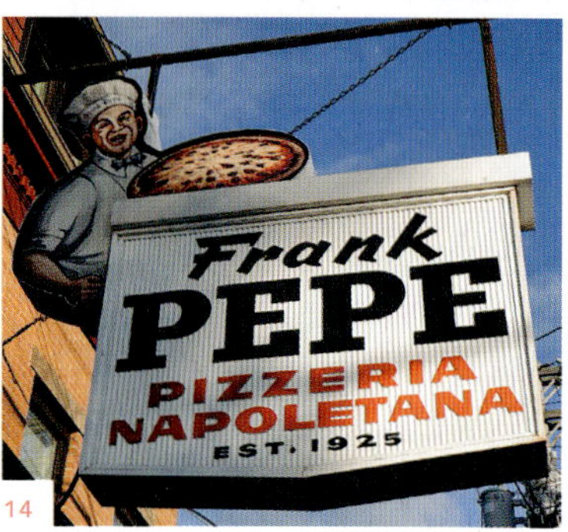

14

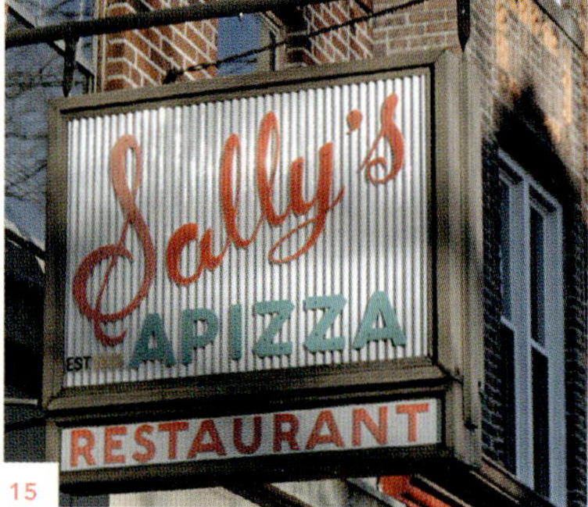

15

If you like your hamburgers with a side of history, then **Louis' Lunch** (FIG. 17) in New Haven will be one of the grandest treats you will ever enjoy. Louis' Lunch has long billed itself as the birthplace of the hamburger: As the story goes, it was a practical creation by Louis Lassen for a customer in 1900 who wanted something fast because he was on the go. Instead of the usual steak sandwiches, the customer was served a patty of ground beef on toast—and the burger was born. Not so fast, say a number of hamburger experts—one of the knocks being that a hamburger on toast, not a bun, isn't really a hamburger. Books have been written on the origin of the hamburger, and we are not going to settle it here. I will say that Louis' Lunch's burger is well worth seeking out, a must for roadside-food completists. The burger here is made from a proprietary blend of five meats and cooked on vertical cast-iron broilers that date to 1898.

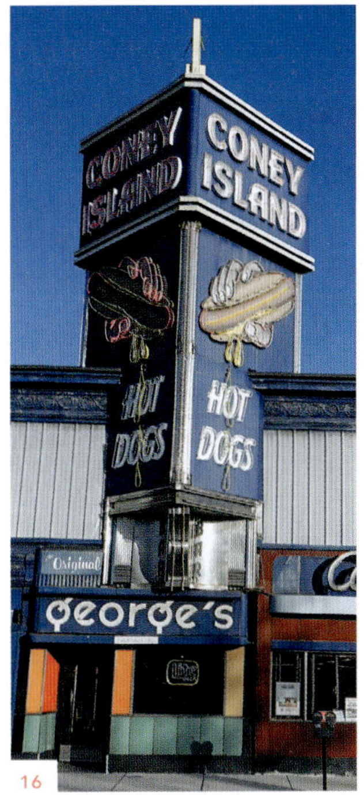

16

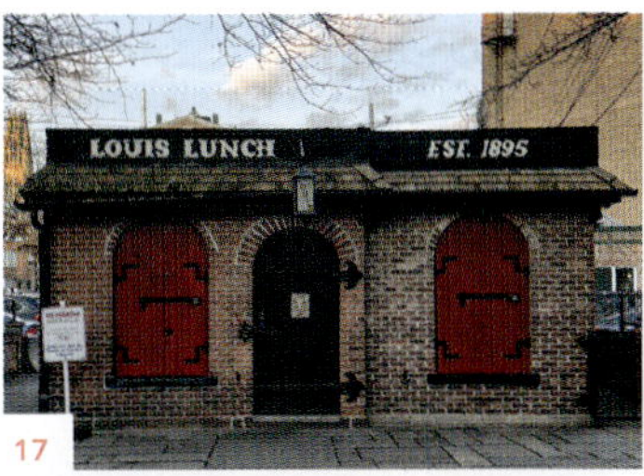

17

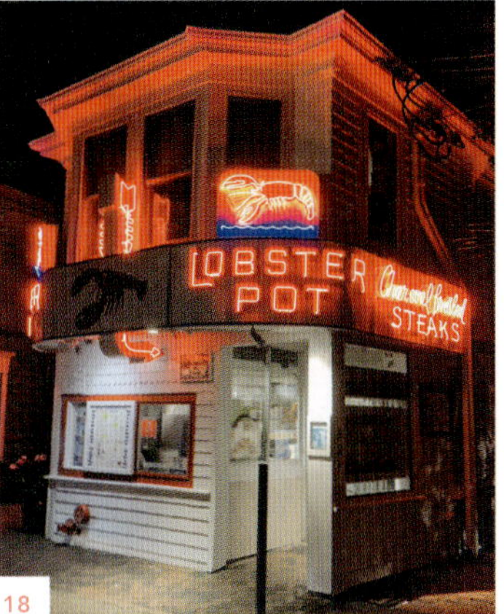

18

In Saugus, Massachusetts, you'll spot 1961's **"Leaning Tower of Pizza"** at **Prince Pizzeria** (FIG. 19), opened by the Prince pasta company. In Boston, you can still see the old North End rowhouse where young "Anthony" was called home by his mom to eat Prince Spaghetti in a long-running TV commercial. Wednesday was Prince Spaghetti Day. The brick house from which mom summons Anthony is still there.

The Lobster Pot (FIG. 18) in Provincetown, Massachusetts, has been reeling in crowds since the 1940s. The McNulty family has been at the helm since 1979, making the restaurant the enduring success that it is, surviving early travails, including a fire in 1982 that almost wiped them out.

While the Lobster Pot's neon is impressive, New England restaurant signage may have found its boldest expression at **George's Coney Island** (FIG. 16) in Worcester, Massachusetts. This eatery is nowhere near Brooklyn, the nineteenth-century cradle of the American hot dog, but Coneys became shorthand for chili-slathered hot dogs. The iconic image on the neon sign was based on the hand of George Tsagarelis, who, with his wife, Catherine, turned George's into an institution. George's marks 1918 as its birth year, even though the family took over about a decade later.

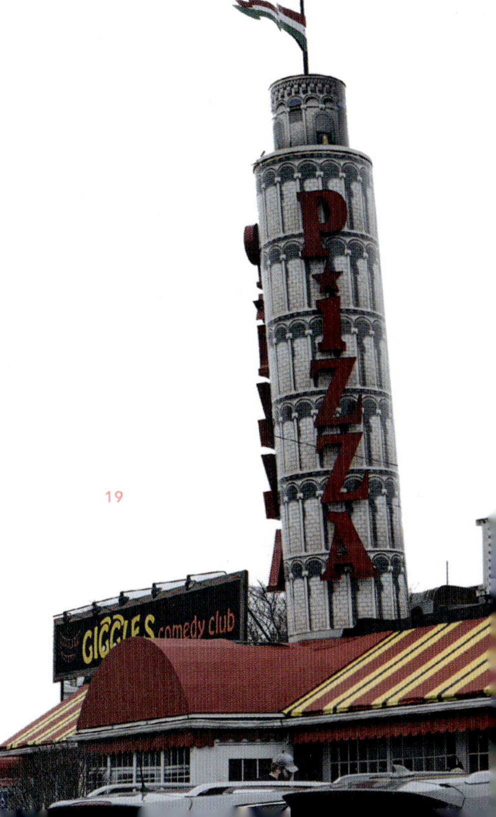

19

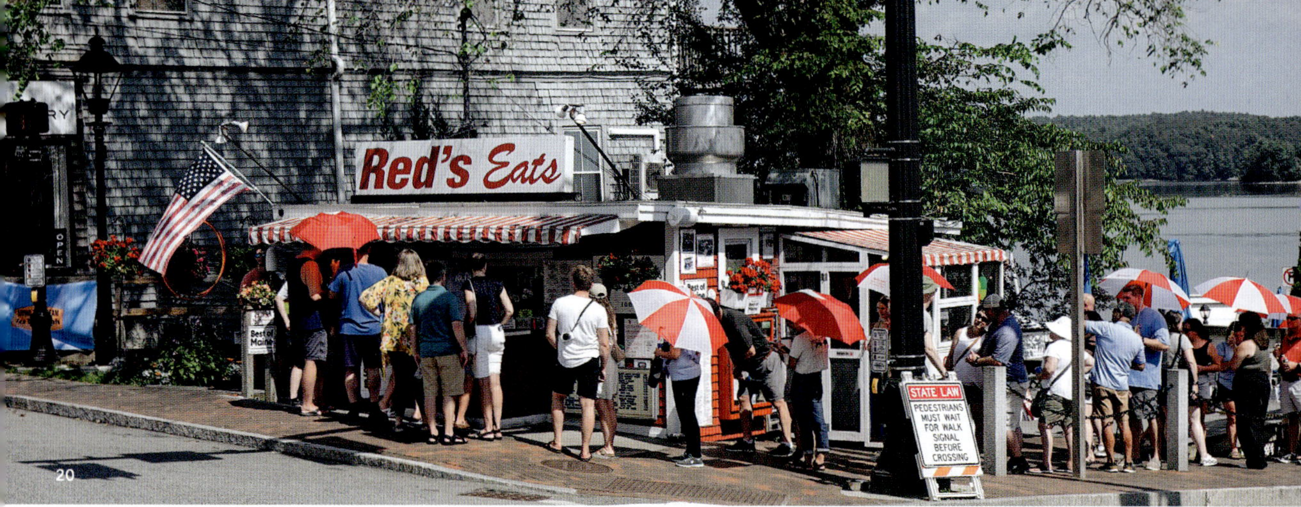

20

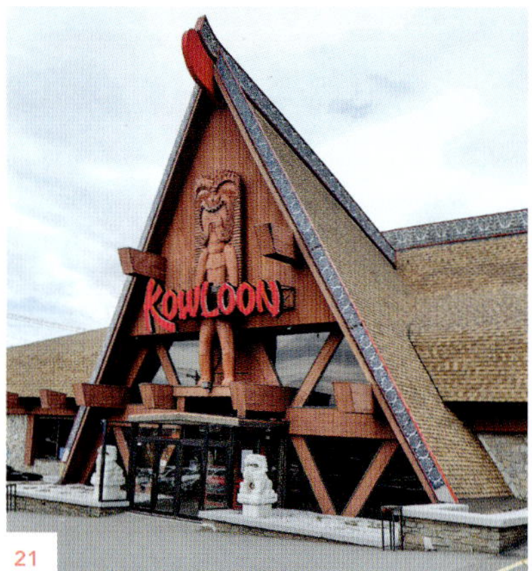

21

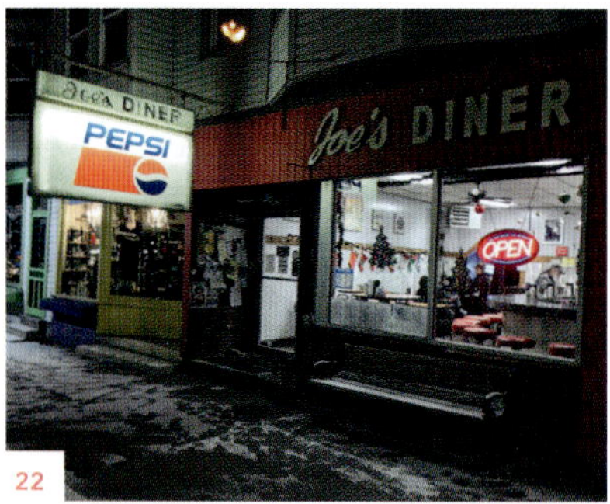

22

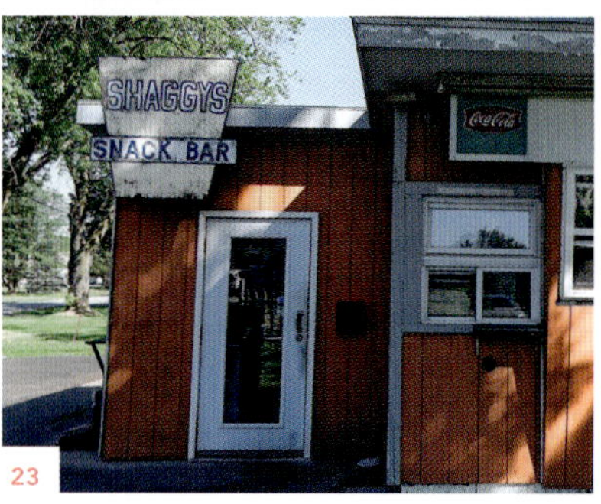

23

Kowloon (FIG. 21) is one of the great survivors of the roadside Americana that dotted U.S. 1 in Saugus, Massachusetts, and the A-frame frontage is breathtaking, something you'd expect in Southern California or Hawaii. Inside, the Chinese restaurant is cavernous, with a warren of evocatively decorated rooms and lounges and seating for twelve hundred. Opened in 1950 as Mandarin House, a modest restaurant to start, the restaurant grew into Kowloon under the ownership of Madeline and William Wong beginning in 1958, and what an experience the place is. Kowloon remains "the soul of Saugus," as Eater.com described it, and is still in the Wong family.

In the Berkshires, **Joe's Diner** (FIG. 22) in Lee, Massachusetts, has simple comforts down to a science. Joe was Joe Sorrentino, who took over the space in 1955 and sold it to Joe and Pam Langlais in 2000—the Joe's name still worked. When it was purchased by Heather Earle in 2013, the Joe's name stayed. I mean, "Eat at Joe's"—it doesn't get any better.

Red's Eats (FIG. 20) is the New England lobster shack of your dreams—and those of many others, one quickly discovers. Each time I get ready to travel on Route 1 to this Wiscasset, Maine, restaurant, patience is the first thing to pack, because the lines are long but the food is legendary, since 1938. The lines exist for a reason—Red's is small and the lobster rolls are huge and beloved. Its popularity, driven in part by its prime U.S. 1 location, also makes it a scapegoat for anger over traffic congestion in the area.

In a region dotted with snack bars, **Shaggy's Snack Bar** (FIG. 23) in Swanton, Vermont, delivers. It's a gem of comfort food close enough to the Quebec border that you can enjoy poutine pizza—french fries on gravy with oodles of cheese. *Scooby-Doo* fans have probably figured out that this was named after Shaggy, the hirsute hipster and best bud of Scoob. The owner, Joe Desrochers, told

BIRTHPLACE OF THE DINER

Wherever the diner is planted, it grows into hearts and finds a permanent berth. People claim it as their own. New Jersey diners are iconic and so many were produced there. New York and Long Island take pride in their diners, to be sure. But the diner as we know it emerged in New England, with a gradual evolution from primitive horse-drawn wagons to the stylish prefabricated diners that defined the form in the twentieth century. Many grand diners can be found in these precincts. Some I've visited include the shuttered **Salem Diner** (FIG. 24) in Salem, Massachusetts; the **Aero Diner** (FIG. 25) in North Windham, Connecticut; the **Modern Diner** (FIG. 26) in Pawtucket, Rhode Island; **Al Mac's** in Fall River, Massachusetts; **The Blue Benn** in Bennington, Vermont; **The Red Arrow** in Manchester, New Hampshire; **The Boulevard Diner**, **Miss Worcester**, and **Corner Lunch** diners in Worcester, Massachusetts; and the **Miss Florence** in Florence, Massachusetts; to name but a few. You'll see many more in your travels.

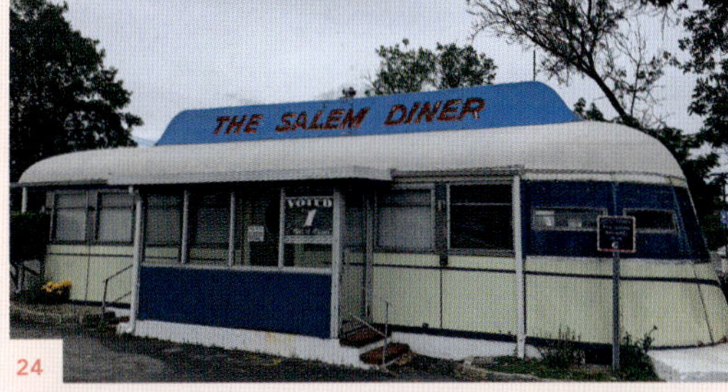

24

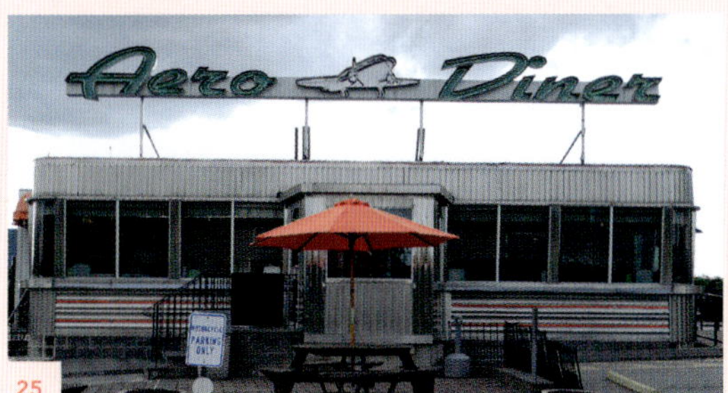

25

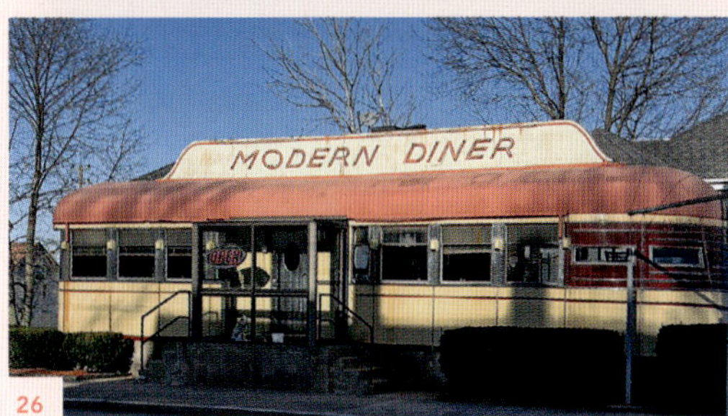

26

Seven Days that children have likened his appearance to that of the cartoon character.

Ah, the french fry, so delicious but almost always shoved to the side of the main dish. A salty afterthought. Not so at **Al's French Frys** (FIG. 27) in Burlington, Vermont, where the fries are the main attraction. It was founded in 1946 by Al and Genevieve Rusterholz, who worked wonders with fried potatoes. Al's has been owned by the Bissonette family since 1983, who expanded the place and broadened its menu while always keeping their eyes on their fries.

The Puritan Backroom (FIG. 28) was founded in 1917 by two Greek immigrants who had arrived here in Manchester, New Hampshire, to work in the mills. Its name was likely embraced to root it in New England tradition, and the menu expanded over the years. The business began with candy and ice cream and takeout, and in 1974, the Puritan Backroom was born with the addition of a dining room in the back. One particular item on their menu has

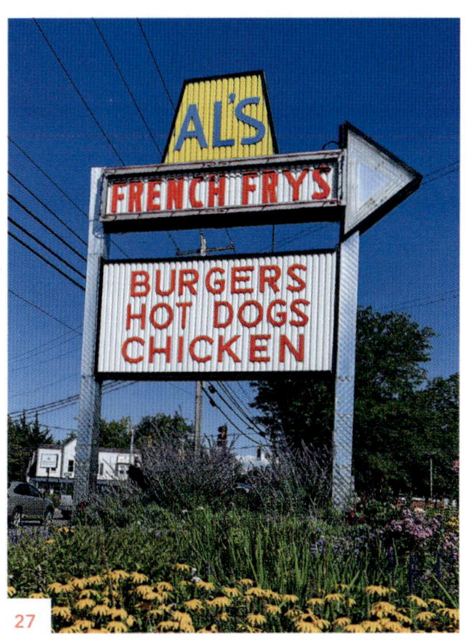

27

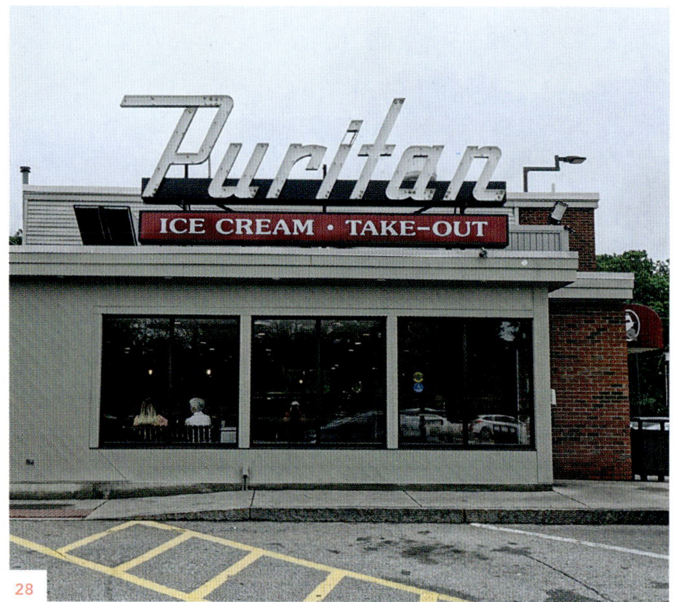

28

made them famous—the chicken tender, first offered here (or anywhere, the story goes) in 1974, and now a common dish and a favorite especially of picky children everywhere. Invariably, the claim of "first" attracts controversy from those contesting it, but Puritan's claim to being the first to use the soft tenderloin part of the bird (along the breastbone) for fried strips seems as solid as Plymouth Rock. There is no debate over the fact that there were chicken fingers or sticks before 1974, but tenders they weren't. What does not attract controversy is Puritan as a destination for presidential hopefuls of both parties during the New Hampshire primary.

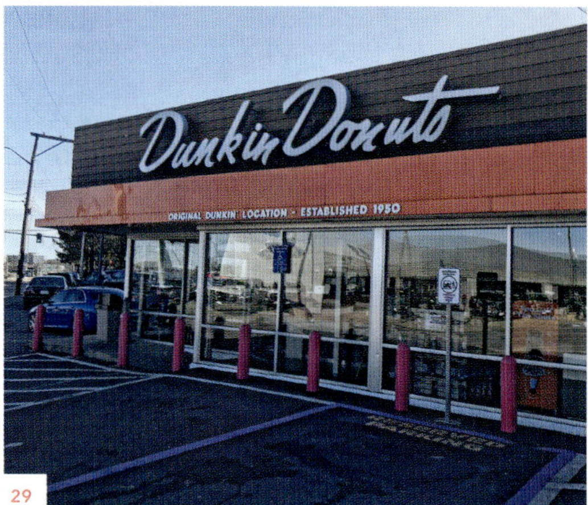

29

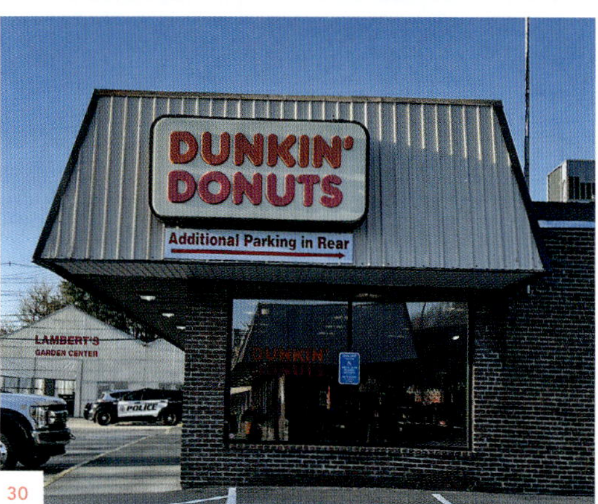

30

CHAINS OF FOOD

It's called Dunkin' these days, and the donuts are still on the racks but not on the signs. **Dunkin' Donuts** was founded by William Rosenberg in Quincy, Massachusetts, in 1948, and was initially called the Open Kettle until he rebranded it Dunkin' Donuts in 1950. Rosenberg is among the great twentieth-century franchise innovators, an entrepreneur who realized coffee and donuts were the top sellers at his lunch-service business at factories and decided that this combination should be the thrust of his new brick-and-mortar enterprise. His chain has grown far and wide from its New England roots, with more than ten thousand stores, but around here, Dunkin' is a hometown spot. It's Dunkies. The site of the original Dunkin' (FIG. 29) in Quincy (pronounced *Quin-zee*) has been renovated in the spirit of the 1950s original, complete with a counter. There are even a couple of Dunkin' Donuts signs from the 1980s that have escaped being upgraded, like this one in Westwood, Massachusetts (FIG. 30). The most sensational survivor, in neon no less, was not in the Boston area but in South Florida; however, it sadly is no longer in public view.

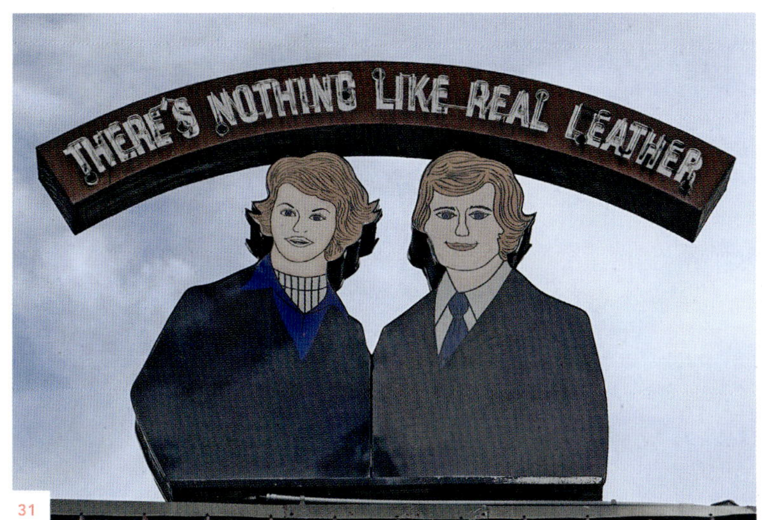

31

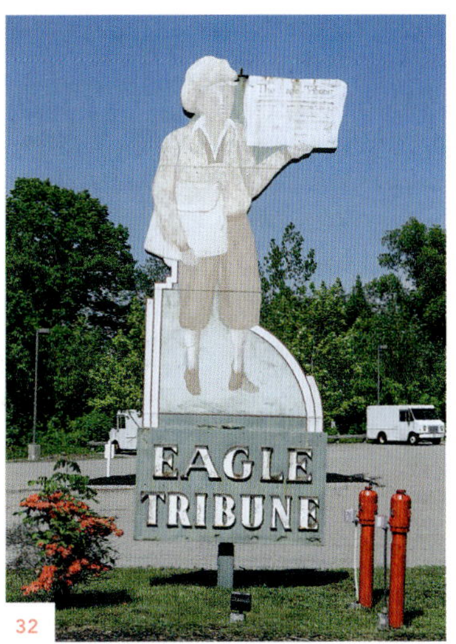

32

MAINSTAYS OF MAIN STREET

Mom-and-pop shops often have the finest examples of design creativity—at least they did back in the day. Here are some of my regional favorites, beginning with a stylish leather-clad couple.

At **Howard's Leather Shop** (FIG. 31) in Spofford, New Hampshire, the 1970s couple sporting leather jackets has long intrigued me. The sign is a replica, but the original couple lurks in the building's basement, mod as ever. It's worth a peek inside for a vintage, family-run department store feel that is increasingly hard to find.

Extra, extra, read all about it! One of my favorite roadside characters is hiding in the parking lot of ***The Eagle-Tribune*** (FIG. 32) newspaper in Lawrence, Massachusetts. Behold the humble paperboy, once the backbone of many a newspaper's circulation department, a job that was a rite of passage for countless children. This delightfully battered sign has survived all the news this forever young fellow has witnessed, and, yet, he and *The Eagle-Tribune* hang on, something many newspapers no longer do.

West End Market (FIG. 33) features a beautiful storefront in North Adams, Massachusetts. The building was constructed in 1919, and the stunning porcelain enamel signage came along later. The Less family long owned the original grocery store.

33

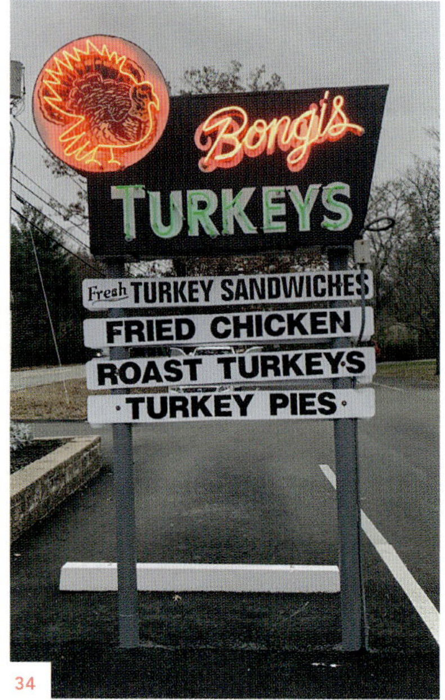

34

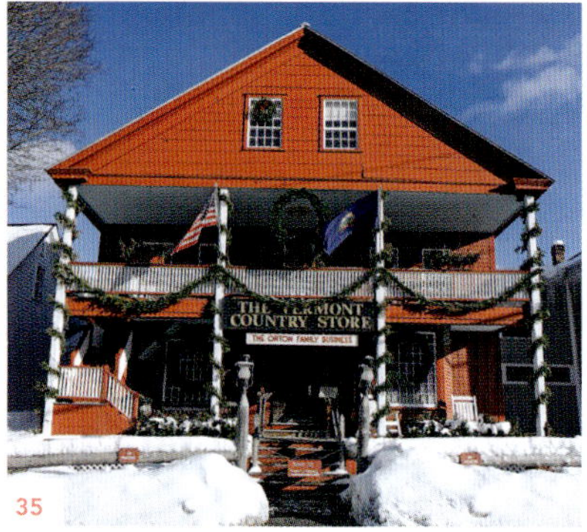

35

Back in 1979, West End Market earned a glowing writeup in the local paper because of the old-fashioned home-delivery service that the Less siblings still offered, just like their pop, Mr. A. A. Less, did in his day. By 1979, North Adams had lost most of its grocery stores. By 1988, West End Market was among the lost, transformed into an art and music gallery, and later an antiques store. And for all the changes, the gorgeous facade has been a constant.

In 2006, Barry and Nancy Garton bought West End Market, and in 2018, they moved their successful legacy business, Brewhaha, here. The Gartons put so much into this place before retiring in 2023.

Bongi's (FIG. 34) may have a turkey on its gorgeous neon sign, but it all began with chickens. In the years before World War II, Italian immigrant Anthony Bongiorno (in time Tony Bongi) and his wife Anna scooped up a 7-acre property in Duxbury, Massachusetts, for $400 and got into the poultry business. After household refrigeration was moving from novelty to necessity, and frozen chickens from other parts of the country were invading grocery stores in the South Shore, the Bongiornos pivoted to turkeys in 1947. Now, it's not Thanksgiving without a visit to Bongi's. The retail business has boomed over the decades, when this area was known as Turkey Row and Route 53 was a dirt road that deposited you onto Cape Cod. Retail got so big that Bongi's no longer raise their turkeys—the White Hollands now come from Pennsylvania—but everything else is the same.

The Vermont Country Store (FIG. 35) is where you can find so many things you didn't think you needed or desired. The store, opened in 1946 in Weston, and then and now run by the Orton family, is also a treasure trove of classic American brands, many of which are hard to find elsewhere.

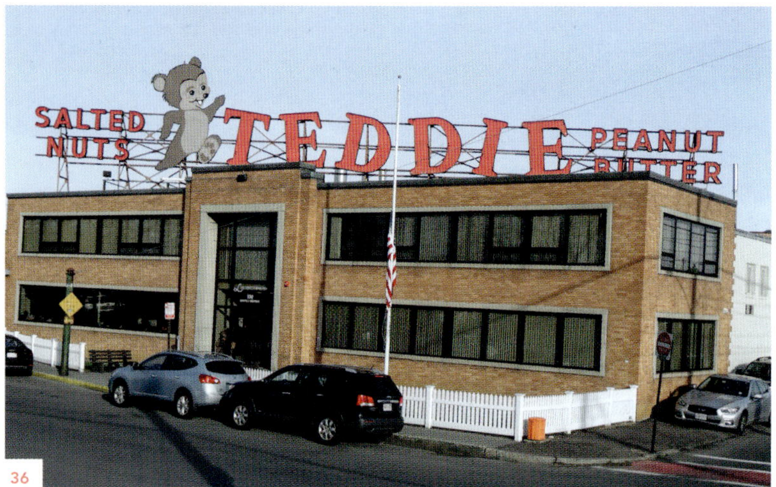

36

Since the Great Depression, **Teddie Peanut Butter** (FIG. 36), a New England family-run company, has been making all-natural peanut butter before that was a thing: All you get is simply delicious ground peanuts—shipped in from the South—with a touch of salt. That's the simple but effective recipe for success at the factory located in Everett, Massachusetts. Well, that and the adorable, ever so cuddly bear mascot.

THE INN CROWD

From mom-and-pop motor courts to Bob Newhart's sitcom inn on *Newhart*, New England has a diverse array of places to stay that have character.

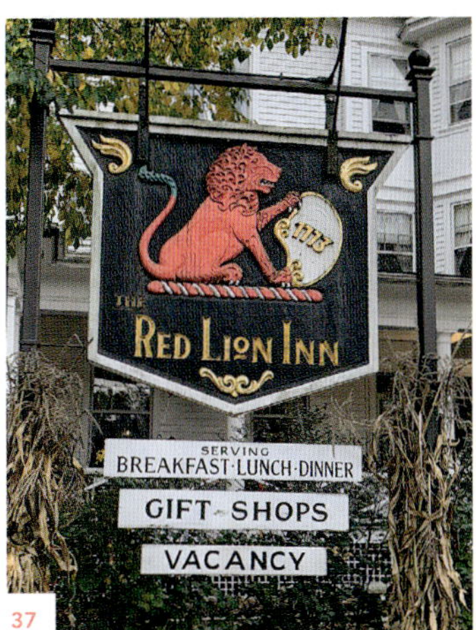

37

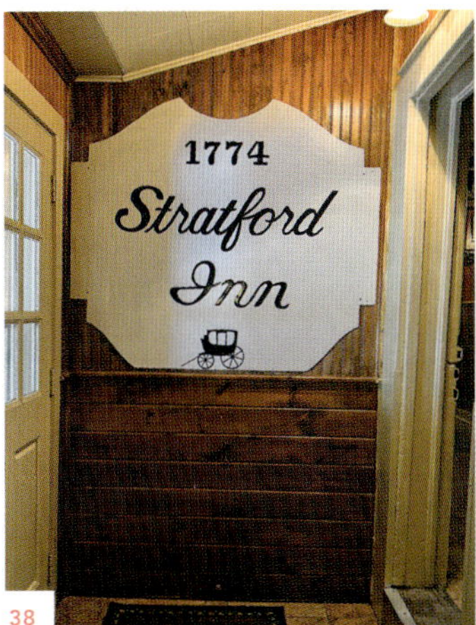

38

The historic **Red Lion** (FIG. 37) is the spiritual heart of Stockbridge, Massachusetts, a perfect setting to complement a visit to the Norman Rockwell Museum nearby. In December, one of Norman Rockwell's famous paintings, *Stockbridge Main Street at Christmas (Home for Christmas)*, is re-created on the streets outside, making it as good a time as any to go.

When I think of New England inns, my television-saturated brain thinks of *Newhart*, and in Middlebury, Vermont, the **Waybury Inn** (FIG. 38) is the stand-in for the Stratford Inn on the Bob Newhart sitcom. I stopped there briefly to check in on the Loudons, and perhaps run into Larry, his brother Darryl, and his other brother Darryl. Well, no such luck, but as I sauntered to the front desk, I announced that I was a *Newhart* fan, and the innkeeper knew the drill. She tipped us off to a Stratford Inn sign that's in the back of the hotel. The inside, of course, bears no resemblance to the MTM (Mary Tyler Moore) Productions set, but there's certainly charm to spare, more than two centuries of it. She also confirmed that Bob Newhart never visited the inn, though he did send along an autographed picture, advising to "take care of my inn!"

▶▶▶ Pull Over!

If the Von Trapp family name sounds familiar to you, an iconic place to stay along the New England circuit is at the **Trapp Family Lodge** in Stowe, Vermont. New Hampshire boasts the **Twin Mountain Campground**, with a sign that's simplicity in cursive, and **Proctor's Lakehouse Cottages**, which has a neon gem. You can salute the **Lord Hampshire** in Tilton, and dive into the pool at the **Rye Motor Inn** (FIG. 39), a retro boutique motel right by the Atlantic Ocean with its history going back to 1956, when it was known as the Surf Haven. The **Maine Idyll Motor Court** in Freeport, and its roadside neon sign, live up to its name. The Marstaller family have been your hosts here since the 1930s.

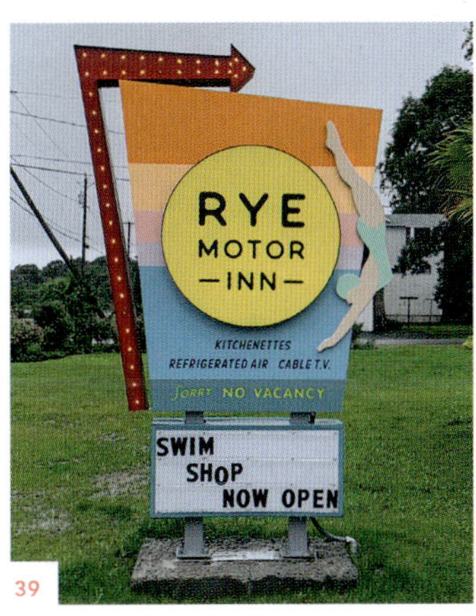

39

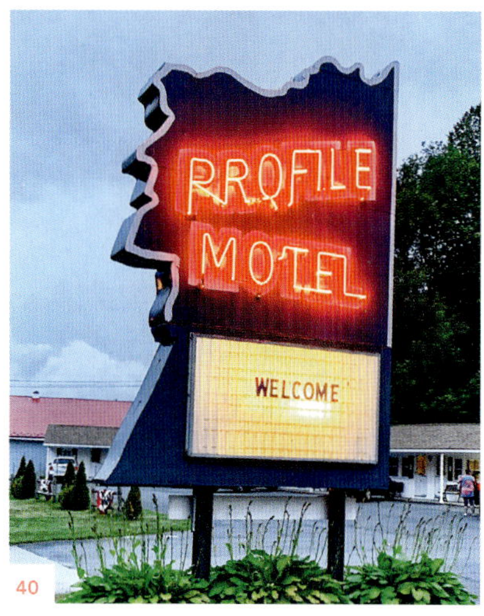

40

One sign in New England preserves a natural feature that was—literally—the face of the state. The **Profile Motel and Cottages** (FIG. 40) in Lincoln, New Hampshire, features in neon the face carved by retreating glaciers millennia ago, a profile in granite that inspired Native American legends, enchanted Daniel Webster and Nathaniel Hawthorne, and symbolized the rugged individualism of a state whose motto is "Live Free or Die."

South Dakota's Mount Rushmore was the work of humans. But **New Hampshire's Old Man of the Mountain**, it's been said, was the work of a higher authority. So when the Great Stone Face came crashing down in the darkness of May 3, 2003, the people of New Hampshire mourned. In his physical absence, the Profile became more powerful. He lives on in the state's license plates, in a mountainside memorial, on coffee mugs, in the imaginations of roadside roamers, and at this motel.

SWEET STOPS

New England and the donut—it's a love affair that's best consummated with a cup of coffee. But some of the sweetest places are also a little bewitching. Read on!

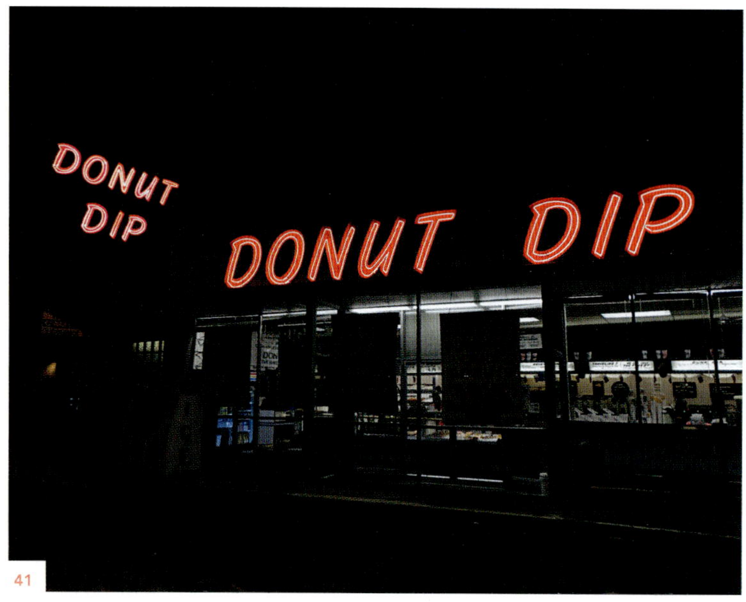

41

In West Springfield, Massachusetts, is **Donut Dip** (FIG. 41) (not to be confused with the other "DD," Dunkin' Donuts). Opened in 1957, Donut Dip is still a mom-and-pop and for years had only one other location. The donuts are made right here, and they're made with love. They are *so* good, and the people here are *so* nice. And this place is a vintage delight inside—enjoy some of the wonderful signs behind the counter, too.

Twin Donuts (FIG. 42) in Allston, Massachusetts, is a survivor—no small feat when you're competing for the hearts

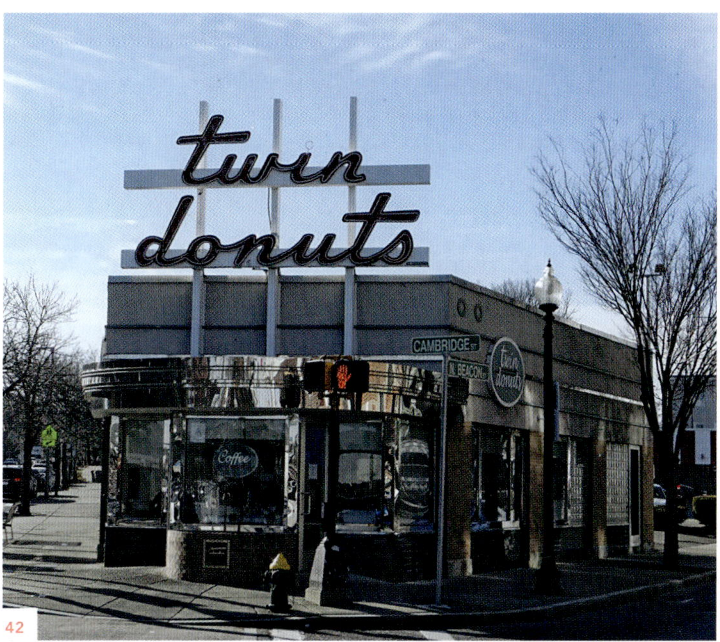

42

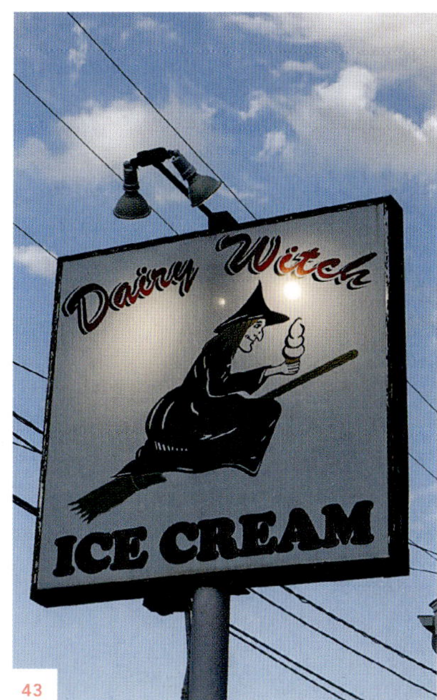

43

and stomachs of carb lovers in Dunkin's ancestral homeland. But don't worry about Twin—the shop, which opened in 1955, often finds itself at the top of Boston donut lists and has a passionate following. Customers come for the donuts and coffee, of course. But surely, they are drawn to the place by its midcentury vibe, its unmistakable authenticity, and its prominent perch at the corner of Cambridge and North Beacon Streets.

When in Salem, Massachusetts, you lean into the witch thing. It makes good business sense. **Dairy Witch** (FIG. 43) is a classic ice-cream stand that took on its bewitching name in 1952 when landowners Beatrice and Peter Polemenako took over a year-old ice-cream stand whose original operators had to move on. The family has run the shop ever since, and they pride themselves on quality dairy treats and friendly service. I was advised to get the "banana whipped frappé" or the crunch coat, often mistaken for peanut brittle, though that's not quite right, since it's bits of peanut brittle mixed with rainbow sprinkles. (Be sure to say hello to the TV Witch—TV Land's **Samantha Stephens statue**, a tribute to the *Bewitched* character, in downtown Salem.)

Caddy's (FIG. 44) in Cumberland Center, Maine, has all the elements of a classic roadside ice-cream stand, but it opened in 2013. It goes to show it's not necessarily how long a place has been around that matters—it's about the intention behind it. And who doesn't love the repurposed Big Boy statue proudly displaying an ice-cream cone instead of his signature hamburger?

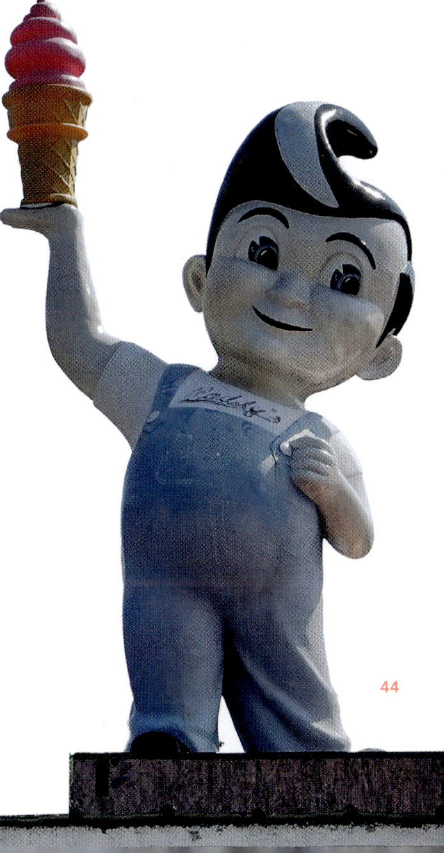
44

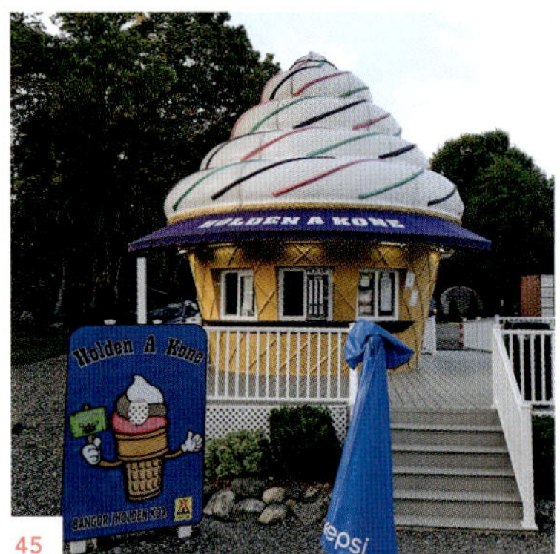

45

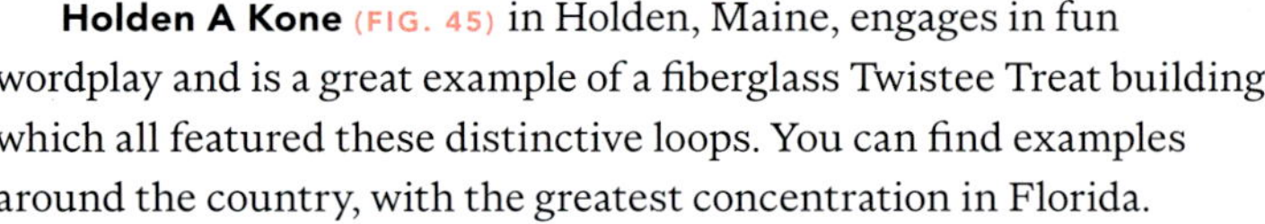

Holden A Kone (FIG. 45) in Holden, Maine, engages in fun wordplay and is a great example of a fiberglass Twistee Treat building, which all featured these distinctive loops. You can find examples around the country, with the greatest concentration in Florida.

Richardson's Ice Cream (FIG. 46) in Middleton, Massachusetts, is not your average roadside stop. It traces its roots to the 1600s, when the Richardson family arrived here from England and began farming, initially just to feed the family. But as the centuries wore on, this became a working dairy farm, and by the early twentieth century, they were in the milk and, later, the ice-cream business starting in 1952. Indeed, you can have a shake and then visit with the dairy cows that helped provide your treat.

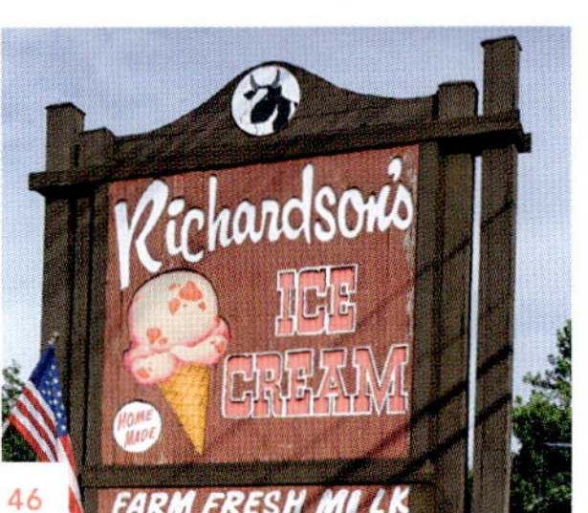

46

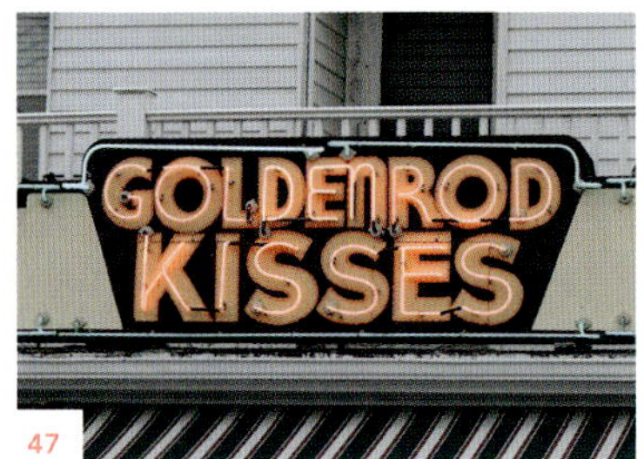

47

We can't leave a New England sweets section without a nod to a candy shop, and **The Goldenrod** (FIG. 47) in York Beach, Maine, has been a treasure for sweet teeth since 1896. Pick up some saltwater taffy—and the Goldenrod Kisses—and head for the beach!

CHEERS!

Neon signs have a certain sizzle. It's science, of course. But it's something much grander than that. They can transport you to a swell time in a town's life when having a bar with an art deco neon sign said something special about your city. Our first examples nails it.

▶▶▶ Pull Over!

Package shops—a regional name for liquor stores, often called "packies"—are sprinkled throughout Connecticut and Massachusetts. Some of the most sensational signage includes the **Old Colony Package Store** in Old Saybrook, Connecticut; the deliciously vintage **H&L Package Store** in Hartford, Connecticut, complete with a Coca-Cola "dot" sign; and **Billy's Package Store,** with its epic "blade" neon sign, also in Hartford.

This beauty still says something special about the Massachusetts city of Westfield, where it graces **The City Hotel** (FIG. 48). There has been a cafe on the ground floor of 43 Elm Street since 1912, when the Daley family opened this hotel. They gave the cafe an art deco makeover a few decades later—check out the curves on the sign, the glass blocks, the porthole windows on the doors, the tile, and of course the futuristic font that seems to have anticipated the Pac-Man fever that would consume America in the 1980s.

The **Anchor Spa** (FIG. 49) is a miracle of sorts, a revival of a cherished New Haven, Connecticut, bar that abruptly closed in 2015 amid a rent dispute with landlord Yale University. Brought back the next year by new owners, the Anchor Spa (returning to its original name) continues a College Street tradition with historic ties to the local intellectuals and the theater scene. The name refers to Anchor Beach in Milford, Connecticut, where the bar first opened in 1933.

Next door is the **Owl Shop** (FIG. 50), where cigar smoke first wafted in 1934. The shop had humble roots as a traditional cigar store that catered to Yale academics, Hollywood actors who appeared at the Shubert Theatre down the street, and anybody else who wanted a good smoke prepared by pros. In the 2000s, the shop morphed by necessity from history-rich-but-shopworn relic into what it is today: a throwback to an era when you could smoke, drink, and listen to good live music inside a cinematically lit, wood-paneled, elegant setting. And no, the Owl Shop has not lost its ties to its days as a simple cigar shop.

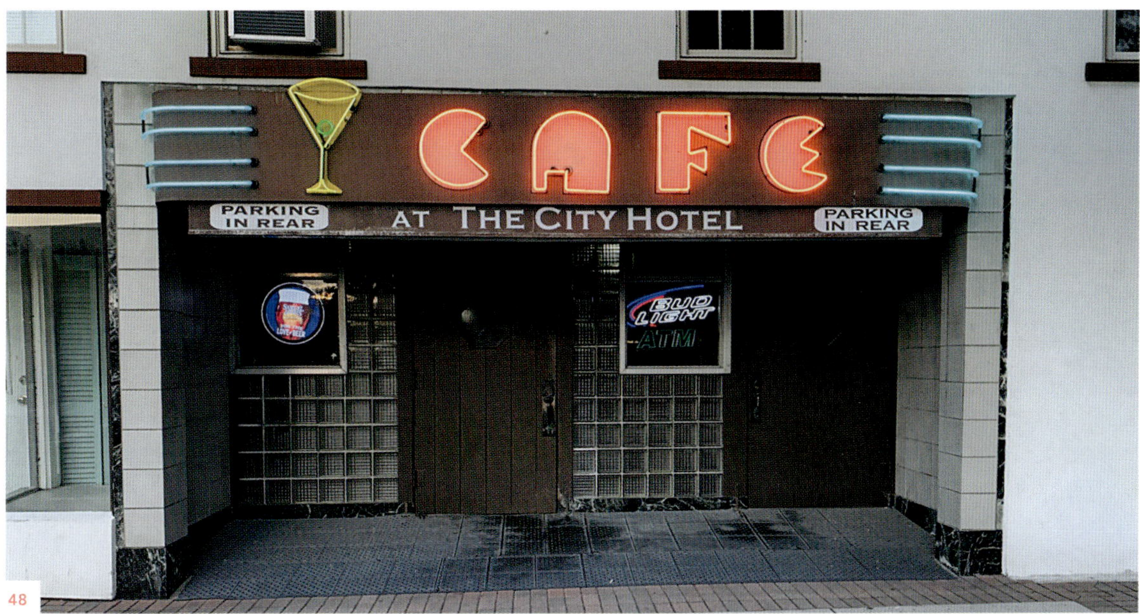

48

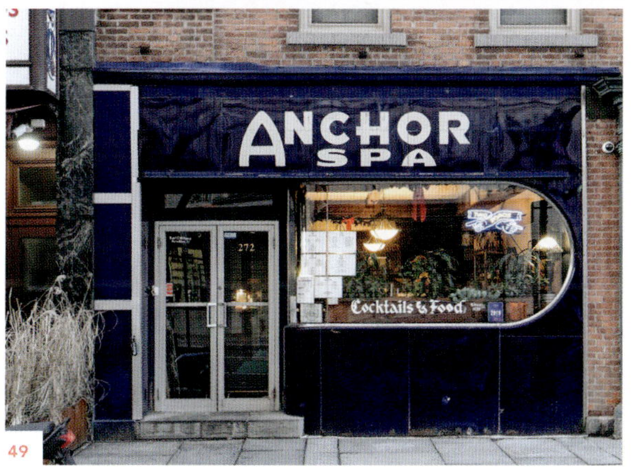

49

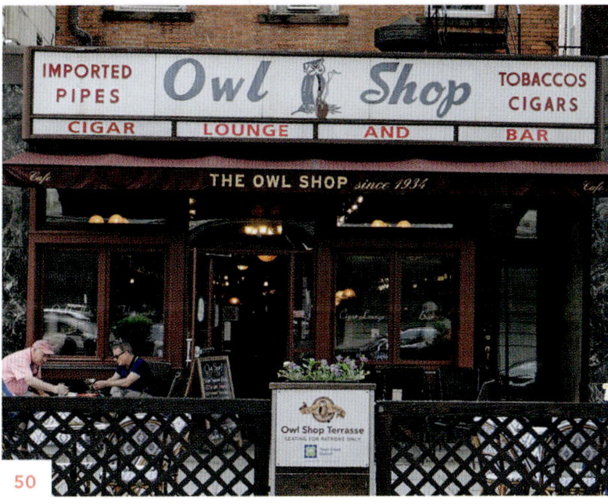

50

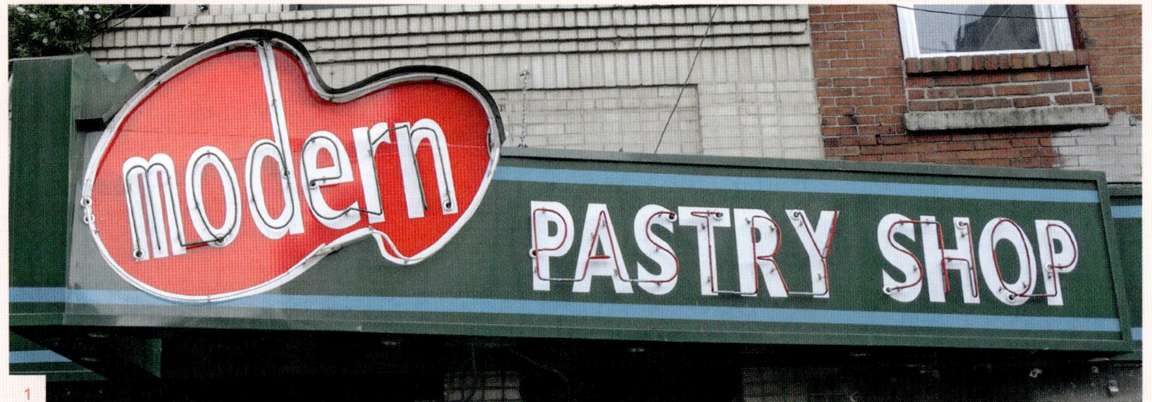

1

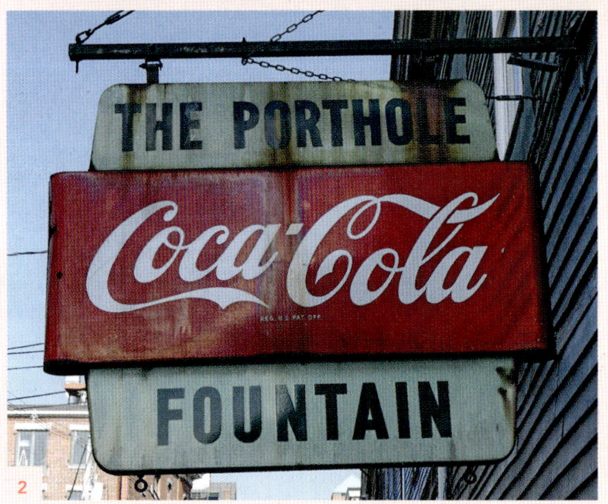

2

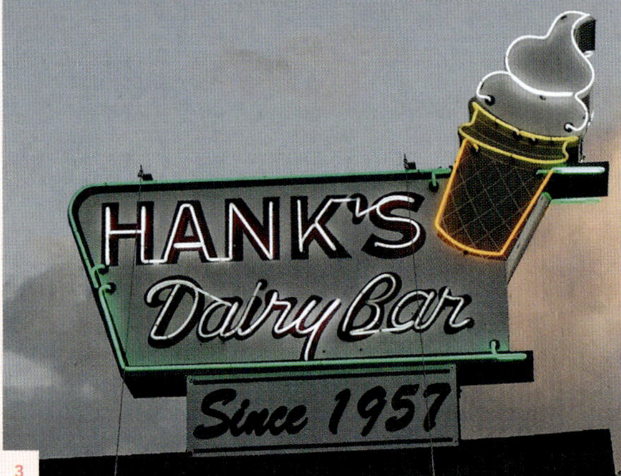

3

PRIDE OF THE YANKEES: VINTAGE VERNACULAR

We have a little bit of everything here—add these to your GPS on your next trip.

1. Modern Pastry Shop, Boston, Massachusetts
2. The Porthole, Portland, Maine
3. Hank's Dairy Bar, Plainfield, Connecticut
4. Carter's Little Liver Pills sign, Brattleboro, Vermont
5. Hotel Hi-Ho, Fairfield, Connecticut
6. Jug Shop, Wareham, Massachusetts
7. Joe's Playland, Salisbury, Massachusetts
8. Simco's, Mattapan, Massachusetts
9. Weirs Beach, Laconia, New Hampshire
10. Moonwink, Manchester Center, Vermont
11. The Freeze, Bennington, Vermont

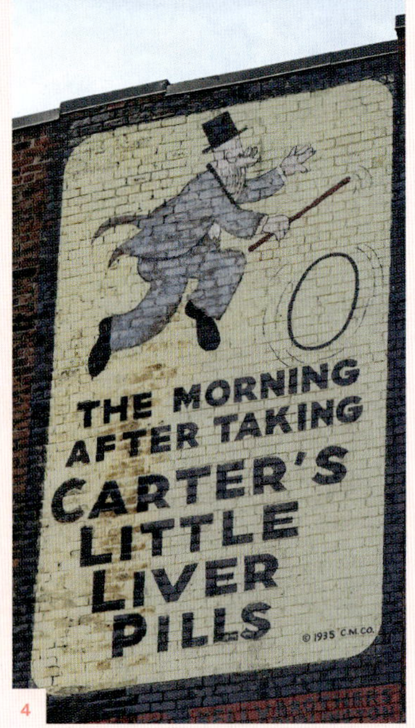

4

HOTEL
HI-HO
5

The
JUG
SHOP
Play THE LOTTERY Here!
6

JOE'S PLAYLAND
ARCADE
TAFFY
COTTON CANDY
DAIRY TWIRL
SKEE BALL
FOOD
7

WORLDS LARGEST
SIMCO
FRANKS
&
PRODUCTS
8

WEIRS
BEACH
9

MOON WINK
10

TF
TASTEE FREEZ
11

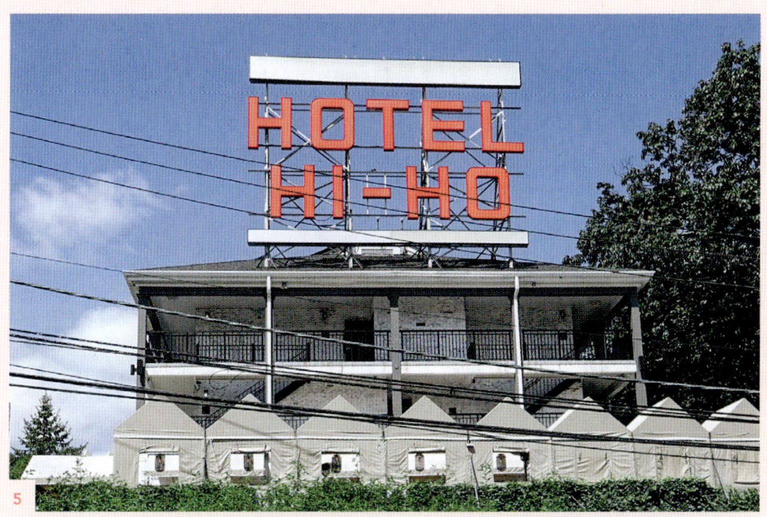

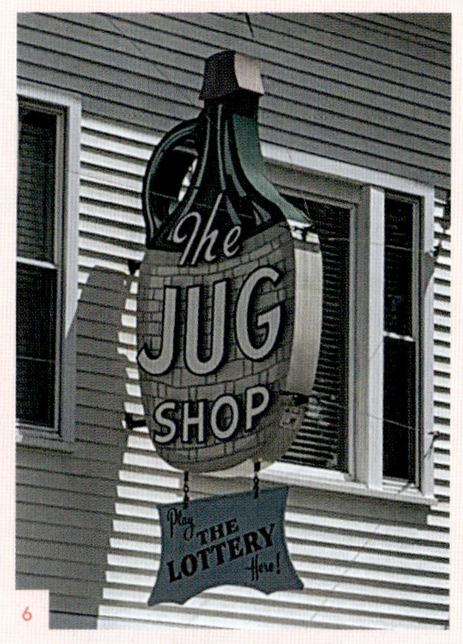

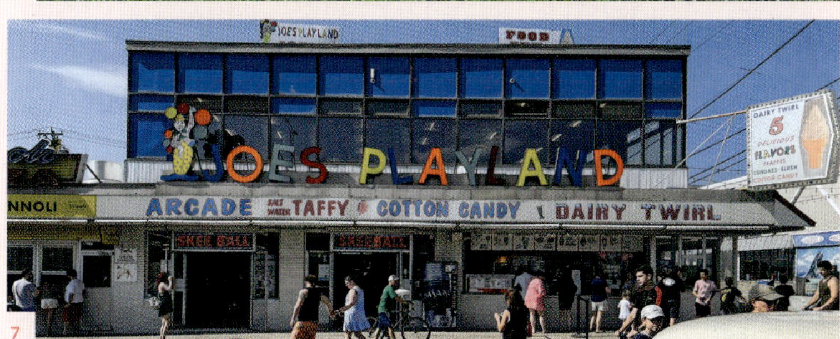

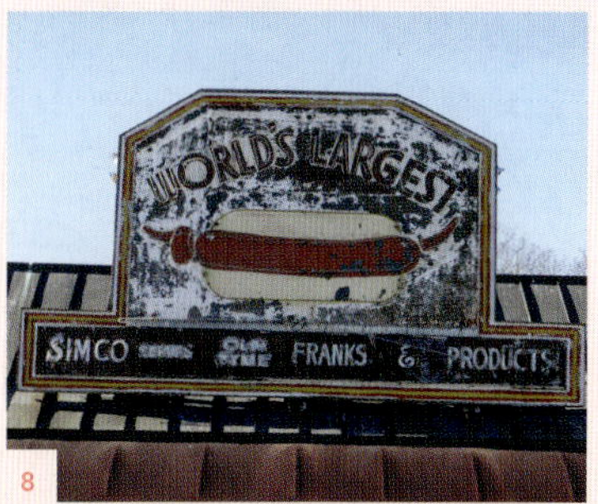

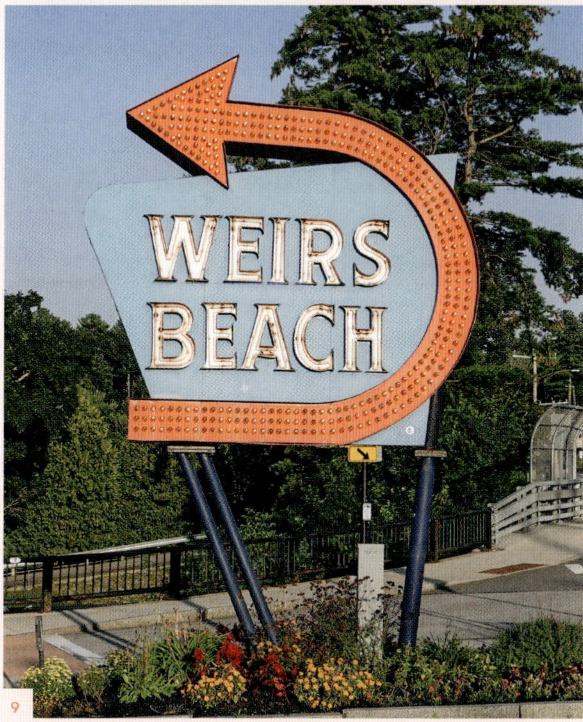

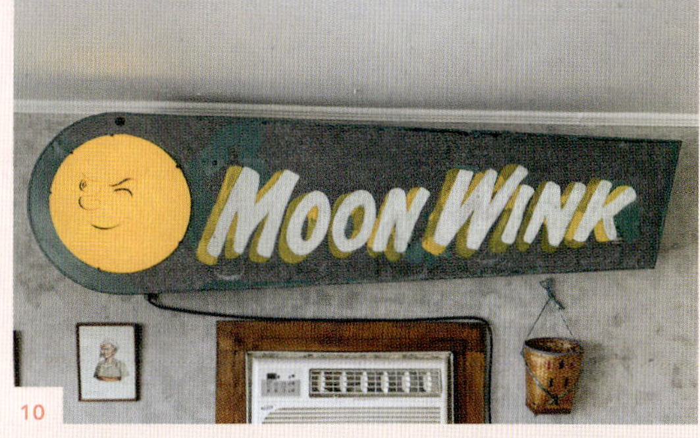

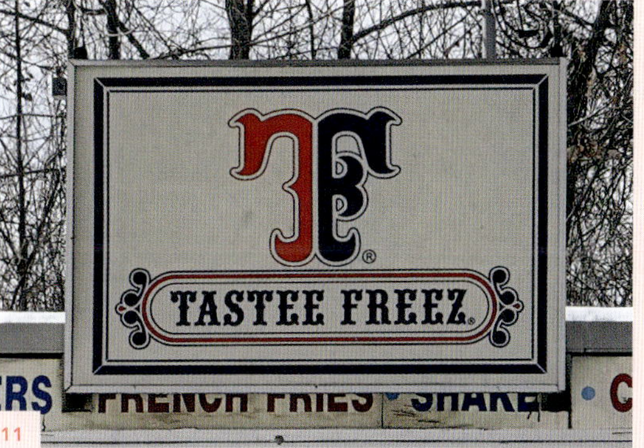

MID-ATLANTIC

DELAWARE · MARYLAND
WASHINGTON, D.C. · PARTS OF VIRGINIA

Some of the gems of the Mid-Atlantic are easy to miss because I-95 is so effective at conveying us to our destinations. But this region has a nice collection of curiosities that merit an exit or a day of exploring back roads. Let's see what we find.

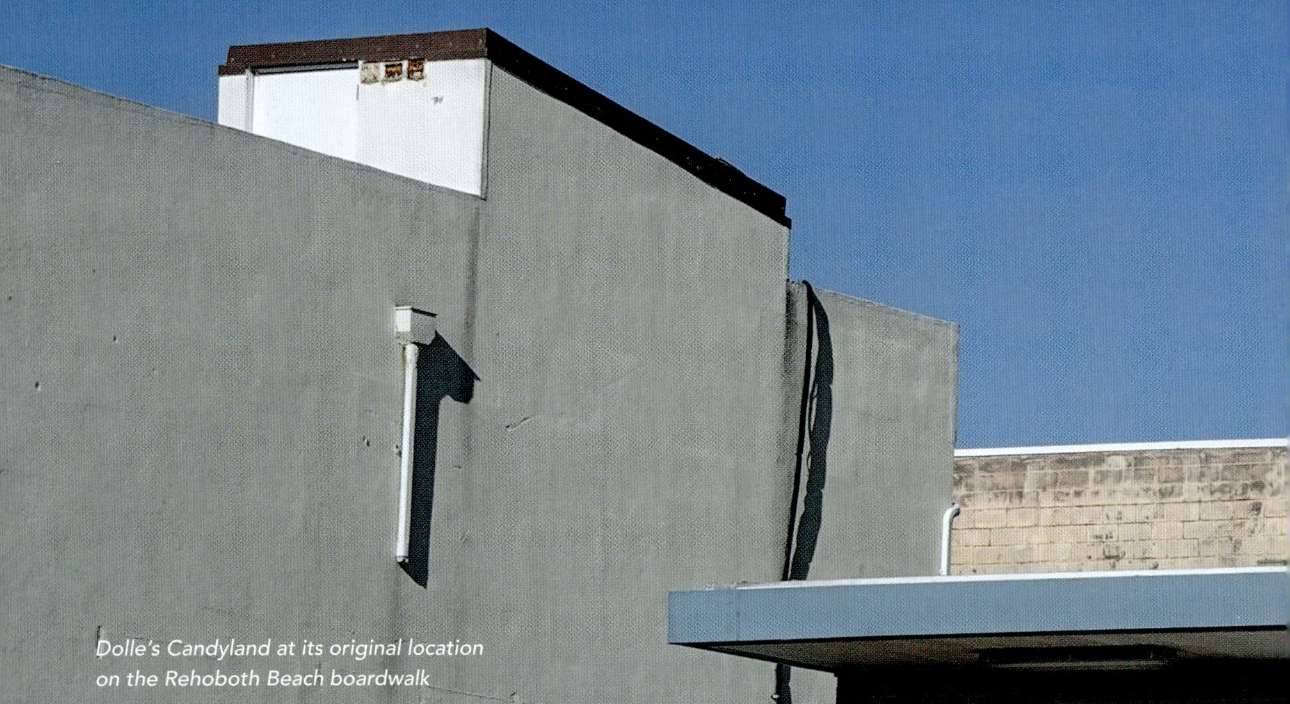

Dolle's Candyland at its original location on the Rehoboth Beach boardwalk

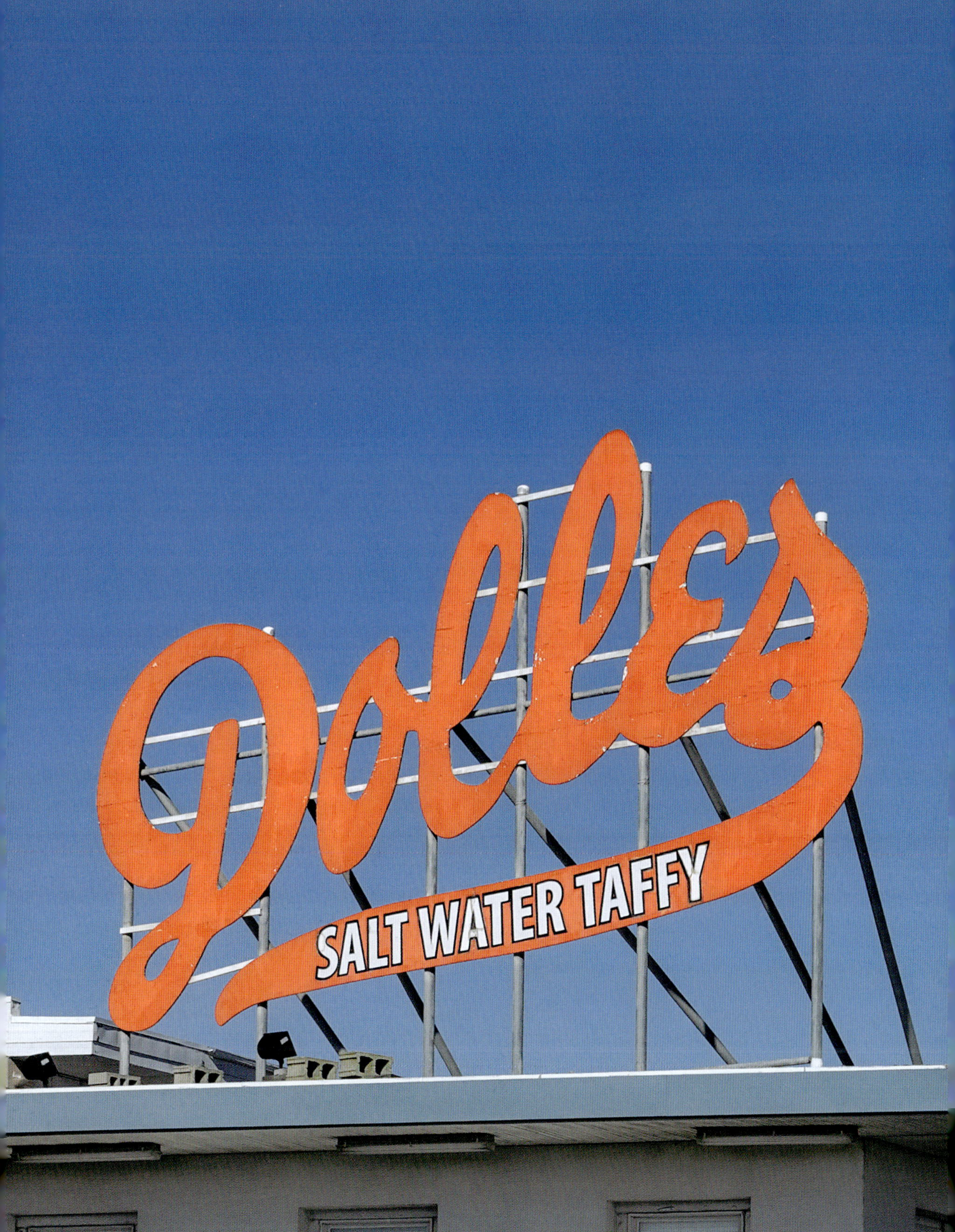
Dolles
SALT WATER TAFFY

ROADSIDE QUIRKS

From monsters (two of them) to Big Boys (one of them) to dinosaurs (dozens of them), these quirky stops demonstrate some of the region's roadside royalty that's easy to miss when you're trying to get somewhere else. This should be your somewhere else.

We've just crossed over from New Jersey and find ourselves in Dover, Delaware. And greeting us in the state that was once known as the "Small Wonder" is a Big Wonder: **Miles the Monster** (FIG. 1). This terrifying 46-foot-tall giant of impressive physique, bold jaw, NASCAR-race-car-toting fist, and red-eyed intensity awaits visitors at the Dover Motor Speedway. A fiberglass golem bursting from the track, Miles is a manifestation of the speedway's nickname, the "Monster Mile," for the challenging course here. He was installed in 2008 to celebrate the racetrack's fortieth anniversary, and he's been causing nightmares—and gamely posing for photos—ever since. Fun fact: An earlier version of Miles the Monster, whose name was picked in a 1990 contest, was a not-so-scary T-rex.

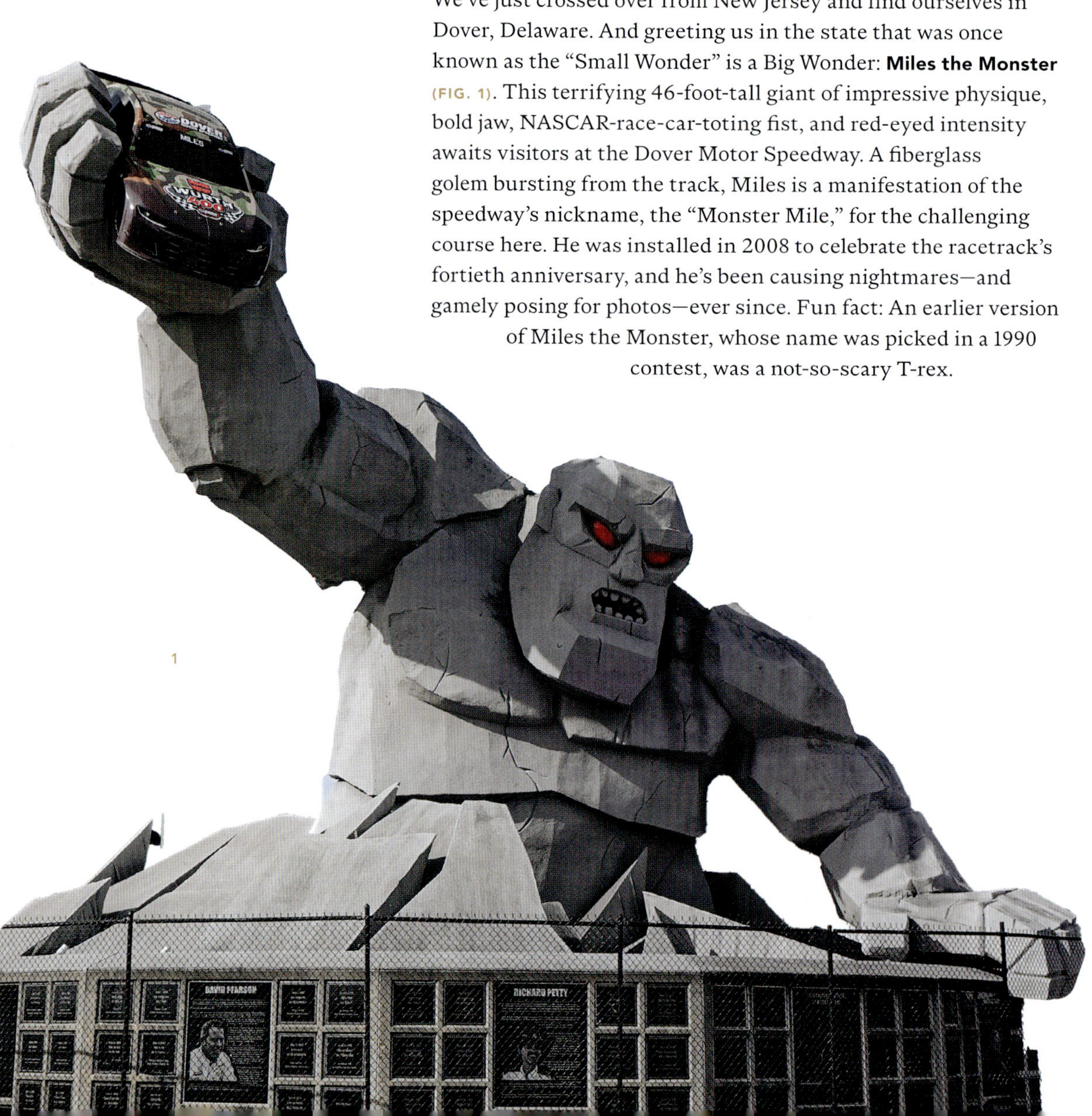

1

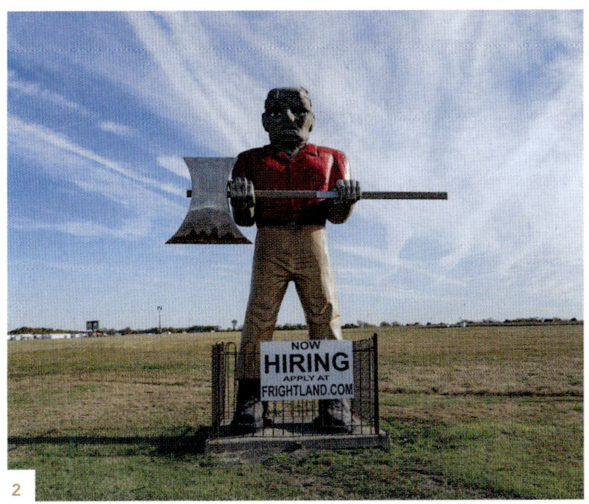

2

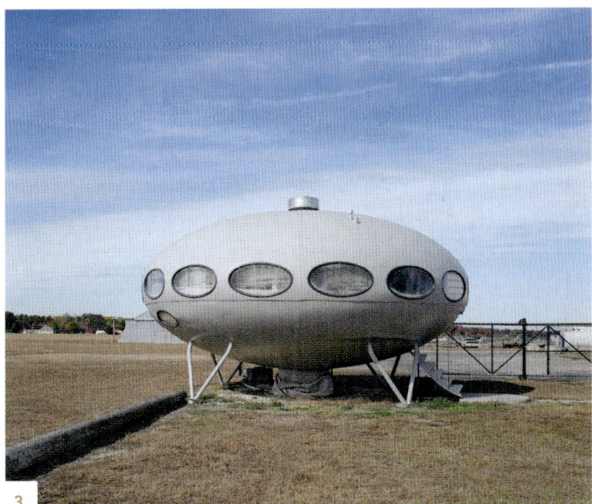

3

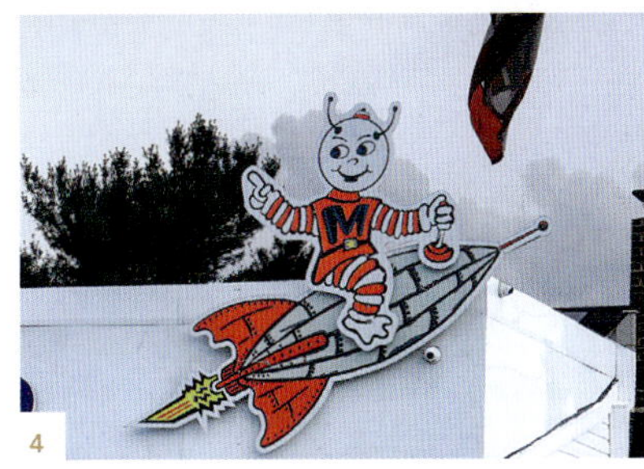

4

Not to paint Delaware in too spooky a light, but I felt compelled to point out that in a field in Middletown stands a giant fiberglass **Frankenstein Muffler Man** (FIG. 2) statue carrying an axe, its tip crimson from, I will only assume, the blood of his victims. This scary fellow is merely here to greet visitors to the Frightland, a Halloween-time horror attraction. Keep an eye out for, or, rather, keep an eye *on*, the silo on the property that's been turned into a giant skull.

Okay, enough frights. How about a toast? The Mid-Atlantic is the turf of **Mr. Boh** (FIG. 5), the proto-hipster mascot who represents National Bohemian Beer, Baltimore's hometown brew.

The official company history states that Mr. Boh was introduced in 1936, just three years after the end of Prohibition. He's a charmer, this gentleman, with luscious locks, a single knowing eye, a smirk, and a mustache, making him the envy of urban dandies who could only dream of sprouting a handlebar so refined. And he's "married" to the **Utz Girl** of potato chip fame. They'll surely have the most adorable children.

In the Northeast, we visited a "UFO" house (see page 15)—and another **Futuro House** (FIG. 3) has roosted in Milton, Delaware. Perhaps that's where the Moonman landed. He's the out-of-this-world mascot for **Moon Air HVAC** (FIG. 4) in Elkton, Maryland. The character makes appearances at community events and parades, and is a hit with kids of all ages, myself included.

Moonman is "perhaps one of the more recognizable mascots in the HVAC industry," according to the *Air Conditioning Heating & Refrigeration News* in a profile of owner Steve Moon and his character, which he said he

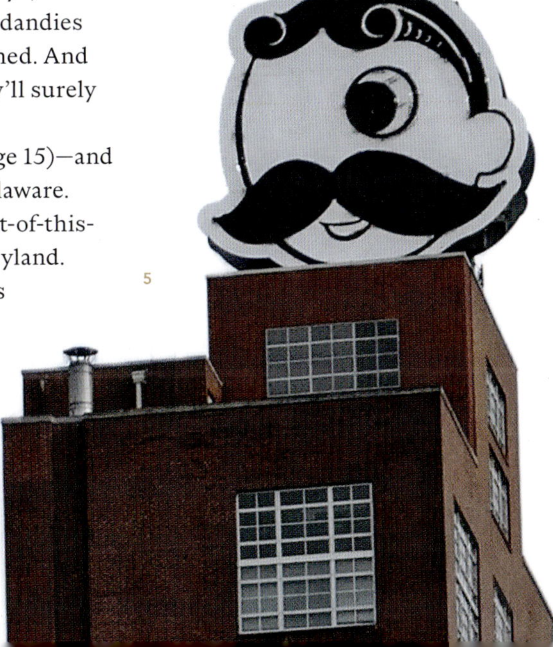

5

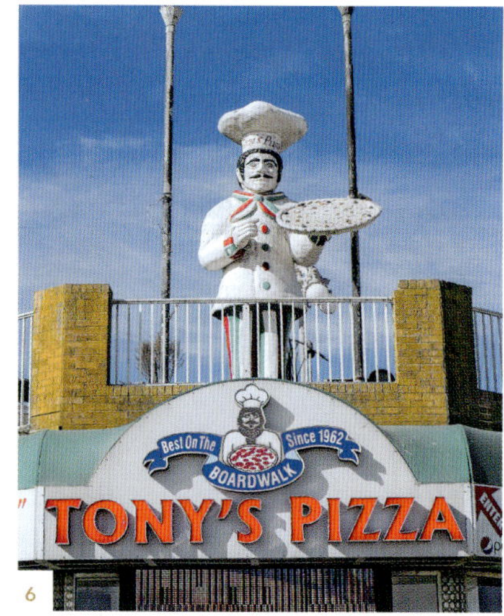

6

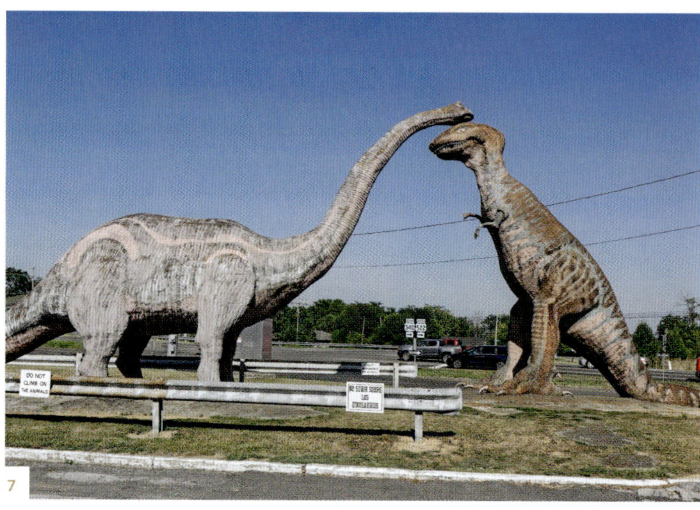
7

borrowed from his father's heating and air business in Virginia. This is a niche category for sure, but one that, like any, can benefit from character-driven branding. (Head to page 102 to meet another, far more famous, Moonman.)

A pizza chef towers over **Tony's Pizza** (FIG. 6) in Ocean City, Maryland. (Tony's twin, Vince, is a longtime curbside pizzaiolo at **Vince's Pizza** in Rochelle, Illinois.)

A roadside giant that's hard to miss is the bright yellow **Crash Test Dummy** (FIG. 8) outside the Maryland Department of Motor Vehicles in Glen Burnie, Maryland. The big dummy has been demonstrating the virtue of buckling up since 2012. In the 1980s, Crash Test Dummies became pop-culture icons, along with McDonald's Mac Tonight and Bud Light's Spuds MacKenzie, and the wisecracking characters achieved a cultural cachet that is most vividly concretized in this spot.

Another must-see in the region is **Dinosaur Land** (FIG. 7) in White Post, Virginia, a 1960s mom-and-pop attraction of the highest order. The park has kept growing since Joseph Geraci founded the tourist stop in 1962. Still in the same family, the park now features over fifty fiberglass dinosaurs "roaming" through a rambling, hilly park, with other creatures, including a giant King Kong and a gigantic octopus, to capture your attention. You can even step inside a menacing shark.

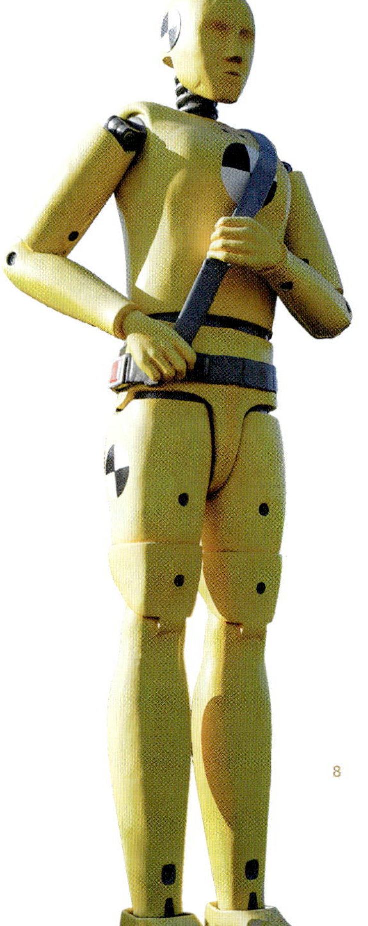
8

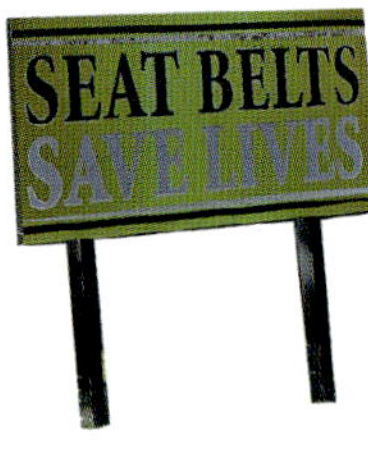

ROADSIDE EATS

The Mid-Atlantic offers us an interesting mix of iconic mom-and-pop restaurants, along with an increasing number of places that feature barbecue and Southern comfort food as we work our way south. Here's a sampler platter of vintage (and one vintage-inspired) spots across the region.

While visiting any one of these restaurants, you'll find it hard not to chat with whatever stranger is sidled up beside you, and that's part of what makes these places such treasures. They were "third places" before such a term became urban-planner speak for a gathering area that's not your home or your place of employ but a separate location where you can mingle at your leisure. At a mom-and-pop eatery, we meet one another on humble terms, equal subjects of the lunch-counter workers, gathered to nourish our needs for sustenance and companionship.

Let's start our tour at the old-school **Blue & White Carry Out**, a mere ten-minute walk from the colonial charms of King Street in Old Town Alexandria, Virginia, but it might as well be a world away. It's certainly not a travel-guide chestnut, nor is it likely to be the first recommendation your hotel concierge will offer. But the Blue & White is a winner with its utter simplicity and charming Coca-Cola privilege sign, the sort given out by companies for free in exchange for perpetual promotion of their brands.

Its standard dishes are all hearty breakfast fare and Southern comfort food; the fried chicken, pork chop, and hamburger steak sandwiches are popular.

Bring your cash—plastic and chips are no good here. There's a line out the door when this place is hopping, which makes sense given its miniature size and grand reputation among locals.

Nearby is another old business painted in blue and white and with a bright future though a much shorter past: **Goodies Frozen Custard & Treats** (FIG. 9) is nostalgic by design.

Its proprietor is Brandon Byrd, whose ice-cream business began in a 1950s van. He graduated to brick-and-mortar and purchased an old ice-house substation—from the days when people kept iceboxes in their kitchens and needed regular ice delivery—and turned it into a charming purveyor of Wisconsin-style custard and other sweet goodies.

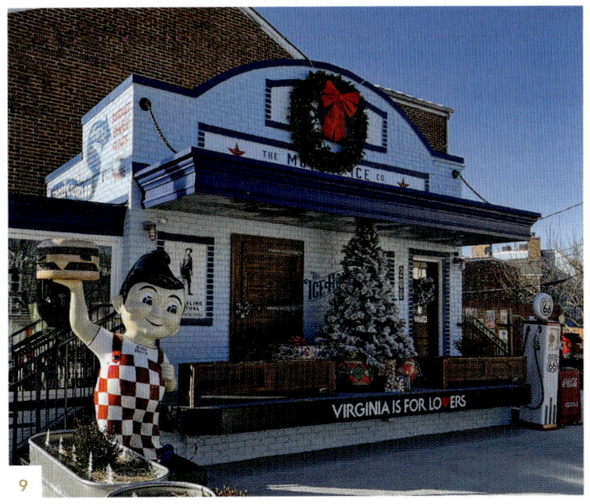

9

Opening a small business is never easy. Opening this cute stand during the pandemic, when few people were walking outside their homes, is heroic, something we risk forgetting as the years go by. Thanks to Byrd, we have this gracious tableau here in Old Town Alexandria, very much in the spirit of the community where history is everything and everywhere.

There's a cute if self-destructive pig in Old Town Alexandria, a neon beauty touting **The Dixie Pig Bar-B-Q** (FIG. 10). That restaurant is long gone, replaced with a highly regarded Greek restaurant called Vaso's Kitchen. Kudos to the new hands for keeping a bright trace of the old in such good condition. Preserving a sign that outshines your own name is a commitment, all right.

We move on now to Arlington and check in on our friends at the charmingly monikered **Weenie Beenie** (FIG. 11). Dating to the 1950s and the last holdout of a small chain, the roadside stand specializes in hot dogs, including those ever-popular half smokes, as well as North Carolina–style barbecue. Weenie Beenie has carved out a secure place in popular culture, appearing in a Zippy cartoon and serving as the presumed inspiration for a Foo Fighters song.

The stand is named for Bill "Weenie Beenie" Staton, a man who knew his way around a pool table and played with the greatest names in the game, including Minnesota Fats.

History runs deep, too, at **Ben's Chili Bowl** (FIG. 12), one of the most cherished vintage restaurants in Washington, D.C. Barack Obama and countless other luminaries have dined at the restaurant, open since 1958. The storefront is smoking, as are the chili dogs. (Get the half smoke. Trust me.) I first visited in 2013 and make it a point to drop by whenever I'm in the area. I'm not alone in that. A book released in 2024, *Breaking Barriers with Chili*, goes so far as to call Virginia Ali, born in 1933 and the wife of Ben, the restaurant's late founder, the "Matriarch of D.C."

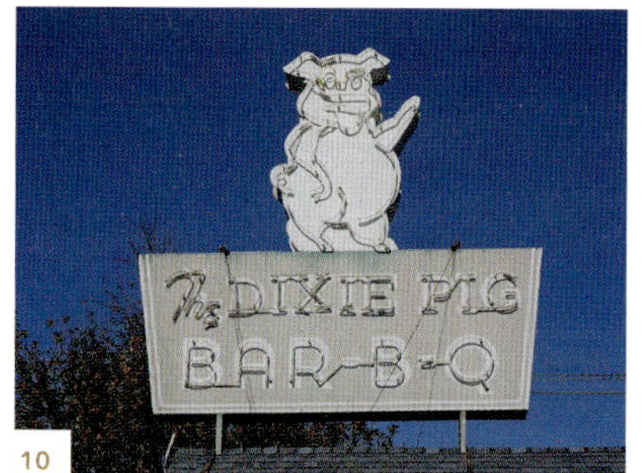

10

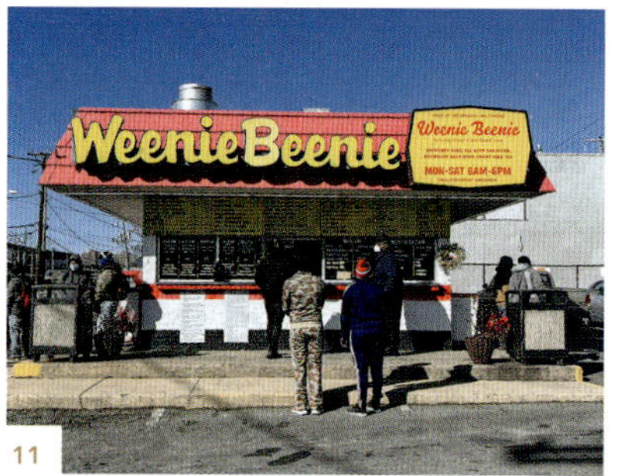

11

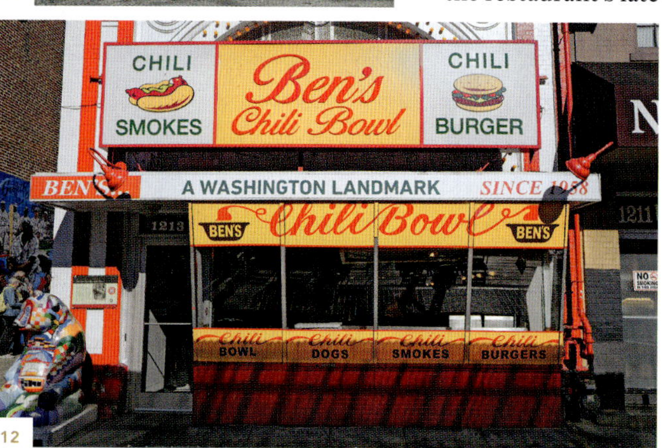

12

The Black-owned business stayed open amid the unrest of the Civil Rights era, stuck with the U Street neighborhood during down times, and has emerged as one of America's greatest mom-and-pop restaurants. Step into the restaurant with its all-original interior, the photos of celebrities and political icons dotting the white walls, and inhale the intoxicatingly redolent grill, whose bounty earned Ben's a James Beard Award. Oh, and don't forget to have a milkshake before you go.

Waffle Shops (FIG. 13) are an (almost) vanished icon of The District. The small chain of shops, noted for its curvy neon signage and art moderne design flair, was a staple in this town for much of the twentieth century. When developer Douglas Jemal purchased the site of a beautifully intact Waffle Shop on Tenth Street NW in the mid-2000s, he relieved preservationist alarm by saving architectural remnants for reassembly elsewhere.

While it took years for the relics to resurface, Jemal delivered on his promise, building a tribute to the Waffle Shop (with a fresh neon sign) nearby. That building attracted a pizzeria, **Stellina**, which, as a nod to the big neon sign that competes with its own smaller one in an adjacent entrance, offers waffles along with its slices. The Waffle Shop is flanked by an old Lord Baltimore gas station and the rebuilt Hodges Sandwich Shop, another defunct Capital City eatery. This special staging is all the handiwork of Jemal, a developer with the heart of a preservationist.

One last taste of the old-school Waffle Shop chain can be found in Alexandria, Virginia, where the distinctive signage still shines. Inside, an oasis of leather stools and terrazzo floor wraps you in mid-twentieth-century restaurant comfort.

A ways away in Annapolis, Maryland, is a restaurant steeped in local political pedigree—**Chick & Ruth's Delly** (FIG. 14). Since 1965, the delicatessen has been dishing out inventive sandwiches and has become a requisite stop for powerbrokers, whose visits are memorialized with a sandwich all their own. Former state governor Larry Hogan can stop by anytime to enjoy his "Hogan's Hero," for instance—a cheesesteak with American cheese and grilled onions. The adventurous can sign up for colossal challenges, like consuming impossibly large milkshakes and sandwiches.

Let's head next to Laurel, Maryland, one of those bucket-list cities where you can find the former **Little Tavern hamburger stand** (FIG. 15), now called Laurel Tavern Donuts, the storybook cottage of comfort food you see here—and whose new iteration still includes tiny burgers made with the original recipe. The Laurel location of this defunct hamburger chain opened circa 1940 and people kept "buying 'em by the bag," as the slogan went, until this store closed in 2006. The owners of this treasure now are Will and Jin Kwon, who bought it back in 2008.

Harry F. Duncan began the business in Louisville, Kentucky, in the mid-1920s, at the height of America's slider craze. Duncan soon moved Little Tavern headquarters to the Washington, D.C., area, where dozens of these baby Tudor temples to tiny hamburgers thrived. He became a very rich man, as many have by betting on our collective love of burgers. Many of his cute little buildings are gone, but here, there's still roadside charm to spare.

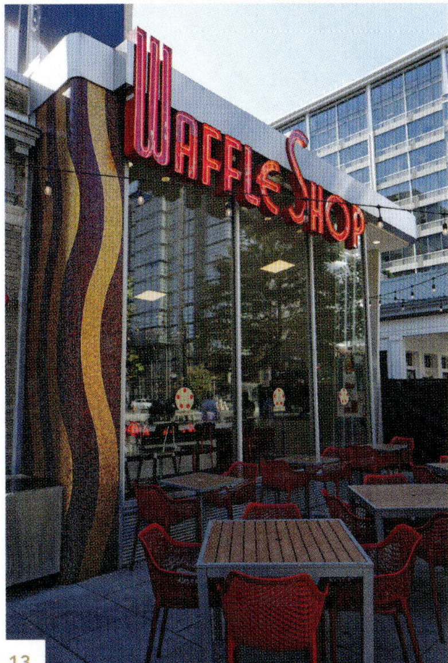

13

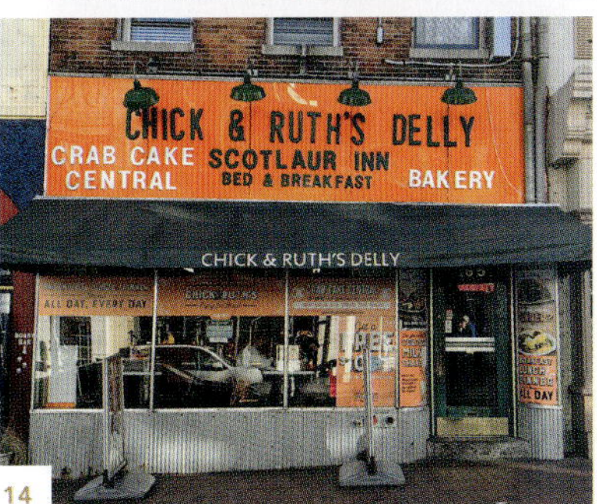

14

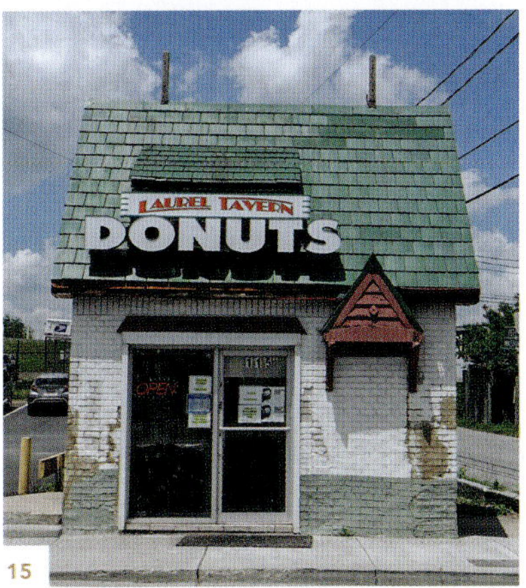

15

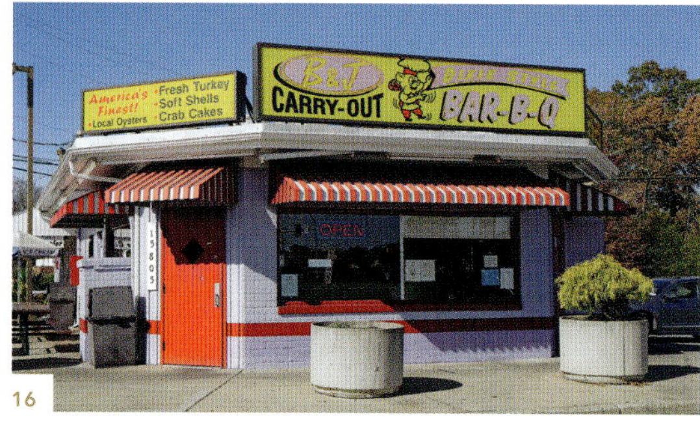

16

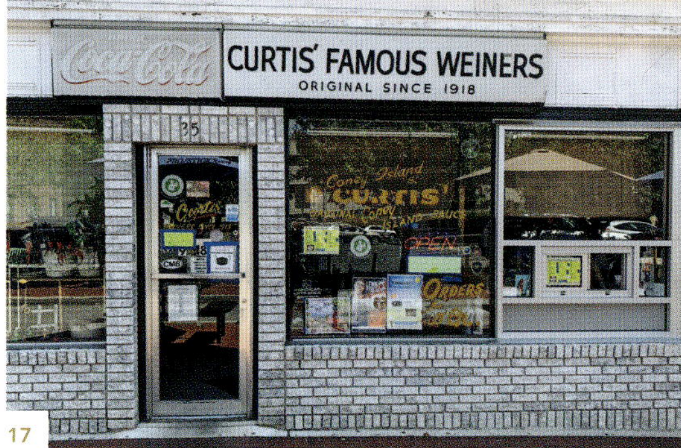

17

For those who like to mix politics with their nostalgia, the **Charcoal Pit** (FIG. 18) in Wilmington, Delaware, opened in 1956, makes a good detour. The restaurant's hometown was the subject of a droll *New York Times* headline: "After Centuries of Obscurity, Wilmington Is Having a Moment."

That headline, from December 2020, topped a story about how President-elect Joe Biden's hometown was in the spotlight. And that spotlight was shared by restaurants he's known to patronize, like **Walt's Chicken Express** and **Claymont Steak Shop,** institutions in their own rights, but special attention is heaped on the Charcoal Pit, which a Roadfood.com reader declared as "the most Roadfood-esque place in the state."

As the Mid-Atlantic bleeds into the South, the number of barbecue joints rises along with the temperature. A nice stop for some 'cue—and ice cream to wash it all down—is the **B&J Carry-Out** (FIG. 16) in Accokeek, Maryland. A simple building with a bold presence, the B&J is a reliable spot for grub, a bit of a diversion from the interstates, but that's the beauty of seeking it out.

So far in our travels, we've stayed within the orbit of Washington, D.C., but Maryland is a long state, and toward the western end is a road-food gem that merits the extra mileage: **Curtis' Famous Weiners** (FIG. 17) in Cumberland has been serving hot dogs since 1918—a time when America was going hot-dog crazy with "Texas Wiener" places opening left and right, a fever that has never really subsided—and has been in the Giatras family the whole time. The restaurant's name is that of an old employee, Pete Curtis, who was a Greek immigrant like the Giatras family. Owner Gino Giatras told me the name "Curtis" had a nice ring to it, even if he wasn't an owner.

The obligatory chili sauce flavors varied from place to place, and Curtis' has never strayed from its original formulation. "We have people that come that are sixth, seventh generations. So I'm a third generation, but I'm feeding seventh generations," Giatras told me. The hot dog to get comes with brown mustard, chili sauce, and raw diced onions. Just say you want your dog "with," and they'll take care of the rest.

18

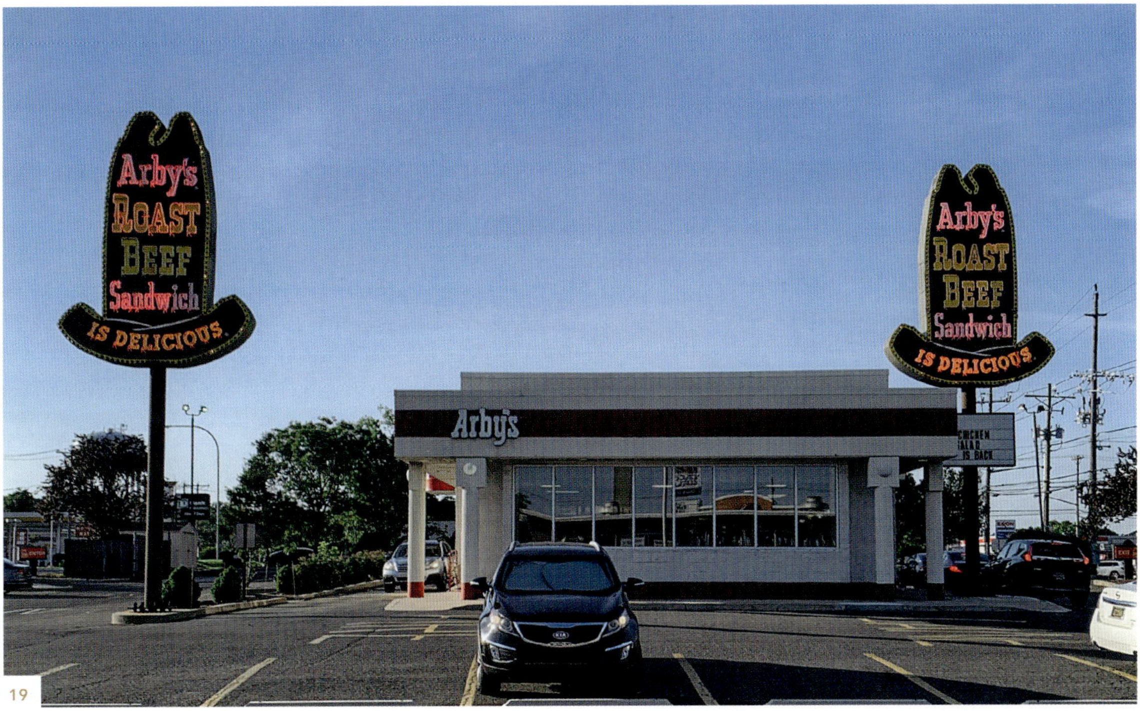

19

We drive east and leave Maryland again, and cross over from the serene Brandywine region of Pennsylvania into Delaware, where this chapter began. We encounter a taste of the garishly delicious—an **Arby's** (FIG. 19) restaurant with not one but two vintage 10-gallon-hat signs. This store sits on an island on the Concord Pike, a historic and vital throughfare, and the signs are siren calls to motorists on either side of the road. There's another vintage hat nearby, on Kirkwood Highway in Wilmington, that is a necessary detour for the Arby's enthusiast.

Perhaps one of my favorite stops in Virginia is the **Knotty Pine Restaurant & Lounge** (FIG. 20) in Front Royal, its facade a comforting slice of roadside Americana. Inside, the dreamy counter, with two lovely hues of blue separated by chrome trim, is a stunner. The RCA clock works perfectly right where it is, even if it's far from art deco. (I adore the 1968 RCA logo, especially when it's accompanied by the words "Color TV by . . ." as seen at many motels.) And the dining room itself is a cozy space filled with booths and surrounded by, appropriately enough, knotty pine walls.

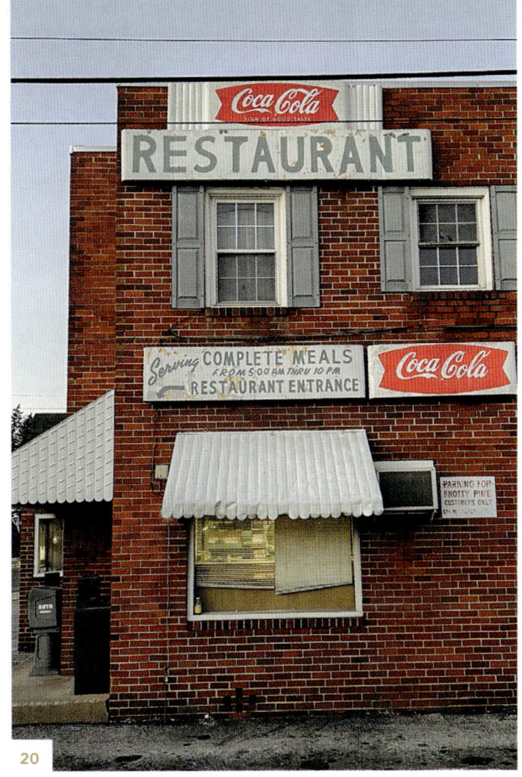

20

CHAINS OF FOOD

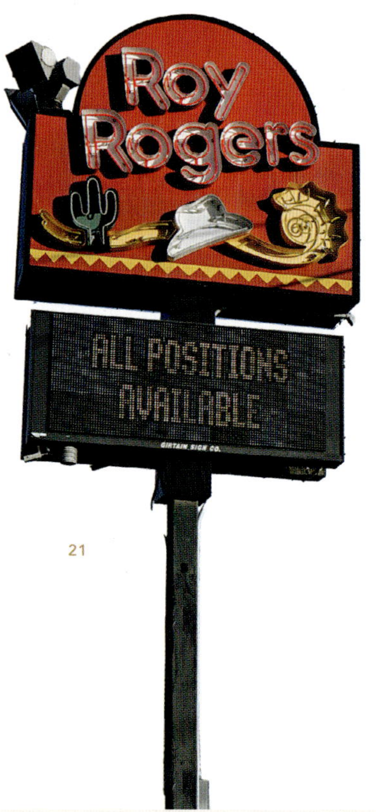

21

Starting in 1968, movie cowboy Roy Rogers agreed to lend his name to a chain of fast-food restaurants, **Roy Rogers** (FIG. 21), offering roast beef, then deemed the next big thing after burgers and chicken had their moments. The chain grew out of the short-lived RoBee's House of Beef restaurants, which got slapped with a lawsuit from the already-established Arby's.

The Roy's chain opted for covered-wagon neon signage in those early years. Those that survive have been repurposed, including this one (FIG. 22) at Roney's, a former Roy Rogers in Milford, Ohio.

Roy's grew to hundreds of locations and spread across much of the country—Roy himself appeared regularly in commercials and made appearances at restaurants. ("Say howdy to fresh food," went a 1978 jingle that still rattles in my noggin at random moments.) Alas, the chain got roughed up in a game of corporate pinball, and only a few dozen stores survived the jostling by the late 1990s. Most of the survivors are clustered in Maryland.

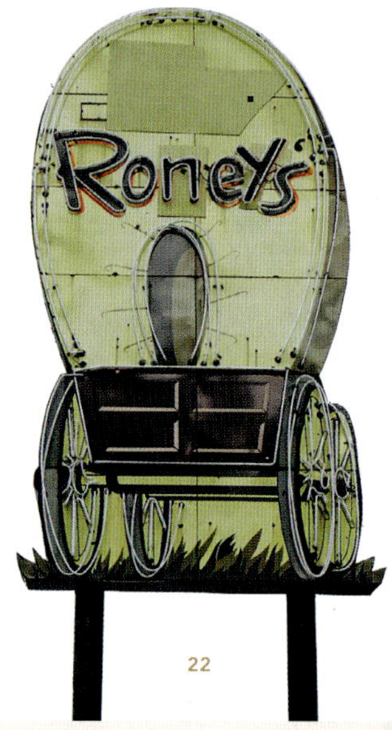

22

HEY, THAT LOOKS FAMILIAR!

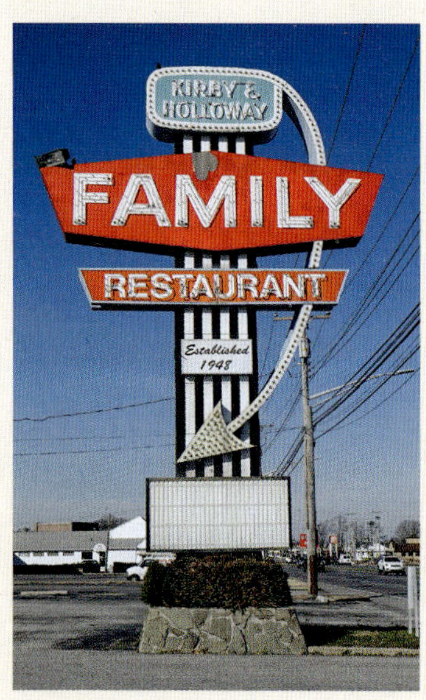

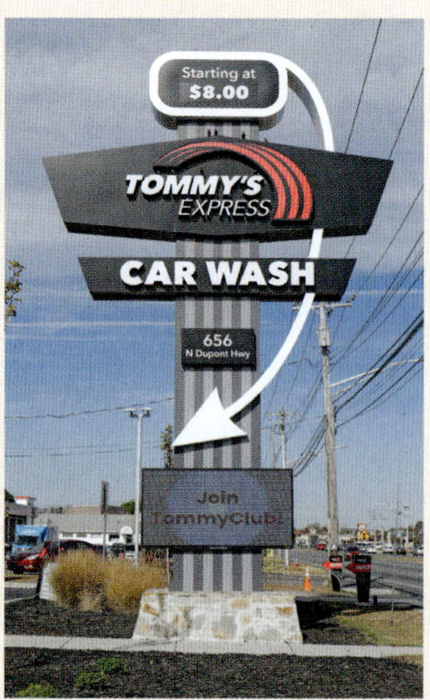

The Kirby & Holloway Family Restaurant in Dover, Delaware, had a fantastic midcentury sign, which I photographed in 2020. The restaurant dated to 1948, and had been shuttered since a fire in 2014. When I drove by again, in late 2024, I was delighted to see the sign wasn't entirely gone but had been repurposed to promote a car wash. Car washes often have some midcentury design flair, so this seems to work here.

MAINSTAYS OF MAIN STREET

A beautiful TV repair sign from a time when people actually bothered to get them fixed. A small appliance store with a rich history, and new owners who sell plants but appreciate the storefront's past. Mom-and-pop shops may be small, but they have big stories behind them, and so do those who work every day to keep them alive.

The sign for **O'Donnell's TV** (FIG. 23) in Baltimore captures the elan of that early era in the 1950s when TV was new and exciting with a force akin to smartphones and social media in our time, not quite the "vast wasteland" that former FCC chief Newton N. Minow famously claimed. It's a throwback to a time when TVs had tubes and our instinct was to fix, not ditch, our sets.

I first visited **Buck Appliance Co.** (FIG. 24) in Baltimore in January 2019, and the shuttered shop was a gem in the rough. Well, it's now a diamond again thanks to the good folks who run the plant shop that's taken root here, Fells Point Cultivated Creations.

This storefront is the legacy of Milton Buck, who spent his eighty-four years on earth in the Baltimore area, and for much of that time he sold appliances and furniture from this dreamy art deco storefront, sheathed in creamy, porcelain enamel tile and elegant lettering.

His legacy survives not only in this shop but in the lives of the people he served and their descendants. Described by the *Baltimore Sun* as a "solid friend" of the city's Polish community, Buck helped countless Polish immigrants get on their feet when they arrived in America.

In a nice touch of kismet, Buck himself was an avid gardener, so it's lovely that a hobby that brought him happiness is celebrated at Cultivated Creations, which has plans to do even more restorative work to the fabulous facade.

A trip to the cleaners is a chore, but dropping off your shirts and slacks at **Harry Louie Laundry & Dry Cleaning** (FIG. 25) is a joy. The shop in Dover, Delaware, has been in business since 1949, moving to its present home in 1953. It stands alone, surrounded by the ghosts of old buildings now paved over for parking lots.

Moving on to brighter times, supermarkets with neon lighting are a rare sight. On the American road, it's hard to top—literally—the **Giant Food** (FIG. 26) sign in Laurel, Maryland. It is one of two stepsibling supermarket chains by that name in the region.

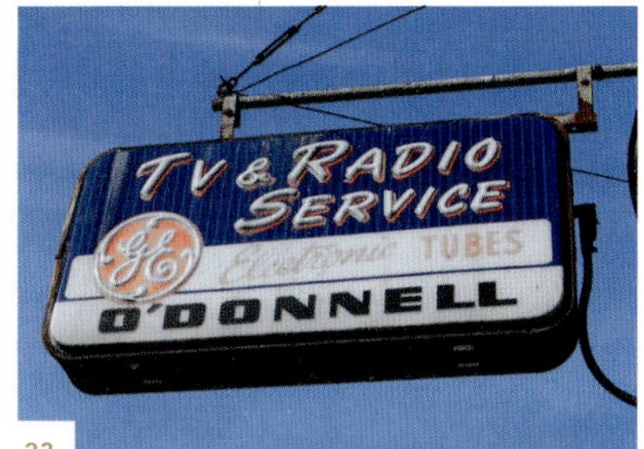

23

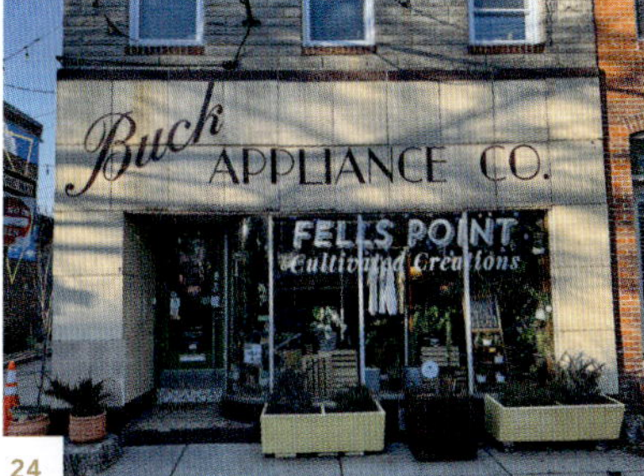

24

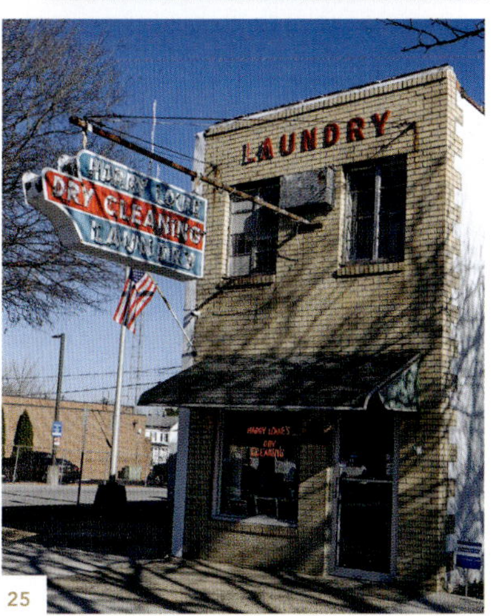

25

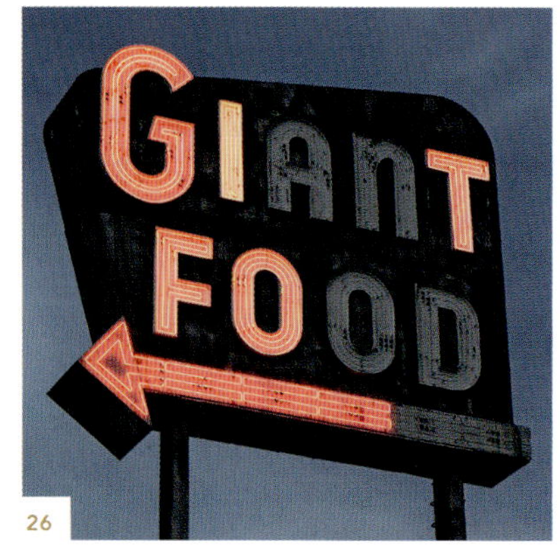

26

The store has a curious footnote in political history. This shopping plaza is the location where Alabama governor and presidential candidate George Wallace was shot by a would-be assassin and left paralyzed on May 15, 1972. This Giant also had an incidental glance with the horror of 9/11—according to the *Baltimore Sun*, Flight 11 hijacker Mohamed Atta, who had spent time in Laurel, sent a $5,000 wire transfer from this store to another September 11 terrorist in the lead-up to the attacks.

Silently witnessing all this history, the sign, jaunty and bold, has been a symbol of this town and a dramatic marker for this shopping plaza, which opened in 1965. Long may it stand, because you'll never see its kind again.

THE INN CROWD

As a road-tripping young adult, besotted with the freedom my freshly paid-off car offered, I resolved to return to New York from my trip to Savannah, Georgia, by staying off Interstate 95 as much as I could. Or at least, staying off it when my pre-GPS internal hunches suggested traffic warranted a detour. This trip was my first real encounter with U.S. 301, which deserves a book of its own one day.

U.S. 301, stretching from Delaware to Florida, was once a trusted path for early motorists seeking the relief of tropical realms. Today, it bears evidence of this forsaken role, in the lonely motels and desiccated downtowns along its path, manna from guidebook heaven for the archaeologically minded motorist.

And it's here that we'll make our first stop as we explore places to hit the sack on the road.

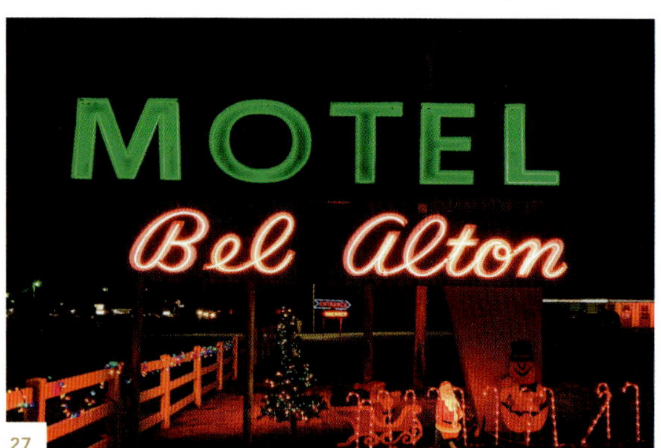

27

One of the biggest cases in point is the **Bel Alton Motel** (FIG. 27), perhaps the grandest survivor of what was once a gaggle of motels on this Maryland stretch of U.S. 301.

At the Maryland terminus of U.S. 50, a coast-to-coast highway that drops you in Ocean City, and, in the other direction, will deposit you in Sacramento, there was for decades a nominal taste of Texas—the **Alamo Motel** (née Motor Court) (FIG. 28).

Opened in 1946 and a pioneer in the mid-twentieth-century transformation of Ocean City into a seaside vacation oasis, the Alamo

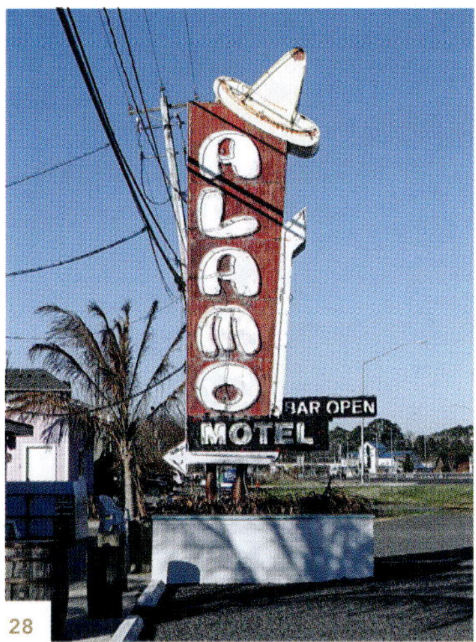

28

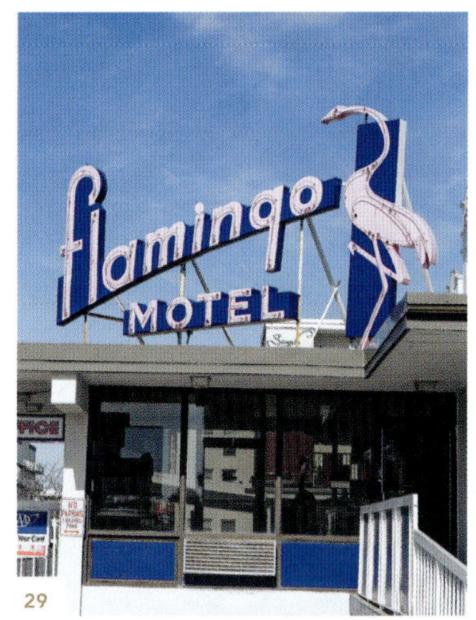

29

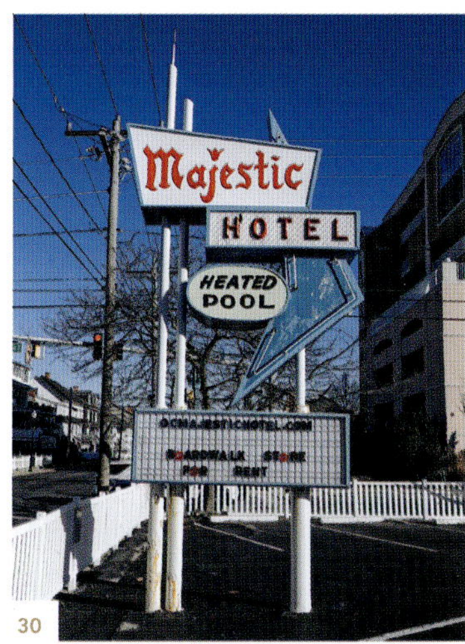

30

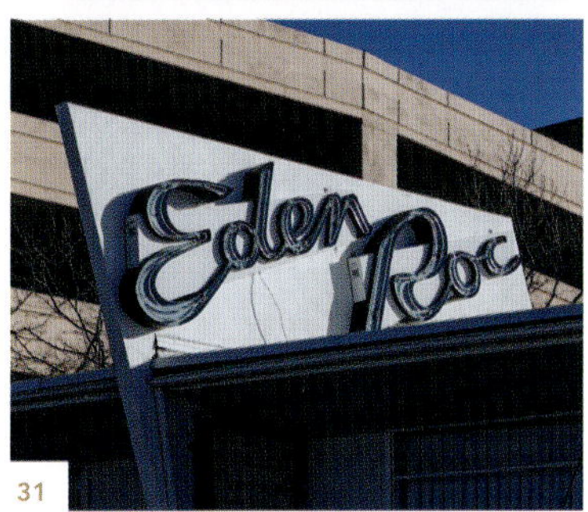

31

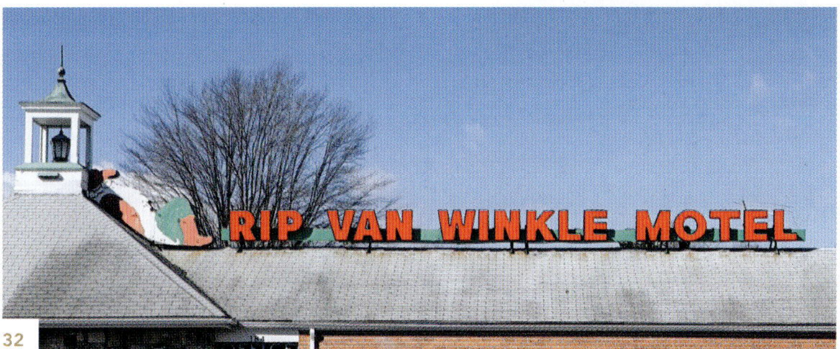

32

followed the arc from awesome to atrocious, a familiar journey in the hospitality world. But the bones of the motel were good, and a new owner set it on a fresh course several years ago, erasing the indignities of time and preparing it for a new era. When it changed hands again, the fantastic sign vanished, and the pastel-heavy renovation was slathered in black paint.

Remember the Alamo next time you're in Ocean City, along with other gems like the **Flamingo Motel** (FIG. 29), **The Majestic** (FIG. 30), and the **Eden Roc** (FIG. 31), a name (and style) that conjures Miami Modernism, trading Collins Avenue for Baltimore Avenue, different mise-en-scène but a kindred swagger.

Before we turn in for the night here, I'd be remiss not to mention the **Rip Van Winkle Motel** (FIG. 32) in Warrenton, Virginia, which features Washington Irving's multidecadal napper lounging in roofline repose. We are far from the Catskills, where Irving set his character to slumbering, only to awake twenty years later to an unfamiliar world. Van Winkle, like Sleepy Hollow and the Headless Horseman, another outgrowth of Irving's imagination, makes for an apropos motel name.

SWEET STOPS

From the countryside to the shore, these stops offer opportunity aplenty for ice cream, candy, and other sweet treats. First up is a store that hasn't been a Dairy Queen in more than fifty years but still looks the part.

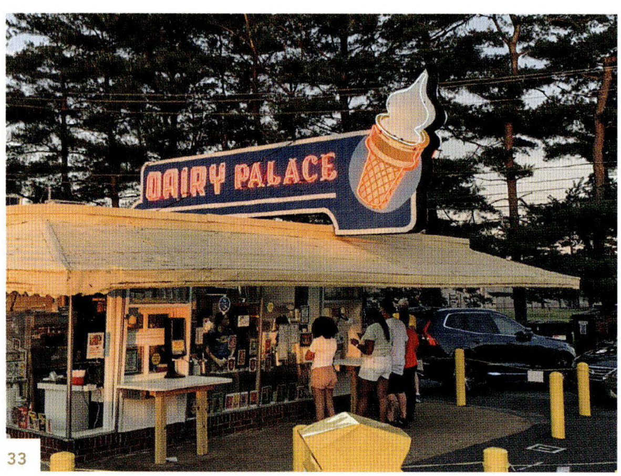

33

The **Dairy Palace** (FIG. 33) in New Castle, Delaware, began as a Dairy Queen in 1954 and assumed its present name in the 1970s, the sign modified but retaining its classic form. Except for the cars, this could be the 1950s.

Dairy Palace has been listed on the National Register of Historic Places. The large shake is called the Monster and is so thick and rich it comes with a spoon.

For ice cream of regional flavor, it's hard to beat **Dumser's Dairyland** (FIG. 35), a small chain that dots Ocean City, Maryland, with seven locations, tracing back to 1939, when Gladys Dumser first sold ice cream in this seaside town. Initially called Bernie's Dairyland, the name was switched to Dumser's after Gladys divorced Bernie Thrush and married Pete Dumser.

Main's Quality Ice Cream (FIG. 36) is long gone, but the vintage neon sign remains in a building that is a registered landmark in Middletown, Maryland. Founded by C. F. Main, the business—whose phone number for decades was simply 110—changed hands many times. Ice cream was made here until the late 1960s and sold here until the shop finally closed in 2002.

After sixty-two years, it seemed in the fall of 2019 that the **Dairy Corner** (FIG. 37) in Winchester, Virginia, was finally licked. The Pack family, keepers of the soft-serve machines since 1986, was closing shop because the children of the founders, who opened the store in 1957, wanted to sell the property.

Well, Rob Landis wasn't going to let this treasure of roadside Americana vanish. Landis owns a power-equipment business just down the street, and after admiring the historic business for a quarter century, he couldn't make sense of this street—called Dairy Corner Place, no less—without its namesake. So, he put his money where his heart is, and he bought Dairy Corner.

▶▶▶ Pull Over!

For other requisite Ocean City boardwalk food, make sure to get the fries at **Thrasher's**. While **Phillips Seafood** has closed its signature home in Ocean City, you can still sample it elsewhere, including the **Maryland House** rest stop on Interstate 95, a perfect pit stop for McCormick's **Old Bay Seasoning** merch. How I relish the childhood memory of inhaling the invigorating smell of McCormick-made spices and seasoning wafting over Inner Harbor from the long-gone Baltimore plant.

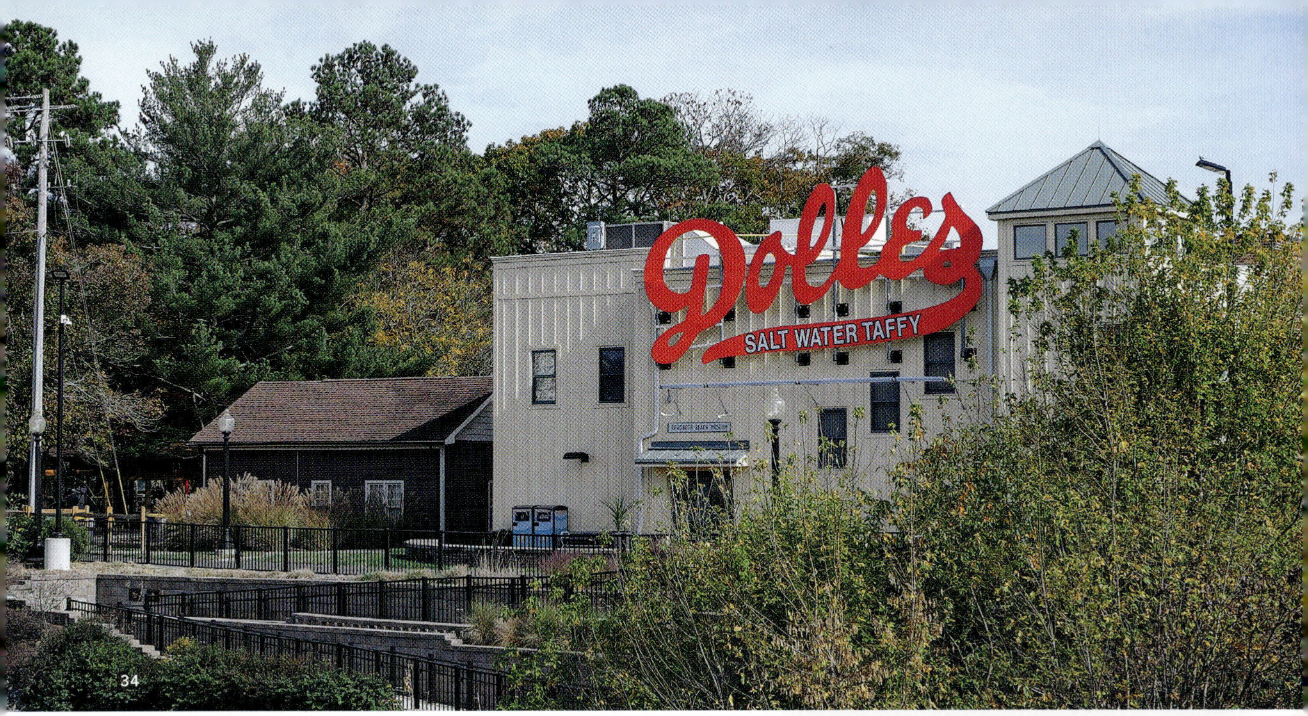

34

In the spring of 2020, despite the pandemic that would sink many a small business, he opened Dairy Corner for its sixty-third year and even brought back employees who'd lost their jobs the previous fall, the *Winchester Star* reported. The building's charm, signage with Coca-Cola "dots," makes the experience all the sweeter. "The goal is to do everything the same," Landis told the *Winchester Star*. "Everybody loves it just like that, including myself, so we're going to keep it how it was."

We've had our share of ice cream. How about some candy (though our story is a little sour)?

A corner of the world that had not changed since 1962 did so in a big way in 2021, when the gigantic sign for **Dolle's Candyland** on the Rehoboth Beach boardwalk (see photo on pages 72–73) was taken down. The business, which opened in 1927, purveys treats like saltwater taffy, caramel popcorn, and chocolates.

Earlier in 2021, owner Tom Ibach, facing a steep rent increase, moved his shop a mere 50 feet away, into an existing family candy store that now carries the Dolle's name and on a much smaller sign in the familiar cursive. The business isn't done; nor is the sign, for that matter. It's an icon, and it's impossible to imagine this town without it. See it at its new home at the **Rehoboth Beach Historical Society & Museum** (FIG. 34), which features a wonderful collection of local vintage signage.

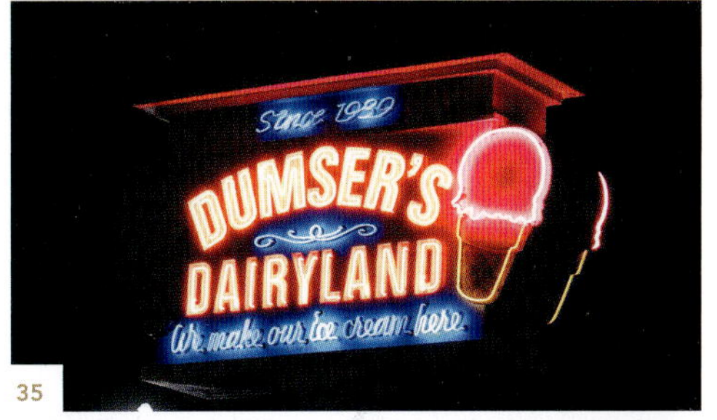

35

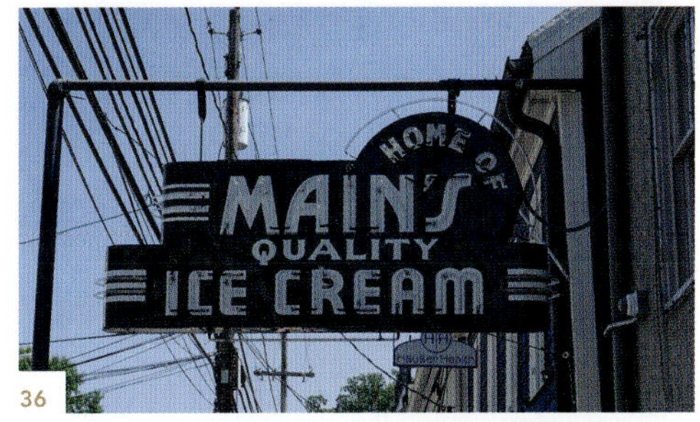

36

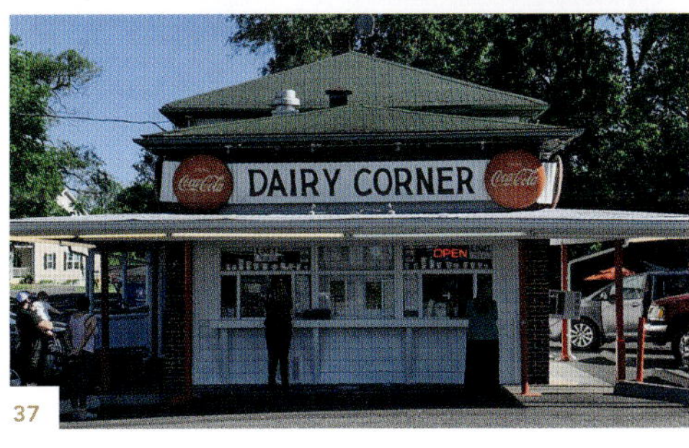

37

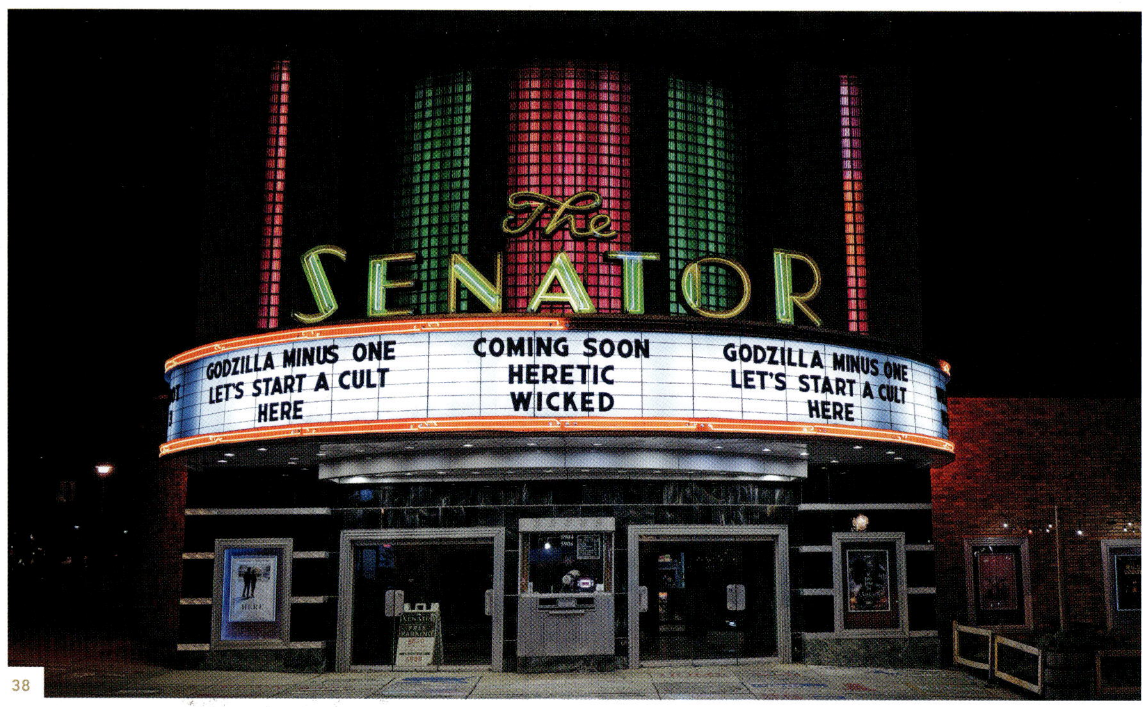

38

ON WITH THE SHOW

Our theater section here has a small but mighty selection to enjoy in the region, a mix of ornately restored gems, a classic drive-in, and one that has found a new use.

The movies on a marquee instantly date a picture with pinpoint accuracy, and my photo of the **Senator Theatre** (FIG. 38) in Baltimore, Maryland, preserves pop culture's *Wicked* moment of 2024. The Senator screened its first film in 1939, and has since seen its share of happy endings, dramatic twists, and nail-biting cliffhangers, both on and off the screen.

The biggest cliffhanger perhaps came in 2009, when the theater closed, foiled by foreclosure. But the Senator never became a forlorn husk, a beautiful ruin, as with so many of its architectural kin coast to coast. The people of Baltimore wouldn't stand for it, and the city itself saved the damsel in distress by buying the Senator and getting it into the caring hands of the Cusack family.

Today, the sumptuously renovated and expanded Senator boasts three screens, including the grand 40-foot silver one in the main auditorium. The theater is still equipped with its 35-millimeter film-projection suite, so classic movies can be seen as they were in their heyday. Those projectors were put back to work one glorious night in October 2013, when the theater reopened after its multimillion-dollar makeover. All it needed for the big bash was some *Hairspray*, and beloved Baltimore native John Waters obliged, screening his 1988 film for a crowd of hundreds.

Those who want to see a movie outdoors in the Maryland area are in for a "reel treat" at **Bengies Drive-In Theatre** (FIG. 39) in Middle River. The sign features the Googie style (see page 297 for more), a kindred spirit of the Malta Drive-In from the Northeast (page 35). Bengies opened in 1956 and looks the part. And here's a neat gift for the roadside enthusiast: You can rent the screen to send a giant message to somebody you love. You can also rent the theater's sign marquee to double down on your message.

The charms of Cumberland, Maryland, are many, and the **Embassy Theatre** (FIG. 40) is high on this list. The theater, which opened in 1931, traces the boom, bust, and, for a fortunate few, boom cycle of many a downtown theater. In its day, the Embassy was "the family theatre with popular prices," as the marquee still reads. But the most popular price of all is free, and television was just that in the 1950s, so the Embassy closed. Rather than fall into adult-film dereliction, the Embassy was absorbed into a downtown store, its marquee preserved, surviving long enough to become a historical curiosity and object of preservationist reimagination. Today, it thrives as a showcase for the stage and the arts.

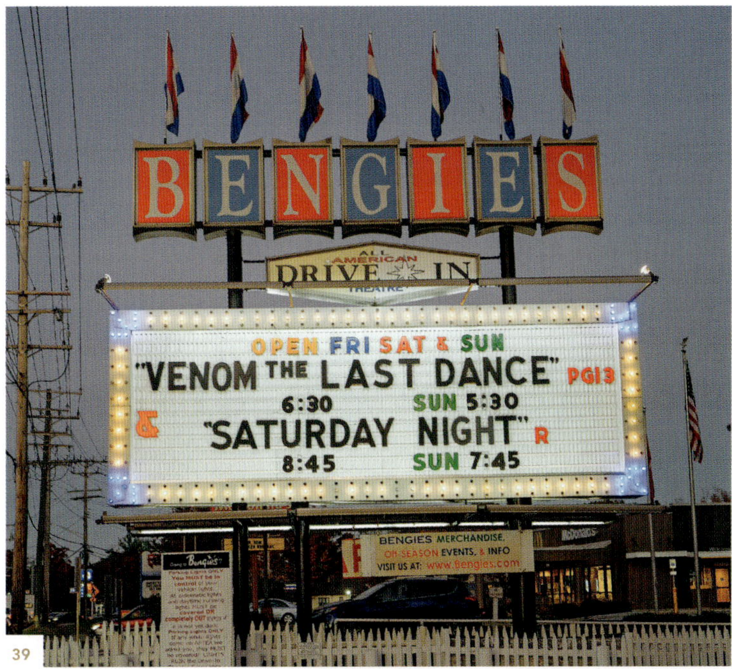

39

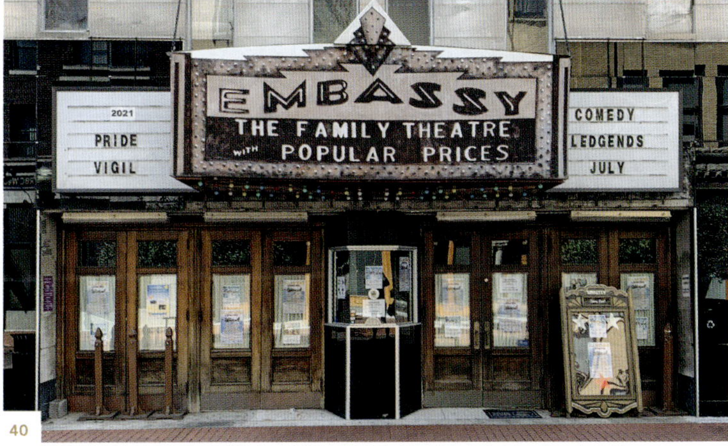

40

CHEERS!

The Wilmington, Delaware, area has a batch of old-school beer signs that have caught my eye, and they offer little lessons in brand history. In Washington, D.C., we'll visit a storefront that's a barrel of fun, but whose future is again up in the air. And there's more, so let's get hopping!

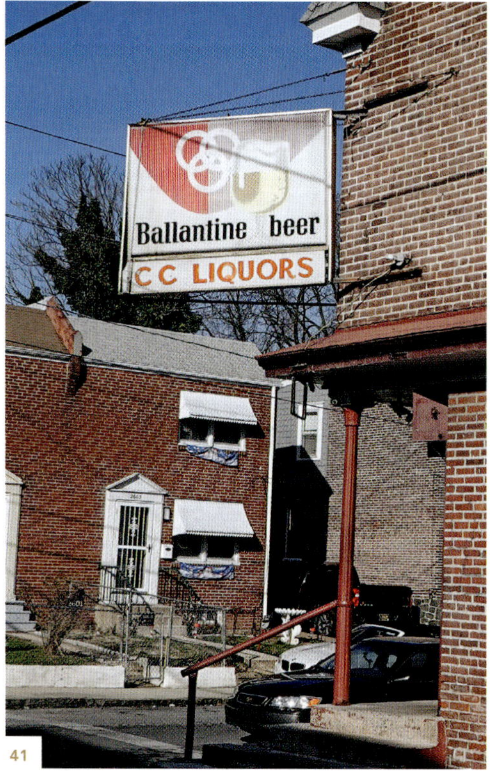

41

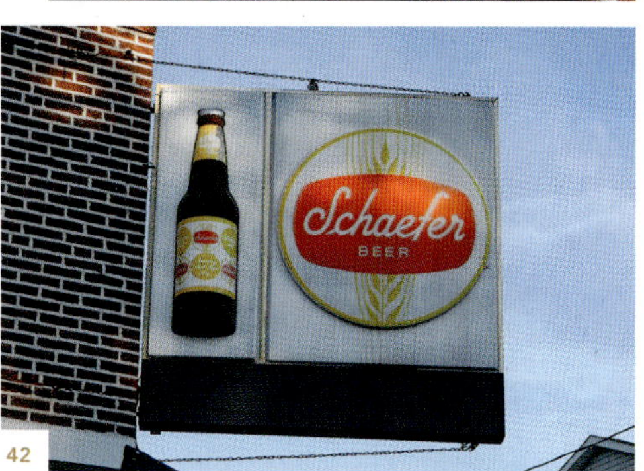

42

Wilmington, Delaware, is something of a preserve of classic beer signage. Behold a remarkable survivor for **Ballantine Beer** (FIG. 41). P. Ballantine and Sons Brewing Company was founded in 1840 in Newark, New Jersey, and reached its cultural zenith in the 1940s through the 1960s, impossible to miss in commercials, magazine ads, tavern taps, and bodega fridges. Yankees fans remember the "Ballantine Blasts" (home runs in announcer Mel Allen's parlance) from the days when the brewery sponsored the Bronx Bombers on radio and TV.

Ballantine ended that million-dollar-a-year-plus arrangement in 1967, and that presaged problems that would leave Ballantine Beer not so much flat—it made a mean IPA, actually—as flatlining. By 1972, Ballantine closed its Newark operation and was sold, eventually becoming a ghost haunting nostalgic conversations about the years after World War II.

Neighbors of this store in Wilmington say this sign has been here "forever." I'd say this old sign has more than faithfully served the brand, wouldn't you? *Frasier*'s Martin Crane, Frasier's dad and a fan of Ballantine, would be proud.

Schaefer (FIG. 42) is another old-school brand represented in Delaware signage. It was a once-ubiquitous beer brewed in Brooklyn until the company, which was founded in 1842, doubled down on its then-new Lehigh Valley operation in Pennsylvania, and on March 29, 1976, New York's rich history of beer-making all but ended.

Schaefer was such a part of the culture with its iconic jingle "the one beer to have when you're having more than one." Basically, if you intended to get drunk, grab a Schaefer. I didn't pick up on that nuance as a child, naturally. I just liked the jingle.

Schaefer faded away and remains a vestigial presence, still discoverable by those who look for it. You'll still see the occasional Schaefer sign in the windows of old dive bars. In Wilmington, Delaware, a corner liquor store proudly displays a rare privilege sign for Schaefer, seemingly from its 1960s or 1970s heyday.

Washington, D.C.'s **Barrel House Liquors** (FIG. 43), a fabled folly of form following function, is a liquor store with a wooden barrel for an entrance. The barrel's future was cast in doubt when the business—which dates to 1945—moved to a smaller space next door. An outlet of Foxtrot, a gourmet grocery-store chain, moved in and preserved the signage and the barrel. Alas, Foxtrot had closed along with the rest of the Chicago-based chain at this writing, and the barrel's future is again undetermined.

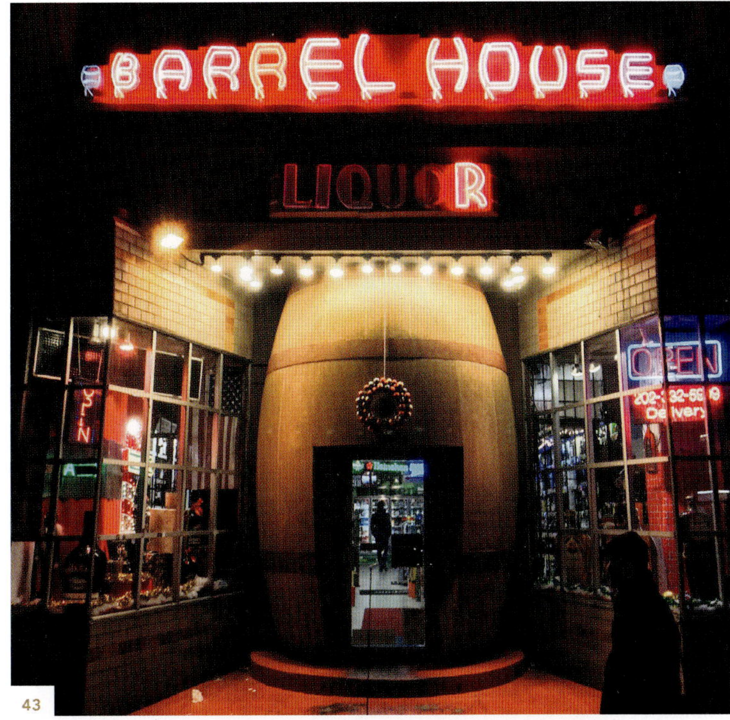

43

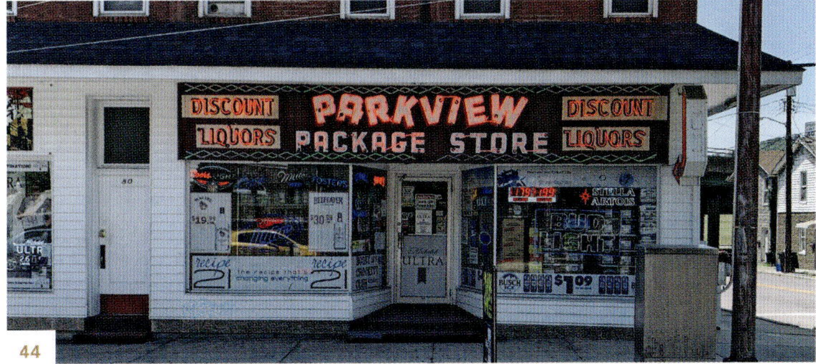

44

We leave the immediate environs of The Beltway for the western edges of Maryland, where Pennsylvania is just over the border and a country road will take you to West Virginia in no time flat. In Cumberland one of my favorite signs in America can be found, the **Parkview Package Store** (FIG. 44), a jaunty jumble of lettering that easily compels a smile.

Baltimore's **2 O'Clock Club** (FIG. 45) is something of a celebrity sign on Instagram. It's especially popular twice a year, when most Americans are confronted with the time change and at 2 a.m. we spring forward or fall back by congressional fiat.

The club is a highlight of The Block, Baltimore's red-light district. It was once an internationally known center of burlesque, and the 2 O'Clock Club was long owned by the legendary Blaze Starr, the "Queen of Burlesque."

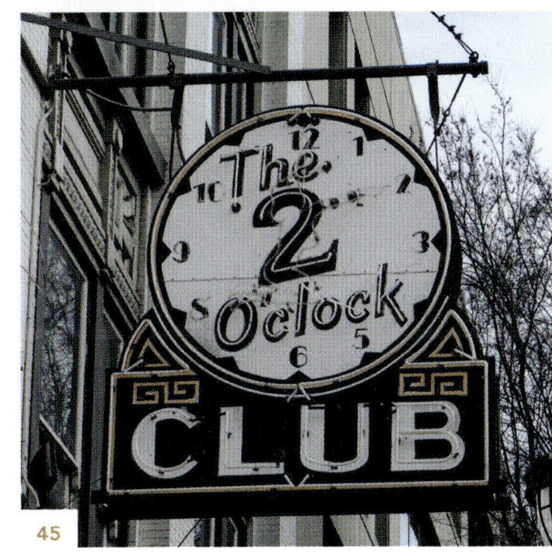

45

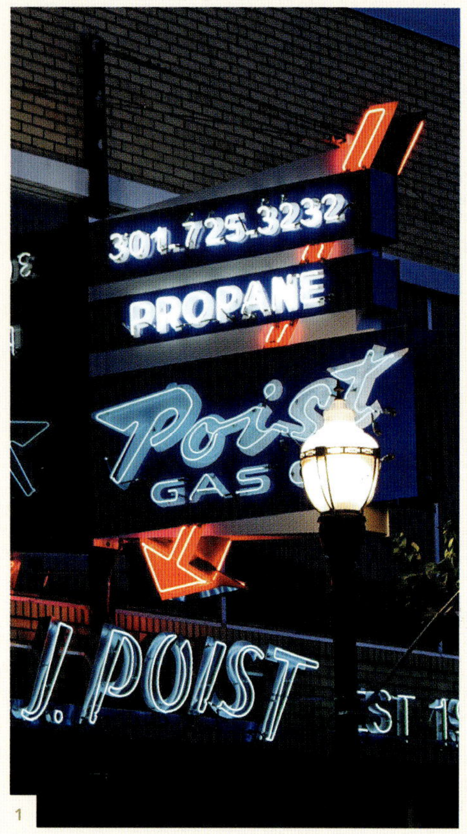

1

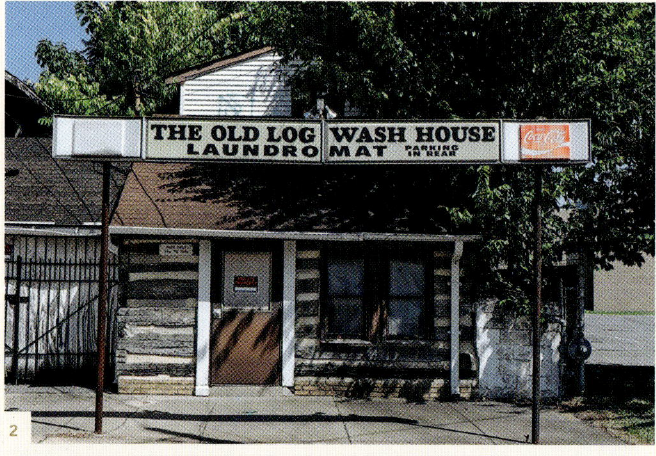

2

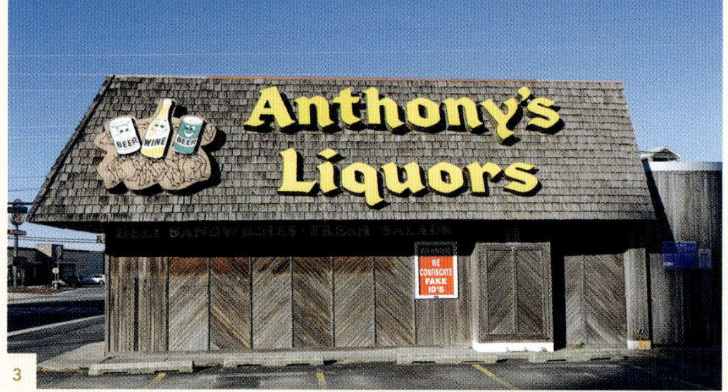

3

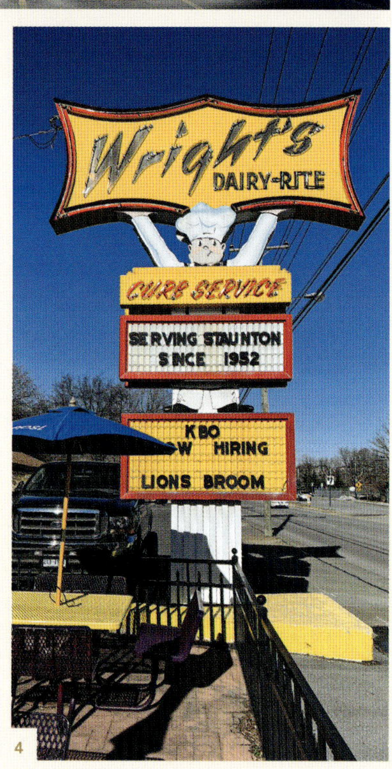

4

BUT WAIT, THERE'S MORE!

Here's a sampling of signs that you'll want to find in your travels through the region.

1. H.J. Poist Gas Co., Laurel, Maryland
2. The Old Log Wash House Laundromat, Frederick, Maryland
3. Anthony's Liquors, Ocean City, Maryland
4. Wright's Dairy-Rite, Staunton, Virginia
5. The Cumberland Motel, Cumberland, Maryland
6. Baby Jim's Snack Bar, Culpeper, Virginia
7. Kline's Dairy Bar, Harrisonburg, Virginia
8. Veterans Liquor, Beltsville, Maryland
9. Cape Motel, Cape Charles, Virginia
10. Doc's Motor Court, Colonial Beach, Virginia

CUMBERLAND
MOTEL
STOP
5

BABY
Jim's
SNACK
BAR
6

KLINE'S
DAIRY
BAR
7

VET'S
LIQUOR
BEER & WINE
ICE
MARYLAND LOTTERY
SEAFOOD & CRABS
BREAKFAST
LINCOLN
8

CAPE
MOTEL
NO VACANCY
9

DOC'S
MOTOR COURT
OFFICE
10

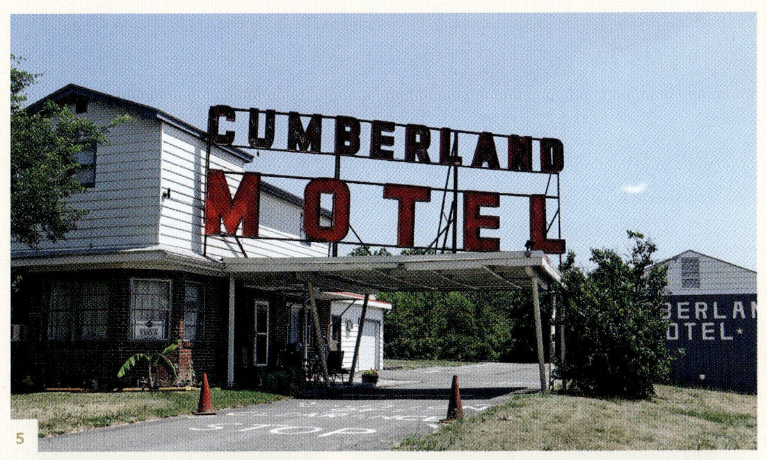

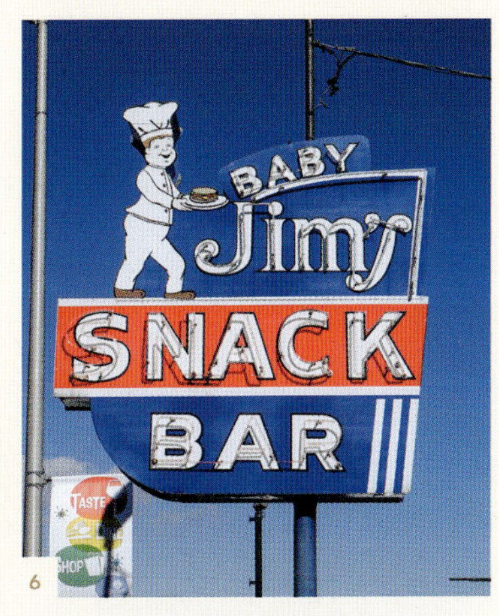

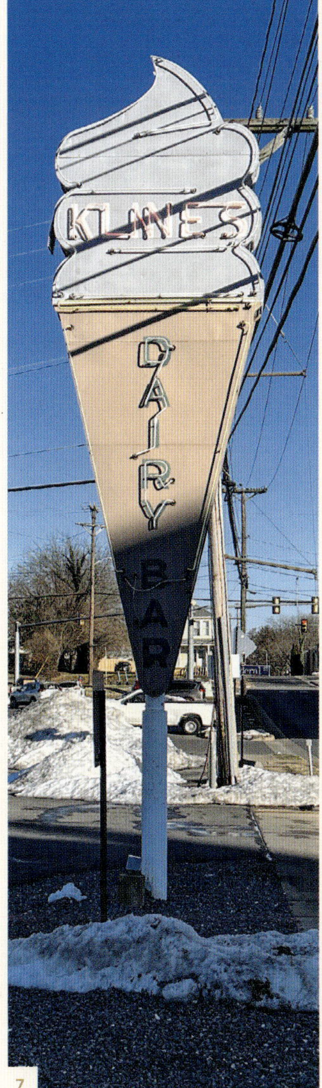

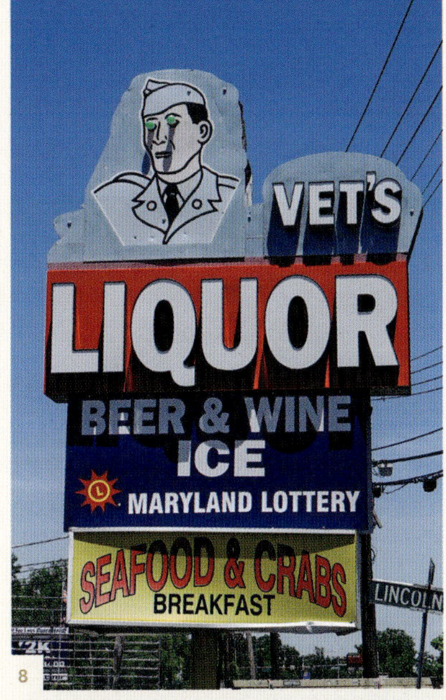

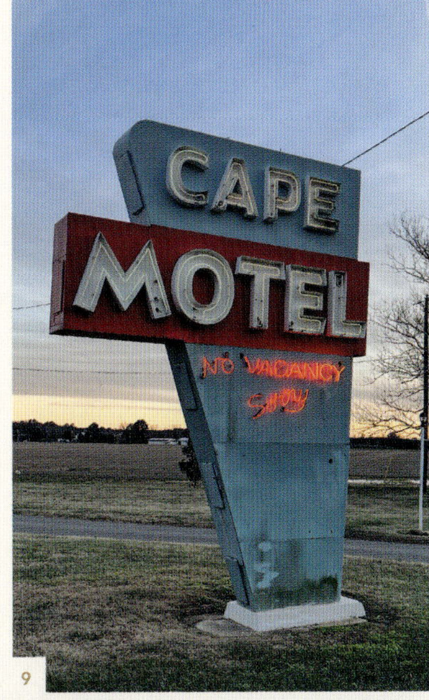

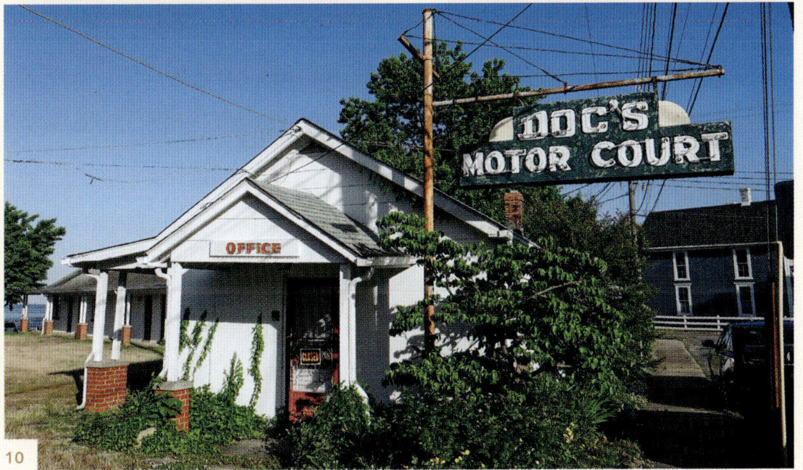

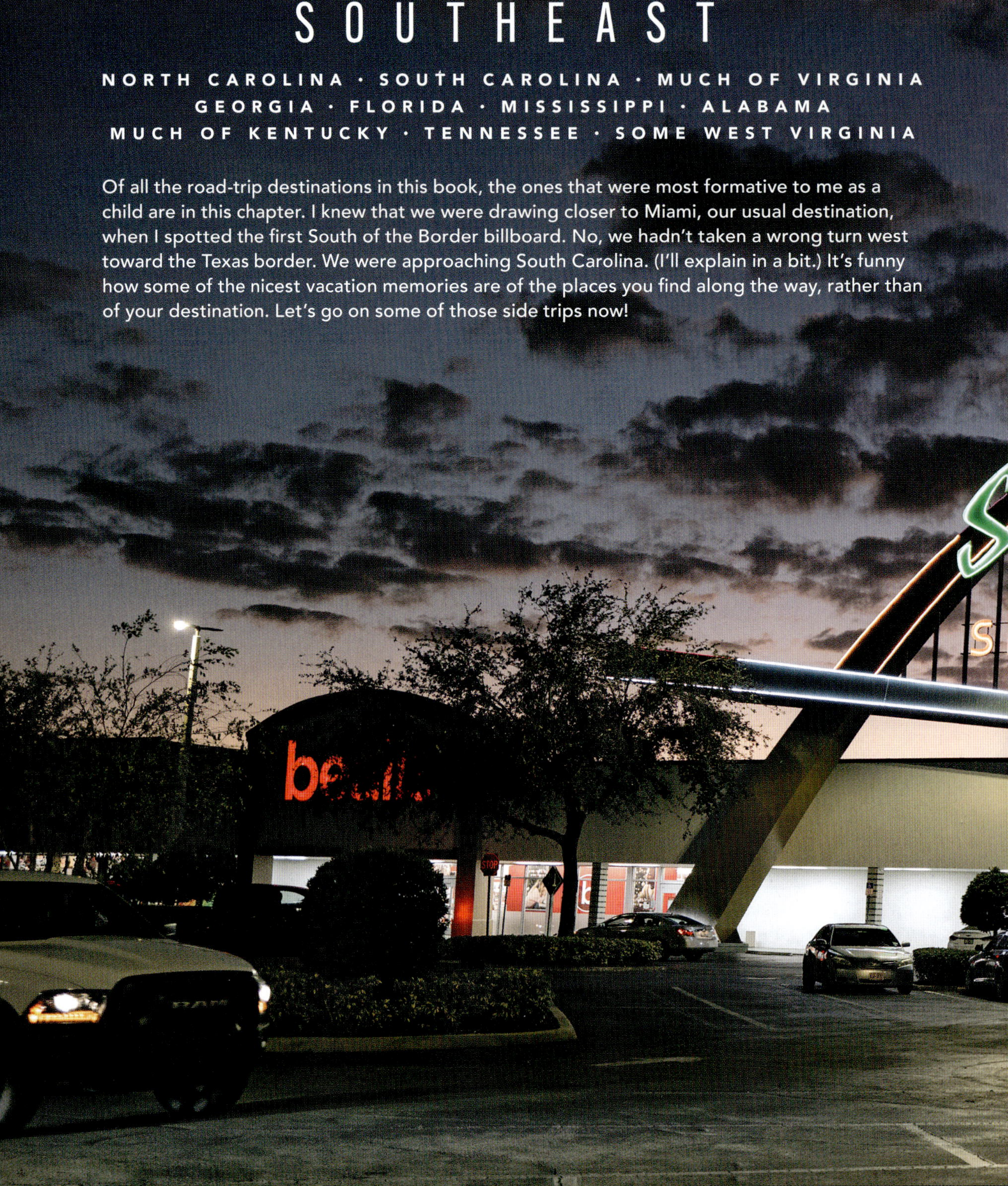

SOUTHEAST

NORTH CAROLINA · SOUTH CAROLINA · MUCH OF VIRGINIA
GEORGIA · FLORIDA · MISSISSIPPI · ALABAMA
MUCH OF KENTUCKY · TENNESSEE · SOME WEST VIRGINIA

Of all the road-trip destinations in this book, the ones that were most formative to me as a child are in this chapter. I knew that we were drawing closer to Miami, our usual destination, when I spotted the first South of the Border billboard. No, we hadn't taken a wrong turn west toward the Texas border. We were approaching South Carolina. (I'll explain in a bit.) It's funny how some of the nicest vacation memories are of the places you find along the way, rather than of your destination. Let's go on some of those side trips now!

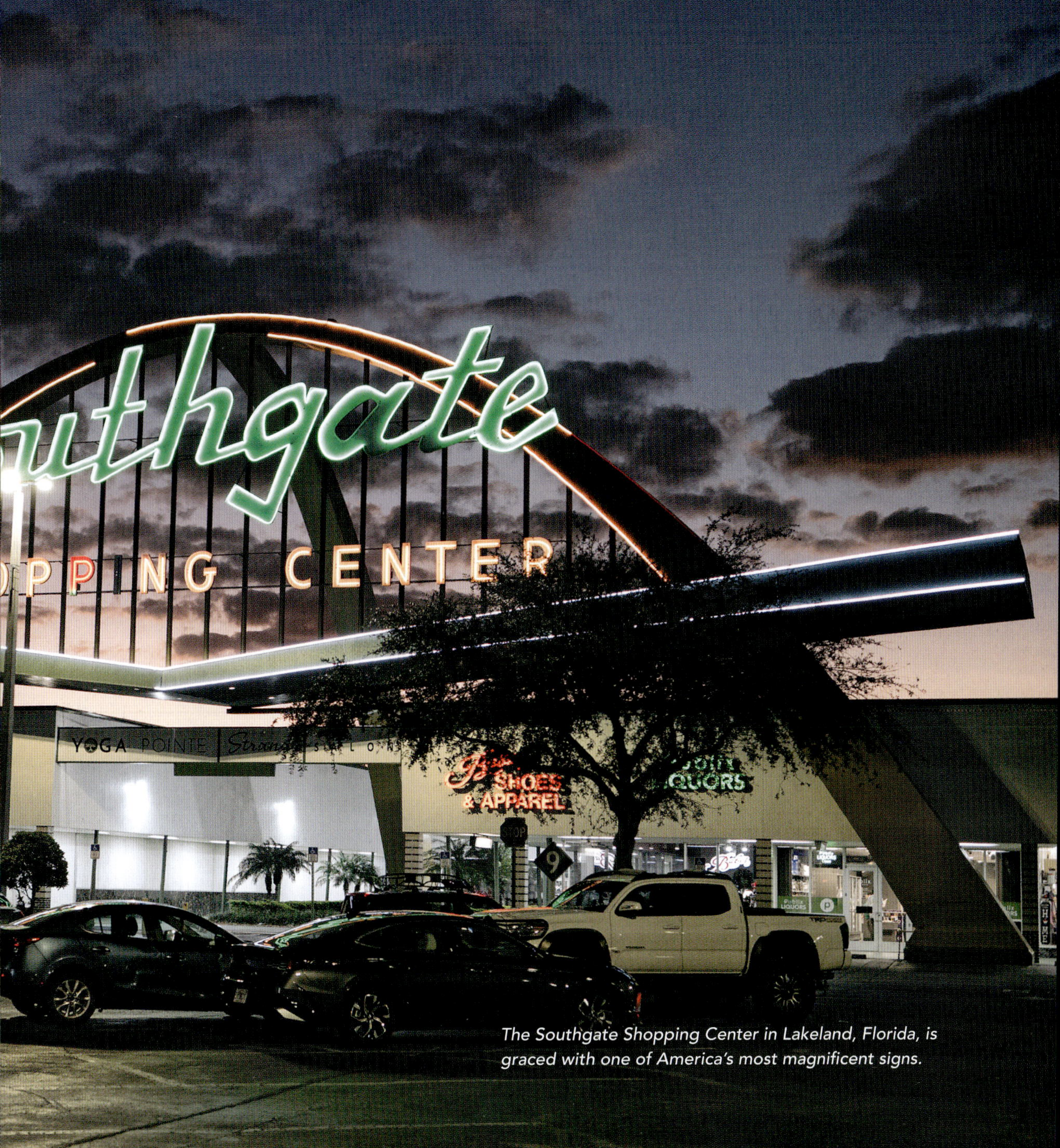

The Southgate Shopping Center in Lakeland, Florida, is graced with one of America's most magnificent signs.

ROADSIDE QUIRKS

Is that a giant sombrero off of I-95? Why is there a giant peach in the air? I can get an oil change . . . in a dinosaur? Wait, mermaids are real? I can walk into an alligator's jaw to see more alligators—and then soar over pits teeming with them? Why, we're only getting started. Read on!

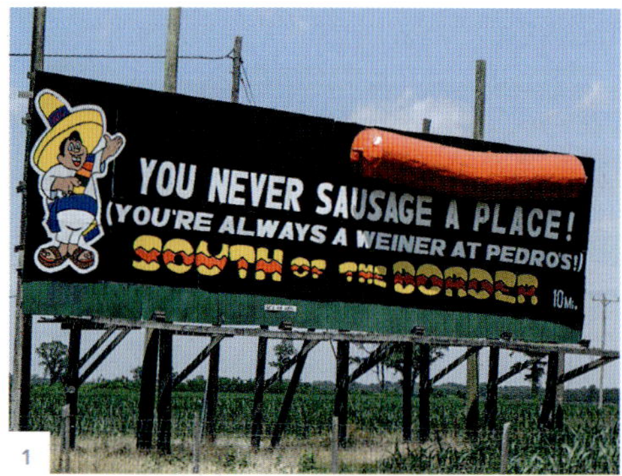

1

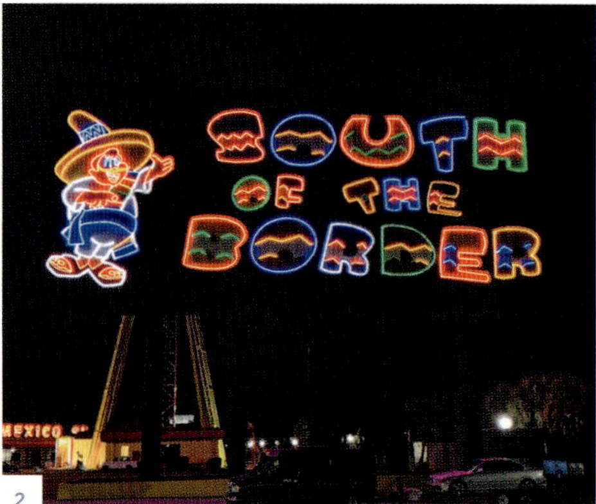

2

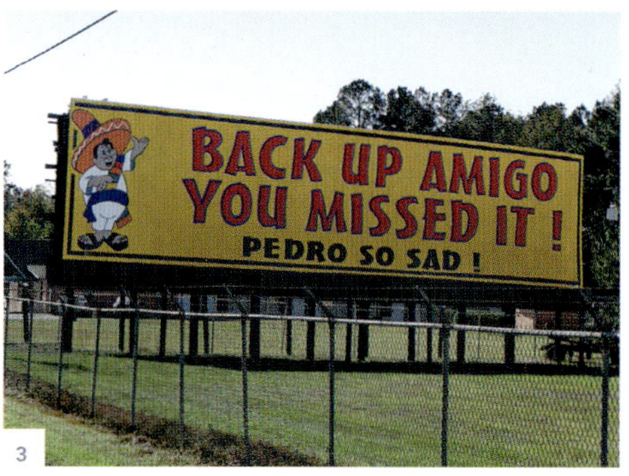

3

South of the Border (FIGS. 1, 2, 3, 4) is more than a flamboyant pit stop on Interstate 95: It placed me on my roadside journey when I was little more than a toddler. The South of the Border experience begins well before you reach Dillon, South Carolina, just "south of the border" from North Carolina.

SOB, as it's cheekily abbreviated, is advertised in punning billboards for hundreds of miles in either direction of I-95—you know, "Pedro's Weather Report!: Chili Today—Hot Tamale!" The billboards provide the interminable drive a tantalizing terminus, a destination promising merriment amid the endless exits for the mundane—gas stations, restrooms, and fast food.

When I was a child, I-95 was a corridor of magic that dropped you in the promised land after a day and change's drive. When you were a Cuban American kid from New York on summer break in the 1980s, that promised land was Miami Beach. And seeing Pedro, the ersatz Mexican mascot, was a sign you were about halfway there.

But as exciting as Miami was as a destination, nothing came close to the thrill of the first Pedro sighting. My family and I played a little game—be the first to spot the huge sombrero observation deck off in the distance. Even more thrilling was being the first to call out a Pedro billboard sighting.

At Pedro's, a hodgepodge of homey delights awaits, a dizzying array of gift shops, arcades, restaurants, pavilions like the reptile lagoon, and a hotel with a Pleasure Dome (it's a pool in a geodesic structure). Oh, and fireworks, plenty of bang for your buck here. I've never stayed at Pedro's, because the experience to me is all about pulling over, buying a souvenir (the obligatory bumper sticker, perhaps), grabbing a bite, and hitting the road.

Pedro traces its roots back to 1949, when Alan Schafer, a successful beer distributor based in Dillon, South Carolina, started a beer stand that was just south of the border with North Carolina's Robeson County, which had banned alcohol sales. A roadside marketing maven, Schafer slowly grew his business, eventually importing souvenirs from Mexico. The official history is that he brought on two men from Mexico to work as bellboys, and people started calling them Pedro and Pancho, and, in time, simply Pedro. Combine that with its location straddling two states—mail kept coming in labeled "south of the North Carolina border"—and the name and Mexican theme coalesced.

Schafer was born into a Jewish family in Baltimore. They settled in Dillon, South Carolina, and it's from this rural community that Schafer built a roadside empire, starting with suds before he added salsa. "He was the greatest marketing mind in the twentieth century in South Carolina," Kevin Geddings, a marketer who worked for Schafer, told the *Tampa Bay Times* in 2001. "This is a gentleman that never finished college and he built one of the biggest tourist attractions on the East Coast from scratch."

In those days, the road trip was a novelty, and architectural imagination was the honey to hook the motorists. The roadside oasis—and its central gimmick, a stereotypical jolly Mexican man—emerged at a time when questions of cultural appropriation had not gone mainstream, when in fact the roadside was awash with fraught depictions of groups, including Native Americans, and South of the Border has come in for its share of criticism. The Schafer family has always pushed back, often citing Alan Schafer's Civil Rights–era commitment to diverse hiring practices and its welcoming of all visitors in a time when segregation's ugly grip had not fully let go.

To this author, there's an innocent, endearing quality to this place that's hard to resist, a total lack of malice in its landscape of sombreros and sarapes far from the U.S.'s actual border with Mexico. But not everyone feels this way, and I understand that. For me, this feeling of emotional warmth is fueled by my own nostalgia for South of the Border and the deep associations with my family and our trips to Miami. Whenever I'm here, I'm four years old again, unburdened by the world's woes.

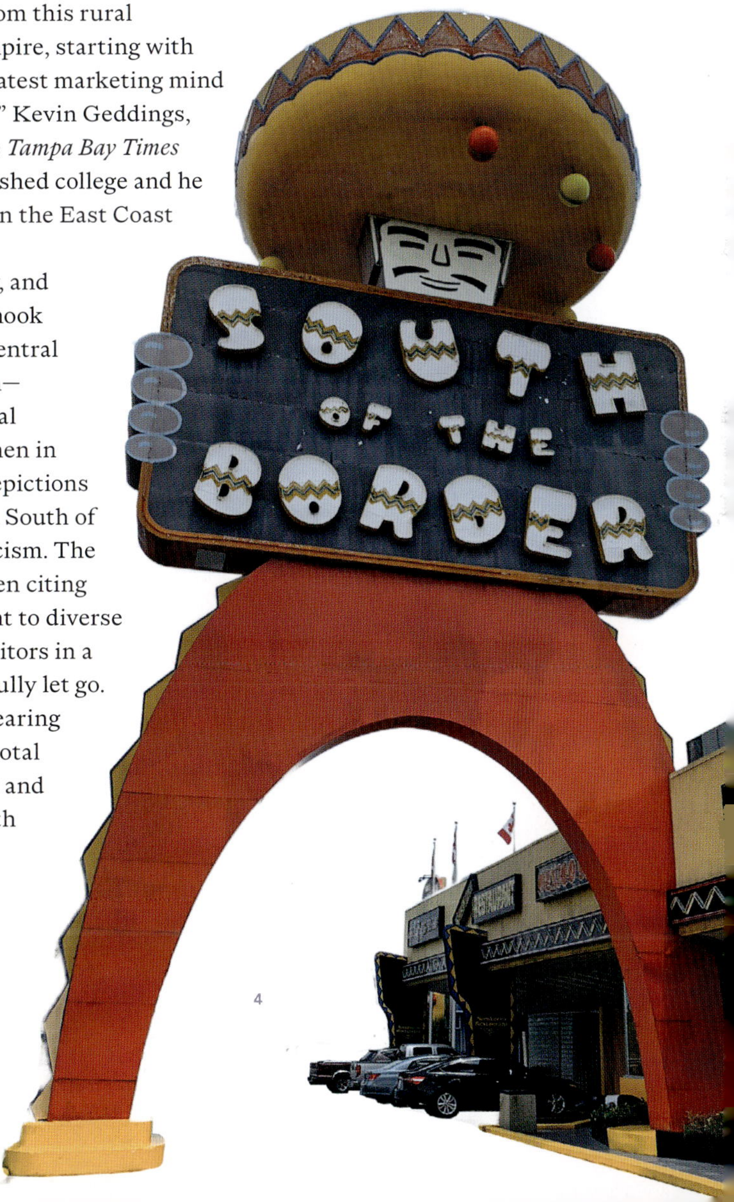

4

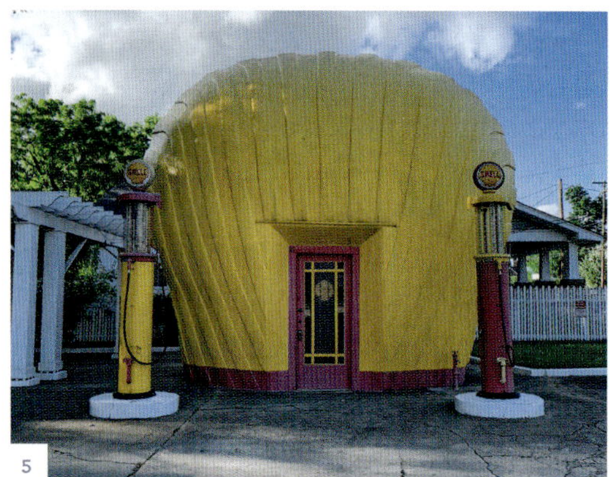
5

Gassing up is a given on any road trip, but it's sure more pleasant when the architecture fuels your imagination. Behold this former **Shell station** (FIG. 5), built in 1930 for the Quality Oil Co., the local distributor of Shell gasoline in Winston-Salem, North Carolina.

What better way to introduce the public to the Shell brand than to build a structure that is a big yellow scalloped shell. Who needs a sign when the building is the sign? This may look like a shell, but it's actually a duck, an academic name for buildings that resemble the product they sell. The "duck" term comes from the beloved Big Duck on Long Island (see page 11). Here, it was Shell's logo that underwent the duck treatment.

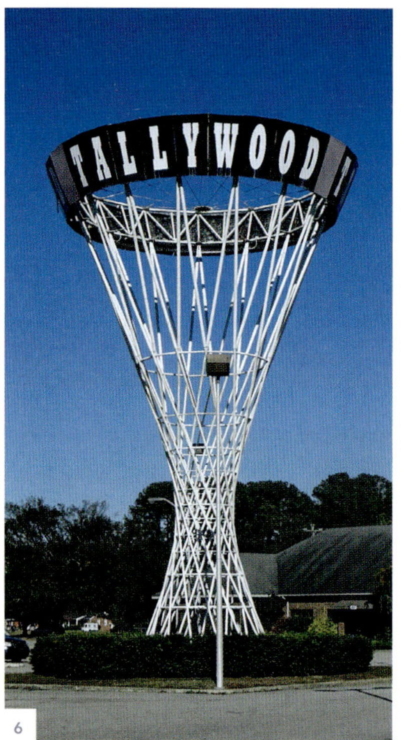

6

This building managed to survive long enough that it was placed on the National Register of Historic Places in 1976, and was restored two decades later by Preservation North Carolina, which once made this 150-square-foot structure a regional office. It is said there used to be eight of these Shells in the Winston-Salem area, but this is the last one—lucky duck.

South of the Raleigh area is the towering **Tallywood Shopping Center** (FIG. 6) sign in Fayetteville, North Carolina, a local landmark. The original shopping center, which dates to the early 1960s, was demolished and rebuilt with a Publix, the Southern supermarket chain, as an anchor. An architectural survey of modernist architecture in Fayetteville likened the tower to the base of an Isamu Noguchi Cyclone Table, expanded to gargantuan proportions. The nearly 50-foot-tall structure still stands, a remarkable relic from the early 1960s.

Catalog showrooms were a way of life in America that seemed to fade away in the 1990s, as Internet commerce began to rise. **Best Products** (FIG. 7) was one of the finest examples of the breed, and unlike the bland structures that housed the likes of Consumers and Service Merchandise, Best took showroom architecture seriously—and literally outside the box, destroying it.

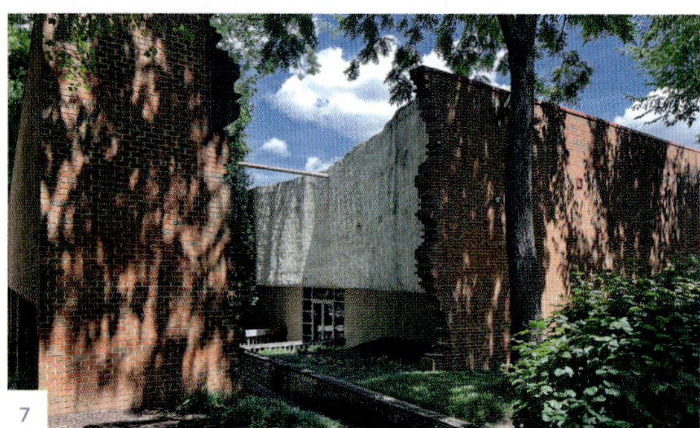
7

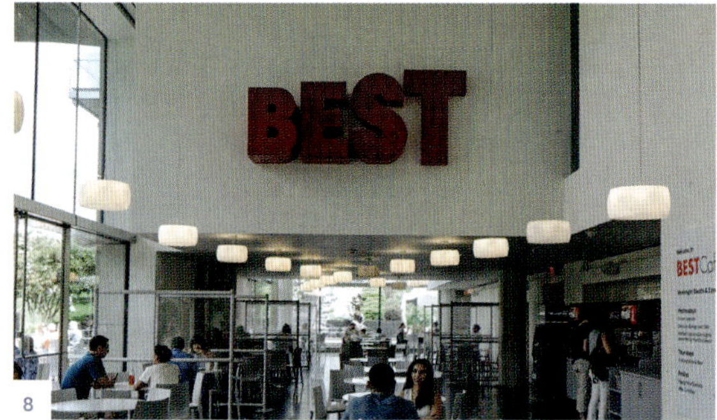

8

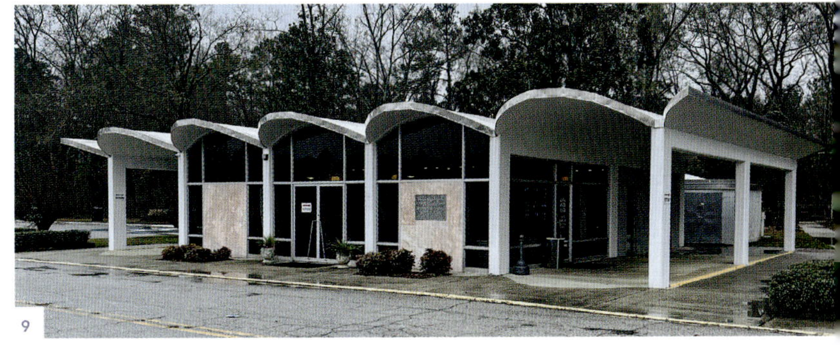
9

Tapping the architectural firm SITE to design showrooms that reflected the environmentally rooted style of the time, Best stores attracted attention by appearing in various stages of decay, abandonment, or outright destruction. Though Best Products itself imploded in the late 1990s, this showroom in Richmond, Virginia, remains, with the building intentionally cleaved open, trees springing from within. This temple to consumerism is now a house of worship.

The Best experience can also be appreciated at the Virginia Museum of Fine Arts in Richmond, where the stylish **Best Cafe** (FIG. 8) sells on-brand souvenirs, including this Best logo magnet, which is now affixed to my refrigerator.

Georgia's welcome centers (FIG. 9) are eye-catching—my favorite is the very first one, on U.S. 301 in Sylvania, a modernist multi-arched facade of aluminum and glass. The elegance extends inside, where, among other things, you can take a picture with an impressively realistic cutout of Jimmy Carter. (Plenty more Carter later in this chapter.)

Its presence on 301—and not 95—is another reminder of the preeminence of 301 as a vital north–south road before the interstates opened, draining vitality from the smaller roads—and the communities they pass through.

Florida has grand roadside attractions, of course, logical in a state whose economy is powered by tourism. It's hard not to marvel at the smile-generating audacity of what's billed as the world's largest orange. At a reported 92 feet wide, 60 feet tall, and 35,000 pounds, **Eli's Orange World** (FIG. 10) in Kissimmee, Florida, is a fascinating fiberglass fixture in the pantheon of great Florida tourist attractions. Eli Sfassie moved to Florida from Indiana and opened a Texaco station near Disney World just as the Magic Kingdom opened in 1971.

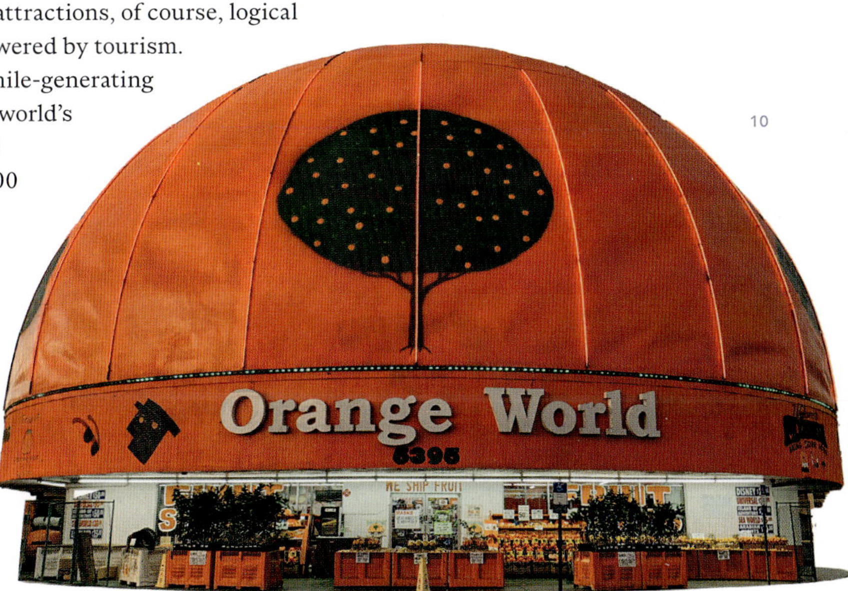

10

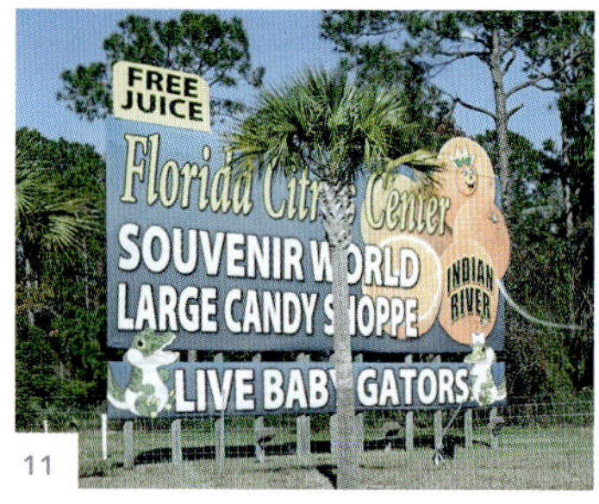

11

▸▸▸ Pull Over!

One of the joys of Florida road trips is finding unusual stops where history and kitsch meet. To wit: The abandoned **Florida Welcome Center** in Ormond Beach along I-95 was a neat adaptive reuse, housed in a former Dairy Queen. **The Florida Citrus Center** (FIG. 11) in St. Augustine dwells in a former Stuckey's, the beloved roadside convenience chain that is in comeback mode (more on that on page 108). The citrus center features live gators (not for sale), orange merch (very much for sale), and free, fresh tiny cups of OJ (priceless).

But Sfassie almost lost his shirt in the gas-station business until he started to sell souvenirs from the mechanic's bay, and that's when he began to partake in the magic of the Central Florida tourist boom of the 1970s. In 1988, he had the sweet idea to turn his shop into a giant orange. He paid $6,000 to a maker of outhouses for the privilege, he told the *Tampa Bay Times*. Business boomed—it was an astronomical return on his investment. I mean, how could a self-respecting tourist pass up a chance to enter a giant orange?

The irony of a big fake orange where orange groves once bloomed was not lost on Sfassie. He told the great Florida writer Jeff Klinkenberg that he missed the aroma of the orange blossoms from the groves, long since paved over for parks, shops, motels, and attractions like the Big Orange and the Giant Wizard, a neighbor of Orange World.

During Hurricane Charley, in 2004, a tropical gust may have flung the wizard's crystal ball onto the defenseless Orange World, leaving a big dent, Kathy Franco, Sfassie's daughter, told the *Herald-Tribune* in 2008. The ball was never found. It's an appropriate tall tale in a town where big is good.

These homey orange-juice attractions and tourist stands touting live alligators are part of the Sunshine State's charm, what folks call Old Florida.

A paradise found—or better yet, crafted—flourishes at **Sunken Gardens** (FIG. 12) in St. Petersburg. In the early 1900s, it was just an ugly sinkhole. George Turner and his wife, Eula, could see something others could not in the roughly four acres of muck.

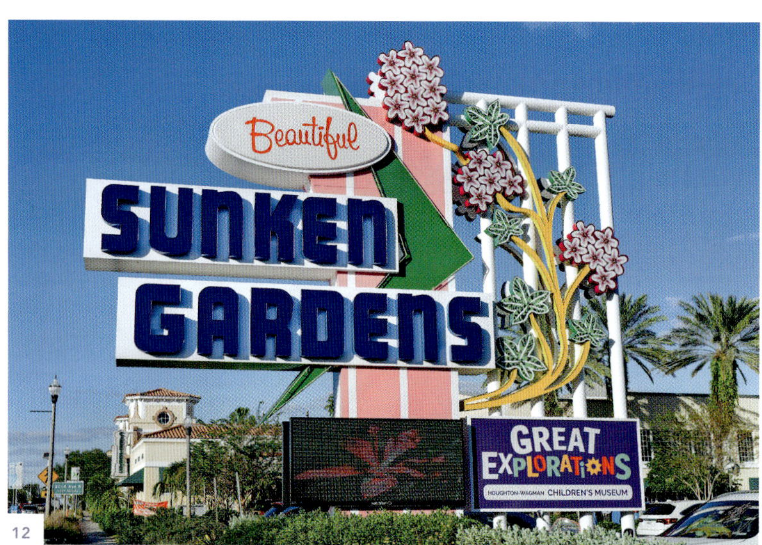

12

Turner was a plumber and horticulturist who gardened for fun, Jennifer Tyson, Sunken Gardens' education coordinator, explained to ABC's *Localish*. He knew he was standing over gold—a rich organic soil that could become the foundation of a glorious tropical garden. And that's exactly what happened. The attraction grew to include an apiary, a visitors center and gift shop, and more.

Sunken Gardens, like so much of Old Florida, declined as the twentieth century wore on, and decimation in the

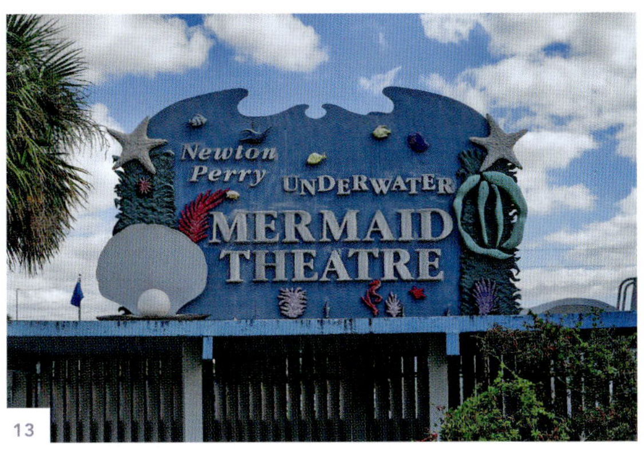

13

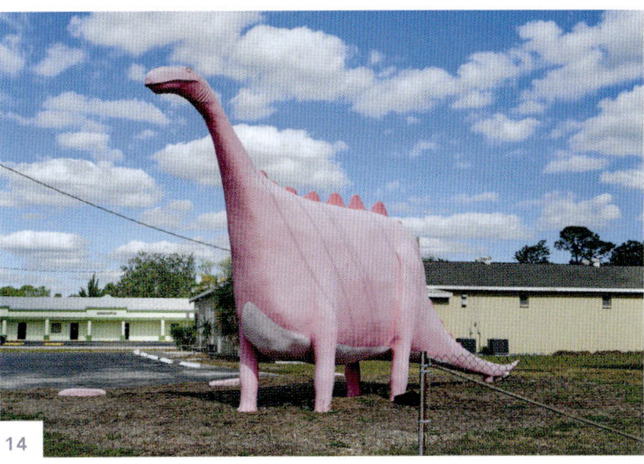
14

service of development was the unseen but feared menace. St. Petersburg rescued Sunken Gardens by buying it in 1999, and later declared it a historical landmark.

Now, we head to the City of Mermaids—and dinosaurs. Perhaps the ultimate representation of twentieth-century roadside Florida is the **Weeki Wachee Mermaid Show** (FIG. 13) in Weeki Wachee Springs State Park. Swimming in fresh, spring-fed waters pumped into an aquarium, well-trained performers dressed as mermaids have been delighting visitors since 1947. The attraction may be midcentury vacation escapism, but you're actually in a natural attraction, Weeki Wachee Springs.

If your car needs a tune-up while in the area, be sure to stop at the gigantic concrete auto shop shaped like a dinosaur in Spring Hill, Florida. The 1960s concrete structure, at 47 feet tall and 100 feet long, is yabba-dabba delightful and is cared for by **Harold's Auto Center** (FIG. 15). (After going "underwater" with mermaids, why not go "in the belly" of a dinosaur. That is Old Florida for you.) Nearby, also on U.S. 19, is a smaller dinosaur called **Foxbower** (FIG. 14), the name of the former family-run taxidermy museum in Spring Hill.

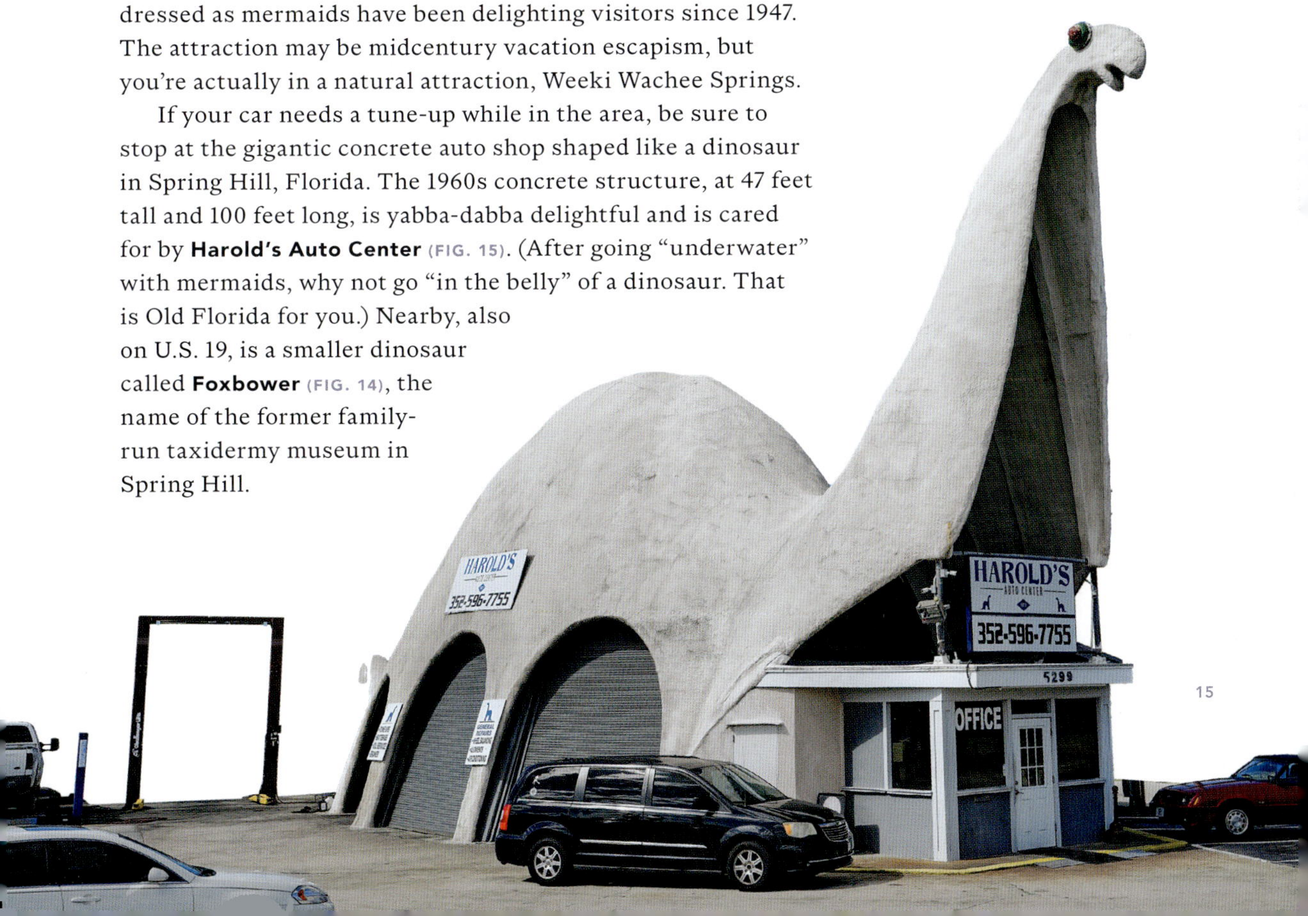

15

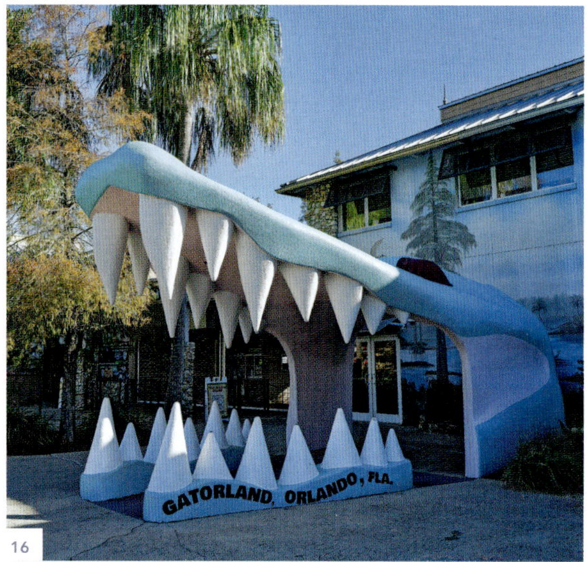

16

In Orlando, dating to 1949, **Gatorland** (FIG. 16) is one of those rest stops that captures the postwar road trip in all its delicious kitschy glory. I mean, you walk in through a big alligator jaw! In the early 1950s, this attraction was known as Snake World and Alligator Farm, but it hit poetic pay dirt with a 1954 rebrand as Gatorland. (Snakeland sounds a little sinister, no?) Faced with those familiar existential threats, Gatorland has adapted and thrived. Inside are alligators, crocodiles, snakes, and uniquely Floridian learning experiences that have kept up with the times. The Screamin' Gator Zip Line will have you screaming as you soar over crocodiles and alligator breeding marshes. Opened in 2024, Croc Rock Adventure combines rock climbing, zip-lining, and a swing-bridge crossing.

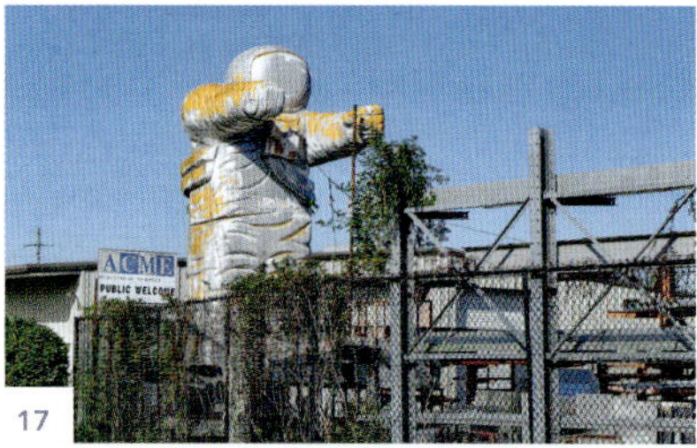

17

Alligators, mermaids, and dinosaurs. What's missing? Well, we're in Florida, so . . . *astronauts*. I could not take you to Florida without a nod to NASA. In Sanford, Georgia, I'd like to introduce you to the **Moonman** (FIG. 17), who landed here after his high-flying days representing MTV as the cable network's mascot at the 2004 MTV Music Awards in Miami. His rock-star days behind, he is enjoying retirement at Acme Industrial Supplies.

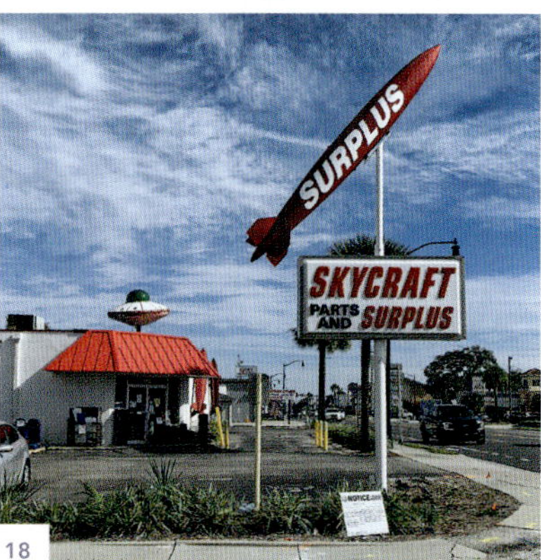

18

We've got UFOs nearby, too, at **Skycraft Parts & Surplus** (FIG. 18), an electronics emporium in Orlando. The business, opened in 1974, took off to a new location in 2021 but brought along its famous rooftop flying saucer (at left is the former location).

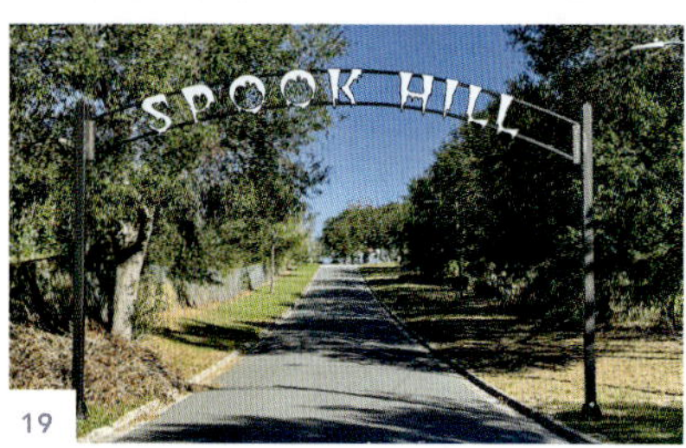

19

Let's add to the sense of otherworldliness and stop at **Spook Hill** (FIG. 19), a gravity hill in Lake Wales, Florida, marked with a cartoon ghost explaining one of the legends behind it. (The local elementary school avails itself of Casper's friendly image.) Park your car in neutral and become part of an optical illusion that is a beloved tradition first touted, not surprisingly, in the road-trip-loving 1950s.

Billboards for **Coppertone** (FIG. 20), featuring the Coppertone Cutie, were once mainstays of road trips to sunny places. Those billboards are long gone, but there's one place where you can still see a giant depiction of the spokeschild—the cocker spaniel tugging at her swimsuit bottom, exposing her tan line—and that's Miami, Florida.

The sign used to say "Don't Be a Paleface!" and "Tan . . . Don't Burn." She'd been there since 1959. By 1991, that message was all shades of wrong—politically incorrect and decidedly health unconscious, so the brand's parent company wanted to junk it. Not so fast, preservationists said. They managed to save it from the side of the doomed Parkleigh House apartment building, itself soon reduced to rubble. She sat in a Hialeah warehouse for a few years and eventually moved back to Biscayne Boulevard. And then, in 2017, Hurricane Irma struck and damaged the sign. Thankfully, it was restored and even improved by signage plastic surgeons. Today, the Coppertone Cutie, forever three years old and three stories tall, towers over Biscayne Boulevard.

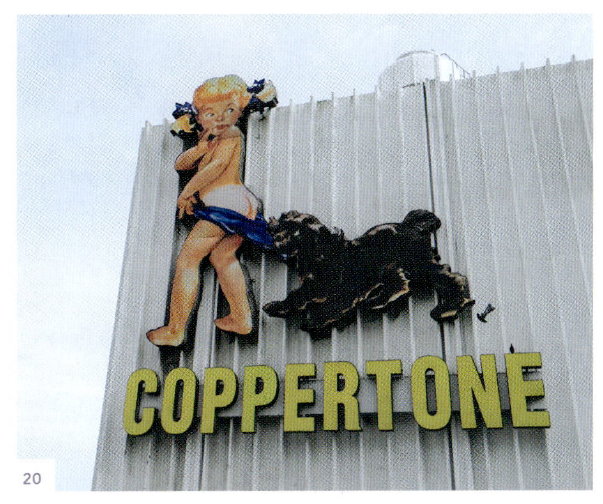

20

We're going to head north again, now to Georgia, where we're about to witness perhaps the biggest roadside grin in America. (Well, Tillie in Asbury Park, New Jersey, might protest; see page 13.)

Plains, Georgia, is famously the hometown of former President Jimmy Carter. Carter-related historic sites abound in this town, but perhaps the most iconic artifact of Carter's 1976 successful quest for the Oval Office is the **Smiling Peanut** (FIG. 21). This statue can make anyone smile, except maybe the former president, who reportedly disapproved of the depiction—surely with a wink and a grin.

The statue was featured at a Carter rally in Evansville, Indiana. It then wended its way to Plains, first sitting outside Carter's election headquarters downtown, which you can also visit.

After a mishap with a motorist in 2000, the peanut was fixed up and moved to its present location on Georgia 45 near Carter's church, where he famously taught Sunday school and mingled with well-wishers into his nineties. The guts of the peanut are made of wooden hoops encased in chicken wire, and the shell is made of polyurethane foam.

Another essential Plains stop is **Billy Carter's Service Station.** It no longer serves motorists, or reporters seeking a memorable quote at his gas station—or perhaps a swig of his infamous Billy Beer—but its well-curated exhibit is a window into the post-Nixon, pre-Reagan America of disco, leisure suits, and a former peanut farmer turned president who "lusted in his heart," as he told *Playboy* magazine, but loved his adored wife, Rosalynn, with all of it.

21

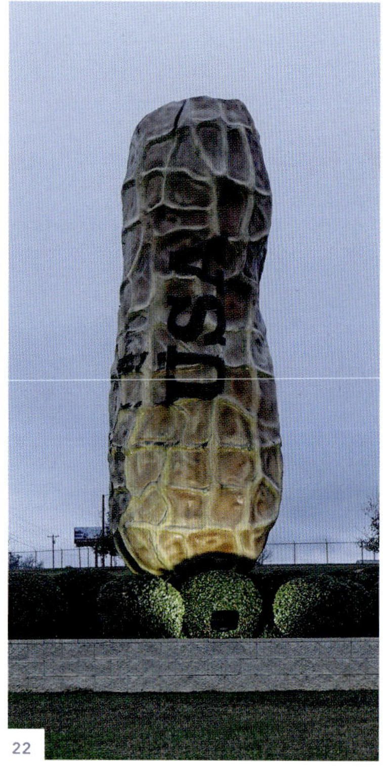

22

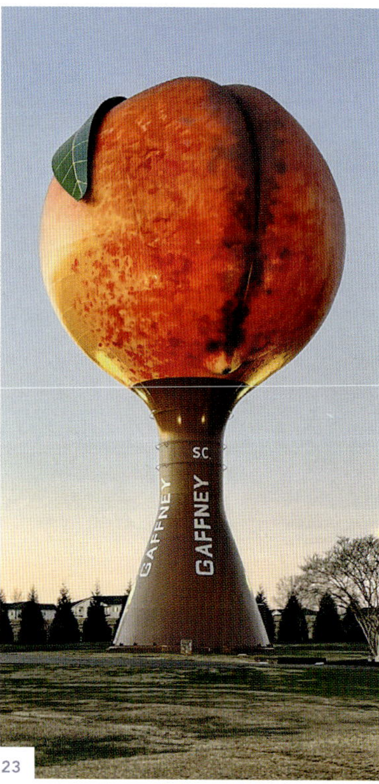

23

Since we're in peanut country, let's head to Dothan, Alabama, which bills itself as the peanut capital of the world and is home to dozens of peanut character statues, their attire matching the business where they are placed. Dothan is also home to a **giant peanut** stamped with the initials USA (FIG. 22), which was once on tour across the country.

We move from peanuts to peaches a couple of states over in Gaffney, South Carolina, where the 135-foot-tall **Peachoid** (FIG. 23) appears to be mooning motorists on Interstate 85. The water tower, built in 1981, instantly draws oohs, aahs, and, of course, snorts, with cheeky nicknames like "The Moon Over Gaffney."

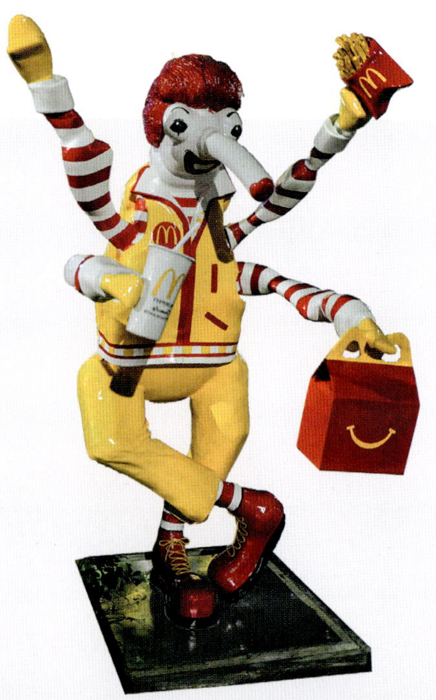

BUGGIN' OUT!

Peanut farming came to Enterprise, Alabama, because of the dreaded cotton-destroying boll weevil beetle. But rather than curse this little upender of the local industry, Enterprise has come to venerate the bug, with the Boll Weevil Monument downtown and a series of quirky boll weevil statues along the so-called Weevil Way.

The boll weevil statue that fascinates and terrifies me is **Ronald McWeevil**, who holds down the fort outside a McDonald's in town, offering passersby a Happy Meal. For those already cursed with coulrophobia, or fear of clowns, the sight of a clown-insect hybrid might turn them into entomophobics as well. Those who fear both clowns and insects would be wise to keep on driving.

Giant depictions of local food are a show of pride and marketing that are featured throughout this book. For sheer ability to stop traffic, one has to admire **The Big Chicken** (FIG. 24) at the Kentucky Fried Chicken in Marietta, Georgia.

In 1963, S. R. "Tubby" Davis opened Johnny Reb's Chick-Chuck-'N'-Shake, for which the towering chicken was built. The restaurant eventually morphed into a KFC, and The Big Chicken, despite an alleged foe in Colonel Harland Sanders himself, has become a landmark, the very symbol of Marietta for some. The chicken has inspired art and song (a popular a capella group is named after it). The goliath red rooster is commonly used in directions ("Turn left at The Big Chicken!") and is said to be a reliable beacon even for aircraft pilots. The Big Chicken becomes more cherished with every passing year and has survived additional brushes with death. KFC is said to have secretly conspired (after Sanders's death in 1980) to move the 56-foot-tall sign to another location when it looked like this franchise was set to expire. That didn't happen, thankfully.

Over New Year's weekend in 1993, a windstorm damaged the sheet-metal skin of the already deteriorated Big Chicken. Initial indications from KFC that the sign was doomed to demolition were met with a resounding public outcry. In an era just before the mass adoption of email and over a decade before the rise of social media, thousands of people picked up their landline telephones and called 1-800-CALL-KFC to show their solidarity for the Marietta landmark.

Well, the damaged Big Chicken *was* demolished, but was replaced with a perfect replica. In later years, a tornado almost wiped out The Big Chicken; a 27-foot-tall inflatable chicken atop a Church's franchise across the "4 lane" taunted the Big Chicken; and a rival Big Chicken has been built in Georgia! (What the cluck?)

But The Big Chicken of Marietta still stands and has never been better. These days, its eyes move and its beak opens and shuts, as they were initially intended to do. The crude mechanism used in the chicken's early days made such a rumble that it reportedly shattered windows, and it was mercifully turned off.

Many have tried to take on the colonel. Some have thrived, finding their own niches. Others have become vestigial.

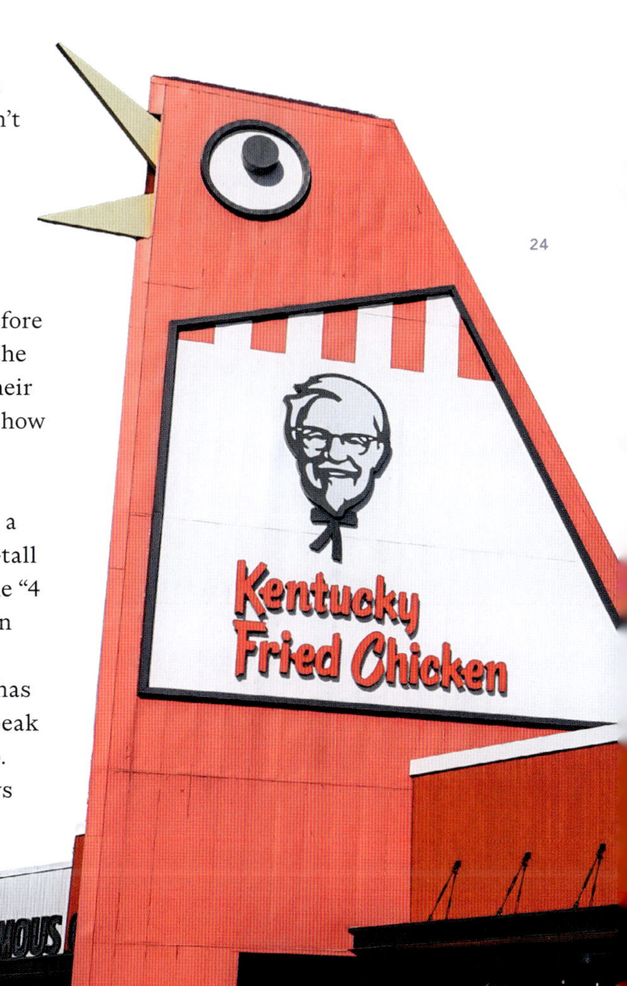

24

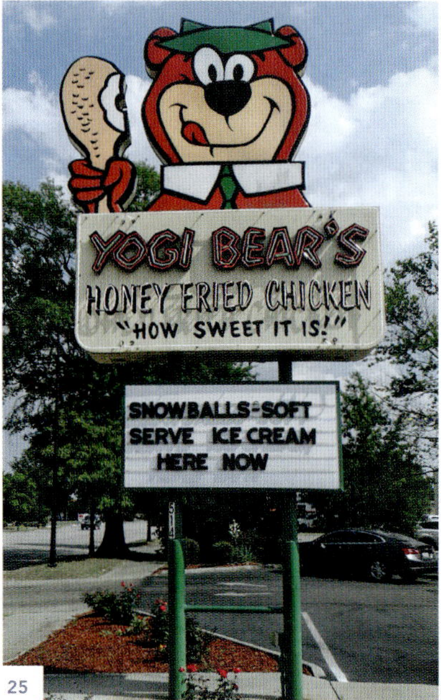

25

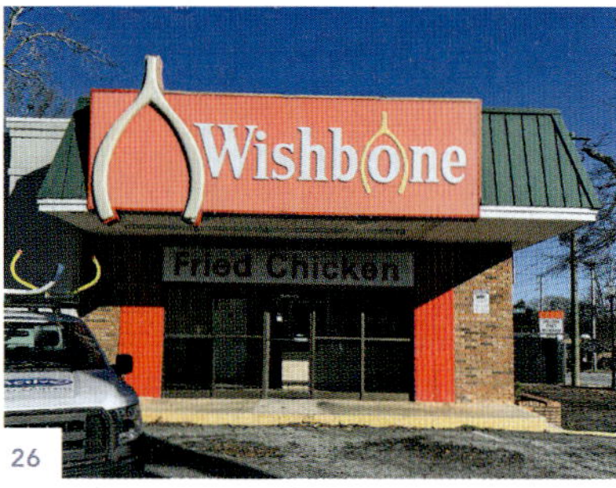

26

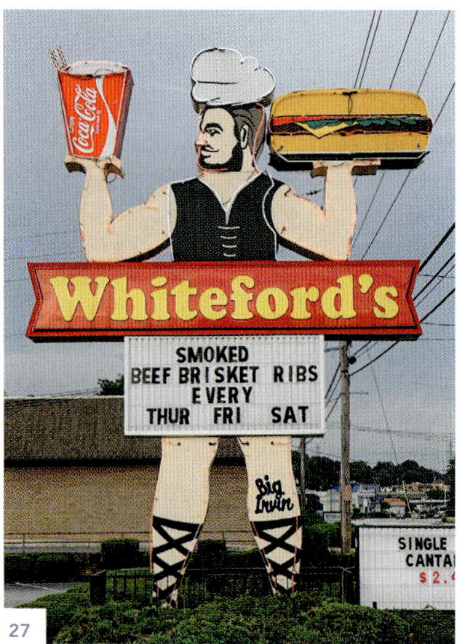

27

Yogi Bear's Honey Fried Chicken (FIG. 25) is down to its last location, in Hartsville, South Carolina, and it's a roadside quirk because, well, it's hard not to love a huge Yogi Bear sign.

The restaurant's slogan is "How Sweet It Is!" That line, of course, is associated with comic legend Jackie Gleason. The founder of the chain is said to have wanted Gleason to be the face of the new restaurants. "The Great One" was the genius behind *The Honeymooners* (perfect, there's the word "honey"!) and even had a character, Stanley R. Sogg, an oleaginous pitchman for No-Cal Chicken Fat (perfect, there's the word "chicken"!). Gleason passed, the *Charleston Post and Courier* reports in an interview with former Yogi partner, Roy Davis, so founder Gene Broome hit upon Yogi as a substitute.

Good fortune was fleeting for the **Wishbone Fried Chicken** (FIG. 26) chain, which grew rapidly in the late 1960s and early 1970s in the Southeast. The chain was proud of its fried chicken, touting its grade A fryers that produced succulent but nongreasy chicken. They even had their own mascot, Captain Wishbone. Today, the chain has almost vanished. Only one survives, in Newnan, Georgia, and it moved from its original location, though the old sign—a cool gigantic wishbone—was still there in 2022.

Whiteford's (FIG. 27) in Laurens, South Carolina, has been around since 1957, and one of the biggest stories in its history happened recently. Big Irvin, as the big-guy mascot is called, switched sides in the Cola Wars, now holding Pepsi instead of Coke. (I visited him during the last of his Coke days.) The local Pepsi bottler worked out a deal that pleased Whiteford's, golaurens.com reported, and soon, the fountains were no longer flowing with "The Real Thing." Although Coke had been the choice here since forever, Big Irvin had only held Coke since 1999—before that, the husky fellow was carrying a more neutral milkshake.

We are covering a wide swath of America in this chapter, and one shortcut to see seven of those states at one time—and still enjoy an old-fashioned roadside attraction—can be to visit **Rock City** high atop Lookout Mountain in Walker County, Georgia.

The boastful claim of "See Seven States" from Lover's Leap is disputable, but it goes that the expanse before you includes Georgia, Tennessee, Kentucky, Virginia, South Carolina, North Carolina, and Alabama. Word spread of Rock City through a roadside gimmick. Taking a page from the Mail Pouch Tobacco campaign (see page 138), the proprietors of Rock City in the 1930s began to paint barns around the Southeast to promote the attraction. "SEE BEAUTIFUL ROCK CITY," the barns blared, and a number survive, like this one (FIG. 28) in Bryson City, North Carolina.

If you're a child of the 1980s, you were likely bewitched by the Cabbage Patch Kids. **BabyLand General Hospital** is the so-called birthplace of the funny-faced dolls that in the America of 1983 became as hot as tulips in the Holland of 1636. So highly sought were the dolls that riots famously broke out in stores in November of that year, an employee at a department store in Pennsylvania waving a baseball bat to ward off hordes of Cabbage Patch–deprived parents. At BabyLand you can adopt your own doll and learn how they came to be, all without losing your dignity in a shopping scrum.

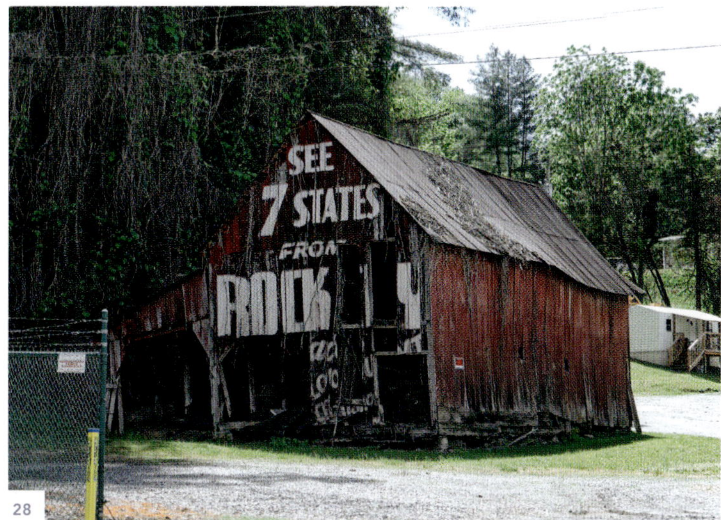

28

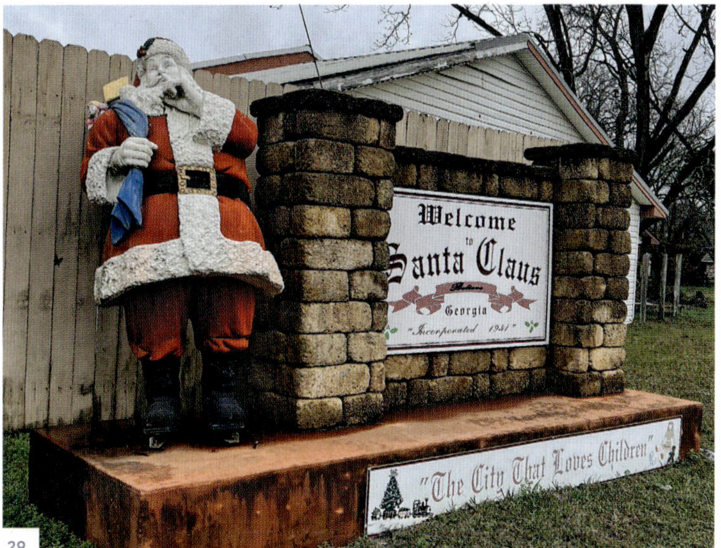

29

Of course we all know that Old St. Nick and his sleigh represent the ultimate shopping experience, and he'd never fail to deliver Cabbage Patch kids. **Santa Claus, Georgia** (FIG. 29)—population about two hundred, if you don't count Santa and his helpers—was incorporated in 1941, the brainchild of a pecan farmer, Calvin Greene, who wanted to sell more pecans, so he figured calling the town Santa Claus might do it. Greene even served as its first mayor, but World War II hit this city like Santa's sleigh running into fog on Christmas Eve, with no Rudolph to guide the town out of trouble.

But Santa is all about faith, and Farmer Greene kept believing. And in the 1960s, the town's second mayor, developer Bill Salem, turned out to be a true believer, too. Salem turned this place into the tidy little city you see today, with street names like Noel, Candy Cane, and Dancer; a community center; a chapel and garden; and even a gas station and convenience store named after Jolly St. Nick.

Got Christmas cards? You can drop them in the Believe mailbox and they'll get a special Santa Claus, Georgia, stamp on them. You can stop in at City Hall, located at 25 December Drive, of course, or check out the museum and gift shop across the street to find something special for the nice folks on your list.

ROADSIDE EATS

There's good road food everywhere in this book. But in the Southeast, we find ourselves with an embarrassment of riches. Pack your appetite—and your sense of wonder.

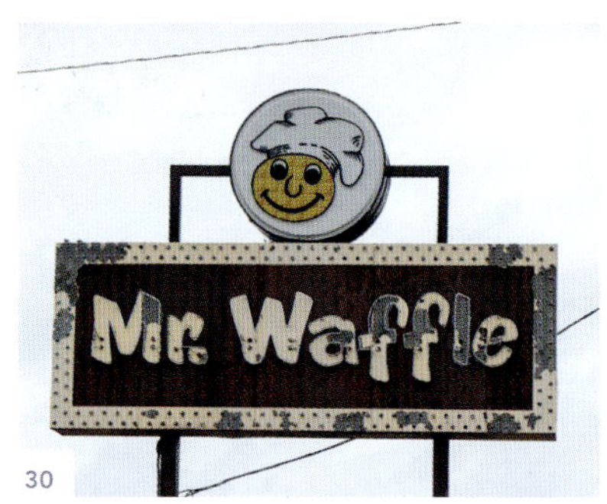

30

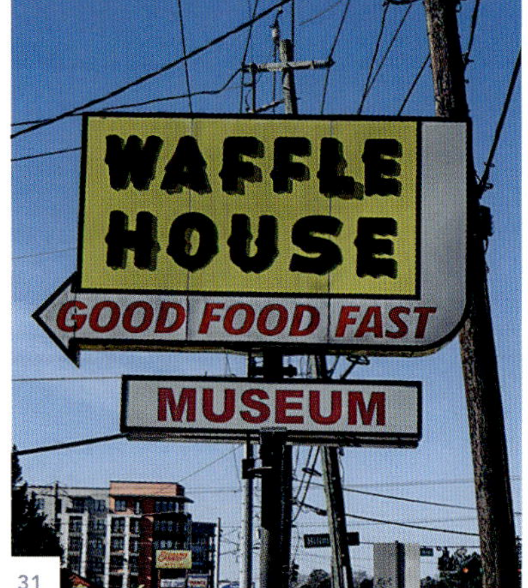

31

32

If you're looking for waffles down South, there's a Waffle House seemingly waiting for you at every highway exit. But there's only one **Mr. Waffle** (FIG. 30). He's right down I-85 from the Peachoid (see page 104) in Gaffney, South Carolina, and he's no slouch in the cute department. He's a yellow smiling griddle face, sporting a chef's hat. Mr. Waffle has been here since March 6, 1975, and hasn't changed much since.

There are too many locations of the chain Waffle House to count in the South, but there's only one that's the first location, in Decatur, Georgia, and it's now the **Waffle House Museum** (FIG. 31). It was here that Joe Rogers Sr. and Tom Forkner opened the first Waffle House on Labor Day in 1955. By 2004, the building was back in Waffle House's hands, and it reopened as the museum in 2008, a re-creation of the original store. Call ahead to book a tour.

One of the South's great homegrown brands is **Stuckey's** (FIG. 32), and in its 1937 birthplace of Eastman, Georgia, you can find a gorgeous mural honoring the institution launched by W. S. Stuckey Sr. Stuckey's became the gold standard for the roadside convenience store in the twentieth century. Practicality met with Southern charm, and a stop meant a good meal, iconic snacks for the ride (like pecan log rolls), souvenirs, and gas. (The "Eat Here & Get Gas" shirt is hard to resist.)

In Summerton, South Carolina, is the last original company-owned Stuckey's, which is undergoing a revival under the stewardship of Stephanie Stuckey, the founder's granddaughter, who has ramped up production of Stuckey's signature snacks (pecan log rolls!) and revived the brand on social media. Stuckey's was once one and the same with the Great American Road Trip and is proudly reasserting that role today.

Of similar DNA but hardly on the rebound is **Horne's** (FIG. 33). The very last one is on the always wonderful U.S. 301 in Port Royal, Virginia. Horne's used to be a chain—"Your highway host for one stop service"—and sold candy, nuts, souvenirs, and a square meal. This location has gasoline as well, and some even offered lodging.

Horne's was founded in 1948 by Bob Horne, a candyman who'd worked at Stuckey's, and indeed, Horne's buildings bear a striking resemblance to the classic Stuckey's stores, among other similarities. This was long before chains thought it was a virtue to hide in anonymous, bland boxes. Horne's, alas, collapsed as travel habits and tastes changed and interstates eclipsed older, long-established highways, and by 1982, the last corporate-owned Horne's was gone. You can still find former Horne's stores here and there. My favorite is near Lawtey, Florida, long shuttered, long decayed, and, alas, likely short on time.

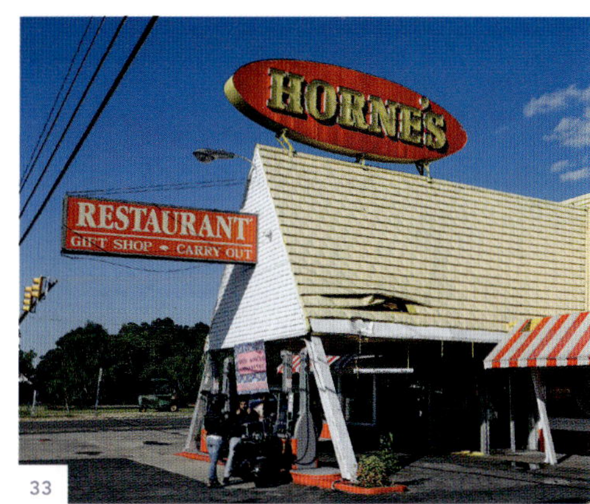

33

We have a lot more ground to cover, so let's bite into it, starting with burgers, hot dogs, and roast beef.

Sure, the **Burger Boy** (FIG. 34), as depicted in the sign, will forever be a carefree scamp in blue overalls, merrily marching along with hamburger in hand. But the Wilson, North Carolina, fast-food restaurant has entered middle age. Burger Boy is that place you wish you had in your town, or the place you used to have that closed long ago. The past is present here at Burger Boy, and that's a good thing. Except for a colorful walk-in area added a few years after they opened on January 22, 1969, it's business as usual.

The *Wilson Times* reports that the hot dogs outsell the burgers four to one, but nobody is talking about changing the joint's name. Like so many great retail stories, Burger Boy began by happy accident, as a clever hack to a frustrating roadblock. Marion Boykin and his business partner were set on opening a lunch truck on Ward Boulevard. The sanitation inspector frowned on the idea, clearly not foreseeing the food-truck explosion that would come a half century later. Burger Boy's founders were determined, however, and with $125,000 they built Burger Boy as you see it today along the boulevard.

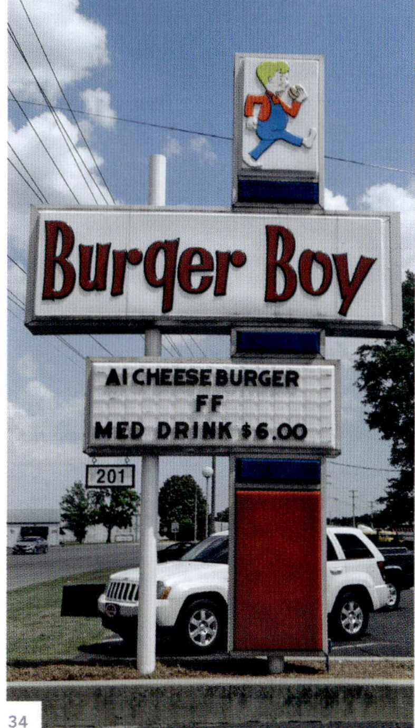

34

Let's head up to Raleigh now for one of my favorite holes-in-the-wall in the South, **The Roast Grill** (FIG. 35). It's a lunch counter tucked in a small house on South West Street that's been around since 1940. Owner George Poniros keeps it simple: hot dogs (charred to perfection), "all the way," with the signature chili, hand-chopped onions, coleslaw, mustard—all washed down with a bottle of Coke. And don't ask for ketchup, please—founder Mary Charles, George's grandma, did not approve, reasoning that the condiment overpowers her beloved chili, still made to her exacting standards. (Her name is etched in the pavement outside!) When you're done (it's hard to have just one dog) you pay with cash, and you find a Tootsie Roll as a free treat with your bill.

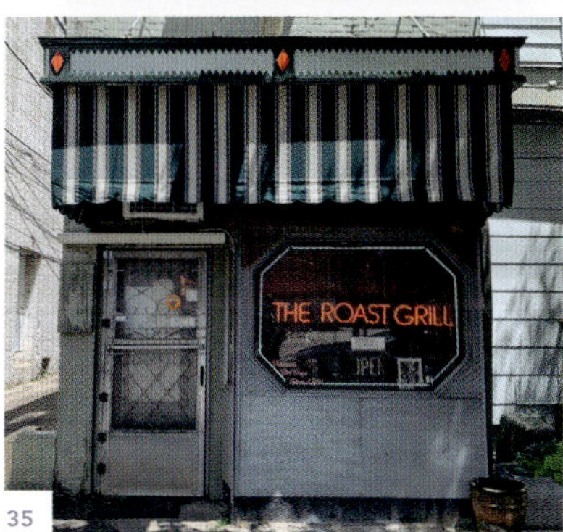

35

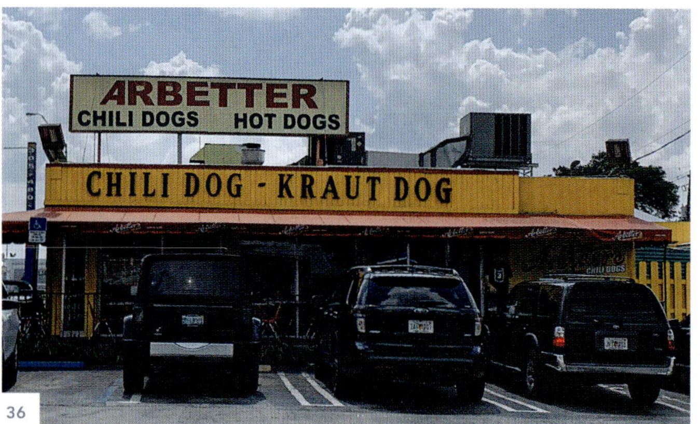

36

No conversation about hot dogs in the Southeast is complete without **Arbetter's Hot Dogs** (FIG. 36). Founded by Robert and Flaminia Arbetter in 1959, this Miami business bopped around until settling at its present location in 1970. A decade later, they sold the stand, which was said to be inspired by the great Joe & Nemo's in Boston. But the family stepped back in by 1990 when Arbetter's as a viable business was almost cooked, and they haven't stepped away from the grill since.

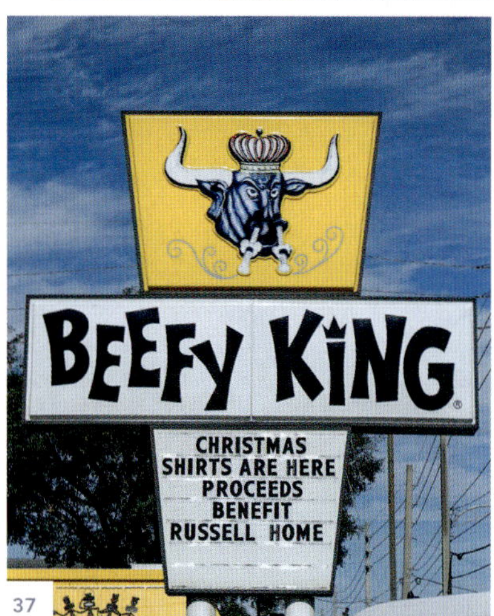

37

Orlando's Milk District is an institution so beloved that maybe this part of town should be renamed the Beef District, or better, Kingdom. This was the first **Beefy King** (FIG. 37) to open, in November 1967, which became the model for a small chain. This is now the last one, an all-too-familiar tale.

The founder, Tom Veigle, sampled a roast-beef sandwich in New York City, and his taste buds savored a business opportunity. Arby's was already erecting its 10-gallon neon hats across the country, and roast beef was a new way to stake a claim on the fast-food gold mine that was postwar America. Orlando fell hard for this place right away.

This very first Beefy King, not long after opening, ended up in the caring hands of Freeman Smith and his wife, Margaret, who escaped Michigan's harsh winters and built this restaurant into a beloved part of life in Orlando. The chain kept growing and then retrenched, leaving the first location as the last one standing.

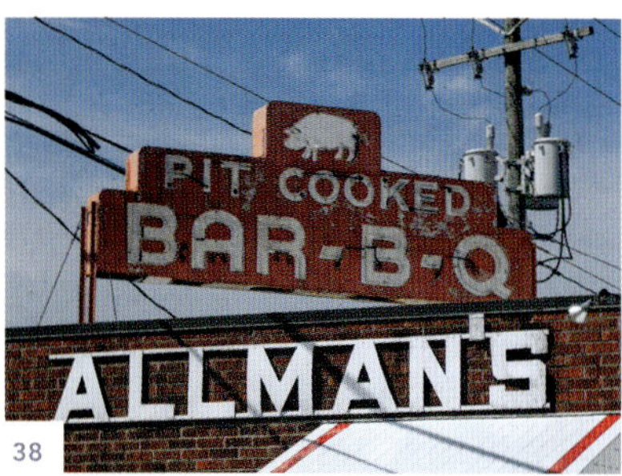

38

The Smiths and their descendants—Beefy King is in third-generation hands now—have kept this place a meticulous time capsule, with the old-timey swivel seats bolted to the tile floor and the vintage decorative plastic room dividers.

Allman's Bar-B-Q (FIG. 38) (1954, neon with a cute piggie on top) is one of the places that make Fredericksburg, Virginia, a comfort-food oasis off I-95. BBQ stands with great signage can be found across the South, like **Bob Sykes Bar-B-Q** in Bessemer, Alabama; **Betty's Bar-B-Q** in Anniston, Alabama, which uses the clever neon sign for the old Goal Post BBQ that once operated here; **Full Moon Bar-B-Que** in Birmingham, Alabama; **Shorty's BBQ** (FIG. 39) in Miami; and so many more.

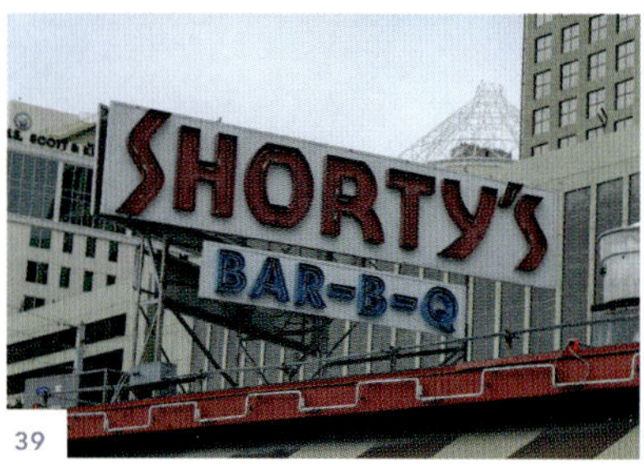

39

Let's move on to cafes, diners, and drive-ins, like the **MoonLight Drive-In** (FIG. 40), a trusted stop on Florida's Space Coast, in Titusville. Once, in this region whose economy boomed during the space race, there were so many places with out-of-this-world names—Astro this, Satellite that. But they've mostly vanished, mere memories like those moon shots of yore.

But here is the MoonLight, christened to capture some of the star power of the Apollo program, a year after President John F. Kennedy's death and five before the *Eagle* finally landed on the moon. It's a special place, a relic of *The Right Stuff* era, and a touchstone in the lives of people who've been coming here for more than sixty years.

In Richmond, Virginia, the space race is alive and well at the **Satellite Restaurant** (FIG. 41). It opened in 1962, the same year NASA astronaut John Glenn became the first American to orbit the Earth.

In Winter Haven, Florida, you'll find **Andy's Igloo Drive-In Restaurant** (FIG. 42). Winter Haven is a special city whose delights including a historic McDonald's sign and a repurposed but unmistakable former Mister Donut. Andy's, like so many classic drive-ins, evolved from an ice-cream stand (the Igloo, opened in 1951 and still there) into a full-fledged drive-in restaurant.

Spartanburg, South Carolina, is the headquarters of the Denny's restaurant chain, but it's also home to one of the most special mom-and-pop restaurants in America. There's only one **Sugar-n-Spice Drive-In** (FIG. 43)—and boy is it nice! "The Spice" opened in 1961. The wavy metal canopy is a reminder of its roots as a drive-in, and makes for a nifty shelter for classic cars on cruise nights.

It's hard to resist pulling over for a shot of the sign for the **Loveless Cafe** (FIG. 44) in Nashville, Tennessee, perhaps snapping a humorous selfie, poking fun at one's personal life.

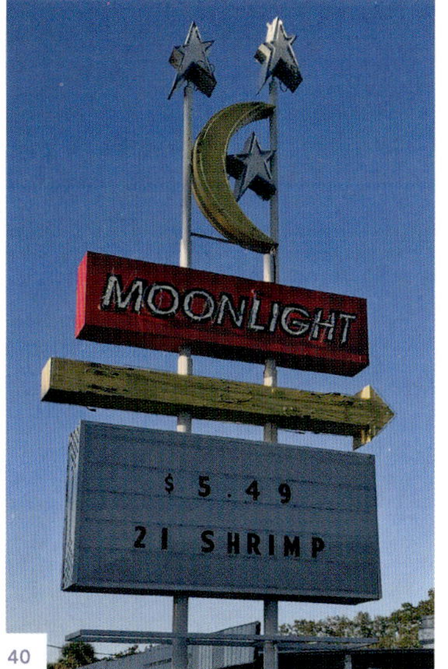

40

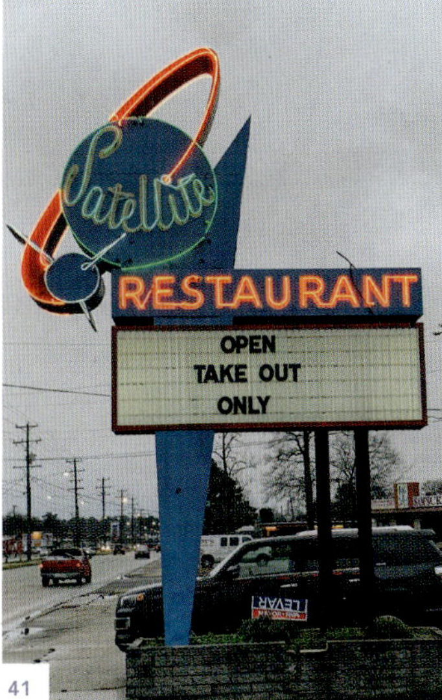

41

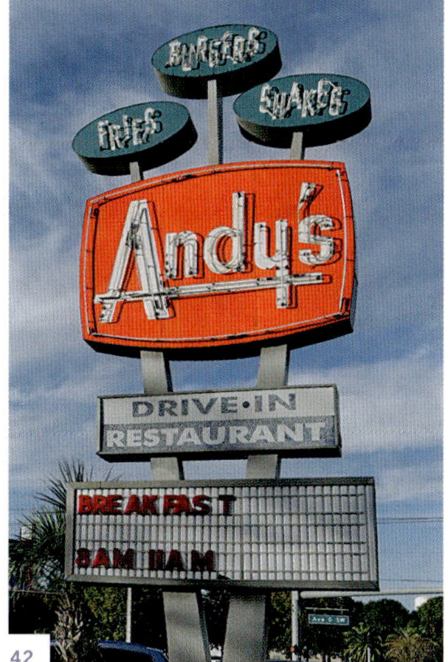

42

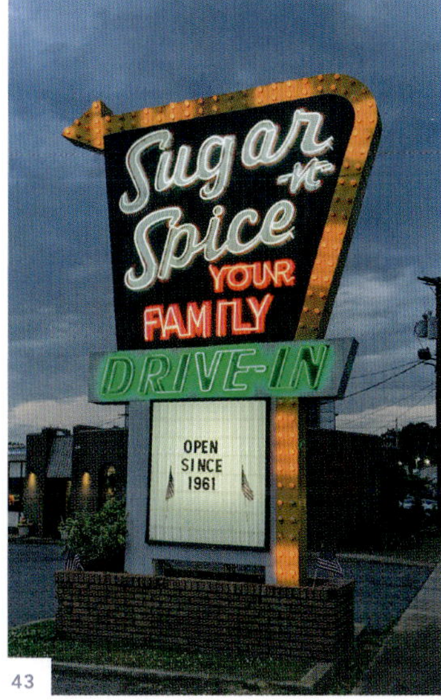

43

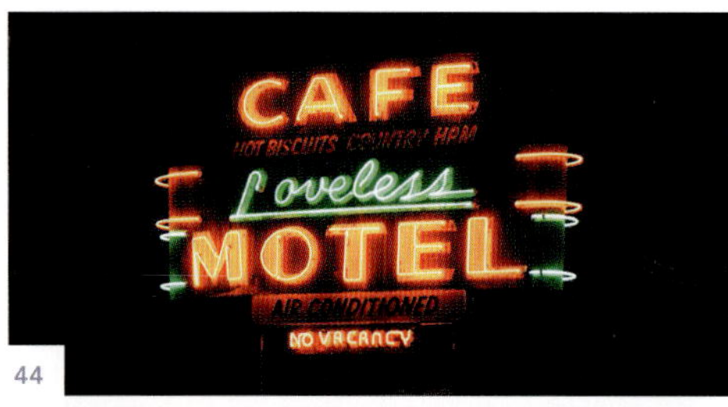

44

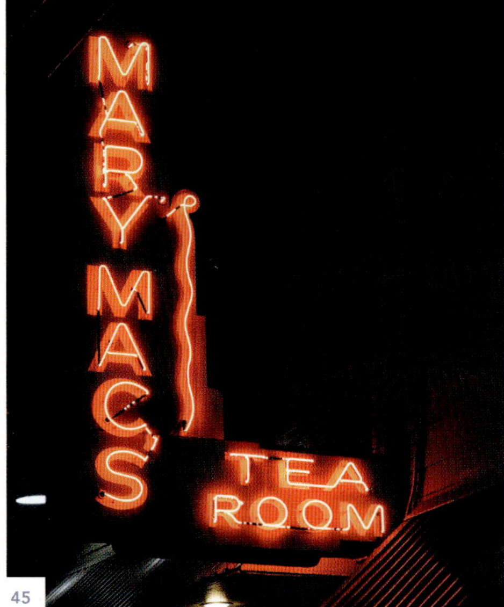

45

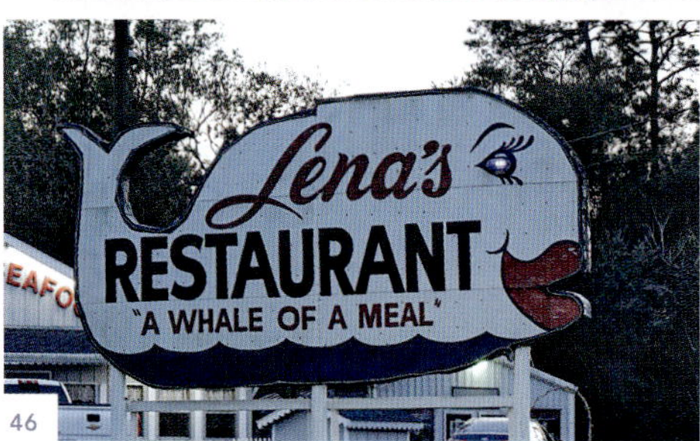

46

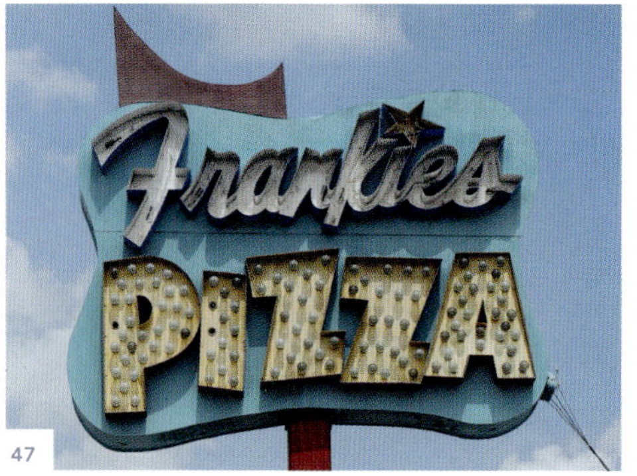

47

Despite the name, there's no love lost here; the cafe takes the names of founders Lon and Annie Loveless, who in 1951 founded an oasis of fried chicken, fresh biscuits and jams, and other comfort food. True Southern hospitality. The couple began to sell their food out of their home along tourist-heavy Highway 100, and realized their home was turning into a restaurant, so why not make it official. The cafe used to accompany a motel, which has been converted into shops.

Mary Mac's Tea Room (FIG. 45) has been a fixture in Atlanta since 1945, and its very name preserves a chapter in restaurant history. This is not a place for refined tea and biscuits but one for Southern comfort food. The history comes in the oft-told story that Atlanta once had sixteen tea rooms, opened by entrepreneurial women at a time when female ownership of restaurants was an affront to societal norms, so they became "tea rooms" instead—sounds genteel enough—restaurants in all but name. This one was run by Mary MacKenzie until 1962, when she turned it over to Margaret Lupo, whose hospitality acumen made it the institution it is today. Tourists, locals, and power brokers alike stop here, breaking bread in one of six dining rooms.

In Silver Springs, outside of Ocala, Florida, **Lena's Seafood** (FIG. 46) is a taste of the New England shore in the Sunshine State. The family that runs Lena's operates a sister restaurant where it started, in Massachusetts. They close up the Florida shop to run the Massachusetts store in the summer, and do the reverse once autumn arrives. This adorable lipsticked whale has quite the jet-set life.

In 1950s Miami, as well as in many places around the country, pizza was an exotic food, something they had up in New York, Chicago, or New Haven. That was about to change. The enterprising restaurateurs of this era realized that pizza—delicious, fun to eat, catnip for kids, ridiculously addictive for all—was a way to make a lot of dough with some dough, cheese, and tomato sauce . . . and be your own boss. The chains like Pizza Hut were just a few years away from forming. Pizza was still the province of the mom-and-pops, and Americans were falling in love with it.

Those enterprising restaurateurs who realized that Miami needed pizza were Frank and Doreen Pasquarella, originally from Ohio. They opened **Frankie's Pizza** (FIG. 47) in 1955 and moved it to a small building on Bird Road in Miami's Westchester neighborhood in 1957, when the area was fairly rural.

Along the Blues Highway, in Tunica, Mississippi, the **Blue and White Restaurant** (FIG. 48) has been welcoming hungry travelers since 1924. In 1937, the restaurant was moved here as part of a Pure Oil service station, and that's the structure you see today. This is a requisite Southern cuisine stop on a tour of the Blues Highway in the Mississippi Delta, though you can no longer fuel up here. (A Blues Highway visitors center can be found up the road on Highway 61.)

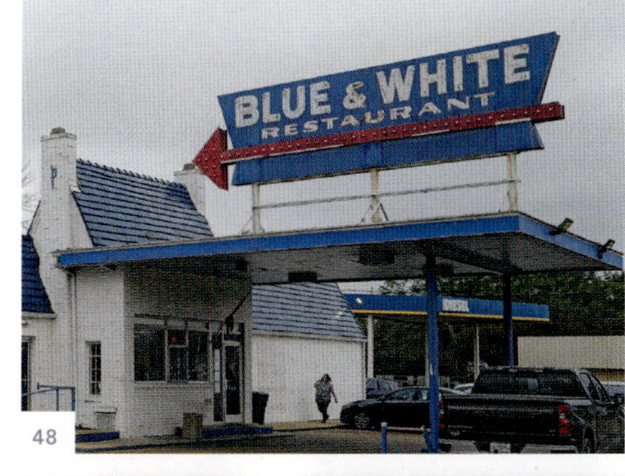

48

On a road trip between Memphis and Nashville, I had to pull over to check out **Loretta Lynn's Kitchen**, the country star's foray into the restaurant business in Hurricane Mills, Tennessee. Earlier that day, as I explored Elvis Presley's home turf in Memphis, **Marlowe's Ribs and Restaurant**'s (FIG. 49) big pink pig caught my eye. The restaurant's limos will pick you up at several hotels in the area, including the **Days Inn Graceland** (FIG. 50), where a neon Elvis performs over the entrance.

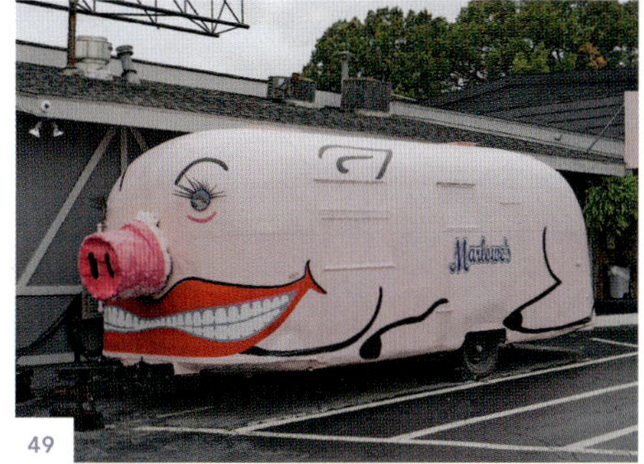

49

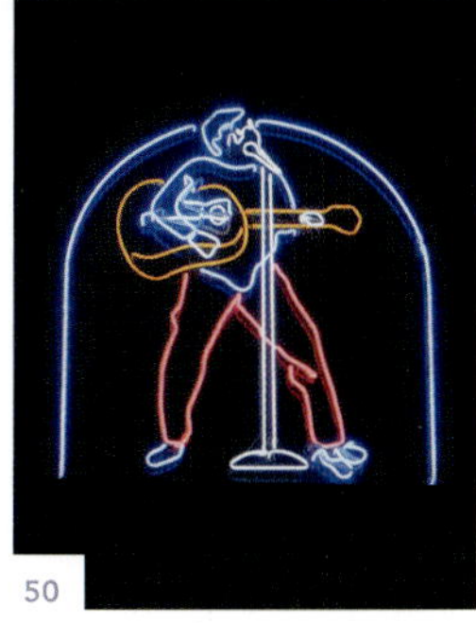
50

MIAMI'S CUBAN FLAVOR

Miami boasts many Cuban musts. For a taste of a specially seasoned Cuban hamburger, aka a "frita," visit **El Rey De Las Fritas** (FIG. 51). Consider having the burger "a la juliana," dressed with savory potato sticks, just like my mom used to enjoy in Cuba from sidewalk vendors in the 1950s.

On visits to Miami as a child, we were sure to stop at **Versailles** (FIG. 52) and **La Carreta** (FIG. 53), two iconic Cuban eateries across from each other on La Calle Ocho. I still alternate between the two on visits all these years later.

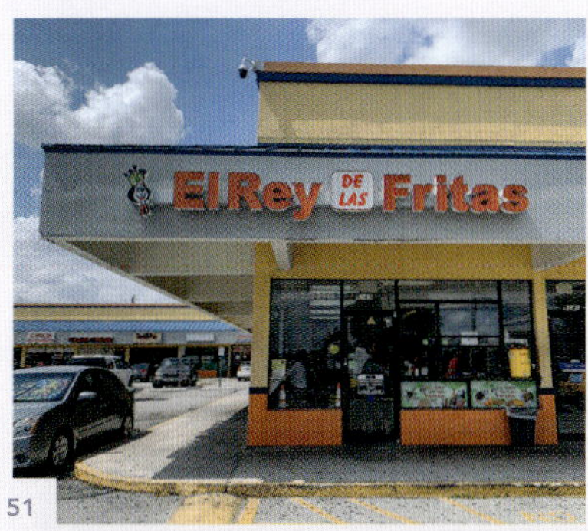

51

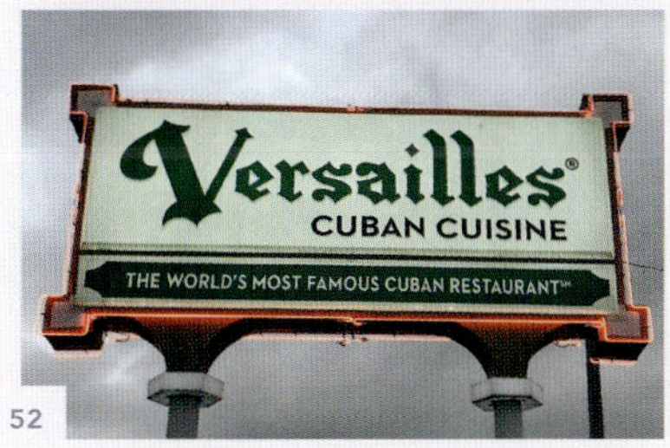

52

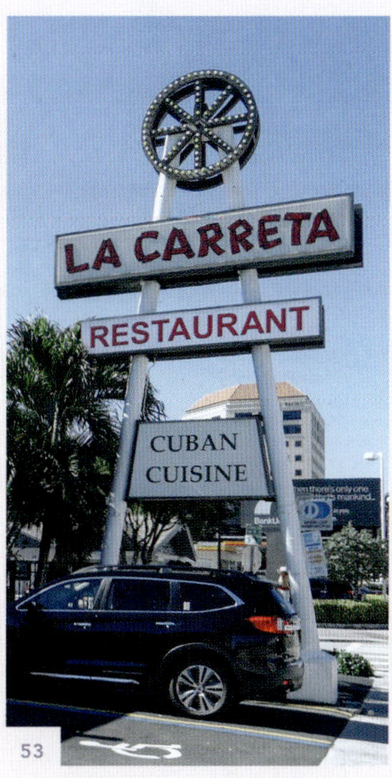

53

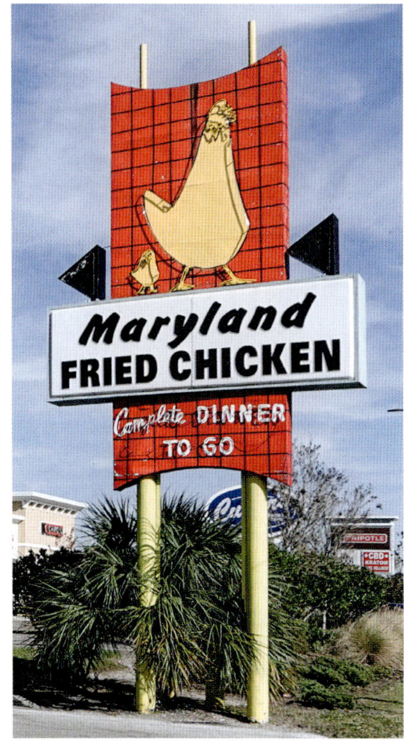

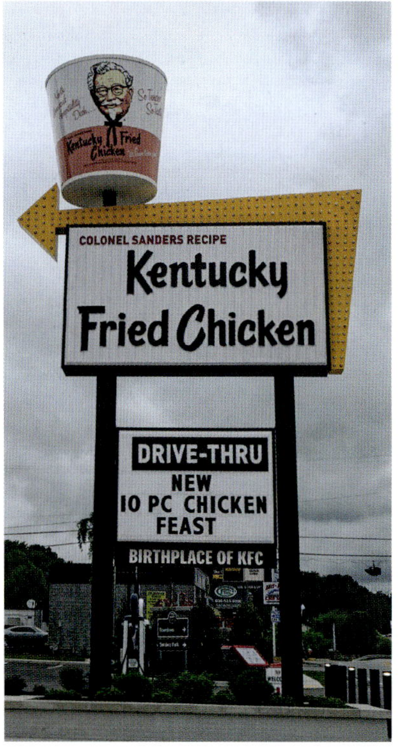

CHAINS OF FOOD

The South has a host of curious fast-food chains, from ones that enjoyed brief periods of growth before falling behind, to others that became household names. Let's take a tour.

Maryland Fried Chicken

While it never quite rivaled the empire built by Colonel Harland Sanders, in its 1970s heyday, MFC was a worthy competitor to KFC. Maryland Fried Chicken was founded in the Orlando area by Albert Constantine, an expatriate from Delaware who opened a restaurant down here in 1958. In 1962, he opened his first Maryland Fried Chicken, in Fern Park, figuring the restaurant's name would appeal to nearby Lockheed Martin (then the Martin Marietta Corporation) workers who had relocated to the Sunshine State from Maryland.

Mr. C, as Constantine was known, was inspired by Sanders's success, impressed by the long lines at a KFC near him. But if the name, with its echo of home and the competing Kentucky Fried Chicken, drew crowds in, then the chicken's quality made them repeat customers, and Constantine's "broasting" method hit the spot—pressure-cooked chicken coated in an herb-and-spice blend that was light on grease and heavy on flavor. The colonel had his secret recipe, and now so did Mr. C.

Constantine grew rich and cashed out when the chain numbered more than two hundred and fifty. But instead of expanding dramatically like, say, Popeye's, MFC retrenched into communities, mainly in the Southeast, with the most in Florida, its birthplace. (Broken chains have a way of retrenching to their home turf, sort of like returning home to die.) There are a roughly a couple dozen MFCs in business today.

KFC

In Corbin, Kentucky, you can visit where it all began—the rest stop where Colonel Harland Sanders first sold his Kentucky Fried Chicken. Sanders built a roadside stop here with cabins and a restaurant, and it's where he nailed down his recipe and method of cooking the chicken under pressure (though not the name, at least not yet).

Today, this is still an actual KFC, but it's also home to a museum and buildings that re-create Sanders's stop. In recent years, a sign with a bucket and a gigantic arrow with chasing light bulbs was reintroduced here, which was the standard signage at many franchises in the 1960s, the era when the chain exploded in growth.

Sanders would grow the chain himself, traveling the country selling franchises. The first was sold to Pete Harman, a restaurateur in Salt Lake City, Utah, in 1952, a key partner and inspiration to Sanders as he crafted the chain's future. The store remains in business, with a small museum and a big bucket asserting its role as the first KFC. (See page 248 for more.)

Sanders's success soon caught the attention of John Brown, who with a business partner bought out Sanders, put him on a salary, made him the official spokesman for the chain and went on a tear growing it.

Through the 1960s and 1970s, Sanders was the famous face of KFC, but no longer its owner. And though Sanders died in 1980 at age ninety, he remains something of a mascot for the chain—he's been made into a cartoon and depicted by Darrell Hammond in commercials but is still one of the most famous faces in America.

The bucket you see in Corbin features the standard 1960s design. The oldest original of this design left in the nation is still attached to a KFC franchise in San Jose, California.

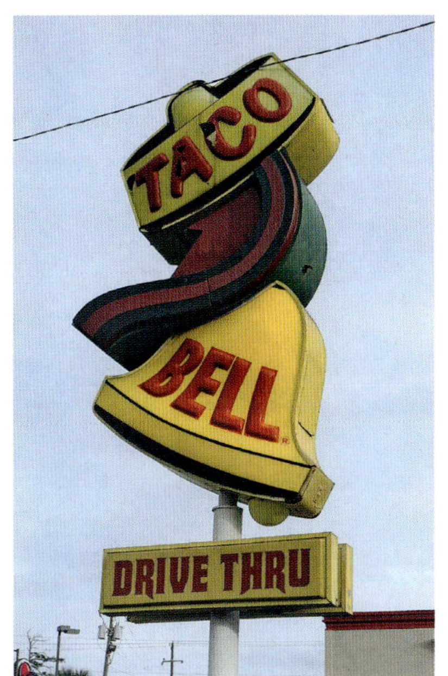

Taco Bell

Yo quiero this sign! I'll share the story of Taco Bell on page 300, but it's worth noting that Savannah, Georgia, has the last of the 1970s-era "sombrero" Taco Bell signs. It's vestigial, tucked away in the back of a remodeled store, but it's an important piece of fast-food history.

Golden Skillet

We've all heard of the Golden Arches, but what about the Golden Skillet? What came to be known as Golden Skillet Fried Chicken was first a popular dish on the Richmond Room restaurant's menu at Thalhimers, a department store in Richmond, Virginia, in 1964. By 1968, standalone stores were opening, the first in Richmond, and then in Petersburg, Virginia.

The menu was the brainchild of C. W. Guthrie, who raised chickens on his Virginia tobacco farm as a kid and loved fried chicken so much he called it "the greatest food in the world," UPI reported in 1981.

The American road once teemed with more than two hundred of these joints. But Golden Skillet restaurants are down to just a handful today.

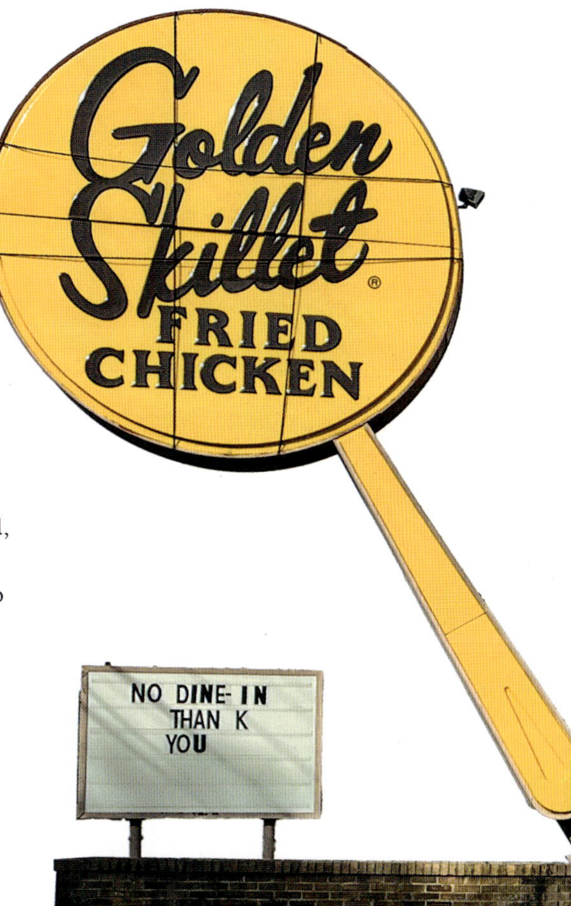

MAINSTAYS OF MAIN STREET

From mom-and-pops downtown to fabulous shopping centers, we are going to cover a lot of gorgeous ground, starting with a story that resonated with me about a Miami storefront I long wondered about—until I finally went in.

For Lourdes Sanchez, dry cleaning is personal. It's etched in her very DNA. Her grandparents ran a distinguished dry-cleaning shop in Havana—La Primera de La Vibora—founded in 1928. It was a business her grandfather loved so much that he was heartbroken to lose it after the Cuban Revolution, and died not long after. But that wasn't the end of the family business—far from it. Living with his young family in the freedom of early 1970s South Florida, Lourdes's father, Justo, a Swarthmore-trained electrical engineer, met Cy Mishkin. Cy was about ready to give up his dry-cleaning business, **Society Cleaners** (FIG. 54), on Southwest Eighth Street in Coral Gables, near the stretch of "Calle Ocho" then becoming known as Little Havana.

Society Cleaners had been around since 1954, before Cuban émigrés began arriving en masse. The fanciful neon of its scripted signage and swanky curves of its architecture offer vivid testimony to its midcentury origins. It was here that Justo Sanchez again took up the family calling. It's a tradition that Lourdes carries on today.

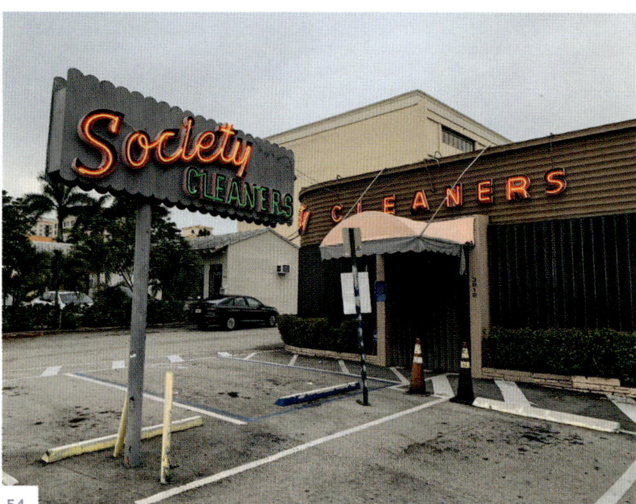

54

For the Sanchez family, it's about the personal touches, like a rush tailoring job for a customer with a looming wedding. Or the many brides Society serves—Lourdes proudly showed off some of the gowns in the back, next to her treasured vintage Hoffman dry-cleaning press.

"I love my business," she declared during my 2019 visit. Her parents' importuning to give it up, just like Cy Mishkin did so many years ago, has fallen on deaf ears. Because what Lourdes is really saying when she says that she loves her business is that she loves her customers. It's no surprise, then, that Society Cleaners is such a class act.

This next place is also glamorous, all right! If I lived anywhere near Dunn, North Carolina, I'd drop off my shirts here every week—and take a picture of their sign every time. **Glam-O-Rama Cleaners** (FIG. 55), a midcentury relic with a fabulously restored sign, is near the Fort Liberty Army base. That explains their "We Do Fatigues" sign.

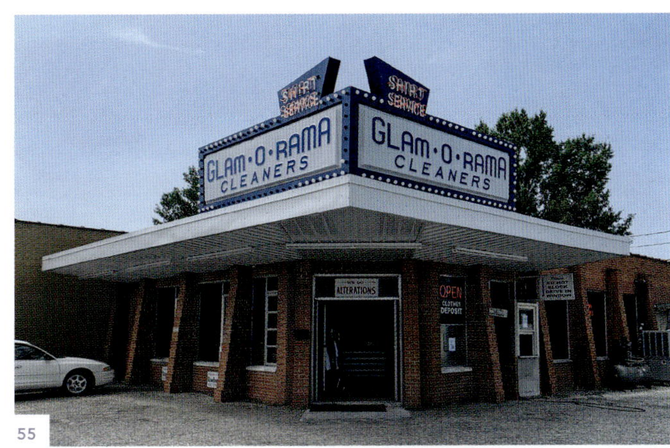

55

We're in the Southeast, of course, but the frontier lore figured big everywhere in the United States in the 1950s, and the **Western Way Shopping Center** (FIG. 56) in Orlando is a reminder of that. The giant neon sign featuring a cowboy on horseback in mid lasso has stood here since 1955, at a time when this part of the city was in indeed the area's western frontier.

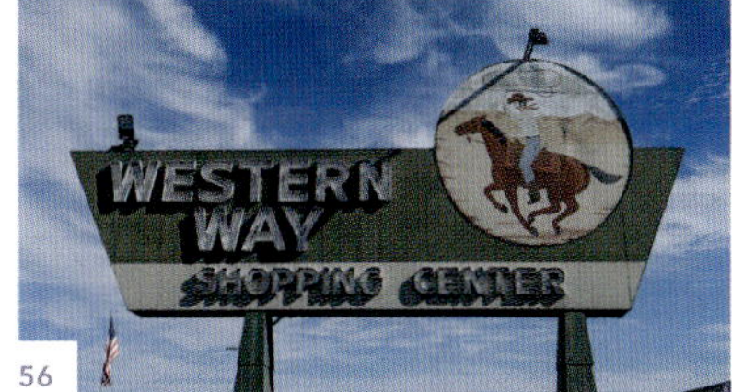

56

The 1957 **Southgate Shopping Center** (see photo on pages 94–95) in Lakeland, Florida, makes an even grander architectural statement with its stunning arch, made famous in the film *Edward Scissorhands*. Once you've seen the Southgate, don't hightail it out of town. Lakeland has many more treasures, including a water tower that takes the cake. Such structures always present opportunities for marketing fun, and the Publix supermarket chain hit the sweet spot in 1982 with a water-tower cake (aka **the Hydrocake**, FIG. 57) outside its production center some 146 feet in the sky. The cake has 8-foot-tall candles that glow after dark!

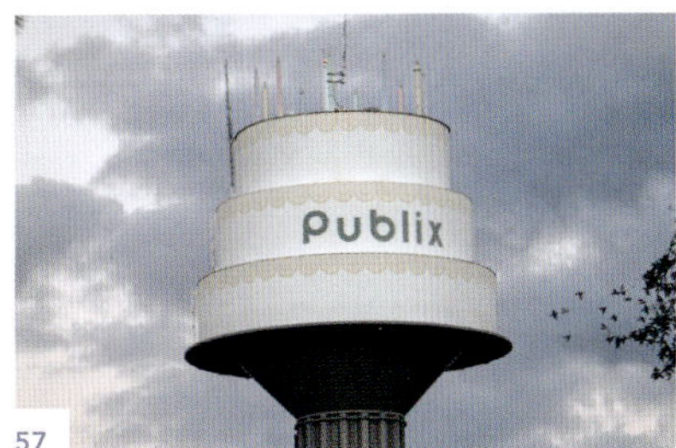

57

On a road trip through Kentucky, I picked up U.S. Route 119 right where it begins in Pineville and followed its meanderings through the countryside along the Cumberland River. Ahead of me were several hit-the-brakes-and-do-a-U-turn moments.

I can't say I know much about **Paul Green Grocery** (FIG. 58), somewhere near Molus along Route 119. The humble business, seemingly long shuttered, has a beautiful Coca-Cola privilege sign and another one on a pole nearby. There were many more abandoned service stations and country stores on the road ahead in this coal-mining country, each with its own mysteries and secrets.

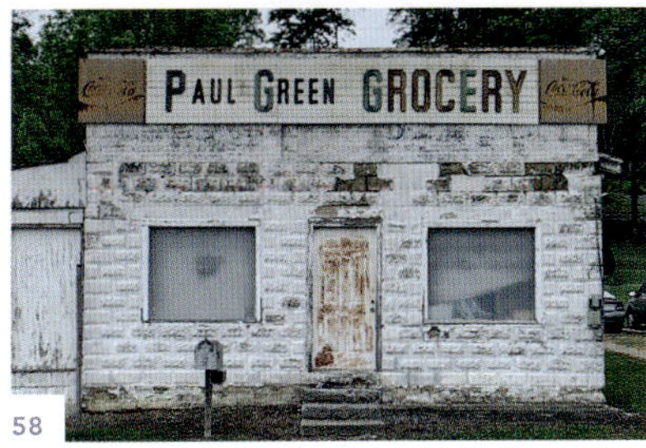

58

The Benton Card Company stopped me cold during another sojourn through the South because of the sign's restrained elegance. **Benton Card** (FIG. 59) opened in 1948 in Benson, North Carolina, and the font is evocative of that era. There is, of course, the lettering—that proto–Pac-Man "C" is something to behold. So is that "A." The legacy of Howard Beasley Benton's business is legendary. He was known as "The King of Posters in the South." Customers have included luminaries such as Aretha Franklin.

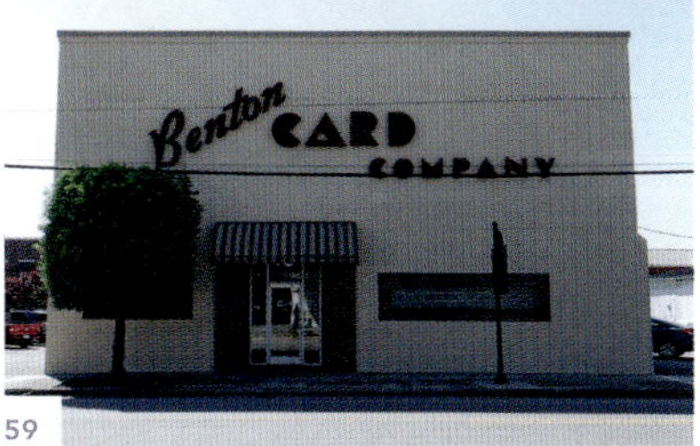

59

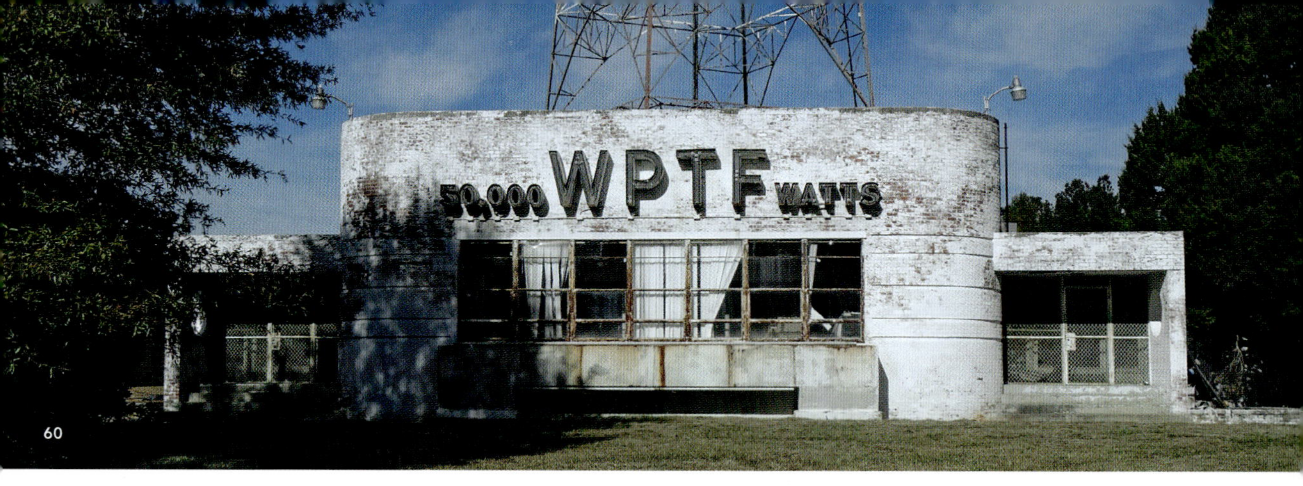

60

ON WITH THE SHOW

We all know that the showiest buildings in town are often movie theaters. And buildings housing TV and radio stations often have a dash of Hollywood. But as you'll see here, even very functional buildings, in some cases those holding technical equipment, can be dressed up beautifully.

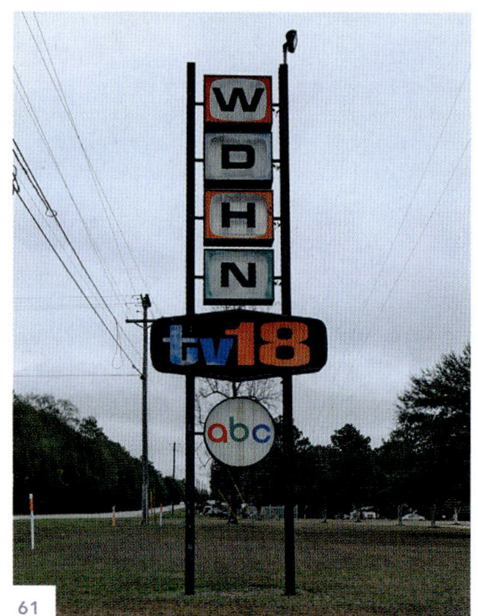

61

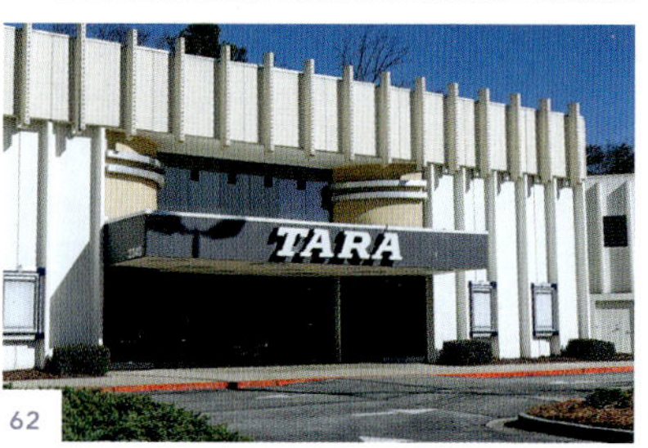

62

WPTF (FIG. 60) has a stunning art deco transmitter building, which is on busy U.S. 1 just outside Raleigh, North Carolina. But while all those watts mean it's easy to dial in the station, the compact marvel of the transmitter building is hard to reach. As I did back in 2016, I had to park across the street, play *Frogger* in traffic, cross railroad tracks, and power through a prickly barrier of bushes to take in this view. It's worth the trouble, though, as you can plainly see.

The neon on the facade proudly trumpets the station and its reach. The call letters stand for "We Protect The Family," a slogan for a life insurance company that once owned the station.

Dothan, Alabama, is home to a wonderful period sign outside the ABC station in town, **WDHN** (FIG. 61). The sign evokes 1970s vibes, with the multicolored ABC logo and the groovy TV 18 branding. (I may or may not have emitted a squeal upon seeing this. Those who road-trip with me may or not be familiar with this sonic phenomenon.)

We can't have a show without a few nice theaters, and I've long been intrigued with the Tara in Atlanta. Named for the fictional estate in *Gone with the Wind*, the **Tara Theatre** (FIG. 62) opened in 1968 as a dazzling monument to modernism.

Looking for a different kind of movie-going experience in Atlanta? Catch a movie under the stars at the **Starlight Drive-In** (FIG. 63), a tradition since 1949 that has morphed from a single screen to multiple screens, offering sharp digital projection.

The **Ashland Theatre** (FIG. 66) in Ashland, Virginia, makes a grand impression, its facade blazing anew, now with LED lighting replacing the neon. This theater opened in 1948 and toward the end of its first chapter found itself on a most-endangered list in Virginia. That's when something remarkable happened: The owner donated the theater to Ashland, volunteers and preservationists got to work raising money, and in 2018, five years after closing, the theater enjoyed its grand reopening. Nowadays, it shows films and hosts events, and guests can partake in liquor in the plush new environment.

The **Henrico Theatre** (FIG. 65) in Highland Springs, Virginia, is another preservation success story. Its run as a movie house began in the art deco glory days of 1938. By the late 1990s, Henrico County stepped in and bought the theater after it closed, turning it into a center for film and culture in this community. This is one I could stare at all day.

On Memphis's Beale Street, buzzing with masterful neon and booming with musical notes, the **New Daisy Theatre** (FIG. 64) is a worthy survivor, as is the Old Daisy right across the street. The New Daisy went through familiar cycles of decline and rebirth. It most recently closed in 2018 but reopened after a renovation in 2023.

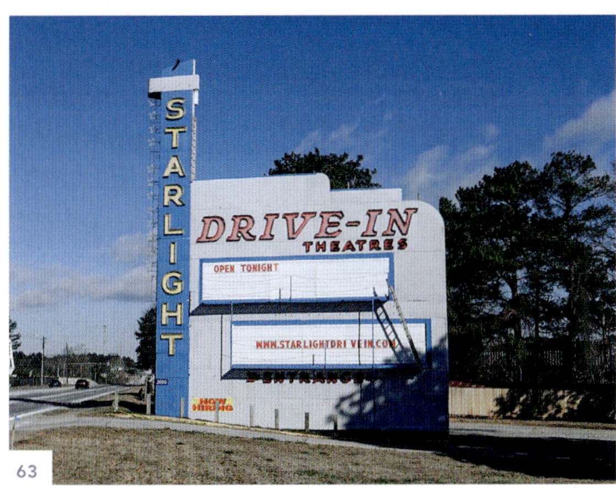

63

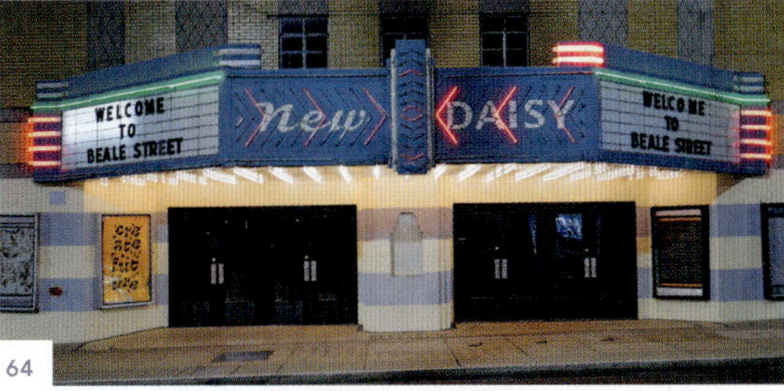

64

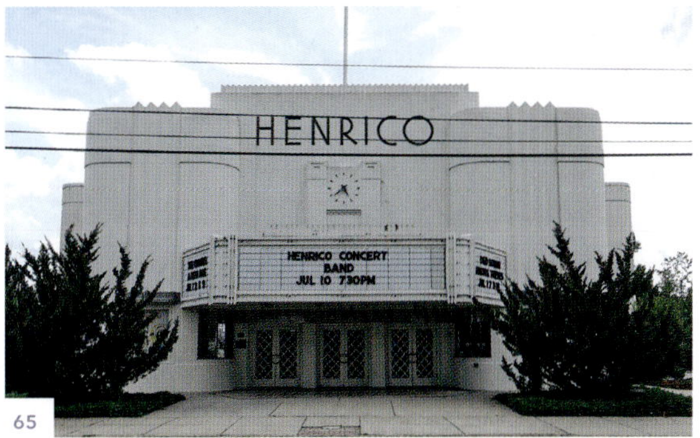

65

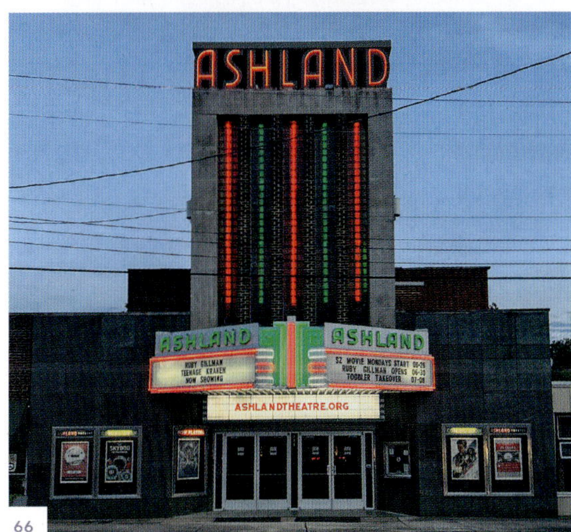

66

THE INN CROWD

There was a time in America when mom-and-pop motels were engaged in a kind of sign war. You had to pull out all the stops to make a motorist pull over. This was clearly a much more interesting time, and here are examples of it. But we begin with one that defies that narrative in a "magical" way.

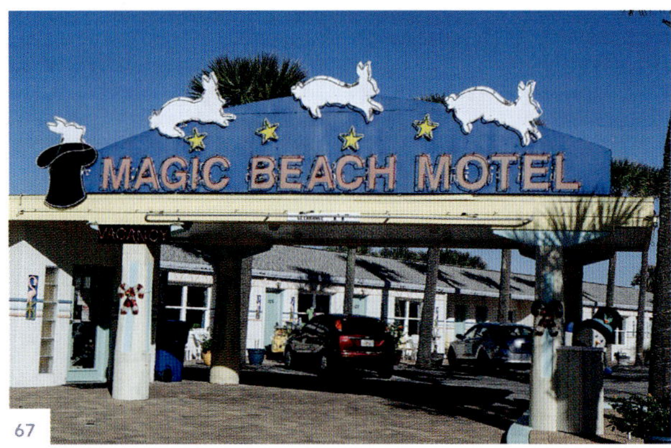

67

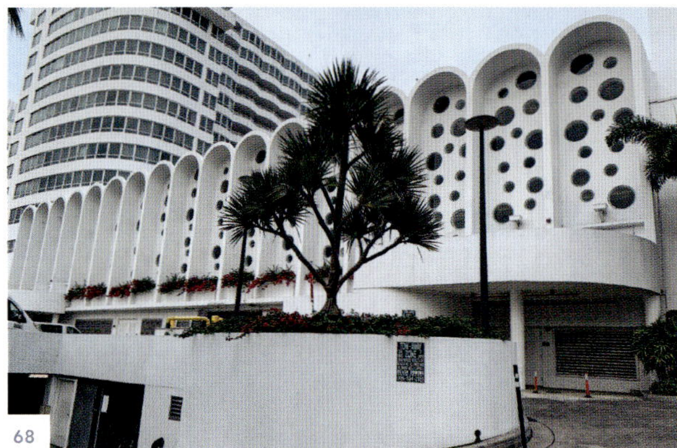

68

The Vilano Beach motel was one of many mom-and-pop motels in St. Augustine, Florida, among the legions of reliable if anonymous havens for weary travelers. Then, something magical happened: Production for the short-lived WB network series *Safe Harbor* came to town in 1999. In the show, Gregory Harrison played a widowed father and the police chief of a fictional Florida beach town named Magic Beach. His mom, played by *Golden Girls* star Rue McClanahan, ran the motel in town, which for the series was named the Magic Beach Motel, and was fitted with a mesmerizing neon sign with a magician theme. In the show, McClanahan's late husband had been a magician. *Safe Harbor* lasted only ten episodes, but more than a quarter century after its cancellation, the **Magic Beach Motel** (FIG. 67) sign remains, now the formal name of the motel itself.

South Beach's art deco and Collins Avenue's midcentury-modern hotels and motels in Miami Beach rightfully get so much of the love. Ocean Drive famously has a stunning lineup of art deco hotels, but it's not only art deco swagger that shapes the Miami Beach of the public imagination. Hotels that came along later, at midcentury, along Collins Avenue, are extraordinary examples of what's known as MiMo, or Miami Modern. Names like the **Eden Roc** and the **Fontainebleau** (FIG. 68), both designed by the legendary Morris Lapidus, come to mind. Other works in different architectural styles defined Miami Beach, one of which is the **Casablanca**, the creation of Roy France.

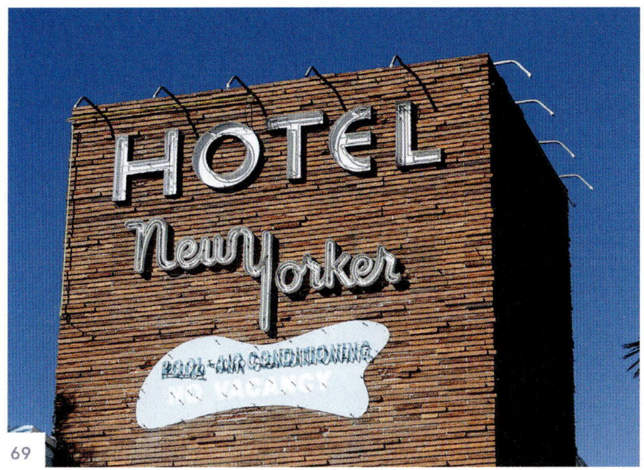

69

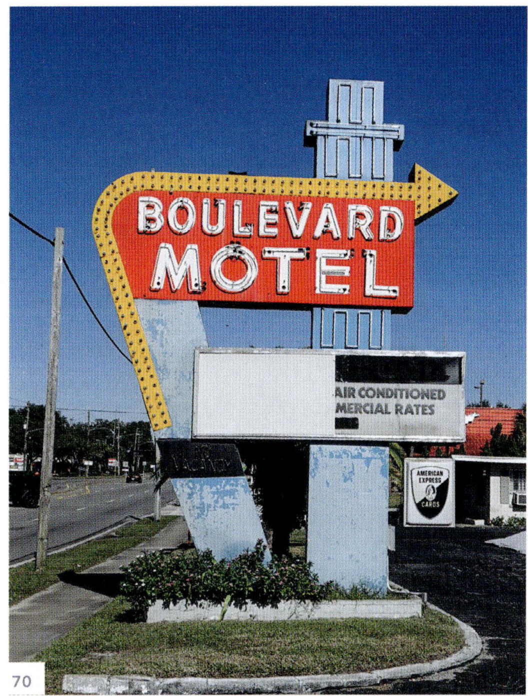

70

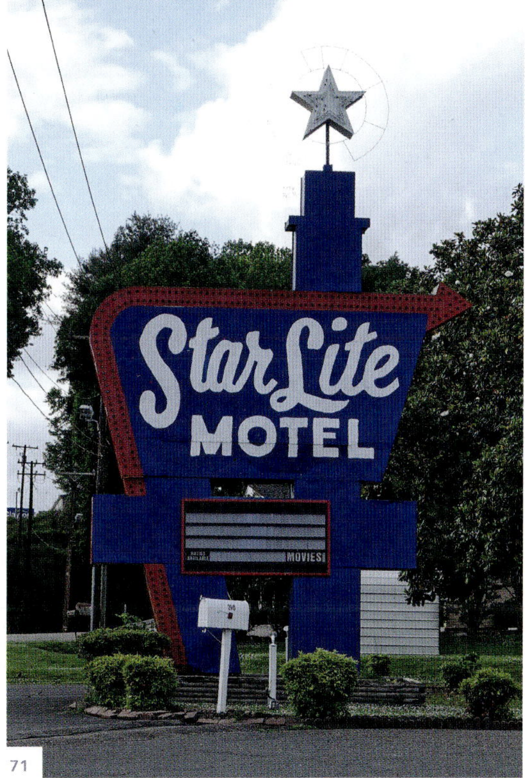

71

Far from Manhattan, **The New Yorker** (FIG. 69) is a boutique hotel on Miami's Biscayne Boulevard, one of dozens of swanky motels and hotels built along the road at midcentury, and a number still exist. The 1953 motel is a beautifully preserved example of MiMo and the work of the prolific and talented Norman Giller, who helped shape the look and feel of Miami in those years. Miami, of course, is often called the Sixth Borough, so closely tied is it to New York.

Motels with signage inspired by that of the old Holiday Inn "Great Sign" (see page 159) still dot the country. The **Boulevard Motel** (FIG. 70) in DeLand, Florida, has a similar sign vibe, one of the most beautiful that's still in existence. Another notable one is the former **Starlite Motel** (FIG. 71), which is also based on the Great Sign. (It's now called Bea's Parkway Inn, an apparent nod to its home of Mount Airy, North Carolina, Andy Griffith's hometown. Fans of the show won't want to miss this taste of fictional Mayberry brought to life, with familiar names like Floyd's Barber Shop and Snappy Lunch.)

The **Moon Winx Lodge** sign, a veritable symbol of Tuscaloosa, Alabama, and a bucket lister for so many roadside enthusiasts, is no more. The Moon Winx goes back a good long while. The lodge, originally labeled a motor court, dates to the 1920s and the sign came along in the 1950s, the work of Glenn House, who sculpted his first name into it.

The Moon Winx holds a special place in the hearts of University of Alabama football fans. Devotees of college football coaching legend Paul "Bear" Bryant

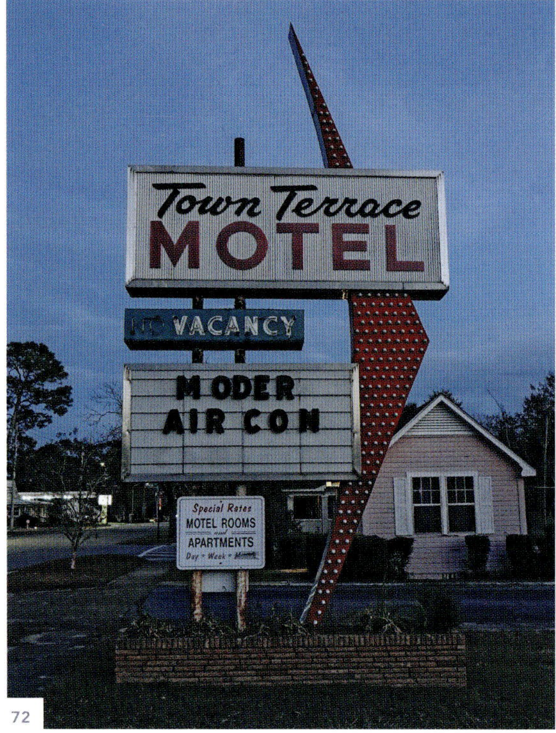

72

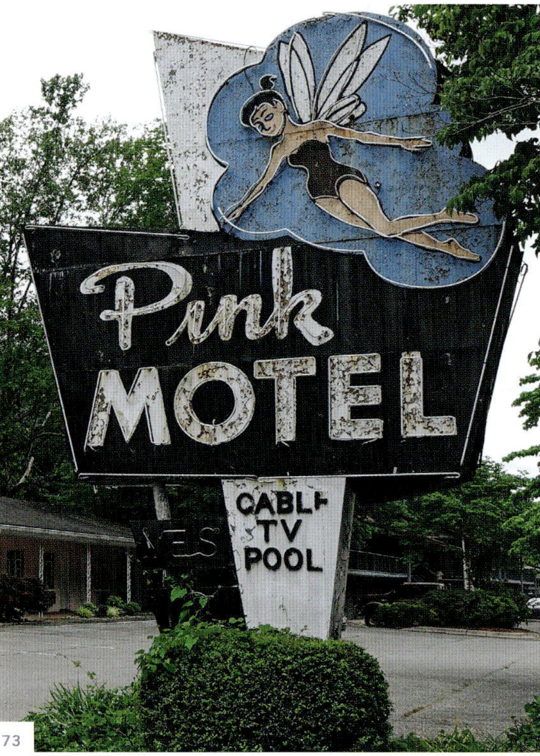

73

know he and his famous players—and many fans—stayed here on Friday nights before home games, according to various accounts. (An old newspaper ad declares the Moon Winx as "Where the Crimson Tide Stays.")

Behold the lovely **Town Terrace Motel** (FIG. 72) in Tifton, Georgia. The motel was once owned by Violet Van Gundy, who in the 1920s received glowing press as Baby Violet, an acting and singing prodigy of early Hollywood cinema. By 1927, a newspaper article described the ten-year-old, said to be a veteran of Hal Roach comedies, as a "reformed actress" who had become a child evangelist with her brother, Jack, after the family heard famed preacher Aimee Semple McPherson on the radio.

The young Van Gundys' ministerial work brought them to Tifton, Georgia, years later, and they decided to stay in town and go into the motel business, now ministering to the needs of travelers.

The Pink Motel (FIG. 73) is perhaps the most whimsical part of the tourist hospitality empire created by Lois Queen Farthing in Cherokee, North Carolina. Pastels were big in the 1950s, and she told an interviewer that she'd traveled to Florida and taken in the pastel wonderland that was the Sunshine State. She chose the color pink because of, well, her laundry. The Sylva Laundry kept mixing up linens amid the area's postwar hospitality boom, and she figured the best way to ensure her new motel didn't suffer a similar fate was to make her laundry distinctive. Pink is a good way to do that! Her pink motif also extended to the motel's paint job, the bathroom tile, and even the soap and toilet tissue once upon a time. Oh, and how did Tinker Bell land on the sign? Thank Farthing's little daughter, Lyna, who, like many a 1950s kid, was smitten with Disney's *Peter Pan*. In their aesthetic collaboration in 1955, this mom-and-daughter duo sprinkled some fairy dust near the Great Smoky Mountains, and we're all still entranced.

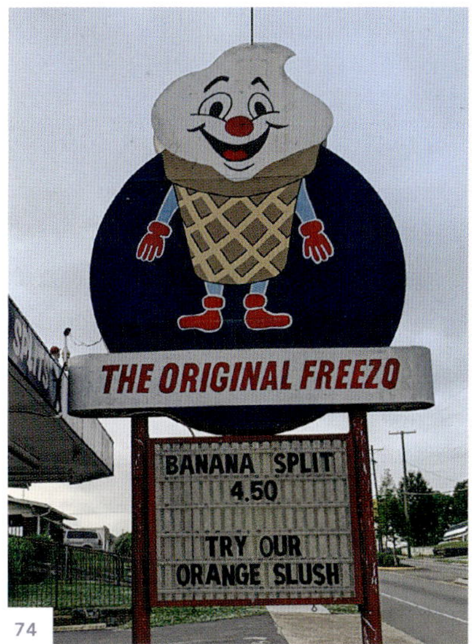

74

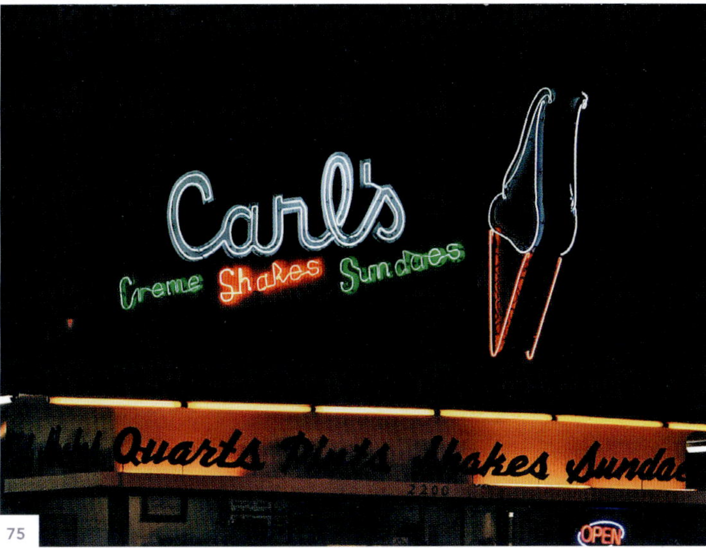

75

SWEET STOPS

Mom-and-pop ice-cream stands are essentially a public health necessity to get through the region's broiling summers. Here's a handful that are more than up to the job. Plus, we have candy, donuts, and even a fruitcake store. Sweet teeth will be smiling.

If this isn't the happiest place in Knoxville's Happy Holler neighborhood, it's certainly one of the sweetest thanks to our next stop. It's certainly a happy thing that the **The Original Freezo** (FIG. 74) ended up in the hands of Darrell Dalton. When he bought the legacy business a couple decades ago, he briefly contemplated tearing it down to create a large space for indoor seating. Customers set him straight real quick, and he's kept things much the same.

You won't find billboards for hundreds of miles advertising the delicious custard and shakes you can have at **Carl's Frozen Custard** (FIG. 75) in Fredericksburg, Virginia. You just have to know it's there, and once you do, you'll be hooked.

Over the years, I've stopped there with my parents, with my sister and nephews, with lifelong friends. I love letting others in on the roadside secret, though it's far from a secret, really. You'll often find long lines there. Carl's opened in 1947 and remains in the same family. It's even on the National Register of Historic Places, but you don't have to know the difference between art moderne and art deco to know that this place matters.

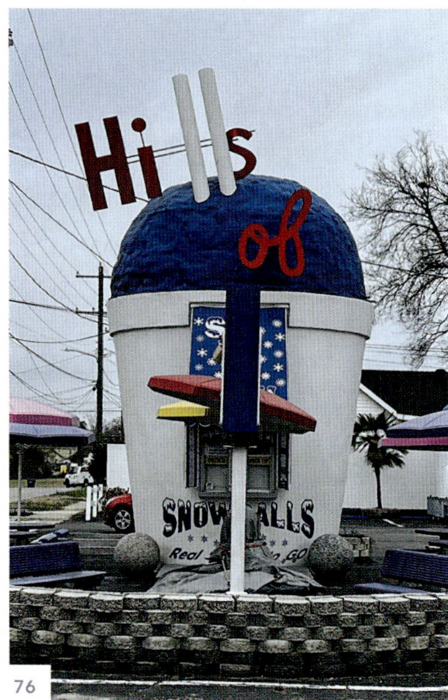

76

Hills of snow in Smithfield, North Carolina, are a rare sight even during the coldest of winters, but **Hills of Snow** (FIG. 76) is there even on the hottest of summer days. The snow in question is the stand's signature snowballs, a creamier version of the snow cones that have quenched many a thirst. The name works on multiple levels—snow, of course, but also hills, a nod to the founder of the business, Tommy Hill, who built the form-follows-function delight in 1984, an addition to his adjacent restaurant, the Chicken Barn.

One of the greatest roadside losses of late was the shuttering of the **Krispy Kreme** in Savannah, Georgia. This store had it all for the vintage-retail enthusiast, beginning with the classic neon sign. Then there's the iconic midcentury building with green tile roof, topped by that Krispy Kreme space-age crown. (You have to love the smiling K's hoisting their donuts, original glazed, no doubt.) Inside, you could help yourself to a white paper hat and enjoy your donut while watching the confections come to life in the bakery behind the window.

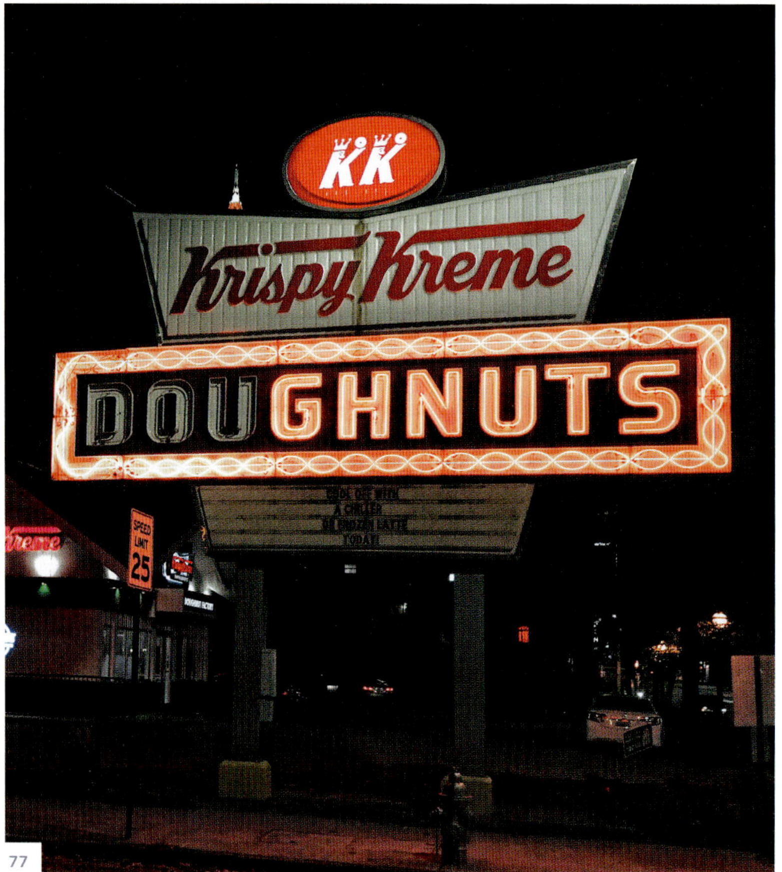

77

The Savannah location hailed from an era when Krispy Kreme, founded in Winston-Salem, North Carolina, in 1937, was expanding throughout the Southeast, before it established itself as a nationally known object of culinary desire. Another one, in Atlanta, Georgia (FIG. 77), and owned by Shaquille O'Neal, reopened after a fire, its sign unscathed but the vintage building not replicated.

Claxton Bakery in Claxton, Georgia, is a real treat if you like fruitcake! In fact, if you've ever had fruitcake, given it as a gift, or, well, regifted it, there's a good chance it came from Claxton Bakery. Or perhaps, back in the day, you sold Claxton Fruit Cake (FIG. 79) as part of a fundraiser.

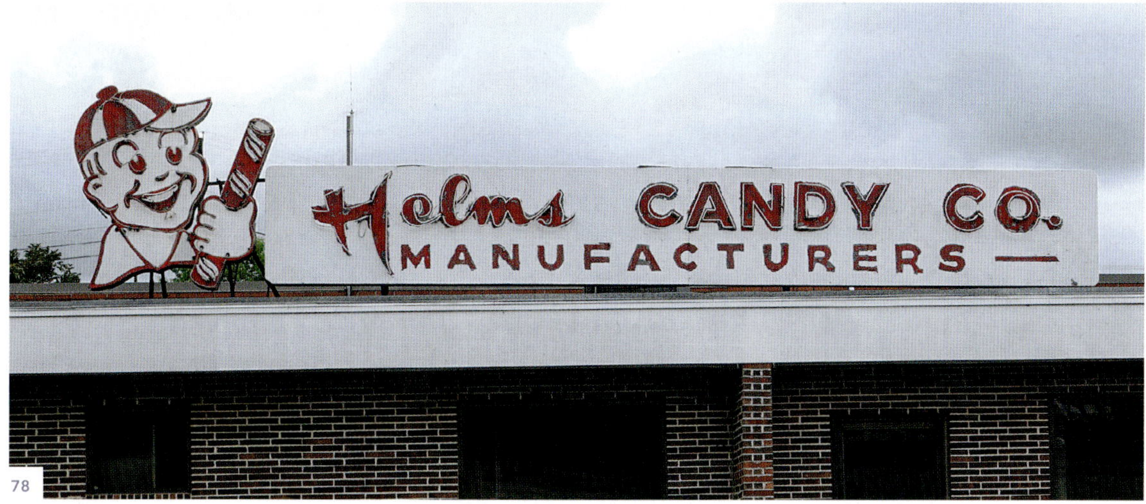

78

Claxton can be found on the aisles of supermarkets around the country, and even on Amazon, but there's something so special about visiting the place where the business began. Savino Tos started it all in 1910, an Italian immigrant who'd toiled as a master baker at a Brooklyn, New York, hotel before moving South. He ultimately settled in Claxton, sensing opportunity here because this community lacked a bakery store.

In 1927, Albert Parker sensed an opportunity here, too. Which is amazing, because he was still a schoolboy, just eleven years old. He made the bakery his life, and when Tos was ready to move on to other things in 1945, he turned the business over to Parker. And Parker, realizing that bakery products were increasingly becoming a commodity selling at supermarkets, pivoted his business to focus on one thing: fruitcake. The rest is holiday history.

A favorite at Christmastime has long been the peppermint sticks from the **Helms Candy Company** (FIG. 78) of Bristol, Virginia. They have been making all kinds of old-fashioned treats since 1909, and the business is now in the fourth generation of Helms family ownership. The signature sweet here is the pure-sugar peppermint stick candies. The local paper, the *Times News*, described the white Red Band candy boxes containing the sweet treat as a symbol of life in this area. But if peppermint sticks aren't your nostalgic weakness, Helms has plenty of alternatives, including such evocatively named delights as Virginia Beauty Stick Candy, King Pops, and Red Band Pillow Puffs.

One place you can buy Helms candy if you want to sample these sugary bits of Americana is the online shop of another iconic retail brand, Ben Franklin (see page 41), whose physical stores have dwindled but are always a joy to visit if you can find one.

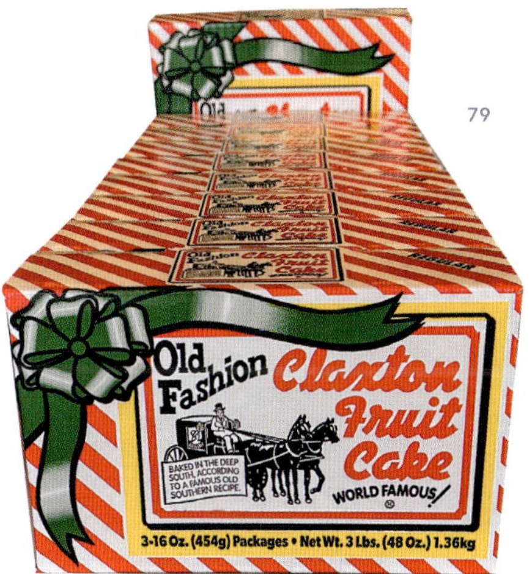

79

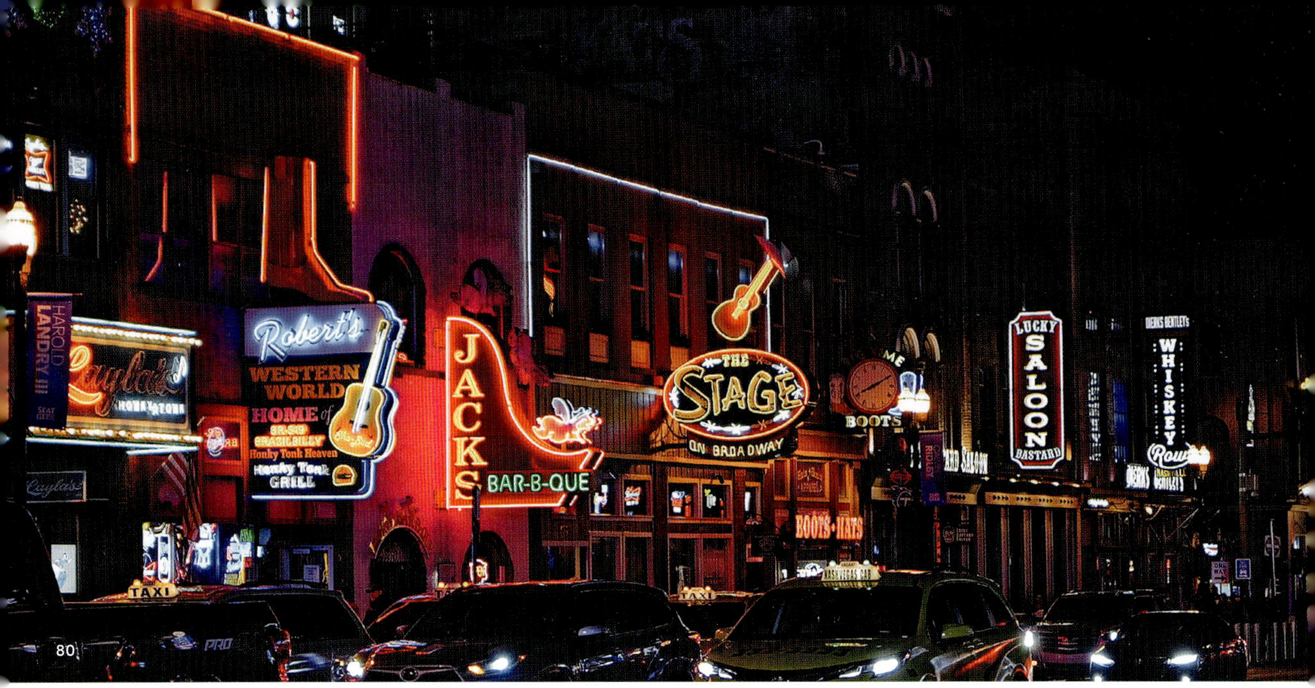

80

CHEERS!

Let's go for a few drinks—and maybe a mojito—as our stops include two classic Miami-Dade businesses.

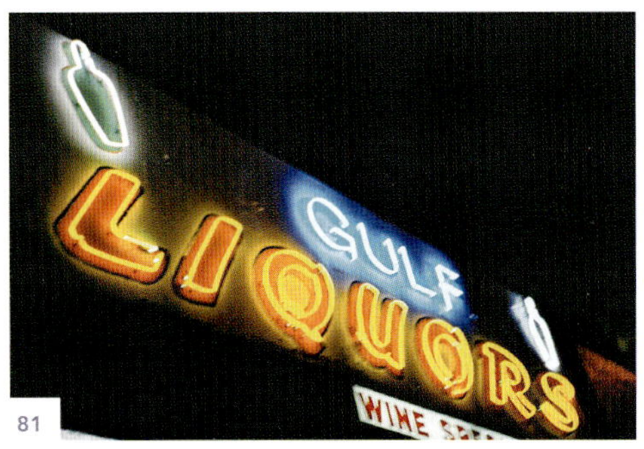

81

Miami Beach's **Gulf Liquors** (FIG. 81) is like a dream, or a memory of another Miami. It's been here since 1950, and the lovely neon sign is a giveaway that this is a legacy business. Miami-Dade has changed all around it, and Gulf Liquors has certainly kept up with the times, modernizing its business while remaining a soothing sign of continuity in a world in constant change.

Over in Miami proper, on the famous Calle Ocho in Little Havana, something remarkable happened in 2014: A nightclub came back from the dead. **Ball & Chain** (FIG. 82) was one of the fabled names of Miami nightlife, which attracted some of the biggest jazz performers from the 1930s to the mid-1950s. In January 1957, the club's owners were in no mood to party. Nor was Count Basie. They didn't pay the legendary performer what he was owed for a string of performances there. His contract called for $13,000; the Ball & Chain's owners coughed up only $5,100. Basie dragged them to court and won a $5,000 judgment. The owners soon after declared bankruptcy and the Ball & Chain was no more. Almost a half century later, the Ball & Chain

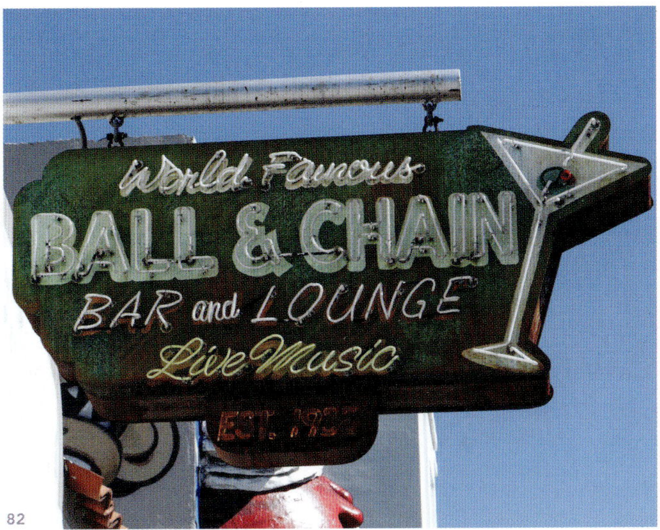

82

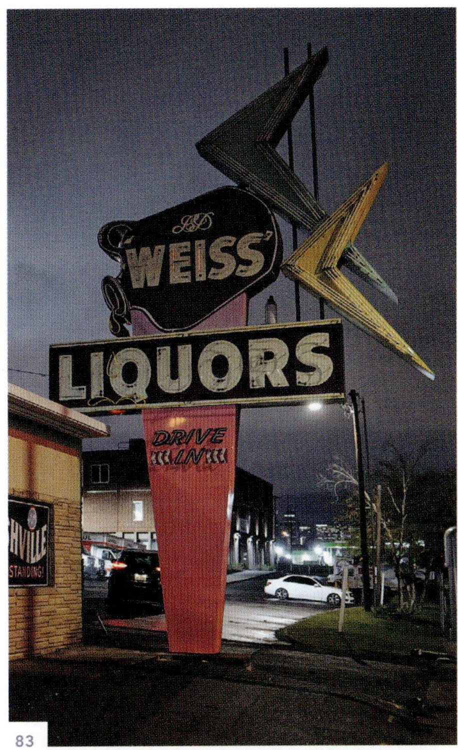

83

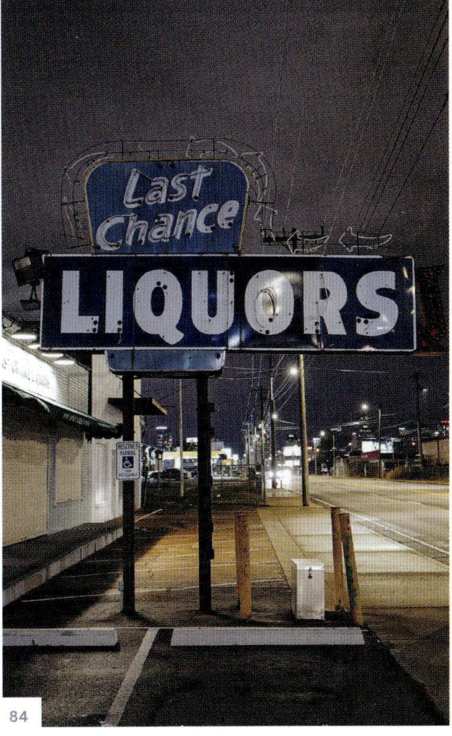

84

returned to the same spot, and a very different neighborhood. In the 1950s, there was a large Jewish community here. In the intervening years, Cuban immigration transformed the neighborhood into Little Havana, and a string of businesses had occupied the nightclub's space, including a decidedly unglamorous furniture store, and then it sat empty. Three entrepreneurs with an appreciation for the neighborhood and the club's history teamed up to revive a long-gone but not forgotten chapter in Miami history, and the Ball & Chain was back, seemingly much as it had been, but now with some Cuban flavor, picking up where it left off during the Eisenhower administration. To look at the sign, you would have never known it was gone.

In Tennessee, I can't recommend enough exploring the historic hearts of Memphis and Nashville, just to bathe in all the neon, much of it new and all of it dazzling. Walks along Broadway in Nashville (FIG. 80) and Beale Street in Memphis are mandatory.

A bucket-list sign for me has long been **Weiss Liquors** (FIG. 83) in Nashville. This gorgeous neon sign was rebuilt after the original was destroyed in a tornado. When I went by, the store was closed (and the neon turned off) after a fire shut the business. Here's hoping that when you go by, that neon jug of liquor will be lit anew.

Appropriately, we end with Nashville's **Last Chance Liquors** (FIG. 84). Back in 1946, when the shop opened, this business was your "last chance" to buy alcohol before entering "dry" counties.

GEORGIA GIRL
DRIVE•IN
1

Parkette
DRIVE IN
CHICKEN
SHRIMP
FISH BOXES
U-HAUL
PAWN
859-ASPHALT
2

Southside
CLEANERS-LAUNDERERS
MOMS ARE LIKE
BUTTONS
THEY HOLD
EVERYTHING
TOGETHER
3

BAR
GEORGE'S #1
LIQUOR
Lounge
PARKING
4

ORANGE BOWL
Lanes
5

MOTEL
6

SKATELAND
COUNTY GLASS
RESIDENTIAL/COMMERCIAL
7

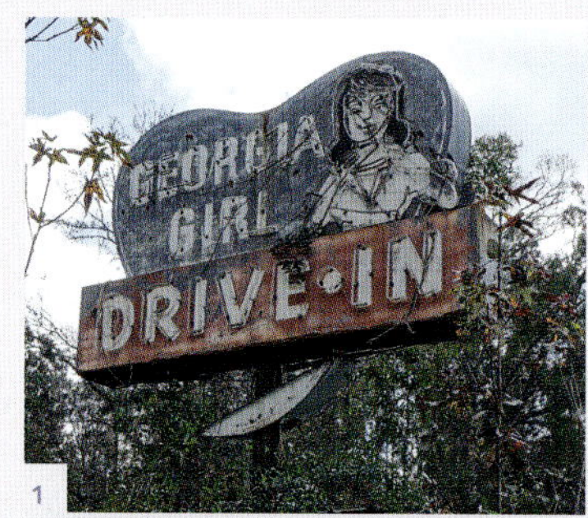

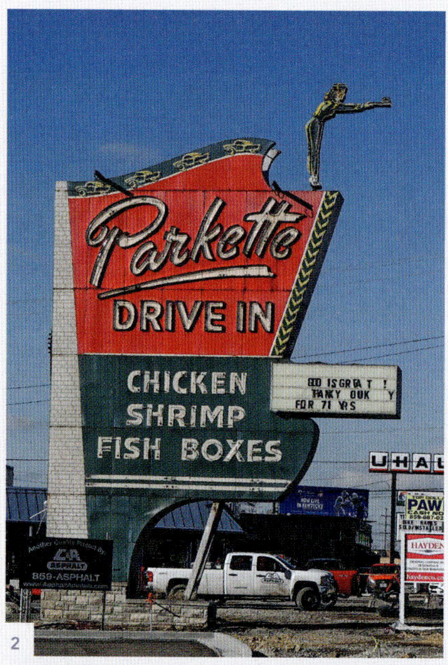

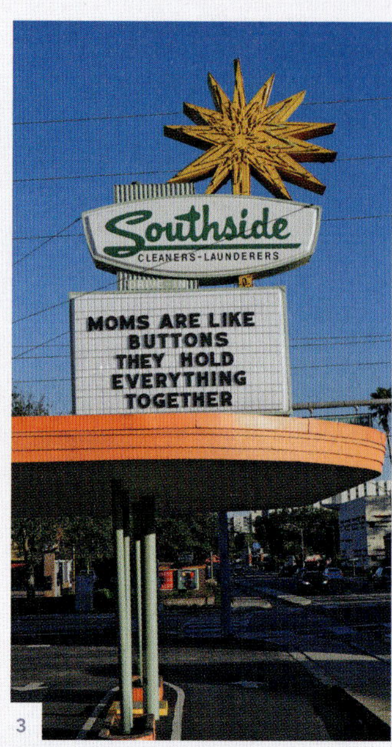

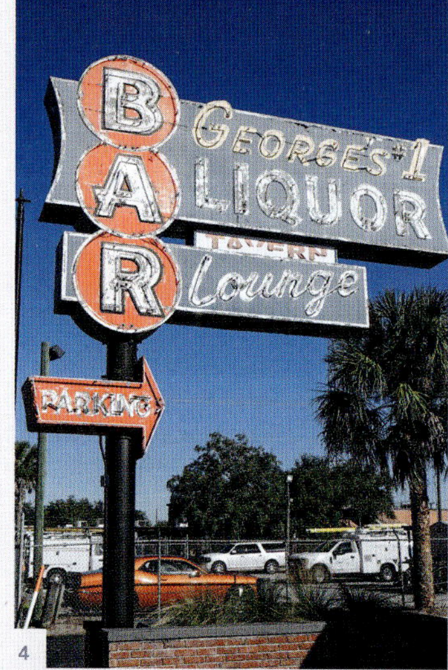

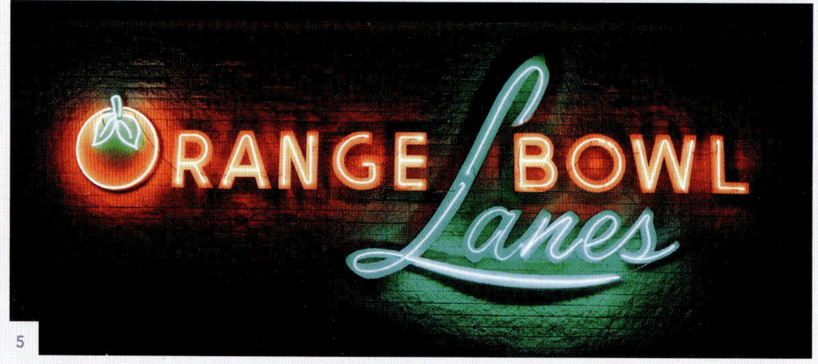

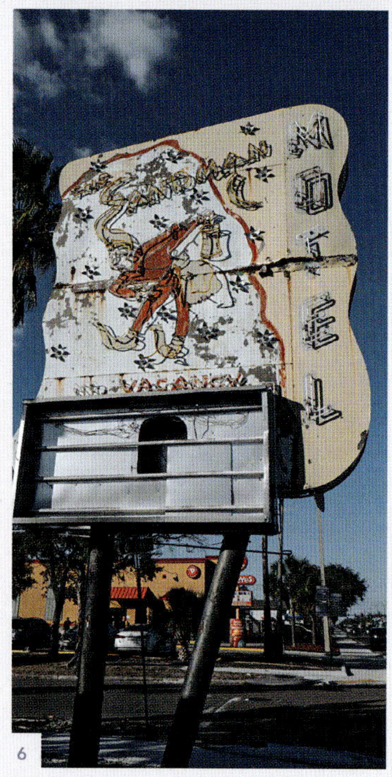

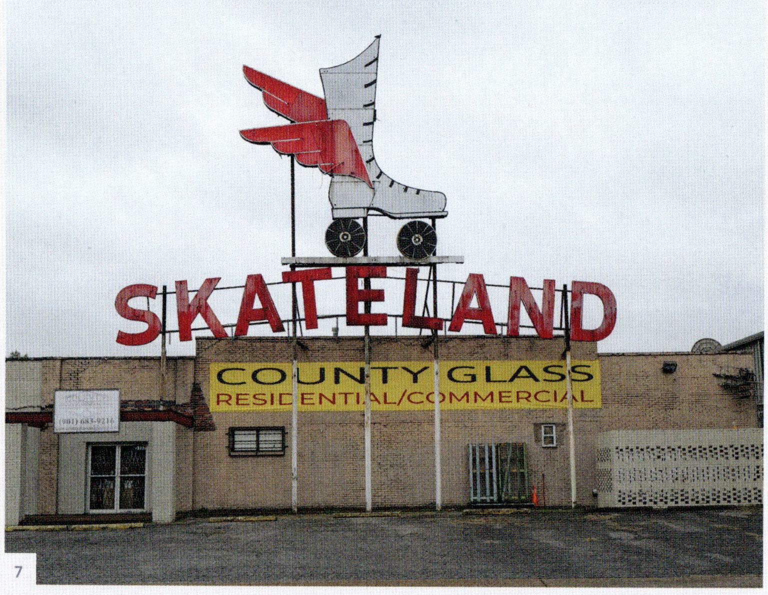

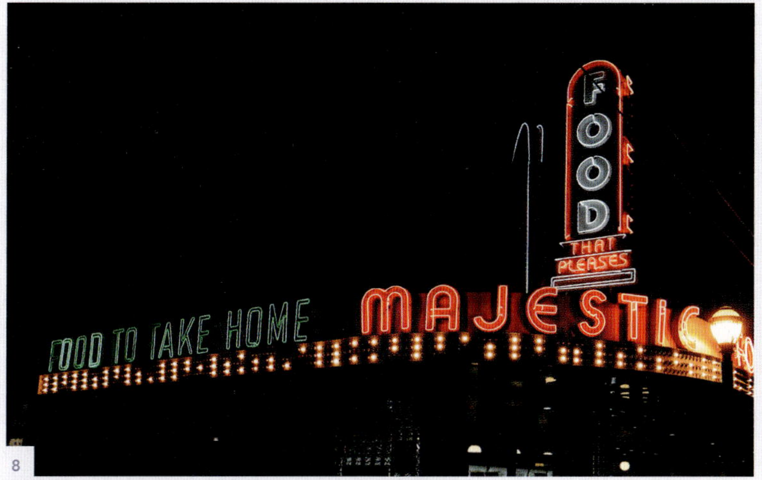

8

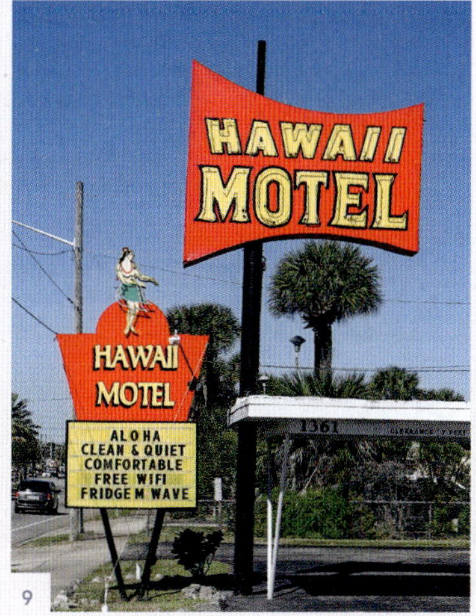

9

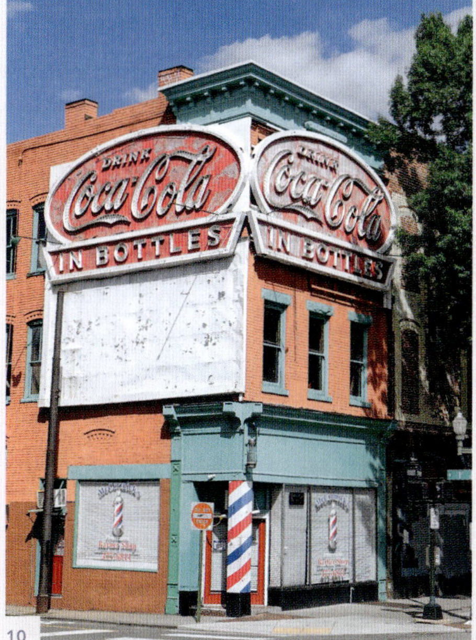

10

SOUTHERN BELLES

Here are some beautiful signs you'll want to seek out in your travels.

1. Georgia Girl Drive-In, Woodbine, Georgia
2. The Parkette Drive-In, Lexington, Kentucky
3. Southside Cleaners, Lakeland, Florida
4. George's Tavern, Sanford, Florida
5. Orange Bowl Lanes, Kissimmee, Florida
6. Sandman Motel, St. Petersburg, Florida
7. Skateland, Memphis, Tennessee
8. The Majestic Diner, Atlanta, Georgia
9. Hawaii Motel, Daytona Beach, Florida
10. Coca-Cola Corner, Richmond, Virginia
11. GMC Strongman, Homosassa, Florida
12. World's Largest Entertainment McDonald's, Orlando, Florida

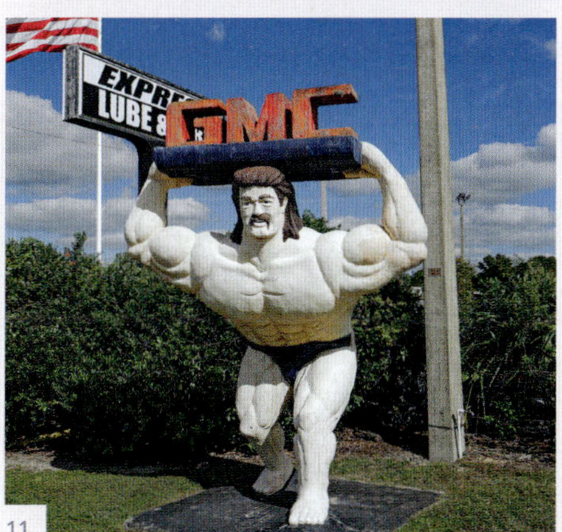

11

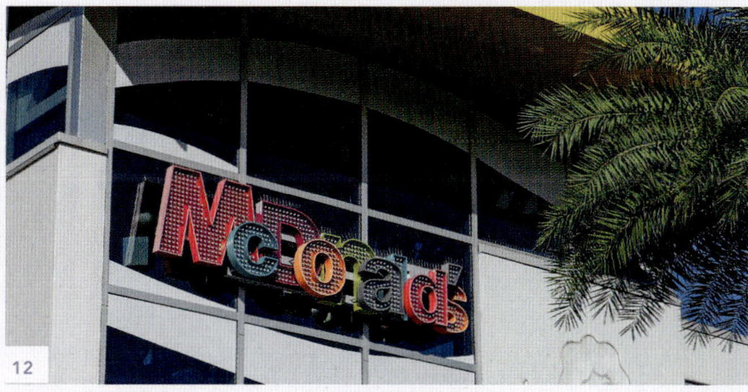

12

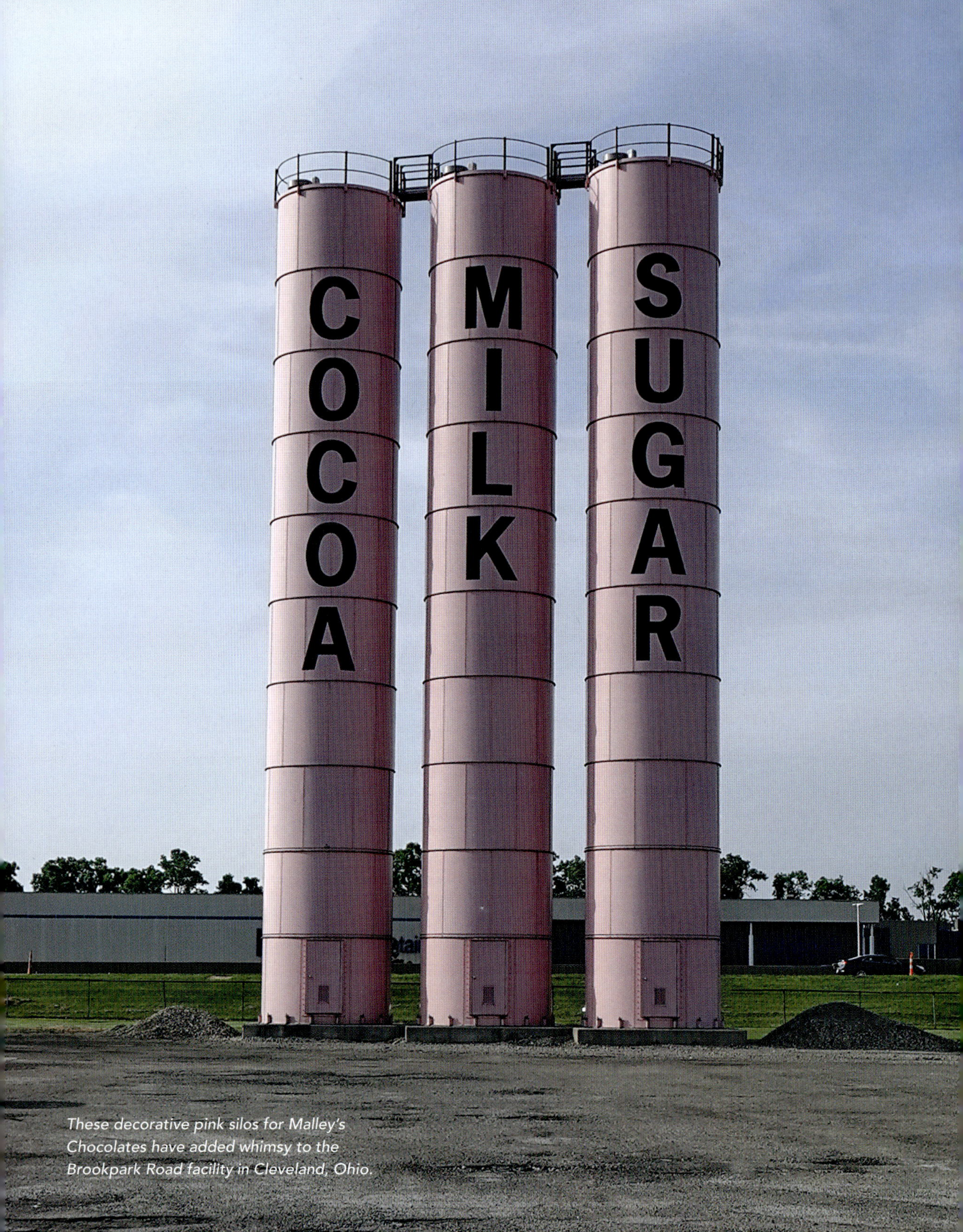

These decorative pink silos for Malley's Chocolates have added whimsy to the Brookpark Road facility in Cleveland, Ohio.

MIDWEST

**MINNESOTA · WISCONSIN · ILLINOIS
INDIANA · MICHIGAN · OHIO
PARTS OF WEST VIRGINIA AND KENTUCKY**

Let's hit play on the highlight reel of my nostalgic travels through the Midwest. In the swath we're covering in this chapter, we will be going to Americana heaven in a very large handbasket. (That's one very specific stop, up ahead.) Indeed, some of the most iconic roadside attractions are clustered here. Let's hit the road.

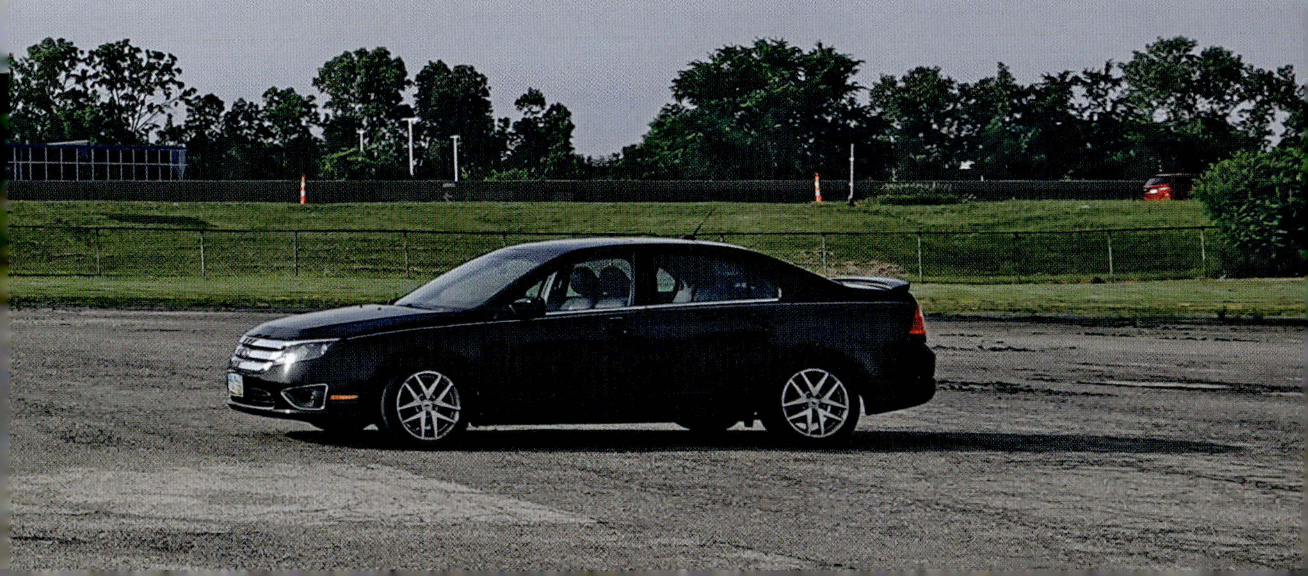

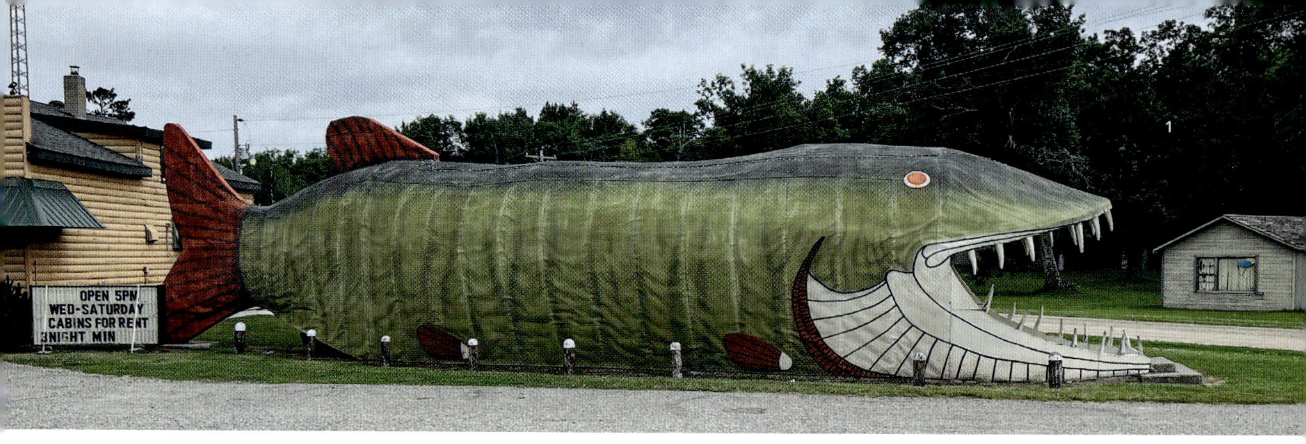

1

R O A D S I D E   Q U I R K S

Where to begin this chapter? The Big Fish Supper Club has reeled me in. It should be no surprise that in the land of Paul Bunyan, we have such wonders to explore.

I was driving along Highway 2 in Minnesota, and nearing the 1950s-era **Big Fish Supper Club** (FIG. 1) just outside Bena, Minnesota, when I, on a whim, cranked up Lindsey Buckingham's 1983 hit "Holiday Road"—the earworm that plays during the opening sequence of *National Lampoon's Vacation*, as dozens of vintage postcards flash by of classic roadside-Americana stops, many of which are places that are no more.

The Big Fish, with its 65-foot-long representation of a muskie, is very much still with us, though you can't go inside the muskie itself like the old days.

Just west of here, in Bemidji, Minnesota, is the home of another spot that's featured in the movie's opening: **Paul Bunyan & Babe the Blue Ox statues** (FIG. 2) have been prompting drivers to pull over since 1937 and are a part of regional folklore.

Minnesota has its share of giant things, and this fellow of green hue is a household name. As the old commercial jingle went, we are going down in the "valley of

2

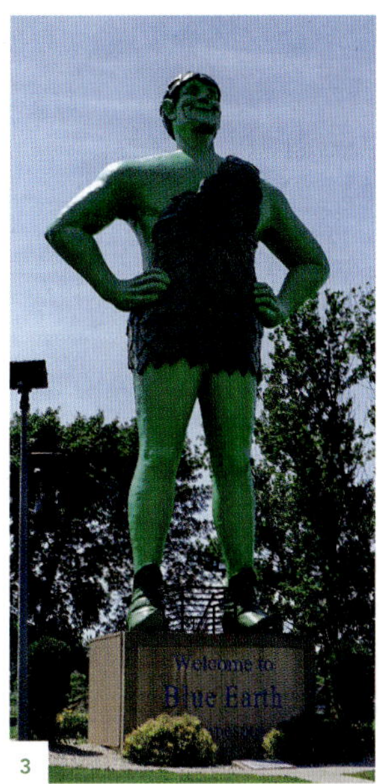

3

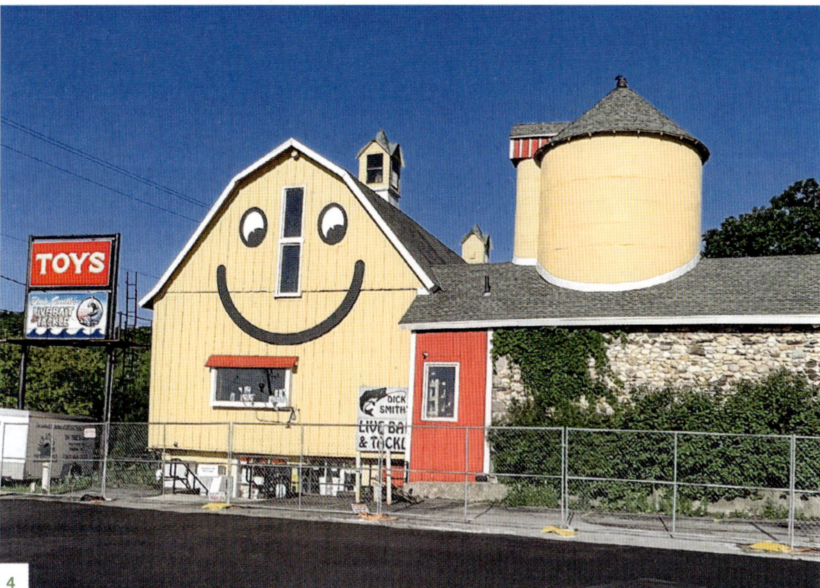

4

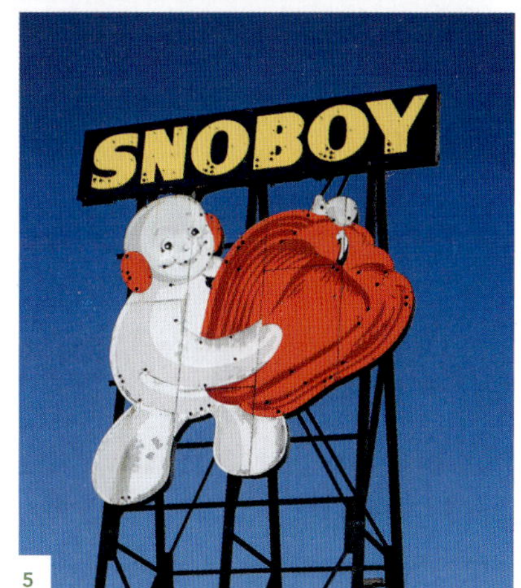

5

the Jolly Green Giant" (FIG. 3) or, more specifically, his statue in Blue Earth, Minnesota. The big guy was installed here on July 6, 1979. The fiberglass statue is big, all right—he weighs 8,000 pounds, towers 55.5 feet tall. His ever-helpful assistant, Sprout, stands nearby.

For some more smiles, **The Smiley Barn** (FIG. 4) in Delafield, Wisconsin, overdelivers. This joyous yellow barn sits along I-94 and can turn any frown upside down. The barn represents one of the brightest comebacks in roadside history. In 2001, after spreading sunshine for decades, the smile on the barn's facade was removed by new owners. Well, almost two decades later, the barn changed hands again and along came the surprise news that the smile was to be restored for a new candy shop and toy store that was to be called The Smiley Barn.

If smiles are the coin of the realm in this part of the book, then the adorable **Snoboy** (FIG. 5) sign in Minneapolis will induce a grin. The Snoboy brand was introduced in 1925 and traces its roots to a horse-drawn fruit-cart business in Tacoma, Washington, in the late 1800s. Snoboy was used on the label of Washington State apples that met certain standards—"picked for flavor," as the company used to say. By dint of corporate merger, Snoboy moved from rainy Washington to snowy Minnesota, where it seems he belonged all along. Snoboy's scaffold sign was erected in 1954 at the site of the former headquarters in Minneapolis, and he's still melting hearts all these years later.

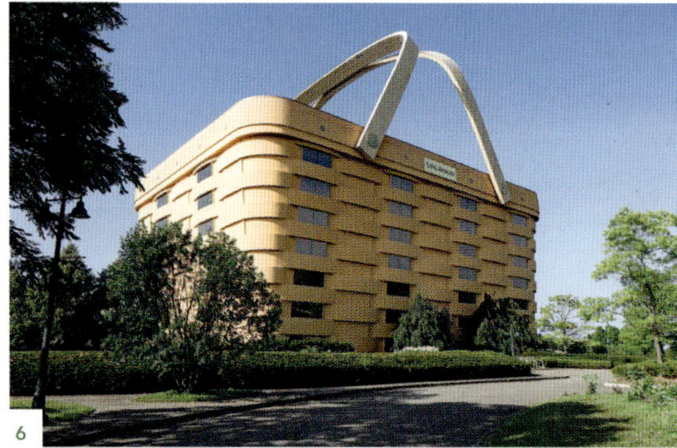
6

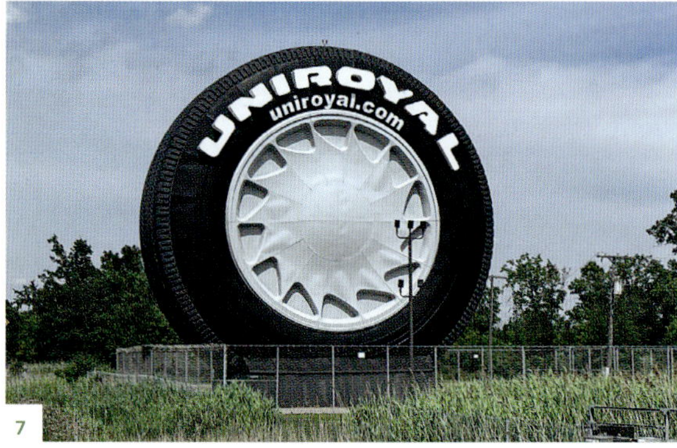

7

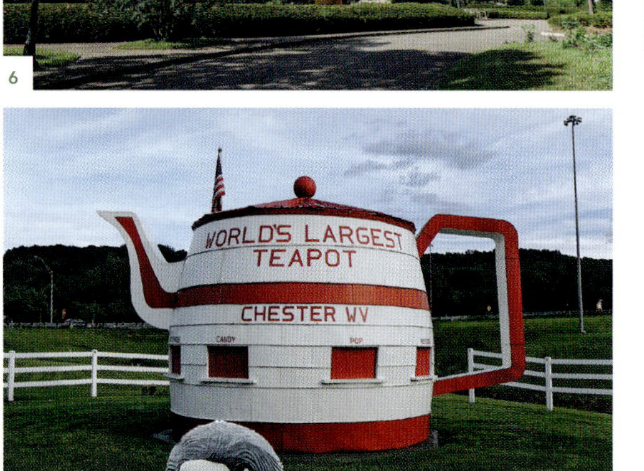

8

9

A lot of Snoboy apples could fit in the **Big Basket** (FIG. 6), in Newark, Ohio. This is a colossal example of novelty architecture, where the building resembles the product the business sells. Dave Longaberger took his family's basketmaking business, the famous Longaberger baskets, and opened the company's headquarters in a $30 million, 180,000-square-foot, seven-story office building in the shape of a basket.

In the late 1990s, Longaberger had tens of thousands of associates selling millions of baskets a year, in a business model described as a cross between Tupperware and Amway. In 2000, Longabergers served as "swag baskets" at the Academy Awards. That year was the company's peak, with a billion dollars in sales, though it was the beginning of the end. The next year, 9/11 happened, and the economy was jolted into recession. Tastes changed. A decade later, sales were down 90 percent.

The company eventually went out of business. Many trace its collapse to Longaberger's death in 1999. The Big Basket serves as a tribute to him and to the pride so many took in making, selling, and buying the baskets. (Related: The World's Largest Apple Basket in Frazeysburg, Ohio, stands outside a shuttered Longaberger store.)

If you're on a road trip in search of big things, pop over to Allen Park, Michigan, to see the 80-foot-tall **Uniroyal Giant Tire** (FIG. 7), a centerpiece of the 1964–65 World's Fair in Queens, New York, that doubled as a Ferris wheel.

As relics of the fair were sold off and dispersed, the world's largest nonproduction tire was hauled west by twenty-two trucks (I'd like to think it was rolled) and placed here near Detroit, the Motor City, an appropriate home for the polyester resin and fiberglass tire, now reflecting Uniroyal branding.

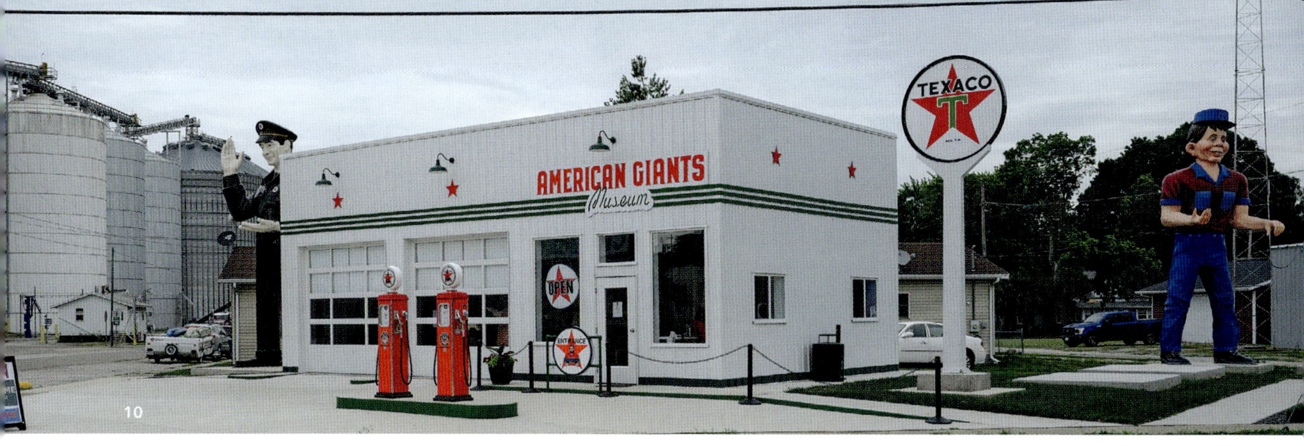

10

We have another foray into form follows function at the **World's Largest Teapot** (FIG. 8) in Chester, West Virginia. The Ohio city that's right across the river is East Liverpool, so you'd think the teapot would have ended up there, what with its British municipal moniker.

But William "Babe" Devon had a ceramic business in Chester. According to the popular telling of the tale, a gigantic Hires Root Beer promotional barrel in Pennsylvania caught his attention. In 1938, he bought it, shipped it here, and turned it into the World's Largest Teapot.

Devon was not selling tea, per se, though he did hire kids to hawk refreshments and souvenirs out of the teapot. His hometown was a great hub of the ceramics trade. (Even today, the famous Fiesta Tableware Company—and its factory outlet store—is nearby.)

Now, it wouldn't be a Roadside Quirks section without a visit with a Muffler Man—or a whole lot of his kin. In Atlanta, Illinois, one of the proudest sights on the skyline (there are more than one) is the **Paul Bunyon Hot Dog Man** (FIG. 9)—aka Hot Dog Muffler Man, a Route 66 must-stop. He moved here two decades ago from Cicero, Illinois, where he stood outside Bunyon's Drive-In. (Spelled "Bunyon," not the traditional Bunyan.) And now has more towering company.

Atlanta, Illinois, is now the home of the **American Giants Museum** (FIG. 10), where you can visit with beautifully restored roadside giants (including a rare Texaco Big Friend). Inside, well-curated panels and additional fiberglass giant-people body parts tell the definitive tale of these roadside wonders. Joel Baker, the museum's founder, has spent years documenting this saga and finding Giants in the wild.

While in Atlanta, say hello to the **Smiley Water Tower** (FIG. 11). His smile set against canary yellow was brought to life in an inspired $175,000 paint job, a (successful) effort to attract attention to the town.

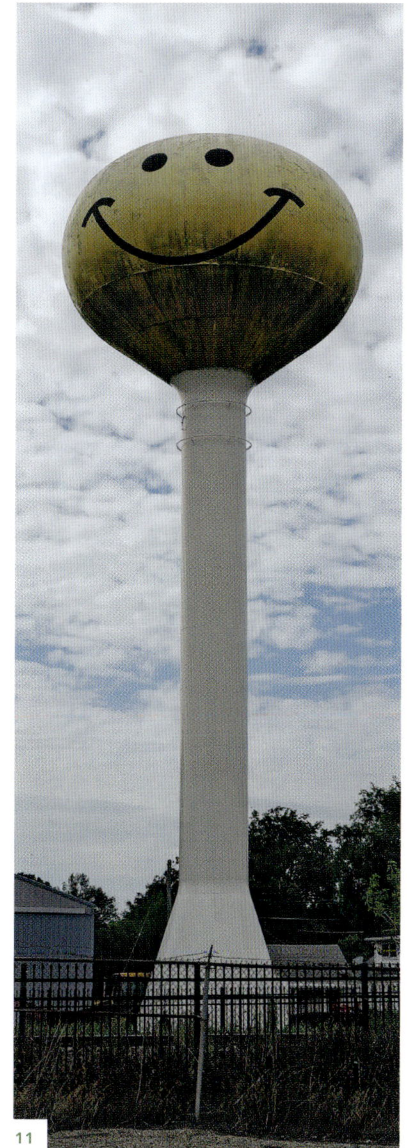
11

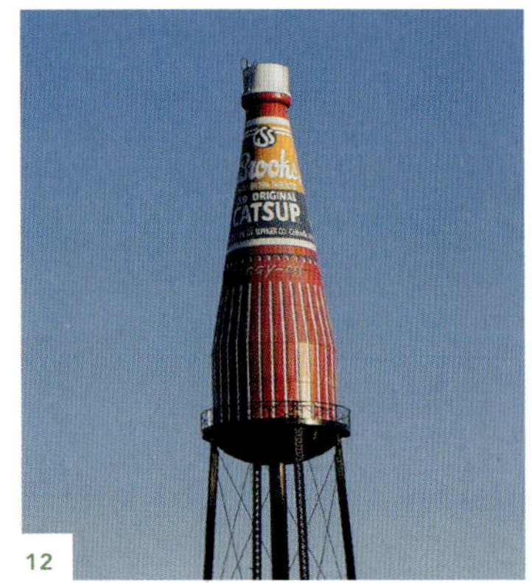

12

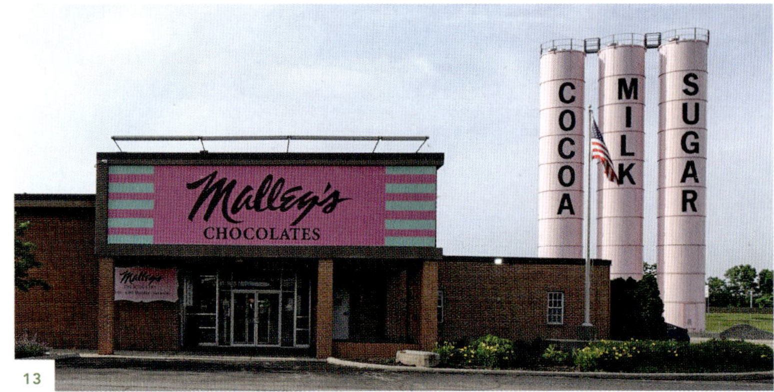

13

Closer to Chicago, the **Gemini Giant** (FIG. 14) had been holding up a rocket ship, and looking over the Launching Pad restaurant in Wilmington, Illinois, since the mid-1960s. The giant was auctioned off in 2024 and then donated back to Wilmington. He was triumphantly reinstalled at South Island Park along Route 66 in December 2024.

If the Hot Dog Muffler Man can use some ketchup—I know, a controversial pairing—he can avail himself of a giant bottle farther down Route 66, in Collinsville, Illinois. That's where the **World's Largest Catsup Bottle** (FIG. 12) can be found, a water tower doubling as a gigantic advertisement for the Brooks Catsup brand that was once made here. The 70-foot-tall bottle (on a 100-foot base) was orphaned after the factory was sold in the 1990s, but preservationists teamed up to raise the money to restore the bottle, and its legacy is further secured by its placement on the National Register of Historic Places.

Now we go from catsup to chocolate—and to three 88-foot-tall pink silos supposedly containing key baking ingredients that stand at an outpost of **Malley's Chocolates** (FIG. 13) in Cleveland, Ohio. When the silos were going up in 2011, a Malley's owner earnestly told a TV reporter that they intended to fill these silos with cocoa, milk, and sugar. Then, in a touch of fancy that Willy Wonka would appreciate, he said the system would require installing an elaborate network of vacuum pumps to convey the raw ingredients into the factory, where the true magic of chocolate making would occur.

But as much as I want this story to be factual, I hate to say it isn't so. The Sculpture Center, based in Cleveland, explains that the fanciful plans remained strictly in a world of imagination.

Illinois is Lincoln country, and tributes to our revered sixteenth president can be found around the state. In Springfield, home to his presidential library and tomb, Lincoln's likeness is especially ubiquitous. A lanky, young, clean-shaven

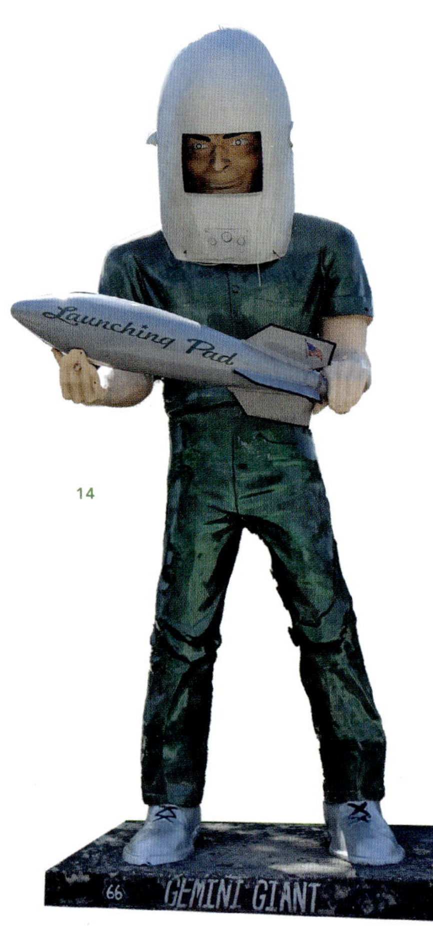

14

Lincoln—the **Abe Lincoln Rail Splitter Statue** (FIG. 16)—first greeted visitors at the 1967 fair at the Springfield State Fairgrounds. But one of the most popular depictions of him can be found in the parking lot of a strip mall in Lincoln, Illinois. There, Abe Lincon reads a law book while riding on the **World's Largest Covered Wagon**.

Note: While in Lincoln, visit the **Tropics Restaurant** (FIG. 15) neon sign, which was beautifully restored in 2018. This sign is a favorite of the Route 66 community. The founder of the Tropics opened it in 1950, inspired by his deployment to Hawaii during World War II, and a future expansion included the addition of the South Seas cocktail lounge. The restaurant is long gone, replaced by a McDonald's, but the sign was happily preserved.

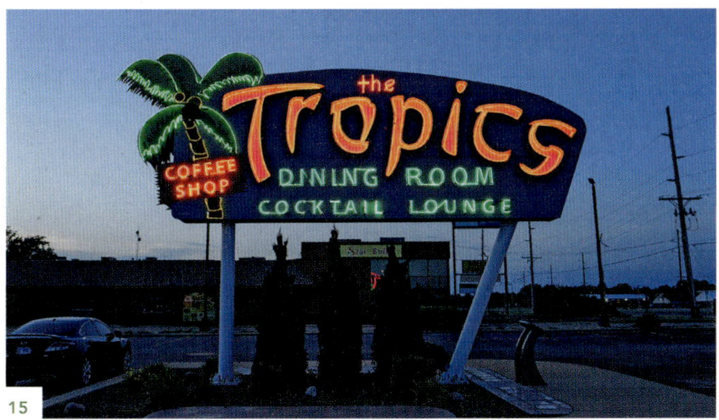

15

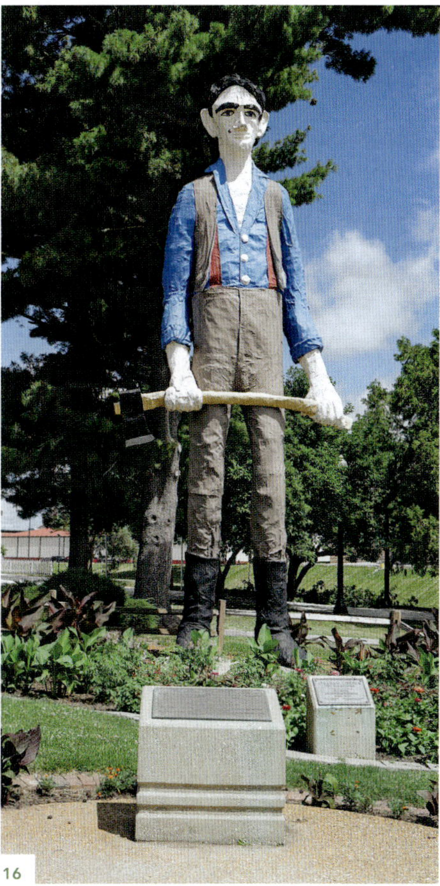
16

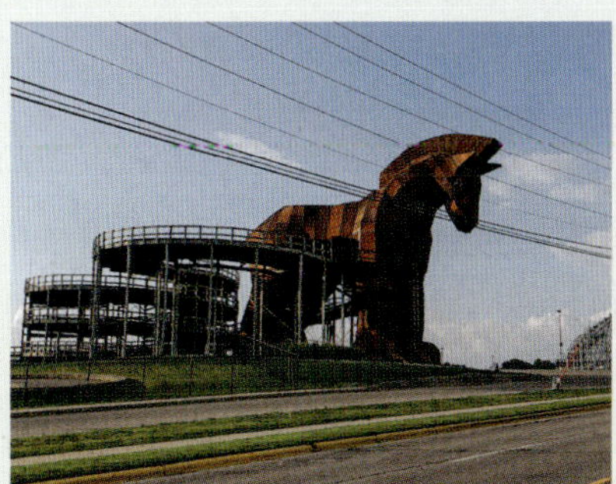

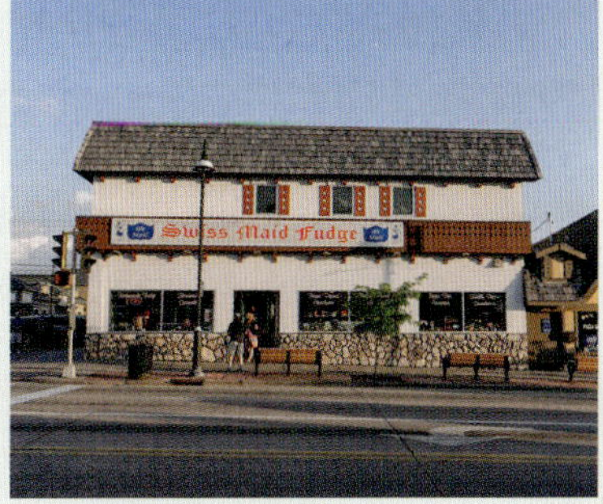

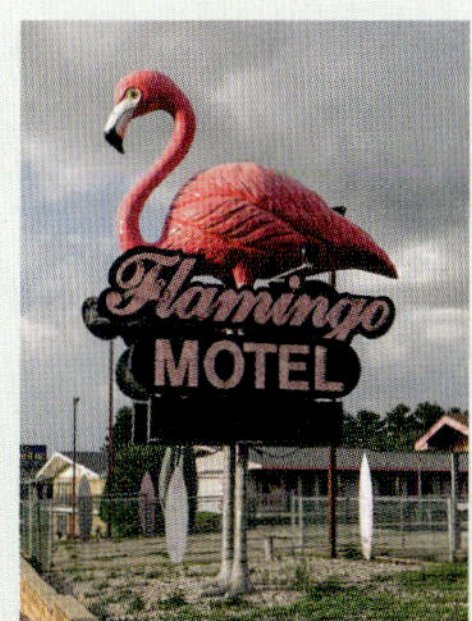

SPOTLIGHT: WISCONSIN DELLS

Oh, how I love the Dells, a vacation paradise forever in the middle twentieth century. It grew as a vacation destination because of the gifts of nature here—water, forest, fresh air—and inevitably, a quirky commercial world grew up around it, with souvenir shops, restaurants, and motels. It's a wonderful, refreshing, nostalgic getaway of super amusement parks and family beach resorts.

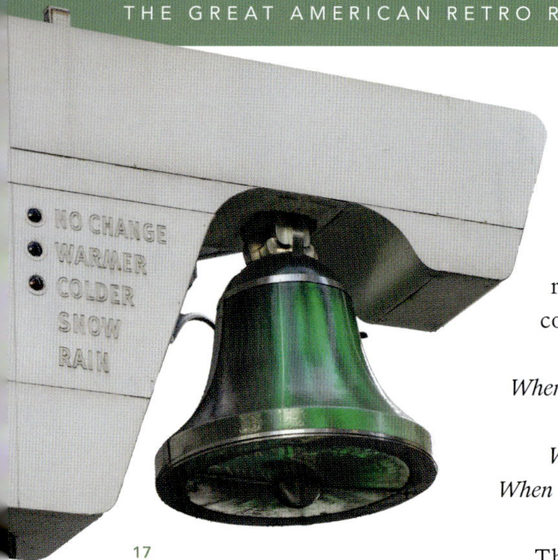

17

A very different take on midcentury Americana is represented by Chicago's **Weather Bell** (FIG. 17), an intriguing relic from a lost time. Long before smartphones gave you weather updates on the go, there was the Weather Bell. The Bell, installed in 1951, would deliver weather reports that at best could be called directional—and the colors told you what kind of weather to expect. To wit:

When Weather Bell is emerald green, no change in temperature is foreseen.
When Weather Bell is glowing red, warmer weather is ahead.
When Weather Bell is flaming gold, a temperature drop is foretold.
When Weather Bell is flashing in agitation, prepare yourself for precipitation.

The Bell Savings and Loan Association emerged as an employee bank within the Illinois Bell Telephone Company before becoming a major banking concern. The Bell S&L is long gone, but the Bell itself survives. There were once nine Weather Bells across Chicago, operated from a control board that was fed information from a private forecasting service.

Starting in the late nineteenth century, barns across the country were painted with ads for **Mail Pouch Tobacco** (FIG. 18), and as the generations passed, they became quaint roadside symbols of a simpler time. One of the most striking survivors of the ads for the West Virginia–based company that I have found is in Osgood, Indiana, but keep an eye out for them wherever you're traveling. They are always—when it's safe—worth a stop. More than twenty thousand of them were painted, so you're bound to spot them. For much of the twentieth century Harley Warrick traveled the nation painting them and was the last of a long line of painters to do so for the company, though surviving barns continue to be touched up in a nod to history, if not tobacco use.

▶▶▶ Pull Over!

Two of my favorite Midwest-based television characters are honored in the Heartland. **Dr. Robert Hartley's statue** (Bob Newhart's psychologist character on *The Bob Newhart Show*) awaits his patients on the Navy Pier in Chicago, and a statue of Mary Richards (played by Mary Tyler Moore on *The Mary Tyler Moore Show*) prepares to toss her hat in the air in downtown Minneapolis, proving she's going to make it after all. Both figures are courtesy of TV Land. In Toledo, Ohio, sitcom funnymen Danny Thomas and Jamie Farr, both native sons of the city, are honored with parks.

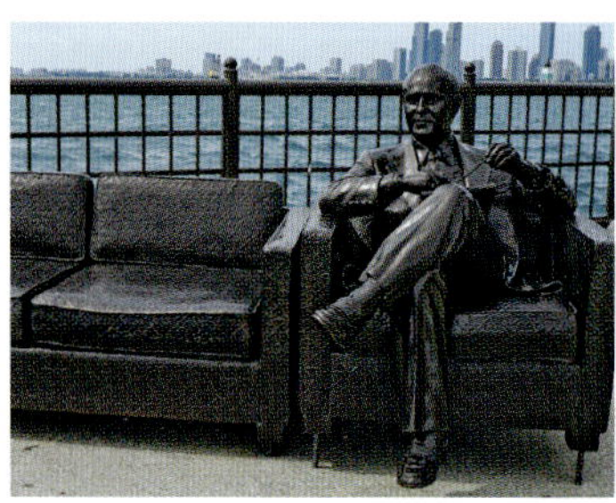

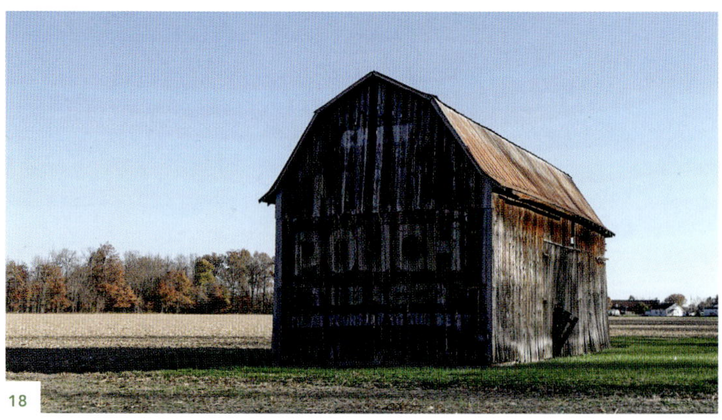

18

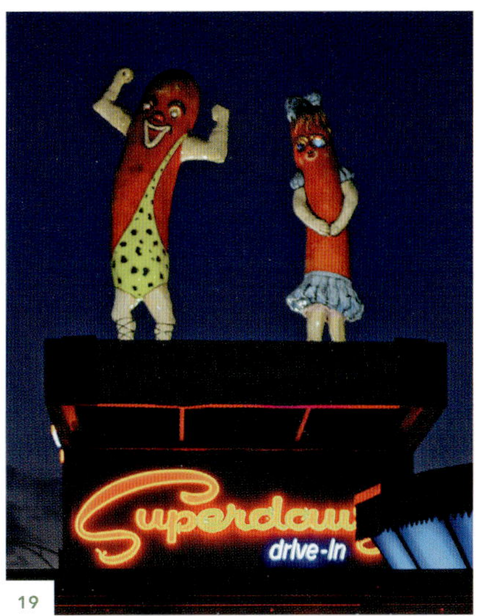

19

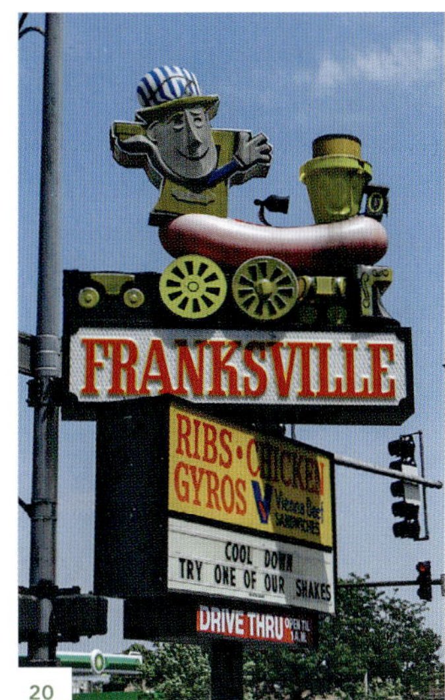

20

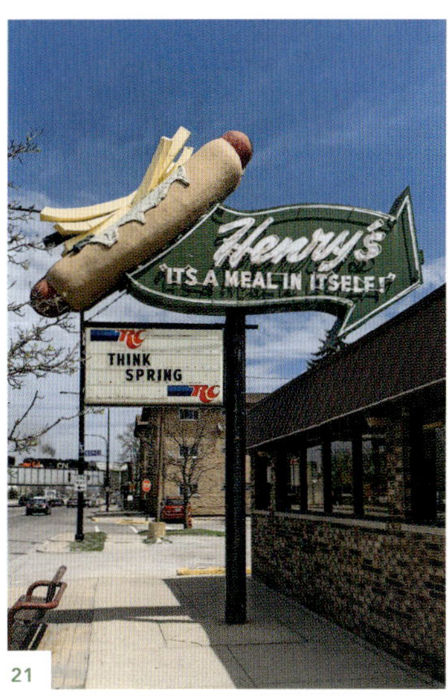

21

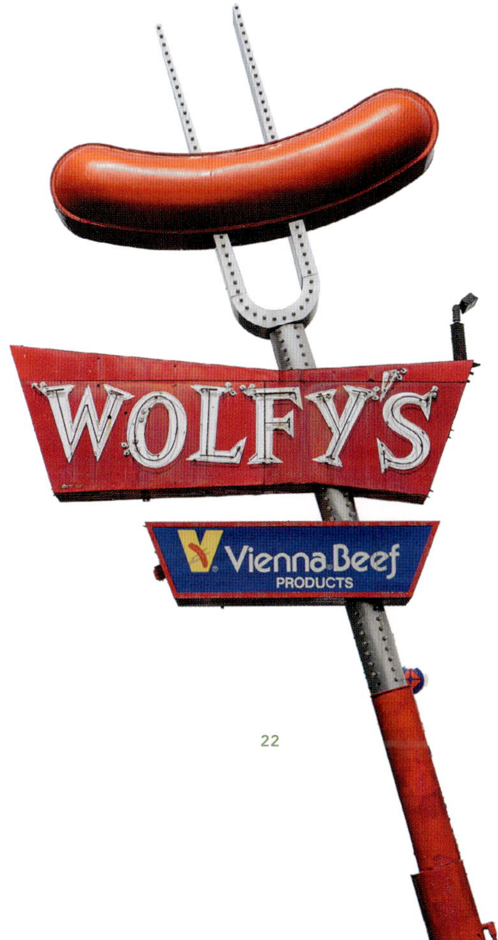

22

ROADSIDE EATS

So much comfort food in this part of the country. Here's some of the best of the region.

If you want a hot dog, your choices in Chicagoland are legion, and you can't wrong with **Wolfy's** (FIG. 22), serving up devilishly good Chicago dogs since 1967.

Superdawg Drive-In (FIG. 19), located in Chicago's Norwood Park neighborhood, may take the bun for the most-cinematic signage. Two 12-foot hot dogs, eyes brightly lit, are perched on the rooftop in perpetual promotion of this Chicago institution, which opened in 1948. They are depictions of the couple that founded the stand, Flaurie and Maurie Berman, and the statues are named after them. In 2024, not long after these photos were taken, the pair was taken down for a "spa treatment," so they'll look better than ever when you visit.

Franksville (FIG. 20) was once a small chain, and is now down to this last location. The sign is a delight, more amusement park than hot dog stand. Another cinematic favorite of mine is **Henry's Hot Dogs** (FIG. 21) in Cicero, an icon of Route 66 since 1950.

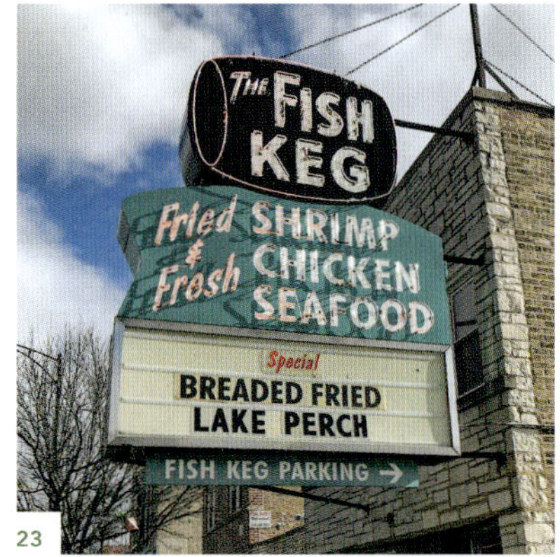

23

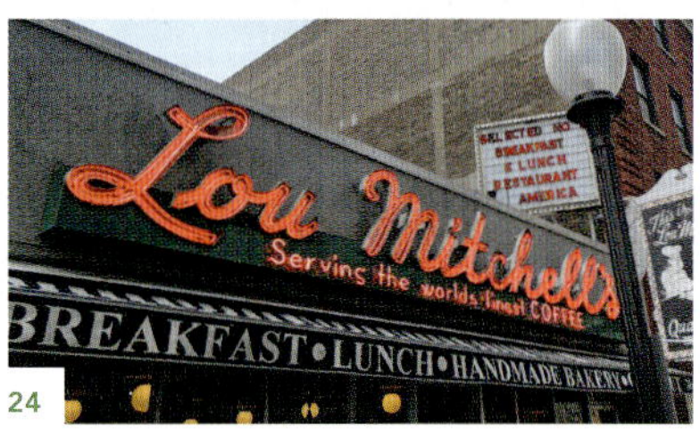

24

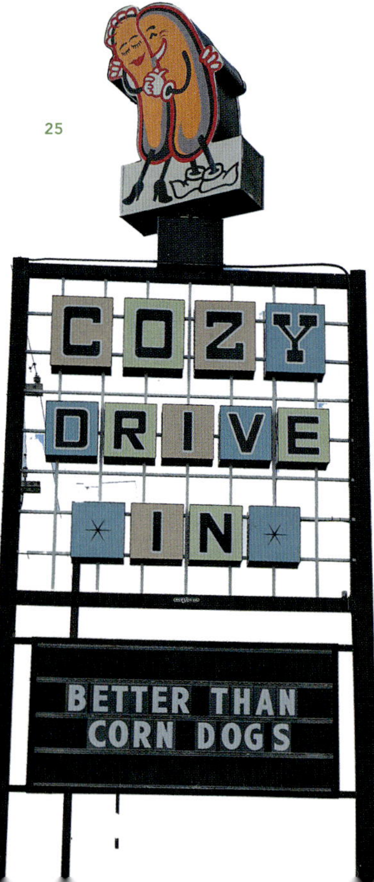

25

Perhaps the most iconic Illinois hot dog stand on Route 66 is the **Cozy Drive-In** (FIG. 25), where its corn dogs (they call them "cozy dogs") have fed legions of roadside-eats fans for generations. (Its founder, Ed Waldmire, made his first big splash in 1946 at the Illinois State Fair, where the hot dog on a stick was a sensation.)

In Niles, Illinois, the hamburgers are the thing at **Booby's**, which opened in 1961. Ronald "Booby" Freedman's cartoon self still keeps an eye on his namesake business. He died a little more than a decade after Booby's opened, and his wife sold the restaurant but remained as an employee until her death in 2014.

The Fish Keg (FIG. 23) in West Rogers Park, Illinois, is quite a catch, and an increasingly rare one these days. The purveyor of fried fish, chicken, and shrimp has been a family-run affair since its first day in 1951.

Chicago's **Lou Mitchell's** (FIG. 24) holds a special place in my heart—and of many Route 66 completists. I began my journey of the entire length of the road with a fortifying breakfast here. Whether Chicago is your launching point or your terminus, Lou's and Route 66 have been together since the very beginning—it was already three years old when the Mother Road was officially opened in 1926.

Dell Rhea's Chicken Basket (FIG. 26) is one of the must-stops of any Route 66 trip in Illinois. Dell Rhea began in 1938 at a gas station. By 1946 it became its own proper restaurant and was well on its way to becoming the road trip institution it is today, but not without a few bumps, like Route 66 being bypassed by a highway.

The legendary **Billy Goat Tavern** (FIG. 27) in Chicago was the inspiration for the John Belushi "Olympia Cafe" sketch on *Saturday Night Live* and a haunt of Chicagoland scribe Mike Royko. "Cheezborger, Cheezborger, Cheezborger. No Pepsi, Coke!" was the famous line from the skit, mimicking what was said at the counter. The Billy Goat Tavern dates to 1934 and has been at its present location on the lower level of North Michigan Avenue since 1964. The "Curse of the Billy Goat" is also tied to the Billy Goat Tavern. The story goes that the bar's owner, Billy Sianis, brought his pet goat to Game 4 of the World Series in 1945, and was summarily ejected by the team's owner for inflicting such a malodorous animal on fans. That's when a peeved Sianis placed the curse on the team that kept them from winning a World Series until 2016. (Disclaimer: tellings of the story vary.)

Another trace of John Belushi's Chicagoland can be found at the **Seven Dwarfs Family Restaurant** (FIG. 28) in Wheaton, Illinois,

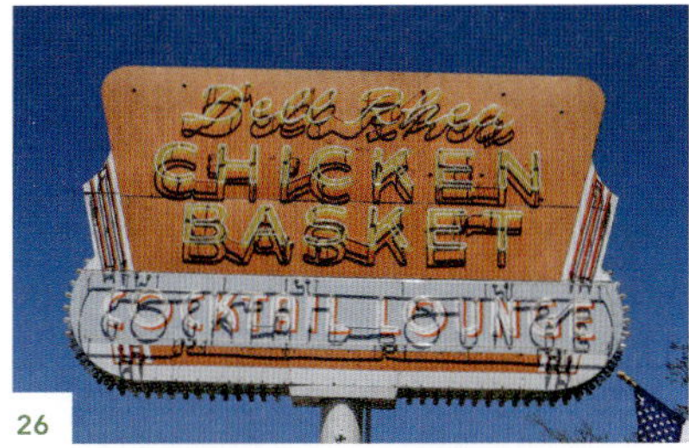

26

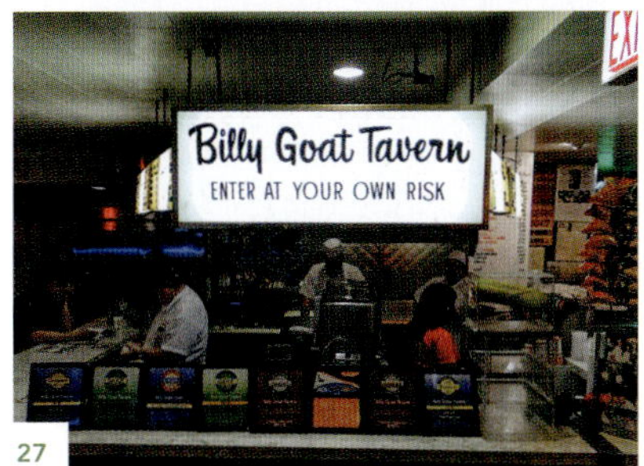

27

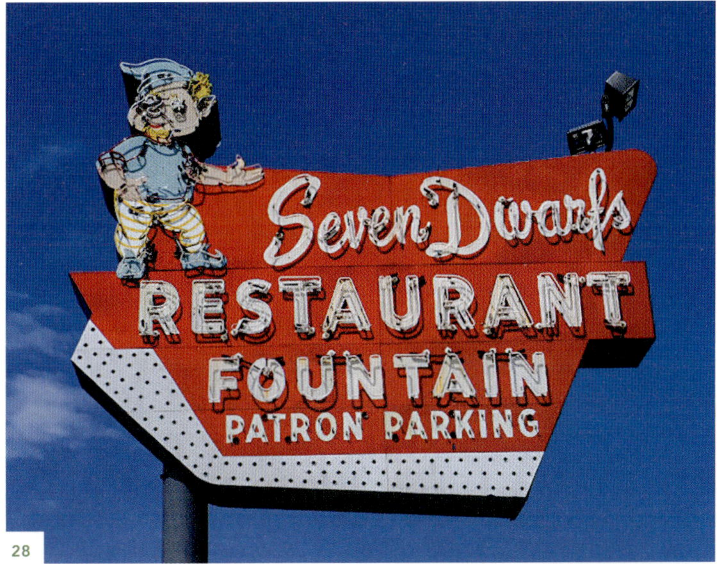

28

where a high-school-aged Belushi was a dishwasher, according to the restaurant's owner. Today you can stop by the restaurant and get your serving of Belushi stories along with comfort food from Sam Sadiku, the proud owner of the eatery since 1978, by which time Belushi was well into his *SNL* heyday, the *Blues Brothers* film only two years away. But the Belushi family has not forgotten their hometown restaurant. Brother Jim Belushi has been known to check in on the Seven Dwarfs. Wherever you look in this 1950s restaurant, there are whimsical murals and other reminders of the enchanting story.

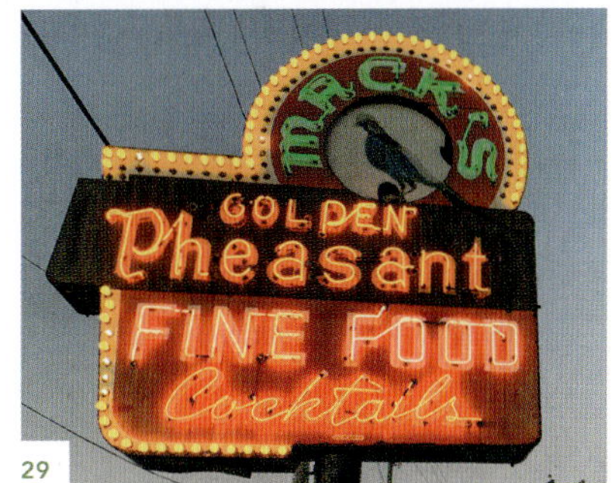

29

Mack's Golden Pheasant (FIG. 29) in Elmhurst, Illinois, was so named because the cofounder, a Czech immigrant named Frank Mack, was fond of these colorful birds. But a more appropriate name might be Mack's Golden Phoenix, because this 1948 restaurant serving hearty Czech-Austrian cuisine survived several brushes with death, two from fires and one from a 1987 flood. It was celebrated as DuPage County's oldest continuously owned restaurant until the end finally came in December 2024.

Hamburger University is the heart of all things McDonald's, housed at its headquarters in Chicago. The McDonald's there is distinguished by its menu, which offers different items available in other countries, a chance to expand your fast-food palate.

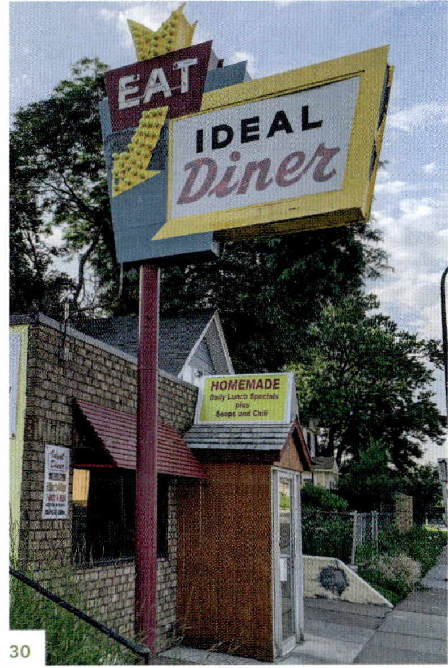

30

Sometimes, a diner lives up to its name. That's a tall order when you're a tiny place—a glorified hut, really—named **The Ideal Diner** (FIG. 30), but its many devoted fans who squeeze into this greasy spoon with "14 stools. 1 counter. No bathroom," as their slogan goes, think the diner's name is spot-on. A staple of

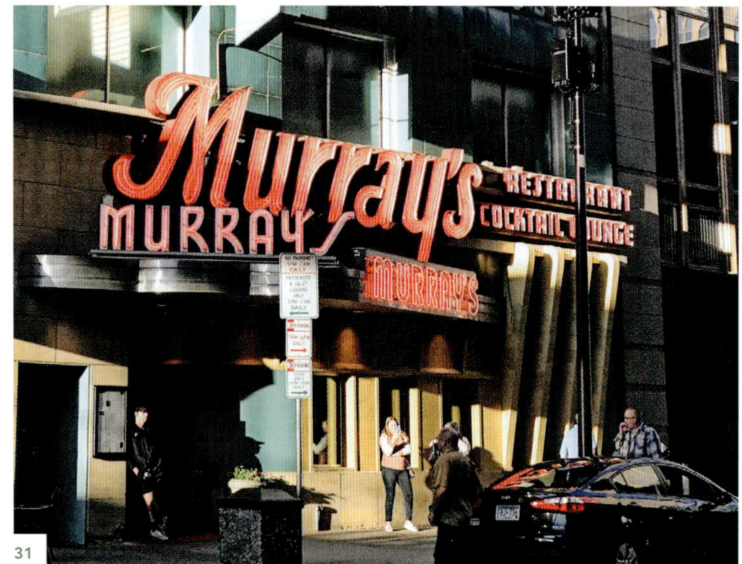

31

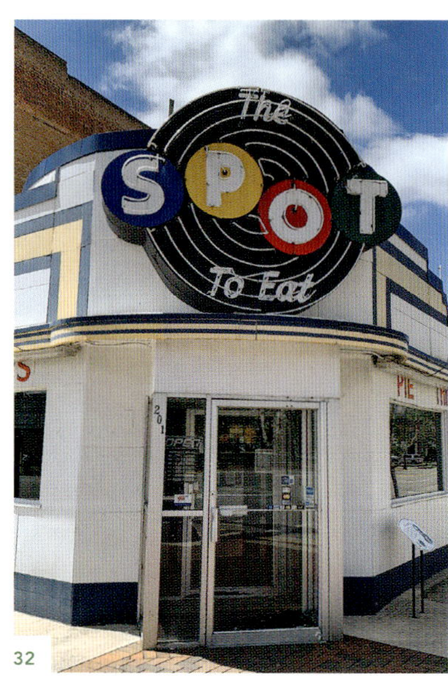

32

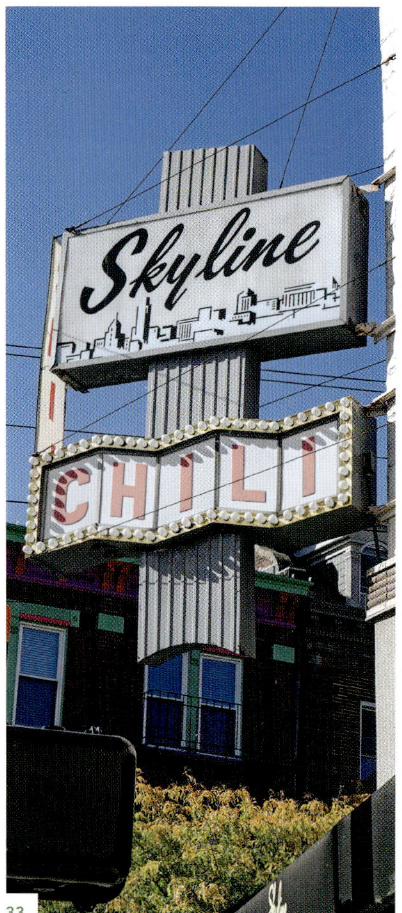

33

Minneapolis's Northeast neighborhood since 1949, the diner was rescued from oblivion by a former waitress there, Kim Robinson, whose mom had also worked at the diner for much of its history. The joint is renowned for its breakfast menu.

Murray's (FIG. 31) steak house has been a fixture of downtown Minneapolis since 1946, and to this day it's a family-run affair. They've managed the delicate dance of staying true to their heritage while also keeping up with the times. The facade is one of the most striking in the nation—and how can you not love a place whose slogan is "Home of the Butter Knife Steak."

In 1907, Spot Miller parked his chuckwagon in downtown Sidney, Ohio, and began to sell vittles at what is now **The Spot** (FIG. 32). The city elders frowned on this shabby chow house, so the wheels came off, the awnings went up, and The Spot became a real restaurant. A new owner named Joe Cook came along a few years later and renamed the restaurant Cook's Spot. The business was such a hit, they eventually cooked up a chain called The Spot to Eat. The chain is now gone and it's back to the original store. The art moderne exterior is a feast for the eyes. And anything you choose to eat—burgers, malts, pies—is a favorite.

Chili on spaghetti? Why, we must be in Cincinnati! The secret sauce has Greek origins, and the meal can be enhanced with everything from shredded cheese, onions, and beans. The biggest exponent of the culinary tradition by far is **Skyline Chili** (FIG. 33), with more than one hundred locations. (I always order the 3-Way—the chili on spaghetti with shredded cheese.) Cincinnati-style chili is also served up at **Camp Washington Chili** (FIG. 34),

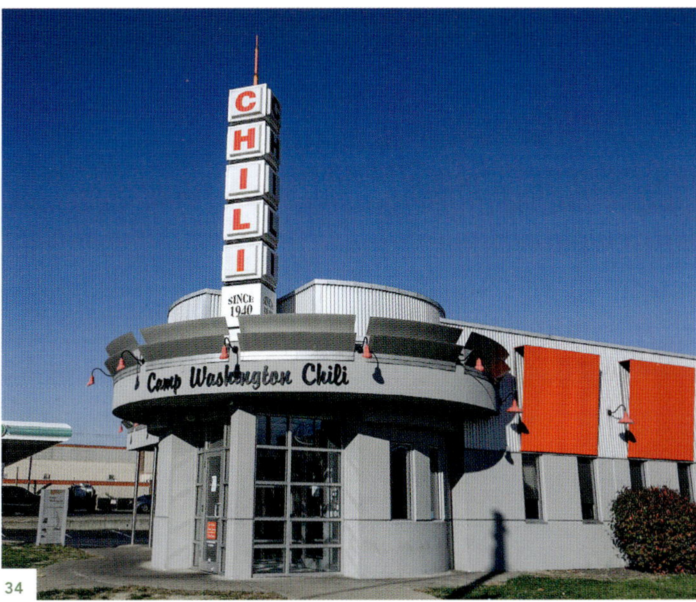

34

which features a notable building not far from the American Sign Museum. The chili can be slathered on hot dogs or, I suppose, anything you like!

The Big Boy is a big deal on the American road. **Frisch's Big Boy** (FIG. 35) was once a major franchisee of the Big Boy brand, along with other regional Big Boys like Manners, Kip's, VIP's, TJ's, Elby's, Shoney's, and many others. They all got the rights to go "Big" from Bob's Big Boy, the parent company, started in Southern California in 1936. Frisch's traces its roots to a Cincinnati cafe in 1905, and a chain eventually formed that allied itself with Big Boy in 1947. Today, Frisch's operates independently of Big Boy International, but retains the rights to the name, the character, and the menu in its Midwest geographic footprint. At press time, the chain was in turmoil following the closure of dozens of locations that had brought down even its original Mainliner restaurant in Fairfax, Ohio, which acts as a museum for the chain.

35

▸▸▸ Pull Over!

Cincinnati has chili joints I love to explore, but when in Detroit, I'm drawn to its slew of slider restaurants, serving tiny hamburgers that pack a flavorful punch, the buildings' elegant moderne structures slathered in soothing porcelain enamel. Behold spots like **The Telway** (FIG. 36), **Bates** (FIG. 37), **Greene's** (FIG. 38), **The Hunter House** (FIG. 39), and **Elmer's** (FIG. 40).

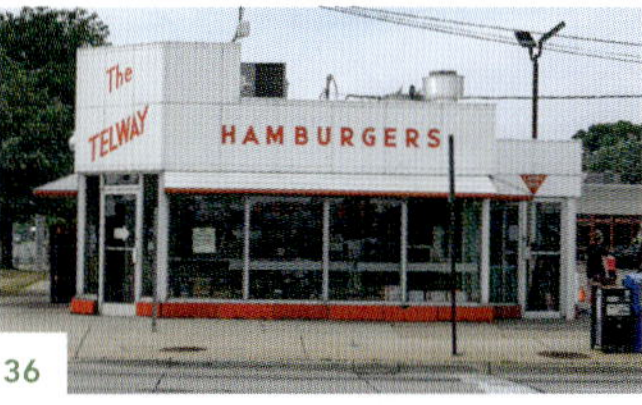

36

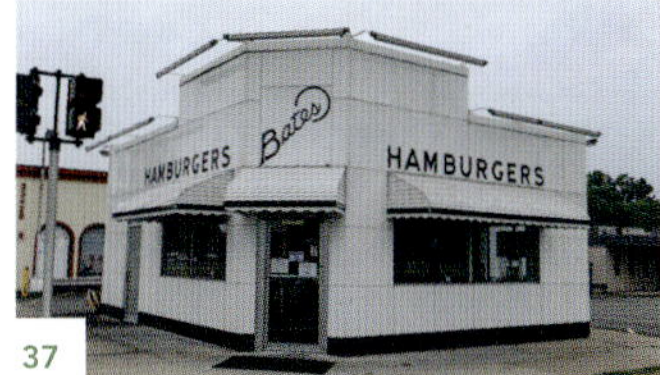

37

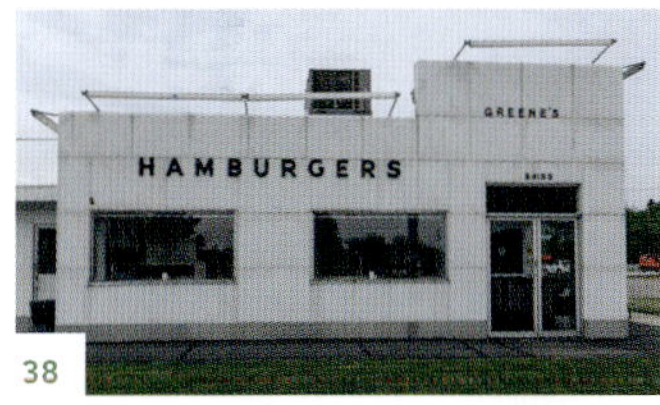

38

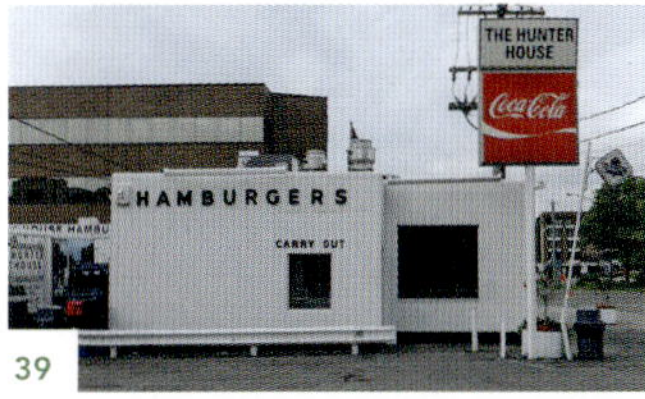

39

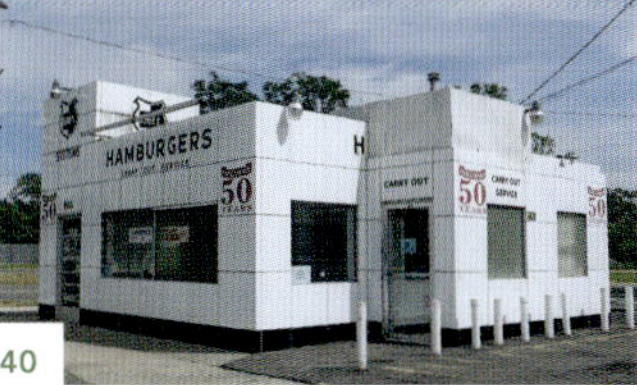

40

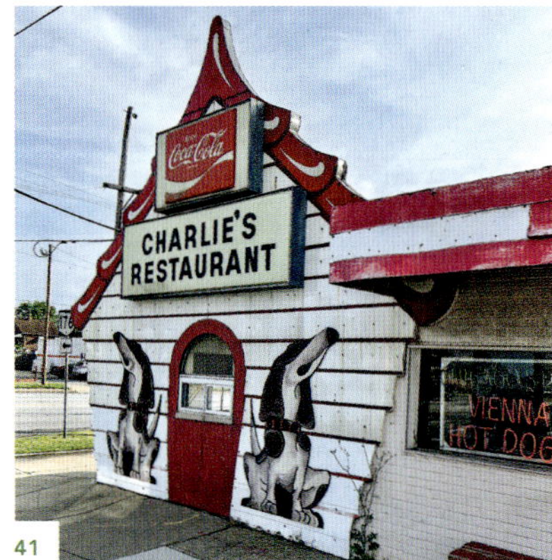

41

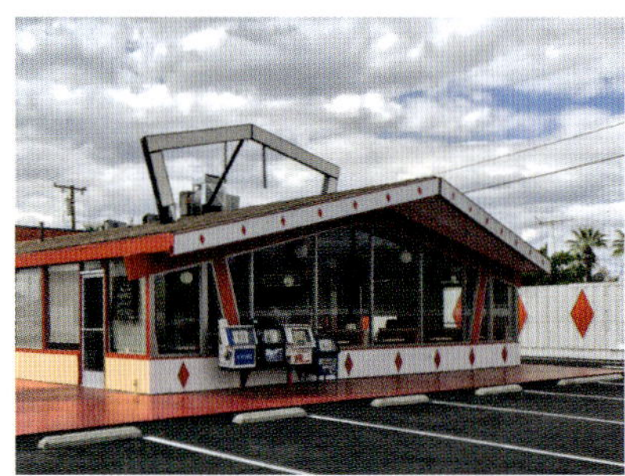

Charlie's Dog House Diner (FIG. 41) in Cleveland, Ohio, which also goes by Charlie's Restaurant, is one of the cutest buildings I've ever visited. This is actually an old Valentine diner that has been expanded and modified, supplied with a charming doghouse facade, complete with two pooches standing sentinel. The Kansas Historical Society, which tracks these old diners, explains this was the first location of the regional Dog House chain in 1952, and it's still here, on 2102 Brookpark Road.

CHAINS OF FOOD

Burger Chef

The Burger Chef, founded in Indianapolis, Indiana, in 1954, was a real contender for the top burger throne. At one point it was leading Burger King in the race to catch up with McDonald's. The chain was a pioneer in many ways, one being the introduction of a Fun Meal for kids in 1973. If that sounds familiar, it's because McDonald's unveiled the Happy Meal six years later. (Burger Chef sued, unsuccessfully.) The chain encountered trouble later in the 1970s, amid overexpansion, bad headlines from a horrific crime at an Indiana store, and corporate upheaval ending with most of the stores being converted to Hardee's. The last store under the name closed in 1996.

One of the finest buildings left is in Rialto, California, so authentic-looking that *Mad Men* location scouts used it as a stand-in for a Burger Chef of the 1960s.

The Burger Chef signage, featuring the chef on top, is another roadside relic to keep an eye out for. One of the better ones is in Petersburg, Virginia, the chef repurposed as a pizzaiolo for Sal's Pizza & Italian Restaurant.

Little Caesars

Pizza, pizza! Little Caesars began as a hometown chain in suburban Detroit in 1959, riding the wave of America's undying love of dough and tomato sauce. Most recognize the Little Caesar cartoon character featured in commercials. But out this way, there are a handful of Little Caesar statues that are fun to see, the first of which emerged in 1962 as franchising got underway. About twenty-two are left, according to roadside historian Debra Jane Seltzer.

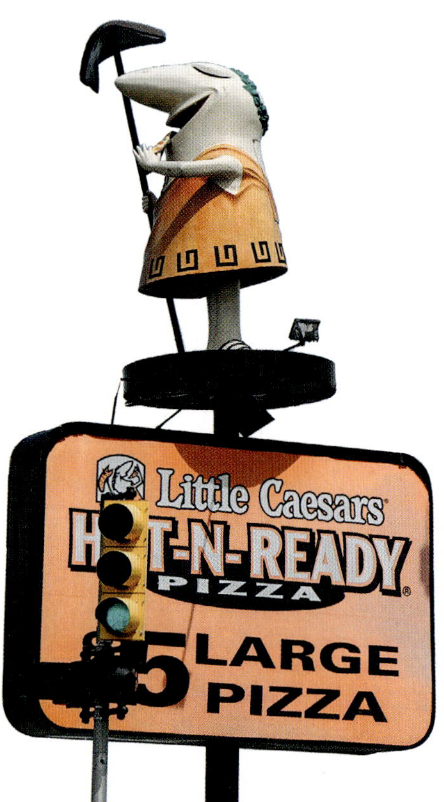

Dairy Queen

On June 22, 1940, the very first Dairy Queen opened at 501 North Chicago Street in Joliet, Illinois. The soft serve was called Dairy Queen, and the queen in question, the oft-cited story goes, was the ordinary cow, without which the product would not exist.

That first DQ was a sensation, and the young couple who managed the shop thought it was a "dream come true" because soft serve does not require laborious hand-dipping, Naomi Mortensen explained in her book on the history of DQ.

From there, the chain would spread far and wide, and today numbers more than six thousand stores. Of those locations, the special ones—the ones where the ice cream just hits better—are the legacy stores that have preserved a taste of the simple charms of the American roadside.

Here is a celebratory tour of some of my favorite DQs.

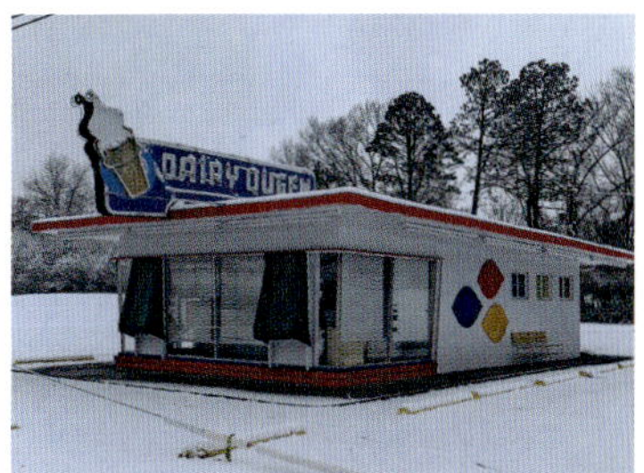

Butler, Pennsylvania

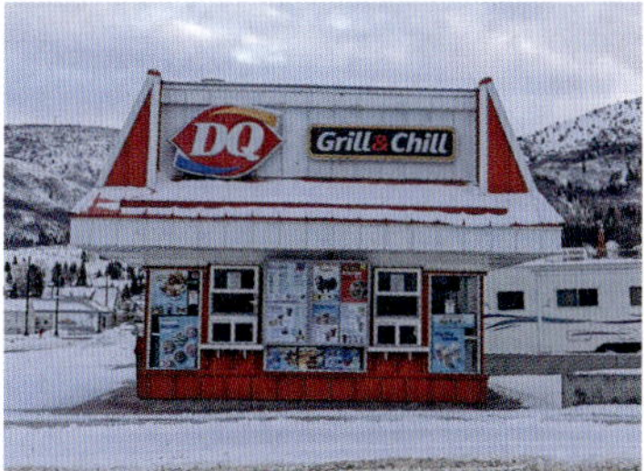

Anaconda, Montana

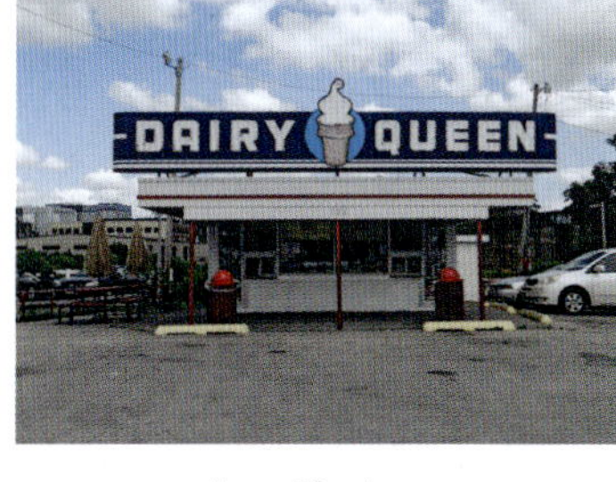

Iowa City, Iowa

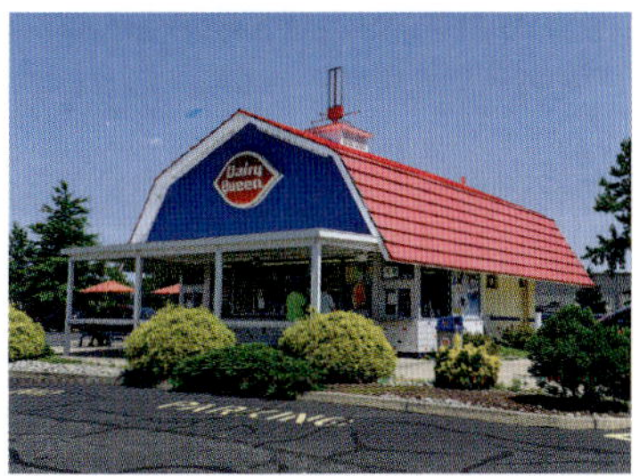

East Windsor, New Jersey

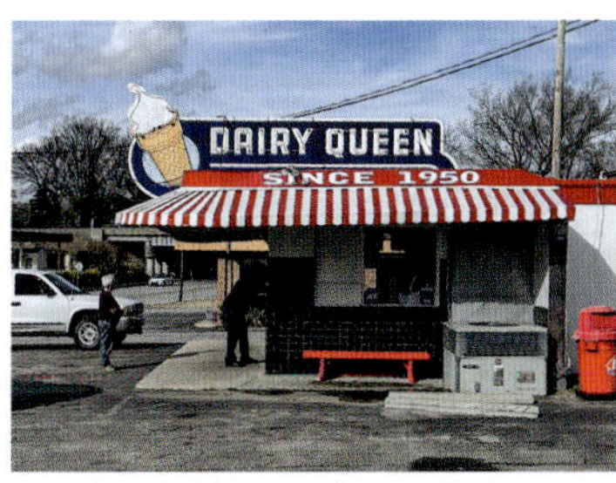

Salisbury, North Carolina

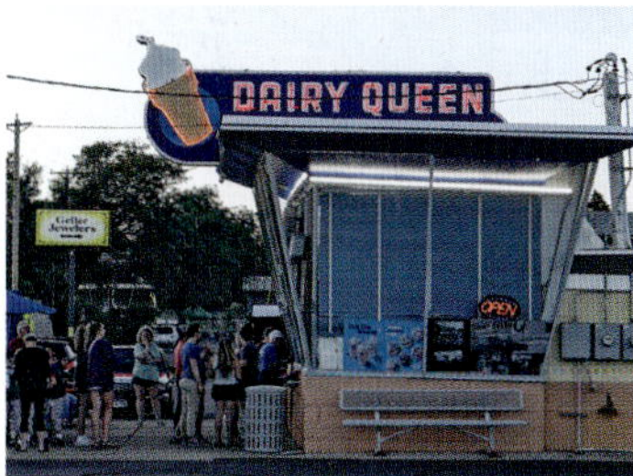

Roseville, Minnesota

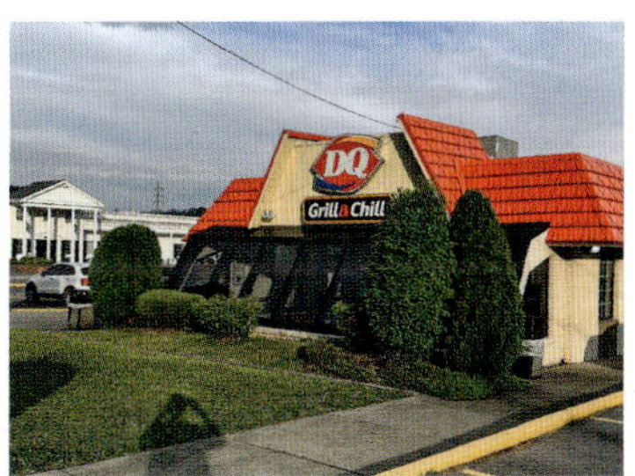

Huntington, West Virginia

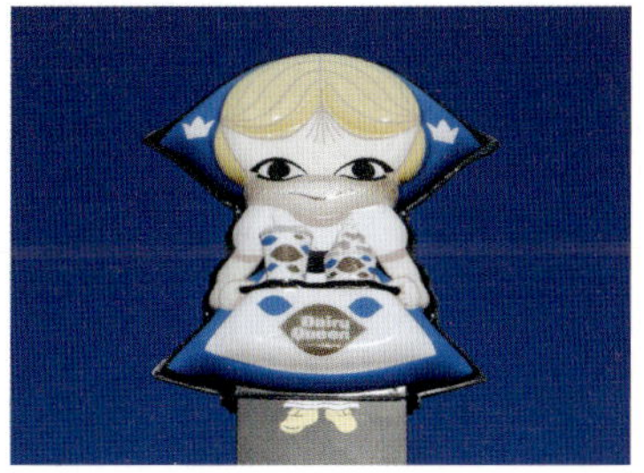

Saco, Maine

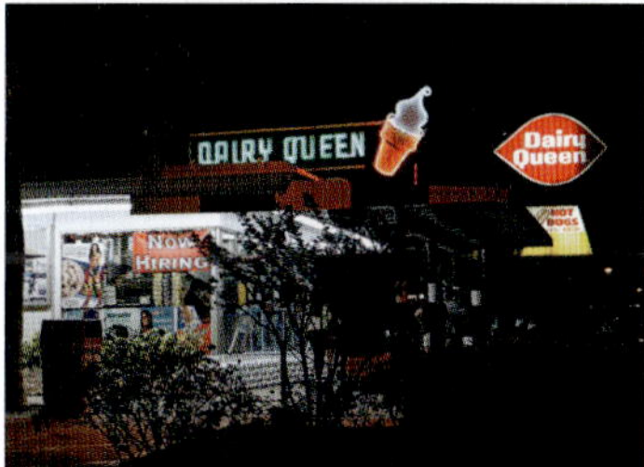

New Smyrna Beach, Florida

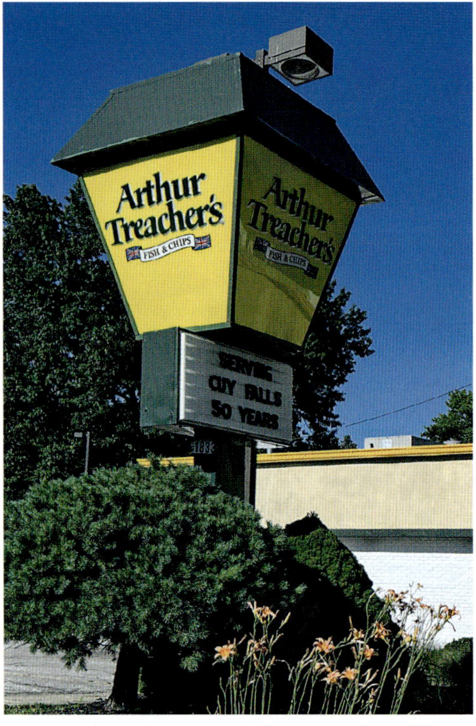

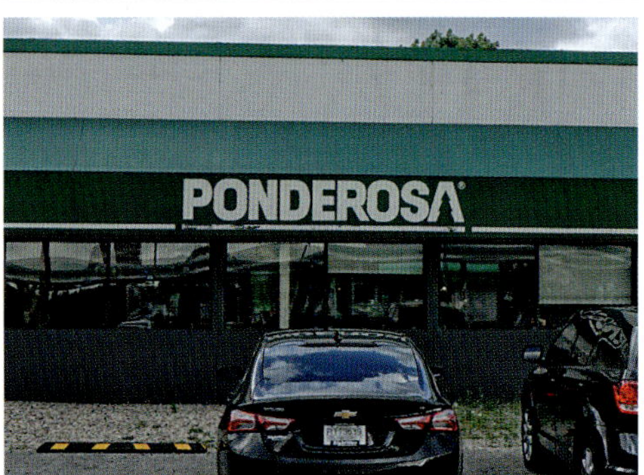

Arthur Treacher's

When you see that yellow lantern with the green top in the distance, in Cuyahoga Falls, Ohio, you're overwhelmed with nostalgia for the 1970s, when the Arthur Treacher's chain, founded in 1969, expanded to more than eight hundred locations and became a staple of American fast food. But Arthur Treacher's lost its way, in part because of the infamous "Cod Wars" of the late 1970s that drove up the price of cod and damaged the quality of the chain's offerings. The chain steadily declined and is now down to a handful, including two standalone restaurants in the Cleveland area as of this writing and plans reportedly afoot for a third. The dapper fellow who greets you is Arthur Treacher himself, a British actor who was born to play Jeeves the butler, and later gained renewed fame as second banana to talk show host and *Jeopardy!* creator Merv Griffin in the 1960s.

Ponderosa

As a child of the 1970s and '80s, the American road offered an endless bounty of buffets, from Sizzler (my family's favorite, every Tuesday night for years) to Bonanza and Ponderosa, both inspired by the TV show *Bonanza* and for decades under shared corporate ownership.

One of the best survivors of the Ponderosa chain can be found in the Wisconsin Dells. This Ponderosa opened on July 31, 1996, according to a clipping from the *Baraboo News Republic*, with seating for 350 along with a banquet room that could seat up to 110. And, yes, there was a buffet. There were about six hundred Ponderosas in business when this location opened. Reportedly, just twelve remain.

Kewpee Burgers

"Hamburg Pickle On Top! Makes Your Heart Go Flippity Flop!" That classic slogan for Kewpee Hamburgers applies not only to the food but to the charming architecture at the Kewpee here in Lima, Ohio. Their iconic square burgers were an inspiration for Wendy's founder Dave Thomas, who differentiated his Wendy's chain with the use of square patties.

The very first Kewpee hamburger joint opened in Flint, Michigan, in 1923, called the Kewpee Hotel, making it one of the earliest fast-food chains, and the second-oldest hamburger chain after White Castle.

In 1928, husband-and-wife team Hoyt and Julia Wilson opened the Lima store, and their shop was so popular that in 1939 they constructed this stunning art moderne building clad in porcelain enamel here on 111 N. Elizabeth Street.

Kewpees once totaled more than four hundred, but today, there are five locations left. The one you see here is the very picture of cuteness overload. Greeting us is cherubic Kewpee, inspired by the Kewpie dolls (note the different spelling) that were all the rage in the early twentieth century and are still cherished by collectors. Kewpee has two siblings inside watching over things.

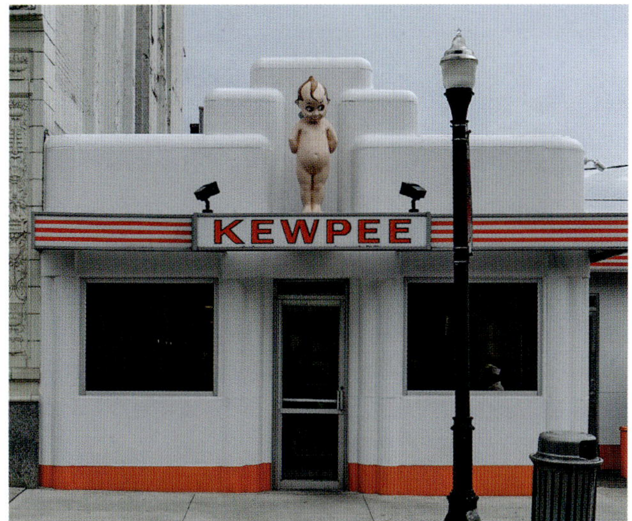

Mister Donut

There was once a great donut war in America. The upstart Mister Donut was taking on Dunkin' Donuts in a battle for the loyalties of caffeinated carb lovers across this land. But this wasn't just any war—this was a family feud. William Rosenberg, Dunkin's founder, did not see donut hole to donut hole with brother-in-law and business partner Harry Winokur about how to run Dunkin'. Bill wanted to grow the chain quickly through franchising; Harry wanted to take it slow. There were disagreements. They parted ways, and Harry went on to found Mister Donut in 1955, with the first shop in Revere, Massachusetts, not far from the first Dunkin' in Quincy.

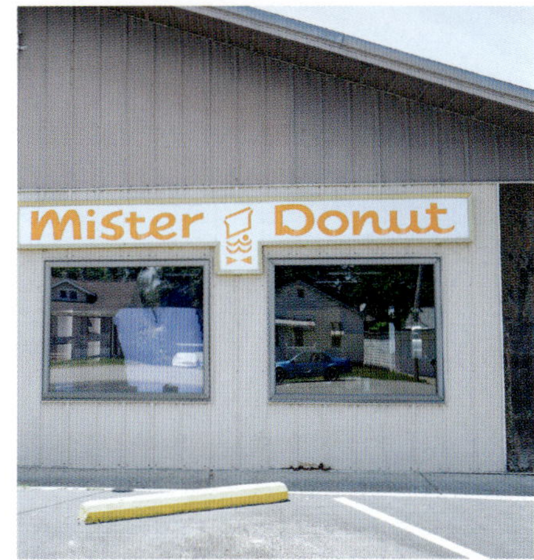

Harry had been so loath to grow Dunkin' through franchising, yet that's what he ended up doing anyway with his Mister Donut, where donuts were dipped, *not* dunked. Mister Donut spread across the country, and later the world, in particular, Asia. Mister Donut eventually fell into the hands of Dunkin's parent company in 1990. Oh, the irony.

There is only one Mister Donut left in the nation (right), in Godfrey, Illinois, but they remain popular in Asia.

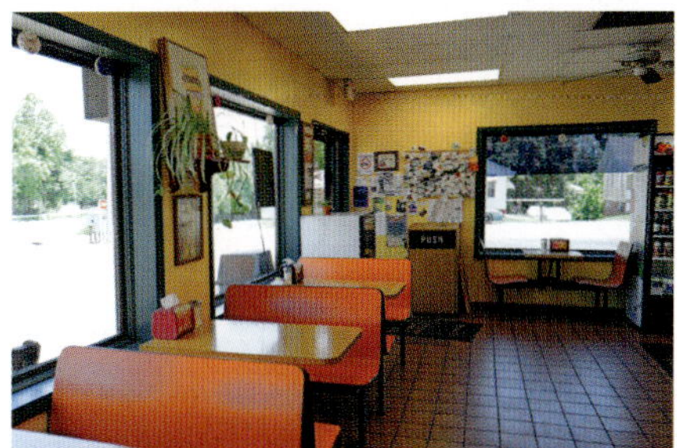

Wendy's

The founder of Wendy's, Dave Thomas, wanted to embrace nostalgia with his restaurants, evoking a spirit of warmth and comfort from "olden times," as communicated to a wide audience in 1969, when he opened the first Wendy's in Columbus, Ohio. His hamburgers were to be "Old Fashioned"—a big square patty of fresh beef, its four corners poking out of the bun—and his daughter (and yes, mascot) Wendy, in

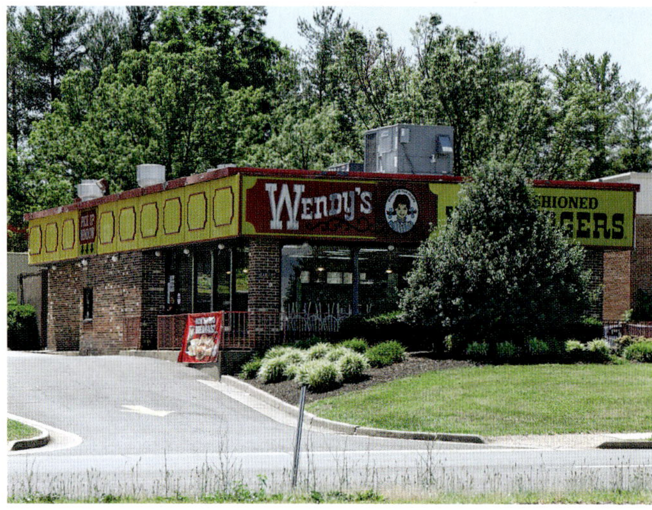

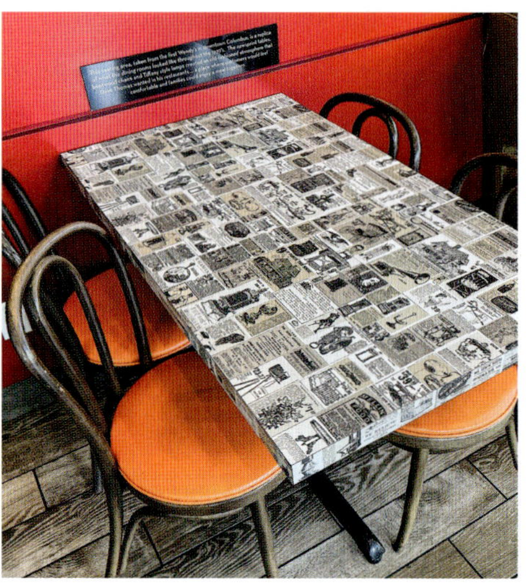

pigtails and a simple striped blue dress, was something out of the imagination of Laura Ingalls Wilder.

The flagship store in Dublin, Ohio, is not an homage to old-school Wendy's, however. It adheres to the modern corporate-dictated look rolled out about a decade ago and slowly adopted by restaurants. But the flagship also features a special dining room that doubles as a museum, including what may well be the last "newsprint table" in use at a Wendy's. Still, I submit that this space, as special as it is, also represents a missed opportunity to rebuild a proper 1970s-era Wendy's dining room.

Not far from the flagship store in Dublin is Wendy's world headquarters. The brick of the building reminds me of that used on older restaurants. What's even more special are the top decorative panels, which mimic those used on the old yellow Wendy's buildings and in the early logo. Yellow Wendy's are down to probably none by now. I caught some of the last ones several years ago down in Delmarva. And in downtown Columbus, at the site of the long-gone first restaurant, a plaque denotes the history that transpired there.

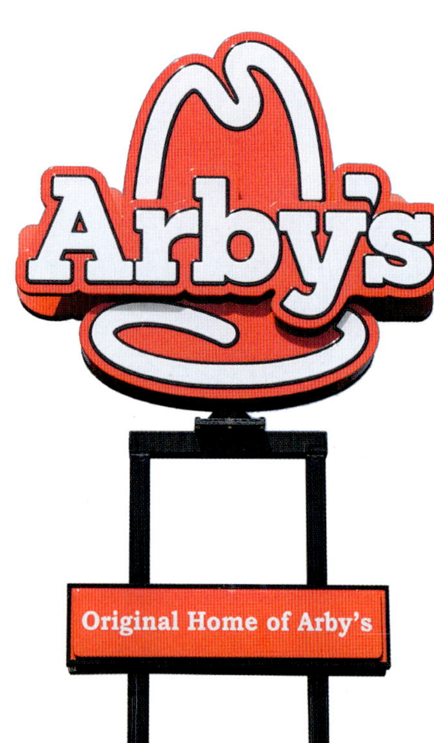

Arby's

July 23, 1964, was a delicious day in the history of American fast food. It's when brothers Forrest and Leroy Raffel opened the first Arby's on Route 224 in Boardman, Ohio, which is now designated as "Meat Town USA." Their very names are preserved (concealed, really) in the brand name: Arby's stands for the RBs, or the Raffel Brothers. An advertising campaign in the early 1980s implanted the now-unshakable idea that Arby's stands for America's Roast

Beef, yes, sir! Perhaps that's the case in some unsung marketer's mind, but it's actually a sly nod to Forrest and Leroy. Arby's started out in the Conestoga wagon building in Boardman, which is still there. Its roots as an Arby's are unmistakable. Now there's an operational Arby's restaurant across the street. (The Hollywood, California, hat at right is at a now-defunct location.)

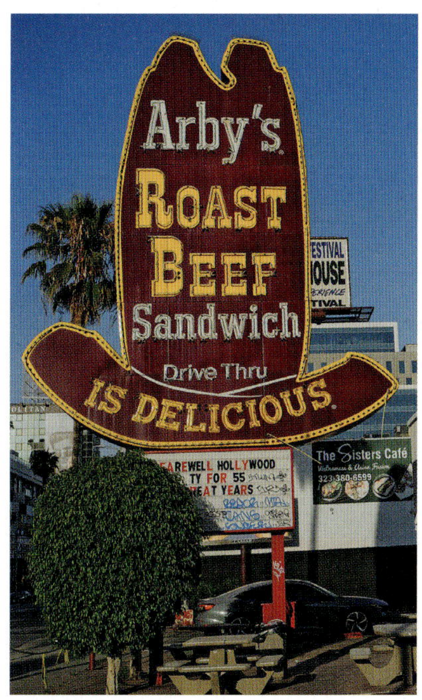

Burger King vs. Burger King

The rare building at center right is a lovingly preserved Burger King franchise, which opened in 1965 in downtown Naperville, Illinois. Burger King in recent years has leaned into its heritage and has discarded the 1999 logo in favor of an iteration of its more burger-like logos that were first rolled out in 1969.

Burger King, the chain, began in 1953 as Insta-Burger King in Jacksonville, Florida. A pair of entrepreneurs quickly saw the potential of flame-broiled riches and fired up the chain to become a fast-food colossus, and called it Burger King. The chain's national march hit a snag in Illinois, where in the early 1960s it stumbled into the realm of a local restaurant that was also called Burger King (bottom right), in Mattoon, Illinois, but that had no connection to the chain. The Mattoon store had registered the trademark with the Illinois Secretary of State before the other BK arrived in Illinois and assumed that all of Illinois was its exclusive territory.

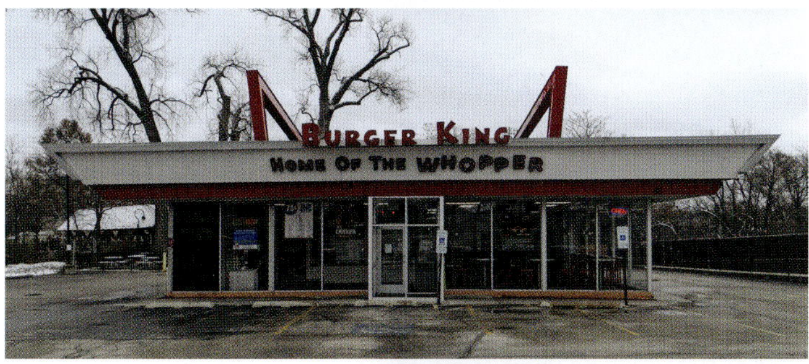

The thorny legal dispute between the two Kings ended with a court-ordered compromise—Burger King, the chain, could not open an Illinois location within 20 miles of the Mattoon mom-and-pop, unrelated Burger King (bottom right), which Gene and Betty Hoots bought in 1952 when it was called Frigid Queen, a seasonal ice-cream place. They turned it into a year-round burger joint, and the queen became a king of burgers. You'll never find a Whopper, Whopper Jr., or Whopper anything on the menu. You will find "Hooter" burgers that are a play on the family name. If you want the chain BK experience, and if you are in Mattoon, about 20 miles away, you'll find the nearest Burger King, the chain, in Tuscola, Illinois. In a 1998 newspaper interview, Gene Hoots said that despite all the years that had passed, he still feels like Burger King pushed him around. As he put it, "We are not a Burger King. We are *the* Burger King."

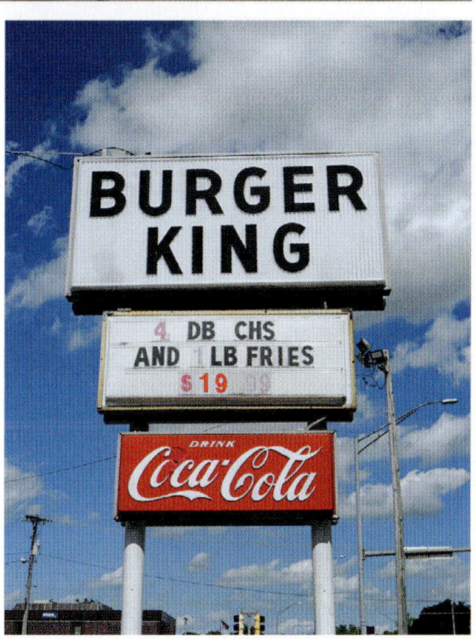

MAINSTAYS OF MAIN STREET

Here you will find many pictures of determination, with shops surviving because of families who believe in their businesses and communities. We'll also see notable examples of ingenuity—but we'll begin with a wonderful example of adaptive reuse.

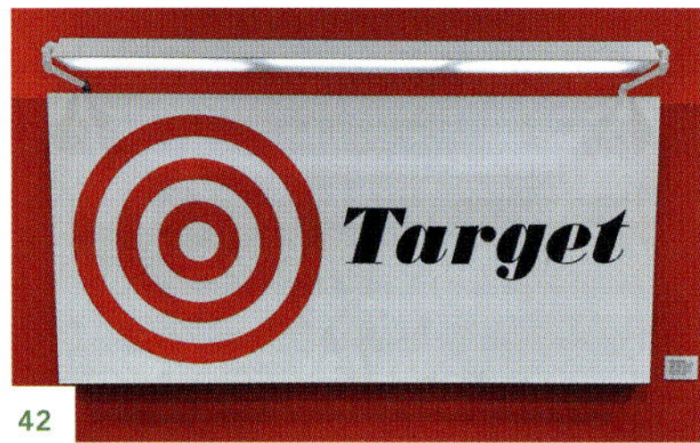

42

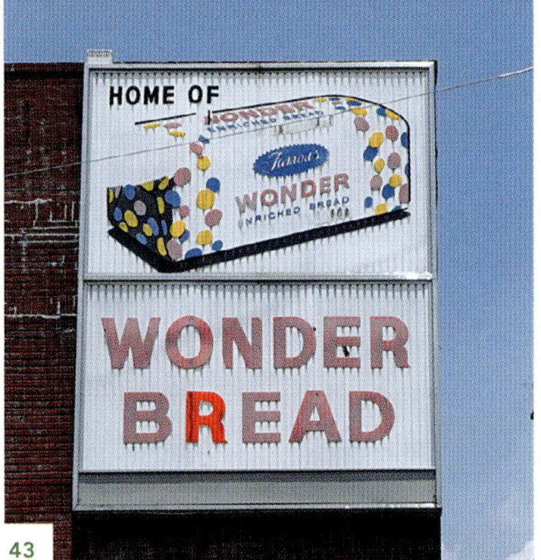

43

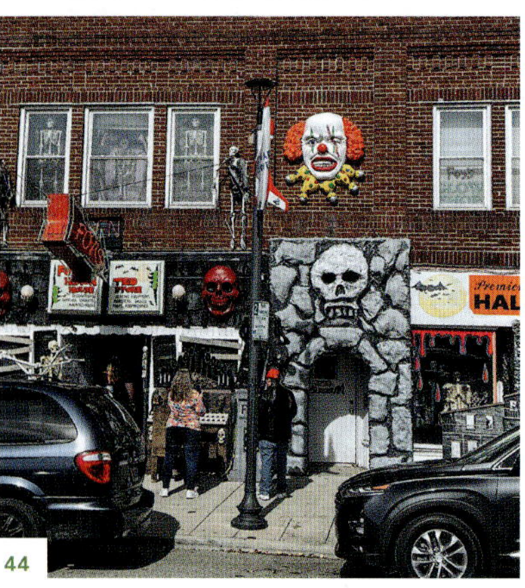
44

I always love visiting the first (or sadly, last) of anything, and the very first **Target** (FIG. 42) opened in Roseville, Minnesota, back in 1962. To see the store from the outside does not suggest anything vintage, but if you step inside, you'll see a sign with the original logo and a little tribute to this store's pioneer status.

Another "slice of America" is Wonder Bread, with its own delightful iconography. In my carb-friendly childhood, Wonder Bread was always in the pantry. As a youngster, I didn't know sliced bread came in any other color but white! Wonder Bread's old jingle called it "just a little slice of America," something we are reminded of at the **Wonder Bread Lofts** (FIG. 43) in Columbus, Ohio.

The Wonder Bread factory in the Italian Village neighborhood was where the famous white bread was made. By 2009, the ovens were turned off for the last time here, when the public realized that white bread was no longer a standby in America's kitchens. But the 70,000-square-foot building wasn't going anywhere, and an idea emerged to name it **Wonderland** and turn it into a cultural complex.

That idea had a run-in with reality, and by 2013, the building had found its next and current calling, becoming the Wonder Bread Lofts. The developer, Kevin Lykens, preserved important historical touches on the inside and outside, most notably the old signage.

No, we are not in Salem, Massachusetts, or Sleepy Hollow, New York. We are in Fairborn, Ohio, a small city just outside Dayton, where the tell-tale heart of the **Foy's Halloween** (FIG. 44) empire beats downtown.

In storefront after jam-packed Main Street storefront, Mike Foy oversees a family emporium that is the stuff of dreams (or the fuel for nightmares) for Halloween enthusiasts. These stores are stocked with masks of all kinds, costumes for all ages, enough treats to make sure no tricks are played on you, a haunted-house store with everything you might need to make your own, and on and on it ghouls—uh, *goes*.

It all began in 1929, when Albert Foy, Mike's grandfather, opened a five-and-dime store here, a downtown staple of yore.

Over the years, the Foys were slowly bewitched by Halloween, and we were left with spooky shopping spectacle.

Pride Cleaners (FIG. 45) is a stunning example of Googie architecture (see page 297), adding a dash of Jetsons sophistication to the corner of East Seventy-Ninth Street and St. Lawrence Avenue in the Chatham neighborhood of Chicago since 1959. The South Side building has hardly been touched since, making it a perfect time capsule of this optimistic style of architecture. Architect Gerald Siegwart's creation has been justly praised by critic Lee Bey as "one of the city's finest and most exuberant examples of postwar modernism." Siegwart's thinking, explains Bey, was to create a structure that conveyed the modern advances in dry cleaning that offered customers faster, more efficient service.

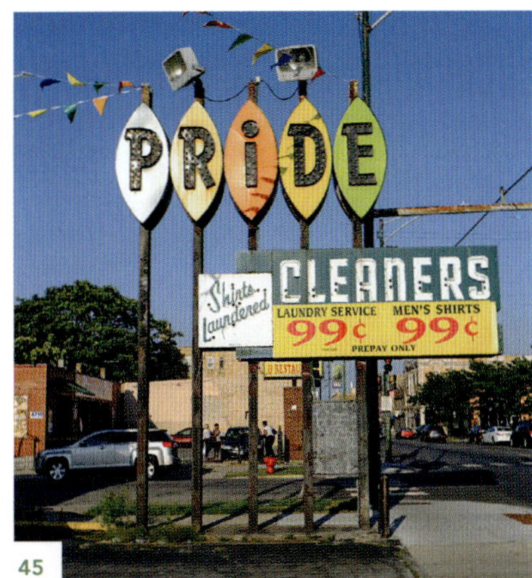

45

Starsiak Clothing (FIG. 46) is a storefront gem across from Chicago's Polish Triangle, yet for many years, this storefront was obscured. Starsiak was a popular suit shop in a Polish neighborhood from 1916 to 1981. But everything changes, and as new ethnic groups moved in, Starsiak closed. "It's time for a change, to give the neighborhood to somebody else. We took it from somebody else, so give it to somebody else," the clearly poetic owner Alexander Starsiak, who lived upstairs and died in 1994, was quoted as saying in a piece syndicated by the New York Times News Service in 1981. All these years later, his name—and legacy—are back on display along the old Polish Broadway, at 1205 N. Milwaukee Avenue.

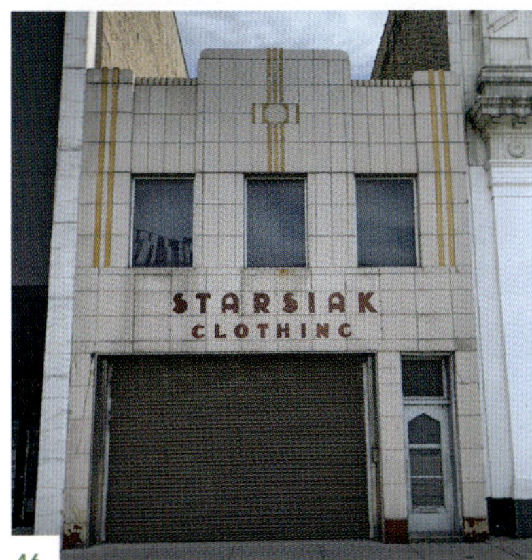

46

The spectacular **Central Camera** (FIG. 47) has been doing business in Chicago's Loop since 1899, now in the third generation of family ownership. America was once dotted with thousands upon thousands of photo shops, the familiar Kodak logo in the window. Their numbers have dwindled mightily, but those that survive embrace their heritage while keeping up with the times. Central Camera is one of those extraordinary survivors.

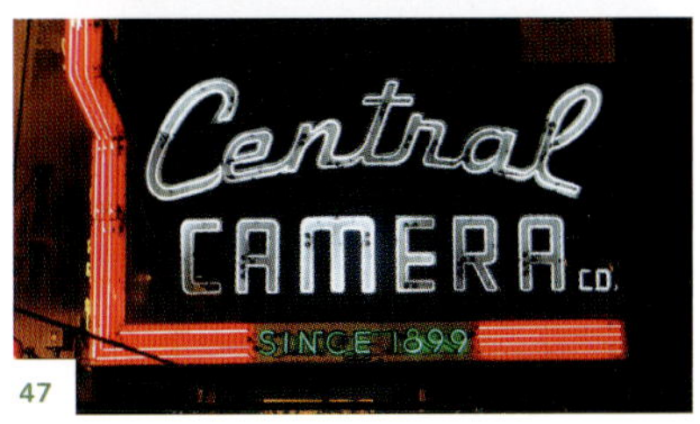

47

SPOTLIGHT: GREYHOUND

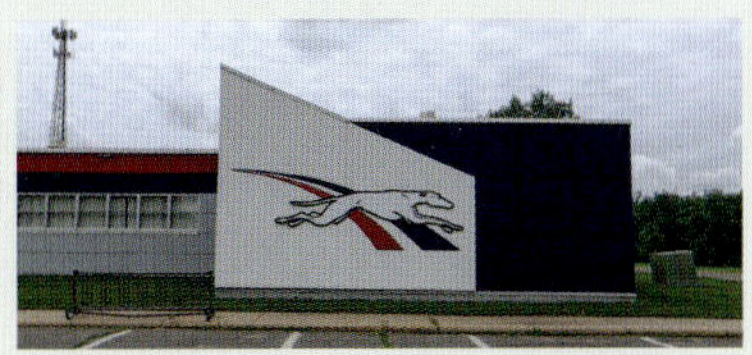

Greyhound was one of the great names that opened up America to travelers. A Greyhound station in your downtown was an important place, usually graced with impressive architecture. The Greyhound Museum is at the site of the bus company's founding, in Hibbard, Minnesota. One of my favorite souvenirs, a brass greyhound paperweight, sits on my desk at *Retrologist* headquarters.

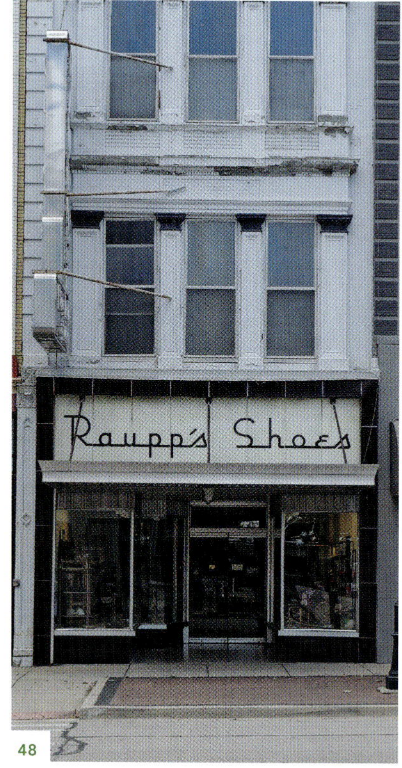

48

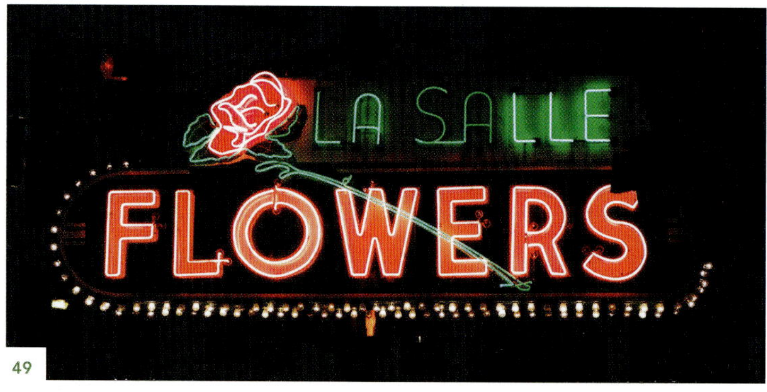

49

La Salle Flowers (FIG. 49) has been a part of Chicago since 1936. Its neon sign is one of the great roadside symbols of the city, and one of the nicest of its kind anywhere in the nation, with an impressive set of chasing light bulbs. The restored sign enjoys a prominent corner location, having been moved to that spot to comply with a 2012 city regulation.

Raupp's Shoes (FIG. 48) is that family-run shoe store that has long been gone from your hometown, the one you remember fondly, the one you wish you could still visit. Your version of Raupp's might be gone, but Raupp's is not—it's still here in downtown Decatur, Illinois, where it's been since 1909.

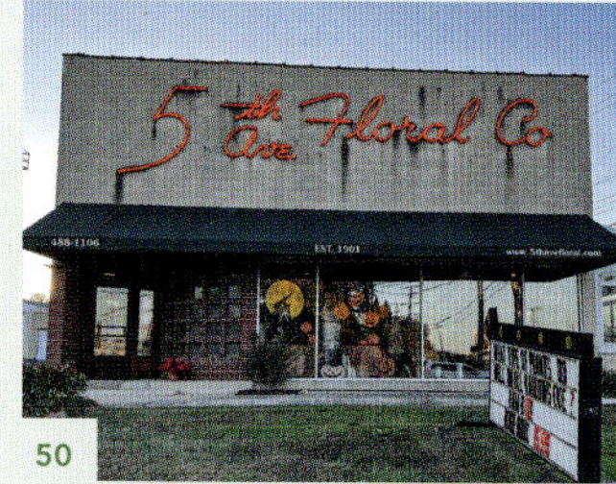

50

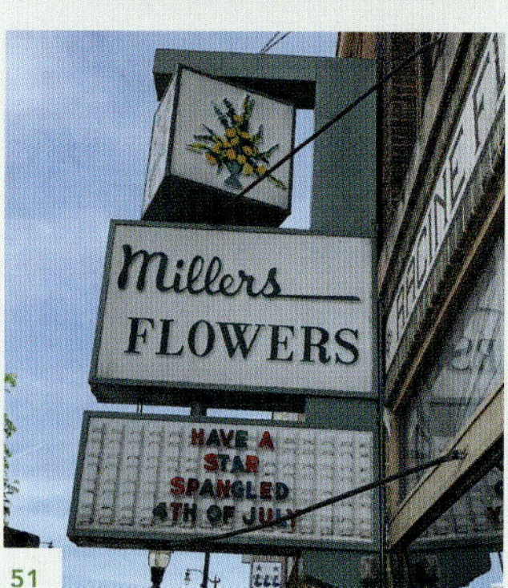

51

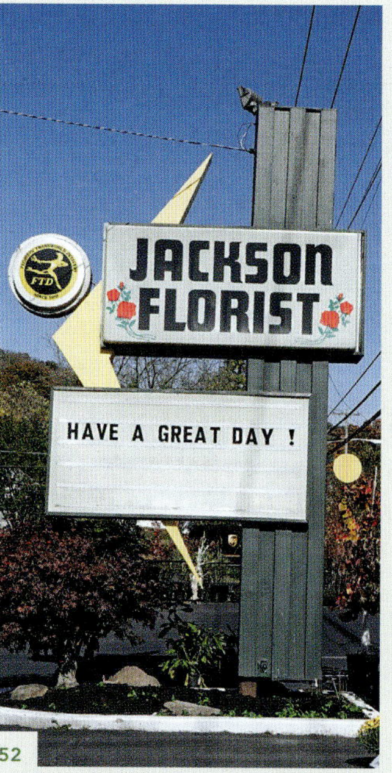

52

FLOWER POWER!

How can you not love a flower shop with a gorgeous sign? Here are three more I'm thrilled to share with you: **The 5th Avenue Floral Co.** (FIG. 50) in Columbus, Ohio, founded in 1901, doesn't sit on Fifth Avenue—it moved here in 1946 but kept the name. The swanky neon script and simple structure make for a bold presence. **Jackson Florist** (FIG. 52) in Covington, Kentucky, has a stunner of a sign complete with the old-school FTD logo, and a history dating to the late nineteenth century. **Miller's Flowers** (FIG. 51) in Racine, Wisconsin, has been a proud family business since 1908, when it opened as Racine Floral Co.

An amazing sign featuring a happy clown still points toward the 26 acres of family fun at **The Camden Park Amusement Park** (FIG. 53) in Huntington, West Virginia. Camden Park is thriving, but alas, **Kiddieland Amusement Park** in Melrose Park, Illinois, is a memory, a nice one. It closed in 2009, the victim of a family dispute, and a Costco now sits in its place. Its various rides were auctioned off and dispersed, but fortunately the sign that stood at the entrance, featuring Jack and Jill forever playing, was saved and placed on the side of the Melrose Park Public Library.

Sullivan's Barbershop in Cudahy, Wisconsin, sits in the historic location of the Sullivan Cigar Shop, founded in 1934 by Joe and Mary Salvatore. "Sullivan" gave the Salvatores cover in a time when having an Anglicized name was seen as an advantage. When the Ripsteins took over the space in 2021, they kept the old neon sign outside as a tribute not to Mr. Sullivan—there never was one here—but to the Salvatores. Ain't that America?

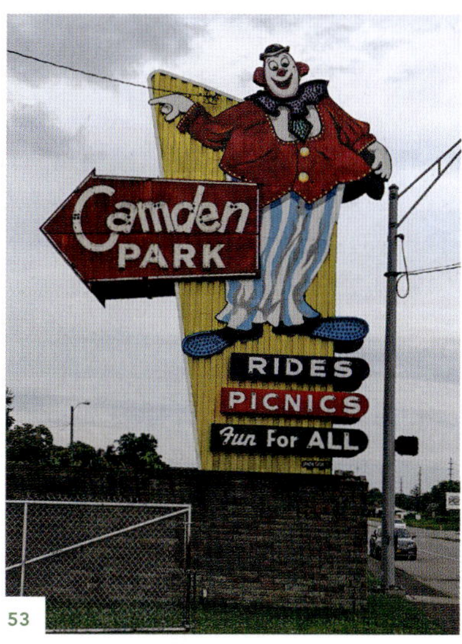

53

ON WITH THE SHOW

We have great movie houses in this region, but some of the most cinematic, if you will, are under the stars—the drive-ins are some of the nicest you will see in the country.

Several hundred drive-in theaters survive in America, a huge decline from their peak in 1958, when there were more than four thousand. Those that do survive are in it for the long haul.

The **Elm Road Triple Drive-In Theatre** (FIG. 54) in Warren, Ohio, opened in 1950 as a single screen, and it has since added two more, today brought to life by digital projection. (You tune in to a radio station to listen to the movie.) However, the movies on the screen face quite a challenge—they need to compete with this spectacular sign at the entrance! A columnist for the *New Castle News* once described the sign, said to date to 1962, as "perhaps the brightest marquee this side of Las Vegas."

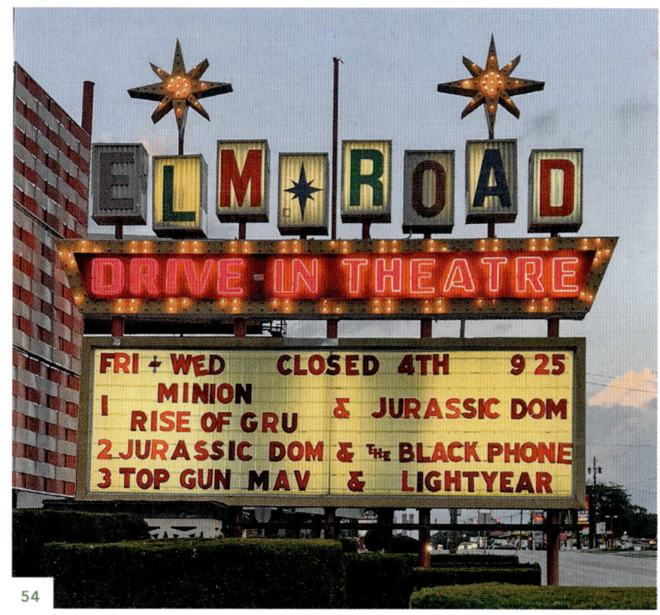

54

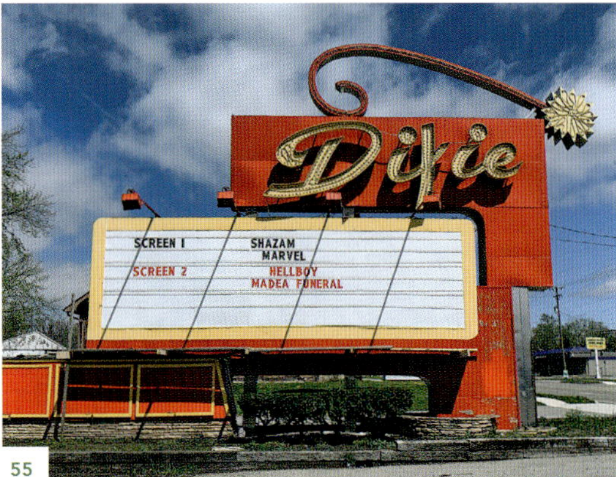

55

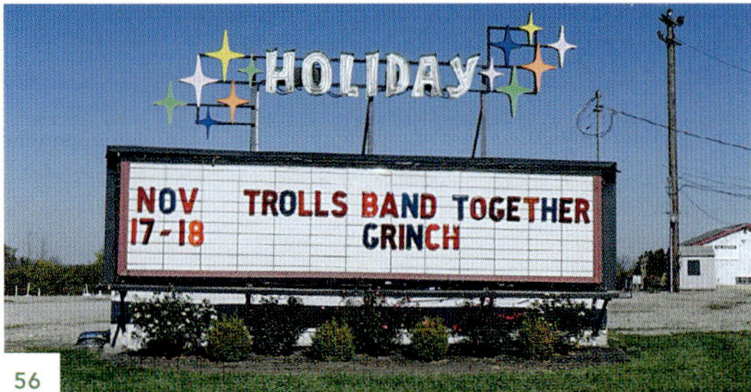

56

The **Dixie Twin Drive-In** (FIG. 55), a jewel of Dayton, Ohio, opened on Friday, July 12, 1957. It was state of the art from the start, with massive screens, RCA "hi-fidelity" sound, and a "beautiful modern snack bar," a newspaper ad enthused the day before. Hollywood hits shown that first night were *A Face in the Crowd*, starring Andy Griffith, and *Living It Up*, featuring Martin and Lewis. By 2014 the Dixie faced an existential challenge if it wanted to keep showing new releases. It was the D-word—*digital*.

The Dixie had to sink $200,000 into replacing the 35 mm film projectors that had served them well for so long, but sink it they did and now the digital system means they're not sunk. The sign was felled in a windstorm in 2024, and as of this writing, plans were in the works to build a new one in the spirit of the old.

The Holiday Auto Theatre (FIG. 56) opened in September 1948 in Hamilton, Ohio, and though its sign is a vintage delight, it also kept up with technology by upgrading to digital projection in 2013.

Some of the most famous marquees you'll see are in the Midwest—hard to get more iconic, for example, than the sweeping **Chicago Theatre**. But I wanted to give some special attention to one that's a little out of the way, but so deserves our love—the epic **Fowler Theatre** in Fowler, Indiana. The mix of color, art deco design, and light are sublime.

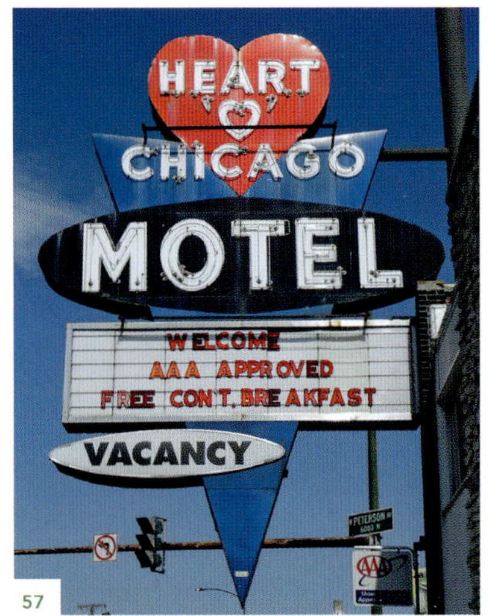

57

THE INN CROWD

Our quick survey of mom-and-pop motels in the region begins with one that has a lot of heart—and has enjoyed new life as a social-media showstopper.

Heart O' Chicago (FIG. 57) is one of the most dramatic survivors of Chicago's motel row. The sign was Insta friendly before that was a thing, with its gigantic heart and typographical quirkiness. Only folks with Grinch-sized hearts are resistant to its allures. The motel opened in 1957 and has been run by the same family ever since. Consistent and caring family ownership is so often the key to the endurance of these places. Owner Scott DeGraf told WGN-TV that the DeGraf family was initially hired to do the concrete work on the hotel, but when the developer bailed, they took over the project, figuring they'd keep it for a couple of years.

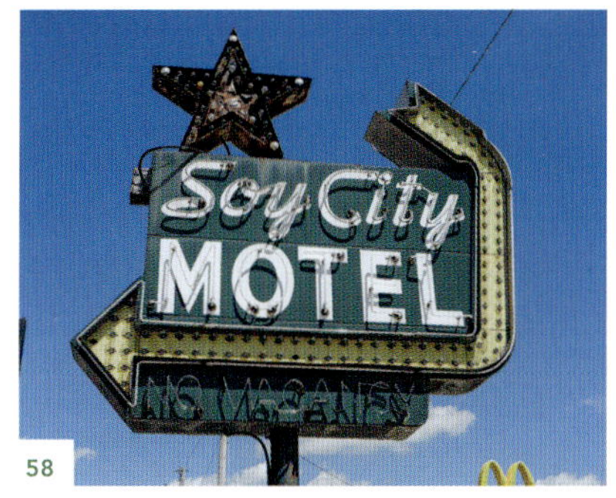

58

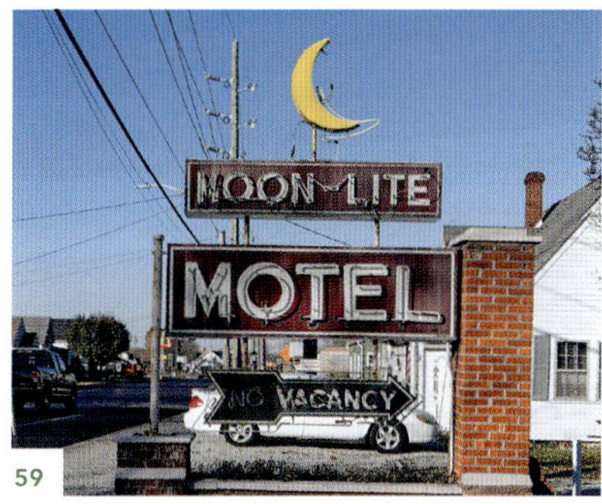

59

Mom-and-pop motels dot the region, and a fair share still have their original signs. I submit the **Soy City Motel** (FIG. 58) in Decatur, Illinois, and the **Moon Lite Motel** (FIG. 59) in Versailles, Indiana.

SWEET STOPS

Some of America's finest ice-cream parlors await you in the Midwest. Let's not worry too much about calories—hey, road-trip eats don't count, right?—and begin our tour.

"By never changing, we'll always remain different." That's long been the credo at this national treasure: **Lagomarcino's** (FIG. 60), a wondrous ice-cream parlor and confectionery shop in Moline, Illinois, and Davenport, Iowa. The business was founded in 1908 by Italian immigrant Angelo Lagomarcino, and it remains in caring family hands to this day, with Angelo's granddaughter Beth Lagomarcino at the helm.

Margie's Candies (FIG. 61) in Chicago had been in business since 1921. Nearby Milwaukee Avenue is nicknamed the "Hipster Highway" for all the young people rushing past on their bicycles. The neighborhood keeps getting fancier—and pricier. But Margie's remains impervious to those changes. Indeed, it is so beloved that the new ownership has secured Margie's place at this corner for a long time, and those hipsters who cycle by have been known to stop in and savor the offerings of this authentic and charming vestige of an earlier Chicago.

Change will certainly not come from within. Margie's still has its vintage candy display cases, comfortable leather booths, old-timey lamps, and long-silenced tabletop jukeboxes. The place would look very familiar to Paul McCartney and Ringo Starr,

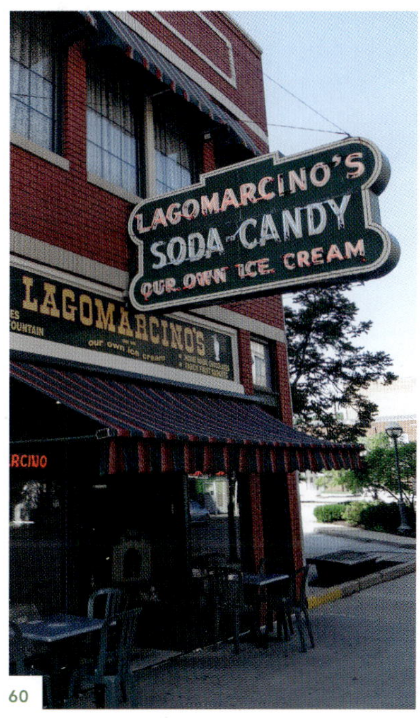

60

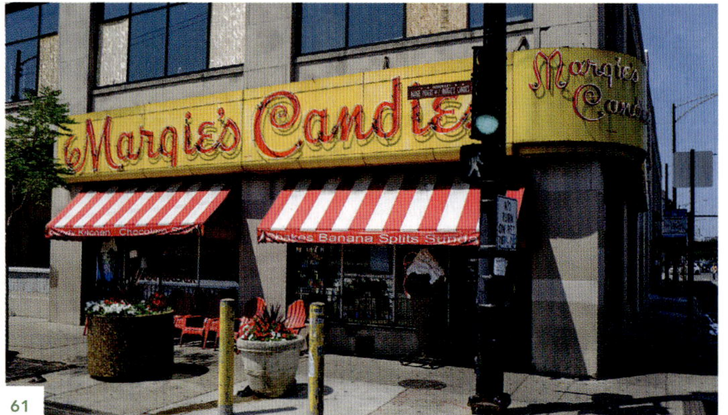

61

should they ever stop in again, for the Beatles famously visited Margie's in 1965 after a concert at Comiskey Park.

Margie Poulos is who the business was renamed for, after she married George Poulos, the son of the founder of the original shop, called the Security Sweet Shop. Today, the shop is owned by their son, Peter, who grew up here. His cradle was concealed by a candy display case. It seems like nothing will change at Margie's for a good long time.

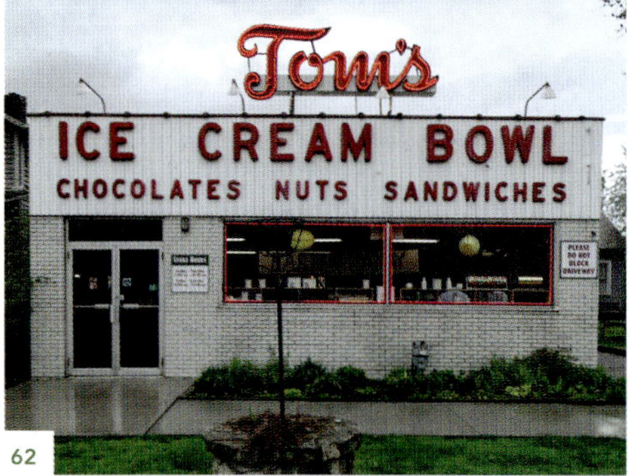

62

Zanesville, Ohio, is known the world over for its pottery. The earth is rich with clay in these parts. But if you picked up *USA Today* on July 24, 1998, you would have learned that Zanesville had another claim to fame—it was ranked the number one place in America to get a scoop of ice cream, and the magical source of such sweet pleasure is **Tom's Ice Cream Bowl** (FIG. 62). Two cousins, Jack and Tom, opened what began as Jack Hemmer Ice Cream in 1948, moving to this spot in 1950. Tom Mirgon bought out his cousin's interest, and by 1957, the shop had assumed its present name. Bill Sullivan took over in 1984, but it's very much as Tom left it—the ice cream still homemade, the nuts freshly roasted.

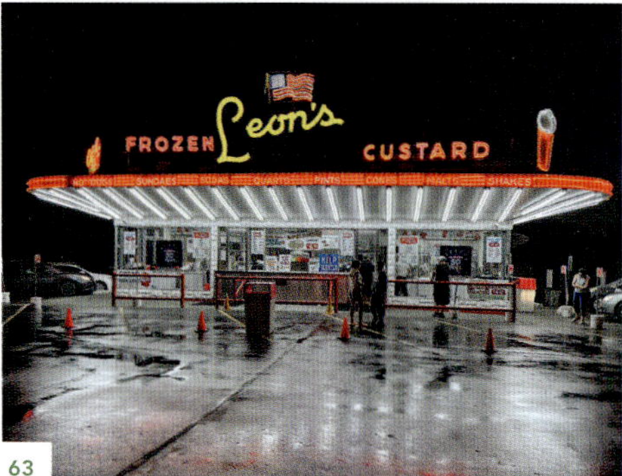

63

In Milwaukee, residents can enjoy some of the best frozen custard anywhere. The popular dish has one of its most cinematic dispensaries at **Leon's Custard** (FIG. 63), which opened in 1942 (this building came along a little later) and is still going strong. I visited after a summer thundershower let up, giving the parking lot a romantic glassy sheen that makes a photographer's heart skip a beat.

For Greek immigrants, one of the most reliable if difficult paths to carving a niche in America was the restaurant business. Greek diners are a well-known and celebrated phenomenon, but the confectionary trade—and paths to ownership of soda fountains and ice-cream shops—also proved a viable conduit to the middle class.

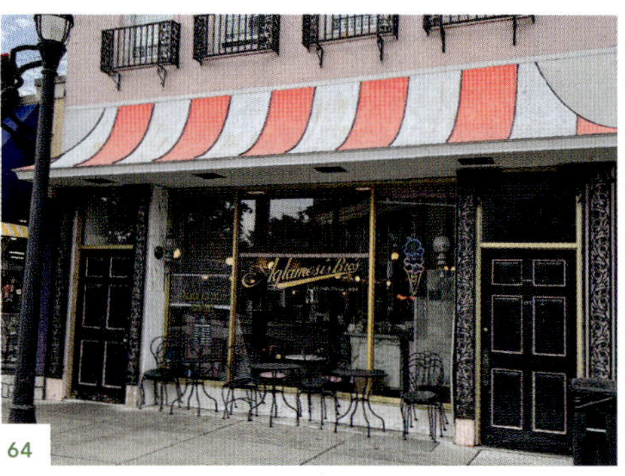
64

With experience in the candy trade, Thomas and Nicholas Aglamesis got into the ice-cream business in the Cincinnati area in 1908. Their shop, **Aglamesis Bros.** (FIG. 64), opened in Oakley Square in 1913. Still in the family, it is the very picture of what an ice-cream parlor should be, from the tile floors to the small, oval marble-top tables and the fancy lamps.

No conversation about Cincinnati-area ice cream is complete without a nod to **Graeter's** (FIG. 65), which traces its roots back to 1870 and has grown into a small chain of ice-cream shops—and you can also find it at supermarkets around the country.

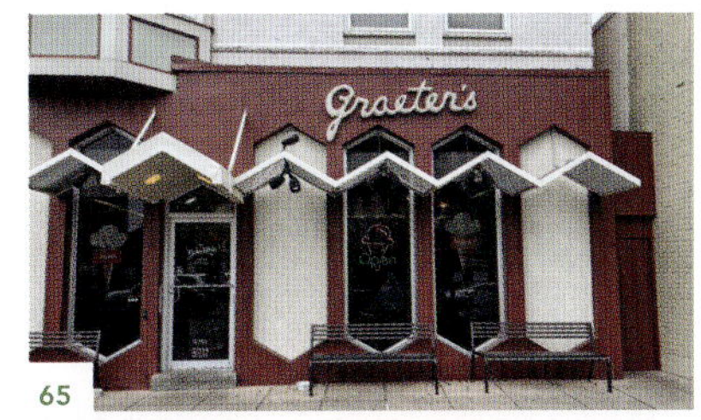

65

Similar praise can be heaped on **Trecaso's Mary Coyle** (FIG. 66) in Akron, Ohio, which is known for its ice cream but offers Italian cuisine, too. It traces back to the original Mary Coyle Ice Cream, an Akron institution founded in 1937, with multiple locales at one point. Coyle herself and her husband, Walter, who started the business, moved to Arizona in 1951 and began a Mary Coyle shop there that recently closed. This particular store, on Highland Square, opened in 1947 and was purchased in 1987 by Michael Trecaso.

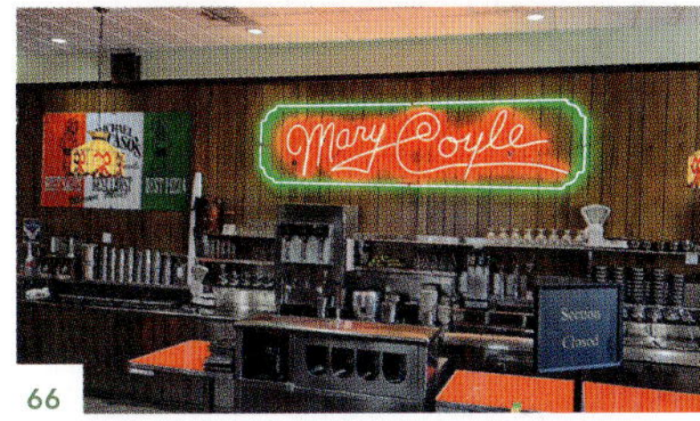

66

In Old Brooklyn, a neighborhood of Cleveland, Ohio, there exists a sign relic from a time when the Peanuts gang created by Charles M. Schulz were promoting bakeries and products affiliated with Interstate Brands. The **Bakery Thrift Shop** (FIG. 67) here is long gone—this building now holds a day-care center—but the yellow sign featuring Snoopy and Woodstock was left behind, which is something of a gift for the kids.

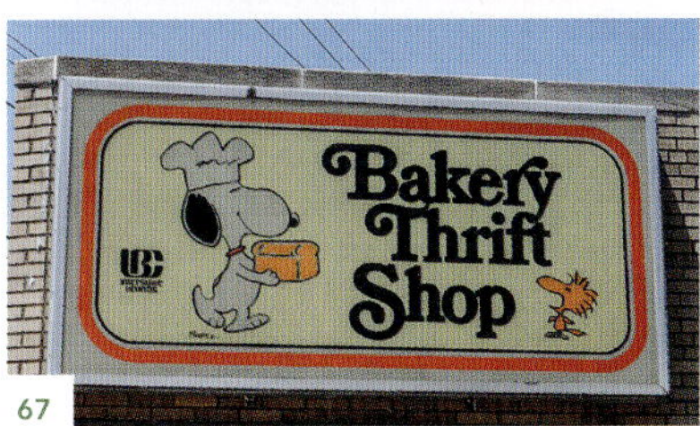

67

CHEERS!

The bars of the Midwest are legion and convey a certain comforting neighborly image—a sign for Old Style swaying slightly outside, and a wooden bar, leather stools, a flowing tap, and a good game on the tube inside. Our first visit, however, is to a spot that's a little swankier, but still oh so Chicago.

For me, no trip to Chicago is complete without a visit to the **Green Mill Cocktail Lounge** (FIG. 68). The Green Mill has a long history, with roots as a roadhouse and then as the fabled Green Mill Gardens. That earlier Green Mill had an actual green mill on its roof—a play on the Moulin Rouge, or "Red Windmill," in Paris. Today, the pedestrian gets to enjoy the sumptuous sign of the cocktail lounge.

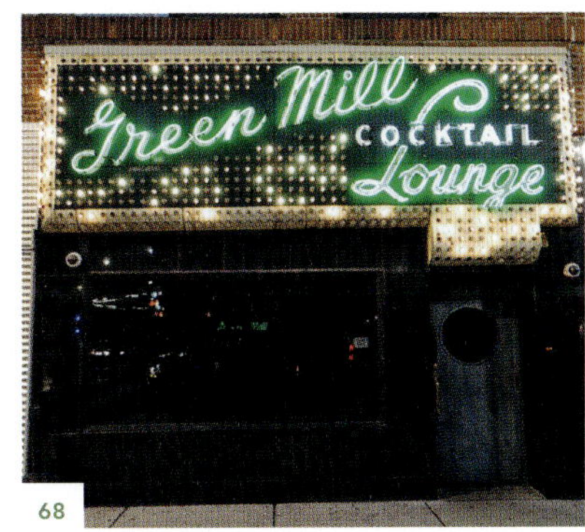

68

Inside, the music lover can slip into a jazz club that's been restored to its Prohibition-vintage splendor, a time when legends of jazz such as Billie Holiday are said to have haunted the place. Mob lore—Al Capone, in particular, is honored with a booth inside—is tied to the Green Mill saga, too. Heroically and presciently

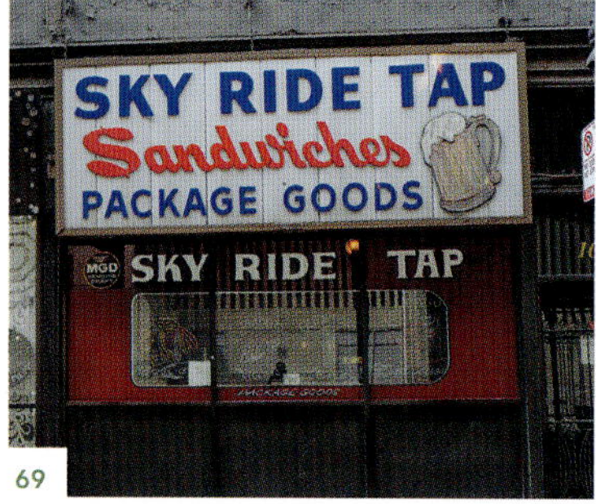

69

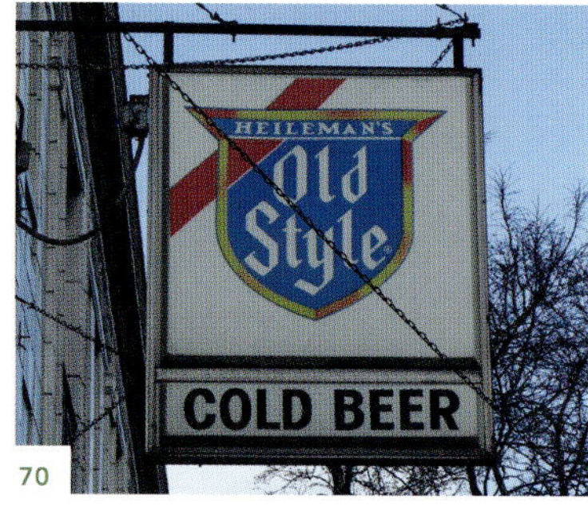

70

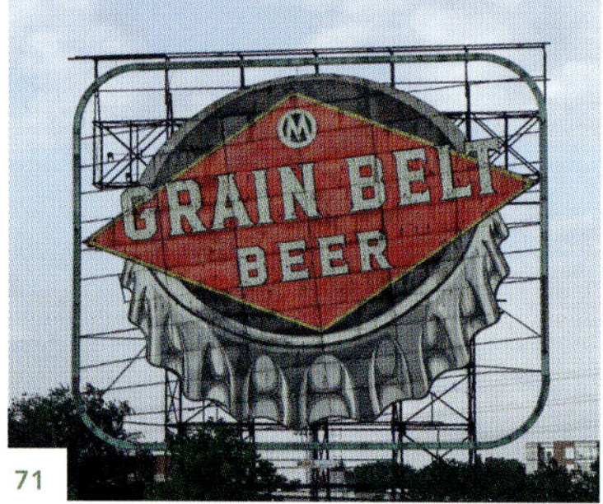

71

restored by Dave Jemilo in the 1980s, when the lounge and the Uptown neighborhood were going through rough times, the Green Mill is today an international destination.

You might think the name **Sky-Ride Tap** (FIG. 69) has something to do with the clanking elevated train up above, but this Chicago dive bar honors a famous ride at the 1933 World's Fair in Chicago. In 1973, Kyriakos "Carl" Damianides took it over and has been here since, keeping this old-school treasure of Chicago's Loop alive through endless ups and downs—and all that clatter from up above. In other words, it's been one heck of a ride.

The **Old Style** (FIG. 70) beer sign can serve as a stand-in for countless Chicago taverns. The signs, though not as numerous as they once were, dangle from dives across Chicagoland. Old Style seems to be one and the same with Chicago, though the beer brand started in Wisconsin, moved to Illinois, before returning to Wisconsin. Beer historian Liz Garibay, speaking to Chicago's WBEZ radio, credits Old Style's longtime Chicago Cubs sponsorship and an aggressive program to give away the signs (even install them) in the 1970s as among the factors that led to their iconographic reach. Given how old they are, I'd dare to call them endangered, a laughable concept not so long ago.

Iconic branded-beer signage pops up elsewhere in the Midwest: Consider Grain Belt beer. Like Old Style in Chicago, you'll spot the signs outside bars here in a blink-and-you'll-miss-it way. But there's no missing the gigantic **Grain Belt Sign** (FIG. 71) next to the Hennepin Avenue Bridge, a treasure of Minneapolis since 1941. It displays a bottle cap on a sign that's 40 feet tall and 50 feet wide. After a long period of dormancy, the sign was repaired, neon tubing swapped out for LED, restoring the nightly spectacle in the sky.

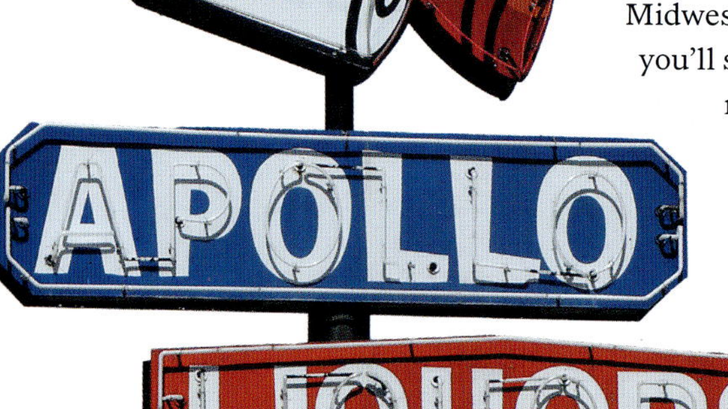

72

On a trip to Minnesota, I had to get to Austin to see **Apollo Liquors** (FIG. 72). The shop, which grew into a chain, was the brainchild of Nick Kolas, a Greek immigrant who founded the store in the aftermath of the Apollo 11 mission in 1969. The Apollo name honors the historic lunar landing and Kolas's Greek heritage.

SPOTLIGHT:

AMERICAN SIGN MUSEUM

You like signs? You like history? You like a good museum? The **American Sign Museum** in the Camp Washington neighborhood of Cincinnati delivers on all fronts and is the best and really only place in the world to see elements of everything being explored in this book in such abundance, good condition, and curatorial excellence. The museum was founded in 1999 by Tod Swormstedt, whose great-grandfather was the founding editor of *Sign of the Times*, the magazine that chronicles the sign business in America that Swormstedt himself would one day edit. Swormstedt took the museum idea from conception to the grand museum that it is today, with spectacular experiences including the Main Street area, which gives you a dizzying feel for American downtowns at the height of neon and incandescence. Perhaps the grandest sign is the restored Holiday Inn "Great Sign" that greets you in the parking lot. Holiday Inn, the motel chain that was founded in 1952, ordered these signs removed in 1982, and not one survives in the wild. The one here (and another at the grand Henry Ford Museum in Detroit) is worth traveling a great distance to admire in person.

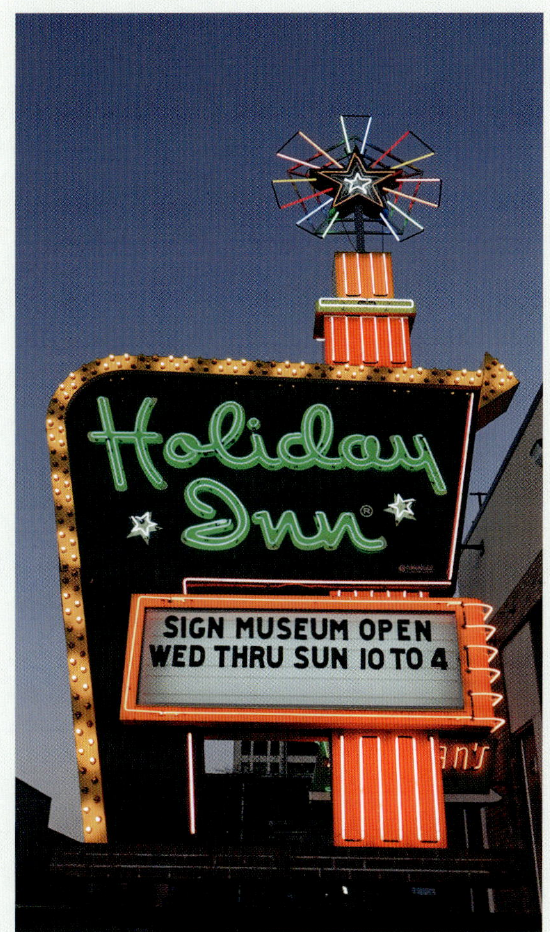

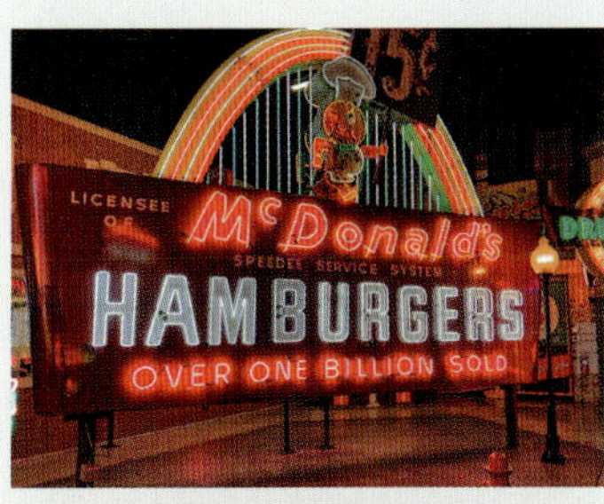

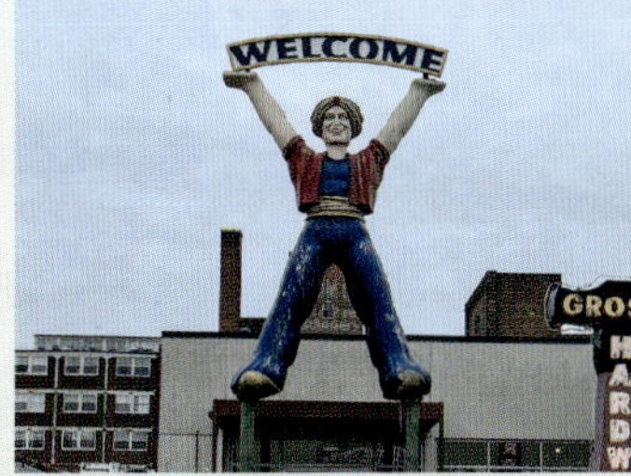

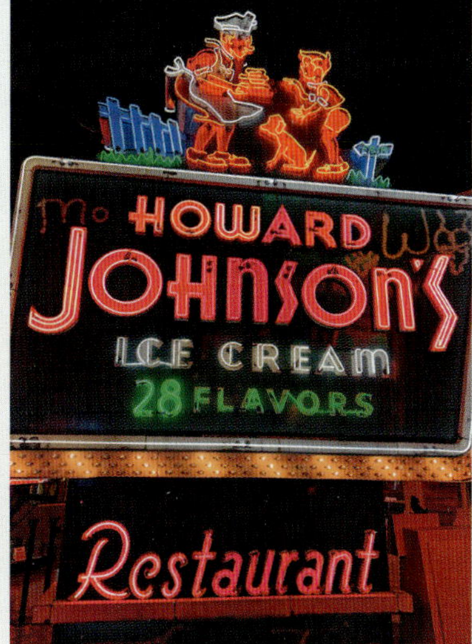

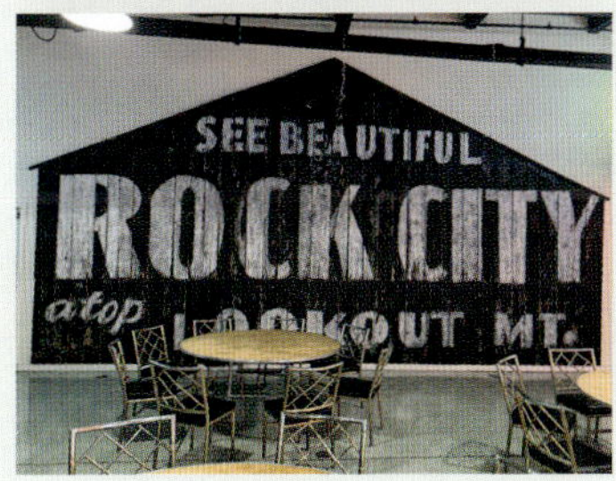

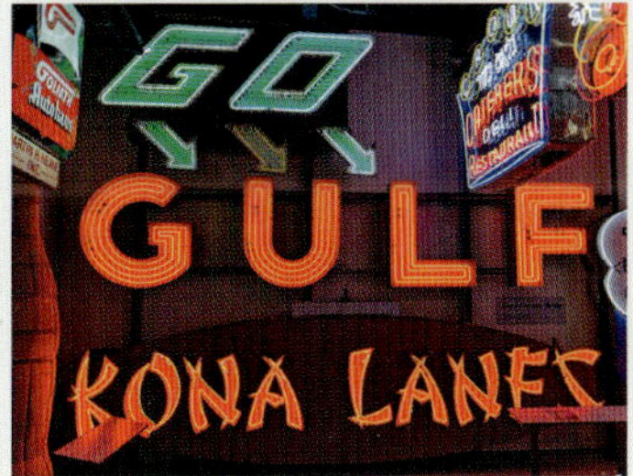

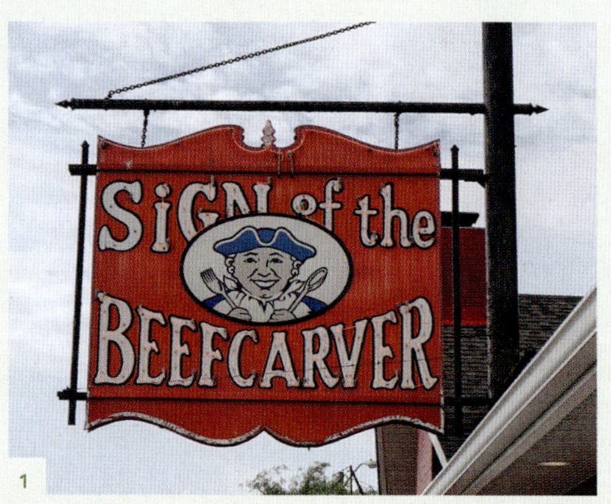

1

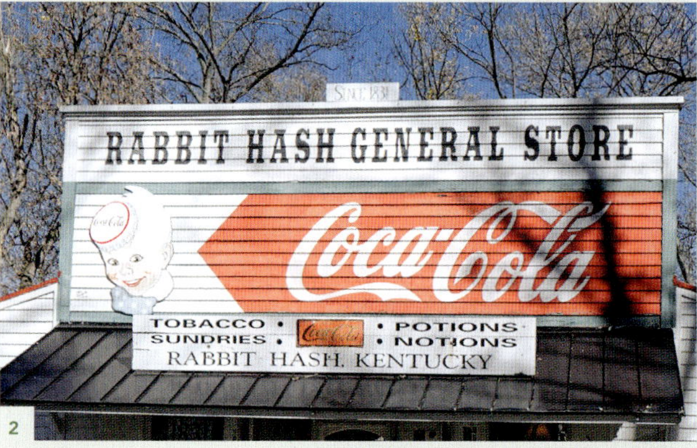

2

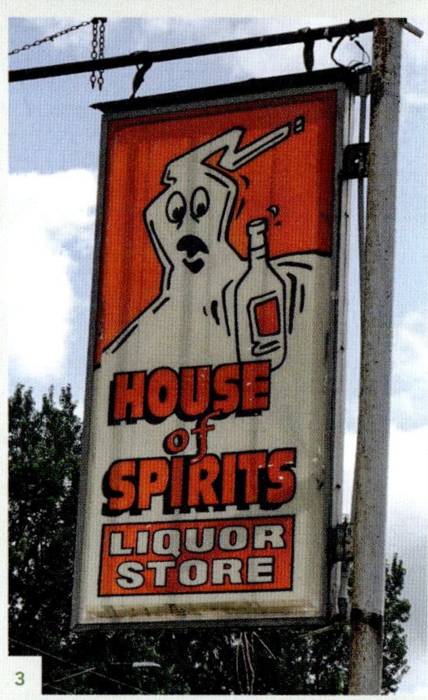

3

SIGNS TO SEEK OUT

These are a few more stops I hope you'll enjoy photographing.

1. Sign of the Beefcarver, Royal Oak, Michigan
2. Rabbit Hash General Store, Burlington, Kentucky
3. House of Spirits, Loyal, Wisconsin
4. Jolly Pirate Donuts, Grove City, Ohio
5. Dellert's Wallpaper & Paint Co., Springfield, Illinois
6. Modern Times, Minneapolis, Minnesota
7. Schlitz globe, Milwaukee, Wisconsin
8. Bonnie Doon Drive-In, Mishawaka, Indiana
9. Leaning Tower of Niles, Niles, Illinois
10. Dairy Land, Mansfield, Ohio
11. Del's Popcorn Shop, Decatur, Illinois

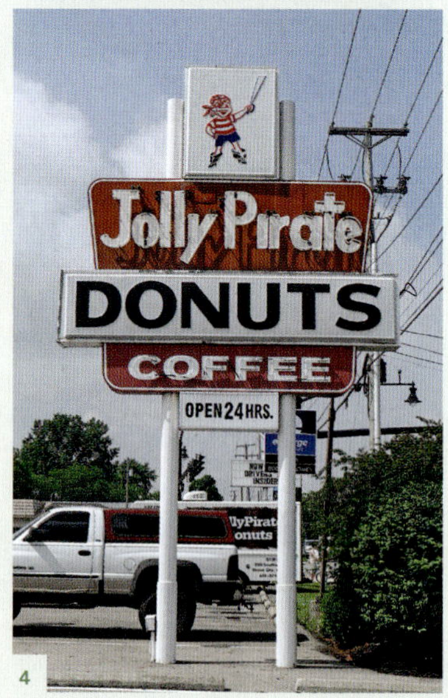

4

Dellerts
WALLPAPER PAINTS
WE HAVE
POOL
PAINT
5

MODERN
TIMES
BREAKFAST
LUNCH
COFFEE·TEA
ESPRESSO
ORGANIC·VEGAN
VEGETARIAN
FAIR TRADE
CARNIVORE
TAKEOUT
HOURS
6

CHLITZ
7

Bonnie
Doon
DRIVE-IN
OPEN
8

9

DAIRY
LAND
10

Del's
POPCORN
SHOP
11

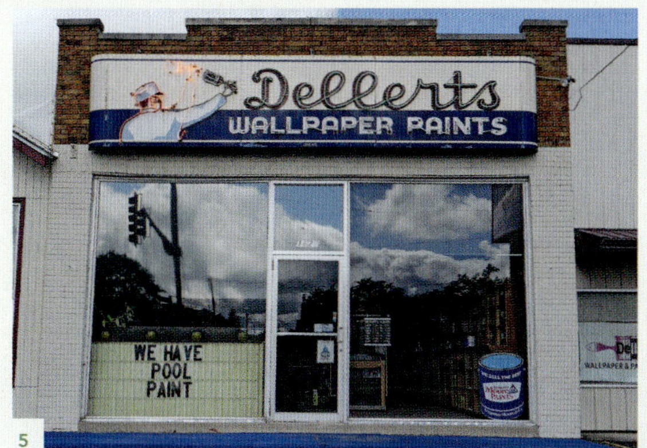

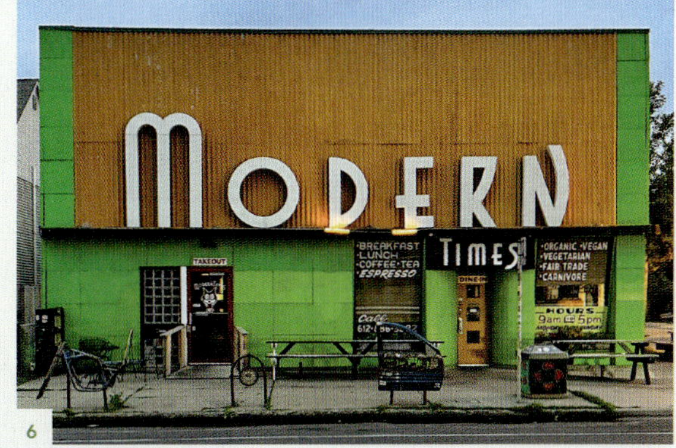

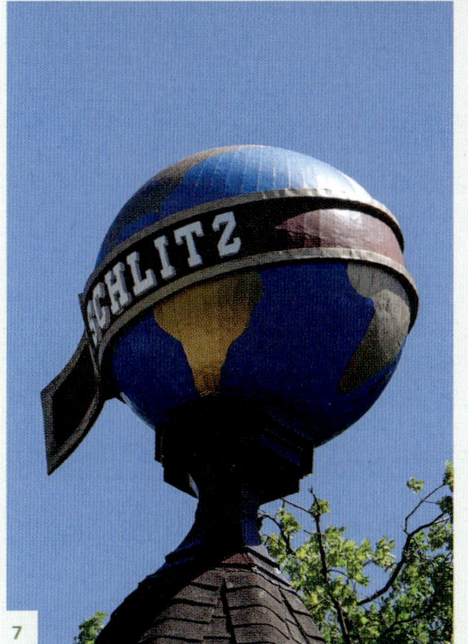

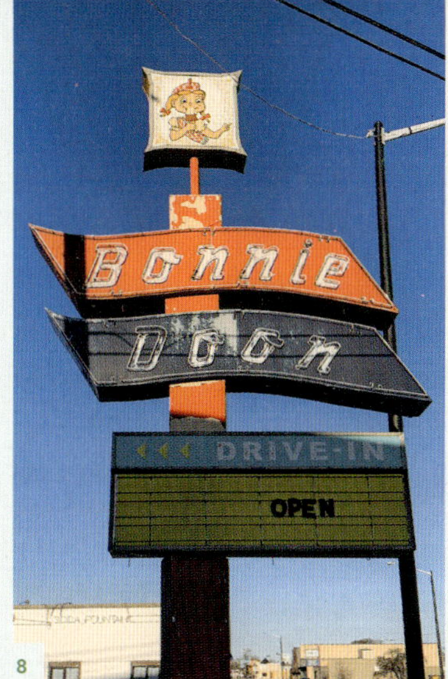

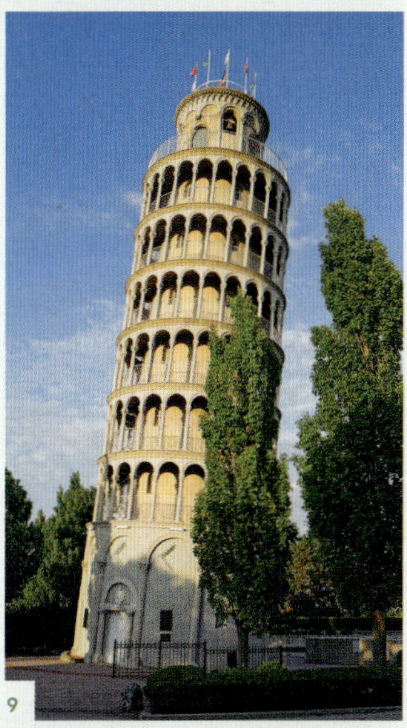

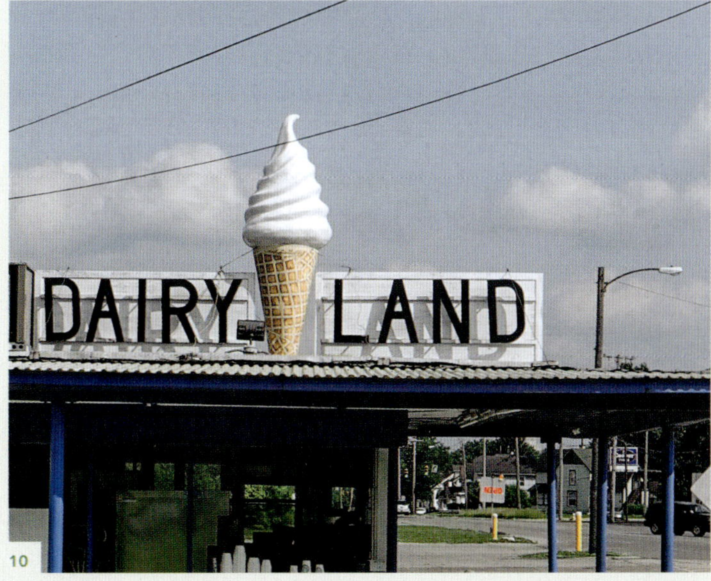

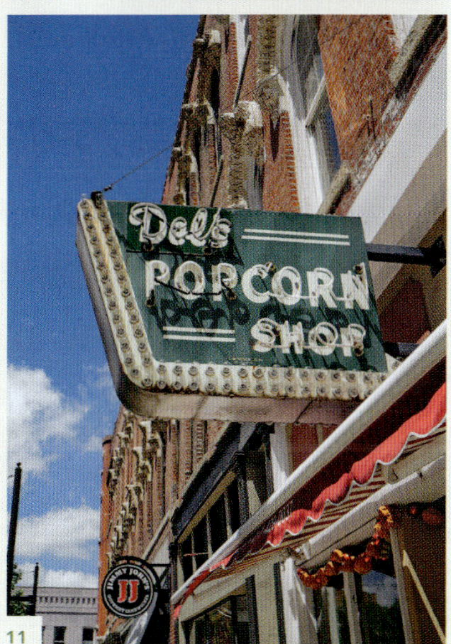

SOUTH CENTRAL

TEXAS · OKLAHOMA · ARKANSAS · LOUISIANA

Come along as we meander the Gulf of Mexico from New Orleans to Galveston, explore deep in the heart of Texas, and make our way across one of the most vivid stretches of the Mother Road, Route 66, in search of giant cowboys, oilmen, as well as Cadillacs and Volkswagen Bugs buried in the Amarillo earth. We'll also revisit relics of our retail past, from a Suncoast video store to a surprising survivor from the earliest days of McDonald's, where fried apple pies have been swapped for kolaches. Oh, and we're doing some shopping at the world's smallest Buc-ee's and a Prada store far from Milan, though your money is no good at either.

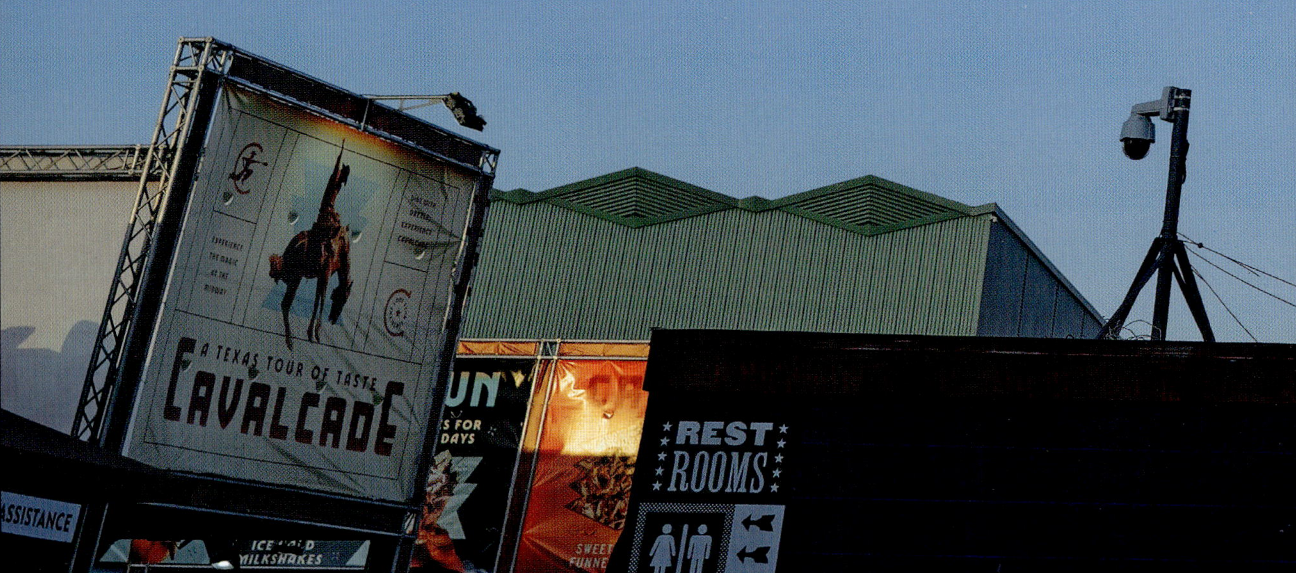

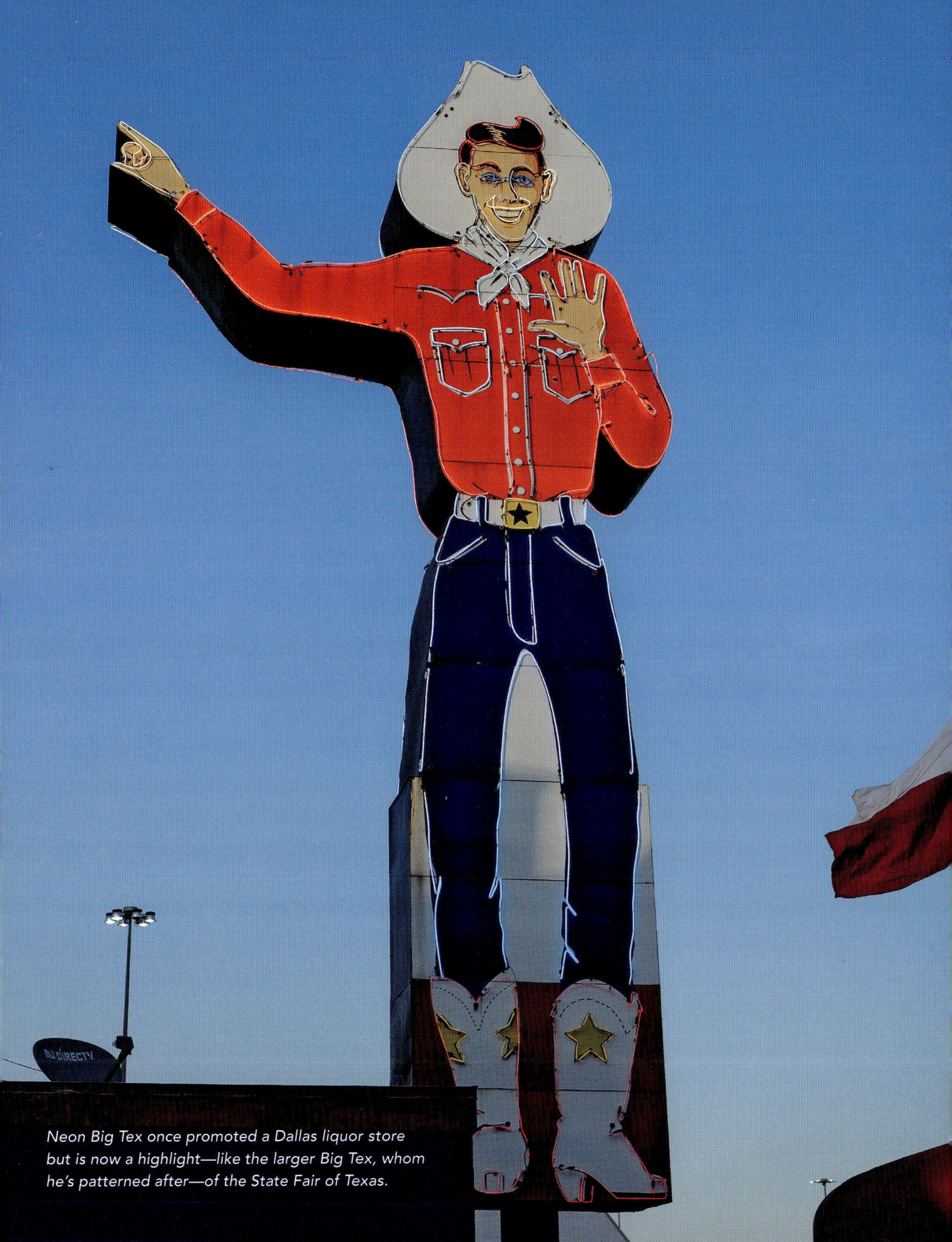

Neon Big Tex once promoted a Dallas liquor store but is now a highlight—like the larger Big Tex, whom he's patterned after—of the State Fair of Texas.

ROADSIDE QUIRKS

The American roadside is teeming with unusual finds, and these are among my favorites. Some of these beauties have serious competition from the stunning, vast landscape but more than hold their own. Where to start? Tulsa, that's where, where we've hit oil!

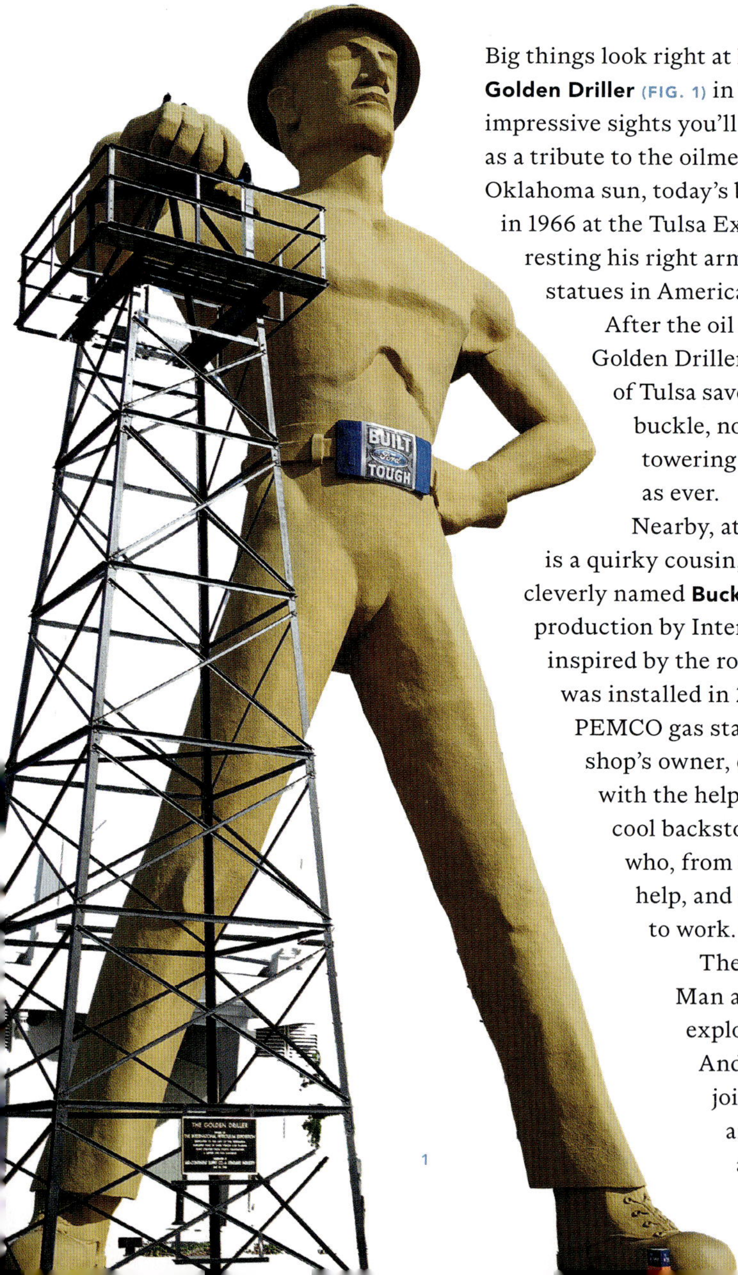

Big things look right at home on the skyline of Route 66. **The Golden Driller** (FIG. 1) in Tulsa, Oklahoma, is one of the most impressive sights you'll see on any American road trip. Built as a tribute to the oilmen who toiled under the unforgiving Oklahoma sun, today's bare-chested Golden Driller was installed in 1966 at the Tulsa Expo Center. Standing 76 feet tall and resting his right arm on an oil derrick, he is one of the tallest statues in America and is Oklahoma's State Monument.

After the oil company that built him went bust, the Golden Driller's prospects dried up, too, but the city of Tulsa saved him (stamping its name on his belt buckle, now covered up by a Ford ad), and his towering bulk and stern visage are as impressive as ever.

Nearby, at **Buck Atom's Cosmic Curios** on Route 66, is a quirky cousin, a Muffler Man space cowboy! The cleverly named **Buck Atom** (FIG. 2) is not from the original production by International Fiberglass, but a creation inspired by the roadside legacy of his older brethren. He was installed in 2019. The attraction sits in a repurposed PEMCO gas station, where Mary Beth Babcock, the shop's owner, executed her out-of-this-world vision with the help of builder Mark Cline and gave Buck a cool backstory—he's a cowboy kidnapped by aliens who, from outer space, saw that Route 66 needed help, and so he landed at the old gas station to get to work. It's working.

The Gemini Giant, the astronaut Muffler Man along Route 66 in Illinois, now has space-exploring siblings of sorts! (See page 136.) And a partner, too, as **Stella Atom** (FIG. 3) joined Buck at Cosmic Curios in June 2024, and Meadow Gold Mac, holding an axe, across the street.

1

Buck, Stella, and Mac are new in these parts, joining familiar faces like the ever-smiling **Blue Whale of Catoosa** (FIG. 4) in Oklahoma. (Like Stella and Buck, the whale has a hat, too—in his case, a cute cap!) This friendly whale sits in a charming sylvan oasis, resting beside a fishing hole. The 80-foot-long concrete structure was built as a gesture of love by Hugh Davis, a nature enthusiast and curator of the Tulsa Zoo, for his wife, Zelta, a thoughtful anniversary present in 1972 for a woman who loved whale figurines. Davis envisioned the whale as the centerpiece of his family's personal land of frolic. Still, outsiders caught on—it's hard to miss a giant blue whale—and for a time, Davis turned the property into a small amusement park, complete with a petting zoo, concession stand, and lifeguards to watch swimmers.

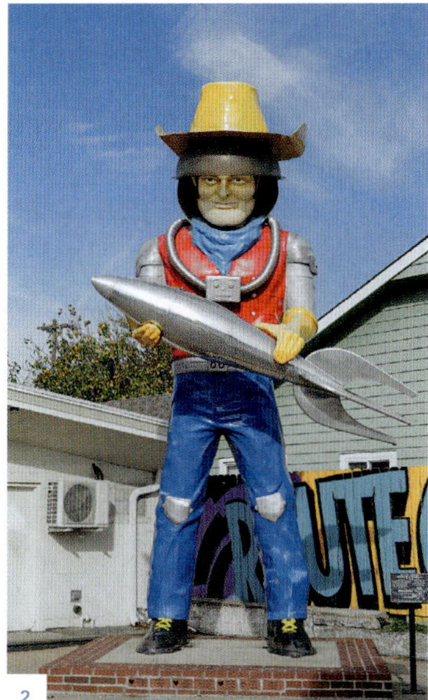

2

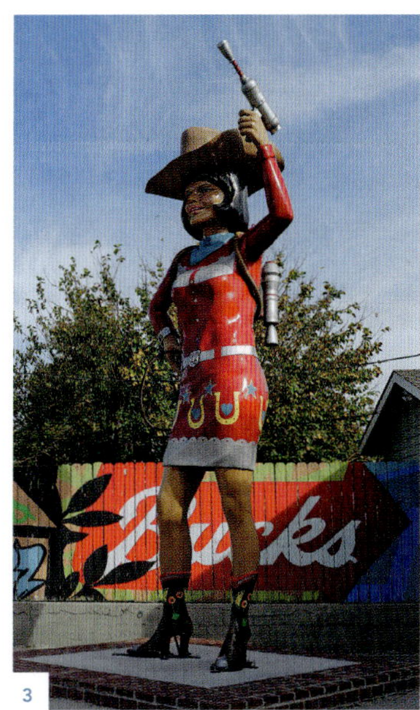

3

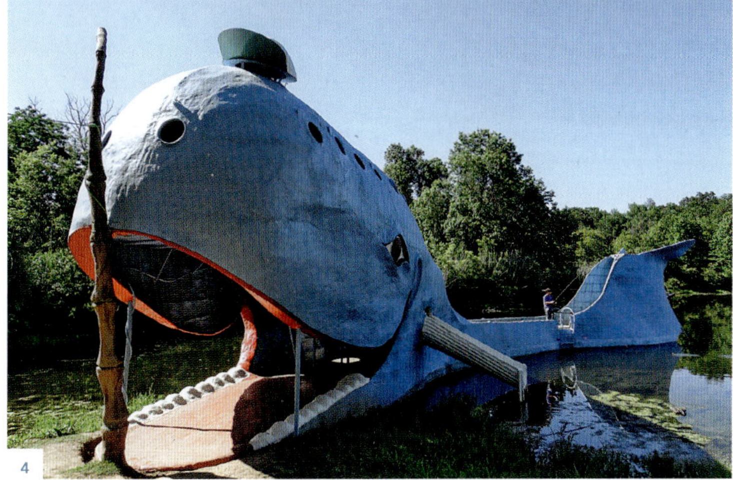

4

Soon, the whole world was hip to it, as the Blue Whale appeared in travel guides and proved an irresistible pull-off point, its fame only growing in the age of social media. Today, Catoosa owns the Blue Whale, and there are plans to build attractions around it, like an RV park and even an ice-cream stand to encourage tourists to stay (and spend) for a while once they've snapped the obligatory pictures and selfies.

We head to the Texas panhandle for some classic Route 66 lore at the **Leaning Tower of Britten** (FIG. 5). Fear not, this is not a slow-motion engineering disaster waiting for a stiff wind to topple it but a marketing coup on a stretch of Route 66 where the desert landscape has long inspired creative expression. This was once an unremarkable and perfectly upright water tower until businessman Ralph Britten purchased it, moved it to promote his truck stop, and tilted it a mere 10 degrees, taking it from banal

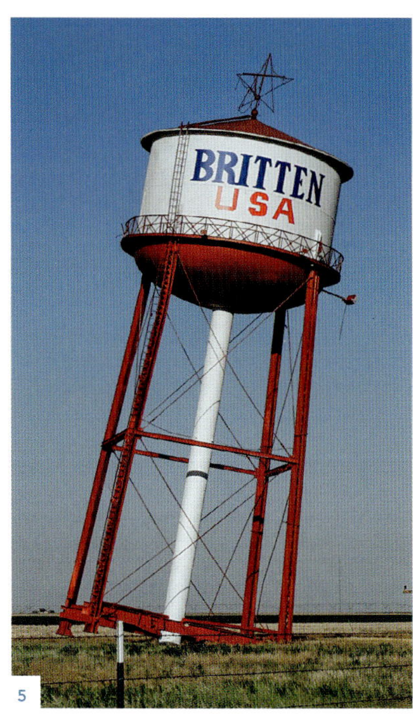

5

to brilliant—and drawing in bucks from curious (and alarmed) motorists here in Groom, Texas.

The Texas horizon has inspired many artists to bury cars in the dirt. **Cadillac Ranch** (FIG. 8) in Amarillo was created by three artists who were members of the Ant Farm art group in 1974 and bankrolled by local millionaire Stanley Marsh 3. The cars perpetually change as the old Cadillacs wither from the influence of nature and humans. Their colors morph with every encounter with a spray-paint-can-holding admirer, contributing to an artwork you can shape—ever so ephemerally.

Nearby, the **Slug Bug Ranch** offers a squat parody of the Cadillac Ranch, but with vintage Volkswagen Beetles buried at 45-degree angles. After a long stay in tiny and more remote Conway, Texas, the bugs have crawled to Amarillo, closer to the Caddies and in a more prominent locale, too, by The Big Texan (see page 173).

Route 66 completists would be wise to stop at the **Route 66 Museum** in Elk City, Oklahoma, teeming with exhibits, neon signs, and more to give you a great feel for the road. (More signage can be enjoyed at the **Route 66 Neon Park** in Tulsa, and, along the entire length, worthy museums, sign parks, and other curated attractions exist—keep an eye out.)

PIXAR'S ROUTE 66

If Route 66 is America's Main Street, then Adrian, Texas, is the heart of downtown. Here is the aptly named **Midpoint Cafe** (FIG. 7). Adrian is heralded as the midpoint on Route 66 between Chicago and Santa Monica and is a requisite stop for children of the Mother Road. Actual kids may get their biggest kick on Route 66 here because the Midpoint Cafe was the inspiration for Flo's V8 Cafe in the 2006 Pixar film *Cars* and the real-life Flo was Fran Hauser, the cafe's owner, who helped put Adrian on the map by embracing its cartographical kismet.

Back east a bit, in Shamrock, Texas, you'll find the **Conoco Tower Station & U-Drop Inn Cafe** (FIG. 6), a beloved Route 66 stop that appears in *Cars* as Ramone's Body Shop. (See the Jack Rabbit Trading Post and the Hackberry General Store on pages 193 and 201 for additional sources of inspiration for the film.)

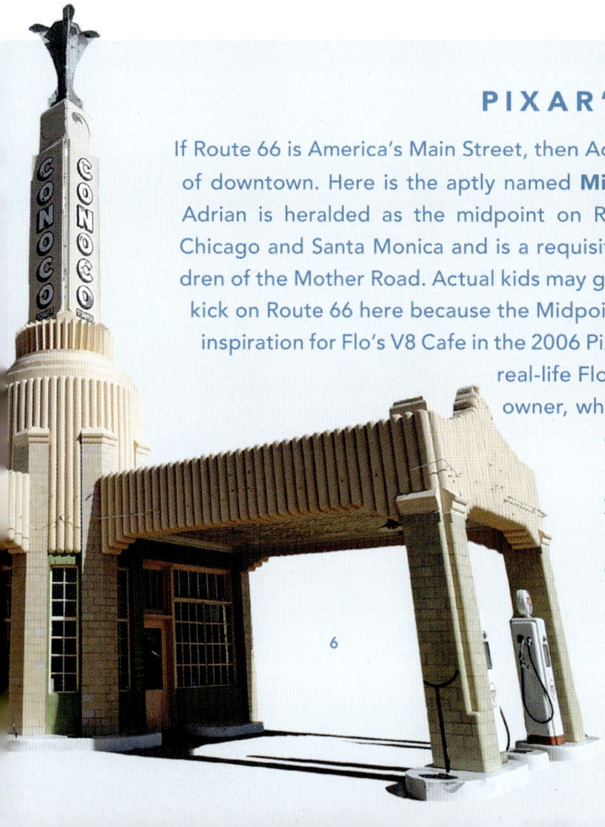

6

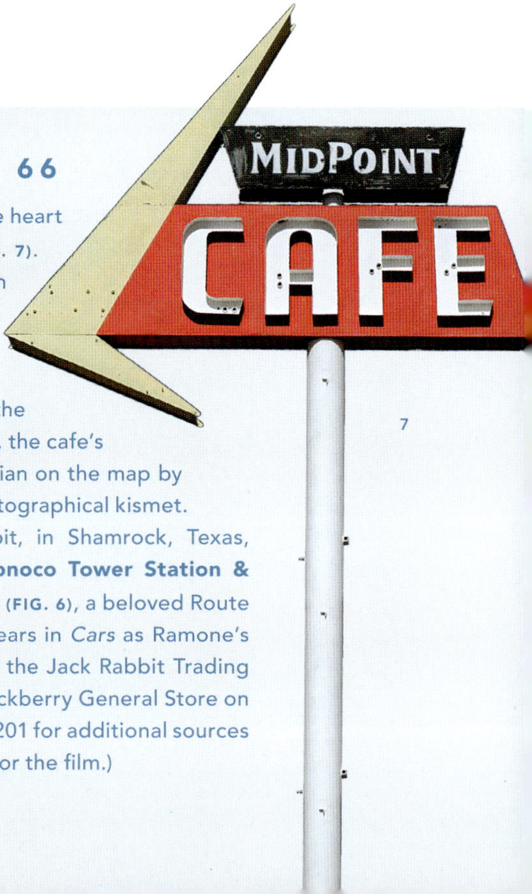

7

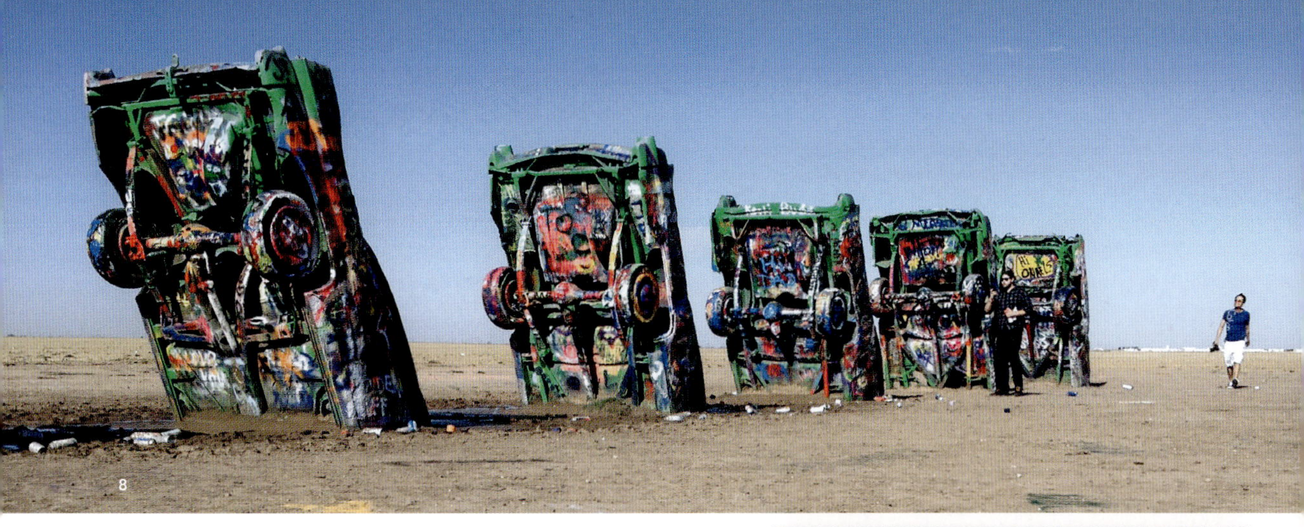

8

Pops 66 is a roadside attraction of the first order and a reminder that a stop needn't be classic to be a classic. Pops opened in 2007, fairly new by Route 66 standards, but the cantilevered gas-pump canopy that juts out of the showroom, which sells all manner of soda pop, is an awesome sight. So is the 66-foot-tall spiral pop-bottle statue in Arcadia, Oklahoma, whose LED lighting puts on a nightly roadside show.

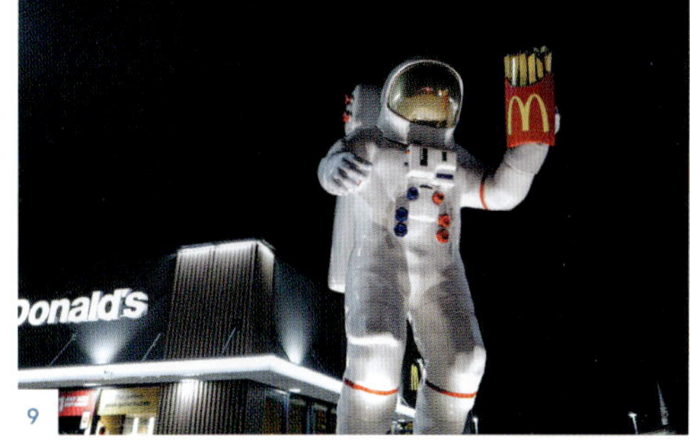

9

We leave Route 66 (for now) and drive across the Lone Star State to the outskirts of Houston, home to NASA's Mission Control Center. I can't recommend the NASA tour enough, but for the fan of roadside kitsch, make sure your car enters the orbit of the Nassau Bay **McDonald's Apollo Astronaut** (FIG. 9) near the Johnson Space Center. That's where you can take a picture of this giant astronaut.

In Austin, **Light Bulb Idea Man** (FIG. 10) once lit the way for the Light Bulb Shop. After the shop closed, DoubleTake, a charity thrift shop, reused it, a bright idea for a secondhand shop. The shop closed in 2024, and the charity it supported was expanding into the space. One can only hope that Light Bulb Idea Man will have a bright future.

Nearby is a super cute rooftop mascot for **Jerry's Artarama** (FIG. 11). Lil Jerry, as he's called, is a stand-in for the beloved founder of the discount-art-supply chain, Jerry Goldstein, who opened the first location on New York's Long Island in 1968, with the goal of bringing affordable and high-quality art supplies to everybody. Jerry got into painting to help kick his smoking habit, picking up the brush instead of a cigarette.

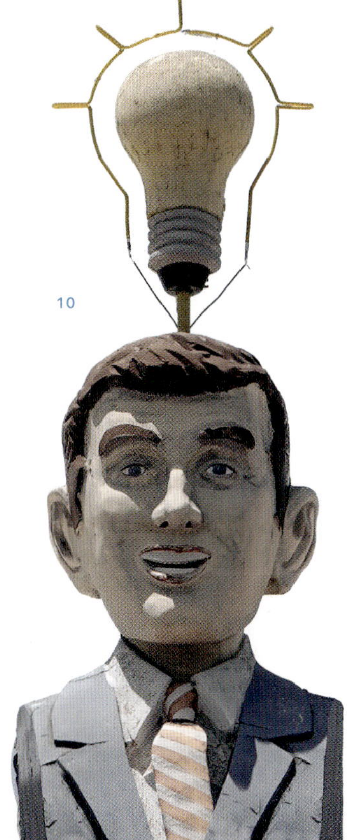

10

11

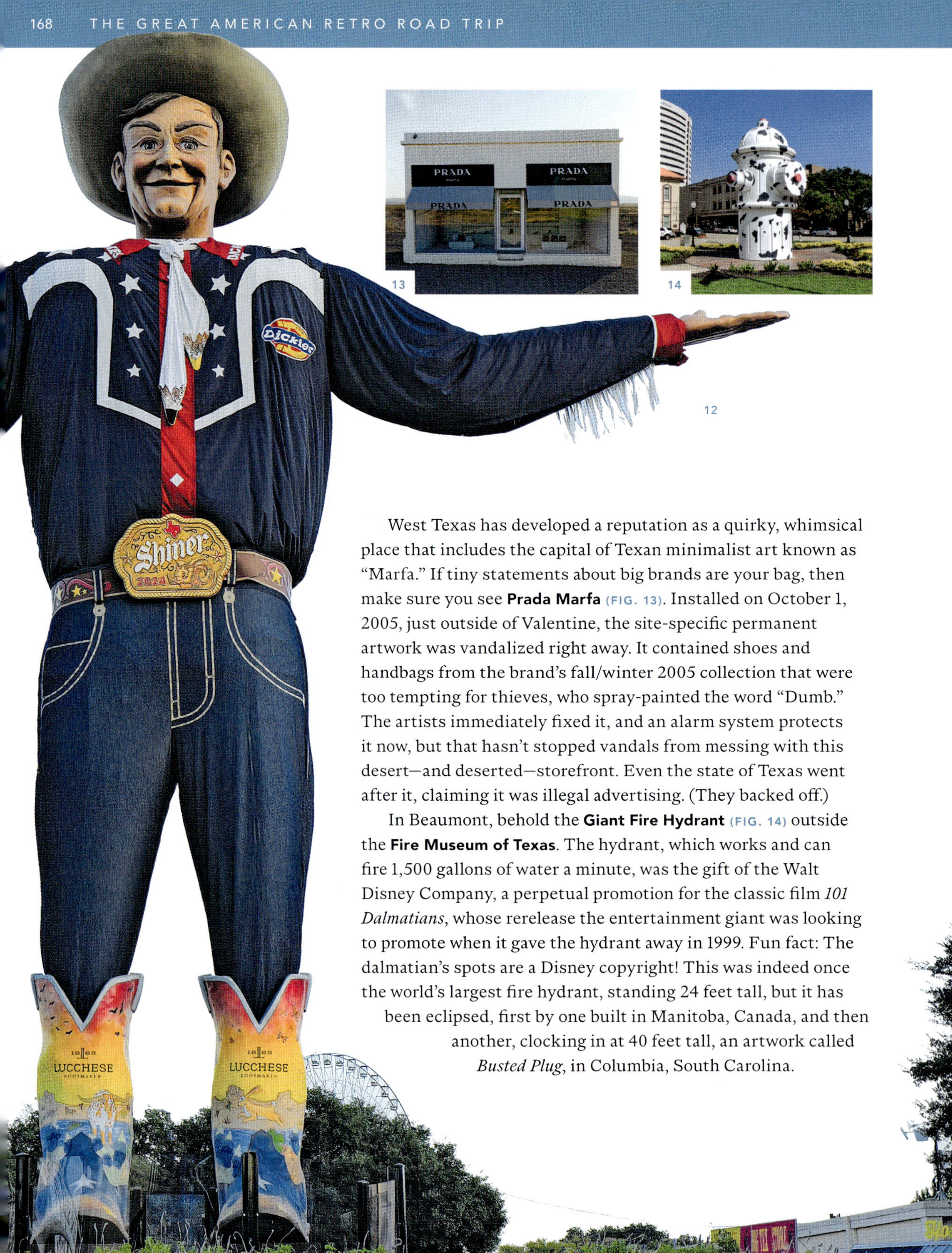

13

14

12

West Texas has developed a reputation as a quirky, whimsical place that includes the capital of Texan minimalist art known as "Marfa." If tiny statements about big brands are your bag, then make sure you see **Prada Marfa** (FIG. 13). Installed on October 1, 2005, just outside of Valentine, the site-specific permanent artwork was vandalized right away. It contained shoes and handbags from the brand's fall/winter 2005 collection that were too tempting for thieves, who spray-painted the word "Dumb." The artists immediately fixed it, and an alarm system protects it now, but that hasn't stopped vandals from messing with this desert—and deserted—storefront. Even the state of Texas went after it, claiming it was illegal advertising. (They backed off.)

In Beaumont, behold the **Giant Fire Hydrant** (FIG. 14) outside the **Fire Museum of Texas**. The hydrant, which works and can fire 1,500 gallons of water a minute, was the gift of the Walt Disney Company, a perpetual promotion for the classic film *101 Dalmatians*, whose rerelease the entertainment giant was looking to promote when it gave the hydrant away in 1999. Fun fact: The dalmatian's spots are a Disney copyright! This was indeed once the world's largest fire hydrant, standing 24 feet tall, but it has been eclipsed, first by one built in Manitoba, Canada, and then another, clocking in at 40 feet tall, an artwork called *Busted Plug*, in Columbia, South Carolina.

If you're in Dallas, make sure you give the **Eye** (FIG. 15) a look, a sculpture of a giant eyeball by the artist Tony Tasset. Located outside The Joule Hotel, the Eye has a twin at Laumeier Sculpture Park in St. Louis, Missouri. Tasset based the eyes on his own, and the sculptures have no particular meaning, so interpret as you see fit.

You can see the Eye and most everything in this chapter any time of year, but not **Big Tex** (FIG. 12), who towers over the state fair in Dallas every year but is otherwise kept in storage. Big Tex has been lording over the fairgrounds since 1952—or, well, 2013. That's because the original statue was destroyed in an electrical fire the year before. The new Tex is one yard taller. During the fair, Big Tex talks (voiced by an off-site emcee), greeting visitors with his classic "Howdy, folks!" and making announcements with a requisite drawl.

Big Tex has inspired everyone from the creators of the show *King of the Hill*—he figured in an episode—to local businesses like Centennial Liquor and Wine, which featured a much smaller Tex in its signage. That **Neon Big Tex** (shown on pages 162–163) ended up in the caring hands of the fair after the liquor store went out of business.

Another midcentury cowboy who is still riding high greets moviegoers at **Winchester Drive-In Theatre**, Oklahoma City's only remaining drive-in theater. Opened in 1968 as the heyday of the drive-in was already in the rearview mirror, the Winchester features a stunning neon sign of Chester the cowboy.

Another big-sign fella you should get to know is **Mortimer Snerd** (FIG. 16), International Fiberglass's official name for this goofy Muffler Man statue. (Mr. Snerd was the creation of ventriloquist Edgar Bergen, the father of actress Candice Bergen, perhaps best known as the star of the sitcom *Murphy Brown*.) Mortimer's been called Happy Halfwit and many folks likely think of *Mad* magazine's Alfred E. Neuman when they see him. His home was **Ken's Mufflers & Brakes** in Dallas.

The **Golden Boy** (FIG. 17) statue isn't roadside Americana per se—it was originally skyline Americana! The statue began life in 1916 perched atop 195 Broadway, the former headquarters of AT&T in Manhattan. By 2005, AT&T was an emaciated long-distance giant, and SBC, one of its offspring from the 1984 phone-monopoly breakup, was growing fast. It swallowed AT&T, took its old name, and saved Golden Boy, moving it to the lobby of its new headquarters in Dallas. It was later relocated to an outdoor plaza at the AT&T Discovery Center, where you can enjoy at eye level what a century ago required binoculars in Manhattan. Wherever AT&T moves next, you can be sure Golden Boy will be along for the ride.

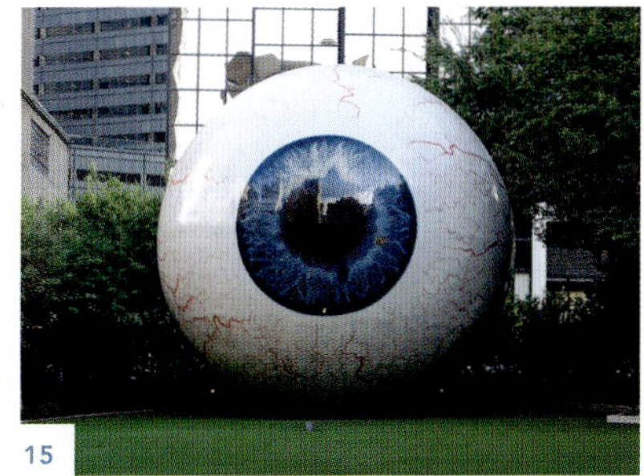

15

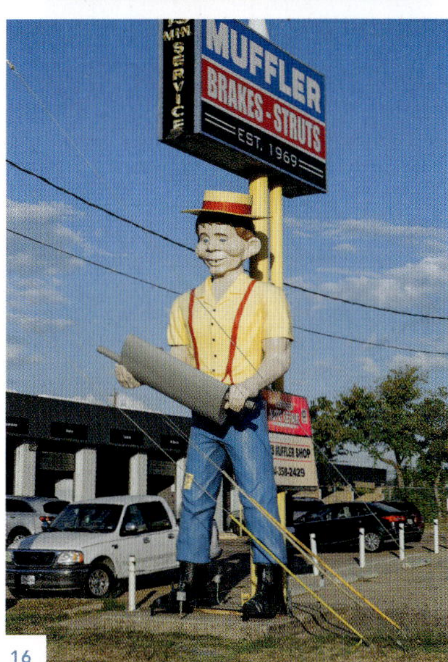

16

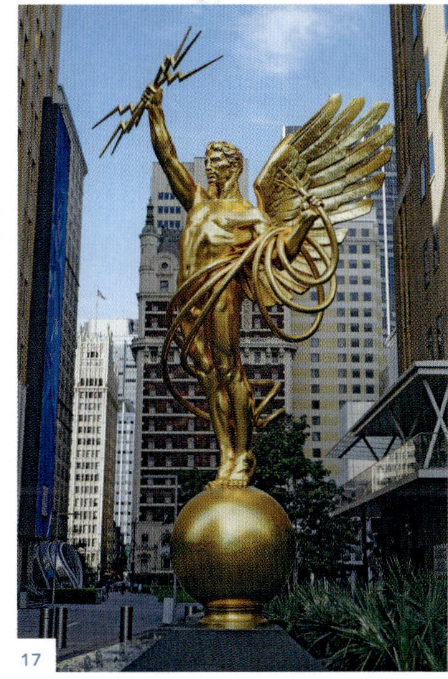

17

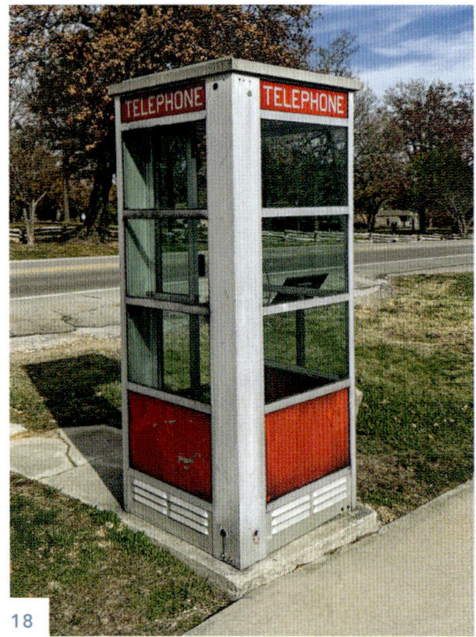

18

The only telephone booth on the National Register of Historic Places—a Superman-ready one from 1959—can be found in Prairie Gove, Arkansas. The Airlight booth was once common all around the country, but this **Prairie Grove Airlight Outdoor Telephone Booth** (FIG. 18) is perhaps the most cherished, and the phone inside still works.

Down in Fort Stockton, Texas, you'll find what was once the world's largest roadrunner (dethroned by one in New Mexico), **Paisano Pete** (FIG. 19), who represents a common bird in these parts, partial to running and walking, depicted in gargantuan dimensions of 11 feet tall and 22 feet long. The brainchild of a former mayor here, Paisano Pete is made of fiberglass and received his name in a contest held when he was a hatchling in 1979. The winner pocketed $50 for their efforts. *Paisano* is Spanish for "countryman" or "buddy," and is a regional nickname for this bird. In 2008, Paisano Pete was briefly sent to prison—for a paint job. Inmates there gave him a new coat after a hailstorm damaged him.

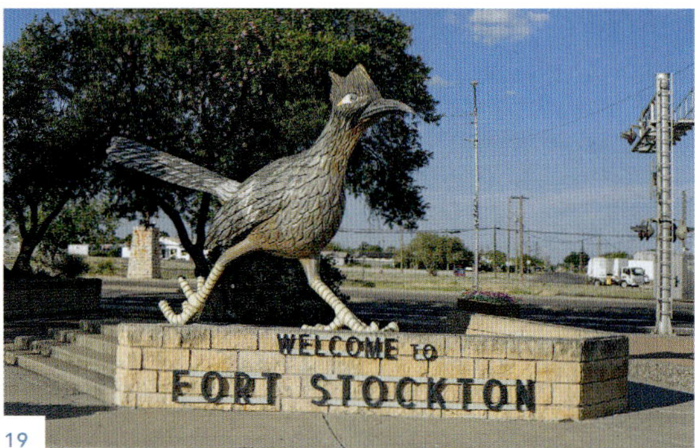

19

In Galveston, you can confront your fear of sharks—or embrace your love of them! Along a short walk on Avenue Q, you'll find a shark head greeting you at **Gianni's Italian Bistro & Bar**, a massive shark mouth inviting you to walk through it to enjoy a screening at the **Shark Attack 5D Theater**, and a **surfer-dude shark** (FIG. 23) outside a liquor store down the street.

One of the quirkiest homes you'll ever see is nearby in Galveston, the **Kettle House** (FIG. 20), a nod to its shape. A restoration project by Michael and Ashley Cordray of Save 1900 Realty, the steel bowl has been a fixture in the area for decades and had its Hollywood moment when it was featured in the HGTV show *Big Texas Fix*. The original owner was Clayton E. Stokley, who worked for a sheet-metal company and acquired a curious spherical building that had been constructed for another project, his daughter told writer Linda Armstrong. Plans to turn it into a store foundered, and it remained a local curiosity until it finally found a role as a comfy vacation rental.

I showed you a couple of **Futuro Homes** in New Jersey and Delaware (see pages 15 and 75), but my favorite may be right here, on the side of a country road in Royse

20

City, Texas, a gleaming orange relic from the Space Age (FIG. 21). These prefabricated structures of a tough fiberglass-and-plastic blend were designed by the Finnish architect Matti Suuronen and produced in Philadelphia. Meant to be a bold innovation in living, they never quite caught on, and fewer than one hundred are said to have been built. This one reportedly belonged at one point to two brothers and fell into a period of neglect before it was spiffed up and stamped with the phrase "Area 276," a reference to the local highway, and, of course, Area 51. These were meant to be tiny homes—often described as ski chalets—and could be fitted with all the conveniences. These days, they mainly serve as fantastical curiosities.

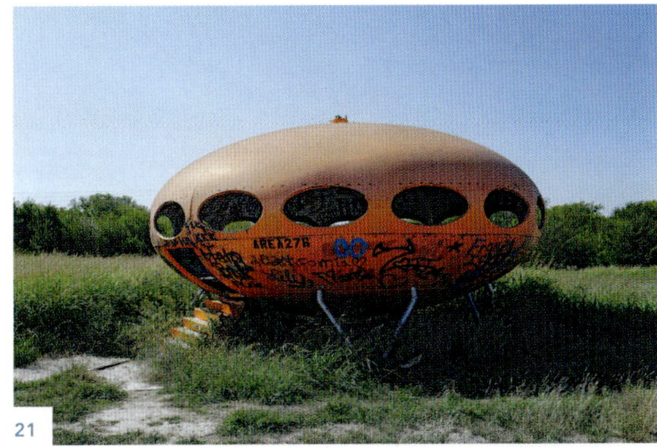

21

From a UFO to a space capsule, the space race moves to Oklahoma, where one of my favorite examples of roadside Americana sits by the side of a road: the **Winganon Concrete Mixer Space Capsule** (FIG. 22). This object of curiosity began life as a cement mixer. The story goes that the truck carrying it was involved in an accident and the mixer landed here, off the side of East 300 Road near Talala, Oklahoma. This happened at an indeterminate date in the second half of the twentieth century (depending on whom you ask), but the thing stayed there long enough that people developed an emotional attachment to it. Those people include artists Barry and Heather Thomas, who in 2011 celebrated their wedding anniversary by visually transforming the mixer into what is now known as the Winganon Concrete Mixer Space Capsule. Yes, with a little paint and the addition of ersatz rocket thrusters, this abandoned concrete mixer became a fascinating example of human imagination and whimsy. And, no doubt, a source of momentary bafflement for passing motorists.

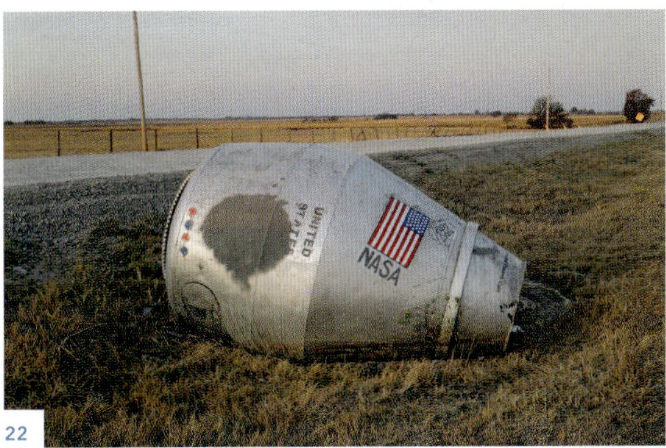

22

Now, a story that will knock your socks off. (Or poke your eye out?) The setting for the film *A Christmas Story* is Hohman, Indiana, a fictional stand-in for the author Jean Shepherd's hometown of Hammond, Indiana. The house—now part of a museum complex—made famous in the movie, based on some of Shepherd's short stories, is in Cleveland, Ohio. Inspired by this infamous movie prop, a 40-foot-tall leg lamp resting atop a 10-foot-tall box marked "Fragile" was installed neither in Hammond nor in Cleveland but in Chickasha, Oklahoma. The reason is a real kick.

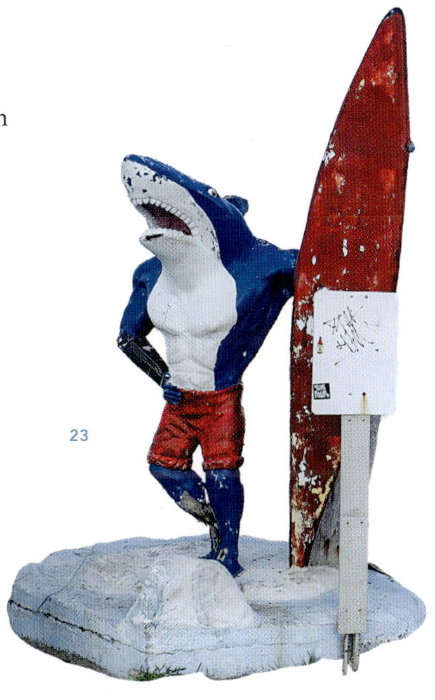
23

In 2020, Noland James, a visual-arts professor in Chickasha, died. But long before *A Christmas Story* came out, he had built his own leg lamp—this one with two legs clad in black hose and a skirt, wearing pumps and topped with a lamp shade made from a wastepaper basket. He long believed his lamp had been the prototype for the one in the film, saying that somebody who would go on to work on the film had seen it in his office and loved it. (The leg also figures in one of the Jean Shepherd stories that inspired the film, and at least one more person claims parentage.) James's obituary, with the story of the lamp, went viral, capturing imaginations everywhere, including Chickasha, where a tourism opportunity was quickly grasped, and, more important, a way to honor a beloved local.

24

The Oklahoman countryside is also home to **Mr. Ed's Grave** (FIG. 25), a quirky tribute to America's most famous palomino, the star of the 1960s sitcom *Mister Ed*, about a talking horse who can only be heard by his long-suffering owner, Wilbur. (Or, to spell it as Mr. Ed pronounced it, *Wiiiilllbuuuur.*) *Atlas Obscura* documents competing theories about the actual horse buried here—one holds that it's Bamboo Harvester, who played the horse on the show; another maintains that it's Pumpkin, a palomino that replaced Bamboo Harvester for promotional engagements around the show.

Whatever happened to Mr. Ed, this is a lovely place for television-besotted brains like mine to visit. Do note that the marker sits on private

▸▸▸ Pull Over!

One of the most interesting sights in Tulsa is a notable skyscraper. As a native New Yorker, I was surprised to see a building reminiscent of the World Trade Center's Twin Towers. Sure enough, the architect of the Twin Towers, Minoru Yamasaki, designed what seems to be a tiny brother of the lost Twin Towers, the **BOK Tower**. Yamasaki's modernist-Gothic touches grace several buildings in America (for example, Rainier Tower in Seattle), but this is perhaps the most striking reminder of the lost towers, and it was a surprise to find it in the Heartland.

property, so, as *Atlas Obscura* advises, get permission first to pay your respects.

The Planters production plant in Fort Smith, Arkansas, is home to a towering **Mr. Peanut** (FIG. 24) of about 30 feet, moved here from his longtime perch in Peabody, Massachusetts, back in 1988, when its future was threatened. Mr. Peanut fans can also visit him depicted in neon in Columbus, Ohio, and as a smaller statue in Suffolk, Virginia.

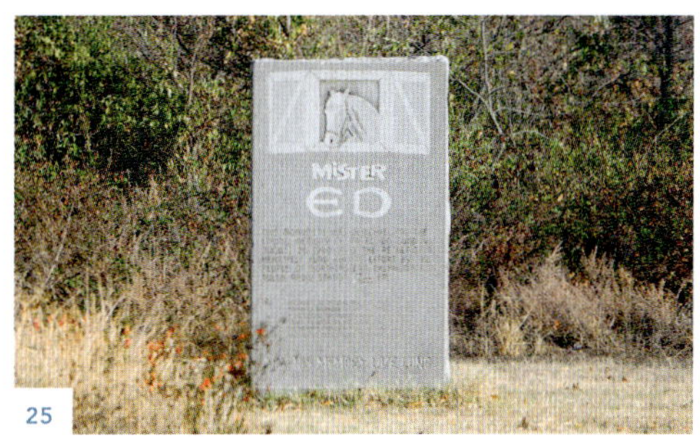

25

ROADSIDE EATS

What are you in the mood for? These selections are some of my favorite spots in the region for a bite of nostalgia.

I first said howdy to **The Big Texan** (FIG. 26) in 2013, on an epic Prairie-to-Pacific adventure on Route 66, and have been smitten with the road ever since. This smiling cowboy is one of the great icons of the Mother Road, and so is the Big Texan Steak Ranch & Brewery the cowboy represents. If your appetite knows no limits, and stage fright is an unfamiliar feeling for you, then step right up and go for the free 72-ounce steak challenge! You have to finish your meal in an hour, and should you succeed—and some have eaten more; at least one challenger had to be stopped for her own sake—you'll forever be part of Route 66 history.

Founder R. J. Lee settled here in the Texas Panhandle, drawn by the lure and lore of cowboy life and a vision to become part of it himself with a grand steakhouse—the Big Texan—which he opened in 1960 and is still in the family. The restaurant moved to its present location in 1971 and was rebuilt several years later following a fire. Today, it has expanded to include an RV Park (and the old motel, turned chic Airbnb) for those looking to sleep off the steak challenge on-site. (The ten thousandth free steak was offered up in 2021!)

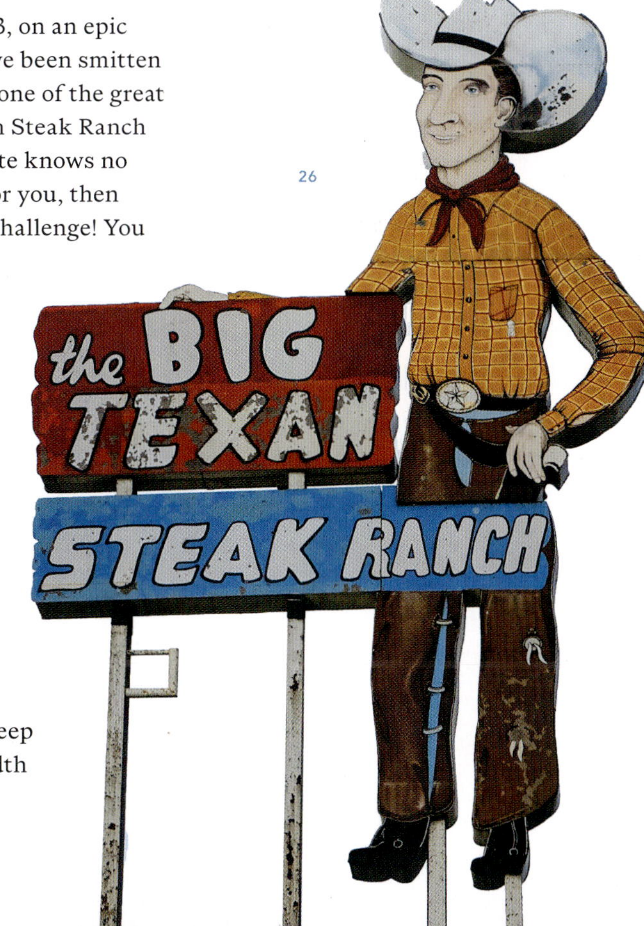

26

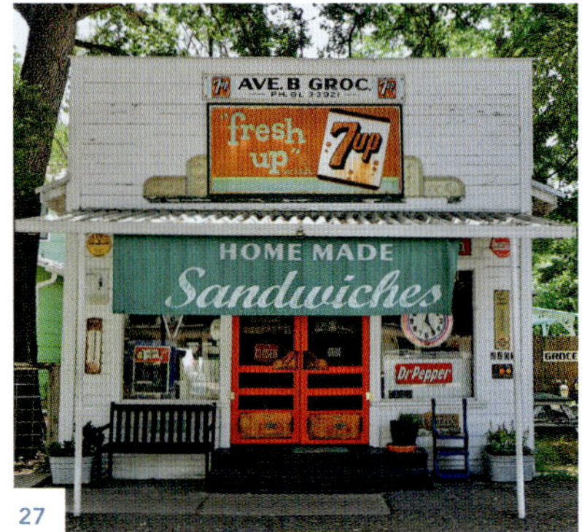

27

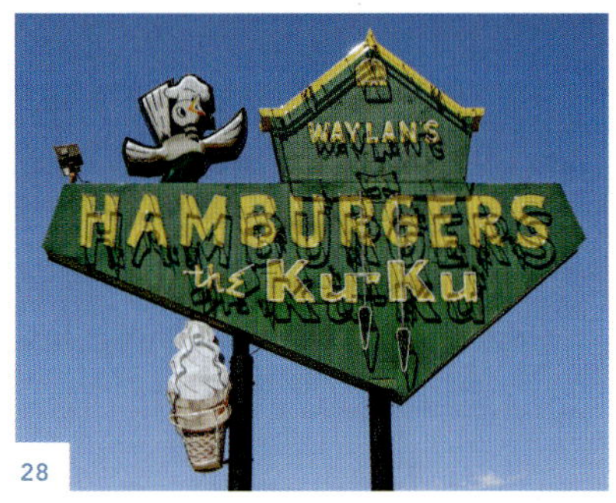

28

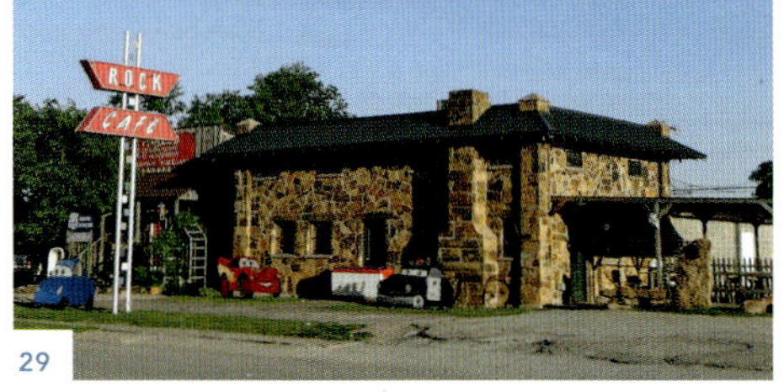

29

Austin's **Avenue B Grocery Store and Market** (FIG. 27) has been around since 1909, long enough to be the Texas city's longest continuously operating grocery store. It's open whenever the "V for Victory" sign is lit in the window. It's gone through ten owners who have all had the love for the place (and the good sense) to leave well enough alone.

Waylan's Ku-Ku (FIG. 28) in Miami, Oklahoma, is the last holdout of what had been a chain of hamburger restaurants. This store—"The Ku-Ku" as it was called—held its grand opening on April 2 and 3, 1966, and talk about a deal: burgers were 15 cents each and the cups of soda at the opening were given away for free.

Eugene Waylan bought the location in 1973 and it still exudes vintage charm, with its clucky mascot showing up in multiple spots outside a building designed like a cuckoo clock but modified in the 1980s with a sunroom. (It was an unwritten fast-food restaurant rule in the 1980s: Must. Build. Sunroom.) Waylan has been quoted as saying he regretted the addition, though business necessitated it, as the Route 66 revival was just down the road.

He needn't worry. Waylan's is a delight. The inside is a homey dining room heavy on wood paneling and plants. Cozy and cute.

One of the "bedrock" institutions of the Mother Road is the **Rock Cafe** (FIG. 29) in Stroud, Oklahoma. Opened in 1939, the Rock Cafe has an appropriate name, both for its rusticated architecture and for its survivor's grit. Fate has tested the Rock Cafe—Route 66's decommissioning,

NOLA NECESSITIES

If you're New Orleans bound, the vintage dining options are overwhelming. Here's a starter pack with nice signage: **Casamento's**, **Commander's Palace**, **Tujague's** (FIG. 30), **The Pearl** (FIG. 31; closed at time of publication), **Crescent City Steak**, and **The Morning Call Coffee Stand** (FIG. 32).

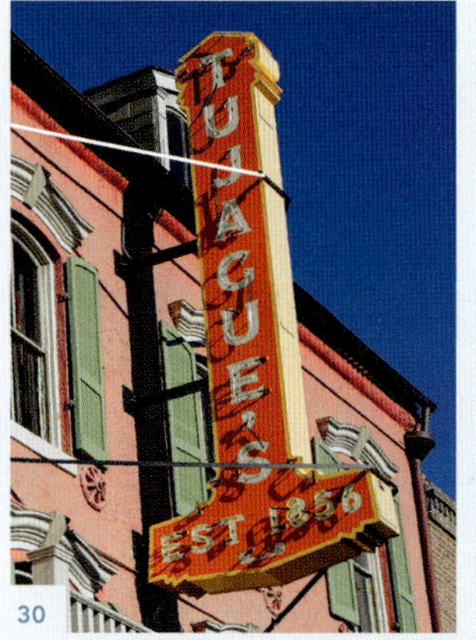

30

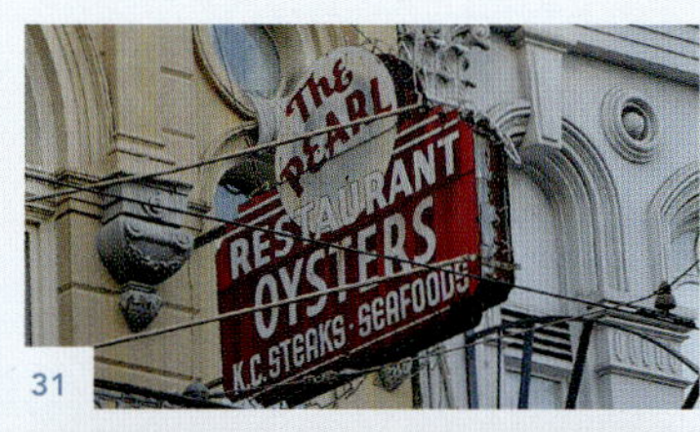

31

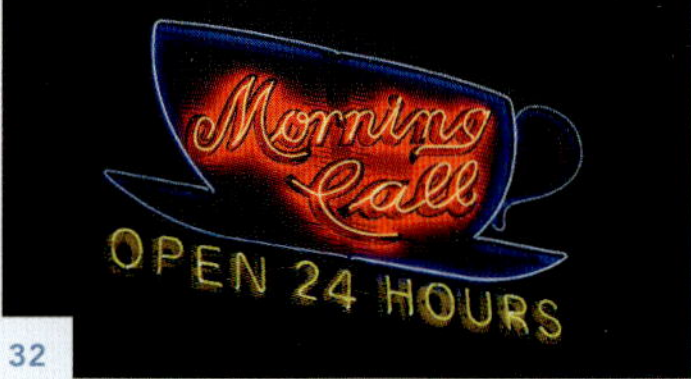

32

tornadoes, closure, a fire that reduced it to its iconic walls. The Rock Cafe—and its indomitable, decades-old grill, known as Betsy—has survived, and today, it sits on the National Register of Historic Places.

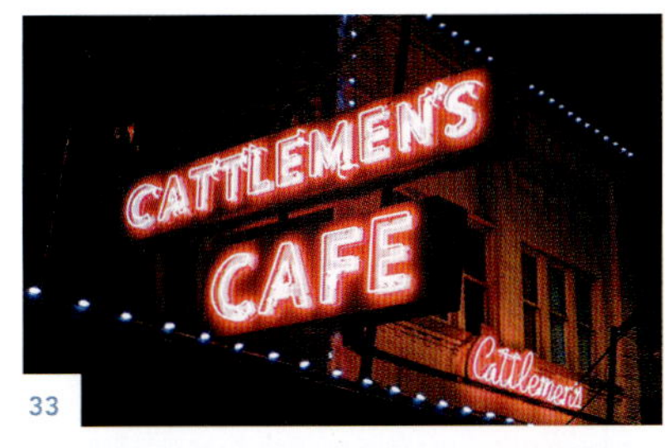

33

Cattlemen's Steakhouse (FIG. 33) in Oklahoma City once served the cattlemen and cowboys of the early twentieth century, and the rich culinary and cowboy history makes it a timeless attraction—and Oklahoma's oldest continuously operating restaurant.

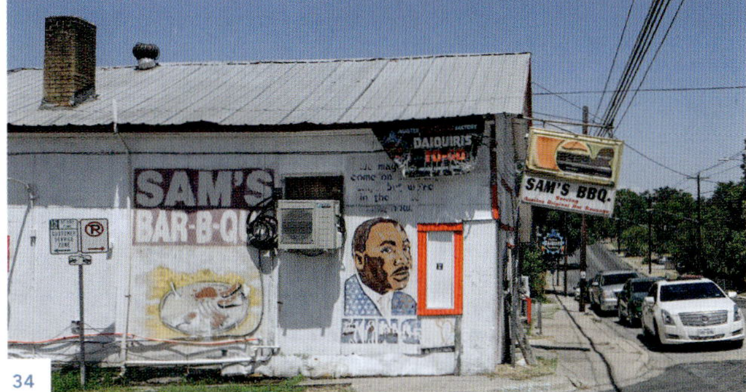

34

So many of these places are survivors, and you can add the great **Sam's BBQ** (FIG. 34), in Austin, Texas, to that list. It was destroyed in a fire in 1992 but was rebuilt into the spot for good food and good company that it is today. Yes, priceless artifacts that testified to Sam's history were destroyed in the blaze, but history itself—Stevie Ray Vaughan was a passionate fan—can never be erased.

BURGER OR BUST

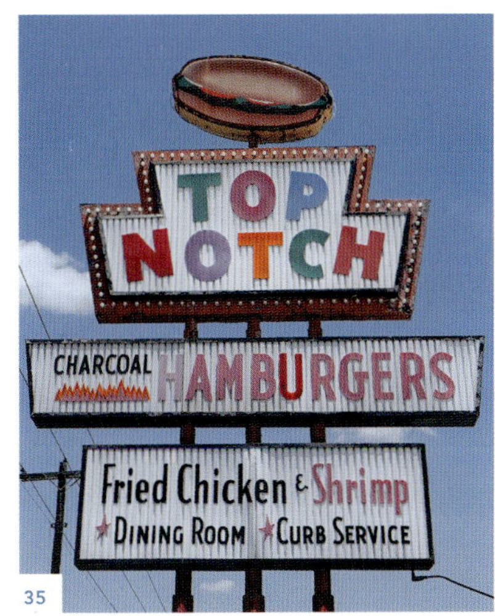

35

"Top notch" is more than a name at **Top Notch Hamburgers** (FIG. 35), and the name and sign miss the epic fried chicken and hand-dipped onion rings. The Austin restaurant dates to 1971, when it opened in the home of a 1960s carhop stand. The carhops never went away, and the menu is frozen in time from the 1970s recipes.

Lankford's began as a simple grocery store in Houston in 1937 (and before that, a fruit stand), and the family lived upstairs. When the second generation of the family took control, Lankford's evolved into an "ice house" (aka a bar serving cold beer) before morphing again, and finally settling into a cozy and satisfying road-food stop, particularly loved for its burgers. Among those who love them is Guy Fieri, and life here has never been the same since the show featured his visit, first aired in 2009, widening the restaurant's renown. Today, a new, second location has been opened by the family's third generation. But rest assured, the original is still the eternal heartbeat of Lankford's.

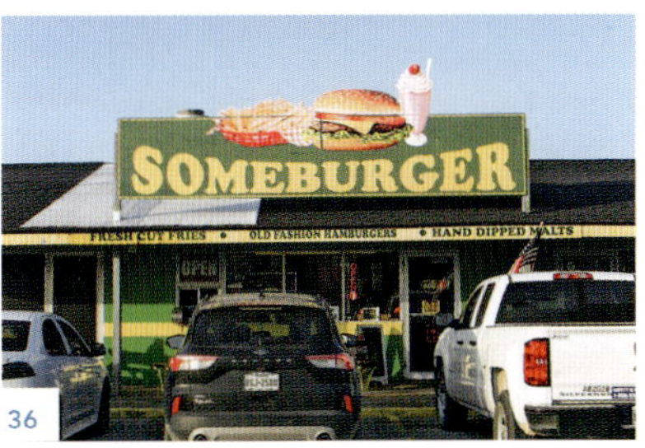

36

Someburger (FIG. 36) has been a Baytown, Texas, institution since 1955, moving to its current location a decade later. The stand once had dozens of brethren. In the 1940s, a chain of restaurants around Austin was known as "Somewhere," with bags emblazoned with the phrase: "I came from Somewhere full of Someburgers." The name Someburger won out.

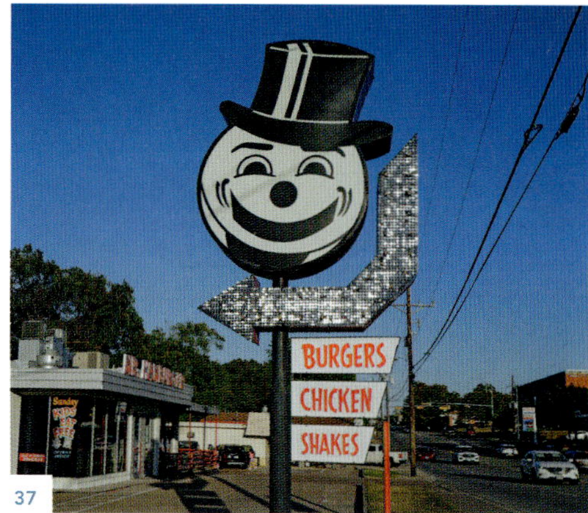

37

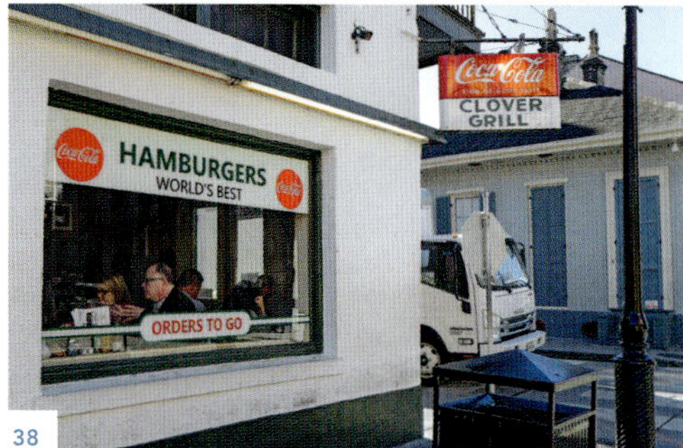

38

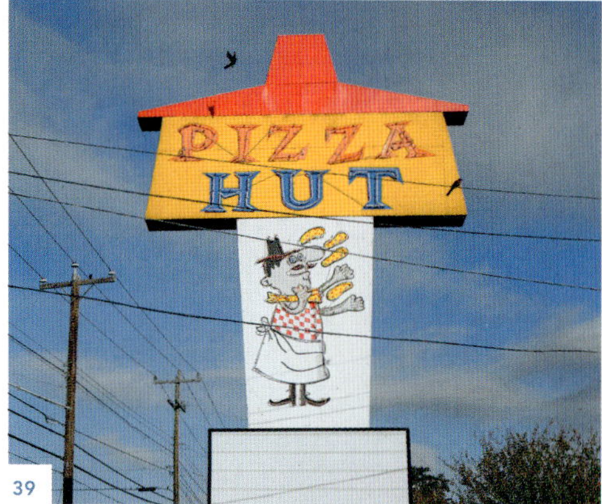

39

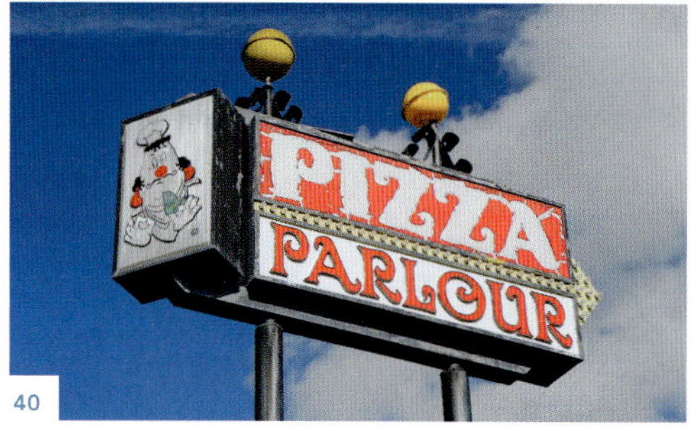

40

Hey, mister! A burger joint in Huntsville, Texas, **Mr. Hamburger** (FIG. 37) first opened in 1959. It closed in 2006 only to be revived by a new owner in 2011, not far from its original home, now in a former Sinclair gas station, but you would never know about the sad interlude. The place feels like it's always been there. Always jaunty is the Mr. Hamburger mascot, a smiley face bedecked with a top hat, his face framed by a bulb-festooned arrow directing drivers to feast on his grill's bounty. (The original Mr. Hamburger sign is inside, displayed as a relic of veneration.) For many released prisoners from the nearby "Walls Unit" state penitentiary, Mr. Hamburger is their first taste of freedom. It's no surprise, then, that the menu has a prison theme, with burgers like Old Sparky (the nickname for the old electric chair at the prison, which is now on display at a nearby museum), Killer, and Warden. It may be grim, but it's the local history, and Mr. Hamburger embraces it.

In New Orleans, the **Clover Grill** (FIG. 38) serves up a heavenly burger. Clover and its workhorse grill are at your service 24 hours a day. Don't be afraid to put it to the test. The restaurant's been here since 1939—and the quaint signage testifies to its longevity.

PIZZA PIZZA!

Home Slice Pizza began in Austin in 2005 and the small chain of New York–style slices has an outpost in the Midtown neighborhood of Houston. Its mascot sports a crown. (**Pizza King** in Long View has a charming character, too, and also wears a crown, with a jaunty bow tie for good measure.)

Texas sports must-see pizza dudes, including America's most famous, Pizza Hut Pete. He survives at the **Pizza Hut** (FIG. 39) in San Antonio, Texas, the last to feature the character in vintage signage.

More vintage vibes can be found at **Pizza Parlour** (FIG. 40) in Alma, Arkansas, which deserves an award for best pizza-parlor font. The very combination of the words "pizza parlour" thrills me . . . it usually means something blissfully old school. Another one that gives those soothing "fontastic" vibes is **Ken's Pizza Parlor** in Athens, Texas.

CHAINS OF FOOD

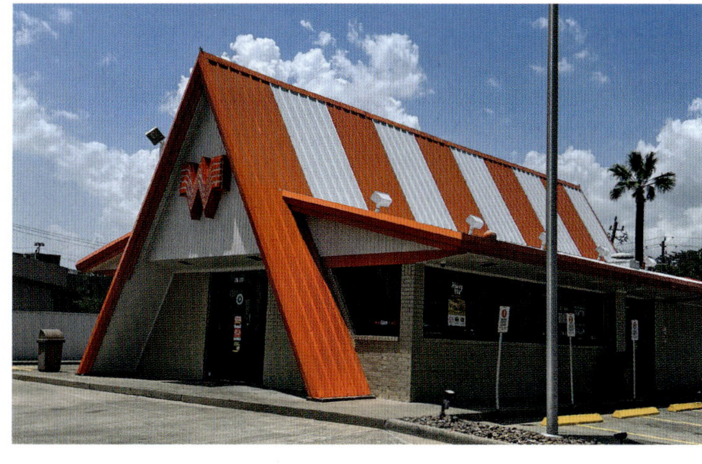

Whataburger

Harmon Dobson founded Whataburger in 1950 with a foolproof premise, the story goes. He wanted to offer a fresh burger so big you'd have to hold it with both hands. And once you took a bite, you'd exclaim, "What a burger!"

Texans took to Whataburger from the get-go, and it spread far from its birthplace in Corpus Christi. In 1959, the chain entered its second state, Florida, and by 1961, the signature orange-and-white A-frame buildings began to appear.

Dobson was killed in a plane crash in 1967, but his widow, Grace, took over and kept expanding the chain, today numbering more than a thousand locations.

Whataburger continues to pride itself on the size and freshness of its burgers, and for hungry night owls, its status since the early 1980s as a 24-hour restaurant helps make it what the state legislature proclaimed a "Texas Treasure."

A PRESCRIPTION FOR NOSTALGIC SOULS

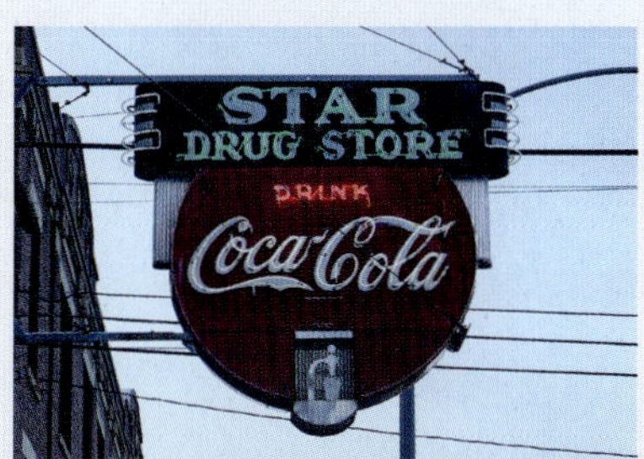

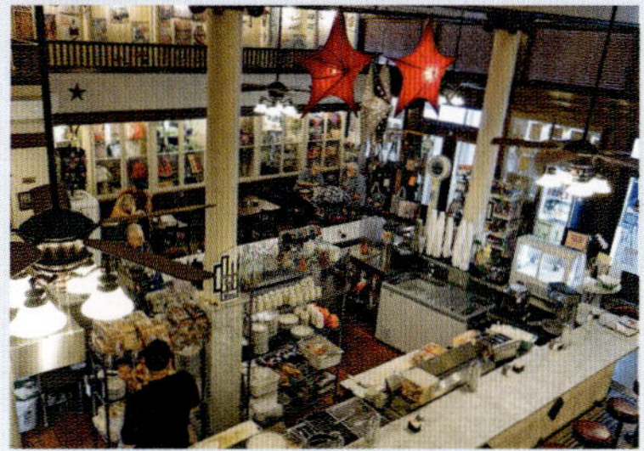

If I were to give the **Star Drug Store** in Galveston a nickname, it would be the Phoenix. The Star was built in a wooden building in 1886, and rebuilt to the same design in brick years later. It has faced endless travails, from epic floods, hurricanes, and a fire that shut it for years. It also holds an important footnote in Civil Rights history as the first lunch counter to desegregate in Galveston in the 1950s.

The store's porcelain neon sign, designed by Jules Lauve, is a regional icon. Its horseshoe-shaped lunch counter makes a lovely place for a hearty breakfast. There's also a second-level balcony, teeming with artifacts and photos, that wraps around the store. In the olden days, according to the store, patients could rest up there after taking their medications so they could be watched for potential allergic reactions. (These days, you'll have to get your prescriptions filled elsewhere, but comfort food is a tonic all its own.)

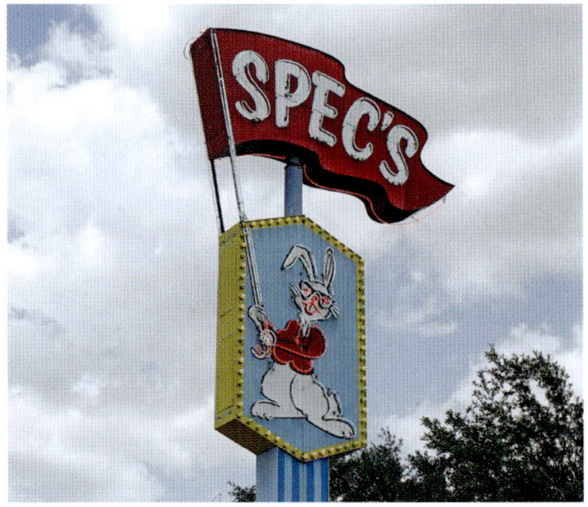

Spec's Wines, Spirits & Finer Foods
This Houston-area chain was founded in 1962 and has spread to more than one hundred locations. It has a wacky rabbit character as its mascot, and he is best showcased at the Spec's on Smith Street, where a gigantic glass dome protects the original sign.

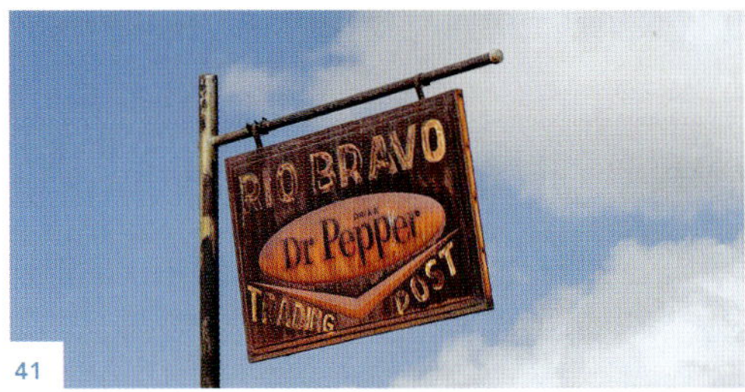

41

WE'RE AN AMERICAN BRAND

Are you a Pepper? In 2024, Dr Pepper became America's number two soft drink, eclipsing Pepsi.

Even as Coke's status as the Real Thing (or, at least the "Number One Thing") seems secure, Dr Pepper can boast it's been playing the long game—and winning. The soft drink that began as a concoction was devised in Texas, and today, the **Dr Pepper Museum** in Waco, Texas, makes an interesting stop. And keep your eyes peeled for other Dr Pepper privilege signage around the state, like this rusty relic in Langtry, Texas (FIG. 41).

MAINSTAYS OF MAIN STREET

Our selective saunter through the Main Streets of the region will take us to chains, some thriving and others not quite giving up the ghost, and to mom-and-pops, fighting the good fight as always.

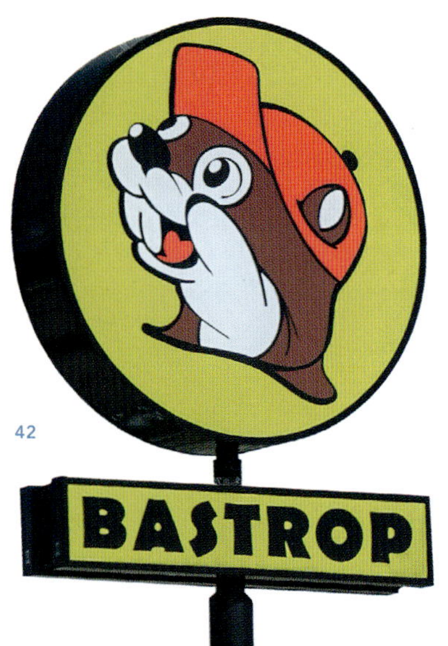

42

I'm just wild about **Buc-ee's** (FIG. 42), which on long road trips has become a sought-out refuge for this weary traveler. The Texas-based convenience-store chain has expanded widely in recent years, using billboard-marketing techniques that helped South of the Border and other roadside attractions grow. With mom-and-pop roots, beginning as a gas station and convenience store in Clute, Texas, in 1982, Buc-ee's moniker draws its inspiration from the name of the founder's dog—Buck—and the 1950s mascot for Ipana toothpaste, Bucky Beaver, who belted out the "brusha, brusha, brusha" jingle. (Curious? It's on YouTube.)

Beyond its cute iconography, Buc-ee's is a true roadside oasis, with a shopping experience that overdelivers in quality grab-and-go food (brisket sandwiches and Beaver Nuggets are highlights) as well as practical considerations for the traveler.

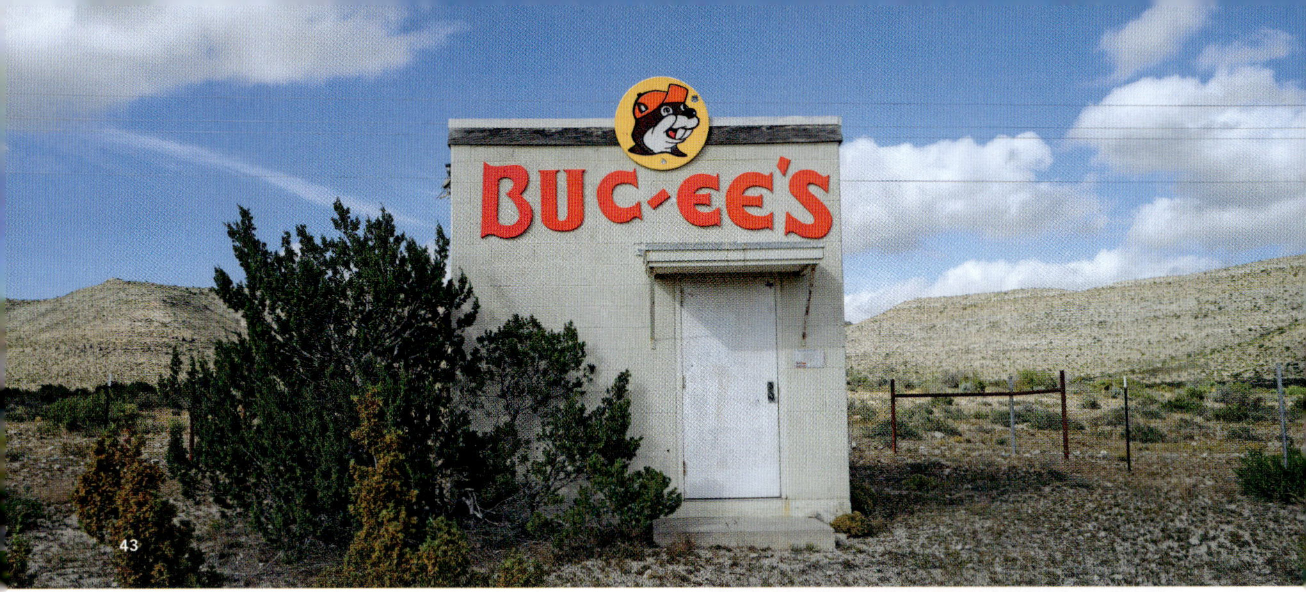

43

Buc-ee's biggest bragging point is its gas pumps—on average, each location has about one hundred of them. That makes gassing up at Buc-ee's a unique and stress-free experience.

Even as Buc-ee's keeps expanding, my favorite may well be deep in West Texas, on I-90 between Sanderson and Marathon. It's a clever art project known as the **World's Smallest Buc-ee's** (FIG. 43). I traveled a great distance to see it. No bathroom, no gas pumps, no Beaver Nuggets. Just pure joy.

One of the grandest drug-store signs you'll ever see is the curved art deco facade of the downtown **New Orleans Walgreens** (FIG. 44), a riot of color and now LED tubing, replacing the original neon. Aside from the technological shift, there have been two big changes here: The word "cigar" was changed to "photo" (itself now anachronistic) and "cafeteria" swapped out for "prescriptions."

New Orleans is also home to **Peaches Records** (FIG. 45), which opened in 1975 and still thrives under the aegis of Mama Peaches herself, Shirani Rae, with familiar iconography from the old, defunct Peaches chain, down to the record crates. Rae enthused about her shop's role as a community hub (local artwork is sold here, too). To her, it's always been about the music, and the people, before profits. Peaches is set within an old Woolworth's that preserves the lunch counter where a historic civil rights sit-in took place.

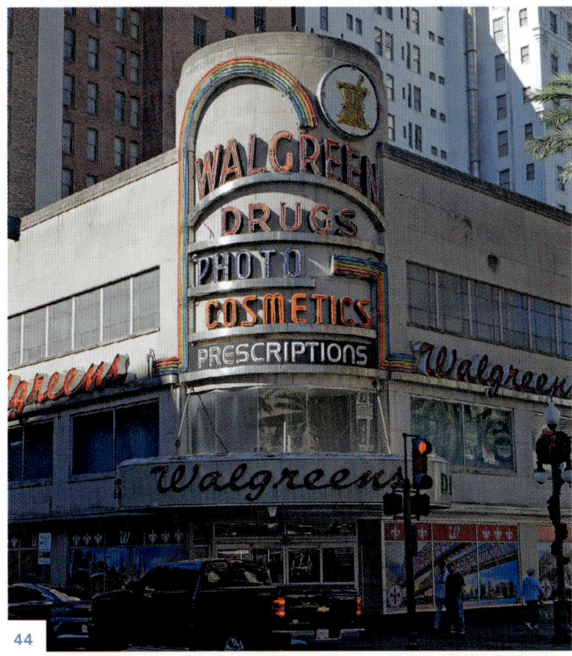

44

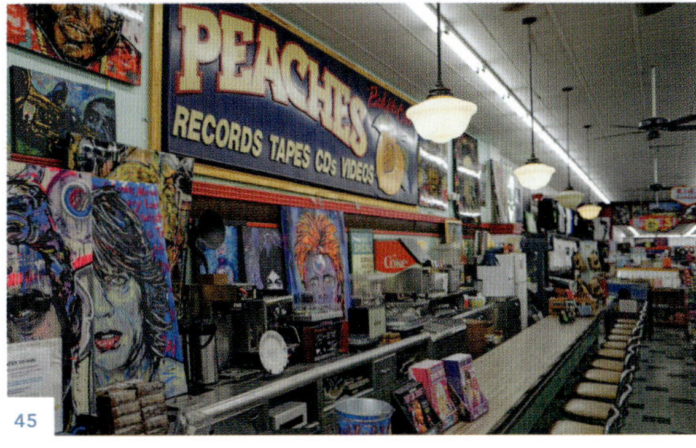

45

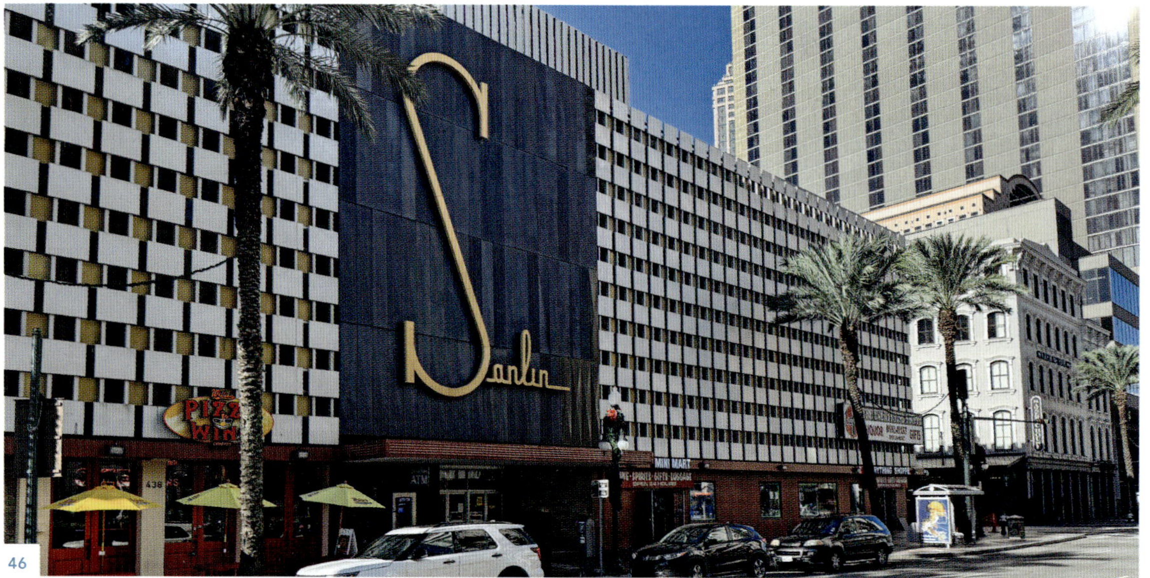

46

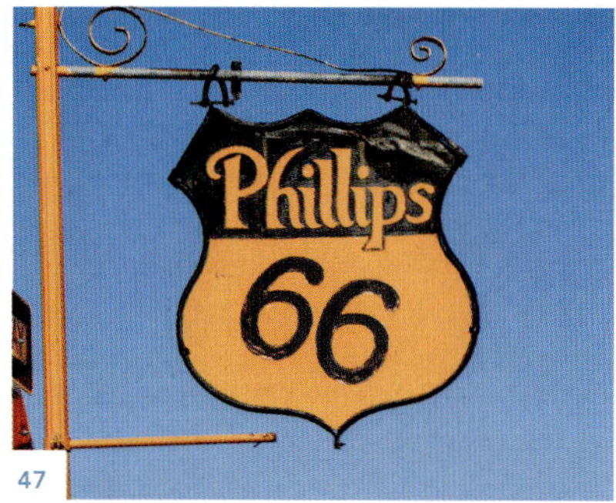

47

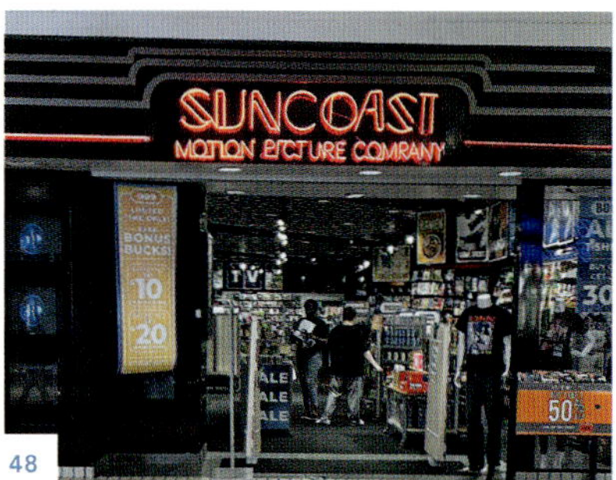

48

The Big Easy knows how to do big signage, and the cursive script of the **Sanlin Building** (FIG. 46) is captivating. The facade conceals a row of nineteenth-century commercial facades, a reminder of how, in the built environment, we are always surrounded by layers just waiting to be discovered, one of the joys of urban archaeology. (**The Delacroix** storefront is another New Orleans beauty.)

Tulsa, Oklahoma, recently declared the capital of Route 66, is teeming with finds, like **Skateland** and **Rose Bowl**. **Broadway Skateland** in Mesquite, Texas, has a fabulous 1950s sign.

The **Phillips 66 Station** (FIG. 47) in McLean, Texas, is a national roadside treasure, lovingly restored and an obligatory Mother Road stop. It'll melt your heart, and it's not far from the fascinating **Devil's Rope Museum,** celebrating the underappreciated wonder (and terror) that is barbed wire.

About ninety minutes northeast of Houston, in the historic oil-boom town of Beaumont, lies the equivalent—for me, anyway—of striking oil. In the Parkdale Mall, one of two remaining **Suncoast Motion Picture Company** (FIG. 48) stores is still putting on a show for shoppers and nostalgists. Unlike the one that survives in Jacksonville, North Carolina, this store still sports its neon sign. Inside, it hardly resembles the Suncoasts of yore—long gone are the racks of VHS tapes and movie memorabilia, though DVDs and Blu-rays can be found aplenty. If you're a plush toy and Funko Pop! collector, you'll find lots to explore here, along with tumblers, T-shirts, backpacks, and other stuff that cinephiles might enjoy but can live without.

Somehow, the sun has not yet set on this Suncoast. There used to be hundreds at the chain's peak. Aside from the odd sign scars in malls here and there, the chain is mostly a memory, heaped in with Blockbuster and Hollywood Video as names that define a different decade. The more things change, the more they stay the same. But in Beaumont, at the Suncoast Motion Picture Company, it's still the 1990s.

A gorgeous vintage sign for a wedding chapel can be seen poking out just off of the Gulf Freeway in Houston. The **Harmony Wedding Chapel** (FIG. 49) has been here since 1965, a Texan spin on the Nevadan tradition of quickie marriages. And perhaps the most momentous nuptials here were in October 1972, when Texas's first gay marriage happened. Two men—one dressed in drag—had obtained a marriage license at city hall, the clerk none the wiser. A minister married them at the chapel, and history was made.

But a predictable maelstrom ensued, the license was revoked, and the couple split up. Gay marriage is now legal across the country, but most who speed by in their cars don't realize the chapel's overlooked footnote in LGBTQIA+ history.

The **Sears bus stop** (FIG. 50) in Houston is an art deco beauty, and the oak tree next to it makes for a stunning combo. This Sears closed in 2020 and at the time of this writing there were concerns about the preservation of this sign. The collapse of Sears has been astonishing: once unthinkable. There were fewer than a dozen left at this writing.

Mac Haik Chevrolet (FIG. 51), also in Houston, features a sign that screams NBC peacock. The peacock is a relic of when former Houston Oilers football player Mac Haik purchased Peacock Chevrolet. After all these years they are still proud of their colorful plumage!

The Daily News (FIG. 52) building in Galveston, Texas, has a stunning painted sign on a white wall that is dramatically lit at night. It reminds us of the importance of the press, and it is a delight that the sign—and this newspaper—is still in business.

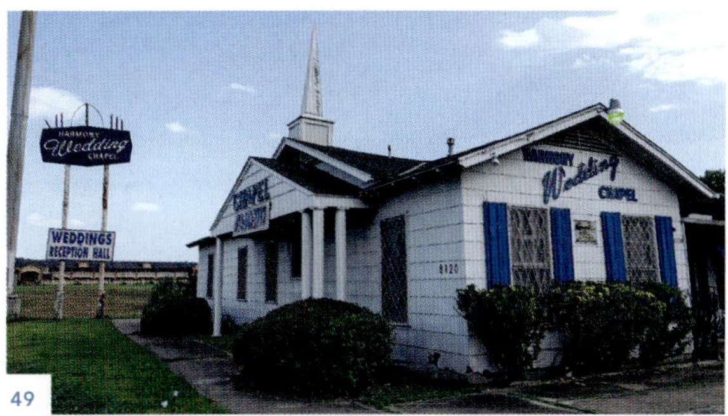

49

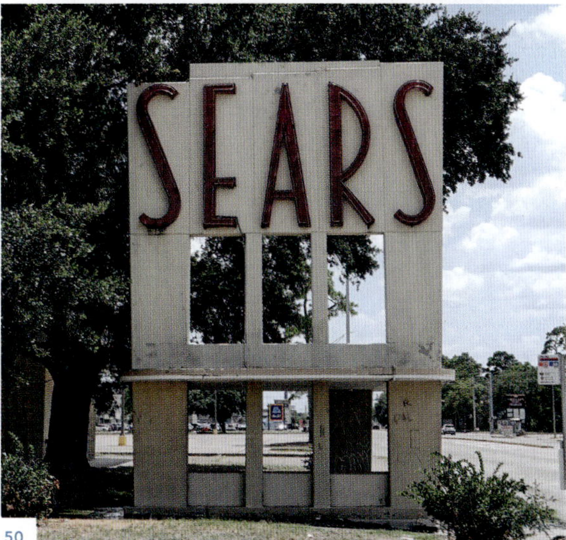

50

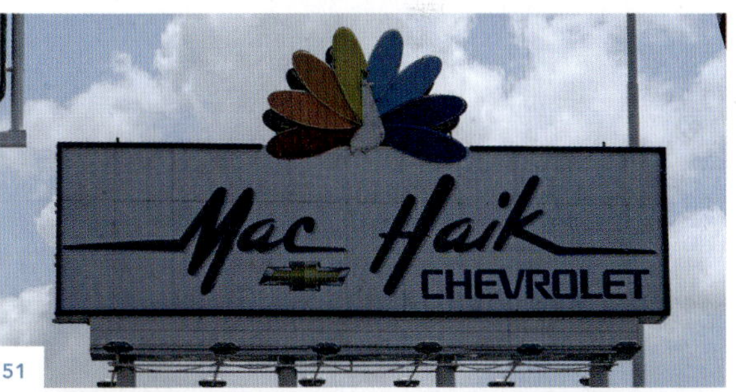

51

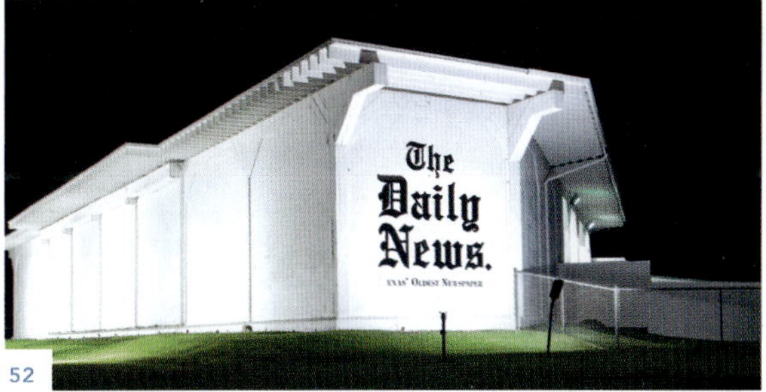

52

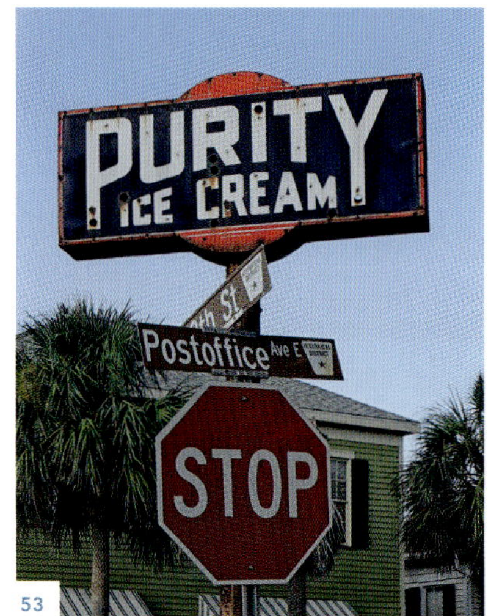

53

Purity Ice Cream (FIG. 53) in Galveston is another ghost brand, but this sign remains, a tantalizing relic in a residential neighborhood.

Once a sumptuous art deco movie palace, the long-closed **Martini Theater** (FIG. 54) in Galveston has been reduced to a ruin, but in its way, a lovely one. The current look, crumbling though it is, is linked to a modernist overhaul the theater received in 1970.

The old mill and elevator for **Yukon's Best Flour** (FIG. 55) in Yukon, Oklahoma, is a Route 66 icon, and the **Shop United** (FIG. 56) sign in Elk City, Oklahoma, is breathtaking.

The Rialto Theater (FIG. 57) in Searcy, Arkansas, opened in the 1920s and got a gorgeous art deco makeover in the 1940s, landing it on the National Register of Historic Places in 1991. It is still an active movie house.

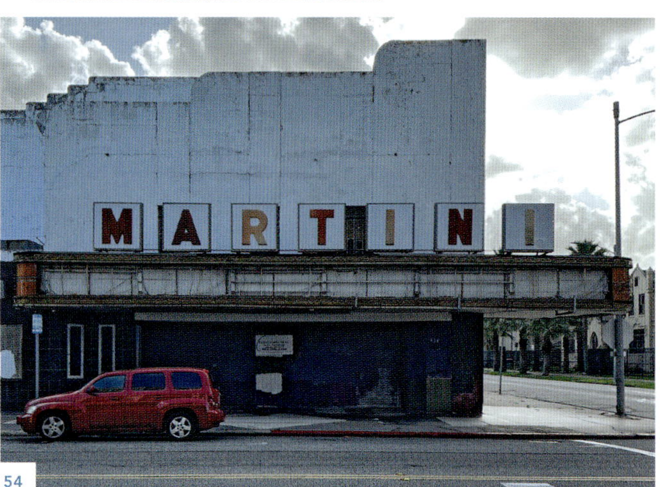

54

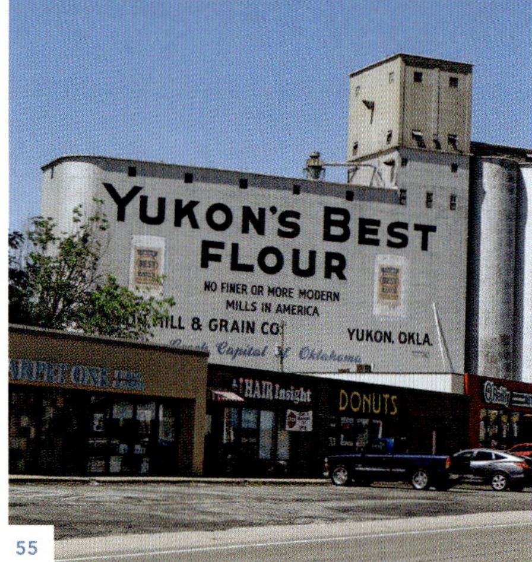

55

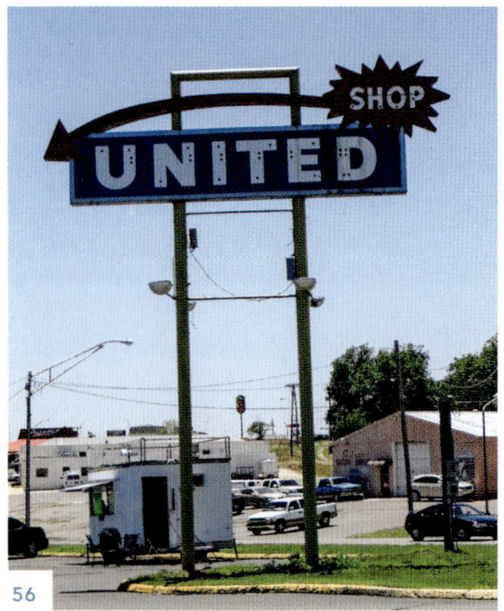

56

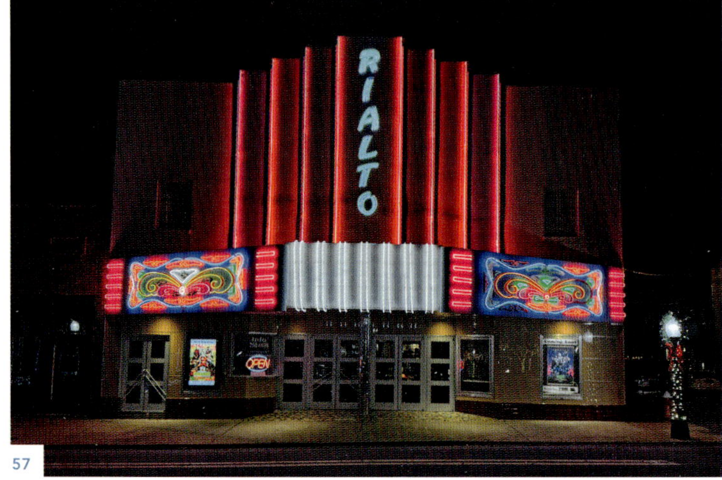

57

THE INN CROWD

Flamboyant vintage motel signs yell "Pull over and shoot!" to me, and I always obey. These two I encountered on Route 66.

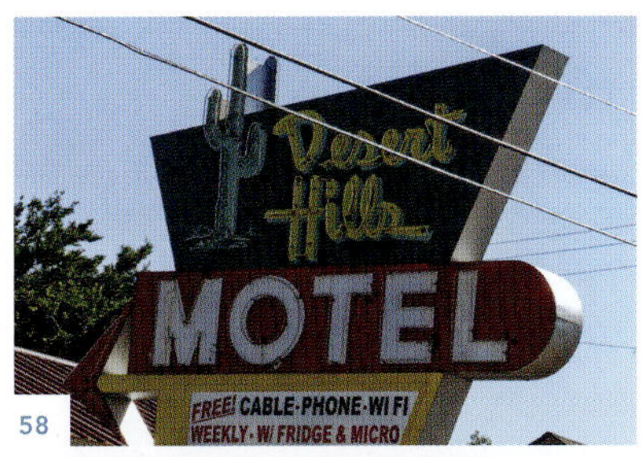

58

The Desert Hills Motel (FIG. 58) in Tulsa, Oklahoma, is one of the requisite photo stops on Route 66. It has attracted moviemakers and photographers (one spent three years photographing scenes reflective of the range of customers who stay in Room 116). The motel's name evokes the arid natural wonderland just beyond.

The Skyliner Motel (FIG. 59) held its grand opening on Sunday, August 2, 1959, a big day in Stroud, Oklahoma. Between 1 and 4 p.m., city folk toured the ten colorful motel rooms and inspected the modern touches like wall-to-wall carpeting, draw drapes, television sets, and even in-room phone service. Owners Jack and Lorene Tarter were proud to invest in Stroud. And the local paper said the sign "dresses up the corner considerably." Its pride is still showing.

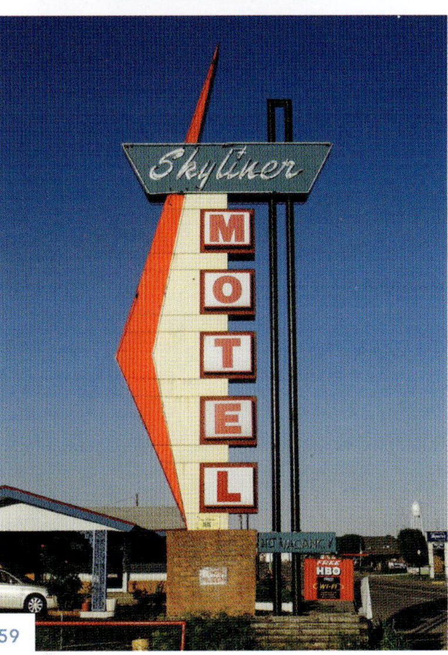

59

SWEET STOPS

From a big neon birthday cake to a grand scaffold sign and the story of a bovine mascot, I present some places for sugary indulgence.

The Meadow Gold (FIG. 60) scaffold sign in Tulsa, Oklahoma, is so gorgeous that it's hard to believe it was ever threatened. The ice-cream brand is still around, even if the sign itself almost disappeared. Route 66 enthusiasts and preservationists intervened, and today it is one of the highlights of the march across the Mother Road.

The historic sign for **Vandervoort's Dairy** (FIG. 62) in Fort Worth, with its cool shades of blue, takes the edge off the Texas sun. Vandervoort's traces its roots back to 1933 and became a

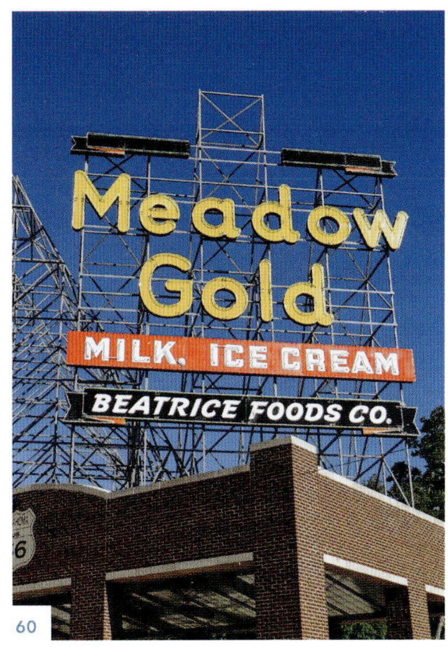

60

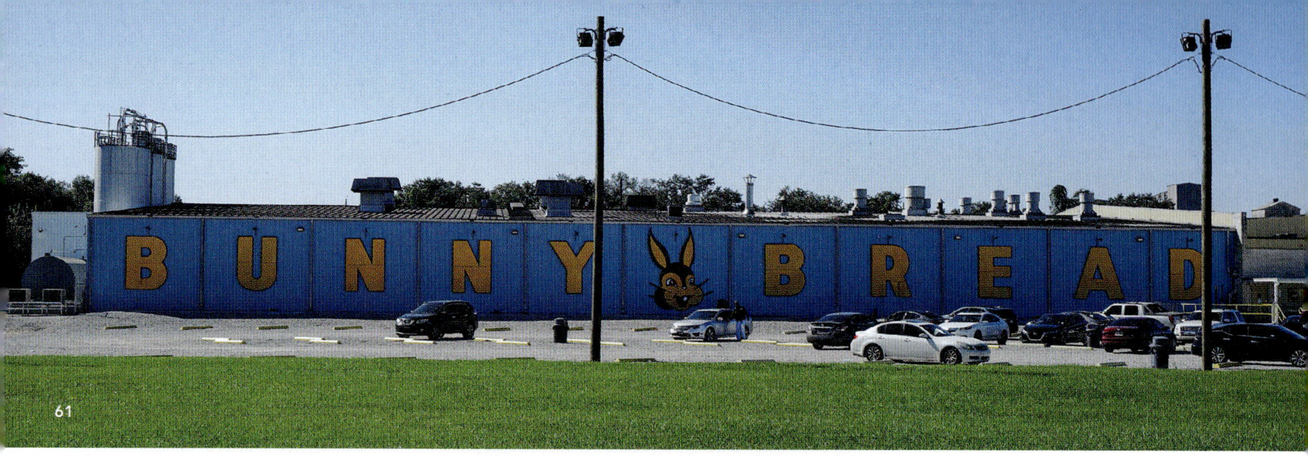

61

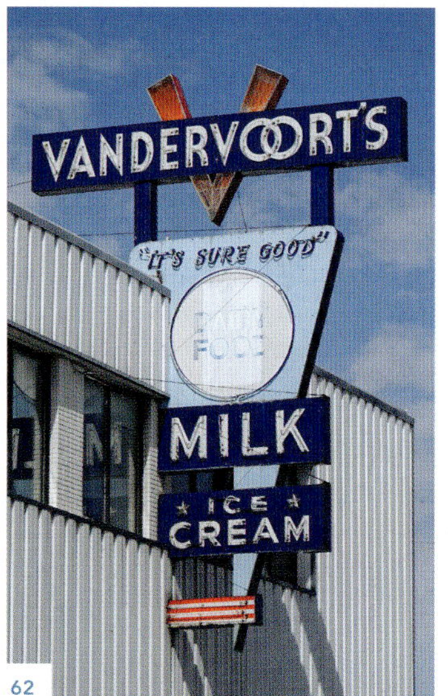

62

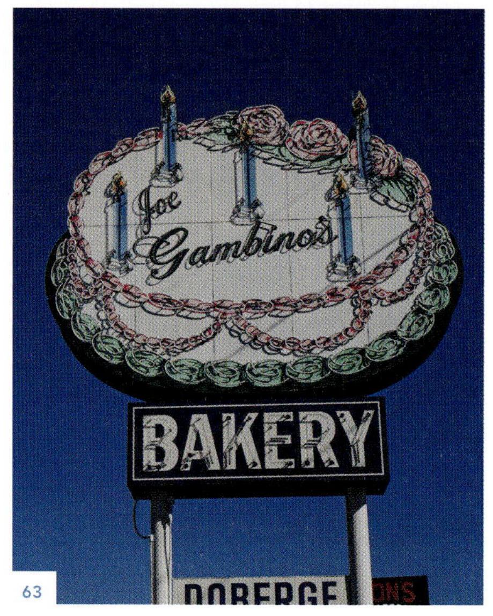

63

major distributor of dairy products in North Texas. Today, Vandervoort's still produces dairy under the aegis of Kroger supermarkets.

Gambino's Bakery (FIG. 63) is a Louisiana institution, a cherished spot to buy King Cake and the home of doberge cakes, the product of Beulah Ledner's fertile culinary mind. She sold her business and recipes to Joe Gambino in the 1940s, and he eventually opened a chain of Gambino's Bakery locations. This one, with the grand neon cake, is in Metairie, Louisiana. (**Paul's Bakery** in Van Buren, Arkansas, is another bakery-sign favorite.)

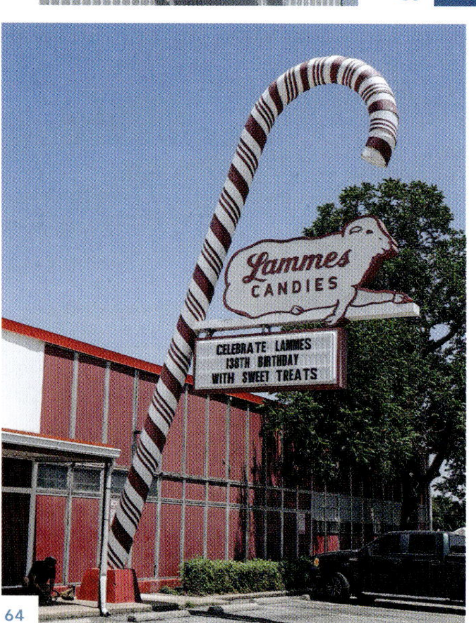

64

Head to the **Bunny Bread Thrift Store** (FIG. 61) in New Orleans, where you'll see a huge sign featuring an adorable bunny mascot. Bunny's native ground is Illinois, and you can see the original neon sign from the founding Lewis Brothers Bakery at the **Bundy Baking Museum** in Urbana, Ohio.

When in the Houston area, you know **Shipley's Donuts**, founded in 1936, has your ace in the hole, and the treats just hit better at the oldest surviving location.

Lammes Candies (FIG. 64) in Austin, Texas, founded in 1885, is surely one of the most charming storefronts you will see in this book, and the flagship location, on Airport Boulevard, is the showstopper. Unsure of what to get? Pick up a Texas Chewie Pecan Praline box and thank me later.

Arandas Bakery (FIG. 66) is a pioneering Mexican panadería in Houston, founded by Jose Camarena in 1993. The mascot chef and feel of the signage give off way-back vibes. The bread is delicious, too.

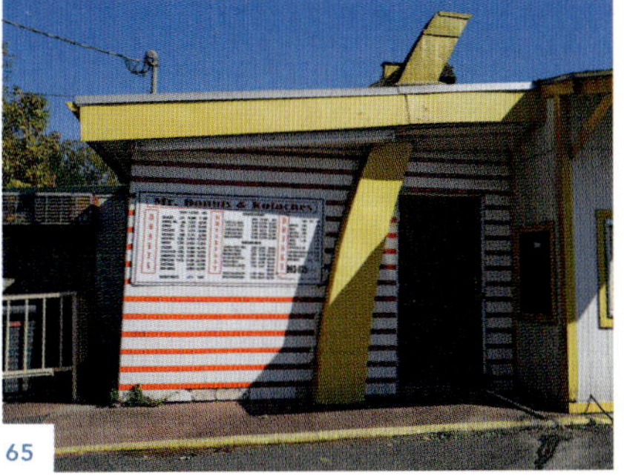

65

66

Mr. Donuts & Kolaches (FIG. 65) in Marshall, Texas, is undoubtedly a fine purveyor of what it advertises. But it made the cut in this book because it's a former "red and white" McDonald's, the style that emerged in the 1950s and persisted until the arrival of the mansard-roofed buildings in 1969. Note the shorn Golden Arches on the building.

Dairy Delights!

Texas has the most Dairy Queens in the nation, and the South Central region of the U.S. has no shortage of ice-cream stands. Some of the sweetest in my book: **Dairy Bar**, Grand Saline, Texas; **Dairy Mart**, Mineral Wells, Texas; and **Barnett's Dairyette** in Siloam Springs, Arkansas.

For old-school ice cream with Sicilian pedigree—aka mouthwatering gelato—**Angelo Brocato** (FIG. 67) is a New Orleans tradition, and still in the same family since 1905.

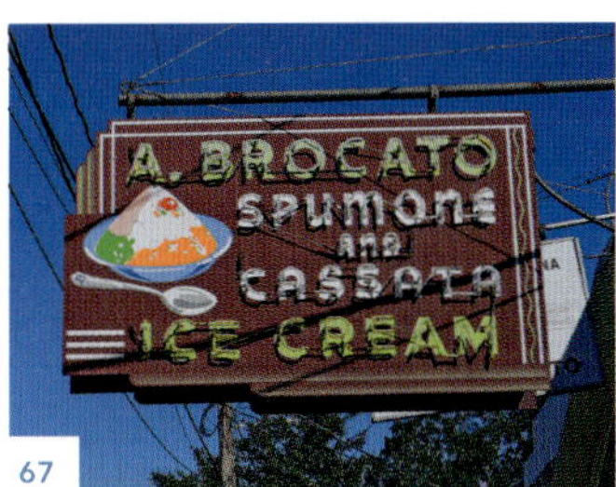

67

BORDEN'S AND THE STORY OF ELSIE THE COW

"If it's Borden's . . . it's got to be good!" So says the neon outside the last Borden's retail ice-cream shop in America, lovingly run by Kackie Lerille in Lafayette, Louisiana. It opened in 1940 and has been carefully renovated to expand the dining room and enhance the vintage atmosphere. (I had one heck of a milkshake along with my chili.) Borden's was one of the great American dairy brands and Elsie the Cow, featured on the facade, one of the great mascots.

Created in 1936 as a cartoon character for Borden's, a real-life Elsie was a star of the 1939–40 World's Fair in Queens, New York, and the Jersey heifer would tour the country on behalf of Borden's until her death—in a truck accident—in 1941. Borden's would go on to have more "real" Elsies, while the original rests in Plainsboro Township, New Jersey, in a grave you can visit. (Fun fact: She was "married" to Elmer of Elmer's Glue fame.)

Her visage can also be found in a mosaic at **Flushing Meadows Corona Park** (FIG. 68), the site of the fair; in stores like **Elsie's Place** in Wallkill, New York; at **Eicke's Restaurant** in Norwich, New York; and at a plant in Tyler, Texas.

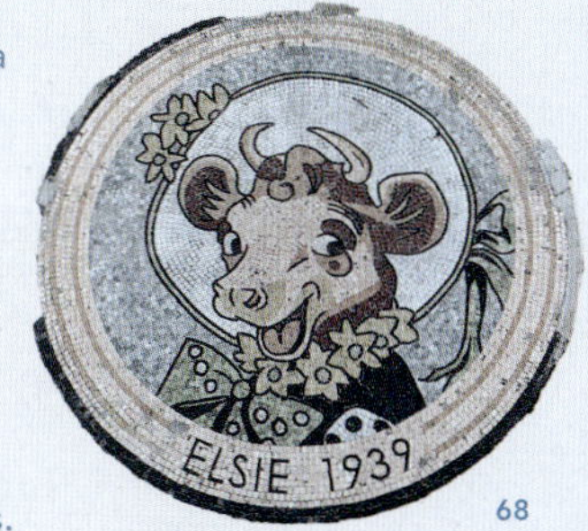

68

CHEERS!

It'll do, this roundup of places for a drink—It'll Do is also the name of one of the bars we're about to visit.

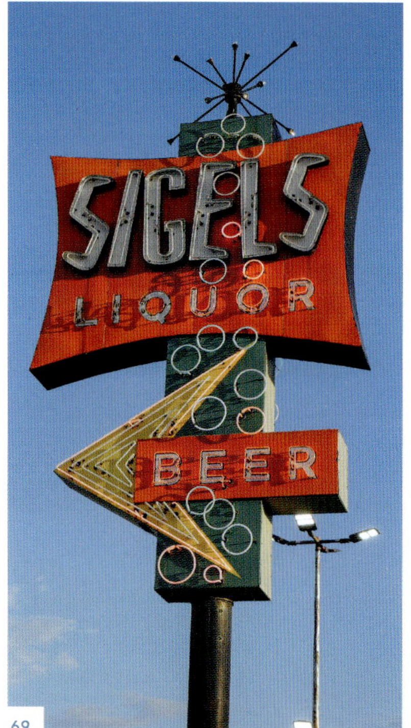

69

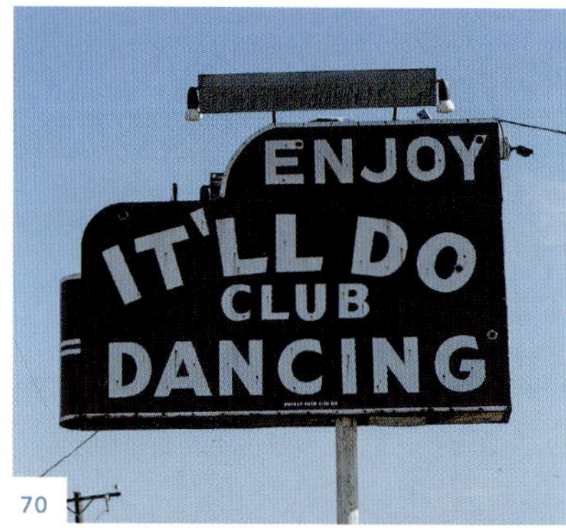

70

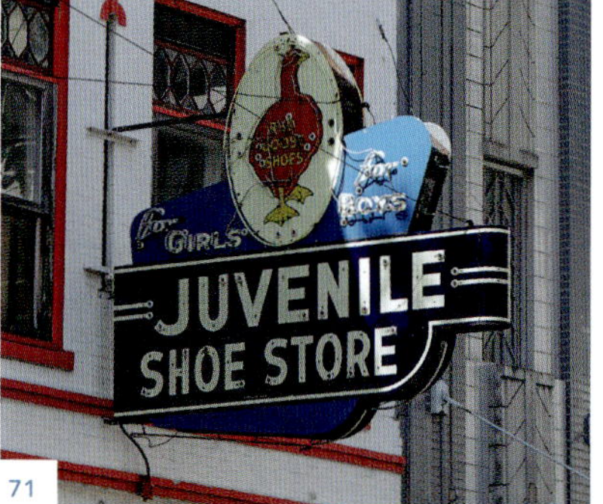

71

Sigel's Fine Wines & Great Spirits (FIG. 69) has one of the grandest neon signs in America. The Sigel's chain went through bankruptcy and was absorbed by Austin-based Twin Liquors, but this sign in Dallas has survived the life-or-death battle, thank goodness.

When in Dallas and unsure where to dance the evening away, just remember this place: **It'll Do** (FIG. 70). This old-school bar didn't get a "liquor by the drink" permit until 1971, when legal mixed drinks were given the legislative thumbs-up. (Sales of mixed drinks had been banned in Texas since 1919, despite Prohibition's end in 1933!)

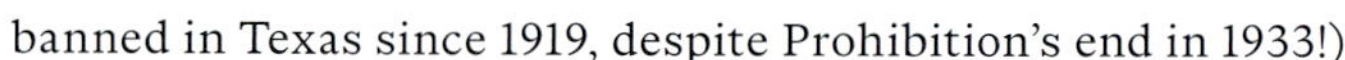

The Red Goose Saloon (FIG. 71) in Fort Worth, Texas, is a wonderful example of function follows sign. This storefront was once a children's shoe store that billed Red Goose Shoes in bright red neon. The racks of shoes have long since been swapped for barstools, but the sign never went anywhere, and its presence was so iconic that the saloon took its name.

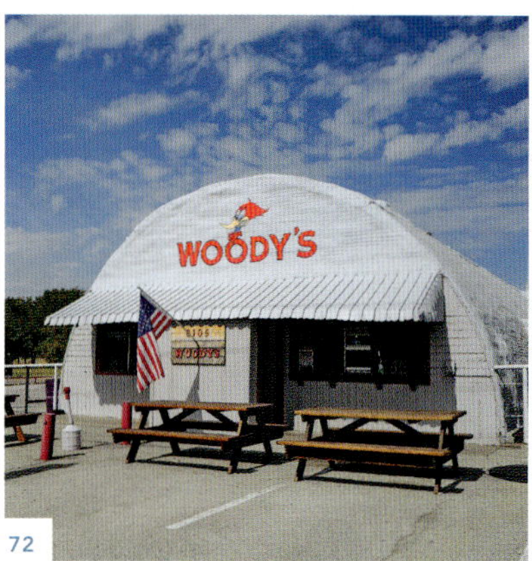

72

Woody's Bar & Grill (FIG. 72) in Mineral Wells, Texas, boasts of serving the best burger in the state. I am in no position to judge that, but I can say that the neon signage and the ode to Woody Woodpecker on the Quonset hut building are a wondrous sight.

One of the great watering holes in the orbit of essential New Orleans corner taverns is the **Saturn Bar** (FIG. 73). The bar changed hands during the pandemic after being run by the Broyard family for decades. Paterfamilias O'Neil Broyard turned the space into the Saturn Bar in 1960 and over the decades it became famous for its quirky decor, the crowd it drew, and the music acts it showcased, if not for the bathrooms that were to be avoided.

Heather Lane and Phil Yiannopoulos took over the Saturn Bar with the goal of preserving its spirit, even if they couldn't hang on to the old artifacts (for instance, artworks that left with the Broyard family) or the corner sign (destroyed by Hurricane Ida, alas, but since remade based on an older one found inside).

Half Moon Bar (FIG. 74) is another NOLA institution with a classic sign, and its walls have witnessed more than we will ever know. A newspaper clipping from 1976 gives insight into the Half Moon of that era. A reporter for *The Daily Advertiser* stopped by the watering hole to assess opinions of the October 6, 1976 debate between President Gerald Ford and his challenger Jimmy Carter—and the reporter wrote that politics was "the spice of life" at the Half Moon, but "most listeners seemed more engrossed in their beer."

For an adult carnival atmosphere, few spots beat the **Carousel Bar** (FIG. 75) in New Orleans, where patrons sidle up to a bar on a slowly moving carousel, taking fifteen minutes to make a revolution! Giddyup! It's located at the historic Hotel Monteleone.

I was intrigued with the facade of the **Gizmo Bar** (FIG. 76) during an early-morning drive through Galveston, Texas. At night, the neon of **Jack's** and the **Press Box** dazzle nearby.

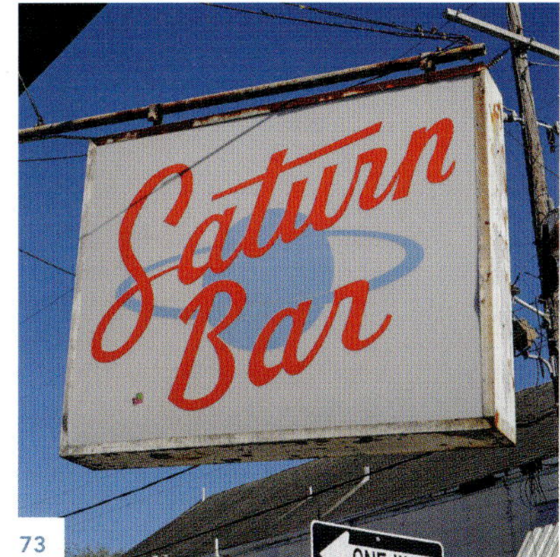

73

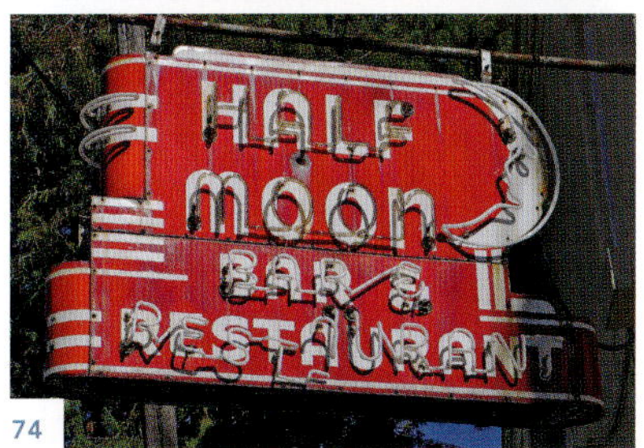

74

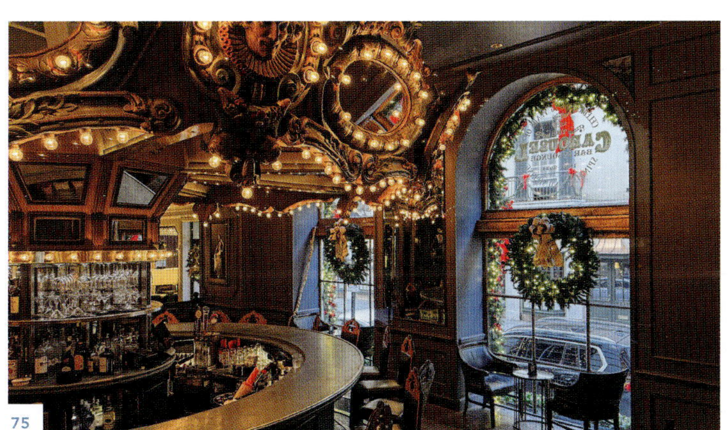
75

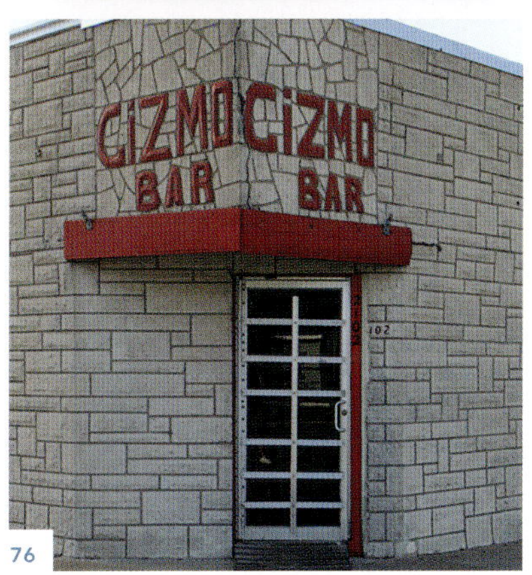

76

Hi-Way
CAFE
1

Dot
Coffee Shop
OPEN 24 HRS.
2

LWORTH 5&10
3

Frostop
ROOT
BEER
4

SAKS FIFTH AVEN
5

Pause Refresh
DRINK
Coca-Cola
Entergy
6

Alright, alright, alright!
Welcome to
UVALDE, TEXAS
Birthplace of
Matthew McConaughey
Oscar Winning Actor
7

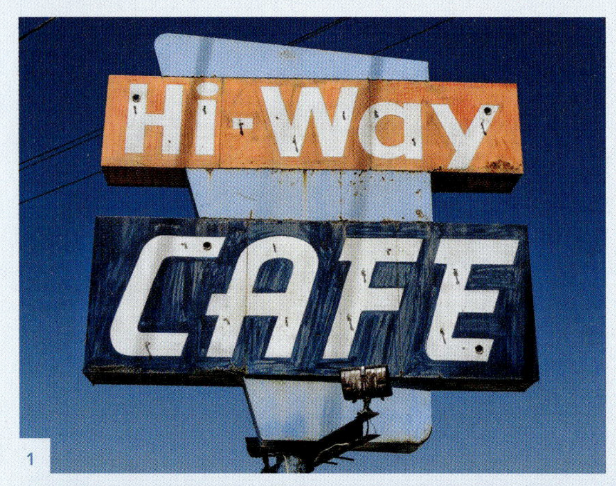

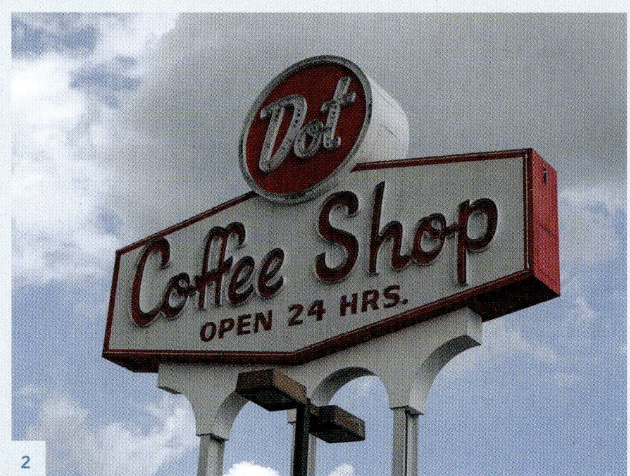

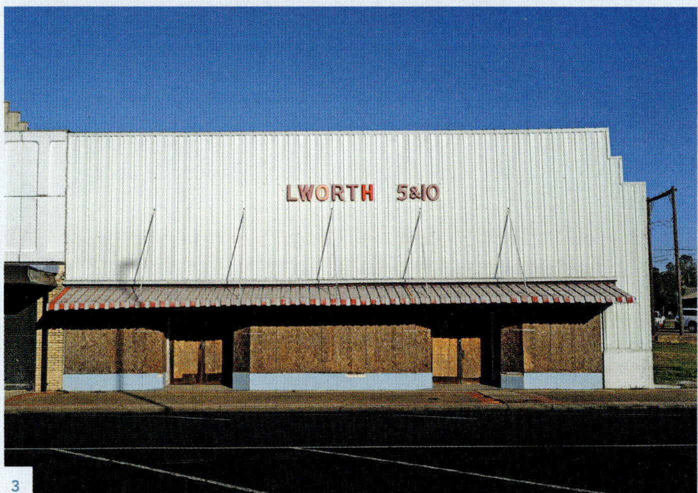

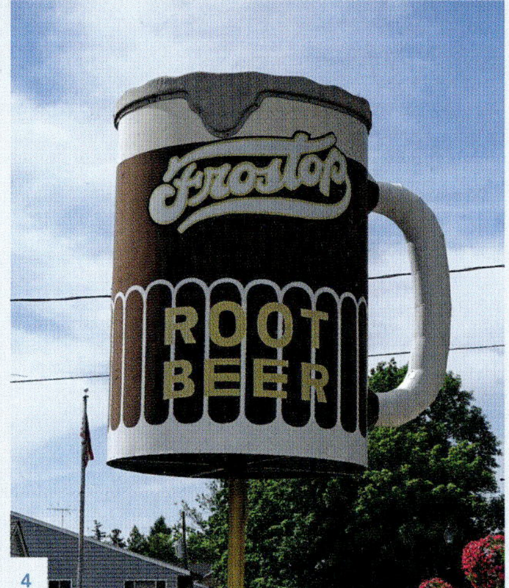

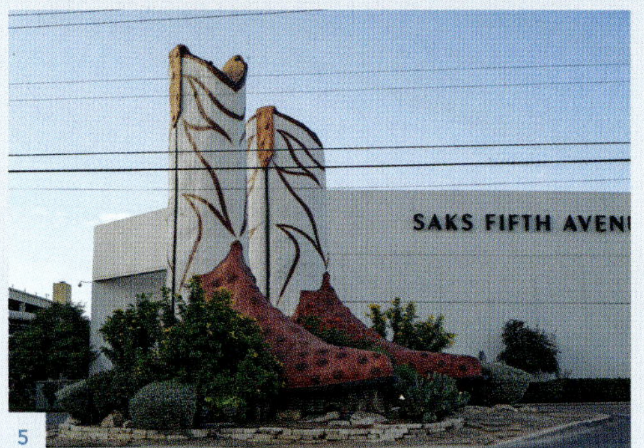

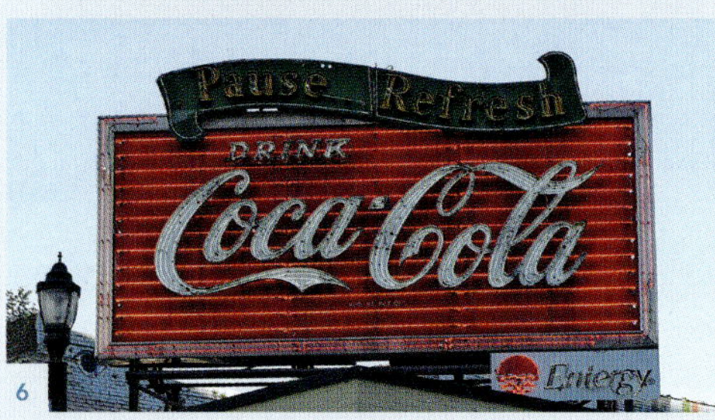

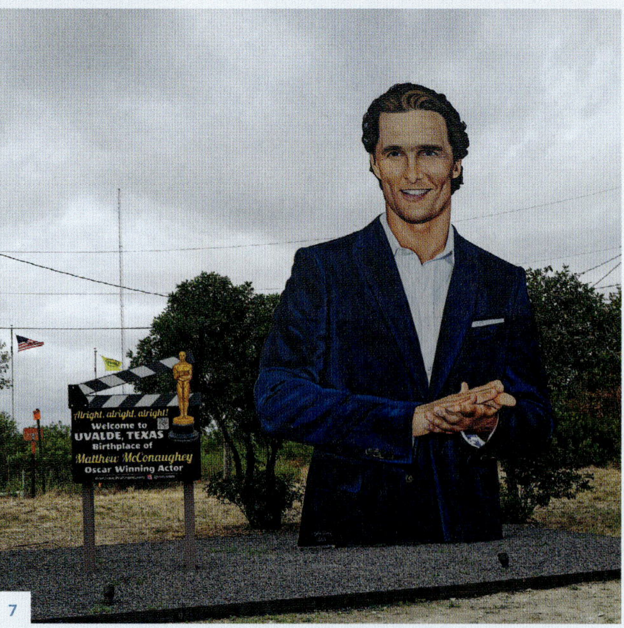

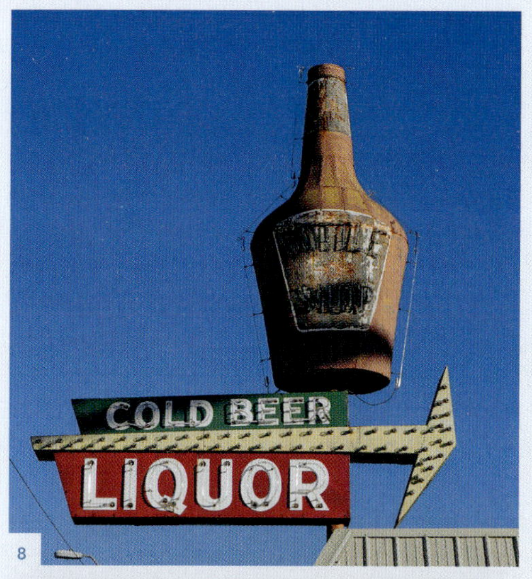

8

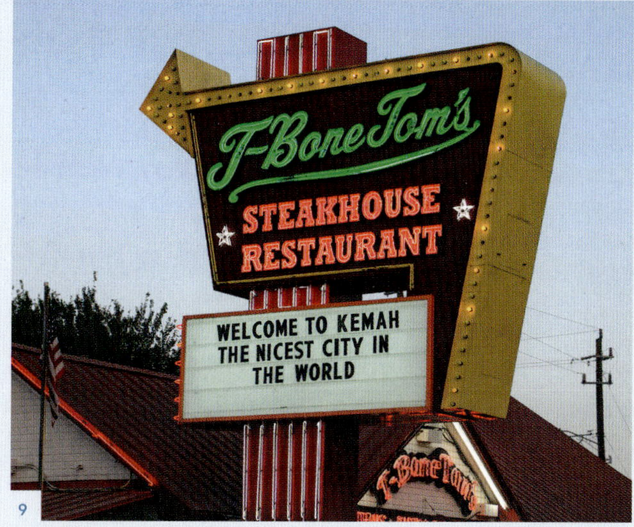

9

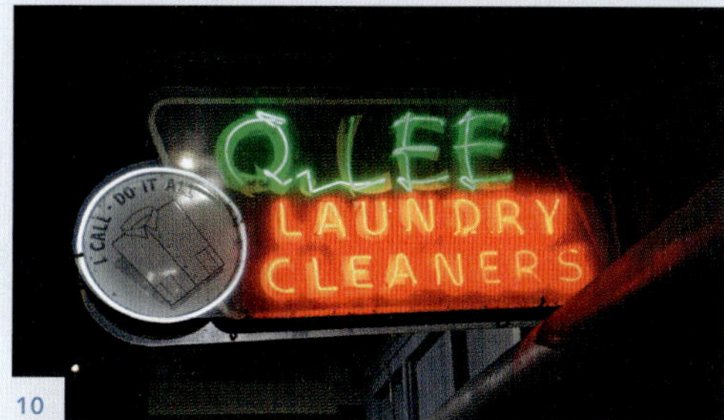

10

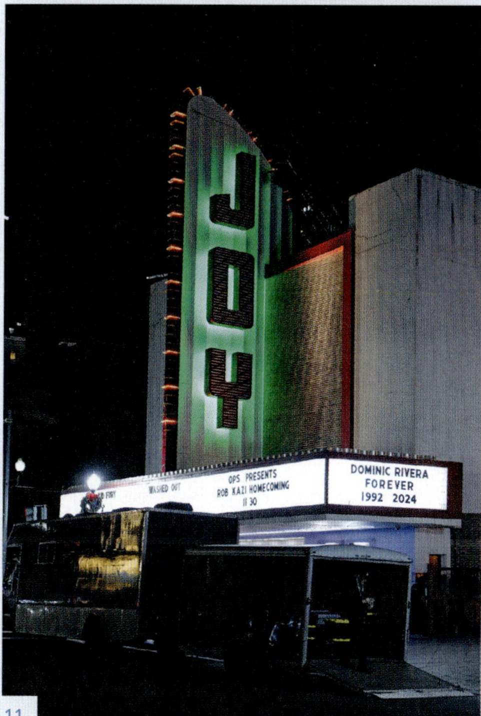

11

DON'T MESS WITH THESE SIGNS!

Keep an eye out for some of these gems as you make your way through the region.

1. Hi-Way Cafe, Vinita, Oklahoma
2. Dot Coffee Shop, Houston, Texas
3. Woolworth's, Texarkana, Arkansas
4. LaPlace Frostop, LaPlace, Louisiana
5. World's Largest Cowboy Boots, San Antonio, Texas
6. Coca-Cola sign, Baton Rouge, Louisiana
7. Matthew McConaughey cutout sign, Uvalde, Texas (McConaughey's hometown)
8. Bottle Shop, Texarkana, Arkansas
9. T-Bone Tom's, Kemah, Texas
10. Q. Lee Laundry & Cleaners, New Orleans, Louisiana
11. Joy Theater, New Orleans, Louisiana

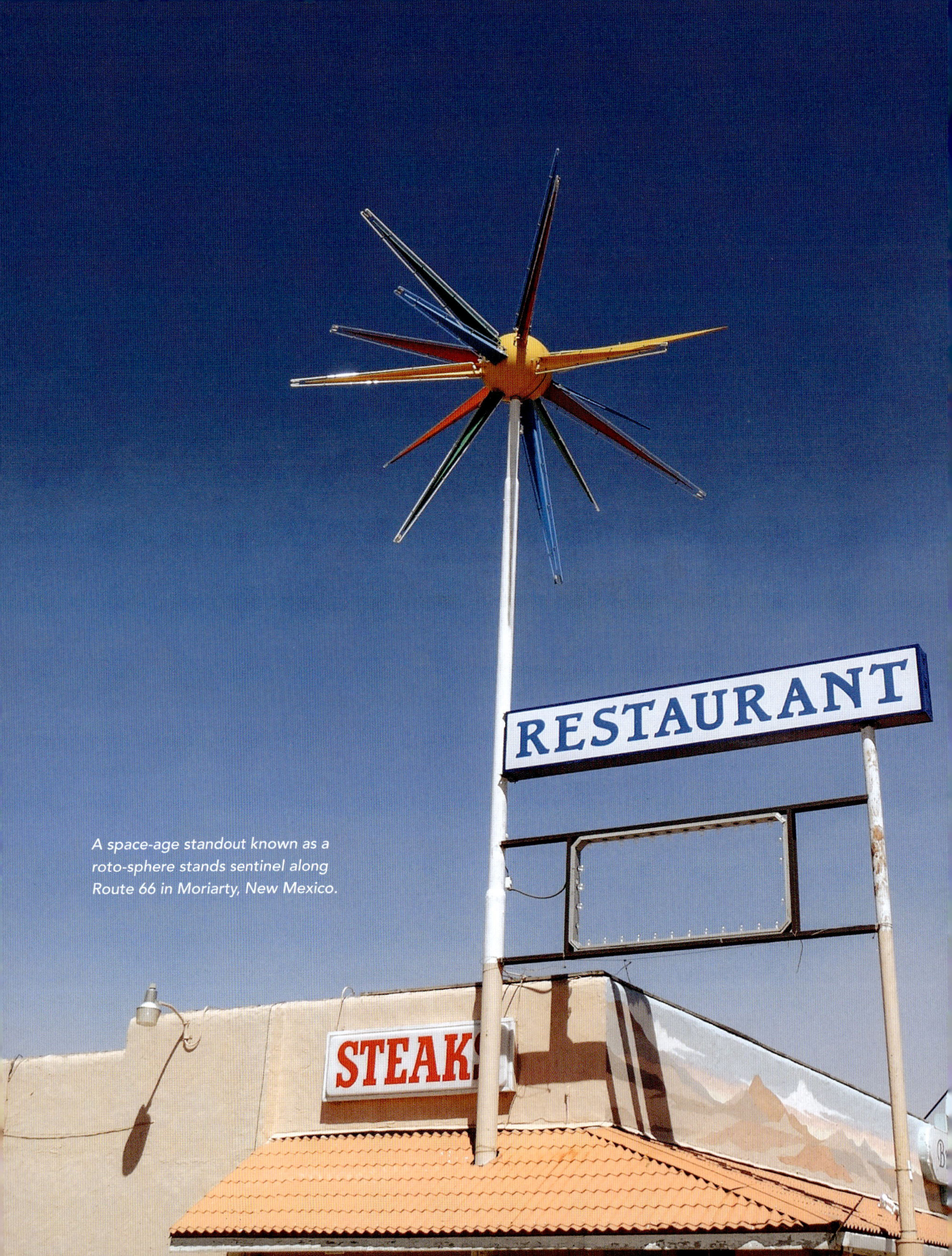

A space-age standout known as a roto-sphere stands sentinel along Route 66 in Moriarty, New Mexico.

DESERT SOUTHWEST

ARIZONA · NEW MEXICO · PARTS OF NEVADA

America is teeming with quirky roadside attractions, but the Desert Southwest has some of the finest—and certainly the most fun. Want to step inside a prehistoric-set cartoon world? No problem. Visit the real-life inspirations for places in the Pixar movie *Cars*? Done. Grab a burrito cooked inside a gigantic (and cute) gopher? Your wish is my command. Get your kicks on Route 66? I wouldn't dare stop you! Enjoy this journey through time, starting with some of my favorite quirks in the nation.

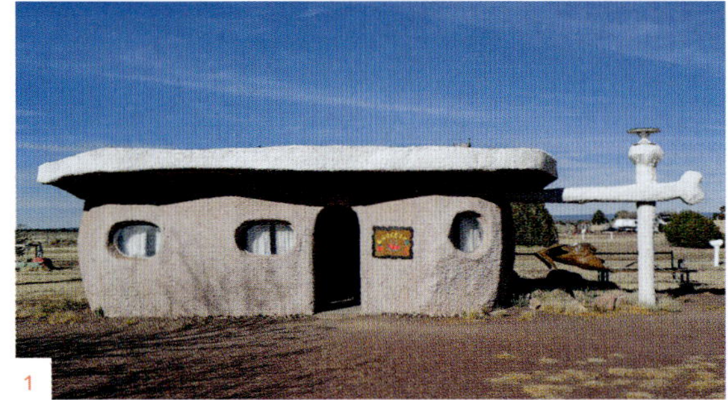

1

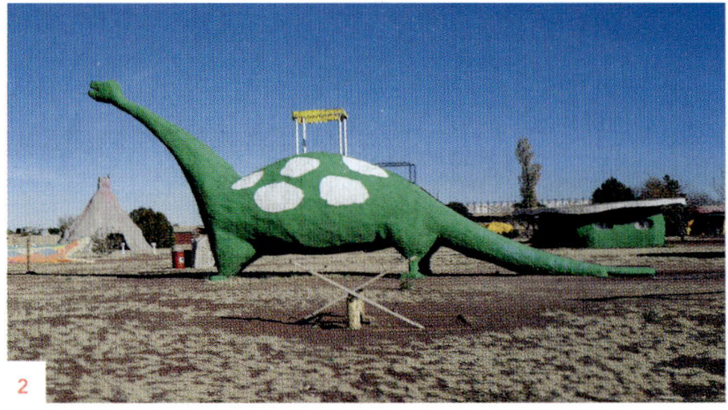

2

ROADSIDE QUIRKS

When prehistoric fact meets prehistoric fiction, you know we're in for a fun time. Then we'll "hop" on over to Route 66 in search of a mythical creature.

3

You'll have a "gay old time" at **Bedrock City** (FIGS. 1, 2, 3)—an attraction based on the classic 1960–66 animated television series *The Flintstones*—located near Williams, Arizona, en route to the Grand Canyon's South Rim. The cartoon was a popular prime-time series on ABC, but like so many early television shows, it became an even bigger cultural force when it entered syndication. Since the local-station reruns began in 1967, *The Flintstones* has probably played somewhere on earth every day, spawning spinoffs, movies, vitamins, cereal, and countless tchotchkes.

Back in 1966, when the show was just wrapping its original run, Woodrow Speckels and his son Francis "Hudi" of South Dakota hit up an idea that was a "page right out of history." Looking for a can't-miss-tourist-attraction concept in the heyday of the family road trip to destination amusement parks, they struck gold—or, rather, stone—by turning life in Bedrock into reality near Custer, in the Black Hills. They opened the very first Bedrock City with the blessing of Screen Gems, the studio that produced the show, in 1966, and it was a smash hit with tourists.

In 1972 came the roadside sequel: Francis and his wife, Linda, opened this branch in Valle, Arizona. They ended up raising their family there, the park a true family affair. The original location in Custer is long gone, but in Arizona, you can still commune with the endearingly familiar characters and buildings from Hanna-Barbera's conception of the Stone Age. You feel a sense of wonder standing outside Fred and Wilma's House, as though you are in the show's closing credits. You almost expect an angry Fred to appear, furious that he's locked out of the house, banging on the door and bellowing, "*Wilma!*" You can also explore the Rubble family house, the Bedrock post office, and so much more architectural fiction turned fact. (Grab a bite at Fred's Diner, in the gift shop.)

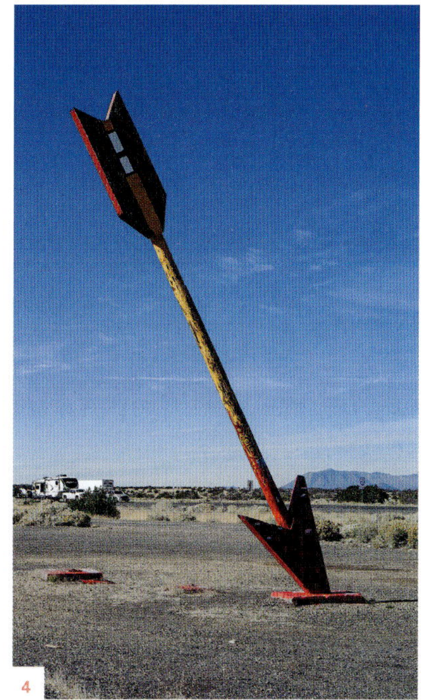

4

Bedrock City, under that name, anyway, closed in 2019 when Linda Speckels—her husband died in 1990—sold the property to Troy Morris and the operators of Raptor Ranch. While they introduced their concept of celebrating birds of prey, the new owners, after talks of demolition stirred a rush of panicked visitors, decided to preserve the artifacts of Bedrock City, quickly realizing the people were making the drive to have a yabba-dabba good time!

Seemingly as prehistoric as Bedrock City is the **Twin Arrows Trading Post** (FIG. 4) in Flagstaff, Arizona. Well, at this writing, we might as well rechristen it "Single Arrow." One of the two giant wooden arrows impaled into the earth collapsed in 2022; when I visited, all that was left was its base. It's a grim sight for one of the must-see attractions of the Great American Retro Road Trip. The derelict tagged buildings offer evidence of what was once a thriving little stop on Route 66. When U.S. 40 bypassed Route 66, the fate of this trading post was sealed. You can spot it in happier times in a scene from the 1994 movie *Forrest Gump*.

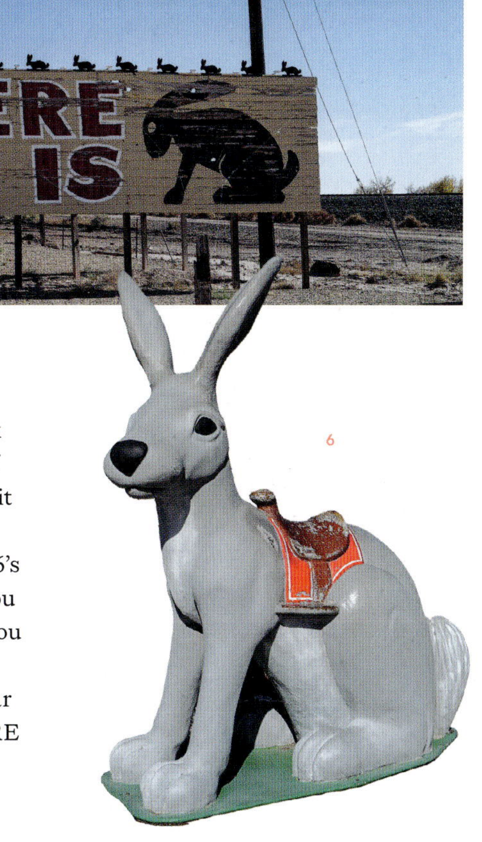

5

6

On a "hoppier" note, Route 66 attractions don't get much more iconic than the **Jack Rabbit Trading Post** (FIGS. 5, 6) in Joseph City, Arizona, where a giant fiberglass jackrabbit greets you, inviting you to hop on for a photo. Like **Wall Drug** (page 220), **The Thing** (page 197), and **South of the Border** (page 96), the Jack Rabbit became a legendary stop by trading on the excitement of anticipation, built by a barrage of billboards compelling (or was it *commanding*?) you to pull over.

These days, the sea of signage is mostly gone, but in Route 66's heyday, each sign ticked off the distance to Jack Rabbit. Once you reached the exit after all that visual bombardment, how could you not pull over for a look-see? And just in case there's any doubt that you've arrived, a gigantic yellow sign—with the now-familiar black silhouette of the rabbit—announces "HERE IT IS!" ("HARE IT IS" was a missed wordplay opportunity.)

▶▶▶ Pull Over!

The Continental Divide captures the imagination, and how could it not? It's amazing to think there is a geographic highpoint where the flow of water divides—to the west it empties into the Pacific Ocean, and to the east, it snakes toward the Atlantic Ocean.

This obligatory stop in New Mexico along Route 66 celebrates the Continental Divide in a town named after the geological feature. The wall is part of the aptly named Top of the World curio shop.

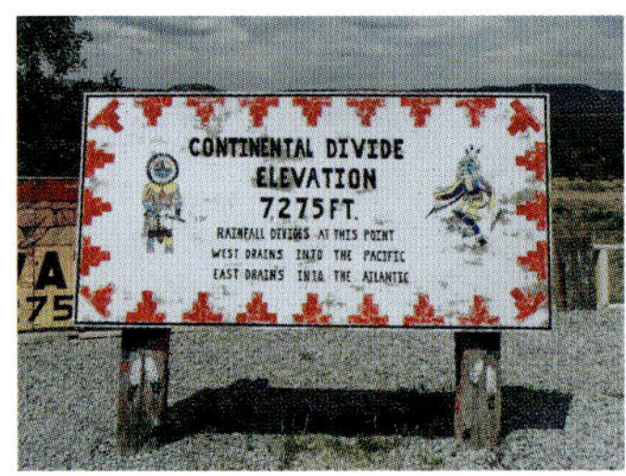

Like so many others, the trading post opened in the years after World War II, when Route 66's homespun attractions were in their prime. Jim Taylor bought what would become the Jack Rabbit in 1949—the trading post's official history states that a statue of a black rabbit Taylor had in his convertible drew the curious, which led to a creative leap in branding (the name) and marketing (the mileage markers).

Back then, the term "trading post" was already an evocative throwback to the frontier days—the only trading that was happening was their souvenir for your cash. The Jack Rabbit was leased and later bought by Glenn Blansett in the 1960s and it's still in the family, run by Cindy and Tony Jaquez.

Fun fact: Pixar's *Cars* immortalized the Jack Rabbit Trading Post, swapping its familiar image for that of a Model T but keeping the words "HERE IT IS" in the forgotten town of Radiator Springs.

Down the road from the Jack Rabbit is the **Geronimo Trading Post,** which boasts the so-called world's largest petrified tree, and a mural in town nearby honors Frank DoBell, who is credited with first selling petrified wood to tourists.

Truth or Consequences (FIG. 7) is a funny name for a town. If it sounds like the name of a game show, you're right. When the *Truth or Consequences* radio show promised it would broadcast its tenth-anniversary program from the first town to rechristen itself after the show, the people of this New Mexico town abandoned the original name of Hot Springs like a hot potato. Put to a vote on March 31, 1950, the name change won in a landslide. And they weren't foolin'. They've stuck with the name to this day.

While most of the eight thousand folks in town were comfortable with the consequences of the moniker makeover, one eighty-five-year-old, quoted in an Associated Press story, was not feeling it, colorfully explaining: "Now who in thundernation can spell this Consequences thing anyway."

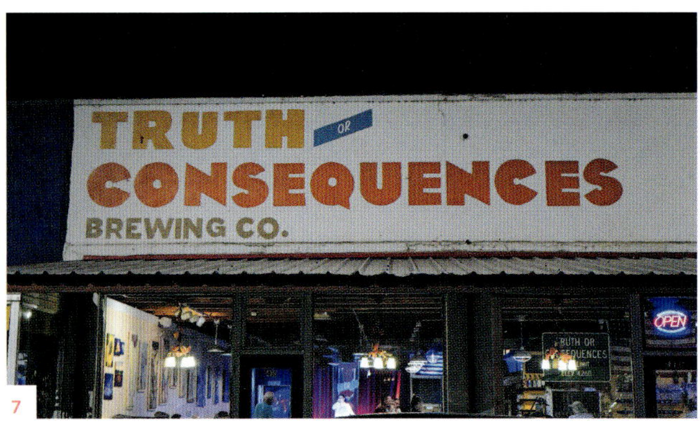

7

That very day, game-show host Ralph Edwards was in town to celebrate, and as promised, the next day emcee the live broadcast of this special episode, beamed across the land. Edwards became revered around here and returned regularly over the next half century to participate in what became the annual "Fiesta" festival, still celebrated here in what the cool kids call "T or C."

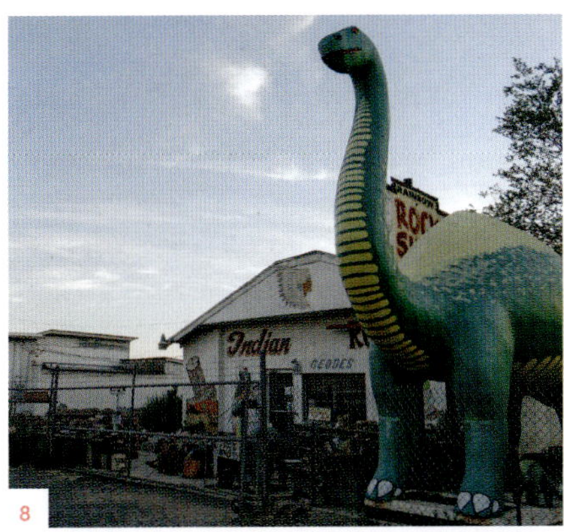

8

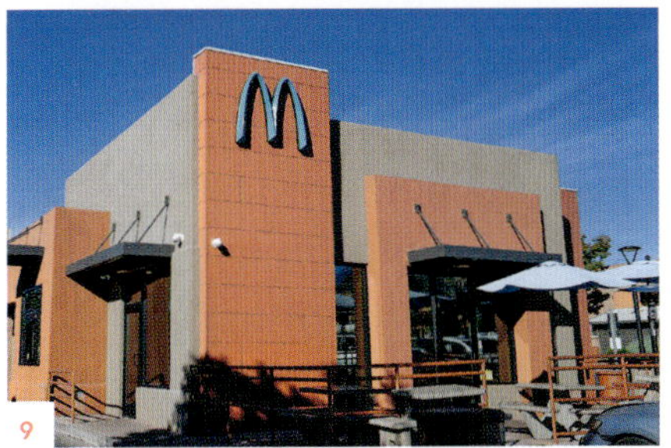
9

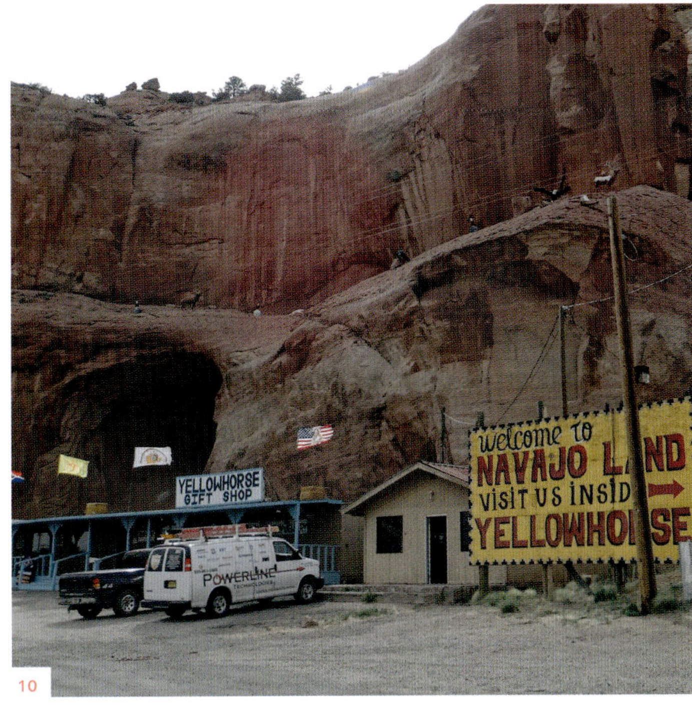

10

The **Pow Wow Trading Post** (FIG. 11) and **Rainbow Rock Shop** (FIG. 8) in Holbrook, Arizona, are throwbacks to the early Route 66 days, capturing the lengths to which store owners went to catch the eye of the motorist—and the kids squirming in the back seat, undoubtedly not strapped in with seatbelts. It's hard to resist the lure of roadside dinosaurs roaming at the Rainbow Rock shop, for example, and you can enjoy some DQ down the street (see page 200).

One of the most dramatic trading posts lies at the New Mexico–Arizona border. The **Yellowhorse Trading Post** (FIG. 10) is set against a bluff, a stunning contrast that captures the natural (and roadside) charms of this place so well, the ephemeral and the eternal.

We see such contrasts all throughout the Southwest. A cool example can be found at the **McDonald's** on Highway 89A in Sedona, Arizona. Here, it's the **Teal Arches** (FIG. 9), said to be a compromise between McDonald's and the city of Sedona in the early 1990s. The story goes that when McDonald's wanted to open here, Sedona was concerned that the chain's traditional bold colors would clash with the earth-toned, red-rock natural beauty of the terrain. The result is a building that in all respects fits in more nicely with nature's designs.

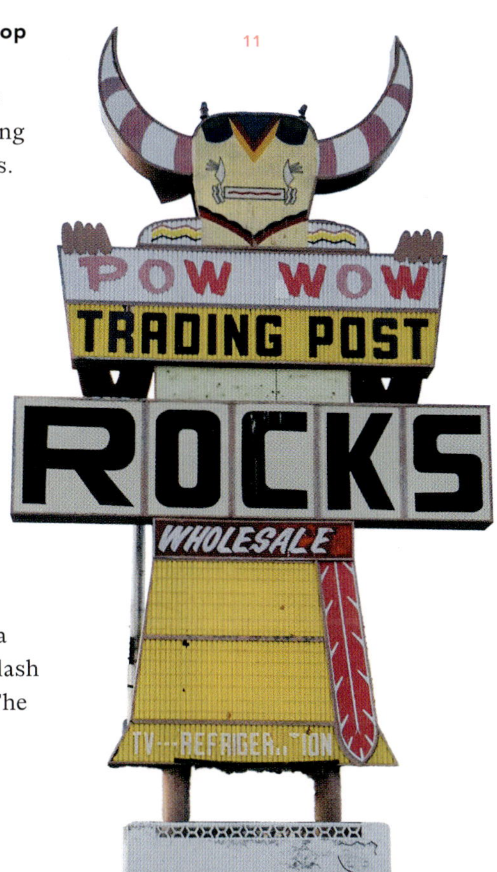

11

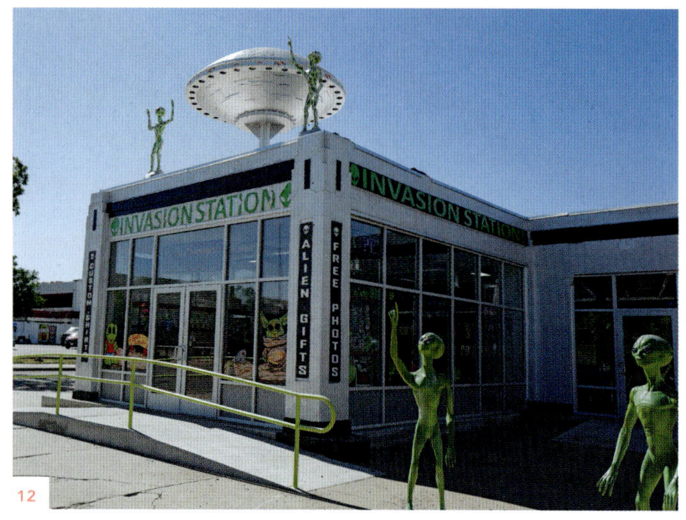

12

This is not the first time McDonald's has compromised in design and architecture in its quest to expand. (See page 299 for examples in Maine and New York state.) If quirky McDonald's locations intrigue you, pop into your GPS the **World's First McDonald's Drive-Thru,** in Sierra Vista, Arizona. McDonald's was a pioneer in countless ways, but not in the area of restaurant drive-thru service. Other notable brands like In-N-Out and even early-seventies-arriviste Wendy's, which branded them "pick-up windows" (see page 147), got into the game earlier than McDonald's. The original mansard building that housed the drive-thru was demolished in 1999 and replaced, but the distinction of being the first Golden Arches drive-thru is heralded on the sign high atop a pole.

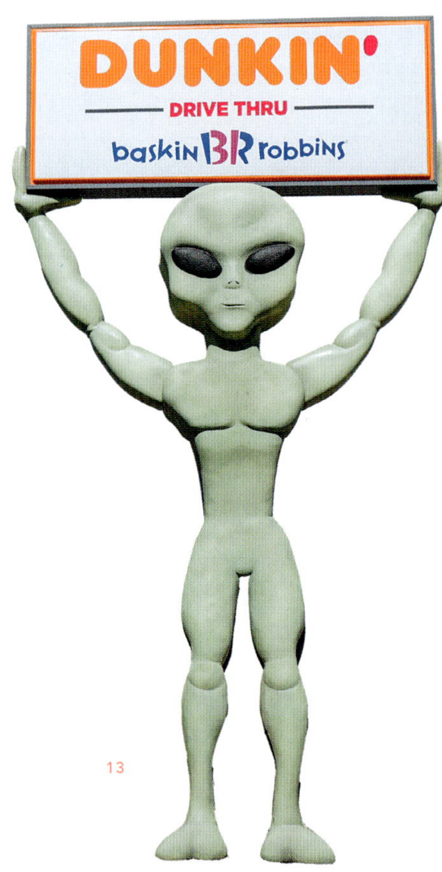

13

This location became the first McDonald's drive-thru by chance. Plans for the first one in Oklahoma City in late 1974 were delayed, but interest had long been building. In Sierra Vista, the operator of the recently opened McDonald's (along the aptly named Fry Boulevard) pitched his location because it would solve a big problem that would also boost sales. Soldiers at the nearby Fort Huachuca Army Base could not be seen in public sporting their fatigues—an old rule about decorum was the reason—so visiting McDonald's during the workday was out of the question for them. It wouldn't be a problem if the military staff could stay in their cars the entire time they were at the restaurant, and so on January 24, 1975, the McDonald's in Sierra Vista became the first to offer drive-thru service. The soldiers were surely lovin' it, and, of course, it was more than fatigue-clad folks who liked the convenience—by the end of the decade more than half of the McDonald's in the U.S. featured drive-thrus. If you love this story, the original glass window from the drive-thru has been preserved and is on display at the Henry F. Hauser Museum in town.

Roswell, New Mexico, prides itself as the home of all things UFO related. The infamous Roswell incident in 1947, in which a farmer found what many called debris from a crashed flying saucer, tickling what became a national obsession with the subject, happened 75 miles away. But the name "Roswell" got attached to it, and the city has embraced its little-green-men heritage, like at the **Invasion Station** gift shop (FIG. 12) on Main Street.

You deserve a break today, as the old McDonald's jingle went. And so do little green men. The McDonald's in Roswell has embraced this town's out-of-this-world theme, planting a **UFO-shaped building** (FIG. 14) on its property, tucked between a glassy PlayPlace and an updated dining room. Silvery alien statues are on hand to greet you. (This would seem like a good town to open a CosMc's restaurant, the new McDonald's store concept named after an obscure McDonaldland alien character from the 1980s.)

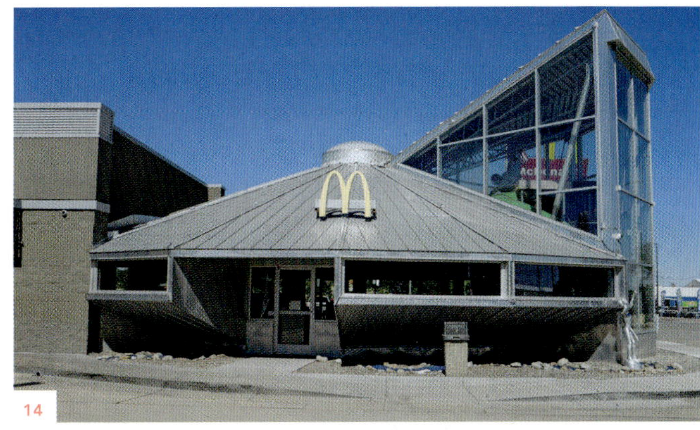
14

You can find depictions of aliens everywhere around here, and the most caffeinated green man is standing outside the city's **Dunkin'** (FIG. 13). Coffee in hand, you, too, can explore museums, exhibits, and many more photo ops that will have you explaining away every mystery with one word: *aliens*!

More than an hour east of here is Capitan, New Mexico, home of Smokey Bear. In 1950, a ferocious forest fire almost claimed a bear cub, whose story of rescue and recovery captivated the nation. The cuddly cub with singed paws was named Smokey, after the Forest Service fire-prevention campaign mascot introduced in 1944. Pay a visit to **Smokey Bear Historical Park** here and keep an eye during your travels for Smokey Bear signs advising motorists of the fire-risk level, often in some of the most beautiful and remote outdoor spaces.

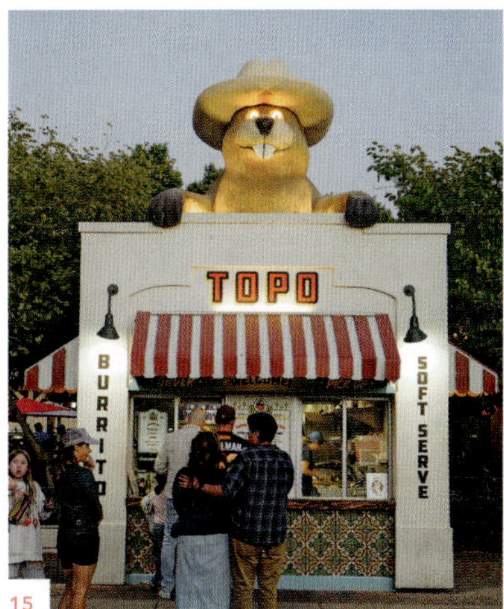

15

Another furry roadside icon who's a new kid on the American roadside scene is Topo, the big gopher who pokes his adorable hat-sporting noggin from behind the parapet of **Topo Arizona** (FIG. 15), a roadside shack serving Mexican food that opened in 2019 but has the moxie of the 1939 American roadside. His website introduces him as being "in the spirit of the great American Road Trip," which particularly endears him to me for obvious reasons.

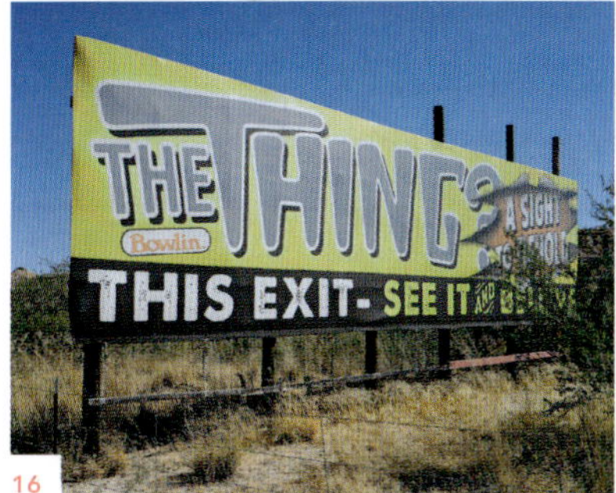

16

Topo is the creation of restaurateur Joe Johnston, who long sought to make his own contribution to mimetic architecture, a piece that would stop traffic, attract tourists, and also cater to locals. *Topo* is Spanish for gopher, the cute but pesky rodents Johnston battled on his family's farm, and so Topo is a nod, too, to the area's agricultural heritage, its tones inspired by the land. PS: His eyes light up and can change colors!

The Thing is . . . have you heard about **The Thing** (FIG. 16)?

The Thing is very much in the spirit of the old-fashioned, mom-and-pop tourist traps—said with love—that once dotted the Southwest. For miles in either direction, billboards beckoned

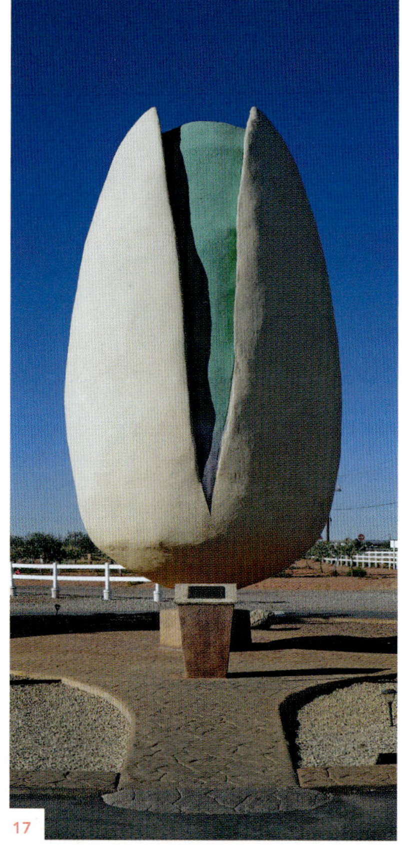
17

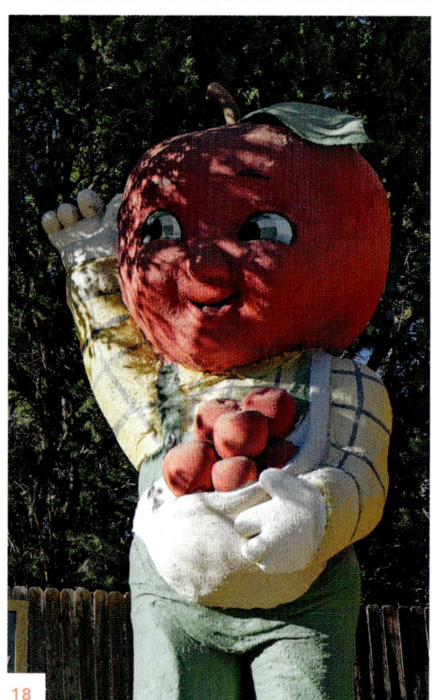
18

motorists to stop and see The Thing for themselves. Until 2018 this attraction had a ramshackle aura to it, three metal structures housing The Thing and an assortment of quirky items, and a gift shop, of course.

That's when Bowlin Travel Centers, the operator of the Shell gas station here and The Thing's owner, spruced up and enclosed the stop, doubled its size, and added a museum that fantastically connects dinosaurs (which everyone loves) and aliens (which everyone loves). And fear not, The Thing was left in peace—never mess with the name on the marquee; it's the same as it's been since the days of founder Thomas Binkley Prince, the first owner of the property, along 1-10 in Dragoon, near Tucson.

What exactly is The Thing? That's a mystery to explore for yourself. The greatest joy is in the journey, and in the satisfaction of driving away from The Thing saying, "Hey, I did a Thing."

The Alamogordo area of New Mexico is one of the most intriguing in the Southwest and there are curiosities here that are sure to compel the long drive south from Albuquerque.

It is here that you can find what's billed as the World's Largest Pistachio, a landmark of **McGinn's PistachioLand** (FIG. 17), built by the son of founder Tom McGinn as a tribute to his pop back in 2007.

It is also in Alamogordo that we can pay our respects to the *E.T. the Extra-Terrestrial* video game. In 1983, hundreds of thousands of the cartridges that Atari couldn't even give away were buried in a landfill. The movie was a blockbuster in the summer of 1982. The video game, however, was a bust for Atari at Christmas 1982, and soon the company, already in a financial tailspin, had to find a place to unload the unsold cartridges.

Some thought the mass burial was apocryphal, an urban legend. But contemporaneous news reports confirmed the games' sandy sepulchral fate, and in 2014, as documentarian video cameras rolled, a portion of the site was excavated, and more than a thousand *E.T.* cartridges saw the light of day. Once the collective curiosity was sated, the site was capped again and said to be encased in concrete, presumably forever. But who knows? Future generations may take another crack at raiding the remains. The salvaged cartridges were auctioned off, and some ended up on display at the **New Mexico Museum of Space History**.

A twenty-minute drive from Alamogordo, the **Old Apple Barn** in High Rolls, New Mexico, might as well be a world away, situated at a higher elevation in an arboreal setting. One of the cutest statues in America, the **Apple Boy** (FIG. 18), stands outside the barn, greeting you with a wave, a warm smile, and a bushel of apples. He's a big boy—more than 12 feet tall. The barn dates to 1941, and inside, it's jam-packed with eclectic country-store merch.

If fruit pies are your thing, about three hours from Apple Boy is **Pie Town**, and it makes a worthy diversion if time allows. **Pie-O-Neer Pies** is also a promising stop, and a colorful thunderbird sign across the street—commanding you to STOP—is a photogenic temptation.

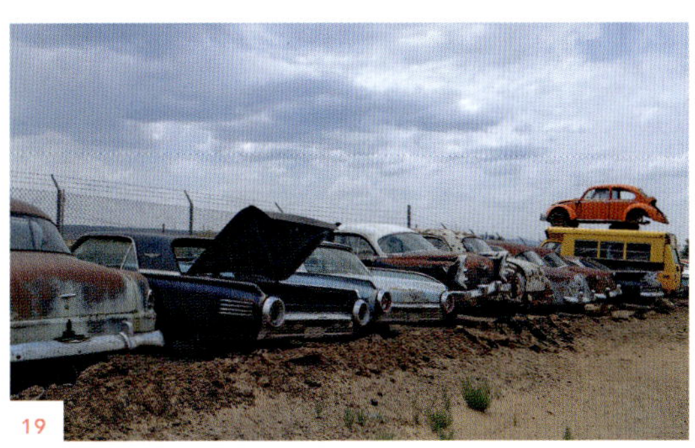

19

These are all great photo ops, but if you have a weakness for rusty Detroit metal, consider stopping at **Oscar's Auto Salvage** in Grants, New Mexico, like stumbling onto heaven for the old cars of Route 66. It's as if every old car that ever ambled down the Mother Road in its glory days came to rest here in this jumble of vintage, crusty, and sun-kissed chrome.

In 2016, brews were added to the mix, and the site can now be found easily under the name **Junkyard on 66 Brewery** (FIG. 19). This is an evocative stop and, in its own way, serves as an unintentional work of art, a distant cousin of Cadillac Ranch (see page 166).

SENSATIONAL SENSORY OVERLOAD

On the way to Albuquerque on a Route 66 adventure, make a detour and explore the **Tinkertown Museum** in Sandia Park, New Mexico.

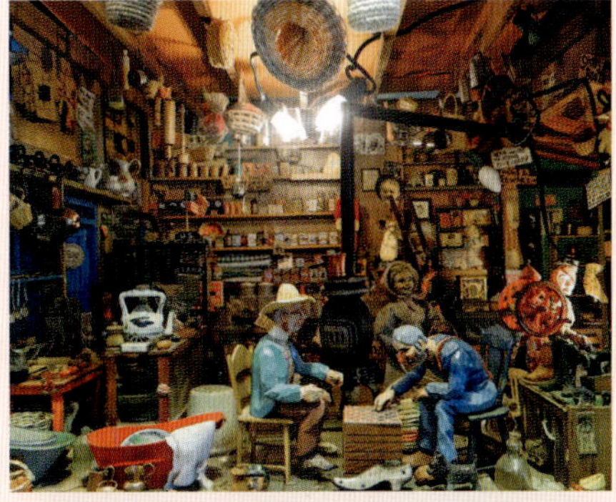

What you see here—and there's so much you could come back dozens of times and not absorb it all—is the work of one of America's greatest tinkerers, Ross Ward. He never formally studied carving or painting, but he was a protean force in both, creating miniature tableaus of nineteenth-century circuses, Western towns, and other scenes of delight and impossibly intricate detail. He was also an inveterate collector of Americana (and countless old glass bottles), and his finds are mixed in with his creations. In fact, how it all plays together is his ultimate act of brilliance.

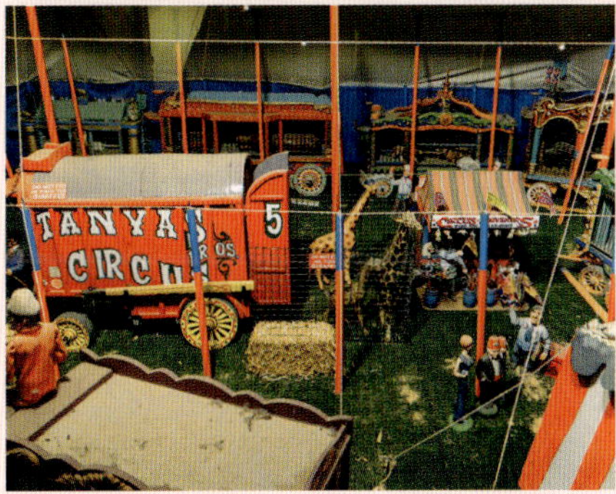

Ward was only sixty-two when he died of Alzheimer's disease in 2002, a cruel fate for a man with such a fertile mind. But his Tinkertown has long outlived him and may well outlive us all—one of the greatest folk-art museums you will ever see.

Just how did he do all of this? He had a funny answer: "I did all this while you were watching TV."

Touché, Mr. Ward. Touché.

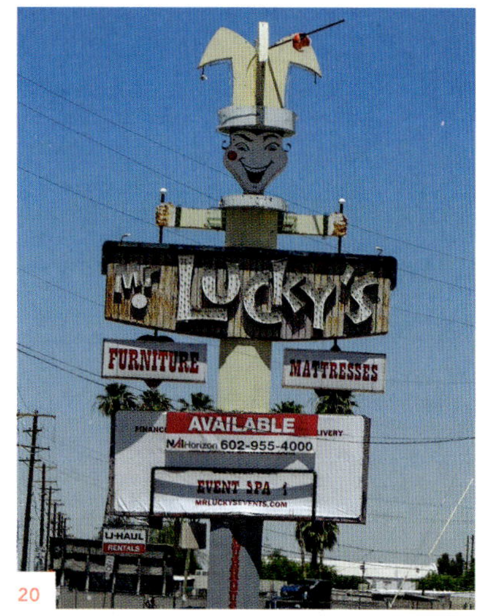

20

The sign for **Mr. Lucky's** (FIG. 20) in Phoenix is the city's unofficial landmark. In 1966, folks were already familiar with the name *Mr. Lucky*, a TV show about a floating casino. And in Phoenix, there was a barbershop by that name. Soon, many thought, there would be a casino in that Arizona city called Mr. Lucky.

The venue and its towering jester were constructed in the dusty western fringe of Phoenix. Casino gambling did not come, but, as luck would have it, something even more memorable was in the cards for Mr. Lucky. It would become a true honky-tonk, attracting legendary names like Glen Campbell and Waylon Jennings and drawing people far and wide who wanted to experience an awesome cowboy bar. Mr. Lucky's closed in 2004 from a lack of cash flow and crowds as Phoenix gradually distanced itself from its frontier roots.

SIGN ME UP

It always hurts when we lose a great roadside sign, but fortunately, some of the classics survive at sign parks, a curated sort of retirement home for signs whose businesses closed or decided to discard them.

A notable stretch of salvaged neon can be found on the **Neon Walk** on Drachman Street in Tucson. One beauty is the **Magic Carpet** (FIG. 21), from a sadly defunct golf course.

Nearby is the beloved and restored sign for the **Tucson Inn** (FIG. 23). The site of the motel now belongs to Pima Community College.

Another extraordinary sign park is the **Casa Grande Neon Sign Park** in Casa Grande, Arizona, a feast for the eyes. One of the signs hails from Holbrook, Arizona. It's a **Dairy Queen "Lips"** (FIG. 22) sign that played a special role: alerting motorists on U.S. 40 of this Dairy Queen's location on the bypassed Route 66. The sign was removed amid a corporate update of the Holbrook store, and by good fortune, the owner donated it to the park. The **Horse Shoe Motel** sign (FIG. 24) is another gem of the Casa Grande park.

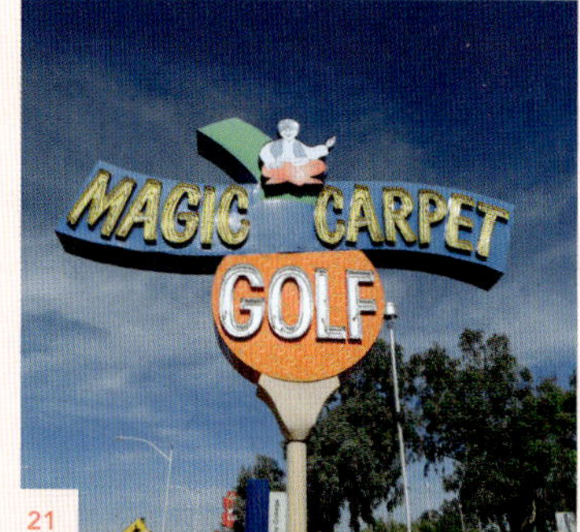

21

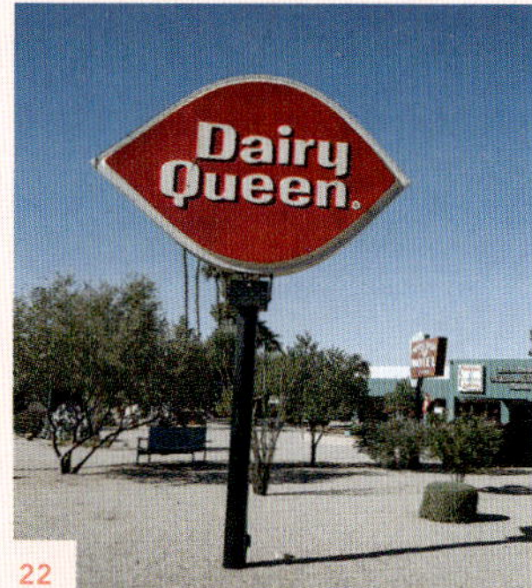

22

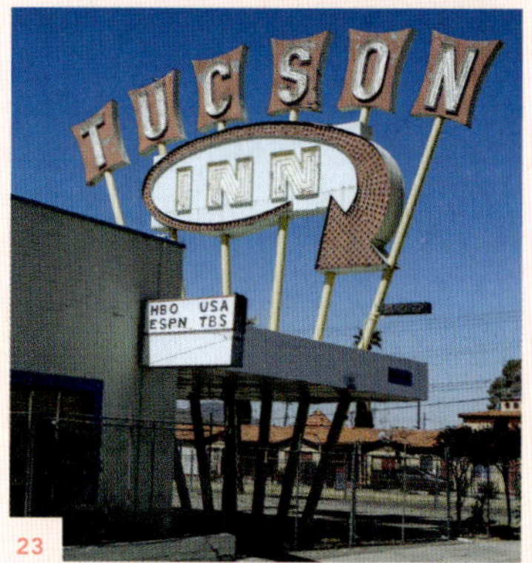

23

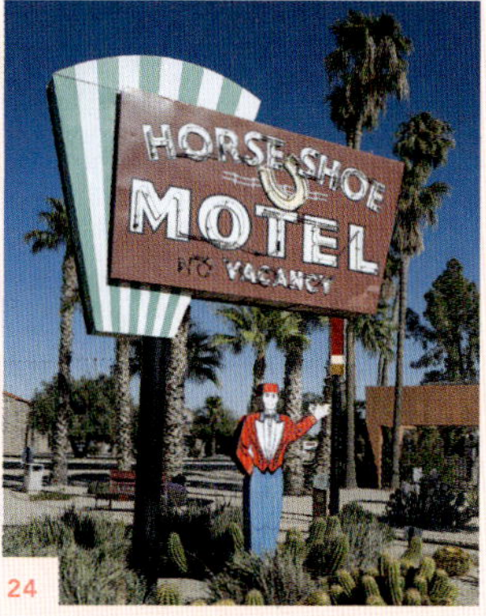

24

Prospectors know a thing or two about luck—and about good fortune not panning out. These gold diggers are a reliable symbol in this region, and one of the most trusty is this statue found outside the Lucky Strike (later Terrible's Hotel & Casino) in Jean, Nevada. This statue (and his on-site twin) were rescued after the casino closed for demolition. One was propped outside the **Pioneer Saloon** (FIG. 25) in nearby Goodsprings, Nevada, and the other was in storage at this writing.

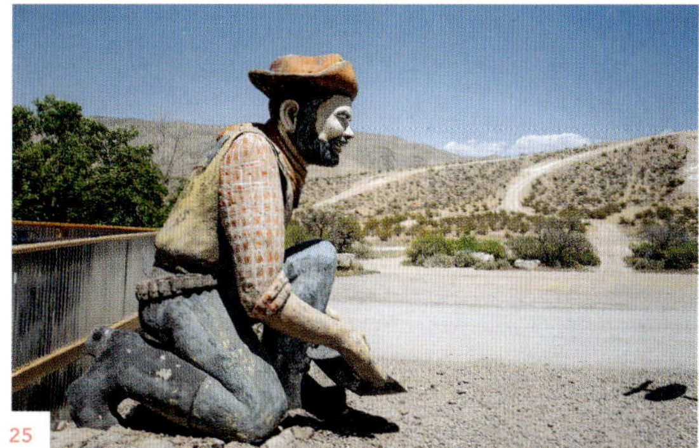

25

The **Hackberry General Store** (FIG. 26) was already a crumbling Route 66 relic when Mother Road icon and artist Bob Waldmire purchased it in 1992 and transformed it into the paean to the road it is today. Hackberry, not far from Kingman, Arizona, was ghosted in 1978 by U.S. 40, the new interstate in the region that drew away the lifeblood of traffic, and the original store closed around that time.

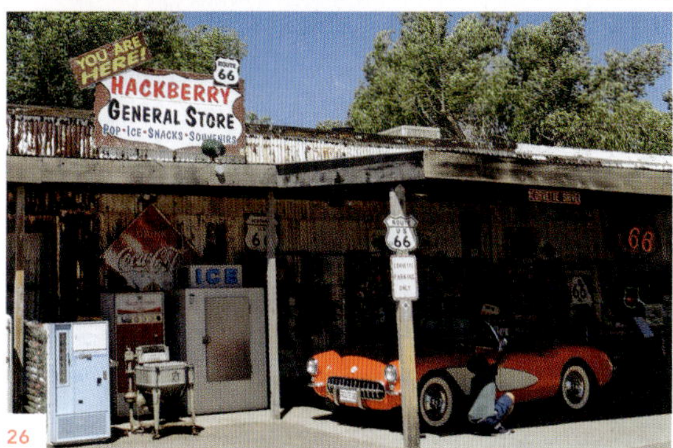

26

Between 1978 and 1992, the Route 66 revival gathered steam even as the road itself headed toward official extinction. Waldmire explored the length of the road in his orange 1972 Volkswagen Microbus and became one of the great champions of its cultural revival.

Waldmire had skin in the game since childhood, as his dad was the co-owner of the Cozy Drive-In (see page 140) in Springfield, Illinois, to this day one of the grand Route 66 stops. You can see his famed Microbus at the Route 66 Hall of Fame in Pontiac, Illinois.

Where do we begin in Las Vegas? It is a town in constant flux, erasing its history and writing new chapters we grow to love until it's time for them to be erased, too.

But not everything in Vegas vanishes. Some of what was salvaged survives at the **Neon Museum Las Vegas**, where so much of the detritus of Las Vegas's glittering age has come to rest, and the iconic La Concha Motel's entrance welcomes visitors. It's an experience you owe yourself—again and again, to appreciate it all. It makes a fine starting point before you set out to prospect for the old stuff that still stands.

Among the rescued? **The Holiday Motel** (FIG. 27), which I captured "out in the wild" just months before it closed. (I adore those old credit-card signs, as well as the juxtaposition of the sign with the pink Cadillac.)

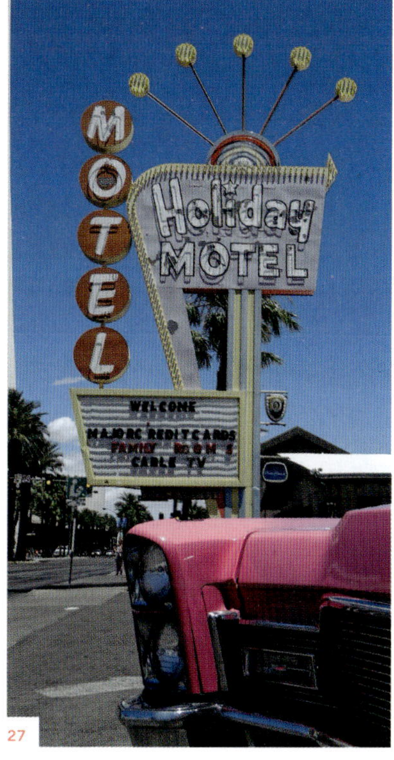

27

The city's most famous sign is also among the most recognized in the country, if not the world, right up there with the Hollywood sign. The **Welcome to Fabulous Las Vegas sign** was installed in 1959, the design of Betty Willis and the work of Western Neon. The sign, which is technically in Paradise, outside the city limits, was placed in a tourist-friendly median in 2008, making picture-snapping both easier and harder, because you must contend with people milling about. Indeed, a parking lot accommodates the great demand for seeing the sign, a sight Willis got to savor when she last visited her most famous creation on her ninetieth birthday. Her daughter told a reporter that Willis thought of it as "the little sign that could."

Fun fact: Willis was never pleased with the execution of the "Fabulous" sign's script. As the designer of the sign, she felt it was not quite as, well, fabulous as she'd envisioned it. Willis was really a master of eye-grabbing signage that stirs the soul, and she also designed the signage for the **Blue Angel** motel, a heaven-sent sign if there ever was one. The motel was demolished in 2015, but the statue and neon sign remain a blessed sight.

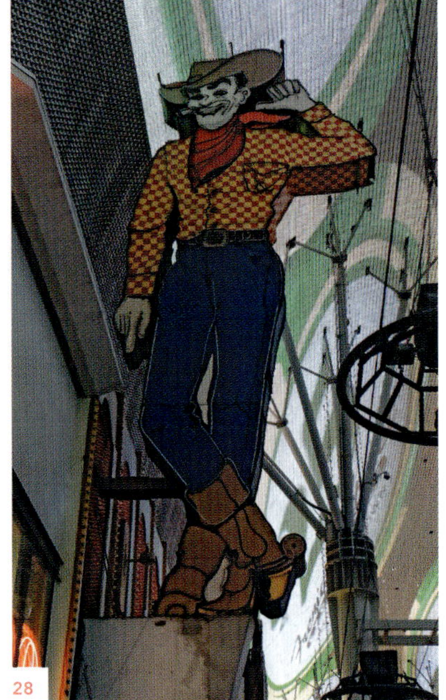

28

If Vegas has a runner-up sign celebrity, I'd vote for **Vegas Vic** (FIG. 28), who was constructed in 1951 to greet visitors to the Pioneer Club casino on Fremont Street and based on a friendly cowboy designed for the Las Vegas Visitors Bureau a few years earlier.

Vegas Vic once waved and even spoke, periodically belting out a mighty "Howdy, podner!" He waves no more and has clammed up, but his cigarette still lights up and his right eye winks. (He was restored in 2023 after complaints that his neon had gone dark, a violation of municipal code in a town that takes sensational scintillation seriously!)

You'll meet the slightly younger Wendover Will in West Wendover, Nevada, in the Mountain West (see page 245). Both were designed by Patrick Denner for the Young Electric Sign Co. (YESCO) of Salt Lake City, and both are icons of their respective terrain.

Today, Vegas Vic sits outside a souvenir shop . . . the Pioneer Club is no more, but you can still visit one in Laughlin, Nevada, where you can meet yet another take on Vic, this one called River Rick. (Vic, by the way, is a married man—his neon sign wife, the perpetually kicking **Vegas Vickie**, now sits inside Circa Resort & Casino Las Vegas.) Vic, since 1995, has been subsumed into the Fremont Street Experience, a glittering corridor that's distinctly Vegas; but Vic seems not quite his old self there, no longer out under the stars but under a canopy.

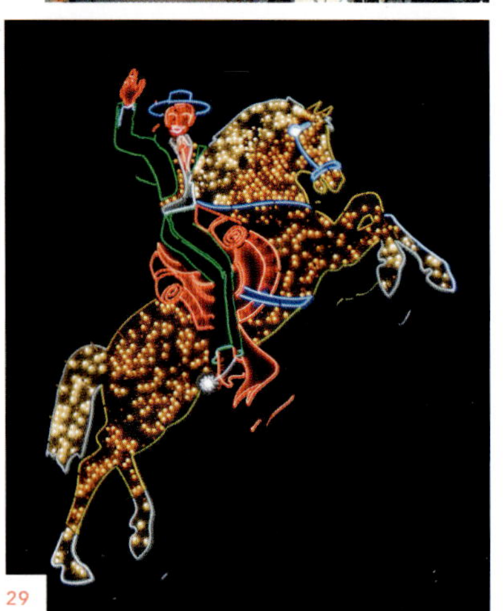

29

Right outside the **Fremont Street Experience** is a flashy cowboy on rearing horseback (FIG. 29) that once belonged to the now-demolished Hacienda Hotel. This vaquero lost his hacienda—and gained all of Vegas's admiration.

A BUCKET-LIST GHOST TOWN

Oatman, Arizona, is one of those mandatory Route 66 stops, and one that made an early impression on me during one of my first road trips. You want to take your time to appreciate what makes Oatman unique: the Old West architecture of this old gold-mining town; the wild burros that roam the roads; the pioneer spirit of the place, perhaps abetted by Oatie, the ghost that is said to inhabit the Oatman Hotel.

If you're traveling Route 66, Oatman will eventually find you, even if you don't look for it. It will always stay with you and call you back whenever you're nearby.

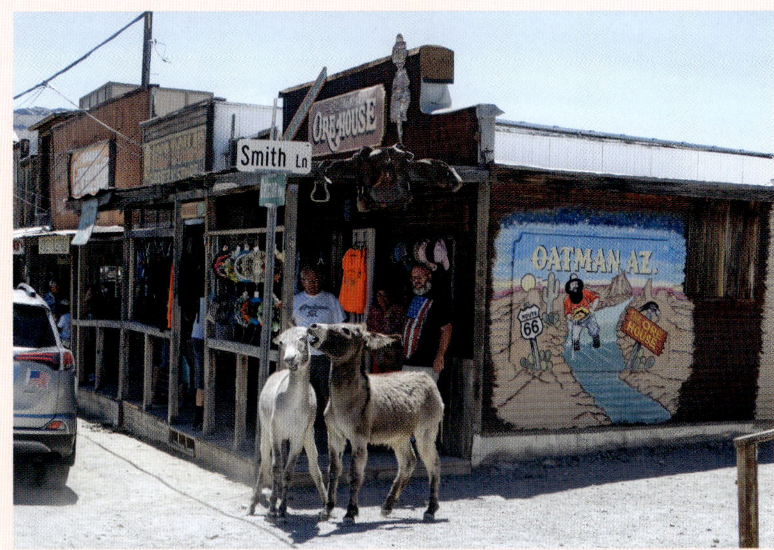

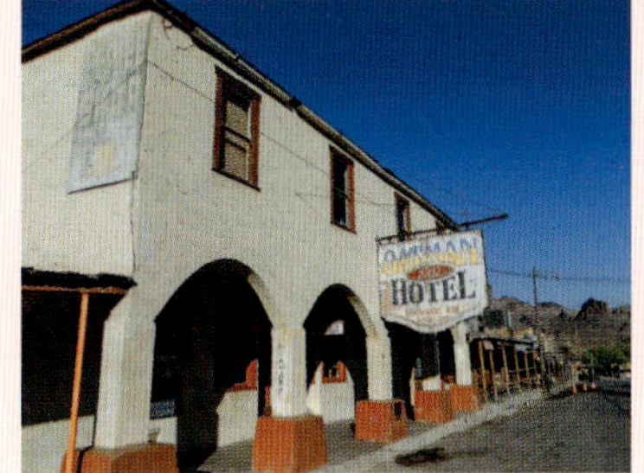

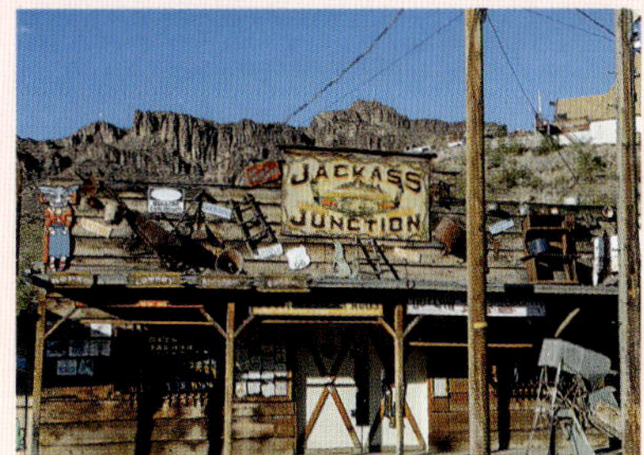

Atomic Liquors (FIG. 30) adopted its name in 1952, at the height of America's fascination with atomic power—and desert test drops not far from here that become tourist attractions. The stunning storefront bottles up the energy of that era, and inside, they make a mean Atomic Cocktail. Atomic Liquor holds Las Vegas's first liquor store license, making it the city's oldest bar. (Though regionally, the Pioneer Saloon in Goodsprings is older. I mention it on page 201.)

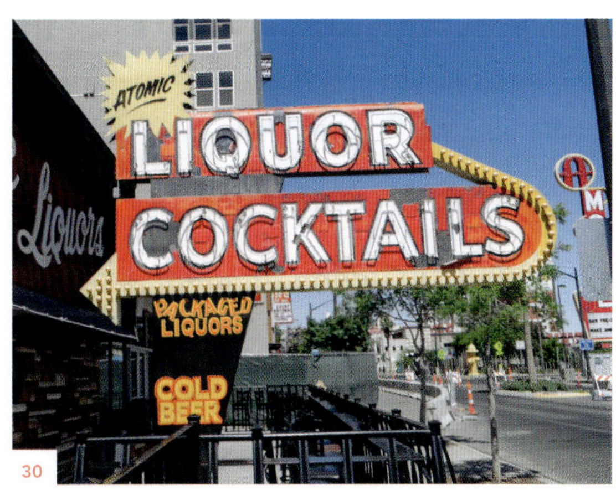

30

ROADSIDE EATS

We'll be zigging on and off Route 66 as we make our way through the region, and if we play our cards right, we might just win the "Sugar Bowl." Read on!

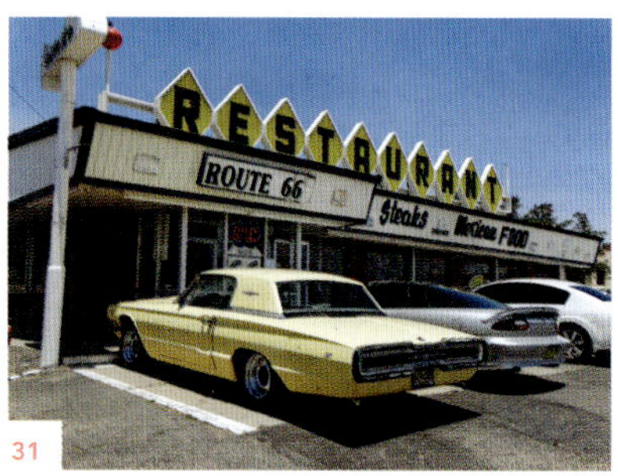

31

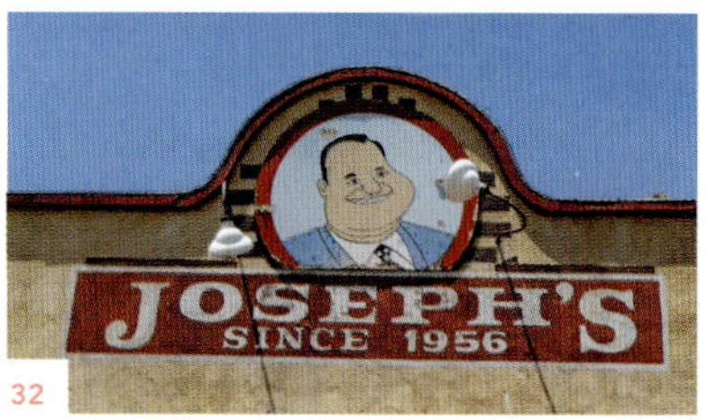

32

When I first set eyes on Santa Rosa, New Mexico, I fell very hard for the town and, in particular, its **Route 66 Restaurant** (FIG. 31). The tableau here—the signage, the canary yellow Ford Thunderbird, the cowboy-attired clientele—is the stuff of American road-trip dreams.

The restaurant opened in the mid-1960s, initially as Lettie's Restaurant—reportedly named for the daughter of the first owner. It sadly closed in 2019, and at this writing still awaits a savior.

Nearby, Santa Rosa's **Joseph's Bar & Grill** (FIG. 32) gives you another hint of what was, in the form of a cartoon of a jolly man who greets you over the door. This fellow is one of the famous faces of Route 66. The "Fat Man" was the mascot of the defunct Club Cafe in town. The owners of the former Fiesta restaurant intended to revive the Club Cafe, but the building was too far gone. So, rather than let the jolly man disappear from the road entirely, his visage was re-created at Joseph's, where it survives to this day. The neon signage for the Club Cafe is now gone. The original Fat Man sign can still be seen at the **Route 66 Auto Museum,** another fine stop in town.

Santa Rosa is also home of the spectacular **Sun 'n Sand Motel and Restaurant** (FIG. 33), a glorious assemblage of signage. By the front door, a vintage pay phone awaits Superman, the booth's only remaining client, and over the roofline, a strip of colorful balls adds to the joyous air. The stunning sign for the motel uses a Zia sun, bringing with it rays of regional culture.

About two hours west, we find ourselves in another great Mother Road stop, Albuquerque. You'd be wise to stop by **Mac's La Sierra** (FIG. 34), popular with locals, and that's because of its superb Mexican food, the vintage ambience, and the friendly staff. It's been here since 1952 and, as the bovine sign suggests, the steak was then and is now a central part of the experience, including the "steak fingers."

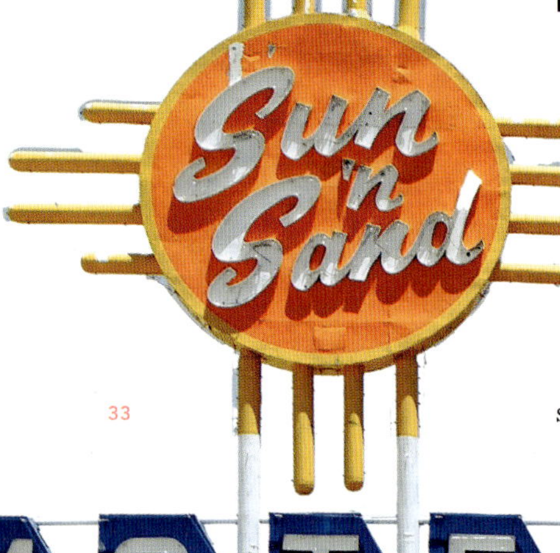

33

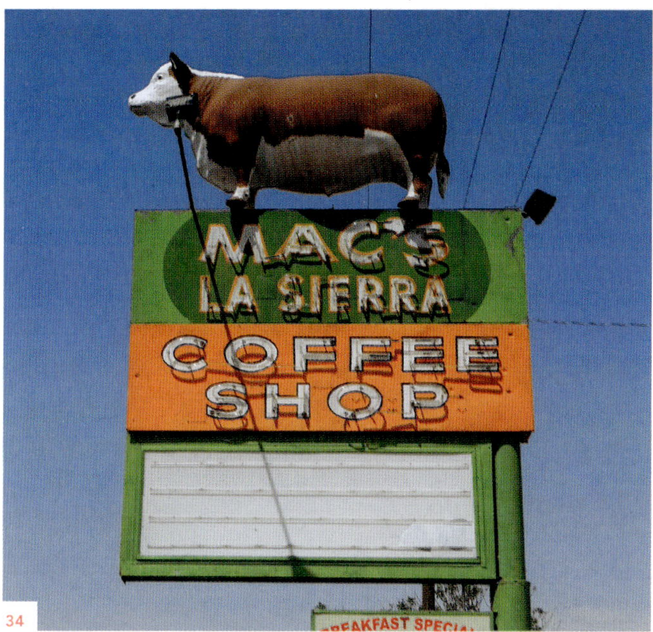

34

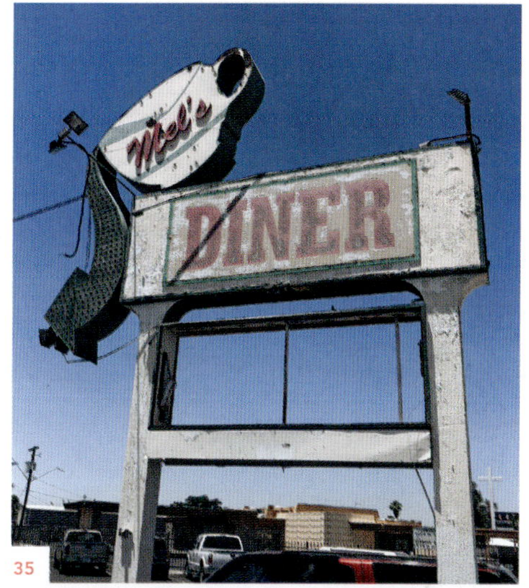

35

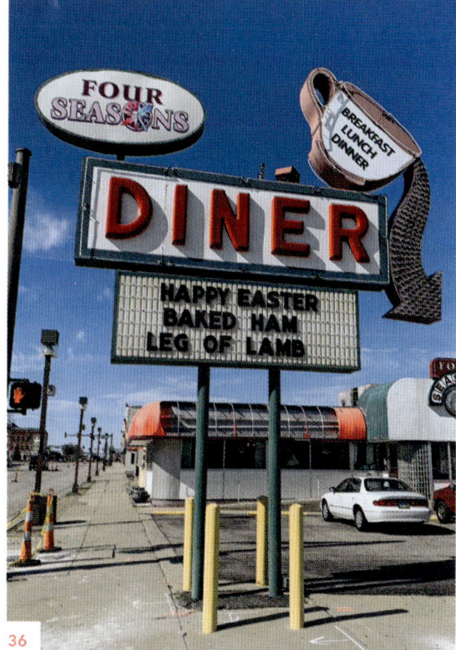

36

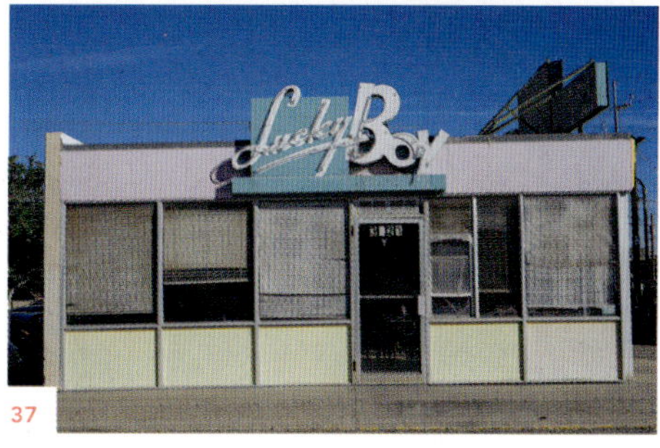

37

If you grew up watching the 1976–85 sitcom *Alice*, **Mel's Diner** (FIG. 35) will be familiar—in fact, this Phoenix-based eatery may rise to the top of your bucket list.

In 2018, I had a fun visit with Emmanouil Stivaktakis, the owner of Mel's. The diner was chosen in the 1970s to represent Mel's Diner, and a shot of the iconic tilting-coffee-cup neon sign briefly appears in the opening credits. At the time the restaurant was called Chris' Diner, but the word "Mel's" was swapped in when the footage was filmed.

When Stivaktakis took over in the early 2000s, he kept getting calls from people asking for Mel. An immigrant from Greece, he'd never seen *Alice* but quickly realized he was sitting on a television-tourism treasure. He renamed the diner Mel's and updated the sign.

The real Mel, if you will, was founder Lester Bammesberger, who opened diners with similar sign designs: one in Bryan, Ohio (now called the Four Seasons; see FIG. 36), as well as one in Fort Lauderdale (still retaining its original name).

The **Lucky Boy** (FIG. 37) in Albuquerque, a reliable spot for Chinese food (and hamburgers) for decades, has one of my favorite signs. In 2021, Lucky Boy enjoyed a lucky pandemic-era boost after it appeared in the Netflix movie *Army of the Dead*. It has a sign twin in a pair of possibly once-connected restaurants in Pasadena, California.

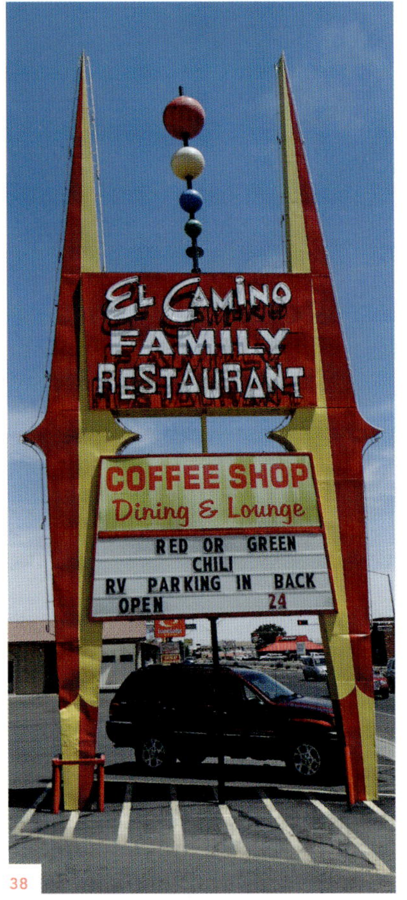

38

The **El Camino Family Restaurant** (FIG. 38) in Socorro, New Mexico, has a glorious vintage sign and interior and is a smart stop on a road trip between Albuquerque to the north and the White Sands National Park in Alamogordo. They have a cozy bar, too, **El Matador**. El Camino opened in 1963, and it remains a time capsule of Camelot America. The nearby **Roadrunner Lounge** is also a magnificent relic.

Seligman, Arizona, as one of the road's great stops, has eye-catching signage like that of the former **Copper Cart** (FIG. 39) restaurant, which opened in the fall of 1952. It was a popular Route 66 stop and boasted in 1958 ads of having "the best coffee" on the road and sumptuous food from its charcoal broiler. The restaurant also sold curios, which you can still find in the town, even though the restaurant is no more.

Seligman banked on nostalgia early, hit by the double whammy of U.S. 40's bypass in September 1978 and the Santa Fe Railroad ending the practice of overnighting crews here in February 1985. Cut off from the precious flow of highway and rail traffic, Seligman embraced Route 66 lore to sustain its economy, and a small but hardy group of local business owners teamed up to make it work.

Delgadillo's Snow Cap (FIG. 40) in Seligman is perhaps the most Route 66 of restaurants. It is a hodgepodge of found Americana, tongue-in-cheek signage, and curiously monikered menu items (dead chicken, anyone?) filtered through the sensibilities of one man, Juan Delgadillo, who founded the restaurant in 1953. Today, it's still in the family—and quirky as ever.

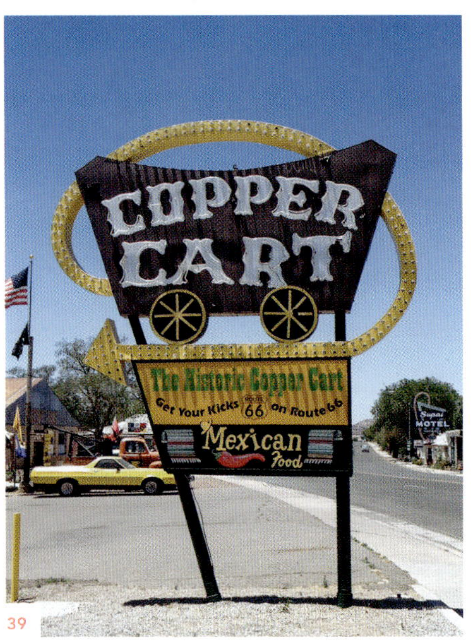

39

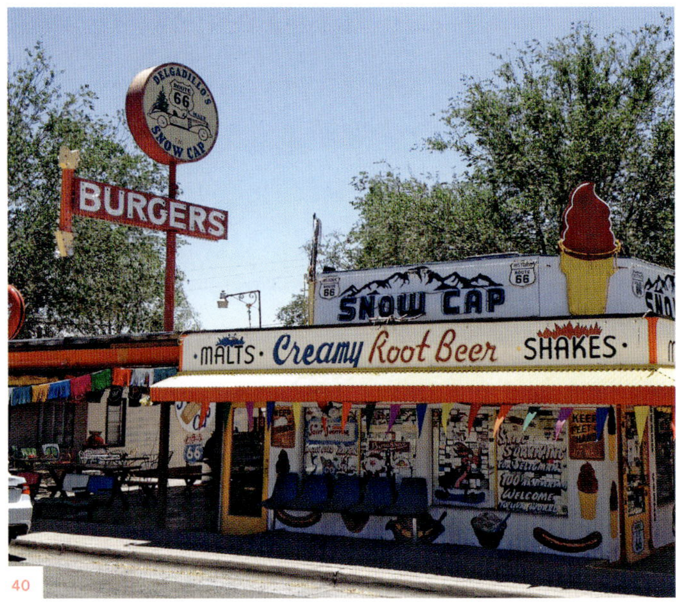

40

Need a haircut? You'd be wise to stop into **Angel's Barber Shop** (FIG. 41), run by Angel Delgadillo, Juan's brother and another titan of the town and the "guardian angel" of the Mother Road. The nonagenarian truly has seen it all, from Route 66's heyday to the last cars to amble down the street before the bypass, and then, to the revival of old Route 66 we are seeing today. All those Historic Route 66 signs you see might not exist were it not for Angel's advocacy. Indeed, to chat with him, as so many awed travelers have done over the decades, is to learn the history firsthand, much like, to go back to *Cars*, Lightning McQueen does from Sally Carrera, a scene that is perhaps the most vivid encapsulation ever of the rise and fall of Route 66. (We are all part of the revival!)

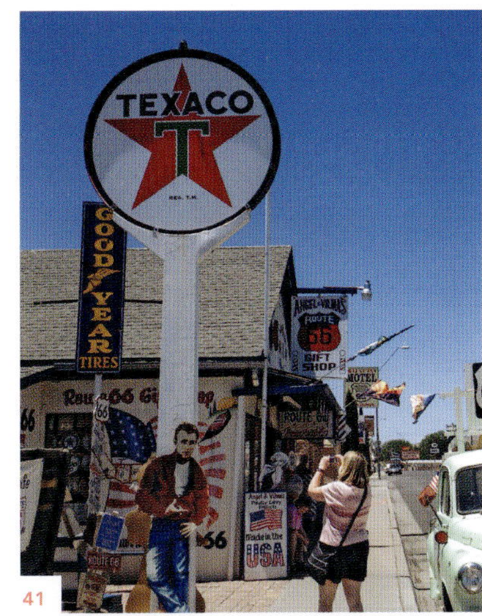

41

Let's wander to Flagstaff, where the **Route 66 Dog Haus** (FIG. 42) delivers hot dogs from its red A-frame building, a former Der Wienerschnitzel (see page 303 for more). Another hot dog hut, called the **Dog House** (FIG. 43), has an elongated neon doggie in Albuquerque. It's a familiar sight for fans of the *Breaking Bad* and *Better Call Saul* television series.

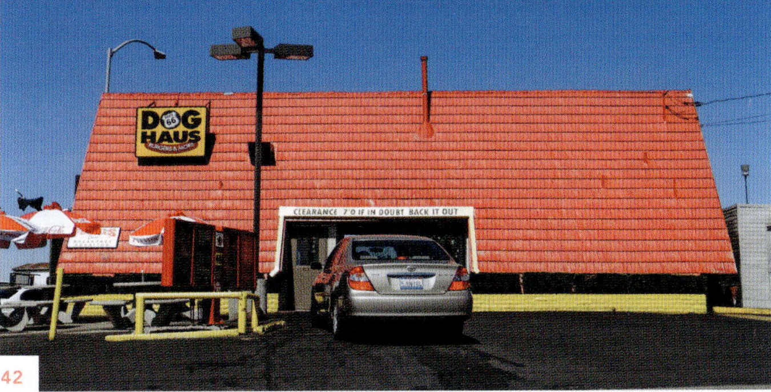

42

MacAlpine's Diner & Soda Fountain (FIG. 44) in Phoenix, Arizona, is a throwback to another time—the 1930s to be exact. It's one of the most extraordinary soda fountains left in the nation, but two other dates are important in its history: 2001 and 2020, both grim years in American history.

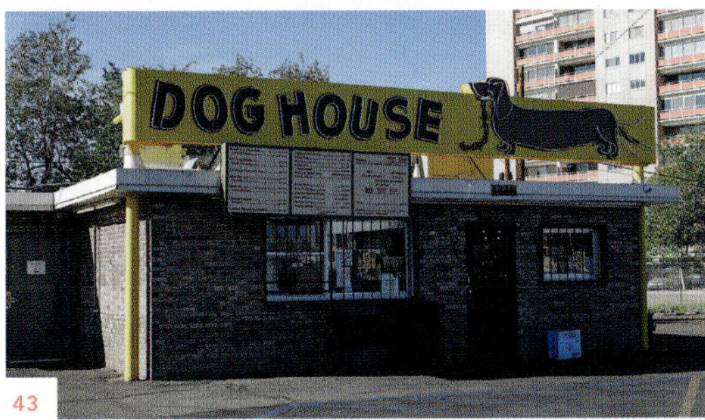

43

Just before 9/11, Monica and Cary Heizenrader saved MacAlpine's from destruction. The previous owner was selling it and poised to auction off its artifacts on eBay before they stepped in. The next nineteen years were fruitful ones. The Heizenraders gave the soda fountain their all, even working second jobs to keep it afloat. Then, the next grim date came along—March 2020, and another catastrophe, this time, COVID-19. They closed for a time, but their efforts to reopen once it was allowed were halting, hit by problems like the labor shortage. And then, there was the horror of Cary's death, listed in his obituary as caused by valley fever and COVID-19.

Ultimately, the family, saying they'd exhausted other options, determined the only way forward was to turn to the public for help, and a GoFundMe has raised tens of thousands of dollars. As of this writing, MacAlpine's is open for lunch part of the week.

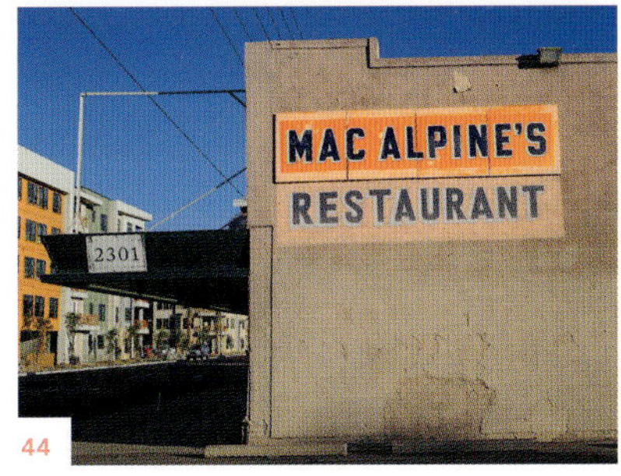

44

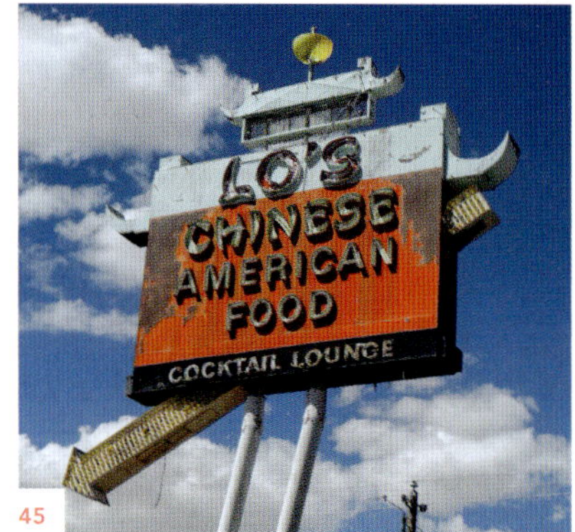

45

Bill Johnson's Big Apple (FIG. 46) was an Arizona institution, a small chain that included this location in Mesa. For some, it was an easily accessible personification of the Old West in a region losing touch with its cowboy roots.

The name had nothing to do with New York City—far from it. It reportedly referred to a dance craze said to be a favorite of the namesake founder of the restaurants, who was also a cowboy, actor, and radio entertainer. He died in 1966, but his restaurants carried on for almost half a century and are much missed. This sign still stood back in May 2018, encapsulating a popular notion of the Old West in a way few signs do, and while it's no longer there, it will return to public view as part of the Neon Garden at The Post in Mesa in 2025.

Lo's Restaurant and Cocktail Lounge (FIG. 45) has been long closed, but its wonderful sign performed decades of yeoman service peeling hungry motorists off nearby Route 66 in Kingman, Arizona.

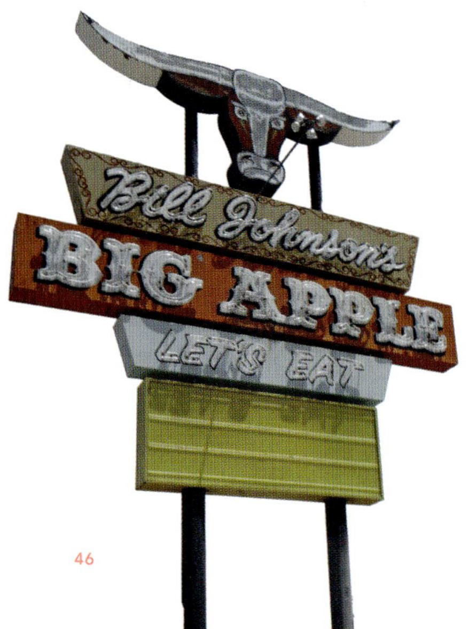

46

In my repeated visits to Kingman, I always check in on the sign for what was once the **ABC Chinese Restaurant** (FIG. 47). By 2018, it had been repurposed, and if you go, you'll find it's changed yet again (FIG. 48), but it still stands.

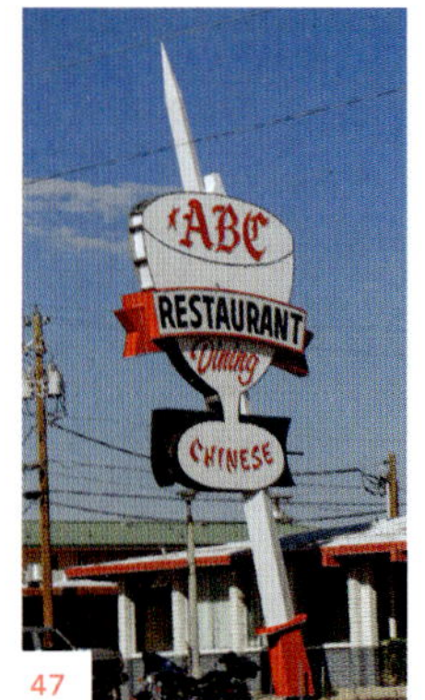

47

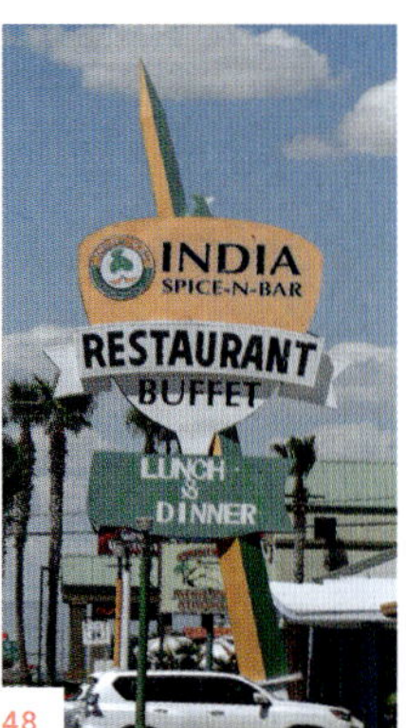

48

TUCUMCARI TONIGHT!

That slogan was emblazoned on billboards, encouraging travelers on the Mother Road (and U.S. 40) to stay in Tucumcari, New Mexico. Today, it is still one of the best-preserved Route 66 towns, with an astonishing number of old motels, restaurants, and other sites that keep you strolling and snapping for hours. An easy fan favorite is the **Blue Swallow Motel**, in operation since 1939.

On a hot New Mexico evening, after hours chasing signs and the need to chase some Z's, doesn't "100% Refrigerated Air" sound like the most delicious thing you've ever heard?

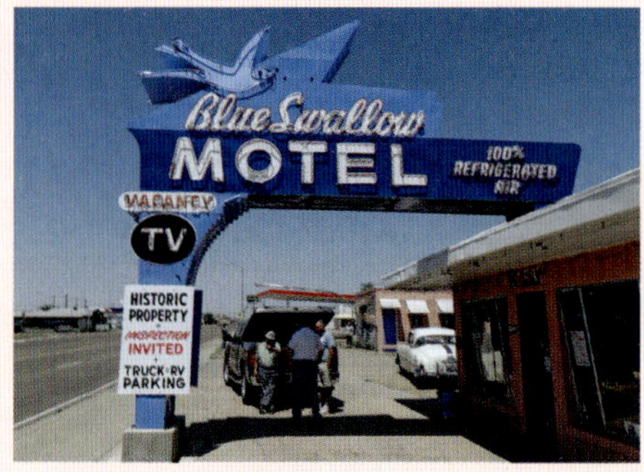

You gotta love the iconic **Blake's Lotaburger Stick Man** (FIG. 49), whose profile is hard to miss in the desert Southwest. Blake Chanslor founded Lotaburger in 1952, born in the postwar incubator period for hamburger stands, with some that would become chains, and others that would remain mom-and-pops—or something in between. Lotaburger would grow into a cherished New Mexico tradition, with dozens of locations serving a highly regarded green-chile burger, in LOTA (large) or ITSA (small) sizes, and a whole lot more, including Frito Pies—it's no surprise that Blake's wound up in *Breaking Bad* episodes.

In Wymola, Arizona, stand the remains of **Nickerson Farms** (FIG. 50). The sign still towers above the desert, casting long shadows on the sandy earth below, the pagoda canopy—which once sheltered gas pumps—another signature of the Nickerson look.

Nickerson was a chain of rest stops from an era when names like Stuckey's and Horne's were a common respite for weary road warriors, offering comfort food, a panoply of nutty snacks, souvenirs, and more. The chain went bankrupt in August 1985 and, yet, here Nickerson's makes its last stand, waiting for its inevitable demolition, by human or natural design. This particular store opened in December 1969, the specialty at its opening was fried chicken, and they were still clucking about it in 1977. A newspaper article noted that fifty people worked here at the start—today, there isn't a soul left, except maybe a photographer in search of ghosts.

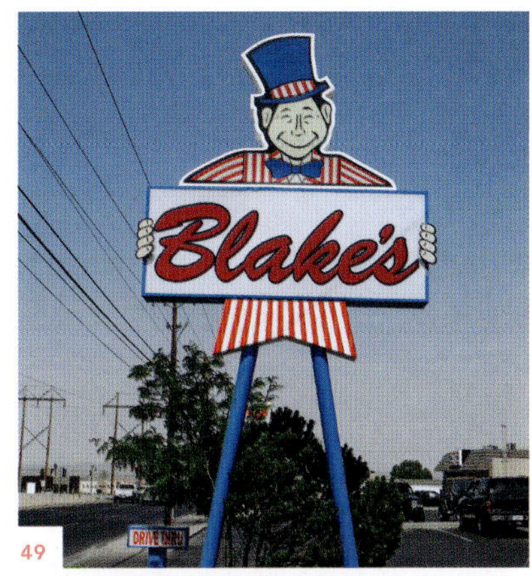

49

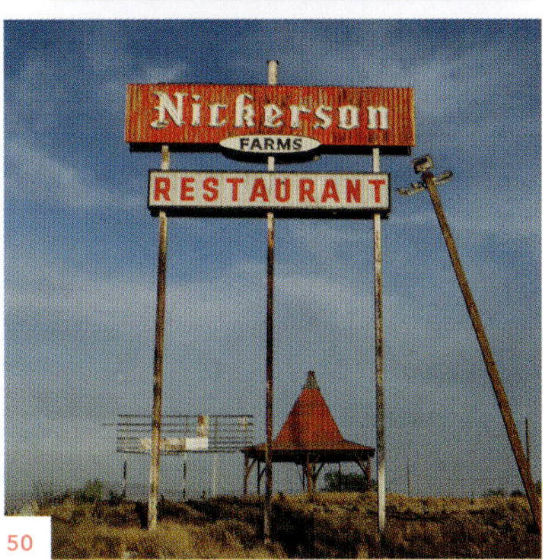

50

MAINSTAYS OF MAIN STREET

From Cactus Candy to a TV king . . . and cheese . . . and stuff . . . we're in for an interesting ride through the region.

Yeehaw! Who doesn't want to buy candy from a smiling saguaro cactus? Take my money! At the **Cactus Candy Company** (FIG. 51) in Phoenix, Arizona, life is sweet and prickly at the same time. The signature sweet here is prickly pear candy, sugar-sprinkled pink gelatinous cubes of deliciousness infused with juice from local cacti. Cactus Candy has been a fixture here since 1942, and its iconic yellow boxes make for an unexpectedly delightful

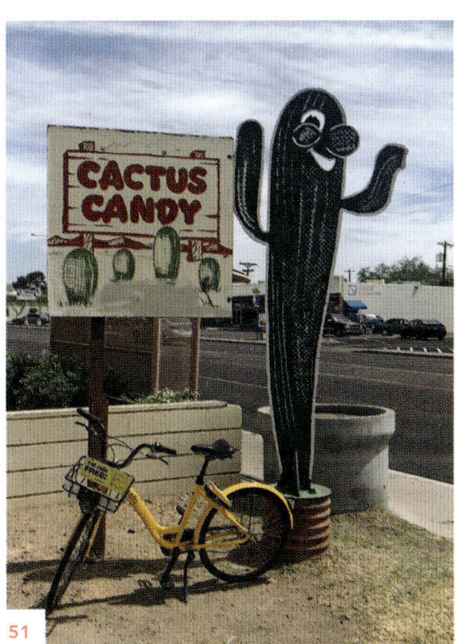

51

BYPASSED, BUT NOT FORGOTTEN

Williams, Arizona's sad claim to fame is that it was the last Route 66 town bypassed by U.S. 40, the flow of traffic diverted away from this wonderful little city.

This happened in 1984—after a hard fight with some lifesaving wins, including securing three exits off I-40—but the town would not be doomed even if Route 66 was officially decommissioned the next year. The Route 66 tourist cavalcade, always a presence, was about to boom, as the road would enter its glorious afterlife.

Williams is home to some of my favorite signs on the road. The **Turquoise Tepee** (FIG. 52), the **Canyon Club** (FIG. 53), **Rod's Steak House** (FIG. 54), and a vintage **Dairy Queen** (FIG. 55), to name some of the gems that make a stop here delightful.

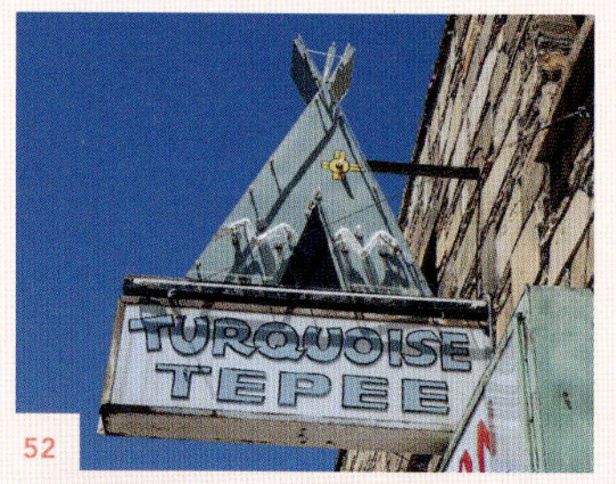

52

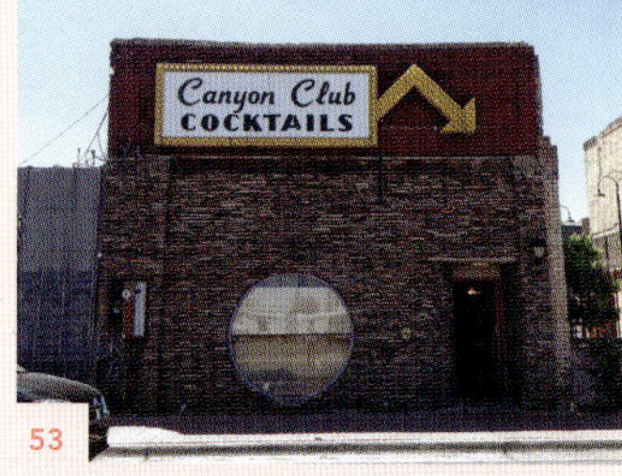

53

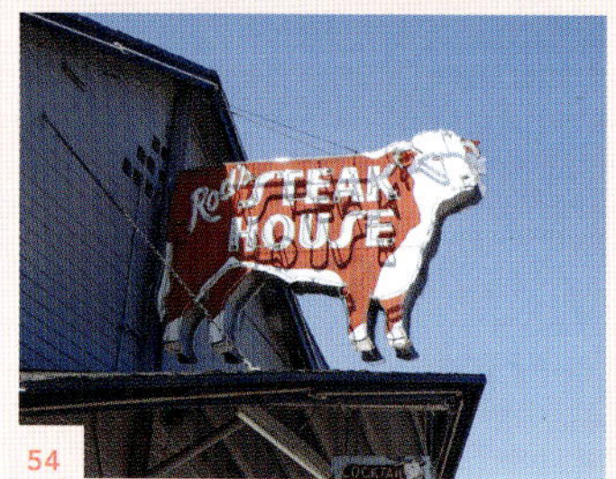

54

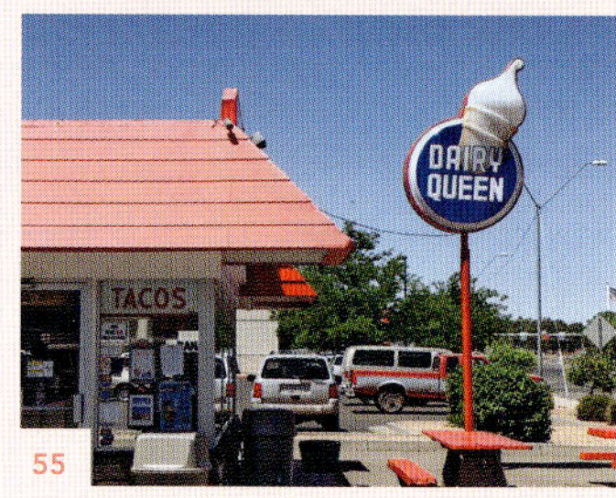

55

▶▶▶ Pull Over!

Kachina Dry Cleaners in Phoenix, Arizona, has been around since the 1950s, owned and operated by the Tsantilas family since day one. Its name and iconography is inspired by Hopi kachina dolls.

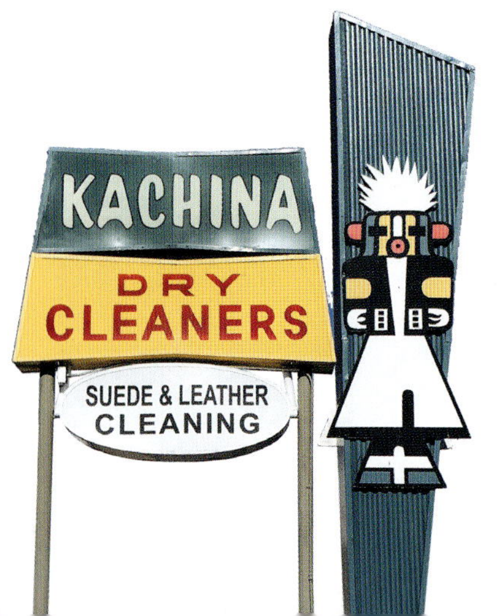

souvenir. Amelio Casciato and family have run Cactus Candy since 1996, and their product line now extends from the sweet to the savory, including salsa and hot sauces.

Casciato traded his work in the roofing business in Pittsburgh, Pennsylvania, for making cactus candy in the desert. He comes from a family of builders who made cathedrals in Italy. Now, he lords over a beloved temple of Southwestern sweetness.

Nearby, I fell for one of the crowning touches of midcentury nostalgia in Phoenix: **Duke Photography.** (FIG. 56) Shown here is the photo studio in 2018, and since, Duke has closed—the photo business said it was moving to a new home—and word was the building was coming down. But in the closest thing we'll get to a picture-perfect ending, the building was reportedly being retrofitted for a new use—a grocery store—and the Duke's neon sign will shine on.

"If you see our sign, that's a good sign." Those words are emblazoned atop the website for **Courtesy Chevrolet** (FIG. 57) in Phoenix, and serve as a reminder of why these signs were built in the first place—marketing! In this case, pulling over in your old car to buy a new one. Indeed, few signs scream 1950s more than that for Courtesy Chevrolet, from the era when Dinah Shore, in spirited commercials, commanded us to "See the USA in Your Chevrolet." The sign is restored and the light bulbs still flash at night—one concession to modernity (and the environment) is that they are now LED, not incandescent.

Cheese 'n Stuff (FIG. 58) has been a savory destination in Phoenix for cheese, meats, and other sandwich essentials—or, for lack of a better word, stuff—since 1949. You can purchase ingredients here from around the world—150 countries by one estimate. That vintage neon sign looks so great today because of a remarkable offer in 2015 by the son of its creator to restore the sign for free! The family that has owned the shop since 1972 credits the restored sign with drawing in business—and how could it not? This is a textbook case of the importance of preserving our retail heritage—it's good for the soul *and* the bottom line!

The **Saguaro Theater** in Wickenburg, Arizona, makes good use of a local symbol and features an awesome marquee (see it on page 216).

If you think the white adobe building and facade neon for Mesa, Arizona's **Watson's Flowers** (FIG. 60) is a showstopper, the pole sign was even grander. Designed by the noted artist Paul Millett, who also created the diving-lady neon sign at Mesa's Starlite Motel (see page 215), the floral beauty tumbled in 2014 but was saved. At last report, it will be reinstalled nearby at the Neon Garden at The Post in Mesa. Watson's merged with a local rival and is happily still in business.

The Watson's sign won't be the only grand flower sign to find a new use—**My Florist** (FIG. 61) in Phoenix long ago closed, but the neon sign still compels a stop!

The **New Empire Food Market** (FIG. 59) in Tucson, Arizona, is a throwback to the small family-run groceries of yore, and the art deco design that envelops it is a gift to all lucky enough to see it. Tun Lim Lee, the longtime proprietor, ran it with his family for six decades before his death in 2017.

This quote in Lee's obituary, from a customer, Armando Alcantar, captures what makes these places truly shine: "It's hard to walk in here because he is no longer here," Alcantar told the *Arizona Daily Star*. "He was like a dad to many of us neighborhood kids. He helped everybody and gave us candy and ice cream."

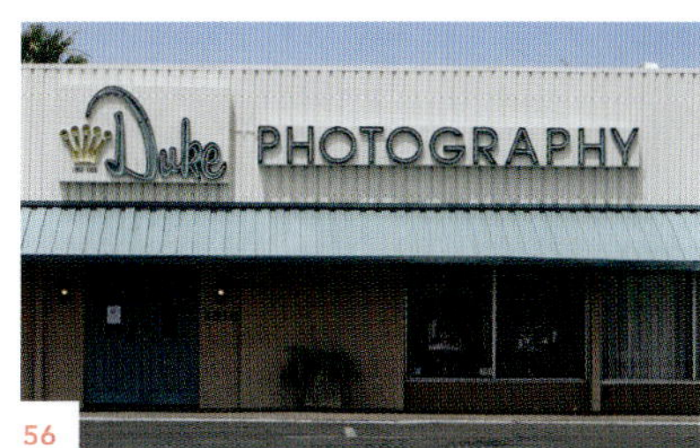

56

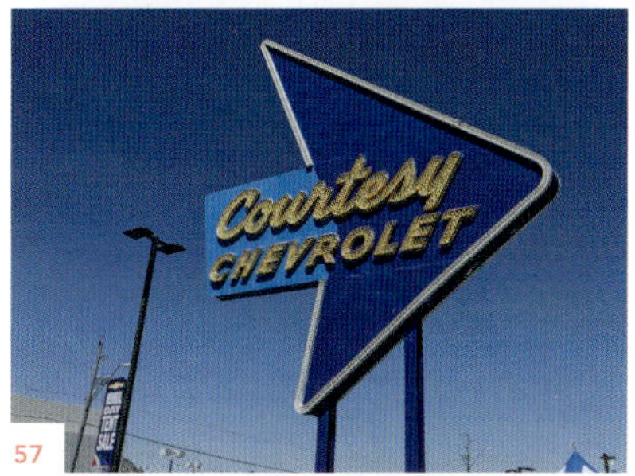

57

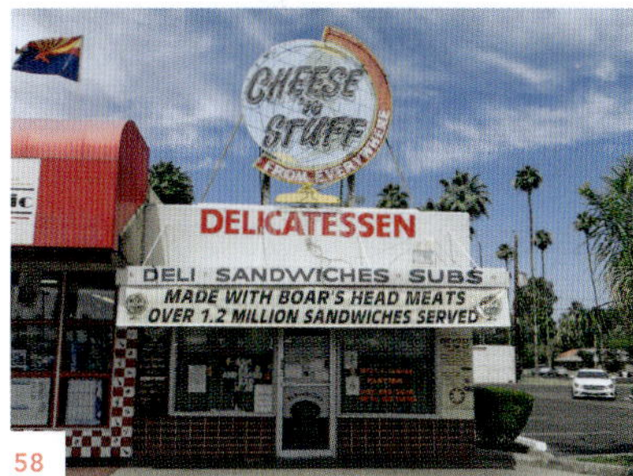

58

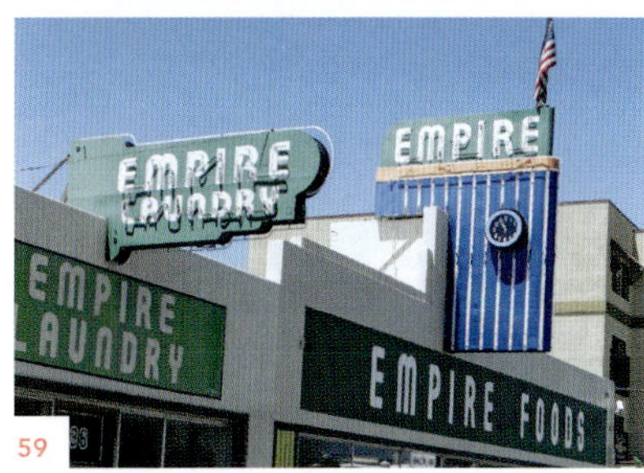

59

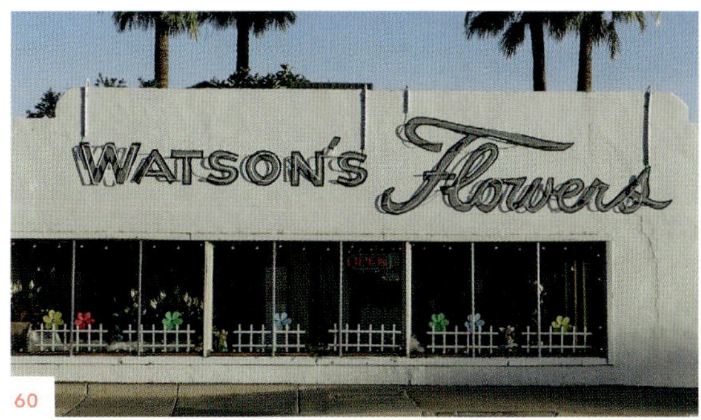

60

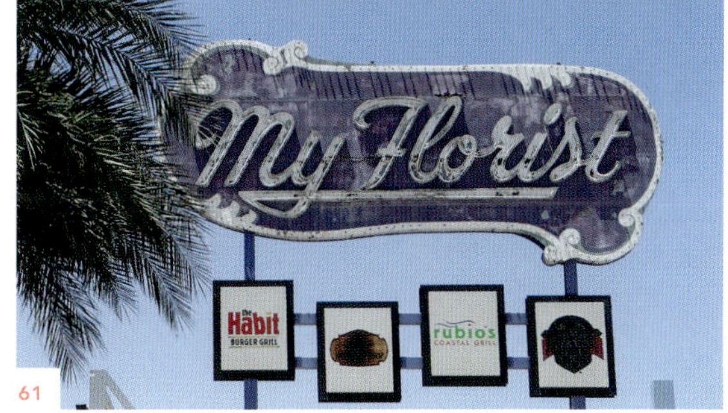

61

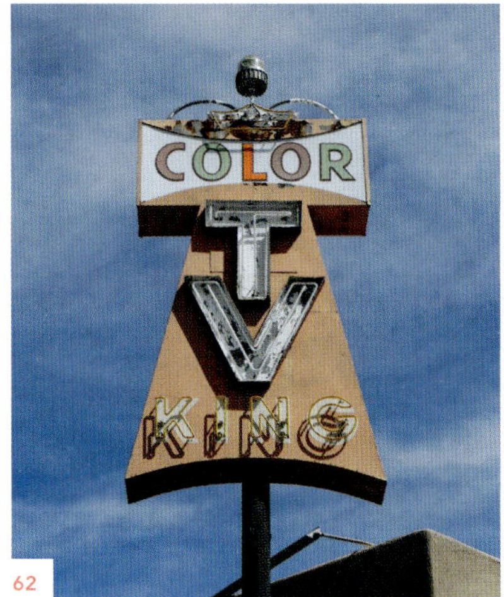

62

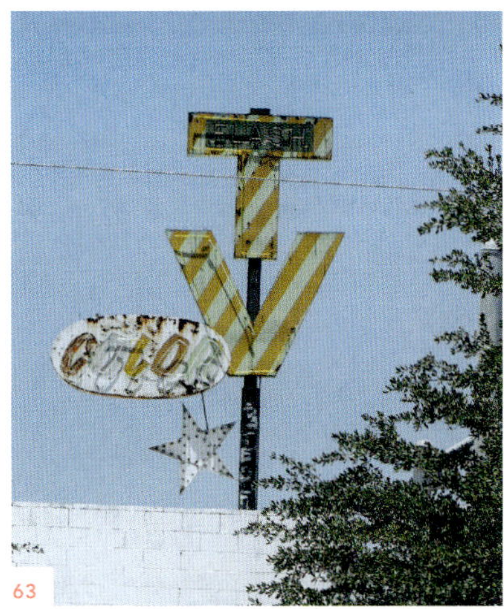

63

In Lee's early days running the market, Jack Fitzgerald was across town, having arrived in Tucson from New York in 1961 without a penny to his name. The next year, he would become a king. His shop, **Fitzgerald Color TV King** (FIG. 62), opened in an era when a color TV was an appliance fit for royalty.

Fitzgerald's legendary salesmanship placed those sets in the homes of his many "subjects" throughout the Tucson region. His throne was in the pages of newspapers and the commercial breaks of the late movie. There Fitzgerald would be, making his convincing pitch among stacks of television sets.

Fitzgerald sold the business in the early 1980s but remained a force in the city's political and civic life. The shop has long been closed, but the sign, which once rotated, remains as one of Tucson's unofficial landmarks.

News flash! Tucson is a great town if you like vintage television signs! In 1965, when **Flash TV and Appliance Store** (FIG. 63) opened in downtown Tucson, color TV was a big deal. The sets were still an expensive novelty and not all network shows had yet switched to color.

I Dream of Jeannie, for instance, debuted that year as a black-and-white show, while *Gilligan's Island*, entering its second season, went color. TV shows opened by promoting that they were "In Color" into the early 1970s. Color TV was a selling point in the hospitality business, too, something RCA turned into a coast-to-coast motel-marketing juggernaut.

So Flash TV made sure to fine-tune their sign with the words "Color TV." Today, the complex is called The Flash, a mixed-use development that preserved the restored sign as its symbol and namesake.

SLEEP ON THE CORNER, OR IN A WIGWAM

Here are two quick stops for the Mother Road completists, and they are just thirty minutes apart. **Earl's Route 66 Motor Court** (FIG. 64) in Winslow, Arizona, is festooned with neon and a plastic sign with the memorable slogan "Sleeping on the Corner!" It's a throwback to the motor courts of yore, such an important part of the road's hospitality history.

You can always spend the night at **Wigwam Village No. 6 in Holbrook**, one of three surviving motor courts that offered concrete teepee-shaped accommodations.

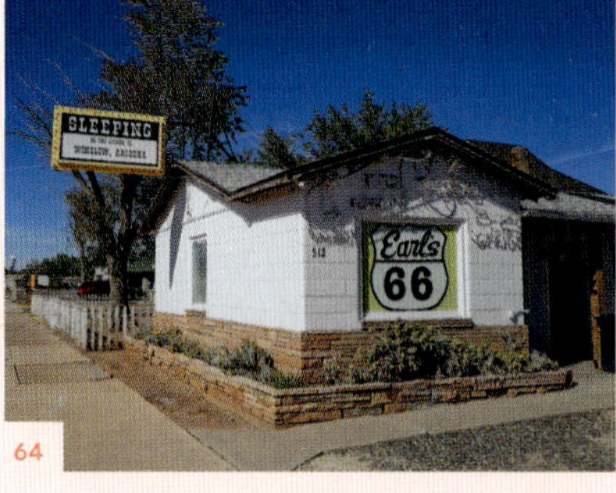

64

THE INN CROWD

Entering Gallup, New Mexico, along Route 66 can feel like a triumphant experience, and the array of vintage signage flanking the road can be dizzying, or so it has felt to me on my visits here.

The Blue Spruce (FIG. 65), closed in 2022 along with a row of other derelict motels, had one of my favorite signs here. Unfortunately, old motels with grand signs often have sad fates befall them. As of this writing, the signs were still there. I can't think of the road without them.

The granddaddy of them all—and very much still here—is the **Hotel El Rancho** (FIG. 66), opened in 1937 and long billed as a playground for the stars. I've been smitten with this place since my first visit in 1999, and its slogan: "The Charm of Yesterday, the Convenience of Tomorrow."

Stars who stayed here back when Gallup was a hub of Western filmmaking have rooms named after them, the story goes, with names like Ronald Reagan (the presidential suite, of course), Lucille Ball, Doris Day, John Wayne, Kirk Douglas (the king suite), and others. Even if you don't stay here, poke your head into the grand lobby or grab a bite at the restaurant.

The shuttered **Hiway House** along Route 66 in Albuquerque was a survivor of a 1950s Southwestern motel chain. Its founder, the developer Del Webb, was one busy guy when this location opened. He was a co-owner of the New York Yankees, and would soon be the father of the famed Sun City retirement community in Arizona (as well as across the country). The sign still stands.

Mesa, Arizona's long-shuttered **Buckhorn Baths Motel** (FIG. 67) opened in 1939. The complex and its mineral waters long attracted tired travelers looking for an oasis along dusty Highway 60, as well as sore and achy baseball players from the Cactus League. Indeed, the Buckhorn was the spring-training base of the New York (and later San Francisco) Giants for more than a quarter century. Founded by Ted and Alice Sliger, the Baths are also home to a still-intact taxidermy collection (Ted was a taxidermist and naturalist as well) that was said to be the largest wildlife museum in Arizona.

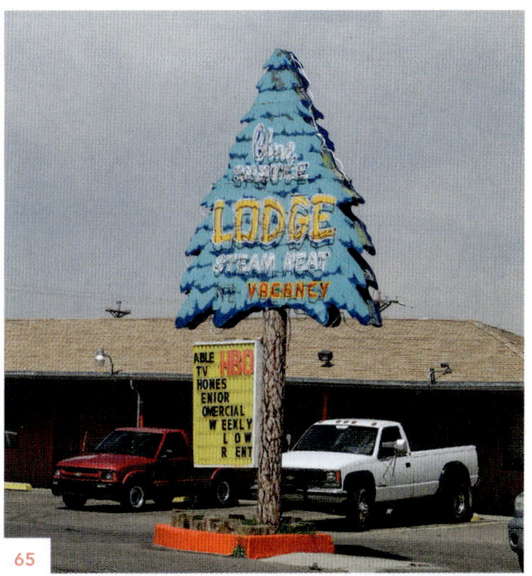

65

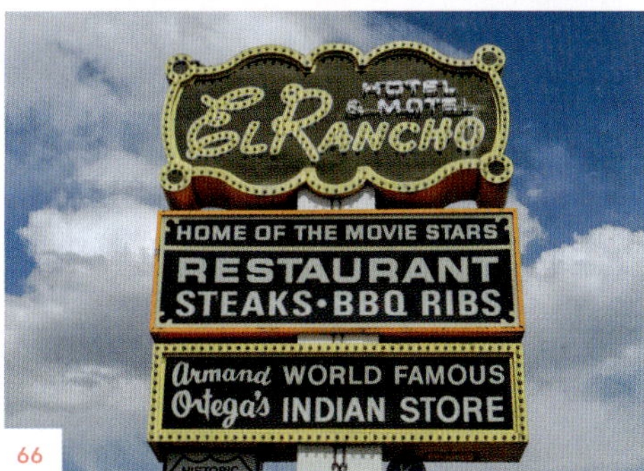

66

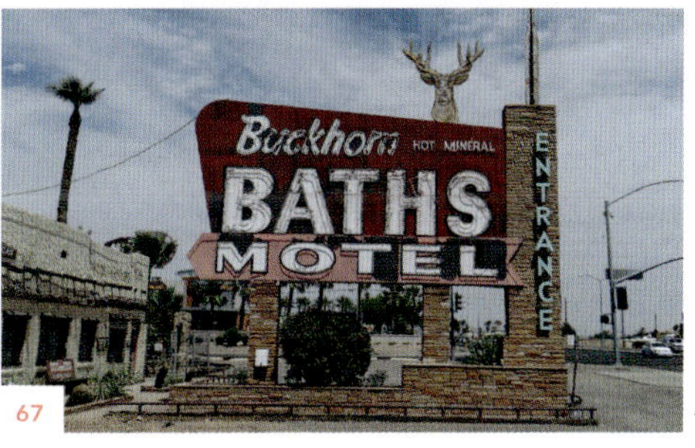

67

And then there are the waters, said to have healing properties, a boast that is conferred a certain credibility when one learns that Alice Sliger lived to 103, sharp until the very end. The Buckhorn closed in 1999, and after years of false starts, was sold in 2017 for just north of $2 million to a group that at last report was assessing the 16-acre property—deeply appreciative of its unique charms—and deciding what to do with it.

IT'S A WESTERN THING

So many motels out this way play off their location in the West. Here are some of my faves, lassoed together:

There are certain names you will encounter repeatedly: **"Sands"** is one, and here is a flag-festooned example in Grants, New Mexico **(FIG. 68)**.

We're out here in the frontier, and the old **Frontier Motel (FIG. 69)** in Truxton, Arizona, heeds the call in dazzling neon and a fun mosaic featuring a jaunty chef, who in 2013 was pointing to a pay phone, appropriately belonging to the Frontier telephone company.

The Highlander Motel (FIG. 71) in Williams, Arizona, has a dramatic sign, one that has been toned down since this photograph was taken in 2013, but still retains its vintage forms.

Supai Village, in Havasupai Canyon deep in the Grand Canyon, is one of the most remote places in the United States. It's accessible only by foot or copter ride—or by mule. The **Supai Motel (FIG. 70)**, on **Route 66** in Seligman, Arizona, is, to put it simply, much easier to reach.

And finally, we see so many motels with "Western" in the name, like **Western Hills (FIG. 73)** in Flagstaff, Arizona, and the weathered remains of the **Western Motel (FIG. 72)** in San Jon, New Mexico.

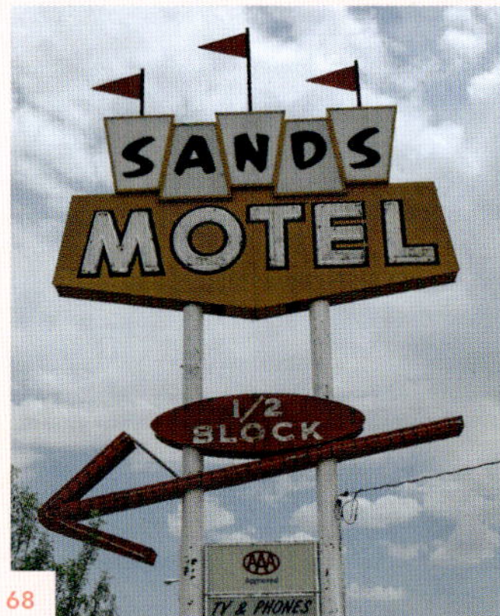

68

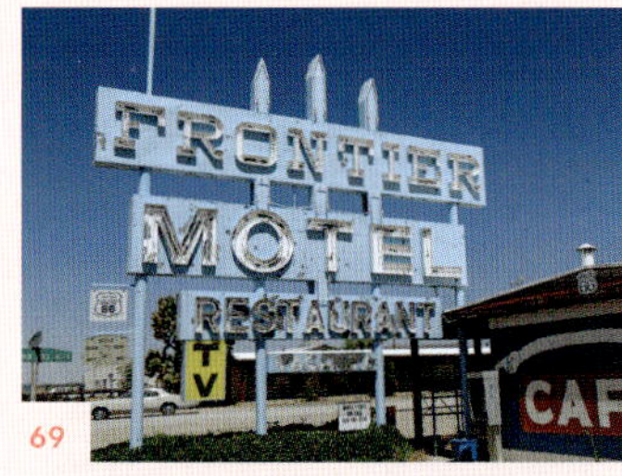

69

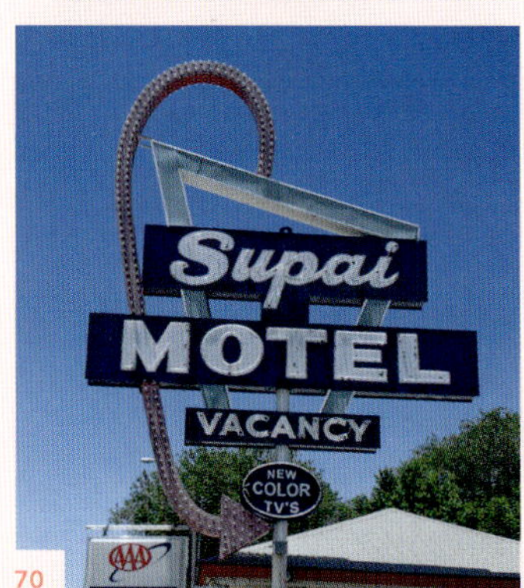

70

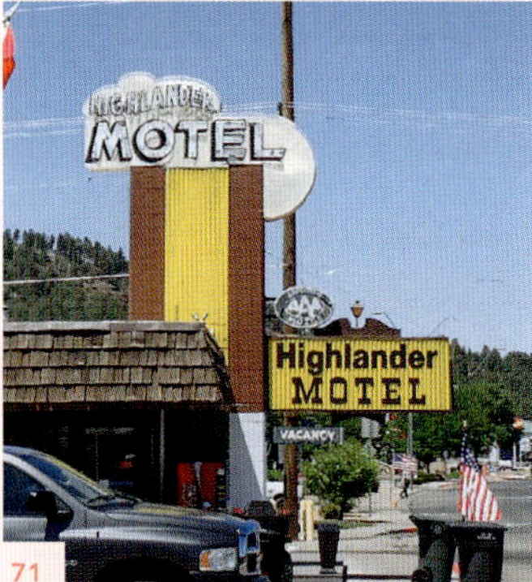

71

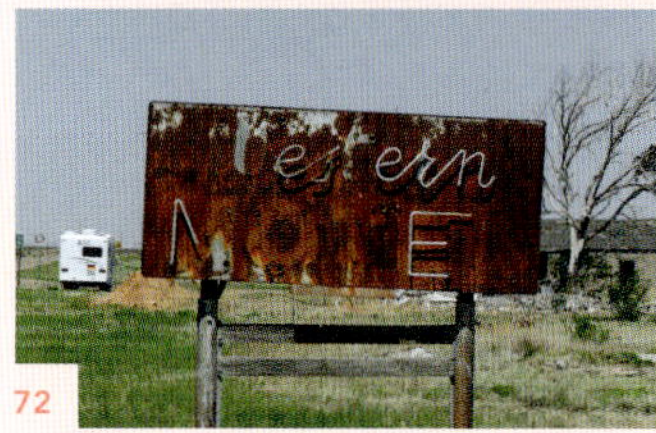

72

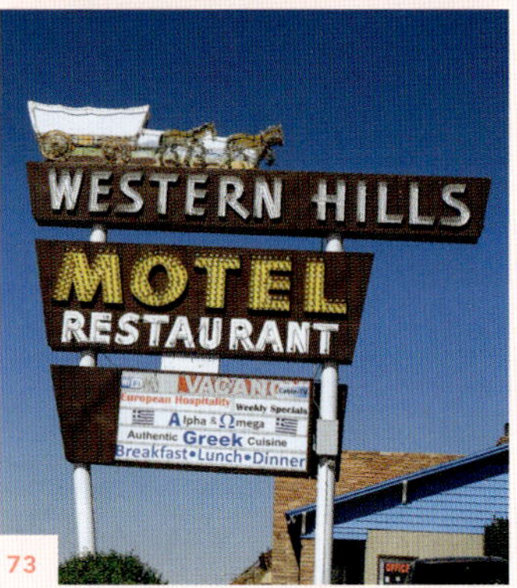

73

Mesa's **Diving Lady** (FIG. 74) is a miracle. She splashes into the water every ten seconds or so, a neon oasis in the Arizona desert. She first did that from 1960 to 2010, when a hailstorm from hell swept through town and sent her crashing to the ground. Preservationists immediately realized what was lost, and rallied a costly and complicated effort to restore the sign using much of the original material.

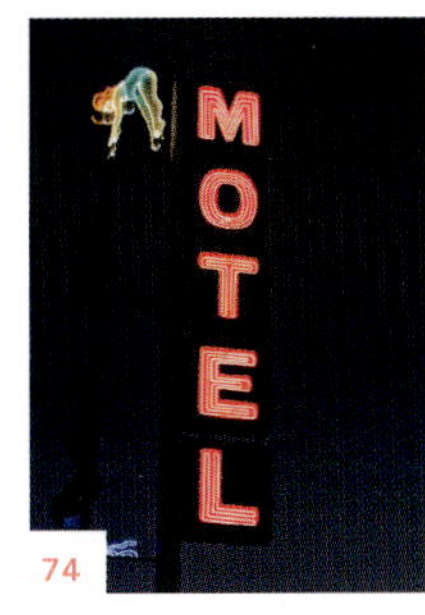

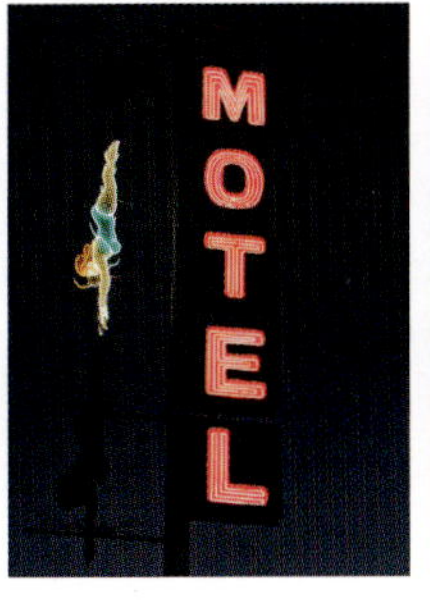

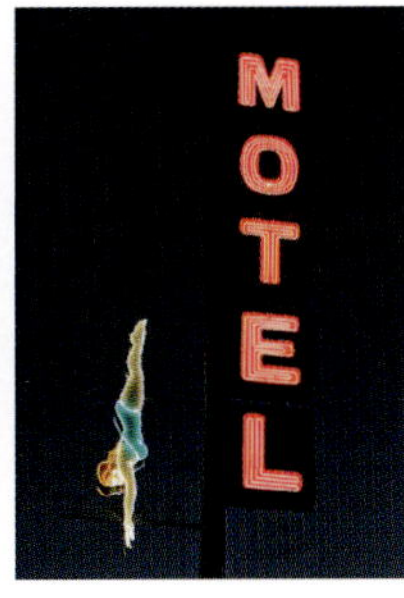

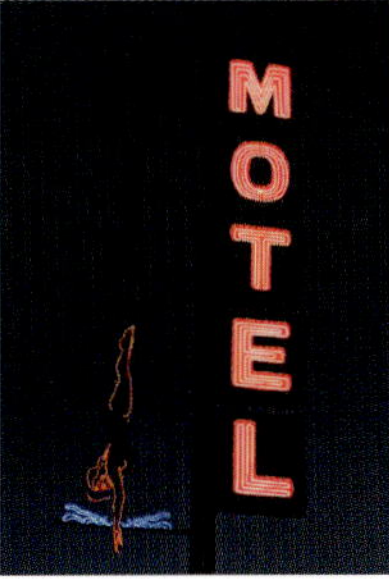

74

She's been diving again since 2013, promoting the **Starlite Motel** as she always has, but not its pool, because it no longer exists. Maybe they'll remove the concrete that filled it in years ago, but that's a small detail.

SWEET STOP

The storefront for our next stop alone is worth the trip. But the backstory—and pop-culture connections—add a richness to the experience here.

Jack Huntress wasn't even in the restaurant business when he realized Scottsdale, Arizona, needed the **Sugar Bowl** (FIG. 75). So he opened this wonderfully colorful ice-cream parlor on Christmas Eve 1958, when Scottsdale was still a recently incorporated city whose downtown was more salty than sweet, the businesses catering to consumers of hard liquor, not soft serve. It was, as its slogan attested, "The West's Most Western Town." The Sugar Bowl grew up with Scottsdale as the city blossomed into the posh resort it is today. The shop is beloved, and the building is a local landmark. It's now in the third generation of family ownership, and in its third generations of local families visiting for sweet bites. The most famous family was fictional—Bil Keane's *The Family Circus* cartoon strip featured the Sugar Bowl, and Keane, who lived close by in Paradise Valley, was a regular and contributed his cartoons—strips that mention the Sugar Bowl are featured on the menu.

75

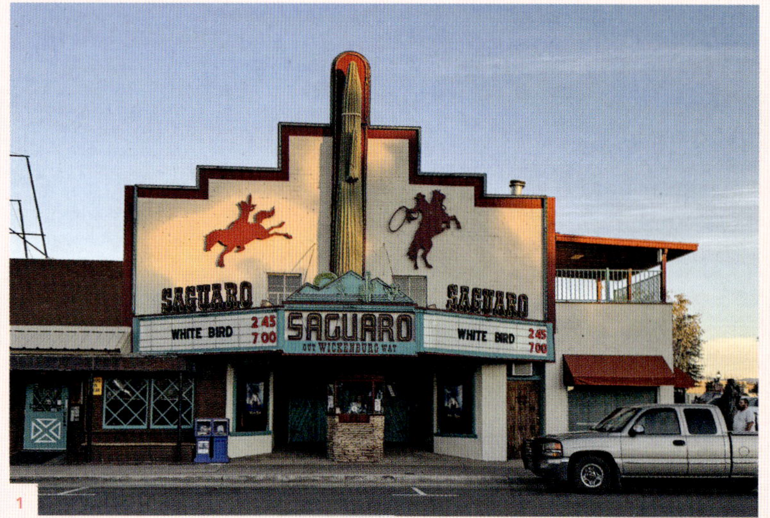

1

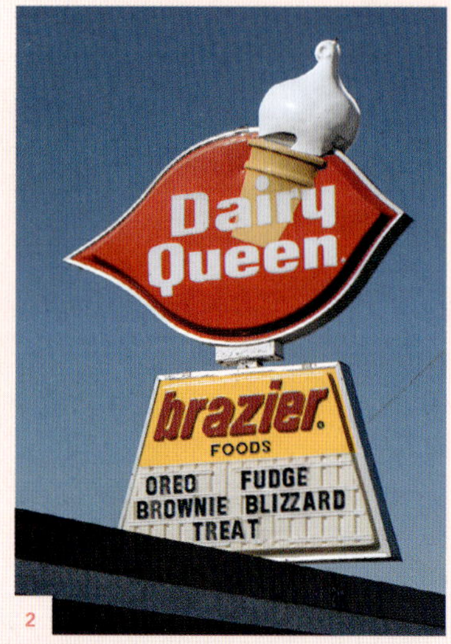

2

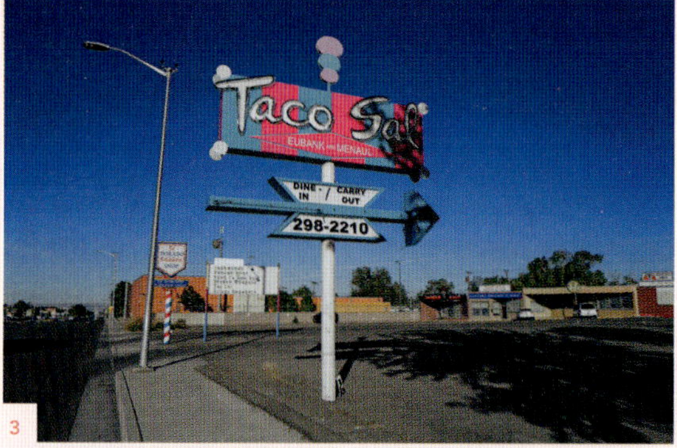

3

THE DELIGHTFUL DOZEN

Mac Tonight. A rare DQ Brazier. Is the Lawless Center for the Saints and Sinners? Enjoy this tour!

1. Saguaro Theater, Wickenburg, Arizona
2. Dairy Queen, Casa Grande, Arizona
3. Taco Sal, Albuquerque, New Mexico
4. Kingman Club, Kingman, Arizona
5. Lawless Center, Las Vegas, Nevada
6. Saints and Sinners, Española, New Mexico
7. Crossroads Motel, Albuquerque, New Mexico
8. KOB-TV, Albuquerque, New Mexico
9. Lincoln County Book Depository, Carrizozo, New Mexico
10. McDonald's mural, Alamogordo, New Mexico
11. Chandler Liquors, Chandler, Arizona
12. Kon Tiki, Kingman, Arizona

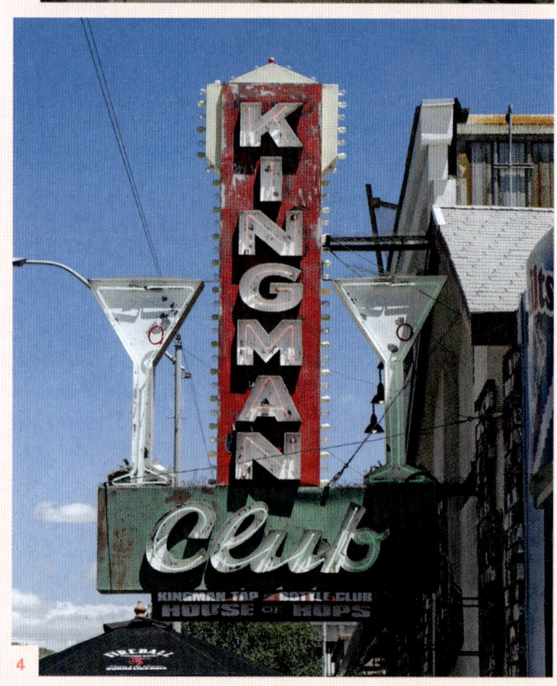

4

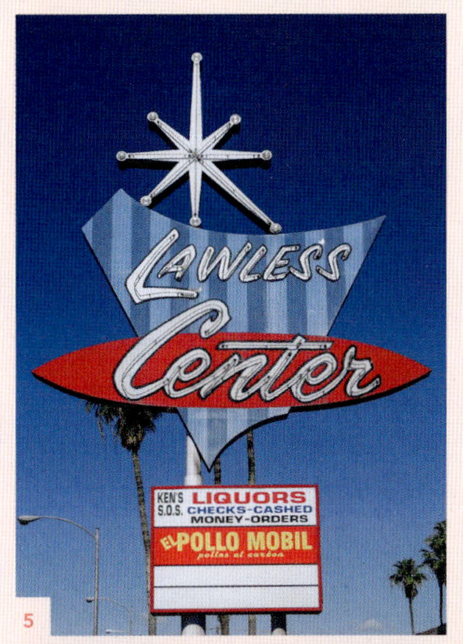

5

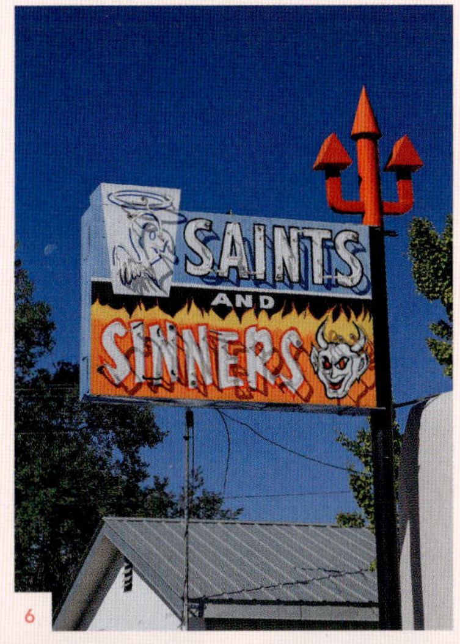

6

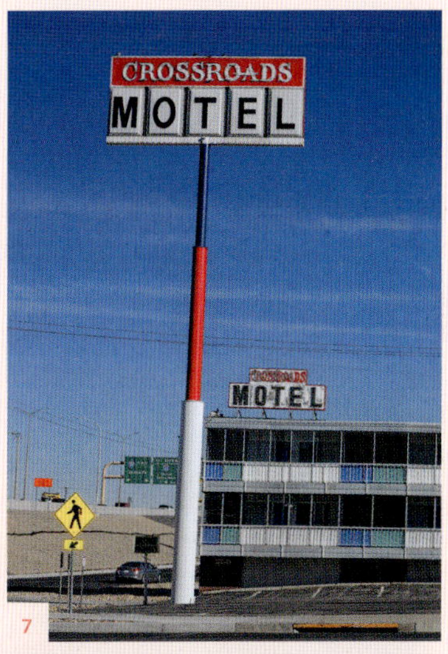

7

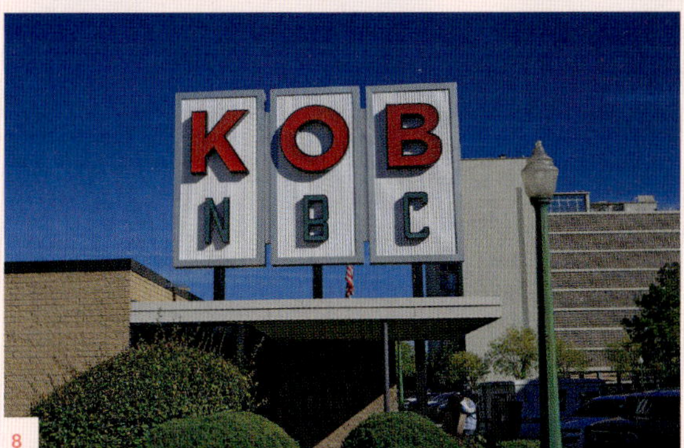

8

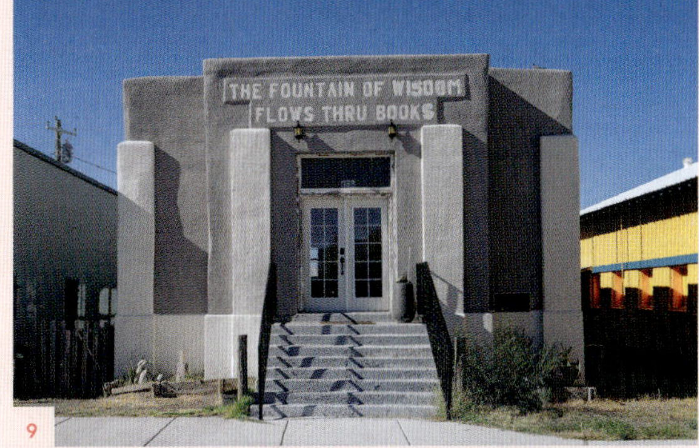

9

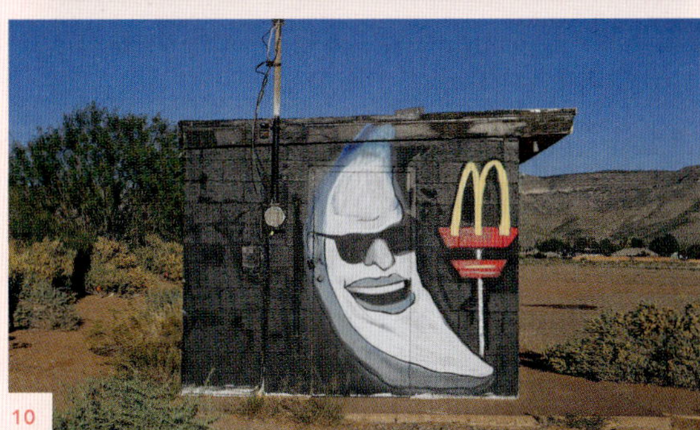
10

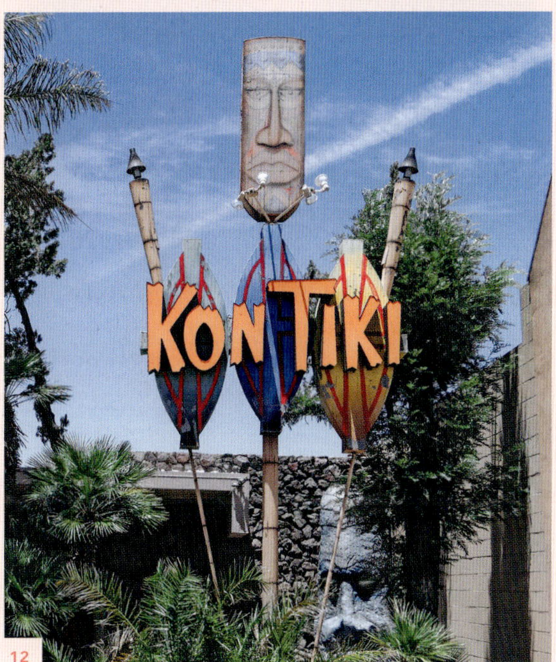

12

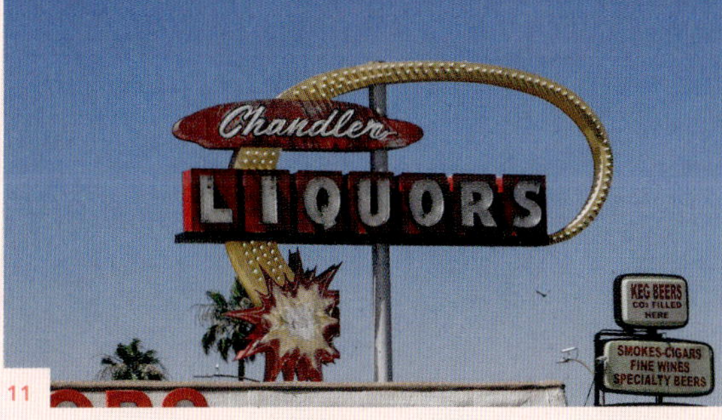

11

HEARTLAND

NORTH DAKOTA · SOUTH DAKOTA · NEBRASKA
KANSAS · IOWA · MISSOURI

From the Lincoln Highway to Route 66, and to countless other places far less known, the Heartland is a broad term. Let's get to the heart of the matter: There is a lot of America—and Americana—right here . . .

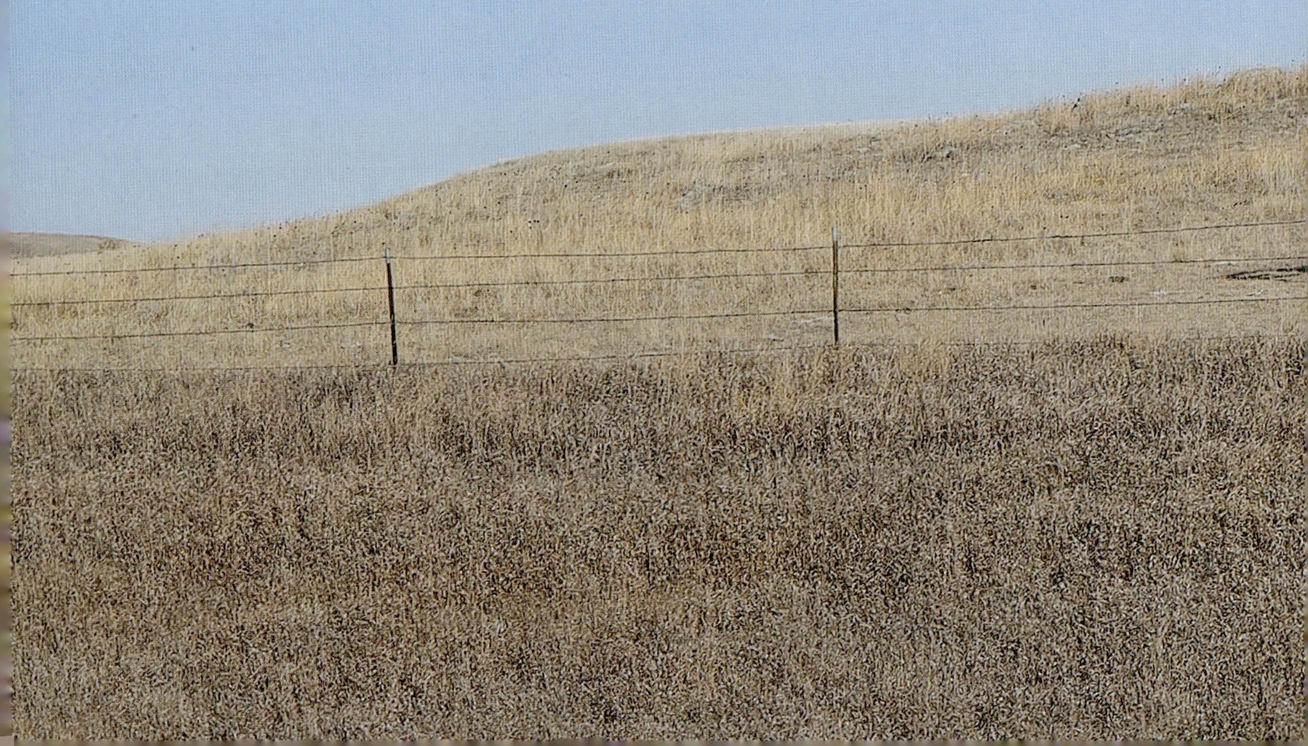

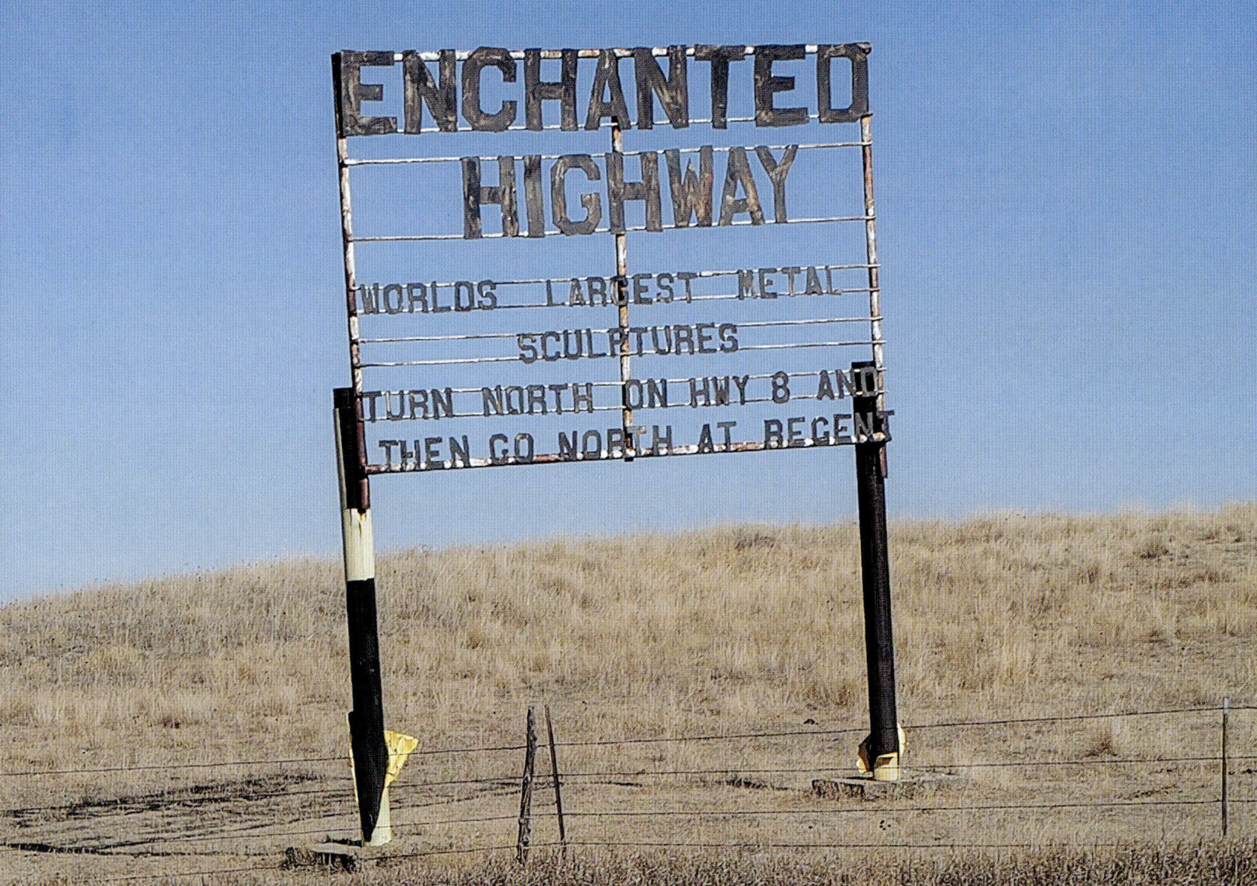

The Enchanted Highway is an adventurous 32-mile drive dotted with giant scrap-metal sculptures in Regent, North Dakota.

ROADSIDE QUIRKS

If there's a place where roadside quirkiness exists with abundance, you'll find it in this region. Wait until you explore the Enchanted Highway's sheet-metal giants, stroll amid Depression-era dinosaurs high above Rapid City, or sip from the most refreshing cup of ice water you will ever taste. It's a big country—and we love big and wacky things created by clever people who should be honorary Wharton summa cum laude MBAs. Enjoy the ride they've created for us.

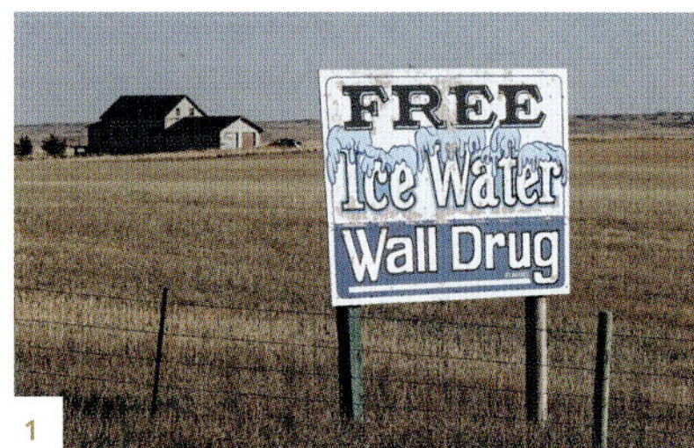

1

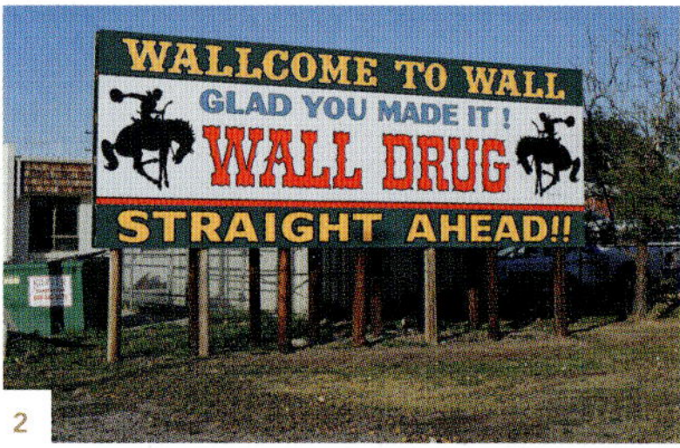

2

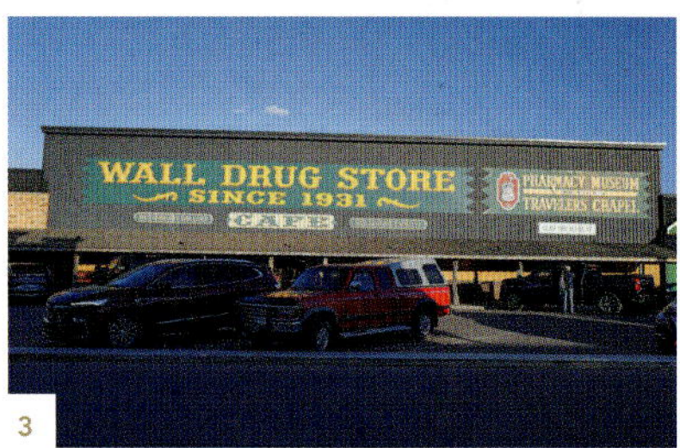

3

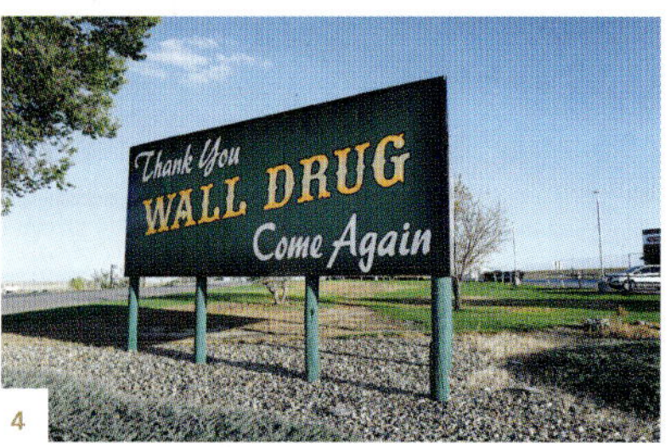

4

If an American road-trip stop is sacred ground—the wellspring of inspiration for countless other roadside entrepreneurs—this is it: **Wall Drug** (FIGS. 1, 2, 3, 4) in Wall, South Dakota. Wall Drug was once a small drugstore in the middle of nowhere. Its doors opened during the Great Depression at a time when life was challenging, and every penny counted. The story goes that pharmacists Dorothy and Ted Hustead (with young son, Bill, in tow) bought the shop in 1931, moved out here, and sank every last cent into the little drug store. They set a self-imposed five-year deadline to make a go of it. By 1936, a business selling tonics for the sick was itself sickly. Just in time, Dorothy had a eureka moment: Put up a billboard on the main highway for the drug store offering visitors free ice water. After all, it gets pretty hot out this way, and she could hear all the cars whizzing by on the highway, as the semiarid desert known as the Badlands gained renown and Mount Rushmore's presidential faces were slowly being chiseled out of rock.

The small sign was inspired by the Burma-Shave roadside ads, then ubiquitous, promoting the now-obscure shaving-cream brand with a series of sequential signs on sticks along the road. Her marketing tonic was restorative, and Ted was soon hunting for more highway spots to place the signs well beyond Wall. The clever billboards—hundreds of miles in either direction—cultivated anticipation to the point where, even if you had a gallon of ice water sloshing next to you in the car, you'd simply *have* to pull over to see what the fuss was about.

Over the years, Wall Drug blossomed from its pharmacy core into a massive tourist attraction, featuring souvenir shops, Western-wear stores, Indigenous jewelry boutiques, restaurants, an art gallery, and curiosities like a massive dinosaur. Oh, and a jackalope statue. The fabled jackalope—an antelope-horned jackrabbit as elusive as Bigfoot and Nessie—is honored in an even bigger way elsewhere in the town of Wall, with a

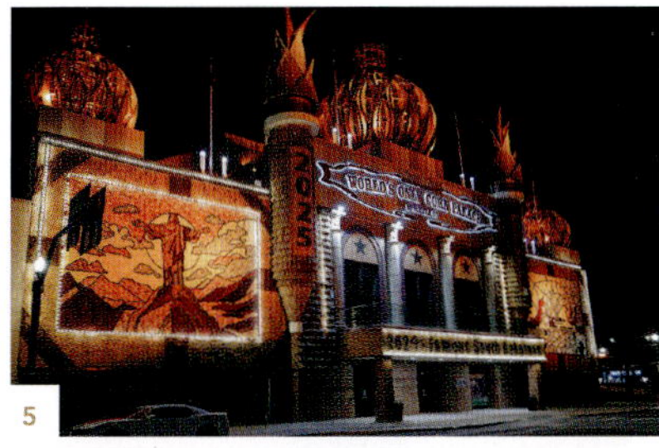

5

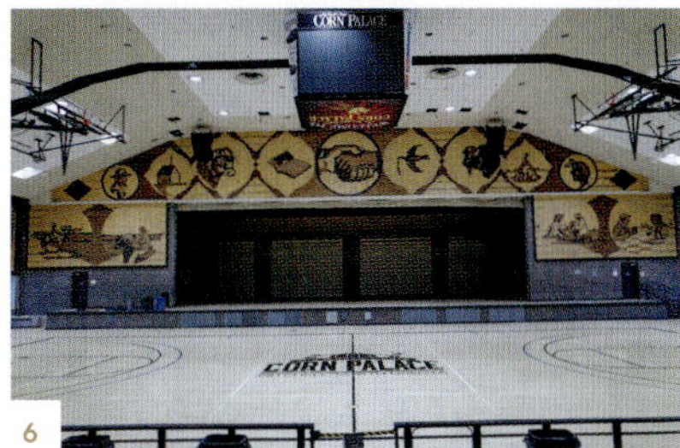

6

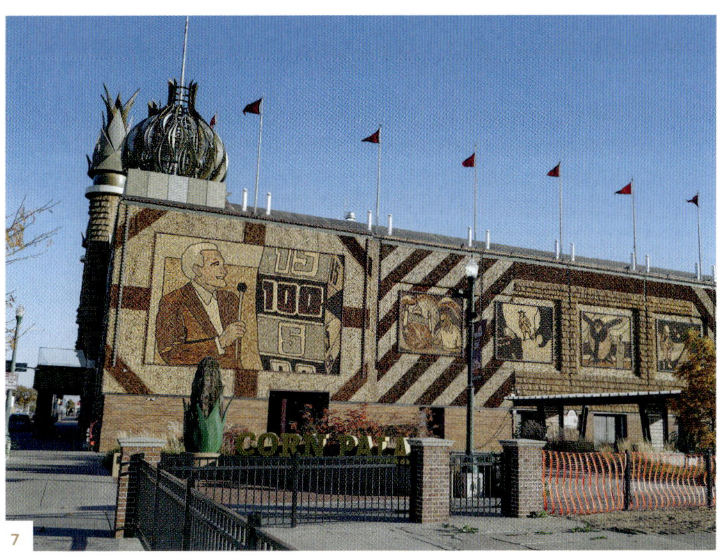

7

40-foot-tall jackalope (FIG. 8) piercing the sky. You can even climb inside the jackalope and admire Badland country from a balcony. After my first visit to Wall Drug in August 1998, I eagerly slapped a "Where the Heck Is Wall Drug" sticker on my tiny Geo Metro, right there in Wall's parking lot, sporting it like a badge of honor.

On that same trip in 1998, I visited the **Mitchell Corn Palace** (FIGS. 5, 6, 7) in Mitchell, South Dakota. When the palace was first built, kernel-encrusted palaces were a showy Midwestern trend, and the Mitchell structure was the biggest and only one that lasted. It is visited by hundreds of thousands of tourists yearly and is a key community hub in this city of around fifteen thousand. This is the third version of the palace on the site, dating to 1921, with the turrets coming along in the late 1930s. The very first palace was built in 1892, proclaiming Mitchell an agricultural wonderland and offering a place to celebrate the bounty of the corn harvest.

The structure displays countless kernels of corn of multiple naturally occurring hues shaped into murals that celebrate the community and its agricultural heritage. Amazingly, these murals are usually switched every year with a fresh theme, an admirable if exhausting feat of artistry and dedication. (I found game show host Bob Barker, who was raised in South Dakota, on a mural during a recent visit.) If you need greater inducements to visit, **Cornelius**, the smiling, 6-foot-tall fiberglass mascot, gamely poses for snapshots. (Nearby, a fiberglass jackalope, **Thunderbunny**, can be hopped on outside the **Thunderbird Lodge** in Mitchell. He was "rehorned" in 2016 after some monster yanked off his antlers, rendering him a mere jackrabbit for half a decade.)

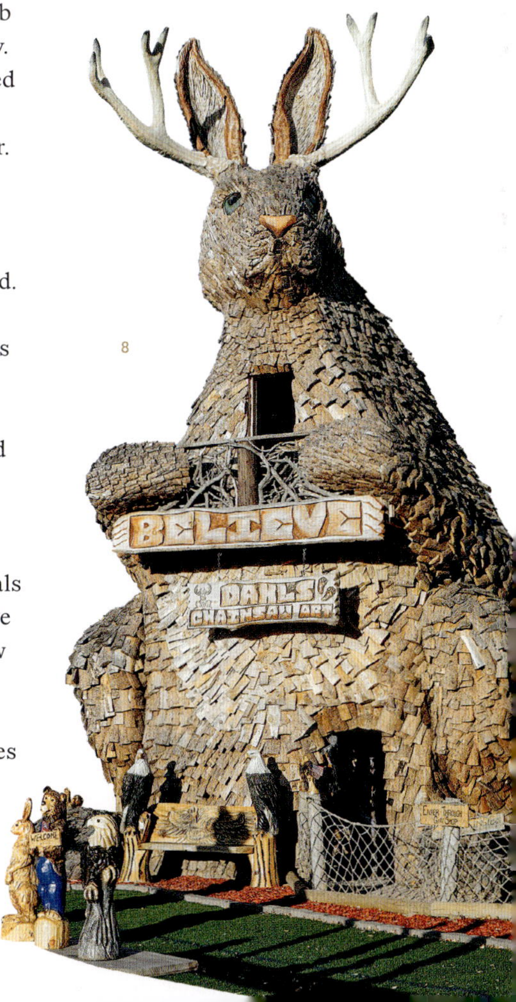

8

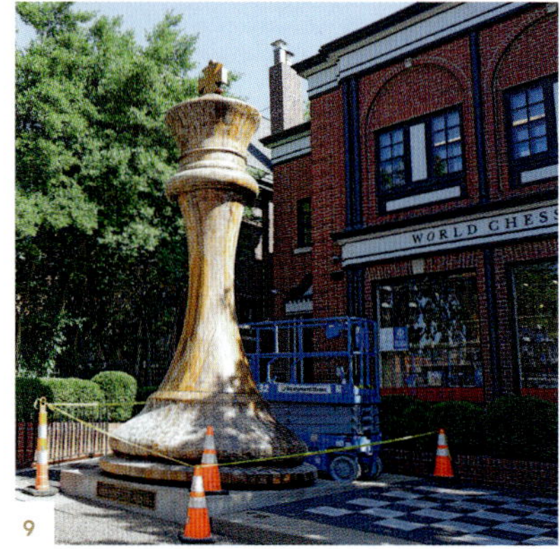

9

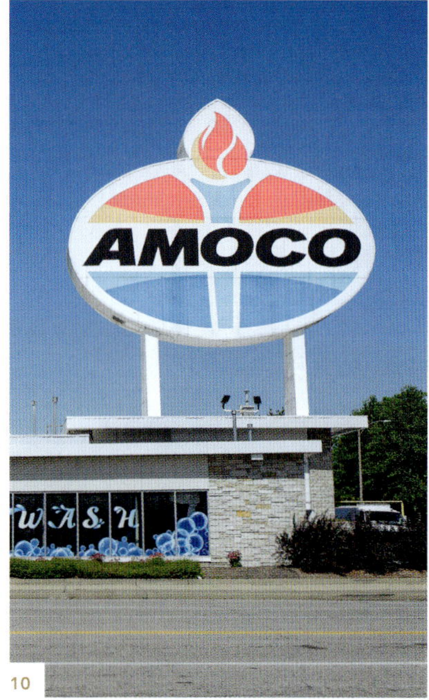

10

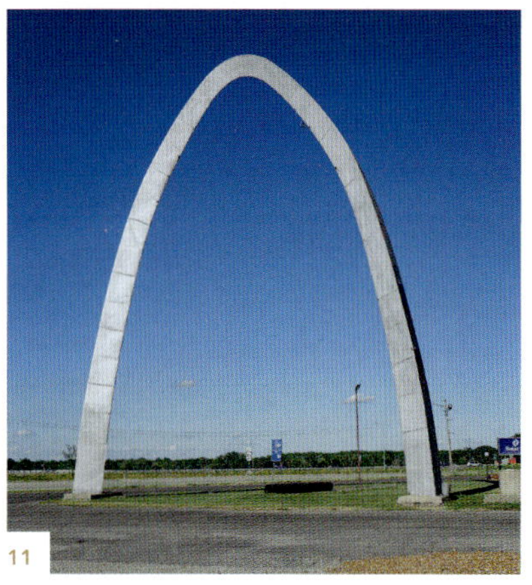
11

Note: Corn enthusiasts will have no shortage of pilgrimage sites in this region of the country—Sac City, Iowa, is home to the **World's Largest Popcorn Ball**, unveiled in 2016. Another big thing waiting to be discovered includes the **World's Largest Fountain Cup** in Cape Girardeau, Missouri. The cup promotes the Rhodes convenience store; the name is where any resemblance to the lost Colossus of Rhodes begins and ends. If you got that reference without having to google it, then, smarty that you are, you'll want to visit the **World's Largest Chess Piece** (FIG. 9) in St. Louis, Missouri, a wooden, 20-foot-tall sculpture of considerable refinement. Inside, well-curated exhibits will stimulate the imagination of chess fans at the **World Chess Hall of Fame**.

Another record-setting structure is near the Chess Hall of Fame—the world's largest **Amoco sign** (FIG. 10) at **Stevenson's Hi-Pointe Amoco station** in St. Louis. Amoco was a Midwestern-based spinoff of the original Standard Oil company. The first large electric sign in this area, a true spectacular worthy of Times Square, was erected in 1923, followed by an impressive replacement in 1932 touting the Standard Red Crown brand, glowing in neon and light bulbs. In 1961, after the station was rebuilt, a new gigantic sign saying "Standard" in the familiar oval-and-torch silhouette was installed, which itself was switched to read "Amoco" in the 1980s as the Standard brand became vestigial. (See page 305 for more.)

British Petroleum purchased the company in 1998 and largely abandoned the Amoco name. Still, the station, rebadged as a BP, kept its large Amoco sign, even as out-of-towners surely wondered why such a large Amoco sign was floating majestically over a BP station. (Locals understood why the Amoco sign was preserved—nobody would *dare* mess with it.) In 2017, BP revived the Amoco brand and it began to make a retail comeback in select markets. Appropriately, this station was converted back to an Amoco. The sign was updated to a refreshed Amoco logo that is very much in the spirit of the previous one. If you step inside the store, you'll see a little Amoco exhibit, an old "Red Crown" lamp hanging above the coffee machine, and friendly employees ready to indulge your curiosity.

St. Louis, of course, is famous for its biggest symbol of all, the **Gateway Arch**, the design of the modernist architect Eero Saarinen, who also gave us the TWA Terminal in Queens, New York (now the TWA Hotel). A fun game to play in the region is "spot the arch," both as it pops up on the skyline in countless photogenic configurations and as signage adopted by businesses across the region, like the **Sharp Shooters Pit & Grill** and the "**Baby Arch**" (FIG. 11), as some call it, just over the border in Vandalia, Illinois, once housing the name of a motel but now standing in pristine isolation.

Vandalia is home to another iconic metallic structure, this one a fiery roadside chimera. The **Kaskaskia Dragon** (FIG. 12) was constructed in 1995, the vision of the owner of Kaskaskia Supply & Rental hardware store, Walt Barenfanger. The dragon faces off with a small knight in shining armor, a David and Goliath–style impasse along I-40. What makes this scene remarkable is that the dragon breathes fire. Yes, the Kaskaskia Dragon is fitted with a hydraulic propane system that's responsive to a token you can buy for a buck at the hardware or an on-site liquor store. The dragon emits flames for ten seconds.

If medieval-inspired frolics have you searching for signs of Middle Earth, **Sir Albert and the Dragon** (FIG. 12) in Regent, North Dakota, will give you a goal to joust for on your journey. This pair is also far better matched than the Kaskaskia Dragon and the puny knight, each standing around 40 feet here. The pair comes from the brilliant mind of Gary Greff, the mechanically inclined (but never trained) merrymaker who put his tiny and remote hometown of Regent on the map by creating a wonderland of scrap-metal sculptures (geese in flight, pheasants on the prairie, Teddy Roosevelt riding again, oh my!) along his **Enchanted Highway**, where his gargantuan works of whimsy have been going up for decades. Sir Albert and the Dragon do battle outside his **Enchanted Castle Hotel**, another Greff creation where you can spend the night in this storybook come to life.

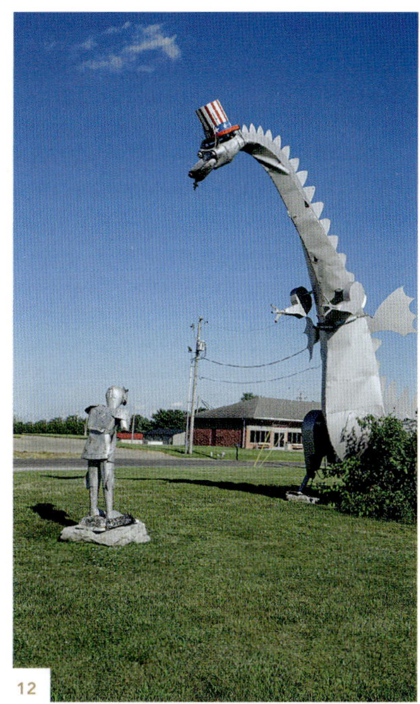

12

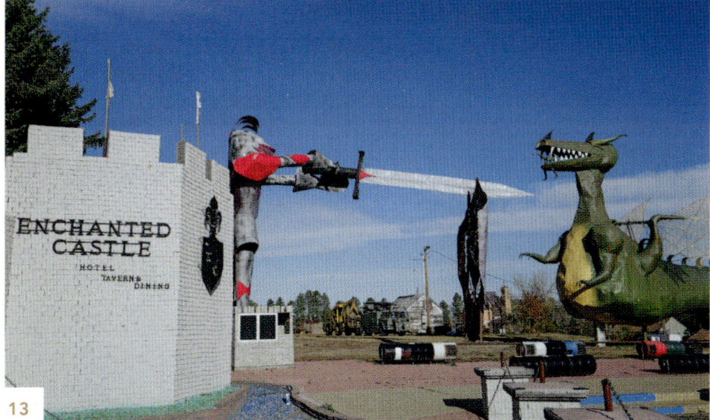

13

The Enchanted Highway also includes Greff's adorable **World's Largest Tin Family** (FIG. 14). The cheery Greff is a dreamer intoxicated by the artistic possibilities of the prairie, but also a doer who gets things off the drawing board. His pieces capture the promise, the thrill, and the sense of limitlessness the American frontier has long represented. They are helping him realize his hopes of reviving his own town's forlorn fortunes. Fairy-tale adjacent, **Storybook Island** in Rapid City, North Dakota, along with **Storybook Land** in Aberdeen, South Dakota, both teem with family-friendly attractions.

From an enchanted highway of giant things, we turn our attention to a 1960s cartoon dinosaur in the Black Hills of

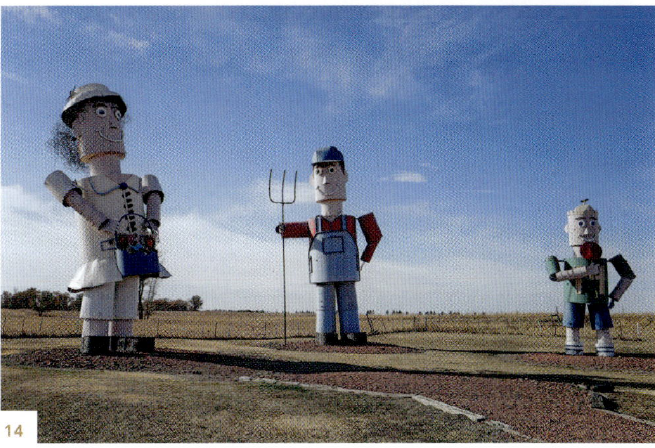

14

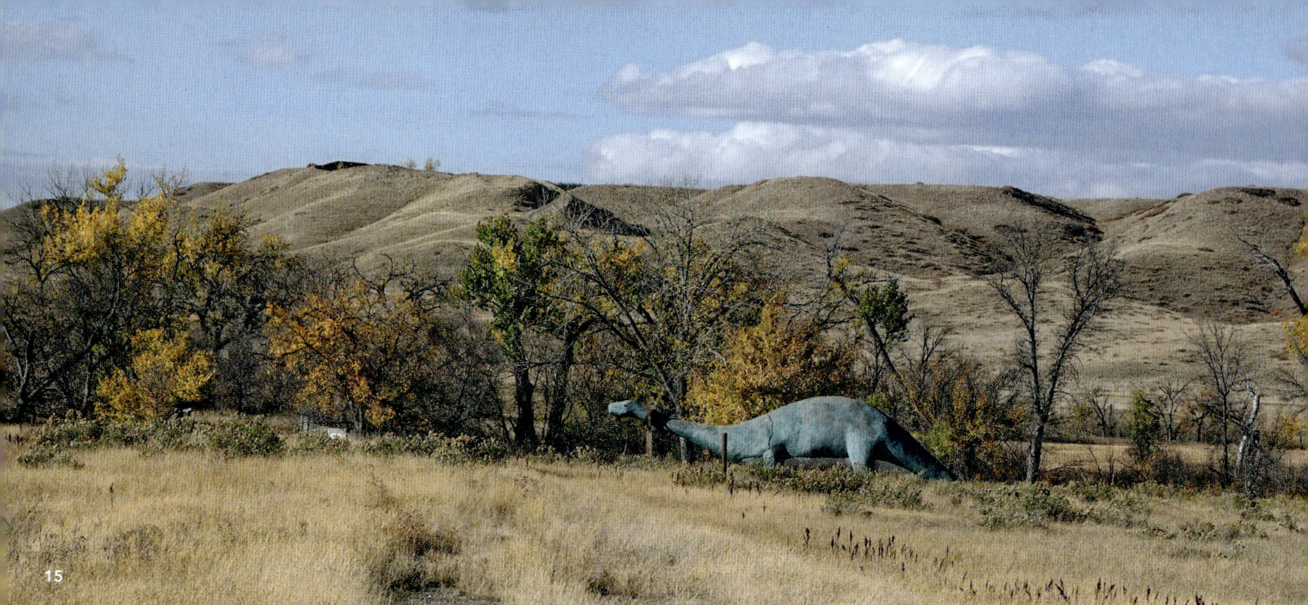
15

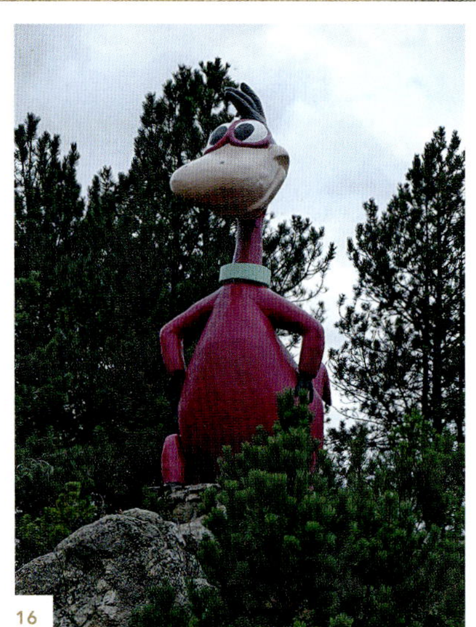
16

South Dakota. Yes, that's **Dino** (FIG. 16) from *The Flintstones*. On page 192, we toured **Bedrock City**, the Flintstones theme park near the Grand Canyon. That park was a spinoff of the original Bedrock City here in Custer, South Dakota, opened in 1966 and shuttered in 2015. Dino is the most prominent survivor from the demolished Custer location, sitting high on a hill, a spotlight shining on him at night. His regal purple hue had been fading, vegetation engulfing him, until Dino was restored in 2024, a tribute to an attraction that entertained generations.

The **Creston dinosaur** (FIG. 15) in Caputa, South Dakota, predates Dino by thirty-three years, and may well be the oldest roadside dinosaur in America and, some say, the loneliest. The dinosaur was constructed for a general store in 1933 to draw in motorists and rail passengers when Creston, now a ghost town, was a thriving little rail town. Today, the dinosaur is the biggest evidence that Creston even existed. The dinosaur languished until engineering students helped rebuild the 60-foot-long reptile in 1998. But the beast is again in decline, its paint fading, cracks reappearing, a frame supporting its neck. It tugs at the ticker to see this beautiful creature in an empty field, a reminder of how brief boom times can be, and at one time there was a lot of pride in this town. When a newspaper article in 1942 mistakenly placed the dinosaur in Caputa, its co-builder and staunchest advocate, Ike Murphy, lashed out for not giving Creston its due. Sad to say, Creston is no more, despite the dinosaur's best efforts.

The Creston dinosaur is about 30 miles south of an attraction that some speculate it inspired—**Dinosaur Park** (FIGS. 17, 18) in Rapid City, South Dakota, and it's still a popular tourist draw. Seven dinosaurs—steel skeletons encased in concrete—stand on

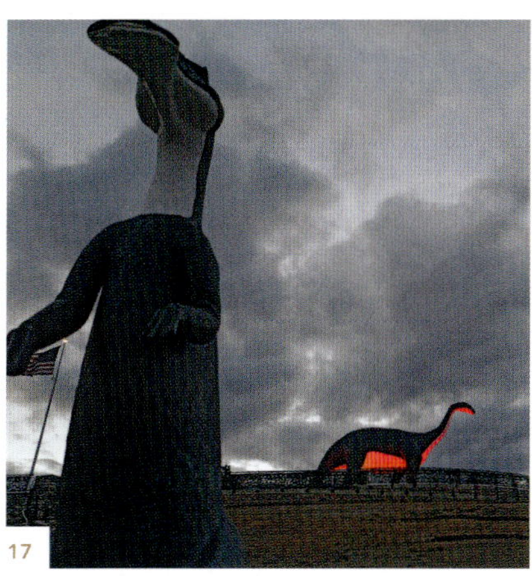
17

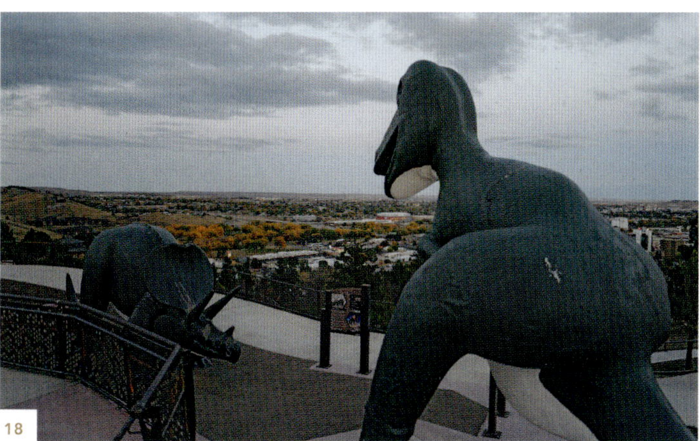
18

land where the real things once roamed. They are the creation of the gifted sculptor Emmet Sullivan, who built Wall Drug's dinosaur in 1959, among other notable prehistoric reptilian statuary in America. Sitting high above the city on a sandstone ridge, the Rapid City dinosaurs make for a stirring sight even if you never walk among them.

Now, pardner, let's skedaddle out of prehistoric times and mosey back to the Old West. On this trip, we will encounter a whole lot of cowboys, and I've lassoed up a sampler pack.

Let's begin our tour with the **Giant Cowboy** in Carson, North Dakota, not a regular stop on the tourist trade but a worthy one for this cowboy cutout that dates to the 1980s. A similar big fella is holding up the **Mount Rushmore Gold Hills Outlet** sign in Rapid City, South Dakota. (You'll also meet a **Giant Prospector** in Rapid City, once the site of a mining attraction run by John A. Aanrud, aka Johnny One Feather.) A giant cowboy points to the **Chute Roosters Restaurant** (FIG. 19) in Hill City, South Dakota. **The Western Holiday Motel** in Wichita, Kansas, features a big cowboy on its sign. I could go on . . . Keep your eye out for those fellas in ten-gallon hats.

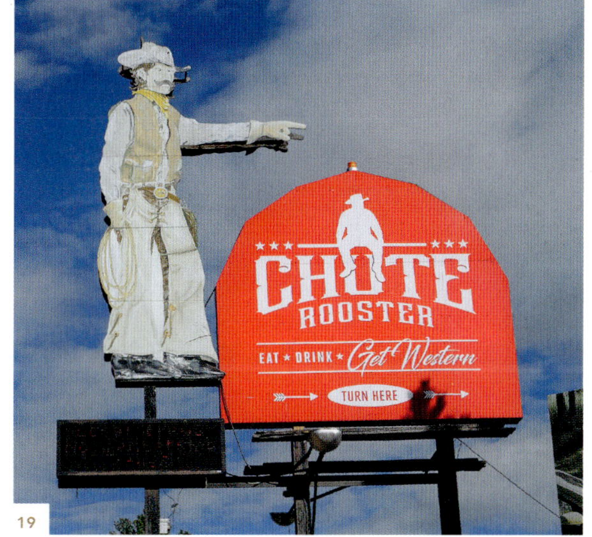

19

But none of these big guys have anything on **Johnny Kaw,** the 24-foot-tall golden wheat farmer of Kansas, a modern myth concocted in 1954, with lantern-jawed lineage traceable to Paul Bunyan and other storybook heroes of the American frontier.

Kaw first appeared in tall tales published in a Manhattan, Kansas, newspaper and written by professor George Filinger to celebrate the town's centennial. Those articles were soon

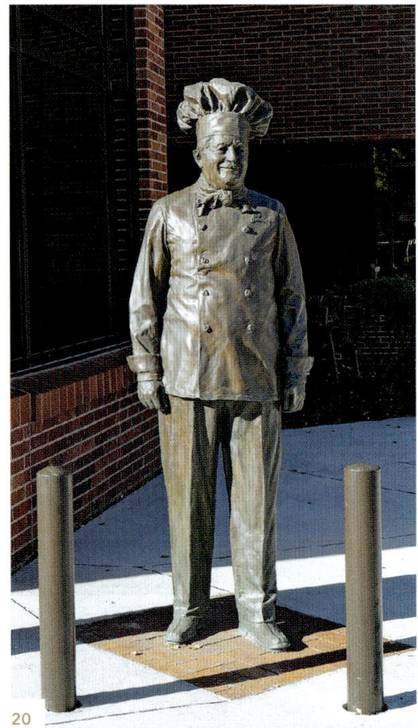

20

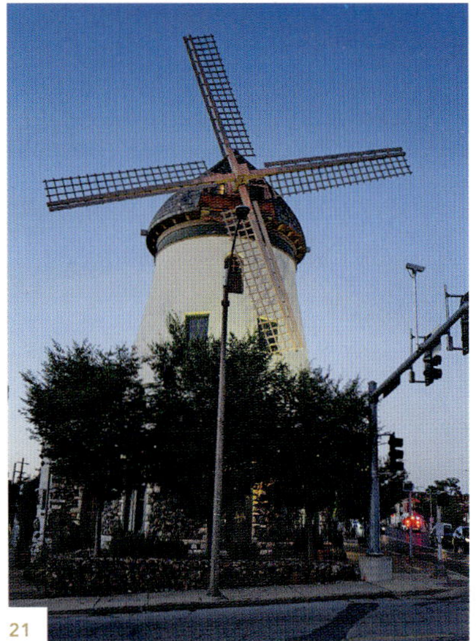

21

anthologized, and the myth of Johnny Kaw took root. A decade later, Filinger led an effort to build a Johnny Kaw statue, scythe in hands (the story goes that he could cut acres of wheat with a single swing), and place it in a Manhattan park. Filinger's imagination imbued Kaw with the protean powers of a deity, ascribing much of the North American landscape to his prodigious strength, vision, and gifts. He even helped scoop out the Grand Canyon, and the earth, moved in giant baskets, formed the basis of America's wheat fields, and the boulders, assembled into the Rocky Mountains. Kaw could even control the weather.

One thing that Johnny Kaw didn't invent is Kool-Aid. That honor goes to the clever and not-at-all-mythological inventor Edwin Elijah Perkins, who concocted the sweet drink in Hastings, Nebraska, in 1927, and the city has embraced Perkins as one of their own. In 2023 the Hastings Museum erected a **Kool-Aid Man** statue outside its building, and the town celebrates Kool-Aid Days every August. (Retrologist pro tip: Great caution is urged standing before any sort of wall in this town—you never know who might burst through yelling "Oh, yeah!" when some random kid yells "Hey, Kool-Aid!") The character first emerged as a smiley face on a pitcher in 1954, until Madison Avenue turned him into the irrepressible Kool-Aid Man in 1975. The original costume and much more Kool-Aid ephemera and artifacts are permanently displayed at the museum.

The power of advertising also made Ettore Boiardi famous, with his line of Italian meals under the brand Chef Boyardee. His company was absorbed by Conagra, and here at the food giant's factory in Omaha, Nebraska, you can visit a life-size **statue of Chef Boyardee** (FIG. 20). You can also visit Chef Boyardee on Conagra's campus in Milton, Pennsylvania, and in 2020, there was a push to honor the famous chef in Cleveland, his home for much of his life, with a statue, replacing one depicting Christopher Columbus.

Our tour of places where Madison Avenue meets Main Street continues in St. Louis. Bevo was the name of a nonalcoholic malt drink brewed by Anheuser-Busch in its hometown of St. Louis. Today, the drink is lost to time, though it flourished from its creation in 1916 through much of Prohibition, until folks got smarter about getting their hands on the real thing, law be damned.

Its mascot, **Reynard the Fox**, survives in statues at the Anheuser-Busch facility on Broadway in St. Louis. But it doesn't take an eagle eye to spot the **Bevo Mill** (FIG. 21), a restaurant and beer garden named for the then-novel drink and opened by August Busch Sr. in 1916, initially as a luxurious oasis for the family halfway between the brewery and the Busch country estate, Grant's Farm. The restaurant, a Tudor-revival affair with a

60-foot-tall windmill, underwent many ownership changes over the years but has stayed true to its hearty Germanic fare. Today it's known as Das Bevo—look for Reynard the Fox enjoying his "near beer" on a stained glass window inside. Fun fact: Irving Berlin immortalized Bevo in a song by that name, bemoaning that it has the "taste of lager" but not the "kick" of the real deal.

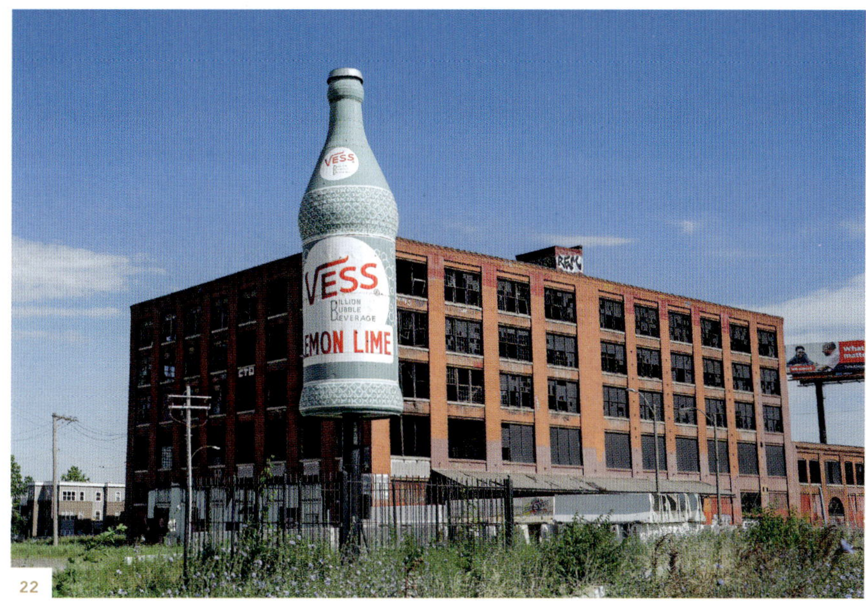

22

St. Louis is a beer town, so you'd think a giant bottle of Bud would be a skyline fixture. But rather, it's a regional soda brand that tugs at nostalgic hearts. The **Vess Cola Bottle** (FIG. 22) sign dates to the early 1950s, and once spun and was neon-bedecked. The bottle ended up in storage after being removed from its original location, and since 1990 the bottle has sat off U.S. 44 near the Dome at America's Center. The soda brand is still in business, with distribution largely in the St. Louis area. Clear across the state, a far less visible but beautiful relic of Vess Cola survives in a ghost sign in St. Joseph, Missouri, on Messanie Street off South Twenty-Second Street.

The big reason to visit St. Joseph is to see the **Pony Express National Museum**. The town also has a relic that testifies to the enduring fascination this short-lived version of express mail still holds: the historic sign for the **Pony Express Motel** (FIG. 23). When the motel closed in 2007 to make way for a development, the sign was salvaged and moved here, near the museum and site of the pony stables, a perpetual reminder of the horseback relay network of mail carriers who served the nation in 1860–61, only to be rendered obsolete by the telegraph at the dawn of the Civil War.

23

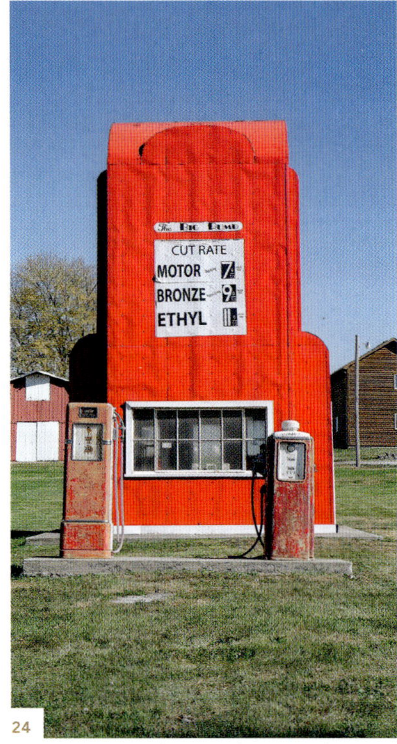

24

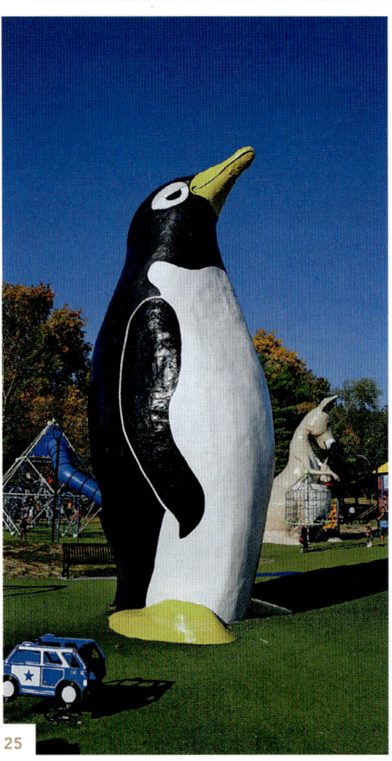
25

The Big Pump (FIG. 24), a lovely piece of mimetic architecture built for a service station, originally went up in Maryville, Missouri, in 1936. The station was busy for years, with four gas pumps and attendants filling up tanks and wiping bugs from windshields along busy Highway 71. It was the vision of Kyle Phares, who wanted a building that mimicked the cutting-edge Wayne computing gas pumps, which displayed the amount of gas sold in dollars and cents. Two of the gas pumps at its opening on May 16, 1936, were of this variety. Customers who bought five gallons of gasoline that day were given a free pint of ice cream for their patronage. Phares got to enjoy his art deco masterpiece for only a few years, dying of a heart attack in July 1941.

Times changed and the new interstate highways drew customers away from old 71. The structure was moved elsewhere in town, reportedly with plans for it to anchor a museum. Finally, in 1994, it ended up on the grounds of the Tri-County Museum in King City, forever celebrating its original purpose, even if gas will never be dispensed from here again.

Think about your obituary. What will it say? Vernon Jones of Kansas City, Missouri, had a fine career as a civil servant in the city's Parks and Recreation Department. But it's *what* he did in that job that ended up in the obituary. In 1965, Jones created the giant fiberglass penguin that lives in what is now known as **Penguin Park** (FIG. 25), inside Lakewood Greenway. He also created fiberglass companions—an elephant, a giraffe, and a kangaroo. Those were just a sampling of the menagerie he left behind to amuse children of all ages—but so many return to the penguin as their favorite, perhaps because of its size, or its outlandishness. Why is it in the middle of a park, people ask? In a 1996 interview, Jones said that he drew inspiration from smaller penguins at a Christmas exhibit in the Midtown neighborhood of Kansas City. He saw how much kids loved the penguins. So why not a large penguin in a playground?

The **Stonehenge** (FIG. 26) in Rolla, Missouri, is hardly a playground, but it does inspire a sense of wonder. It may have you wondering how it ended up here, thousands of miles from the Salisbury Plain in southern England, where the actual Stonehenge monoliths have been a source of intrigue for millennia. The Ozarks Stonehenge has been a roadside curiosity measured only in decades, beginning specifically on June 20, 1984, just hours before the summer solstice. This Stonehenge is a half-scale version of the monoliths, constructed by an engineering team at Missouri University of Science and Technology. They used the school's high-pressure water-jet technology to carve the granite stones, lending them crisp, sharp profiles, unlike the craggy originals, more Donald Judd than ancient Briton. In the spirit of the original, they also built in cool astronomical features, like a viewer for the North Star. To tie both Stonehenges together, John Bevan, a Druid of Gorsedd, attended the summer-solstice ceremony in his signature white robe, to connect with his brethren that year at the real Stonehenge at that hour.

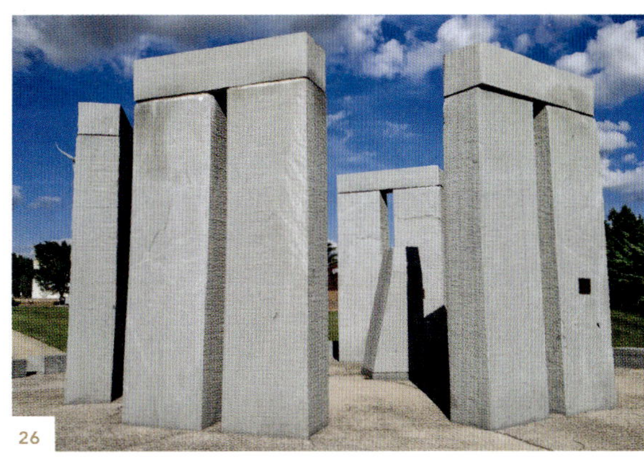

26

Today, of course, we have telescopes for observing the sky, and not long after Missouri's Stonehenge came to be, NASA's Hubble Telescope was sent into low-Earth orbit. Hubble beamed down jaw-dropping imagery that expanded our understanding of the universe. Outside the courthouse in Marshfield, Missouri, the hometown of astronomer Edwin Hubble, for whom the telescope was named, there's a quarter-scale **replica of the Hubble**. Don't try to look through the darn thing, as so many do. It's not *that* kind of telescope.

ROADSIDE EATS

Below is a dizzying array of delicious road food and vintage signage.

Many classic American chains have a good origin story, and **Maid-Rite** (FIG. 27), shown in Cedar Rapids, Iowa, is one of them. It's been said that butcher Fred Angell of Muscatine, Iowa, had whipped together a blend of "loose" meats and spices that was quite savory, and in 1926, Angell opened up his first shop. (Loose meats are sort of like sloppy joe, without the gravy.)

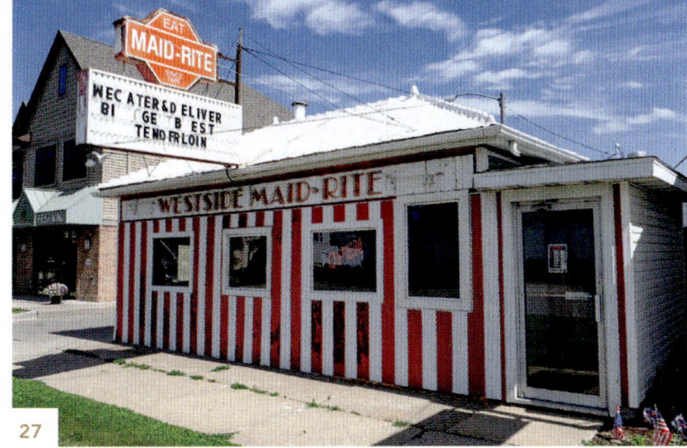

27

At the time, quirky and memorable spellings were a must, so he christened the establishment "Maid-Rite." That first shop grew into a chain with over one hundred stores, with around thirty left today. Loose meats are the signature dish here. This location, in Cedar Rapids, was built in 1935.

When Taylor's Maid-Rite in Marshalltown, Iowa, decided to offer the option of adding ketchup, they put the matter up to a vote first, the ballot being the back of customer receipts, this being poll-minded Iowa, after all. Ketchup won. Still, it caused a kerfuffle among loose-meat traditionalists. So maybe savvy campaigners will avoid the ketchup, unless they are really going for the progressive vote.

In the middle twentieth century, there was a gold rush to acquaint Americans with a range of cuisines, in an era when even pizza was a novelty for some. In 1961, one year before Glen Bell opened the first Taco Bell in Downey, California, DuWayne Engness opened what has been described as the first Mexican restaurant in all of North Dakota, the **Taco Shop** in Fargo. In an article that year, Engness, who said he got the idea while living in California, had to describe the concept to readers, explaining that tacos were eaten like hamburgers. Today, there are two locations.

Scotty's (FIG. 28) was a UFO-themed chain that opened in several Midwestern states before dissolving. The remaining Scotty's are in Scottsbluff, Nebraska (shown here), which opened in 1963, and Idaho Falls, Idaho.

Nick's Hamburger Stand in Bismarck, North Dakota, and Brookings, South Dakota, traces its roots to 1929 and is on the National Register of Historic Places; as is **Steak & Shake**, a beloved national chain with hundreds of locations, including a notable one in Springfield, Missouri, along Route 66.

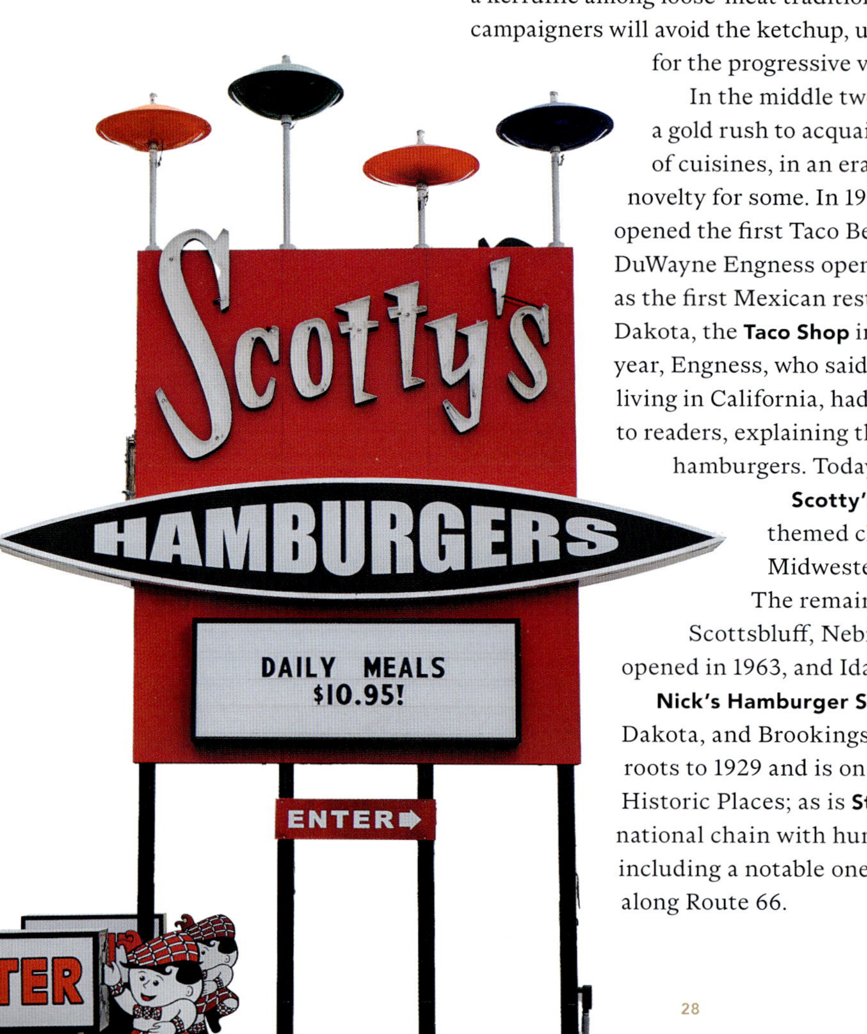

28

THE BEST THING

What's the best thing since sliced bread? Well, this is the standard to which all other inventions aspire because this is where sliced bread began, or at least the commercial application of the slicing machine. The invention was developed by Midwest native Otto Frederick Rohwedder, who set his mind to figuring out how to slice loaves of bread automatically. This brilliant yet eminently practical achievement was greeted with wonderment, suspicion, and derision. The wonderment won out, and soon Wonder Bread loaves (and many others) were arriving in stores, perfectly presliced. The large rooftop sign in Chillicothe, Missouri, where the machine was first deployed in July 1928, is a tribute to the history that has touched practically everyone's lips.

MAINSTAYS OF MAIN STREET

There's a lot to see along a Heartland Main Street, but we'll need gas if we're going to explore all these states, and so we'll start at service stations with a specialty for full service—of the soul.

One of the great privileges of my road-tripping life was the chance to sit down and chat with Gary Turner at **Gary's Gay Parita Sinclair Station** (FIG. 29) in Ash Grove, Missouri. In 2005, Turner and his wife, Lena, became proprietors of the site of the historic Route 66 service station, Gay Parita. A replica was rebuilt—the original long gone, and in a short time, Gary cultivated one of the most soulful stops on America's Main Street. Indeed, when I visited in 2013, I assumed Turner had been there for decades, not less than a decade. The building looked the part of having been there for the ages, teeming with roadside memorabilia and signage, and on a superficial level, it's a perfect grab-and-go Route 66 photo op. But you came here for Gary Turner and his nourishing homilies about Route 66. His welcoming ways (slices of watermelon served right up) were unique, and his gift for conversation and endless curiosity about people were comforting. He had a way of sharing Route 66 lore that was specific to him, and making you feel that you were on the trip of a lifetime. He welcomed you into the Mother Road family, a club you were in, now and forever.

Turner died in January 2015, and his wife followed him several months later. The store seemed doomed for a time, with vultures picking at the memorabilia. Fortunately, members of Turner's family concluded that his legacy was too great to abandon. They took over the stop and, just like Gary and Lena did, continue to welcome tourists and make them feel like they, too, are part of something uniquely American. That's Gary, off camera, still working his magic.

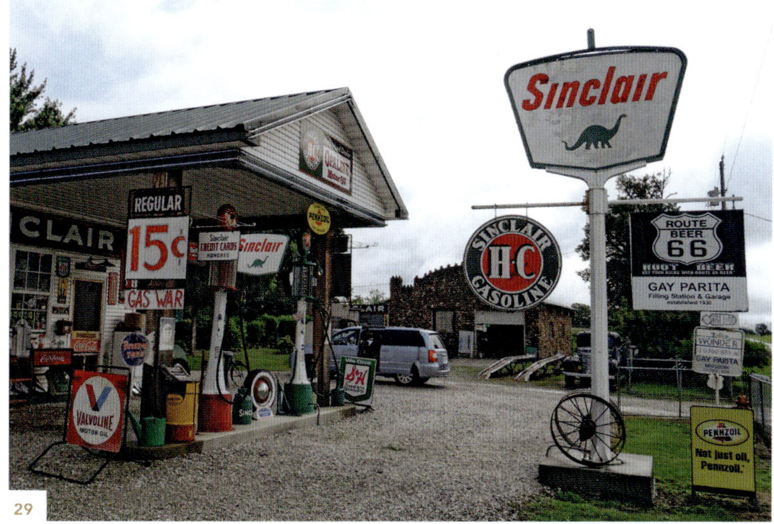

29

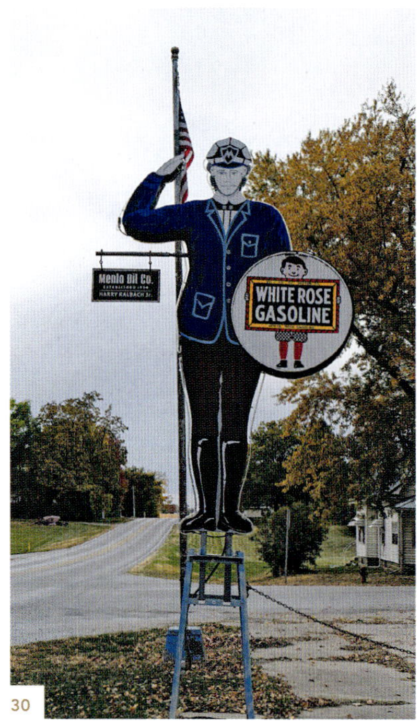

30

Earlier in this chapter, I took you to the epic Amoco gas station in St. Louis, and while it's hard to top the sign, there are plenty of places to fuel up—or where people once did—that make for a retrologist-worthy visit.

For a taste of Amoco's predecessor, Standard, and at a much more human scale, visit the **brick Standard station**, which first serviced cars in the 1920s and now serves the curious as a visitors center in Ogallala, Nebraska. It was lovingly restored between 2002 and 2003 to make it a centerpiece of the town, after last topping off a tank in 1984 and later becoming a repair shop. The station is part of Lincoln Highway lore, a must-stop on your journey along America's first transcontinental highway. Another **former Standard station** also pays quaint corner tribute to the early days of road trips in Ord, Nebraska. In Brooklyn, Iowa, there's a magnificent Standard station sheathed in glazed brick, terra-cotta, and modern typeface—and it's still in business!

Bob's Oil Co. in Grand Forks, North Dakota, is an independent, and has been so since it began under the Torreson's name in the 1950s. The storefront is a glass jewel box topped with bold red letters. The Bob's name came along in 2008—named after a longtime employee who took over the business—but the name change made this place even more dreamy. The fabulous mod sign is a dazzler with the simple word "GAS" in neon. The sign begins with a chasing-light-bulb-covered starburst, with the lights zigzagging down the letters before culminating in an arrow pointing the way to Bob's, and right below it, the term "FULL SERV"—full service—a mystery to younger generations of drivers who never met a gas pump they didn't pump themselves.

HIDDEN HISTORY

As a retrologist, I look in the most unlikely places for vintage discoveries. While at a St. Louis pizza shop waiting for my pie, I was admiring a vintage map of St. Louis that marked landmarks and businesses, and one caught my attention: a cartoon character of a little girl and the term "**Tom Boy**." What was this? It turned out Tom Boy was a regional chain of independent grocery stores that operated under that name and logo. The chain withered away, and most traces of Tom Boy vanished with it, except at the **LeGrand's Market and Catering**, where the neon sign for Tom Boy survives outside, and another sign is inside. Jim LeGrand first worked at the store as a teenager in the 1970s, and after he bought it 1987, he didn't entirely erase the Tom Boy traces. You can explore the retail layers here while picking up some serious bratwurst and so much more.

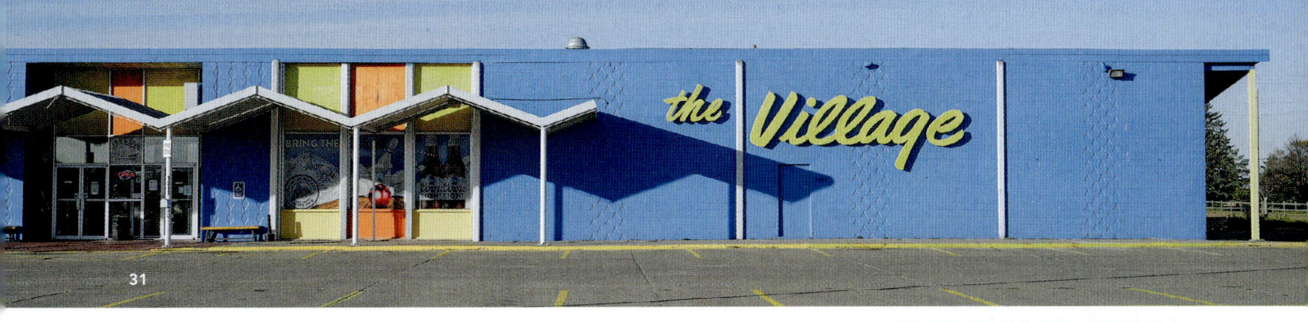

31

They call him the **Old Man** (FIG. 30)—or the Friendly Gas Station Man—and he's been there since the 1930s, waving at enchanted motorists with his endearingly creaky neon mechanical arm. But he doesn't look very old, and that's because he's been well cared for over the years. Originally he was the mascot for the former White Rose gasoline station in Menlo Park, Iowa, a suburb of Des Moines. The White Rose station was founded by Harry Kalbach Sr., who had the idea to install the sheet-metal sign here. The 12-foot-tall gentleman has undergone various rejuvenating restorations but none more luxurious than his overhaul in 2008, when his neon was relit for the first time since the days after World War II. Kalbach's son told the *Des Moines Register* in 2008 that the sign was once used by airplane pilots to orient themselves.

The Old Man is the great symbol of the **White Pole Road**, the local name for U.S. 6, another old and lesser-known coast-to-coast highway full of its own roadside secrets—and now you know one of them.

Crestwood Bowl (FIG. 32) has been a mainstay of St. Louis, Missouri, since 1958 and is a requisite photo stop for travelers of Route 66. The city of Crestwood was in its formative years then, only a decade out from incorporation, as the strip-malling of America was transforming the landscape. There was a lot of really wonderful architecture and signage during this boom, including Crestwood Bowl, the twenty-four lanes of midcentury leisure magic, founded by a group of professional bowlers in an era when the sport was a true national pastime. Among the founders were Dick Weber and Pat Patterson, members of the famed Budweiser team who were featured in many old TV broadcasts of the sport.

Here are a sample of other Heartland lanes that are easy on the eyes:

Village Bowl (FIG. 31) has been a fixture of Aberdeen, South Dakota, since 1960 and is a gorgeous relic of that period inside and out.

Sport Bowl (FIG. 33) in Sioux Falls, South Dakota, strikes a pose, from the pole sign with its tilted cocktail glass to the bold words "SPORT BOWL" beside the sinuous canopy entryway.

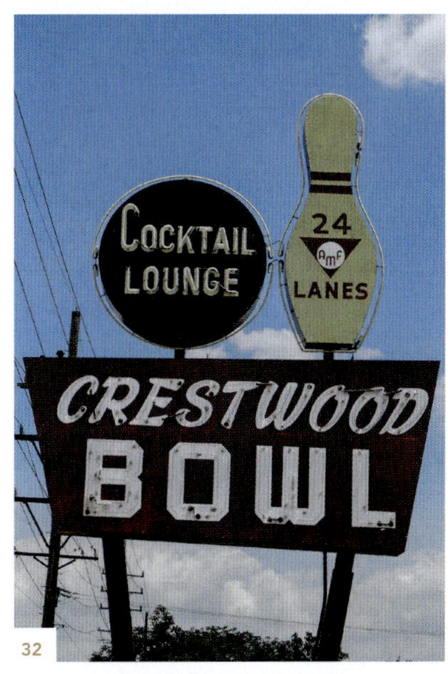

32

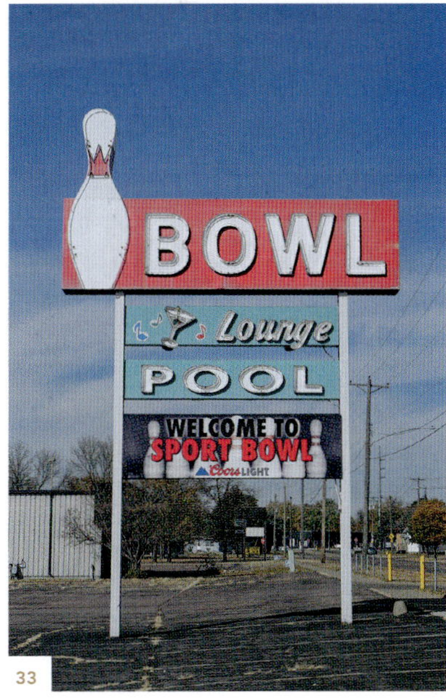

33

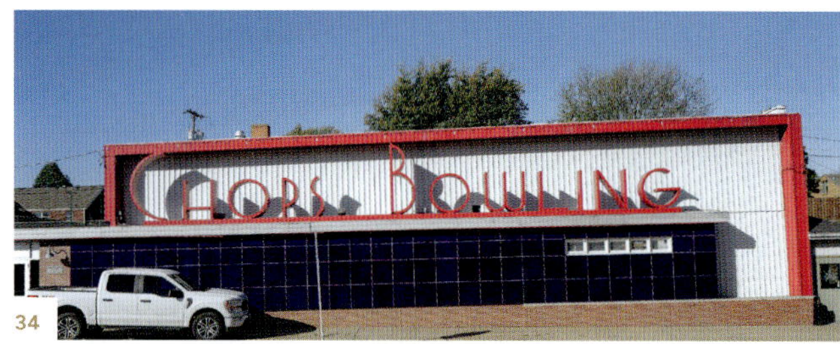

34

Chops Bowling (FIG. 34) in Omaha, Nebraska, has a stunning facade and is the city's oldest-operating bowling alley, according to the local paper, dating to 1950.

William H. Osterburg founded **Who's Hobby House** (FIG. 35) in Rapid City, South Dakota, in 1950; his initials formed the first word of the store's name—"WHO." An owl seemed a logical neon mascot. The hobby shop is still in the same family, but has moved locations over the years. The animated owl sign, constructed in 1951, has been along for the ride every time. (And nearby is the family's Who's Toy House, whose sign also sports a neon owl.)

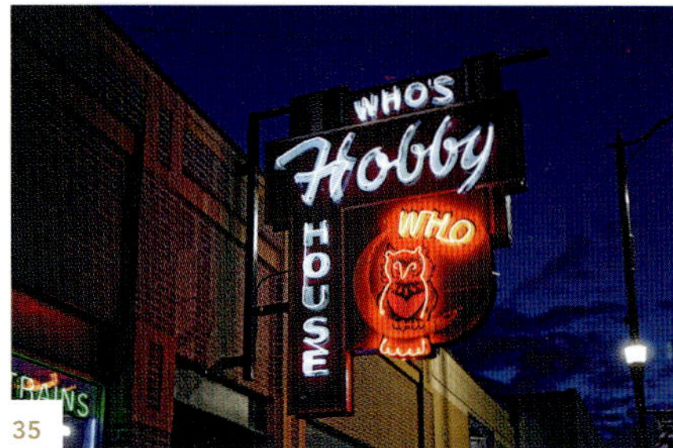

35

The **Val Air Ballroom** (FIG. 36) in West Des Moines, Iowa, has one of the dreamiest facades in America. Opened by ballroom impresario Tom Archer in June 1939, the Val Air captures the romance of an era when Americans loved swooning to live bands. The original ballroom was partially open air, a fact preserved in its name, a portmanteau of Valley Junction and Open Air, according to a history of the venue. The complex was enclosed around 1955 and the majestic building that you see today dates to then, having survived a fire in January 1961. Today it has been reimagined as a popular live-music venue.

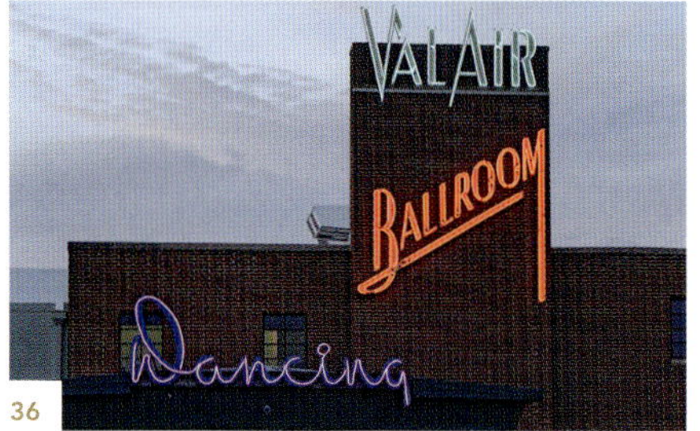

36

ON WITH THE SHOW

A tale of two theaters—one of which has played its last reel.

America swooned for arches in the 1950s and 1960s, from the Golden Arches to the Gateway Arch. In Independence, Missouri, the **Twin Drive-In** (FIG. 37) made its bold statement in 1965, the tail end of such architectural exuberance. It opened as the Kansas City area's largest theater, with enough room for seventeen hundred cars. The theater closed in 2024, and the sign is being restored by the Lumi Neon Museum for exhibition at Pennway Point.

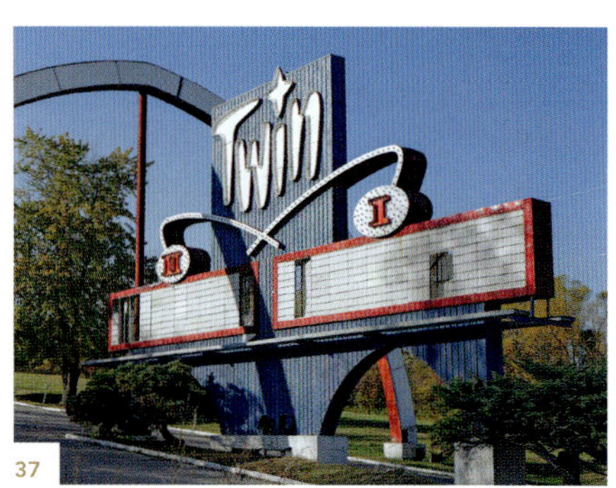

37

66 Drive-In (FIG. 38) in Carthage, Missouri, opened in 1949, during the heyday of the Mother Road and just before television became America's mass leisure activity. By 1985 the theater was closed before being revived in 1998 and has been riding the wave of Route 66 nostalgia in the years since. The National Park Service points out that this theater is especially important because it is still set in splendid sylvan isolation, far from the encroachment of strip malls and civilization that eventually consumed other drive-ins. Its only concession to modernity? The sound is now projected through your FM receiver, though the old metal poles, now shorn of their speakers, remain.

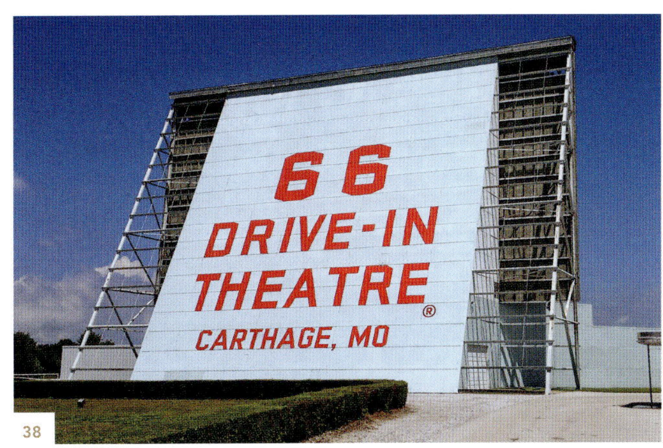

38

THE INN CROWD

These Mother Road motels are a nice place to call it a night in the lap of history.

The Munger Moss Motel (FIG. 40) in Lebanon, Missouri, stole my heart when I saw this epic sign on my first road trip along all of Route 66. The motel was built in 1946 and the sign appeared in the 1950s. The motel was named for the founders of a sandwich shop that used to be here.

Another beloved 1930s "tourist court" is **The Wagon Wheel Motel** (FIG. 39) (née Cabins) in Cuba, Missouri. An icon of Route 66, the Wagon Wheel gives you a feel for the simple roadside stops of yore. The intimate set of buildings are stone clad and cozy-looking. And the neon sign, built in 1947, has achieved celebrity status. There is also a former filling station and cafe on the property. And for Pixar *Cars* fans, the Wheel gets a fictional cameo in the film as the "Wheel Well Motel."

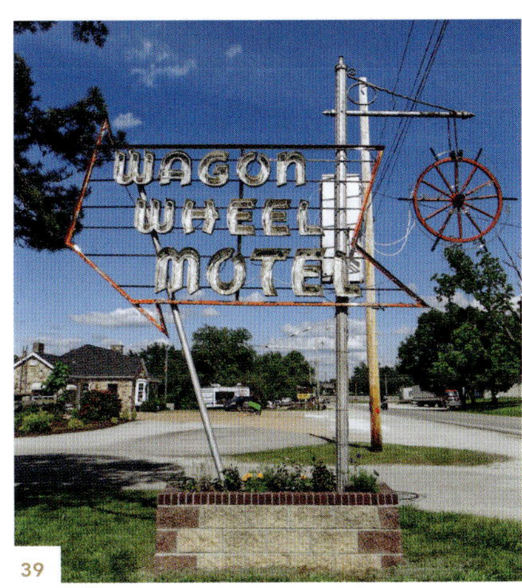

39

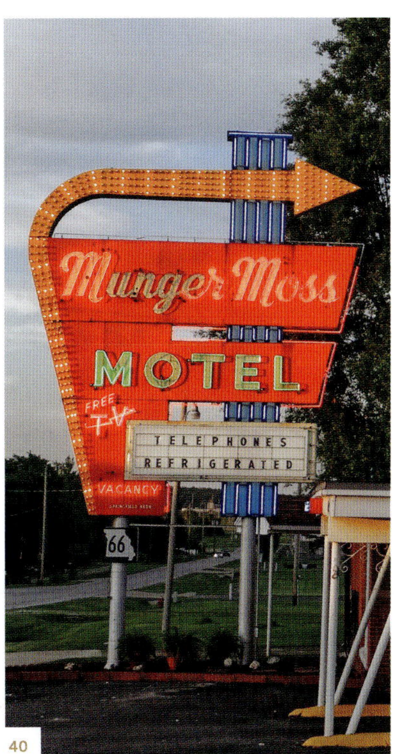

40

SWEET STOPS

We have your share of custards and cakes, but this is the only place you'll find Bionic Apples!

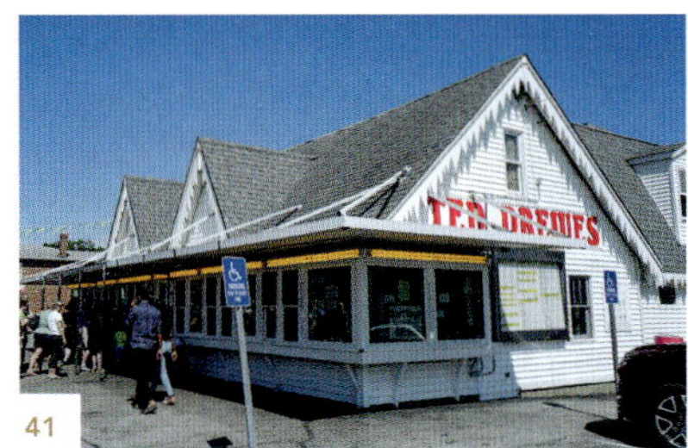
41

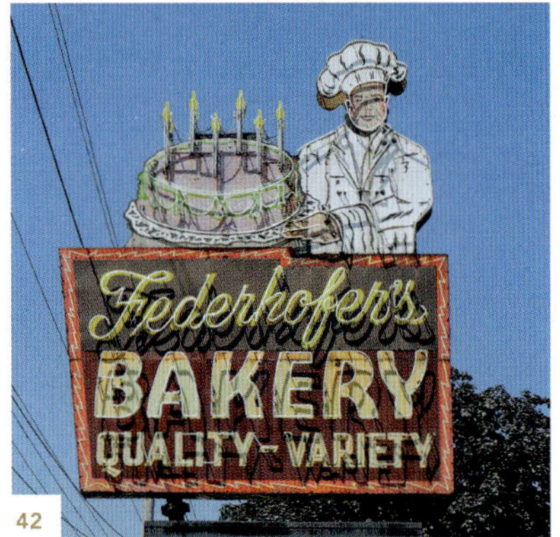

42

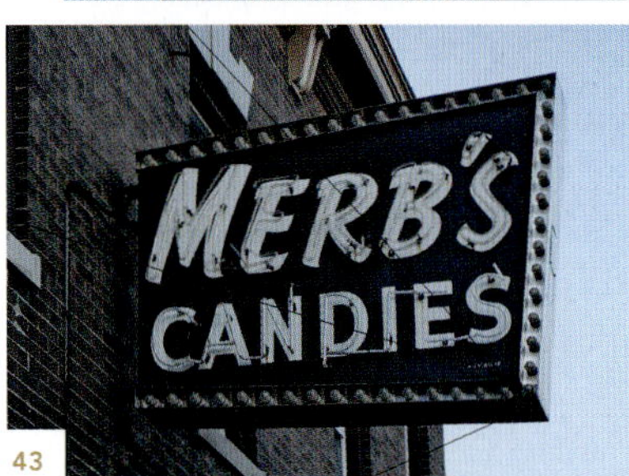

43

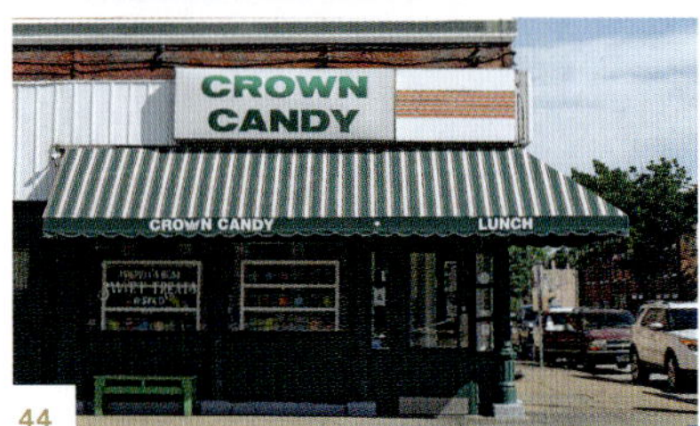

44

Ted Drewes Frozen Custard (FIG. 41) sets the bar high for the ultimate sweet Route 66 experience. There are only two locations and both are in St. Louis, Missouri. It's all delicious, but enjoying a superthick "concrete" shake is essential to a Ted Drewes order. Your server will hand it to you upside down, but fear not; gravity has no effect on it. Ted Drewes Sr. opened the first location in 1930 and ran it until his death in 1968. His son, Ted Drewes Jr., took over and solidified its role as a great American institution. He passed away in August 2024.

Federhofer's (FIG. 42) is another St. Louis institution. Known for its iconic neon sign and selection of baked goods, the store has been around since 1966 under that name.

We stay in St. Louis and visit **Merb's Candies** (FIG. 43), where a proud tradition of candy-making dates to 1921, founded by Emma Merb. It's been run by the same family since the 1970s, when Robert Wright, who was a hairdresser, spotted a newspaper ad for the candy shop and bought it, even though he had no experience as a candymaker. Wright's caramel recipes are still in use, and his signature caramel-coated, pecan-rolled Bionic Apples are still showcased. (The name dates them to the 1970s *Six Million Dollar Man* bionic craze, and there's even a dramatic vintage commercial to go with it on Merb's Facebook page.)

Also in St. Louis is the heart-melter **Crown Candy Kitchen** (FIG. 44), a beautiful shop founded in 1913. It's a heart-stopper, too, known for its "Heart-Stopping BLT," which is stuffed with bacon and was once featured in *Adam Richman's Best Sandwich in America*. You can also skip the sandwich and go right for the ice cream, and perhaps the malt, where you can take on the "five malt challenge." Can you drink five malts in thirty minutes? If you can they are all yours, free, and your name is inscribed in the store for posterity.

Wilton Candy Kitchen in Wilton, Iowa, is one of America's most beautiful candy shops. Candy was first made here in the 1860s, but the business began to take its form as we know it in 1910, when it was purchased by Gus Nopoulus, who with his wife, Mildred, and young family turned it into this priceless institution.

CHEERS!

Here's a handful of places for a little liquid courage—and nice signage—in a region replete with watering holes where everybody knows your name.

Mac's Tavern (FIG. 45) is one of those bucket listers you'll go a long way to see. It's been a mainstay of Davenport, Iowa, since 1934, founded by Bill "Mac" McLaughlin, and has gone through many caring hands since. The tavern's neon sign is exquisite, and the interior, a long cocoon of tin celling, terrazzo floor, and sturdy wood bar, is one of the nicest places for brew and chat you'll find anywhere.

Tim's Chrome Bar (FIG. 46) in St. Louis, Missouri, is a staple of the Bevo neighborhood, with epic neon and escapist retro interiors recalling the 1960s and '70s, appropriate for a bar founded by Tim Pappas in 1977. It was renovated by the same folks who infused new life into the Bevo Mill across the street.

On a drive along the Lincoln Highway, **The Hub Bar** (FIG. 47) in North Platte, Nebraska, proved an irresistible photo stop. In Omaha, **The Nifty** (FIG. 48) and its neon sign live up to the bar's name.

One place I feel compelled to mention, in Vale, South Dakota, is the world-renowned biker bar **Full Throttle Saloon**, showcased on the reality series by the same name (though the original structure seen on the show was destroyed in a fire in 2015). It attracts crowds during the annual Sturgis Motorcycle Rally.

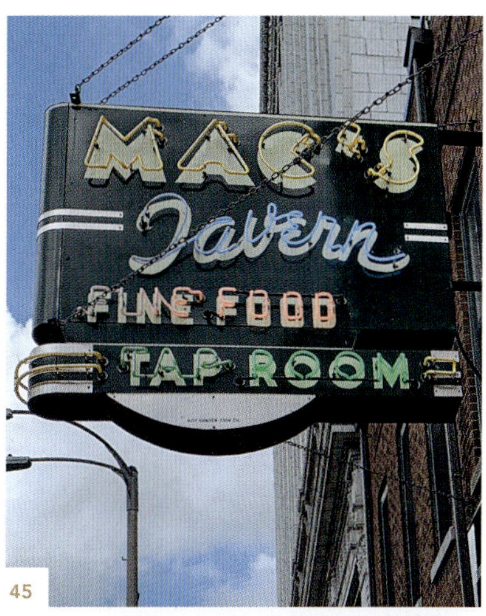

45

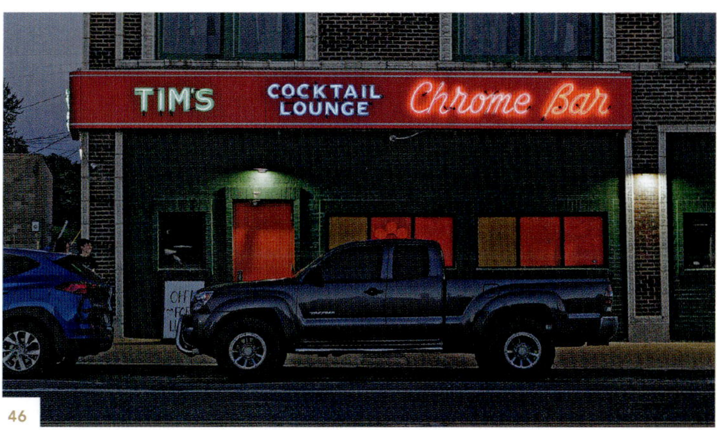

46

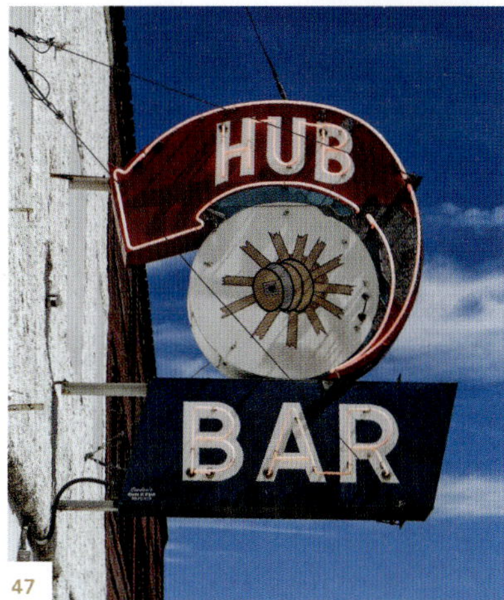

47

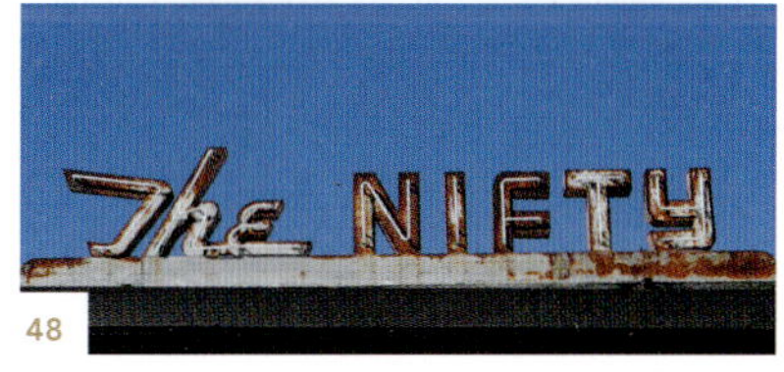

48

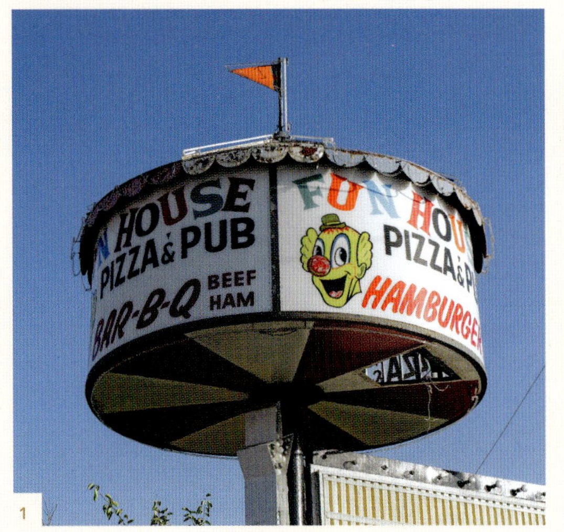

1

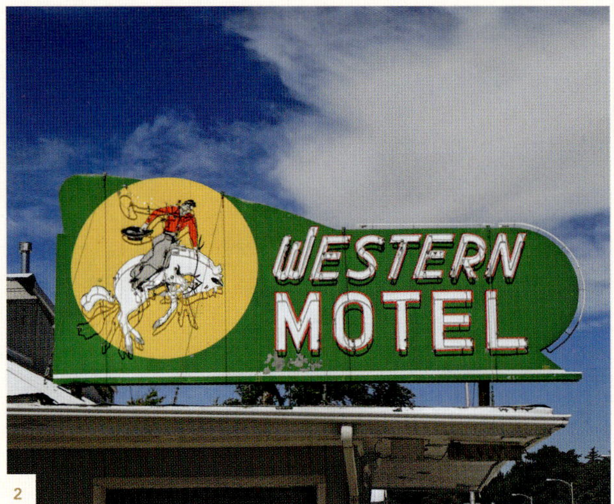

2

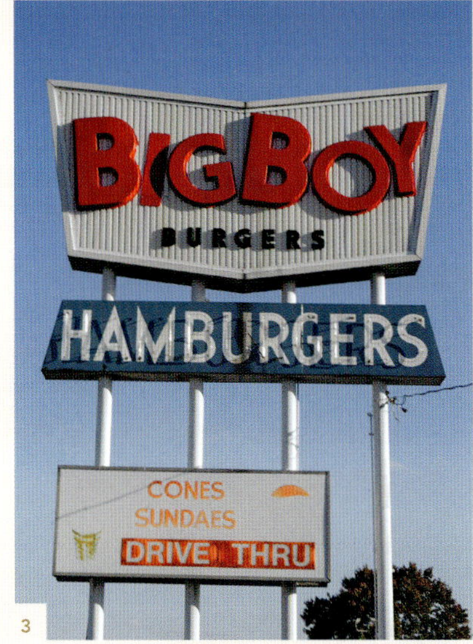

3

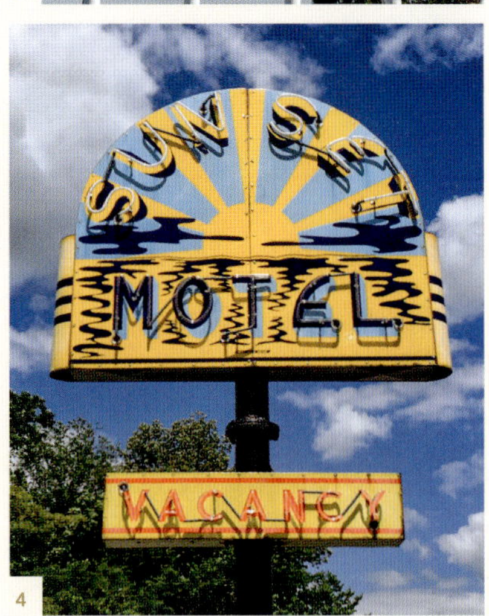

4

HEARTLAND HIGHLIGHTS

Looking for reasons to exit the highway—or take the local roads? These signs may provide the inspiration.

1. Fun House Pizza & Pub, Independence, Missouri
2. Western Motel, North Platte, Nebraska
3. Big Boy Burgers, Independence, Missouri
4. Sunset Motel, Villa Ridge, Missouri
5. Gaslight Saloon, Sioux Falls, South Dakota
6. Sunset Strip Pawn, Sioux Falls, South Dakota
7. Ced-Rel Motel, Cedar Rapids, Iowa
8. Trail Theatre, St. Joseph, Missouri
9. Black Hills Bagels, Rapid City, South Dakota
10. Gates Bar-B-Q, Kansas City, Missouri

GASLIGHT
SALOON
5

Sunset Strip
PAWN
BIKES GENERATORS
CHAINSAWS
ON SALE
6

Ced-Rel
MOTEL
FINE FOOD
7

8

BLACK HILLS
BAGELS
9

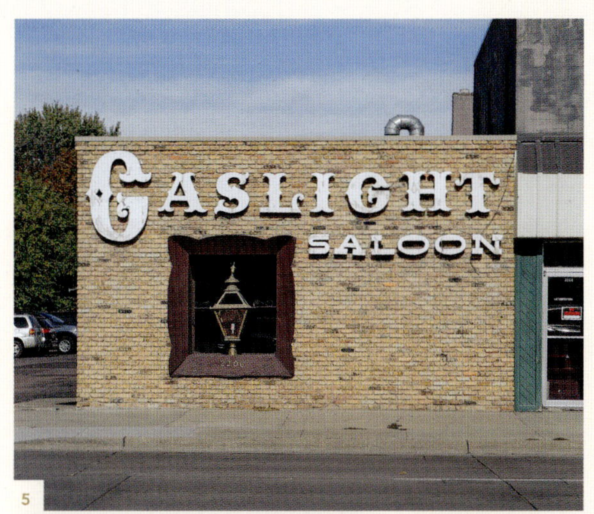

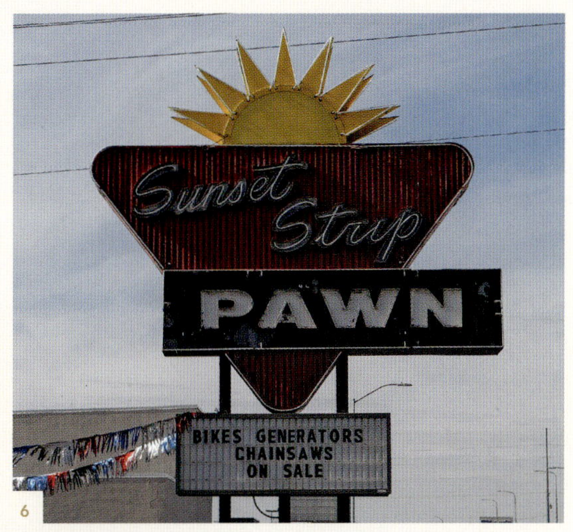

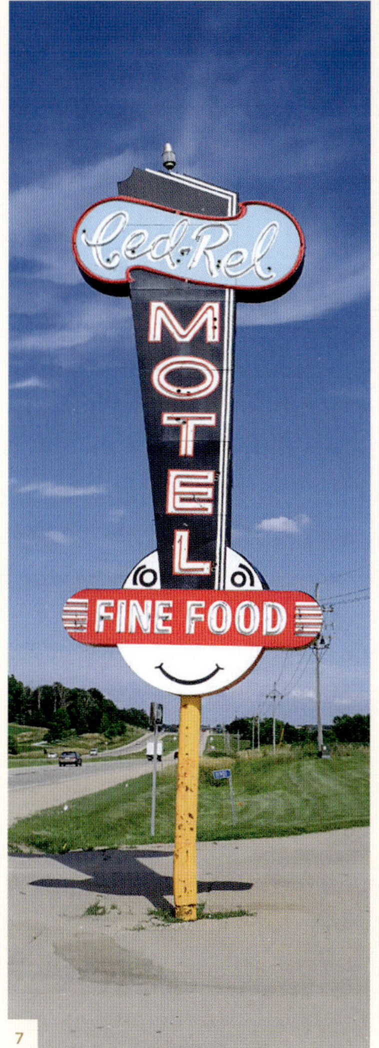

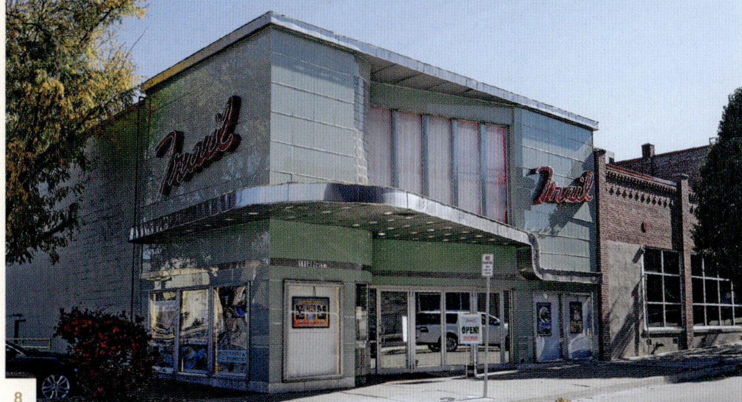

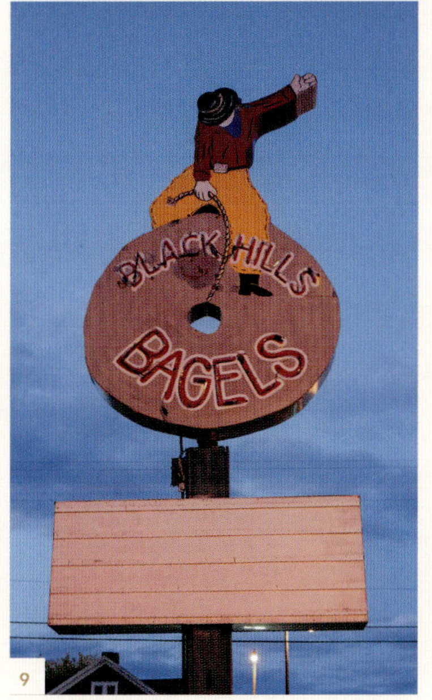

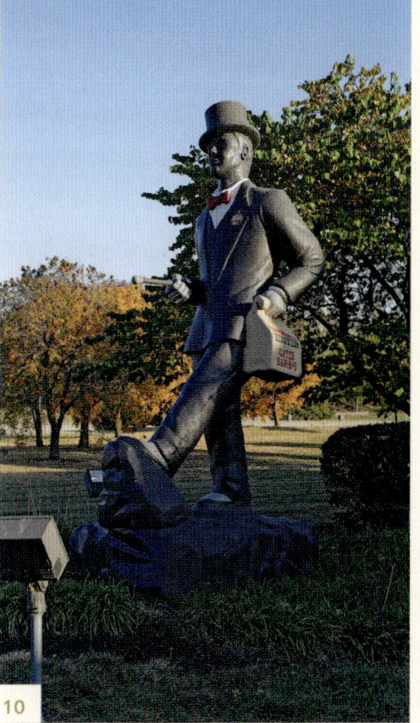

10

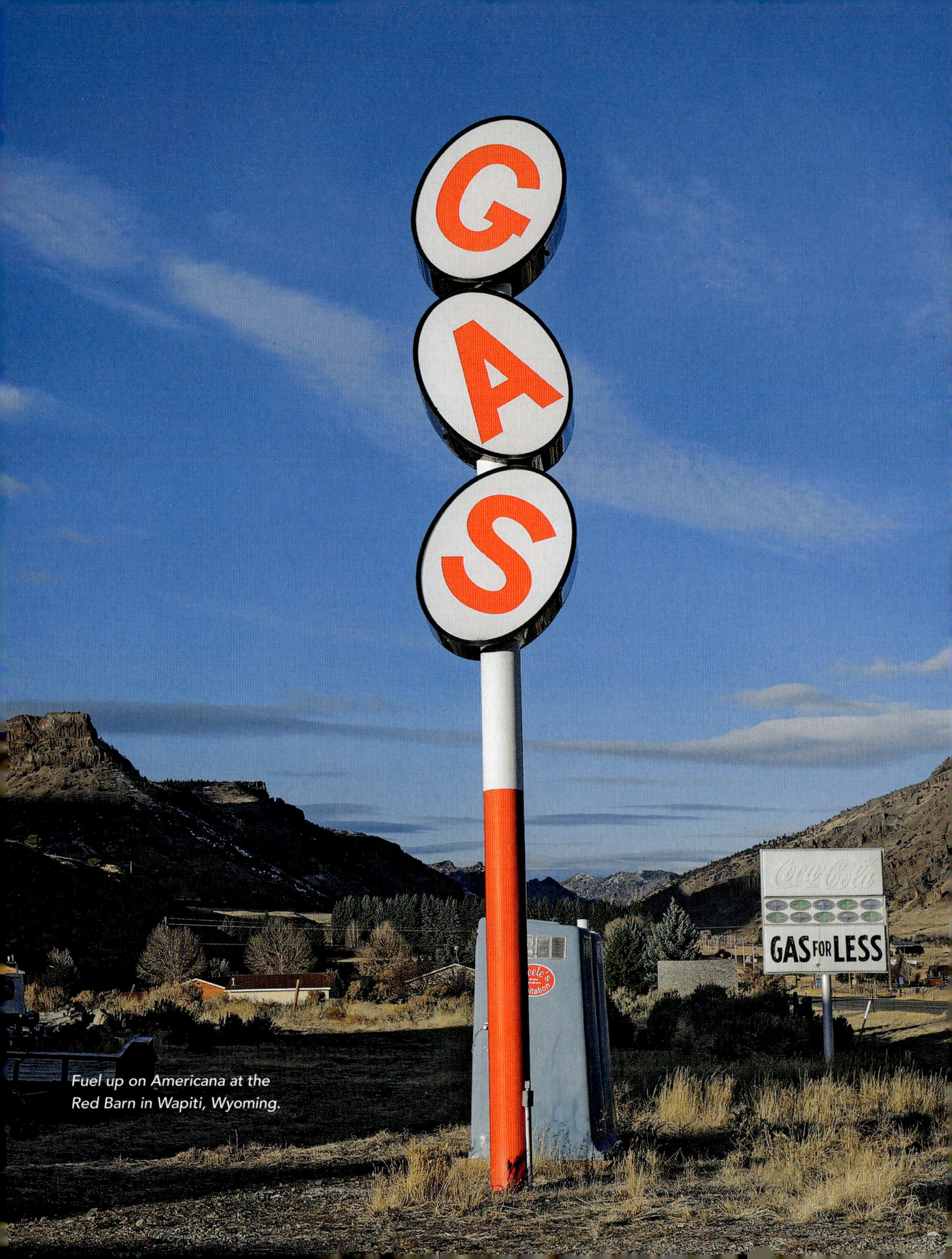

Fuel up on Americana at the Red Barn in Wapiti, Wyoming.

MOUNTAIN WEST

MONTANA · WYOMING · COLORADO
UTAH · PARTS OF NEVADA

Sleep in a potato? Admire a Warhol-approved giant soup can? Dine in a purple turtle? My, what wonders await us in the Mountain West section, including one of the great stretches of neon in the country (in Denver) and a Big Boy statue who stands in splendid isolation. And, pardner, we'll hit a cowboy bar or three on our dusty trail. Giddyup!

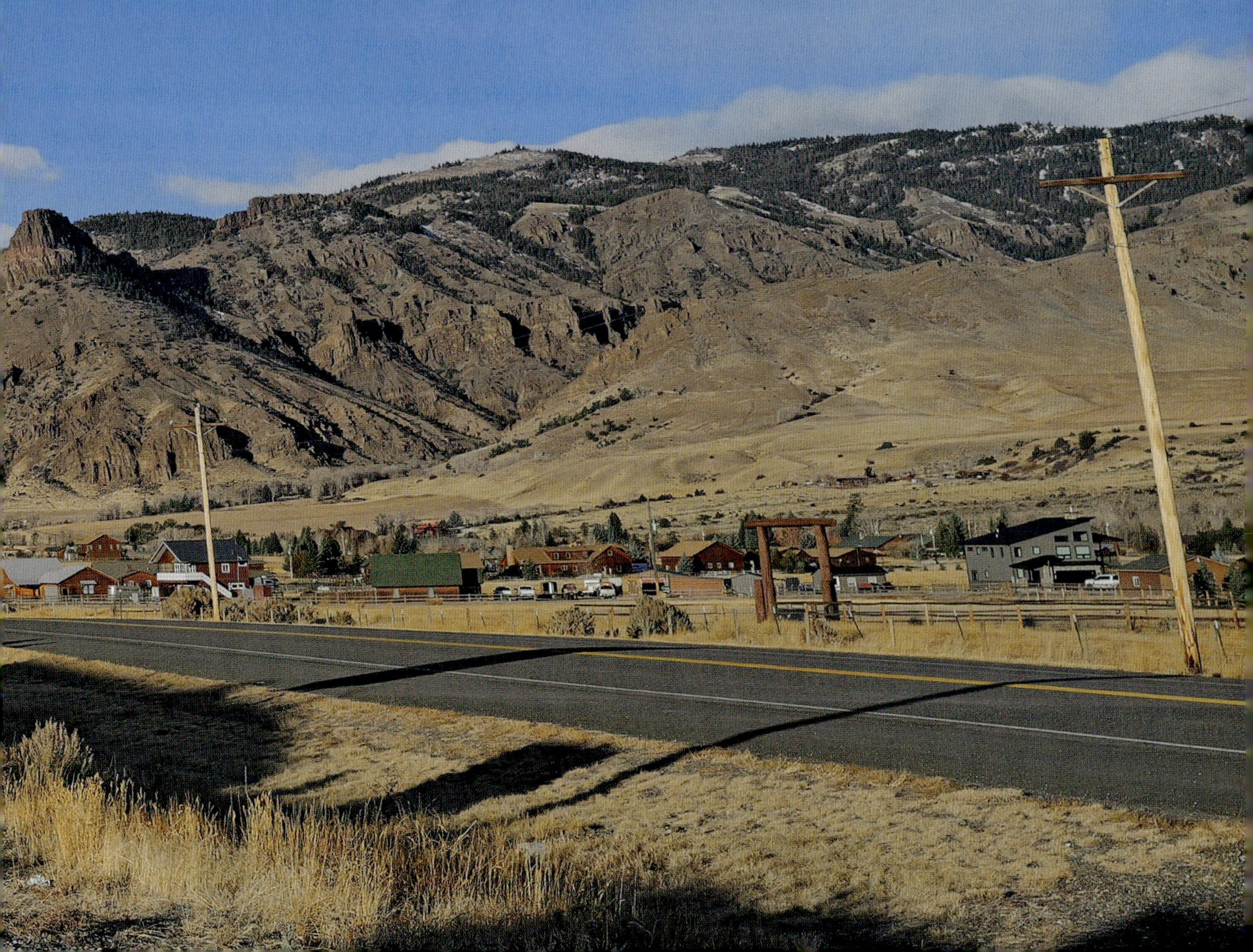

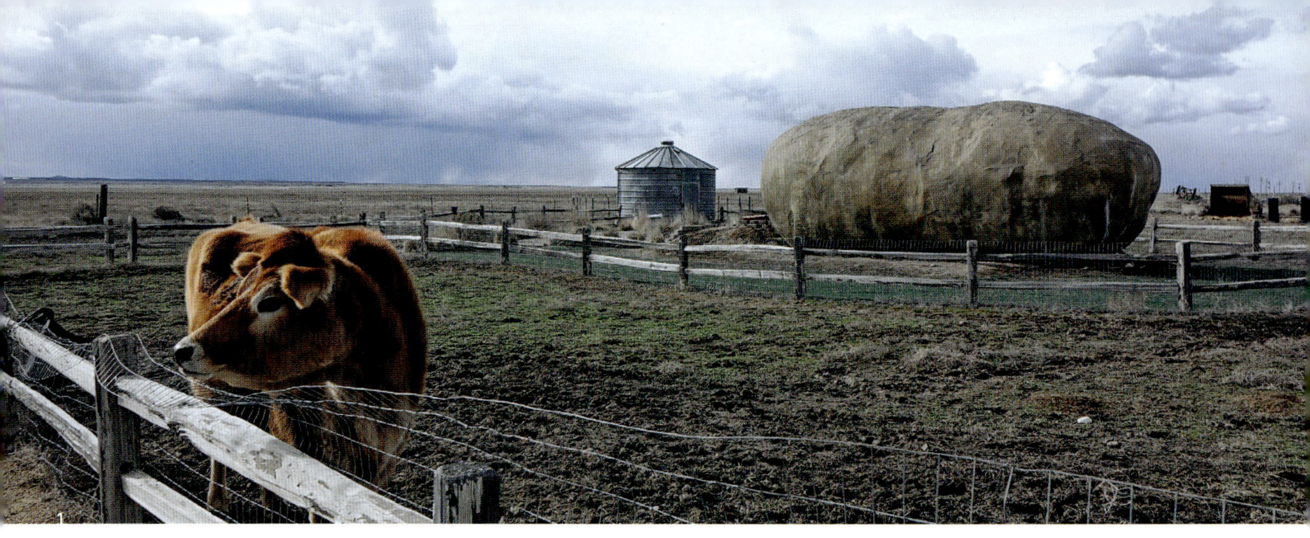

1

ROADSIDE QUIRKS

Some of my favorite stops for big, silly, and just wonderful things are here in the Mountain West. Many of these are far from one another, so plot your trip with care. Now let the travel inspo begin!

What better to go with a plate of Montana beef than a side of Idaho potatoes? Well, the **Big Idaho Potato Hotel** (FIG. 1) in Boise, Idaho, demands to be the main course, all 6 tons of it. You can book overnight stays, and it's surprisingly roomy, coming in at 28 feet long, 12 feet wide, and 11.5 feet tall. But even though you're spending the night in the middle of a 400-acre field, the Owyhee Mountains in the distance and the sweet Jersey cow Dolly as a neighbor, you are far from roughing it. The potato hotel is thoughtfully designed and decorated, the work of Kristie Wolfe, who once toured the country with the giant spud to promote the Idaho Potato Commission. You'll find the comforts you'd expect at a boutique hotel. Just outside is a converted silo, where you'll find the bathroom and a spa with a skylight—and even a fireplace.

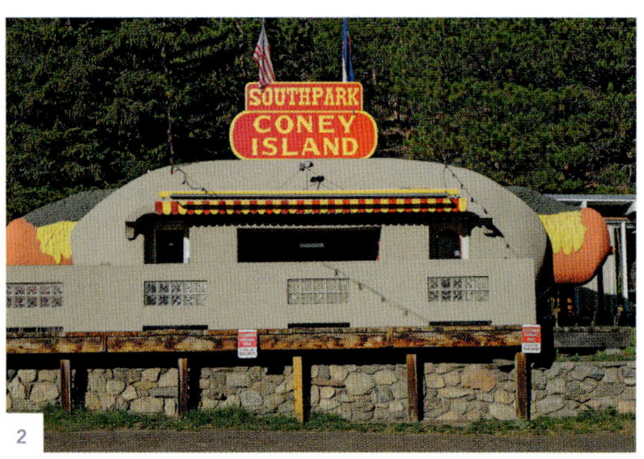

2

Potato lovers, there's more for you: If you'd like to learn more about Idaho's potato-cultivation culture, a visit to the **Idaho Potato Museum & Potato Station Cafe** in Blackfoot, where a massive baked potato—oozing with creamy goodness—is ready for Instagram.

You can also catch a movie under the stars at the historic **Spud Drive-In Theatre** in Driggs, Idaho. The site is marked by a huge potato resting on a vintage flatbed truck.

We'll stick with big food, and among the most famous examples in the Mountain West is **South**

Park Coney Island (FIG. 2) diner in Bailey, Colorado. It sits at the edge of Pike National Forest but began life in 1966 in downtown Denver—along Colfax Avenue, which is still a grand repository of roadside Americana—and was envisioned as the foundation of a hot dog chain. A few years later, the structure was transported to Aspen Park for what would be a thirty-five-year run—only to be displaced by a bank—and was then moved to Bailey. *South Park* fans might recognize it as the character Eric Cartman's home for a time. Historian Thomas Noel has extolled the diner, calling it "the best example of roadside architecture in the state."

Big potatoes and hot dogs might be good examples of roadside kitsch, but they're not fine art. The **Campbell's Soup Can** (FIG. 3) on display at Colorado State University in Fort Collins, however, could fetch a pretty penny at auction. That's because it's signed by Andy Warhol, the pop artist who became a household name by painting soup cans, Brillo boxes, and other supermarket-shelf ephemera. The can—and two others—were cut from a 50-foot pipe and painted by a student, all with Warhol's guidance. The cans were created to honor Warhol ahead of a 1981 campus visit, and for several years after, all three were on display here. One is now in storage on campus and the other was sold to a museum in Japan. The remaining can sits outside the University Center for the Arts. It's under video surveillance, so don't get any funny ideas about adding it to your art collection.

The **Old Town Churn Ice Cream** (FIG. 4) shop in Fort Collins is, in its way, pop art as well. The business is housed in a wooden structure shaped like an old-fashioned ice-cream maker. And so are several sister Colorado ice-cream stands, part of the Little Man Ice Cream chain. In Denver, you'll find ice cream scooped inside a giant milk can, a stainless-steel Constellation jet, and other curiosities.

When I think of road-trip adventures through this region, two giant statues always make an impression. The first is the delightful smiling dinosaur who has become a symbol of Vernal, Utah. **Dinah the Pink Dinosaur** (FIG. 5) dates to 1958 and once welcomed guests to the Dine-a-Ville Motel in town. When the motel became a fossil itself, Dinah was rescued, and she was handed new responsibilities as city greeter. In 2024, Dinah lost her tail after a car crashed into it, but she was quickly fixed up and given a fresh coat of vibrant pink paint. Her lovely eyes move and light up at night. Vernal is home to the **Dinosaur National Monument**, where you can admire the remains of Dinah's real-life descendants, the source of inspiration for her and other dinosaurs you'll spot around town.

The prehistoric creatures that once roamed the Mountain West are memorialized in various ways. I remember the

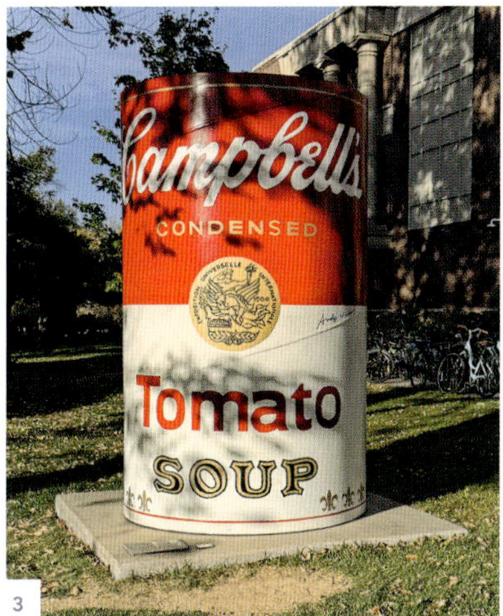

3

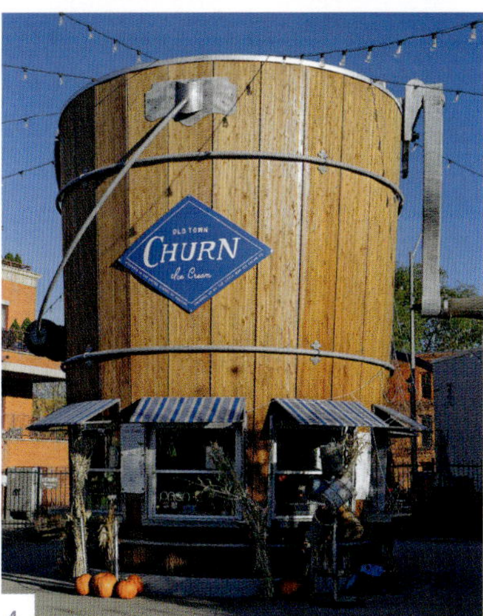

4

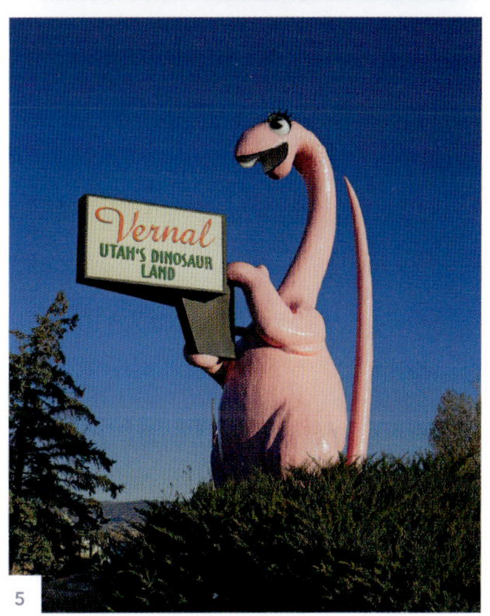

5

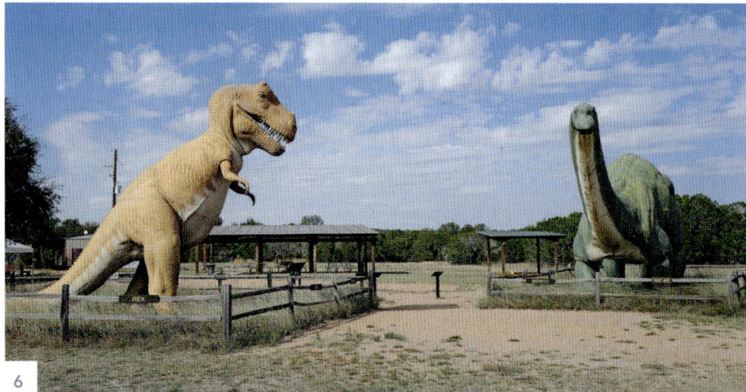

6

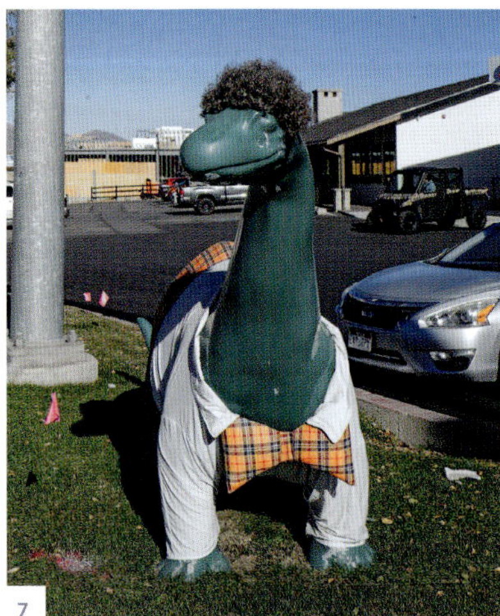

7

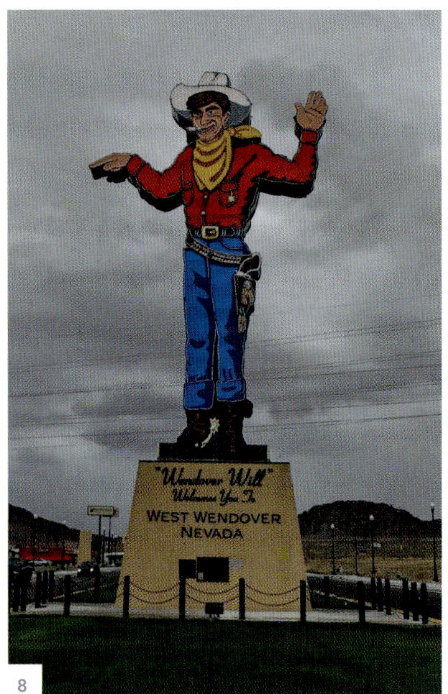

8

excitement I felt when I first spotted a Sinclair gas station during a trip out West in 1998. The oil company takes its mascot inspiration straight from the source of the fossil fuel. A fiberglass **Dino** statue is often plopped outside service stations, usually with kids swarming around it. Sinclair, Wyoming, is named after the oil concern, which has a refinery there. Sinclair is also known for its eye-catching Spanish Colonial Revival architecture, including a water fountain, constructed for what has always been an oil-company town, even before Sinclair arrived. Sinclair has wended its way into pop culture as Dinoco in the Pixar film *Cars* (see page 166 for more *Cars* callouts) and as a part of Sinclair's 1964–65 New York World's Fair exhibit, the statues now adding their own dinosaur tracks to the real ones at **Dinosaur Valley State Park** (FIG. 6) in Glen Rose, Texas.

Outside **Mountainland One Stop** (FIG. 7) in Heber City, Utah, the Sinclair dinosaur (named Octane) gets a monthly makeover by a local schoolteacher, Christine Chappell, who sews dino-sized outfits for the roadside character. Chappell first dressed up Octane to promote a stage production of *Mary Poppins*, but after a positive response, she kept the costumes coming. Octane has been dressed up as everything from a Utah Jazz player to Barbie to the Statue of Liberty. He's promoted school fundraisers, political candidates, and helped celebrate holidays year-round. In summer 2023, Octane boldly sported no clothes. "I'm headed to the Samak Nudist Colony," a sign in front of him read—a reference to an urban legend about a nudist colony in the nearby Uinta Mountains.

The decline of the oil business in Montana indirectly led to the creation of one of my favorite attractions, **Cut Bank Penguin**. Back in 1989, Ron Gustafson and his family were running a furniture business that, like most of the other shops in Cut Bank, had been hit by the decline. He had a stroke of genius to help his store and hometown—the 27-foot-tall concrete Cut Bank Penguin, which stands on an iceberg emblazoned with the words "Welcome to Cut Bank MT. Coldest Spot in the Nation." Gustafson turned the property into a motel, the Glacier Gateway Inn, a nod to nearby Glacier National Park.

There was never any mystery about the origins of the Cut Bank Penguin, but the **Wapiti Big Boy** (FIG. 9) statue that stands in the middle of a Wyoming field has inspired the imagination since it first appeared in 2013. How did the mascot of the Big Boy

9

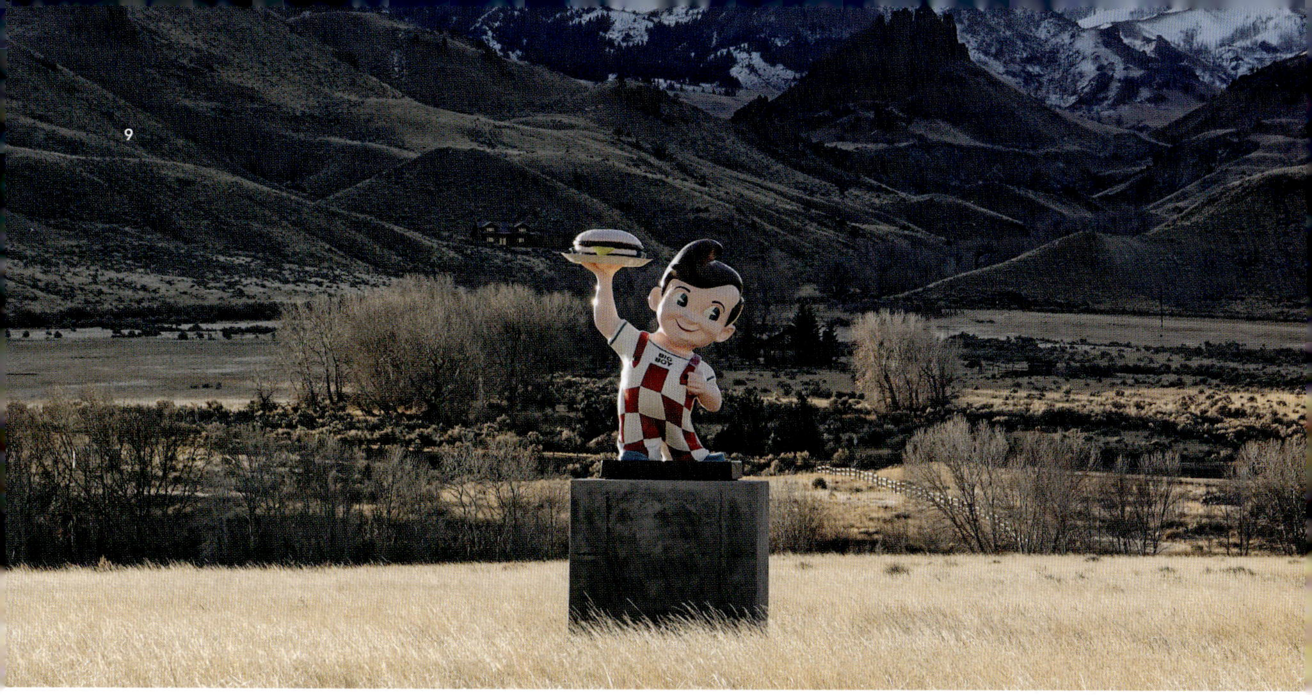

restaurants end up here, far from any of his namesake restaurants? Was he abandoned here? Left as a prank? The theories abounded as its legendary status grew. But the answer is simple: Local artist James Geier rescued him from a Big Boy restaurant in California, restored him, and placed him here, he told the *Cowboy State Daily*. It became a source of fascination adding to the experience of approaching the majestic Yellowstone National Park nearby.

The big boys of the roadside Mountain West, of course, are cowboys, and perhaps the most famous is **Wendover Will** (FIG. 8), who has a hearty howdy for you at West Wendover, Nevada, on the border with Utah. Wendover Will was built in 1952 to draw folks into the Stateline Casino, and his right hand once pointed to the casino. Will was named for his hometown and the casino's operator, William Smith. After the casino's closure in 2002, Will became the property of West Wendover, and he was later moved to his current home after an elaborate renovation. He is listed in *Guinness World Records* as the world's largest mechanical cowboy. Will is such a big deal that he's part of West Wendover's municipal seal. Much like Dinah the Pink Dinosaur and the Cut Bank Penguin, it's a sign that was built initially to drum up sales for a specific business that has morphed into an official greeter, something much bigger and more meaningful than its original purpose.

Wendover Will has an even more famous neon cowboy brother, Vegas Vic, whom you can visit in the Desert Southwest (page 202).

Just east of Wendover lies the vast, hardscrabble loneliness of the Bonneville Salt Flats in Utah. **Metaphor: The Tree of Utah** (FIG. 10) (also known as **Tree of Life**) is an unexpected sign of life in

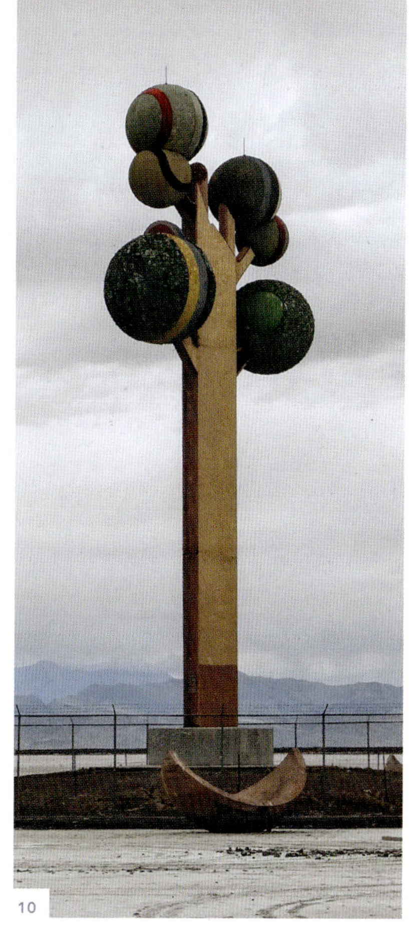
10

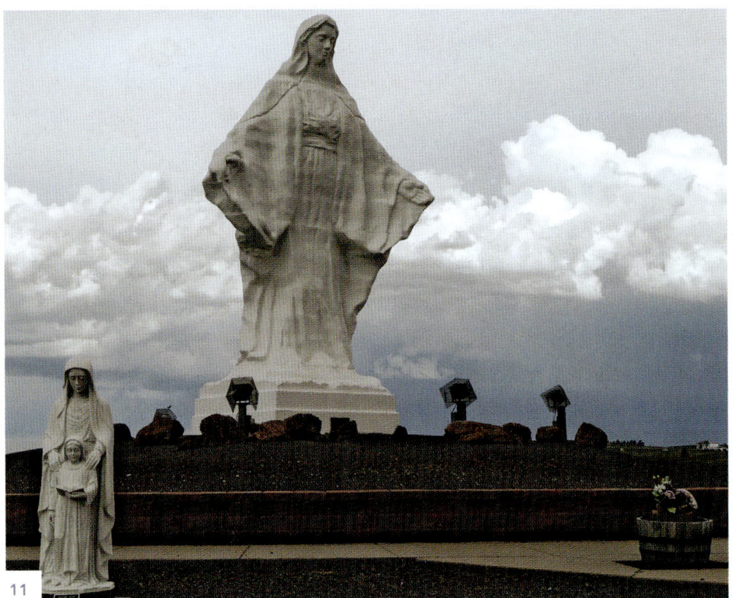
11

such a desolate place. The towering sculpture is planted in the middle of the flats and was built by Swedish artist Karl Momen, who donated the sculpture to the state of Utah when he returned to his home country. The sculpture is made of 225 tons of cement, almost 2,000 ceramic tiles, 5 tons of welding rod, and minerals and rocks native to Utah. At first glance it looks almost like a collection of concrete tennis balls, or giant lollipops. Part of its magic is its abstraction. A plaque on the sculpture quotes Friedrich Schiller's "Ode to Joy," apt words for the feelings this sculpture has the power to generate.

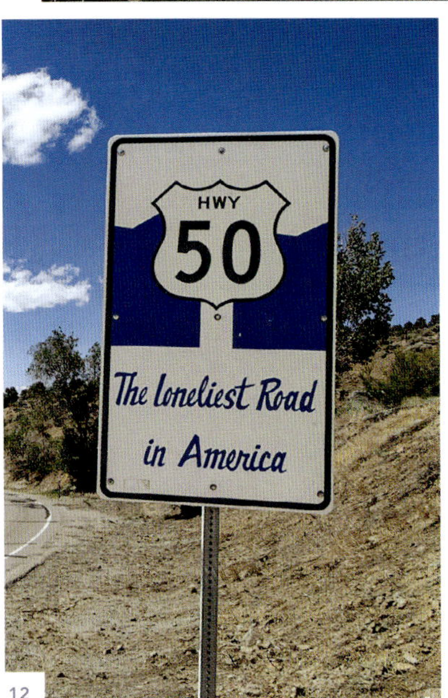

12

Our Lady of Peace Shrine (FIG. 11) in Pine Bluffs, Wyoming, was created by Marjorie and Ted Trefren, a local devout Catholic couple determined to build a shrine to the Virgin Mary, as their state lacked one. After touring some of the world's famed sites of Marian apparitions, the couple settled on a plot of earth between Interstate 80 and Highway 30 at the border with Nebraska. Its prominence meant it would be impossible to miss. They commissioned the Cheyenne sculptor Robert Fida to construct the colossal statue of Mary, towering 30 feet in the sky and weighing 180 tons. The site has only grown since its dedication in 1998, featuring kneelers, Stations of the Cross, and other religious statuary. Marjorie was clear that the shrine was not just for Catholics, and was, in her words, "for people." It is indeed a beautiful place where one can pray or think—or maybe do neither and simply savor a moment of peace.

You'll find plenty of peace along the so-called **Loneliest Road in America** (FIG. 12). It's a stretch of Highway 50 in Nevada that was designated as such in a 1986 article in *Life* magazine. The writer observed there was nothing to do along this desolate stretch and cautioned to steer clear unless you had the right "survival skills." The people of Nevada disagreed, especially the small but vibrant communities along the path, and the state's tourism board embraced the sobriquet, crafting a tour experience highlighting the towns like Ely, Eureka, and Austin.

ROADSIDE EATS

This collection of nostalgic spots is easy on the eyes, with grub that's tempting for the belly. Lots of burger joints here, lots of family histories, and lots of love that's keeping these places alive. You can show some love by stopping at any and all for a bite!

The **Hungry Onion** (FIG. 13) drive-in was a holdover from the early 1960s in Meridian, Idaho, and went out of business for good in February 2022 but lives on in the 1980 Clint Eastwood movie *Bronco Billy*. Eastwood's eponymous character, a stuntman fronting a traveling Wild West show, visits the roadside stand. The Bronco Billy burger remained a fixture on the stand's "secret menu" until the end. According to the *Idaho Statesman*, Eastwood's burger was a quarter pounder with bacon, cheese, and barbecue sauce served on a hoagie roll. You would've wanted to order the onion rings on the side—the place was said to be named after them.

Of similar vintage is **Gem In & Out** (FIG. 14), serving Caldwell, Idaho, since 1961. A trusty menu choice here is the Gem Burger, which features ham and cheese.

In Ashton, Idaho, we encounter a **Frostop Drive-In**, and its giant mug of root beer at this classic drive-in still rotates. This location opened in 1965, during the heyday of the Frostop chain, which once numbered in the hundreds, springing from the first location in Ohio, in 1926.

Mark's In & Out Beefburgers (FIG. 15) opened in Livingston, Montana, in 1954, and the biggest change has probably been the name—from Mart (the first name of the original owner) to Mark, the first name of one of the new owners who took over in 1980. The hamburger is the big draw here, but not far behind is the ice cream from local maker Wilcoxson's.

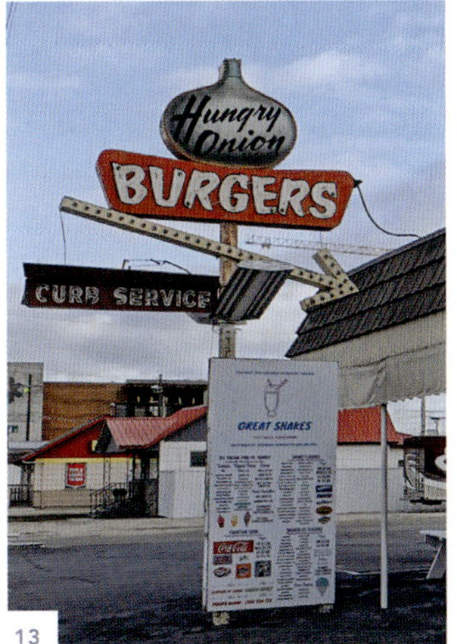

13

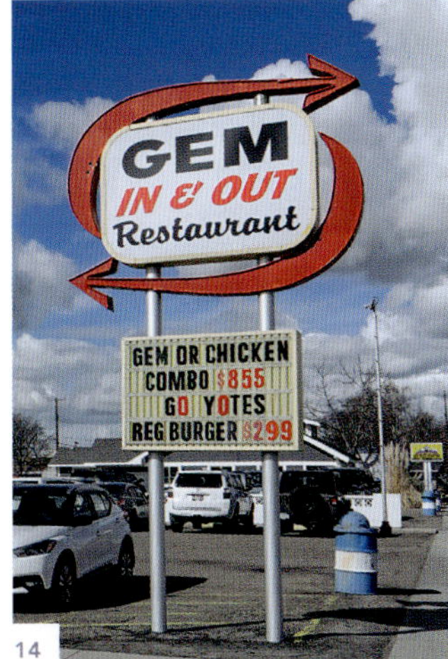

14

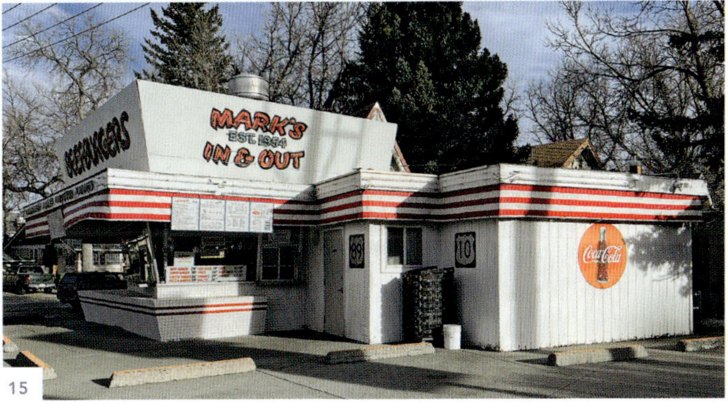

15

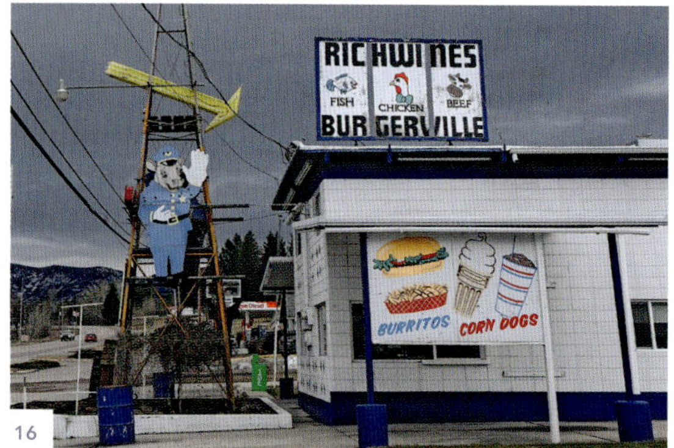

16

In Polson, Montana, get ready to experience something special when you spot the eclectic assemblage of signage for **Richwine's Burgerville** (FIG. 16)—from a windmill to a cow dressed as a police officer gesturing to pull over, a holdover from the very first shack that opened here in 1961. Now owned by Marcia Richwine Moen, the store is known for its high-quality burgers (made from bull meat) and swift, courteous service. It is a treasure of the American road, kept alive on the fumes of love, family, and the life skills the young people who work here learn from Moen, who devotes her life fully to this place. In 2019, Burgerville was the subject of the documentary *Burgers, Fries & Family Ties*, an insightful look at what it takes to keep this place alive and *thriving*. If you get the special burger, you'll get a doohickey (vegetable bites on a toothpick!).

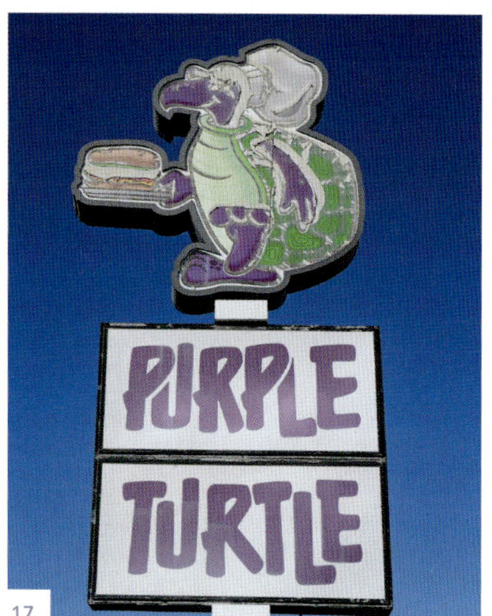

17

Sanford's Grub & Pub in Casper, Wyoming, has a little bit of this and a whole lot of that, an eclectic collection of Americana, perhaps most notably a towering Daffy Duck who greets you. Some call it overkill; I feel like you can never have enough of this stuff.

The **Peach City Drive-In** in Brigham City, Utah, traces its roots to 1937, when Bill Harris founded a malt shop that hit the sweet spot. By 1957, he moved it and transformed it into a drive-in. After all these years, Peach City is only on its third set of owners.

The Purple Turtle (FIG. 17) may seem like a dream, and its founding story can be traced to one. Lloyd Ash kept having dreams about a purple turtle, and he seized upon the idea that it

THE FIRST KFC

This is the first **Kentucky Fried Chicken**. And it's in Salt Lake City, Utah. Something does not compute, right? Well, this is the first place that franchised Colonel Harland Sanders's secret recipe of herbs and spices, in 1952. Pete Harman went into business with Sanders, and their historic collaboration is memorialized in statuary and exhibits at the restaurant, which, though decidedly a KFC, still goes by the name **Harman Cafe**. Indeed, Sanders sealed the deal by cooking up his fried chicken while on a visit to Harman's home, and Harman, convinced it would be a hit, immediately began selling it. Harman even came up with the name "Kentucky Fried Chicken" (a collab with a sign painter) and is credited with developing the "bucket" packaging concept for the chain. Read more on page 114.

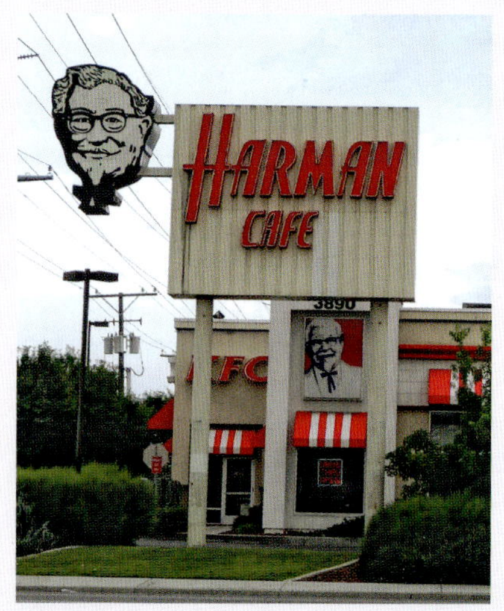

should be a restaurant, according to the local history group. And so in 1968, he founded the Purple Turtle, and it remains a pillar of life in Pleasant Grove, Utah. The current owners, Steve and Amy Cobbley, met at the Purple Turtle and have raised their family there. They don't call them mom-and-pop restaurants for nothing.

Mom's Cafe in Salina, Utah, has been around since 1929 and is as charming as you would expect a place with two neon signs and a menu teeming with comfort food. When former NBC anchor Tom Brokaw wanted to do a report from the Heartland, he ended up here—it's easy to see why.

Leave room in your belly for a visit to **El Bambi Cafe** in Beaver, Utah, with its exceptionally cute sign. The restaurant opened in 1943, when Disney's *Bambi* was offering audiences a sentimental escape from the horrors of World War II. (While in town, **Arshels Cafe** is another notable vintage stop.)

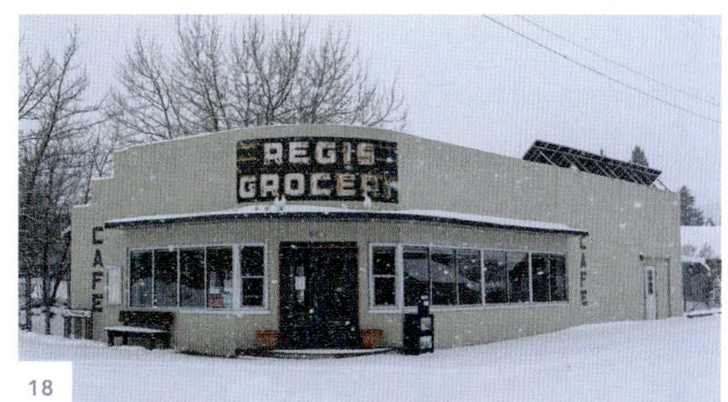

18

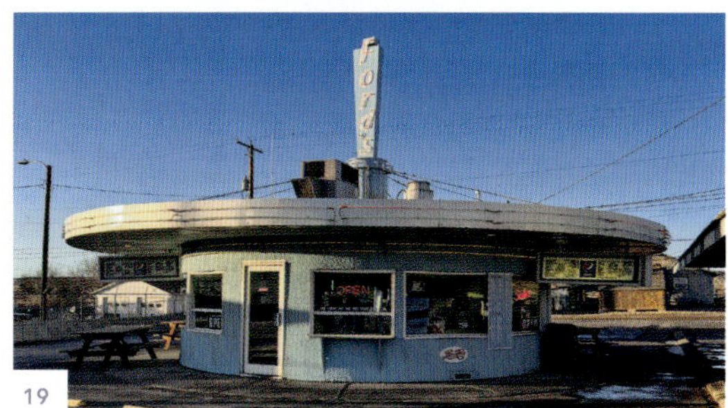
19

The Regis Grocery building in Red Lodge, Montana, is one of the most admirable examples of an adaptive reuse I've seen. Since 2002, it has been known as **Cafe Regis** (FIG. 18), but the owners proudly preserved the old neon sign from 1950. The business, built by Joe and Viola Regis in 1942, was added in late 2024 to the National Register of Historic Places.

I stopped for a burger and shake at **Ford's Drive-In** (FIG. 19) in Great Falls, Montana, which has been here since 1954. We never had to leave our SUV thanks to our carhop. She was continuing the tradition started by Florence Ford and her sons, Bob and Dick, who opened the drive-in in November 1954. The family's foray into the restaurant business in Great Falls started with a diner, but the Fords got hip quickly to the growing curb appeal of drive-ins and had the diner moved and modified to offer drive-in service. Their biggest early challenge? A gas explosion that severely damaged the restaurant in March 1955 . . . fortunately nobody was hurt. How did they advertise their return just a month later? With the phrase "Blowout Opening!"

Today, the round building and gorgeous neon sign make this a perfect spot to drive your vintage Ford—or Chevy or any all-American brand—for a burger and one of their dozens of shakes. And the burger has earned local and national acclaim, too, *Food Network Magazine* naming it as Montana's "ultimate" back in 2009.

Viking Drive-In (FIG. 20) in Boise, Idaho, is a gem from 1965, which proves Vikings can make for nifty mascots. It was an extension of the existing Viking Motel on State Street—the motel is a memory, the Viking, we hope, is forever.

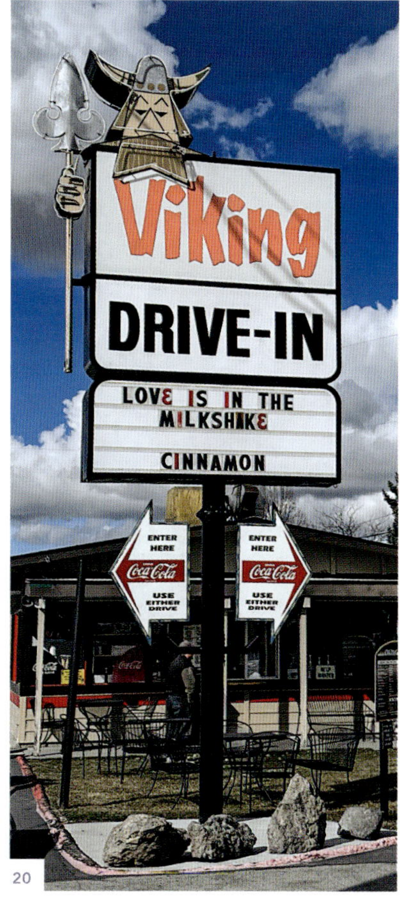

20

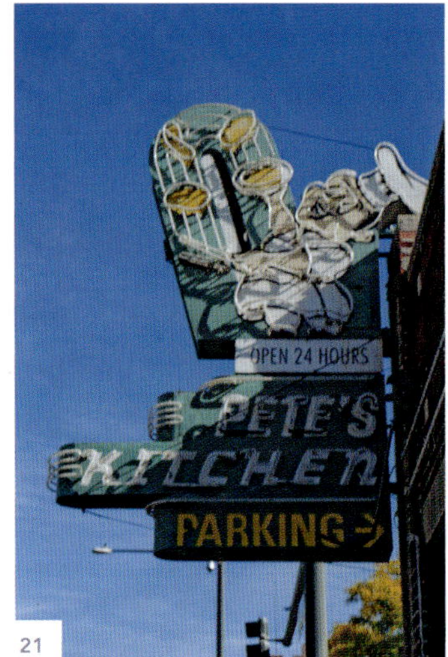

21

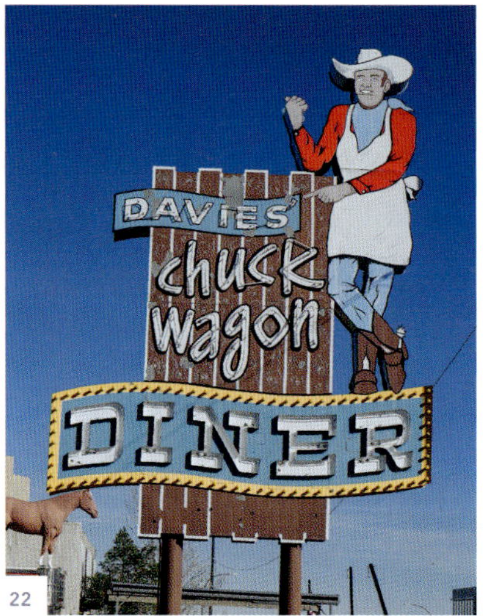

22

Pete's Kitchen (FIG. 21) and its animated neon chef, flipping flapjacks, are West Colfax Avenue mainstays of Denver, Colorado. The sign once read "The Kitchen" until new owner Pete Contos added his name in neon in the 1980s. Contos was a Denver restaurant entrepreneur who left his mark on the city, and in one particular block, has preserved some of Colfax's best and brightest neon. (See the Satire Lounge on page 263.)

Davies' Chuck Wagon Diner (FIG. 22), also in the West Colfax neighborhood, is graced by an iconic neon sign and sits in a Mountain View diner built in New Jersey—since 1957.

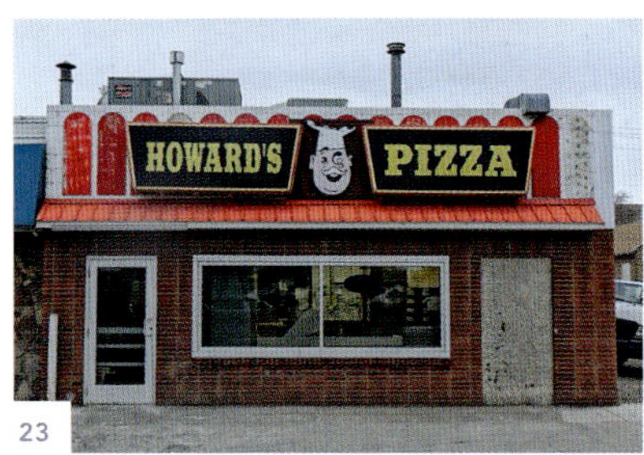

23

Howard's Pizza (FIG. 23) has four locations in Great Falls, Montana. This first one opened downtown in July 1959, with "13 varieties of lip-smacking good pizza." A newspaper ad published that October promised that the pizza here was a specialty and not a "side line," making Howard's a pioneer of America's hearty embrace of pizza in the postwar years.

CHEF SPEEDEE'S IDAHO RETREAT

The **McDonald's in Lewiston, Idaho,** is worth checking out. Though its menu is the same as other locations today, the restaurant doesn't physically look like most of the other McDonald's today. You might think it was actually built in the 1950s or 1960s. Nostalgia for the early days of McDonald's was riding high in the 1990s and early 2000s, when McDonald's built "retro" locations that played off the heritage of the building style from the chain's earlier days. Those "red and whites" as they were called, were mostly gone by the 1990s. The Lewiston store was one of the nicest of this throwback style, with signage echoing the world's oldest operating McDonald's in Downey, California.

Today, a new nostalgia is building for the mansard-roofed buildings that went up from 1968 and into the early 2000s, most of which have been demolished. Will they be tomorrow's "retro" buildings? I wouldn't be surprised. (See more on page 299.)

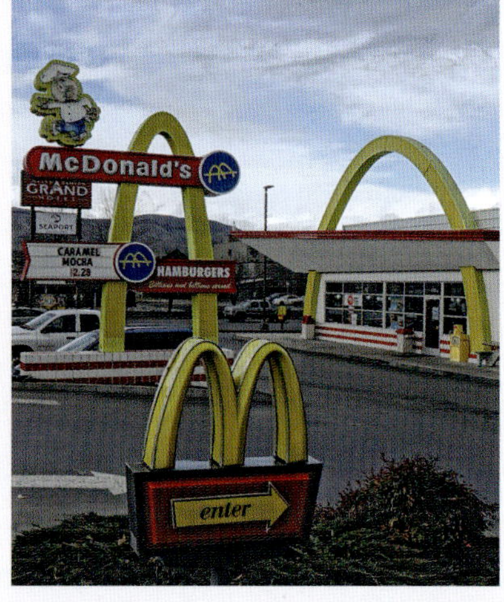

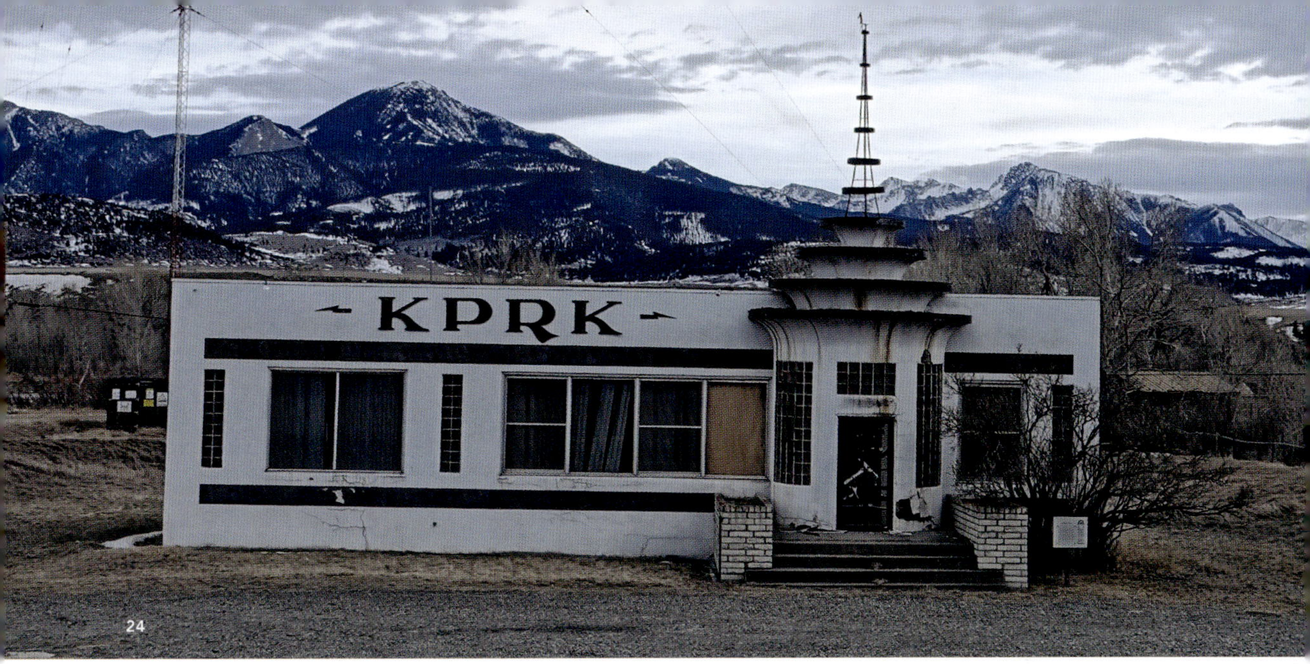

24

MAINSTAYS OF MAIN STREET

Some of the most fascinating places I've ever visited are right here, including a drug store frozen in 1979 and a radio station that could be on a set of a *Flash Gordon* revival, as you're about to see.

This radio station building in Livingston, Montana, could have just been a squat hut or a cement box, nothing fancy. One can imagine an architect being intimidated by the mountain range behind it, and conceding there was no point in competing with nature's designs. Or a general manager, launching a radio station just after World War II, reluctant to spend on form when function is what pays the bills. But fortunately, we didn't have those problems when this art moderne masterpiece was built for the newly launched **KPRK radio** (FIG. 24). Missoula architect William Fox created something so captivating that this building sits on the National Register of Historic Places. When it was added to this list in 1979 it was still a tad young, having only opened in 1947, and the Department of the Interior defended the inclusion of this "belated" example of moderne because the design was so unusual for the area and was so well preserved.

According to the Montana Historical Society, the futuristic style of the building was meant to contrast with the traditional brick buildings in Livingston—a fantastic town with some extraordinary neon—and some awfully nice people I enjoyed getting to know.

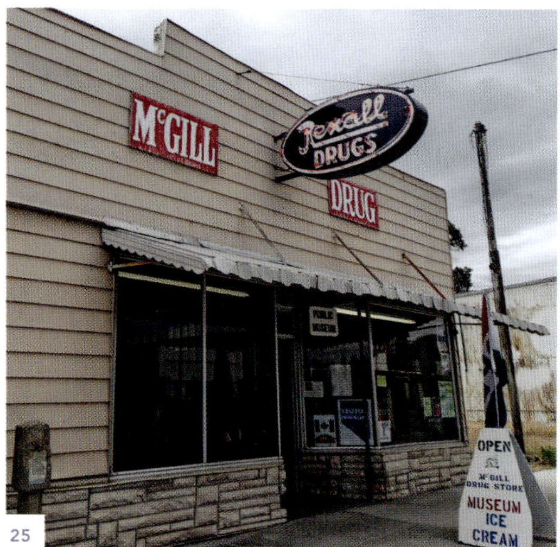

25

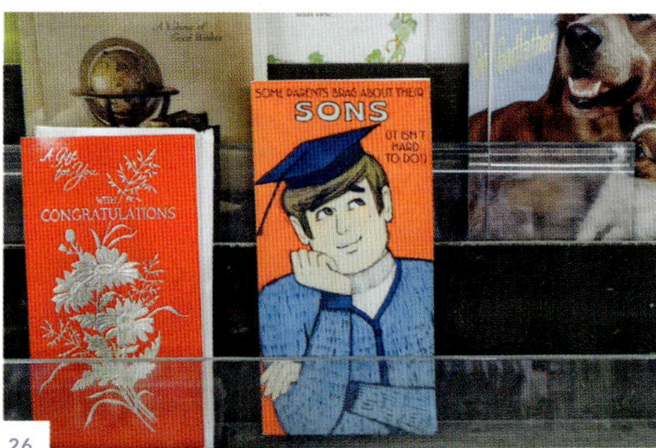

26

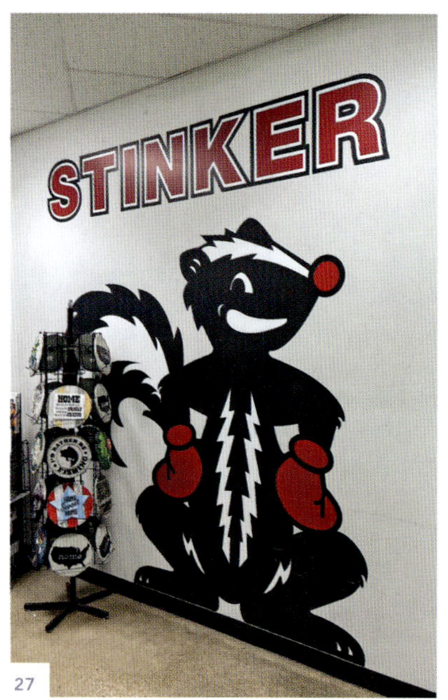

27

It's been a long time since you could catch up on the news of the day and fill your prescriptions at the **McGill Drug Store** (FIGS. 25, 26) in McGill, Nevada, one of the most fascinating places in America. When the store shut down in 1979, its contents were never cleared out, forever frozen in the era of disco demolitions, Jimmy Carter malaise speeches, and odd-even gas lines. As the years passed by, it became apparent that disturbing the contents of this store was a prescription for the destruction of an accidental time capsule of twentieth-century America unlike any other. In the safe hands of the White Pines Public Museum, the McGill Drug Store remains the same as it ever was, and the same as it will ever be.

You can even arrange for a tour. When I was there in 2014, the wonderful Daniel Braddock, the store's curator (who sadly died in 2022 after twenty-three years of devotion to the store), took me around inside the store to see its countless artifacts. Yes, there is a lot of stuff here from the 1970s, but the layers go back to the early twentieth century. Products from the 1950s sit alongside the unsold '70s stock. The store preserved generations of prescriptions and receipts—it offers an invaluable window into society and public health during much of the twentieth century. And the old soda fountain is still there, patiently awaiting the return of Bobby Soxers who will never come back, of course, but would feel right at home if they did.

Stinker (FIG. 27) is a chain of service stations that dot Idaho, Colorado, and Wyoming. They're hard to miss with the skunk mascot, seen here in Donnelly, Idaho. Farris Lind founded the chain in 1936, and adopted the name—and mascot—because Stinker was determined to undercut gas prices at the more established competition, making him the "stinker," so to speak. The chain's popularity was abetted by humorous billboards, the bon mots of Lind's invention. Stinker's website quotes Lind as saying, "I'll do anything for a laugh—and for a few dollars, I'll get hysterical."

The space race of the 1950s and 1960s influenced the roadside in countless ways, and one of the most vivid examples is the **Space Station Gas** station in Steamboat Springs, Colorado. The Sputnik sign dates back to the early 1960s, and the new owners in 2009 leaned into the space-age theme inside the store as well. They had such success with it that a second location opened in Oak Creek, Colorado.

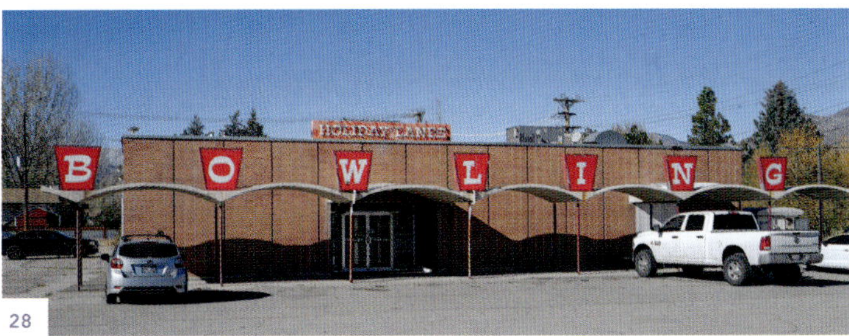

28

Lake Steam Baths in Denver, Colorado, has been the place for a proper Russian bath, a sensational schvitz for what ails you, since 1927. Founded by Russian emigrants Harry and Ethyl Hyman and until recently in the same family, the baths remain a vital part of the cultural landscape in the West Colfax neighborhood. The sign has been called "Colfaxian" for its bright role in the firmament of neon on this street.

Holiday Lanes (FIG. 28) in Heber City, Utah, is a glorious relic, inside and out. It's been in the same family since 1964 and is run by Phyllis Christensen, the daughter of the original owner. The classic malts are still made with the original hand-mixing machines, and locals are known to stop by just for the burgers, even without playing a round.

▸▸▸ Pull Over!

I'm always on the lookout for tokens of our telecommunications past—another way of saying "pay phones." In Joliet, Montana, in 2022, there was still a pay phone branded "USWEST." That's the name of the regional Bell company that served this area from 1984 through 2000, when the company adopted the name Qwest. So this was a hardy survivor. In downtown Boise, Idaho, a phone booth has found a more reliable use—as an ATM. Always follow the money.

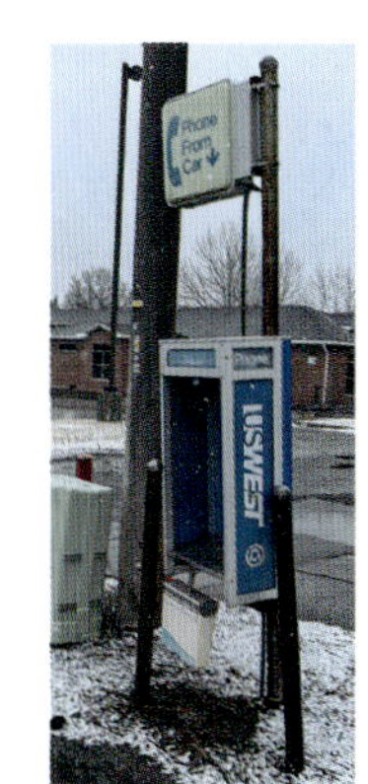

ON WITH THE SHOW

There are some really fine movie palaces here, just a taste in a region with so many, but my favorite might be one run by high school kids. Read on!

Truly a work of art and aptly named, the **Hyart Theatre** (FIG. 29) in Lovell, Wyoming, opened in 1951, a touch of quirky modernism in the Bighorn Basin. The builder was Hyrum "Hy" Bischoff, who came from a family that thrived in the local theater business after toiling as ranchers. The name blends his nickname and the "art" of moviegoing at the time, the palette and brush driving the idea home. The theater, with its elegant typeface and pink behind a vast turquoise metal grid, is an arresting sight. The Hyart began showing films again in again 2004 after a twelve-year hiatus, and remains in the Bischoff family.

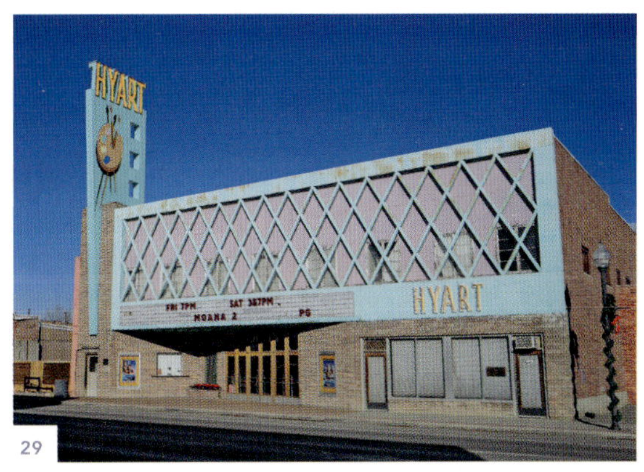

29

▸▸▸ Pull Over!

We've met plenty of Muffler Men in this book, but these muffler shops have their own spin. The **Silent Knight** (FIG. 30) chain in Idaho features a knight in shining armor, promising a silent ride. **Master Muffler** (FIG. 31), shown here in Salt Lake City, is like a superhero of the muffler set, ready to battle the Knight, though, in reality, they are on the same team in giving you a quiet car ride.

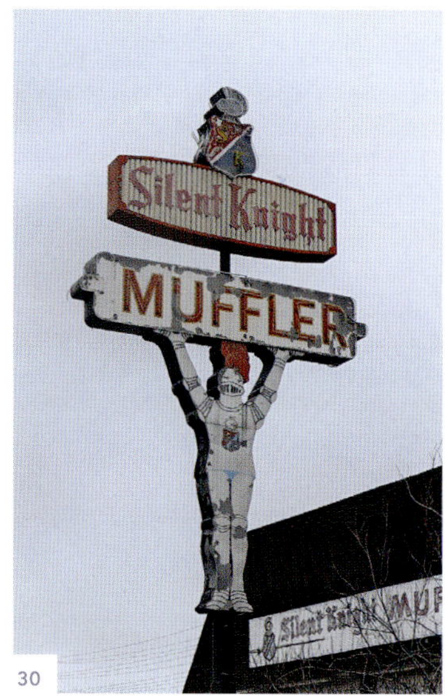

30

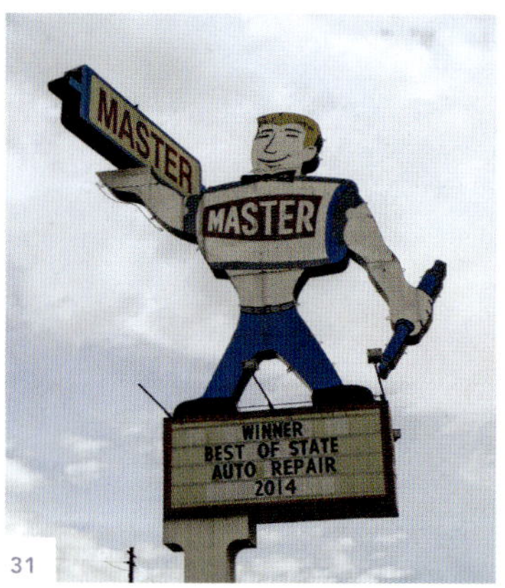

31

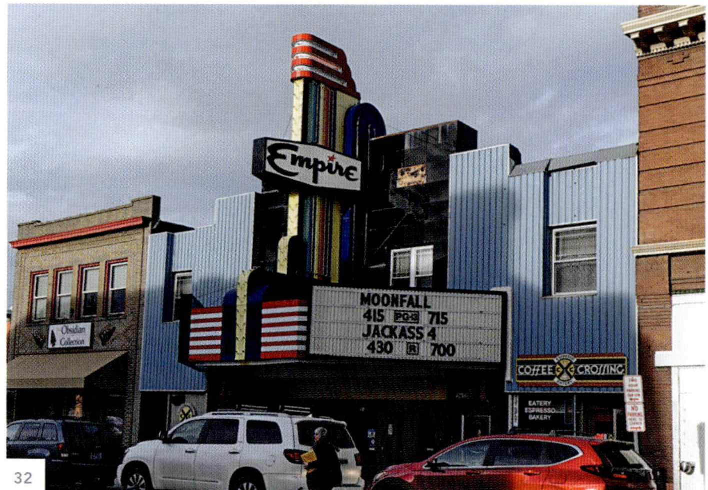

32

The **Empire Twin Theatre** (FIG. 32) is perhaps the nicest gem in the jewel box of a downtown that is Livingston, Montana. Its streamline moderne marquee puts on a show before you ever step inside. Beginning life as the State Theater, the complex adopted the Empire name around 1965, and the midcentury-modern style of the oval Empire sign is a graphic tip-off to the theater's history.

Schoolkids are our future, tomorrow's leaders in training, and in Harlowton, Montana, the kids have skipped a few steps and are running one of the biggest businesses in town, **The Harlo Theater** (FIG. 33). The theater has been open since 1948, back when kids were watching the films, not running the place (with the help of advisers). The theater is owned by the local public school district, and kids can start working at the theater as early as seventh grade. This on-the-job-training for the "reel" world is financed through scholarship money the students receive when they graduate high school, according to the district.

The Roxy Theater (FIG. 34) in Missoula, Montana, is a love-at-first-sight kind of place. Opened in 1937, this theater has endured a fire and the vicissitudes of changing tastes, the rise of television, and now smartphones and streaming. Initially a second-run theater, it briefly became a dollar cinema. Its fortunes turned around when the International Wildlife Film Festival bought it in 2002 and began to pour money, attention, and love into the theater, making it a community hub. Its art deco marquee was long gone—but in 2017, as the theater was turning eighty, the film-festival organization that owns it announced bold plans for the marquee's re-creation, and, to look at it today, you'd think it's been shining this way since day one.

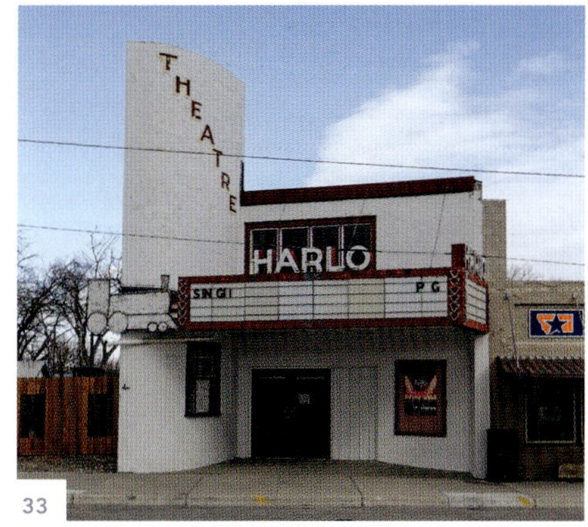

33

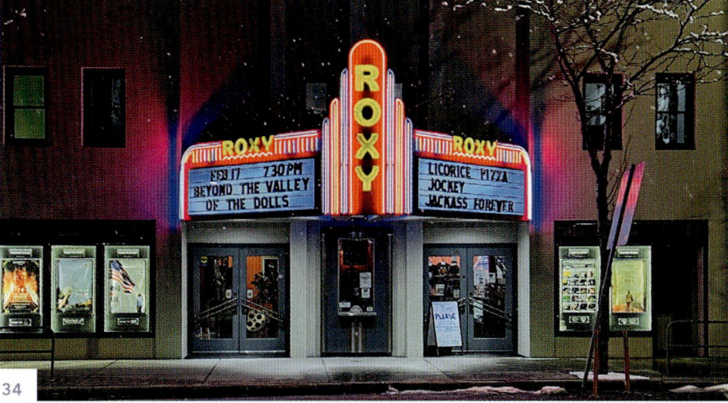

34

Boulder Theatre's lineage goes back to its days as an opera house, assuming its current name and look in the 1930s. Like any theater, it has faced ups and downs, and now is thriving as a popular entertainment venue, its art deco beauty intact.

The Esquire Theatre (FIG. 35) in Denver was closed at this writing, but I can only hope it finds a new role and that its glorious letterform is preserved. Indeed, there are plans for repurposing the structure into a mixed-use facility.

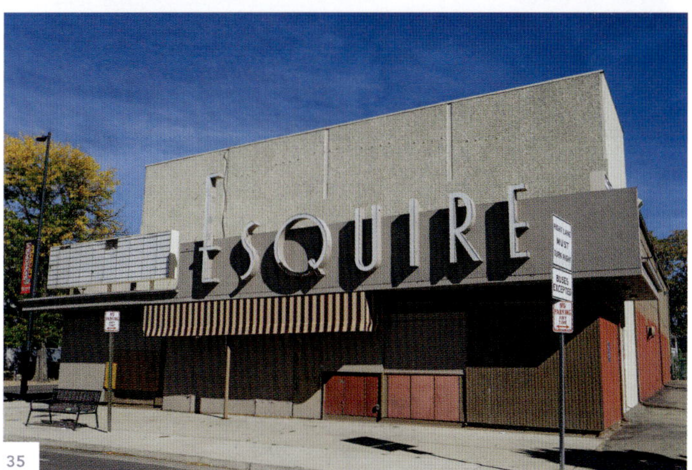

35

GORGEOUS GHOSTS

Ghost signs—faded advertising on the sides of old buildings, often but not always painted over bricks—compel a pull-over. The most classic perhaps are the old ghost signs for Coca-Cola, ubiquitous coast to coast.

Consider the **Eddy's Bread** sign (FIG. 36), which I spotted on a wall in Great Falls, Montana. It's an enticing depiction of a loaf of Eddy's Bread, the closest you can get to enjoying it, as this bakery chain closed long ago. More Eddy's ghosts haunt this part of the country.

Also in Great Falls, a ghost sign for **Owl Cigars** (FIG. 37) lords over the street. Owl ghosts have nests on a number of walls across the country, perpetually promoting nickel stogies.

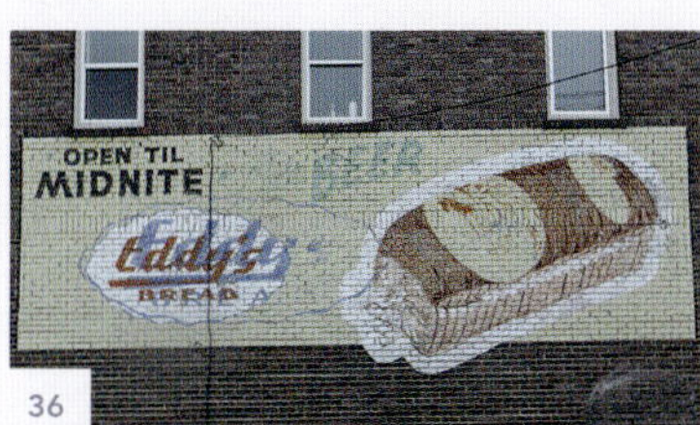

36

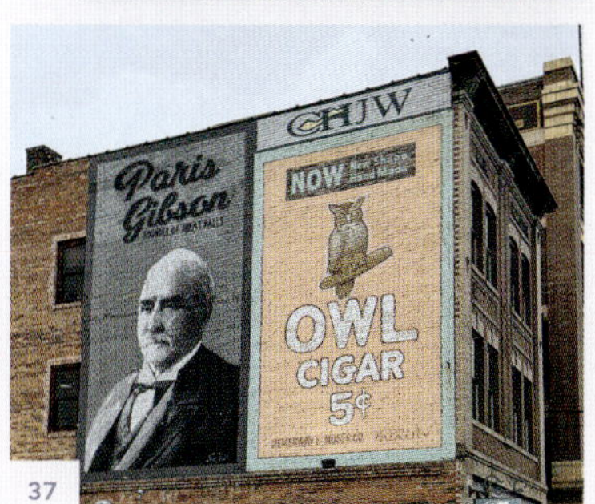

37

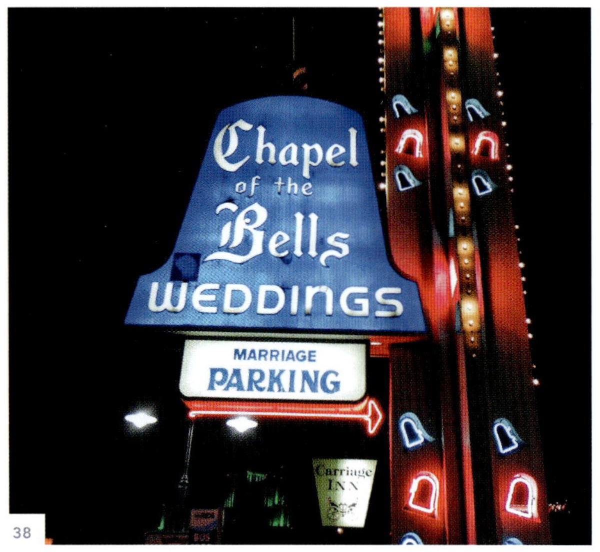

38

Chapel of the Bells (FIG. 38) in Reno, Nevada, was a visual heartbreaker, offering quickie weddings since 1962. Sadly, what was the last drive-thru wedding chapel in Reno closed in 2018. The wedding business used to be a big deal in western Nevada. According to the *Reno Gazette-Journal*, 1978 was the top year, with more than thirty-six thousand marriage licenses issued in Washoe County. By 2017, that number was down to under eight thousand. The Chapel of the Bells was not immune to this trend, nor to the decline of the neighborhood and changing tastes. The bell last tolled on February 28, 2018—two weddings were performed on that day, a happy moment at least for those two couples.

HE MAKES YOUR CARPET (OR TILE) WISHES COME TRUE

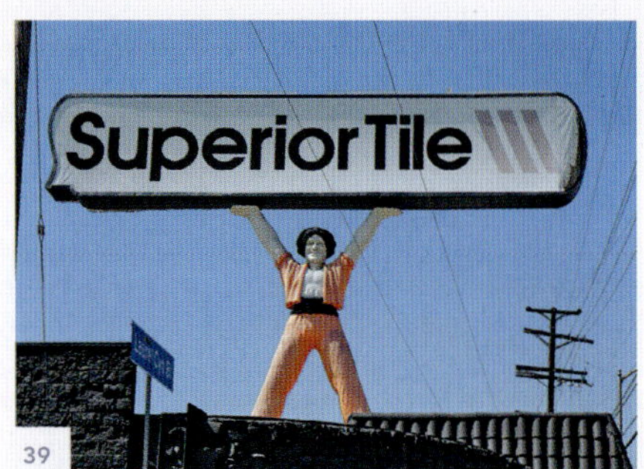

39

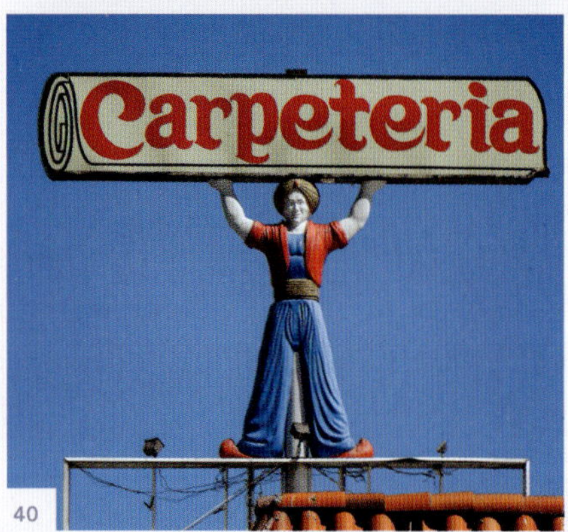

40

In 1999, financial woes pulled the rug out from under the **Carpeteria** chain. But that wasn't the end of Carpeteria. First, there was no erasing the chain's simple jingle from the memories of those who grew up in Carpeteria country: California and, to a lesser extent, Nevada. Second, some owners of individual Carpeteria stores soldiered on after the chain's collapse, and you can still shop at a number of Carpeteria stores today.

But what has largely vanished is the Carpeteria Genie. The chain was launched in 1960 in Canoga Park, California, and the genie, standing 20 feet tall, was soon spreading across California. He was modeled after Ted Haserjian, who with his brother, Harold, founded the chain, a family member told the *Los Angeles Times*. This genie was also a Janus, two-faced, so his smiling visage was in view of carpet-shopping motorists all around him. But by 1989, the genie was on the ropes. Many had been felled in an era of strict sign ordinances, and those that survived weren't as flashy. Today, there are only a handful of genies left. A giant survives in North Hollywood, California (FIG. 39), promoting a tile business. The only one in the wild still holding a roll of carpet bearing the word "Carpeteria" is in Reno, Nevada (FIG. 40).

INN CROWD

Once upon a time in American travel, you could count on finding motels with certain names waiting for you coast to coast, an oasis of neon after a long day on the road. But these were usually mom-and-pops, not chains. They just shared picturesque names like Starlite, Stardust, and Thunderbird.

This particular **Thunderbird** (FIG. 41), in Missoula, Montana, makes my heart soar. The story of the motel traces back to 1957, when Dorcas Rose inherited an old house and some land on East Broadway. She turned the property into a motel that she ran with her husband, Jim, according to an old clip from the *Great Falls Tribune*. By 1965, Mrs. Rose's venture was thriving, and she won an award from the Small Business Administration to salute her hospitality-business prowess. The motel has for decades been in the hands of Thelma Baker, who makes headlines every four years as one of Montana's three electors in the electoral college. But her motel is always in the spotlight, certainly whenever that neon is lit.

41

The **Horseshoe Bend Motel** (FIG. 42) in Lovell, Wyoming, is immortalized in a 1973 photograph by famed photographer Stephen Shore. The motel is currently undergoing revitalization, and its owner, Bobbi Jo McJunkin, is leaning into the motel's vintage vibe and the aesthetic that drew Shore here for a photo. It was taken just after a rainfall on July 16, 1973, with a rainbow in the sky, a period American gas guzzler in the foreground—green in color, not in environmental impact—and the horseshoe sign, seen at an angle, standing off in the distance, casts its reflection on the rain-slickened parking-lot pavement. The sign still stands and is a popular draw as a slice of roadside authenticity in a world increasingly deprived of it.

McJunkin told *Cowboy State Daily* that she'd been offered $50,000 for the sign, a windfall that would go a long way toward underwriting the total restoration of the property. But if you're refurbishing a vintage oasis, losing the sign—or erecting an LED replica—makes no sense.

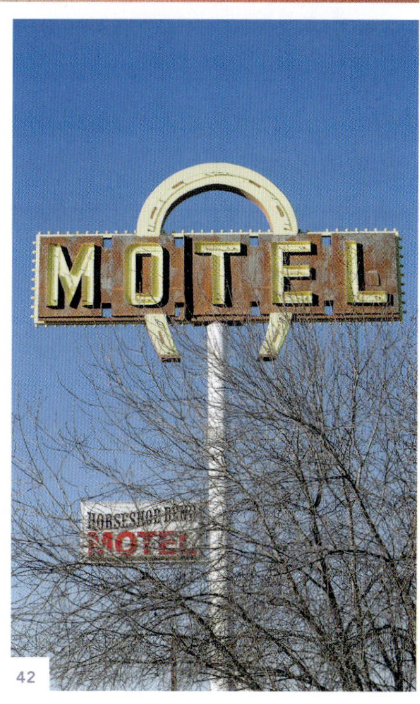

42

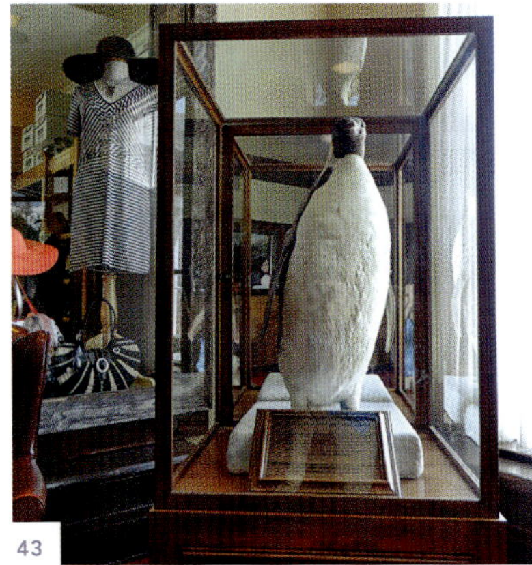

43

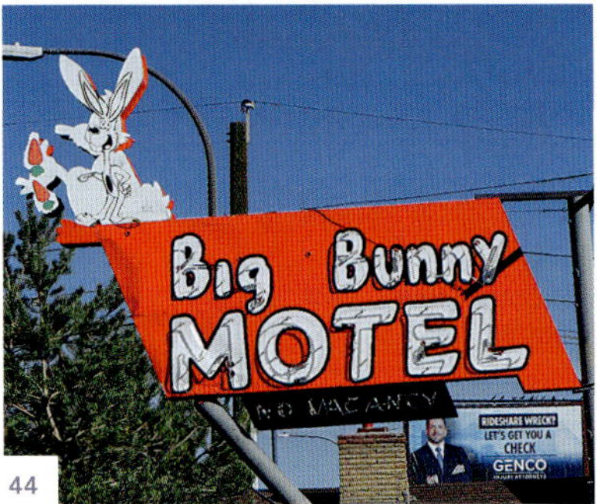

44

And what's this about a Stephen Shore room? McJunkin is renovating the motel's rooms according to a theme—one inspired by Apollo 8 astronaut Jim Lovell, who shares the same name as the town. Another room features a cowboy motif—a fitting choice in the Cowboy State. One will be themed after Mr. Shore and will feature a print of the iconic 1973 photograph taken just outside in the parking lot. I have dibs on the Stephen Shore room.

The Little America (FIG. 43) in Wyoming began as a roadside pit stop on the Lincoln Highway in the 1934, once boasting the greatest number of gas pumps in the nation. A hotel and restaurant sprang up on the property, and the stop became so important that the town is now named after it. The name is a reference to the remote Antarctic station called Little America, an inspiration because of how remote this area of Wyoming was, and indeed still is. (Admiral Richard Byrd's exploration of Antarctica was headline news in those days.) An Emperor penguin became the face of the hospitality chain. An actual penguin was procured to become a live mascot but died before arriving. The penguin was stuffed and is on display in a glass box in Little America, Wyoming.

What's up doc? **The Big Bunny Motel** (FIG. 44) in Denver began life in 1952 as the Bugs Bunny Motel, the modification still evident on the neon sign. The sign made it, unscathed, to almost the new millennium, before Warner Brothers and the motel

BOZEMAN MOTELS

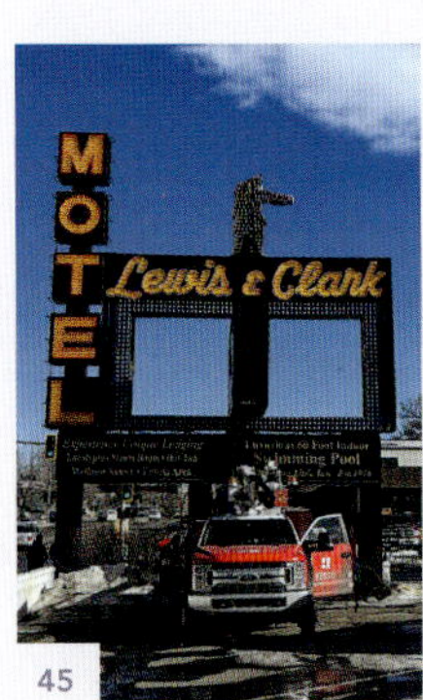

45

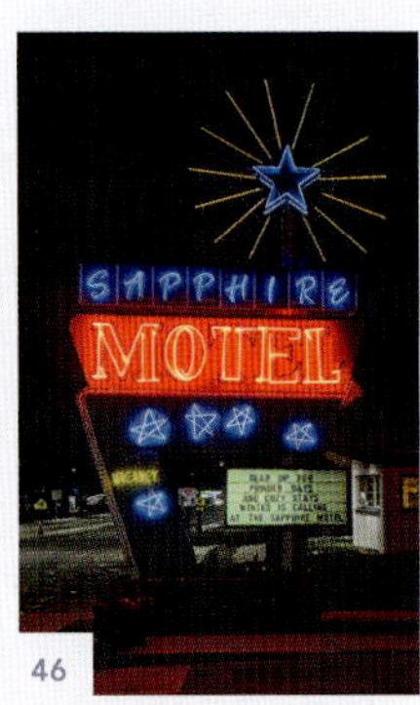

46

Lewis & Clark Motel (FIG. 45) in Bozeman, Montana, has been around since 1976, a tribute to the explorers Meriwether Lewis and William Clark.

Sapphire Motel (FIG. 46) began as a simple tourist court, adopting different names over the years. In 1955, at the height of the motor court era, it became the Travelier Motel and acquired its iconic sign. Brothers Shiloh and Jacob Klatt, whose family owned the property since 1972, took on the motel in 2021, renovated it to distill its swank midcentury elegance, and renamed it the Sapphire. For their efforts they have been rewarded with a Historic Preservation Award from Bozeman for restoring the sign.

The historic **Rainbow Motel** is now known as the **RSVP**, a boutique retro motel as well, but the old sign survived along the road. "Since the sale and subsequent revamp to create the RSVP in 2018, we weren't willing to bid adieu to so much history. So we kept the spirit of the hotel alive with a fresh coat of paint and a stylish rethink to the landmark sign. It still guides travelers to our uber-chic boutique to this day," according to the RSVP's blog. How wonderful is that?

tangled, according to an oft-told tale. As you can see, the modification to the sign was practical.

Hotel Nevada & Gambling Hall (FIG. 47) in Ely, Nevada, is a towering presence in this town, and a reminder that the Loneliest Road in America, which cuts through here, isn't so lonely. It opened in 1929 and was the tallest building in Nevada for two years, which is hard to contemplate when you think of the skyscraping wonders in Las Vegas.

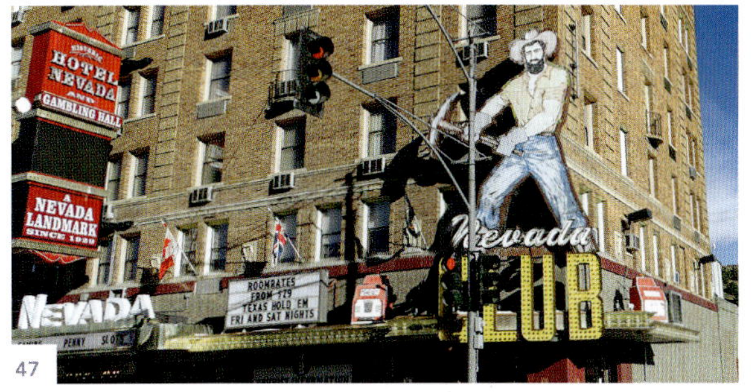

47

SWEET STOPS

Here's a constellation of options for those who love something sweet on the road, beginning with a visit to the Big Dipper.

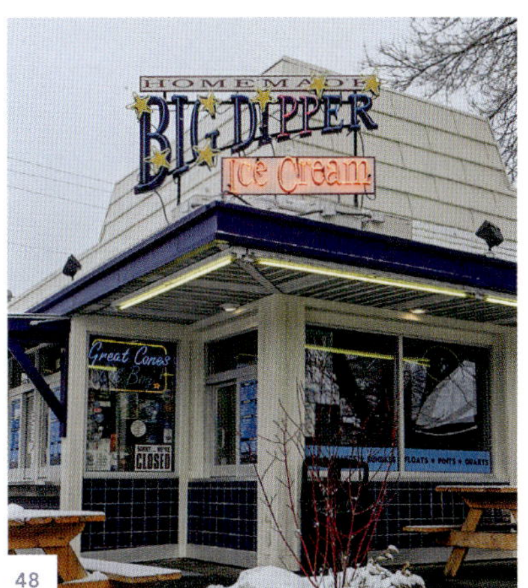

48

Big Dipper Ice Cream (FIG. 48) was founded in 1995 and today sits at a location in Missoula, Montana, that was once a gas station, a yogurt shop, a sandwich shop, and a catering business before becoming home to this charming ice-cream store, famous for its innovative and seasonal flavors, chill vibe, and long lines. Not closing in the winter months was key to the business plan, owner and founder Charlie Beaton told the *Missoulian* in 2008. Beaton got into the ice-cream business because he enjoyed making ice cream, and making people happy, he told the *Missoula Current*.

Big Dipper enjoys a national reputation and has a second location in Missoula, along with stores in Helena, Billings, and Great Falls. And keep an eye out for their truck, aka Cowboy, at events around Missoula.

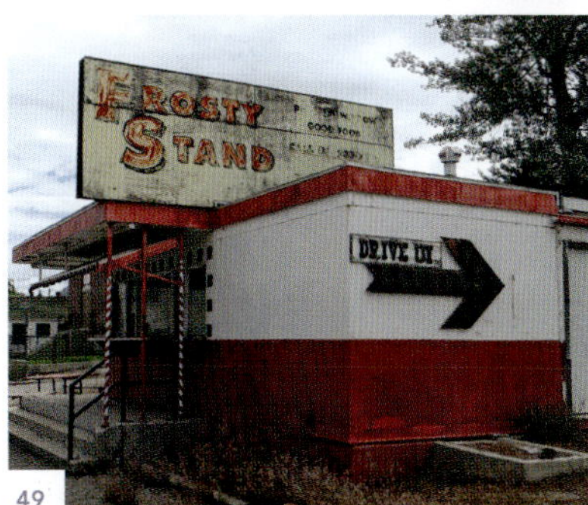

49

The Loneliest Road in America led me to **Frosty Stand** (FIG. 49) in McGill, Nevada, just off Highway 50. This long-shuttered ice-cream stand began life as Bob's Drive-In in the late 1950s. The proprietors were Bob and Flora Drakulich. According to Flora's obituary, they went on to pursue their fortunes in Reno in 1963, and this building went on to become Frosty Stand (though a 1966 classified ad spells it "Frostee"). If there's beauty in neglect, then Frosty Stand has the market cornered.

The Fanci Freez (FIG. 50) is a beloved staple in Boise, Idaho, with another location in Meridian, Idaho. Around these parts, Fanci Freez is ice-cream royalty.

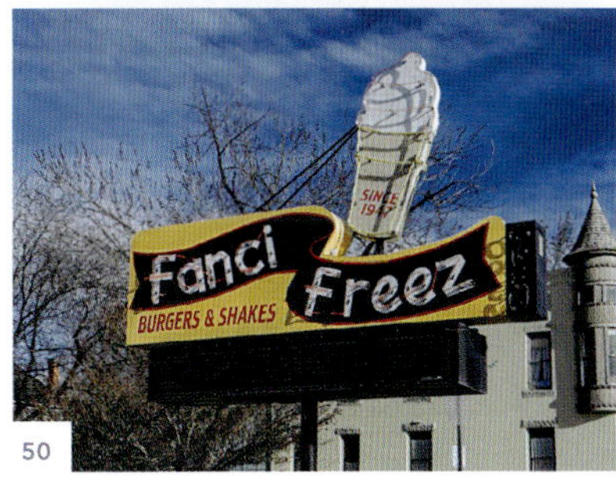

50

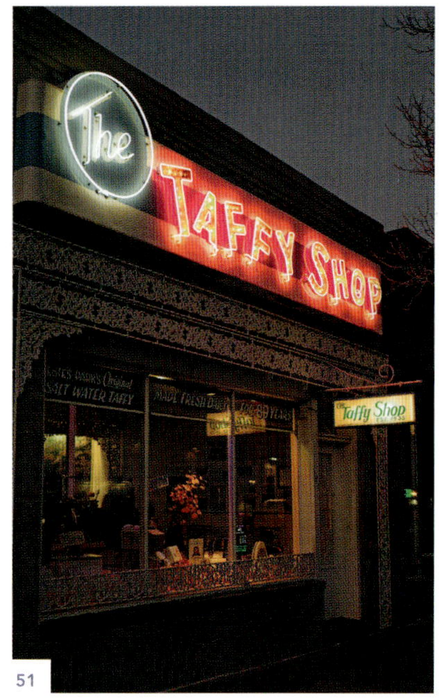

51

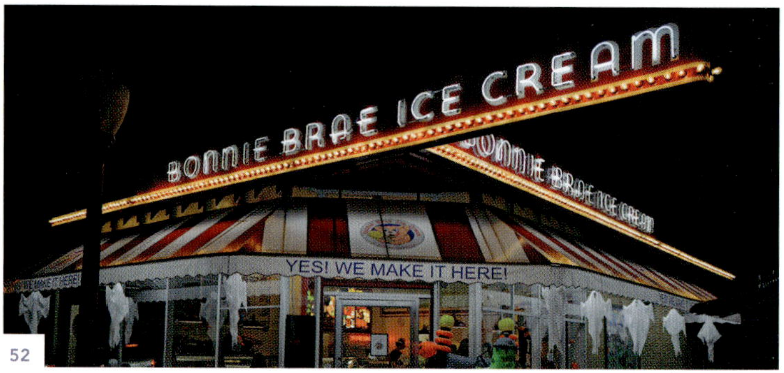

52

The Taffy Shop (FIG. 51) in Estes Park, Colorado, opened in 1935 and only changed hands once, back in 2014. The handover from the founding Slack family to the Igels involved retrieving the taffy recipe from a bank safety-deposit box.

Bonnie Brae Ice Cream (FIG. 52) in Denver, Colorado, was founded in 1986, which seems pretty recent for a storefront dripping with such vintage charm. This was once a Dolly Madison ice-cream store, and the look was simply adapted.

CHEERS!

Mermaids in the middle of Montana? An Irish bar founded by an Italian boxer named Sonny O'Day? Here's to some fun stories up ahead!

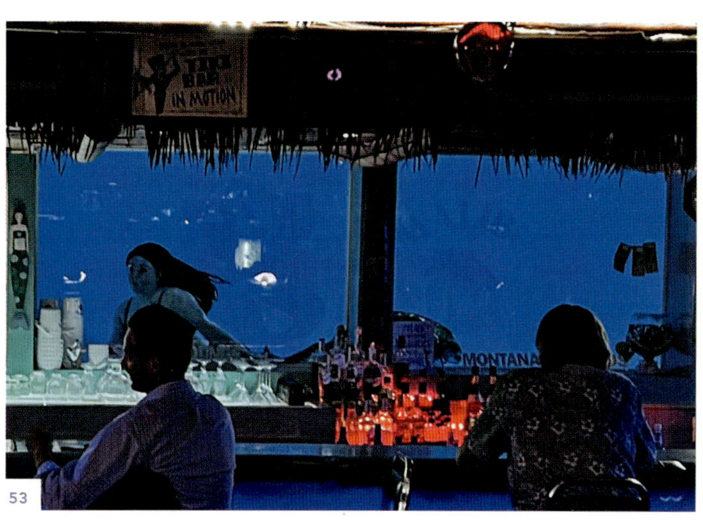

53

When I arrived in Montana for a weeklong road trip in 2022 and showed up with my camera and my questions at vintage spots, I would invariably hear: "Are you going to the Sip 'n Dip in Great Falls?" I heard it so many times that I rearranged my plans to make sure I didn't miss it. The **Sip 'n Dip** (FIG. 53), which opened in 1962, is a unique and largely unchanged tiki bar on the O'Haire Inn's second floor. The hotel has a pool, and a massive glass wall behind the bar looks into this pool. And there, since December 31, 1995, have swum mermaids and, occasionally, mermen, who frolic for captivated admirers at the bar or in the elegant leather booths.

But, alas, I arrived too late, because the year before, "Piano Pat" Spoonheim had died. She tickled the ivories here and sang, mostly American standards—*no rock*—from the age of twenty-eight, in 1963, until her death at age eighty-six. Pat was a famous octogenarian who became a reluctant celebrity and wished that the fame had come earlier, but this single mom who worked two jobs most of her life knew she was loved. There is a tribute to her here—her CDs are for sale and her spirit is very much felt. A magical combination of Piano Pat, mermaids, and a tiki bar in the middle of Montana turned this into a bucket-list destination, with *GQ* famously declaring it the number one "bar on earth worth flying for" in 2003.

Behind the name of shuttered bar **Sonny O'Day** (FIG. 54) is the story of boxer-turned-bartender Carlo Giorgi, born in Italy in 1913. His life took him from Italy to Butte, Montana, where he began boxing at the age of ten. He became a boxer in New York, adopting an Irish name at the suggestion of an agent, who told the young man, "The Irish control the game. Nobody is gonna come see an Italian boxer," according to O'Day's obit in the *Montana Standard*. He returned to Montana and plowed his earnings into running two taverns in Butte. Then, he and his wife, Carra, moved to Laurel, Montana, around 1945 and opened Sonny O'Day, which he ran until his death in 2001. Today it's closed, and I can only hope not forever.

Late into his life, O'Day would hop into the ring and take on men half his age in good-natured bouts. And the biggest day of the year for O'Day was St. Patrick's Day, when guests could enjoy green Pabst beer and corned beef and cabbage. He was born March 8, but he decided to celebrate his birthday on March 17 instead.

Timber Bar's sign (FIG. 55) has become the symbol of Big Timber, the Montana ranching town of 1,650, named after Big Timber Creek. On Interstate 90 you'll see signs featuring the "Timber Logger." The bar has been around since 1957 and for much of that time was under the care of the Fuller family. Melissa and Frank Chounet kept the taps flowing for a decade until selling to Scott and Tammi Laird in 2024. Donnie Sexton wrote a sweet essay on this bar in the *Montana Standard*, calling it "the quintessential watering hole of Big Timber."

Club Moderne (FIG. 56) was not the first bar in Anaconda, Montana, but it holds License No. 001 in Deer Lodge County. The bar is tops in more ways than one. In 2016, Club Moderne was named America's Favorite Historic Bar by the National Trust

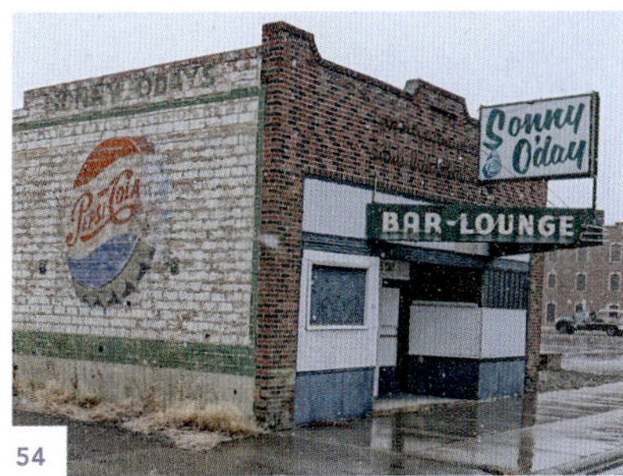

54

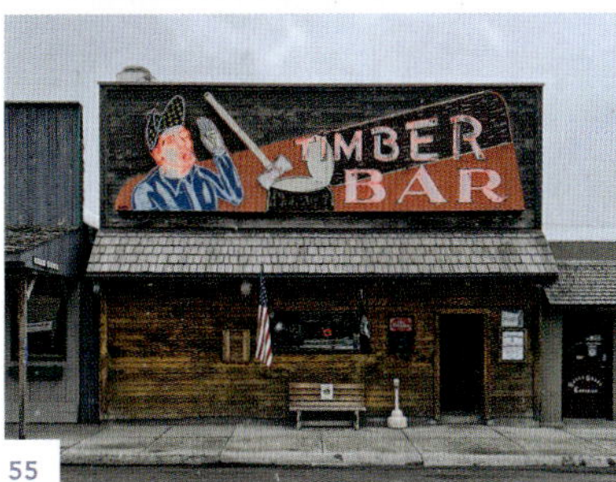

55

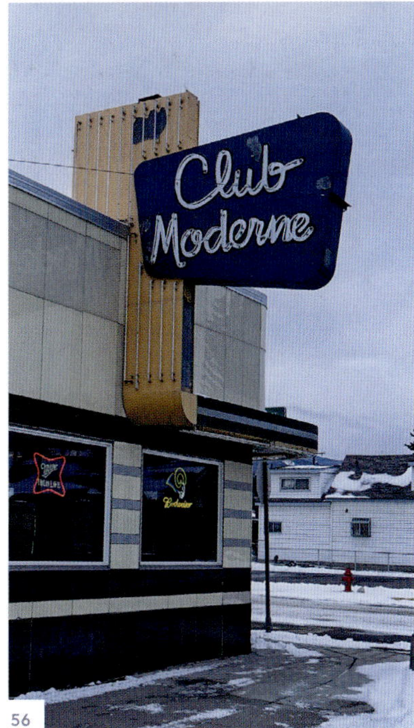

56

for Historic Preservation. It's also number one in a lot of hearts in this community of around 9,500, named after the Anaconda copper mining company founded here in 1881. That was perhaps never clearer than on the evening of October 3, 2016, when grief-stricken residents watched helplessly as The Club Moderne went up in flames. But it would rise from the ashes soon enough.

The Hekkel family, owners since 1997, rebuilt quickly, with many of the original furnishings preserved and the facade restored. This bar's urbane streamline sophistication was the product of the prolific architect Fred F. Willson, who was based in Bozeman and gave that city much of its architectural character. But it was the brainchild of John "Skinny" Francisco. The Hekkels say he had traveled a lot and had ideas about the kind of high-class watering hole he wanted here. John Hekkel, speaking of his desire to rebuild, told the *Montana Standard*: "There's no way I could drive down the street and not see the Club Moderne." All we can say is thank you.

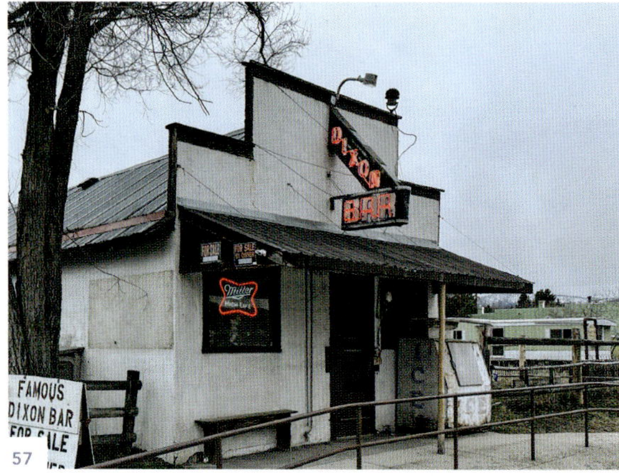

57

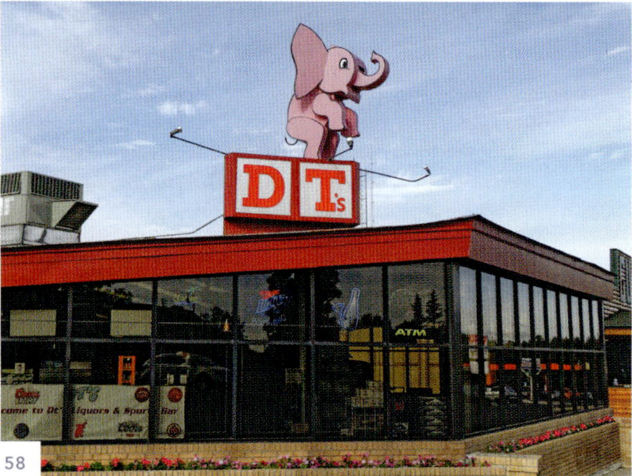

58

The Dixon Bar (FIG. 57) was an unexpected surprise in Dixon, Montana, when I drove past it—what a beauty! This is a state legend that once inspired three very drunk poets to each write a poem about it titled "The Only Bar in Dixon." *The New Yorker* published the poems in 1970.

DT Discount Liquor (FIG. 58) is a bar and liquor shop in Cheyenne, Wyoming, featuring a pink elephant and a name, which when combined would appear to be an inside joke. (The DTs, or delirium tremens, refers to the tremors the body endures during withdrawal from alcohol, and people are said to hallucinate—aka see pink elephants—during this process.) But in this case, there was an actual DT—D. T. Johnson, the founder of this shop, who died in 1968, three years after selling his store.

As we continue our mountain pub crawl, it should come as no surprise to encounter multiple bars with cowboy themes. **Cowboy Bar and Grill** in Meeteetse, Wyoming, was founded in 1893, steeped in Old West and outlaw lore, with tales of visits from Butch Cassidy and more recent dodgers of the law.

Dating to the 1940s, the **Dime Horseshoe Bar** in Sundance, Wyoming, is a biker bar famous for their annual Burnout Wednesday festival—in which they spin their wheels while not moving—since the 1970s.

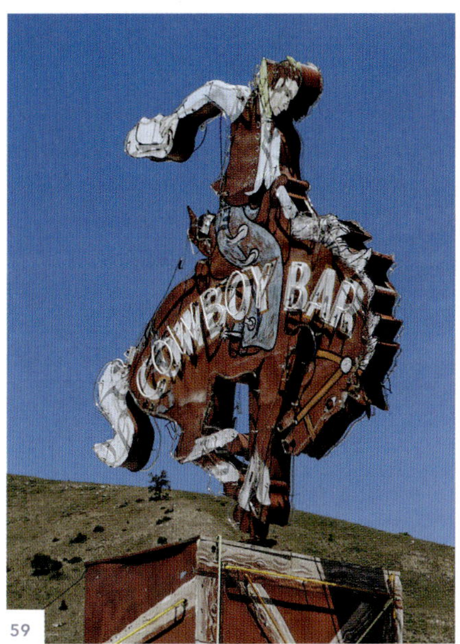

59

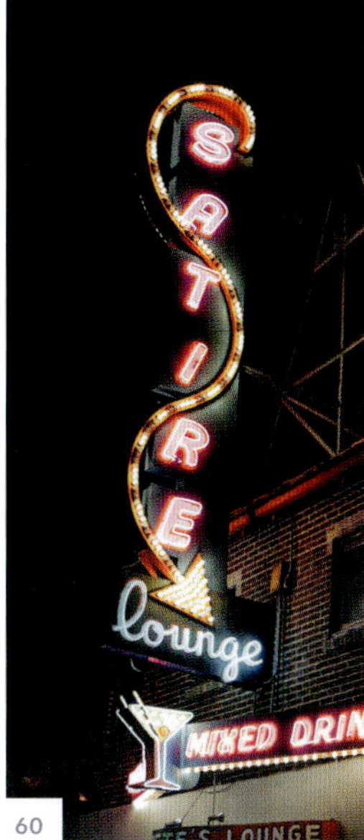

60

Million Dollar Cowboy Bar (FIG. 59) in Jackson Hole, Wyoming, traces its roots back to a bar operated by Joe Ruby in the early 1930s. By the end of the decade, it was the Cowboy Bar and became an oasis of knotty pine and Western character—and characters. It came to take its current form in the 1950s, under the ownership of Press Parkinson, who clad it in neon and had the iconic cowboy built, and remodeled the interior after a devasting gas explosion. But it's the bar's signage that often reels people in.

The music venue and bar **Lion's Lair** in Denver, Colorado, went through a number of names before Jim Lyons bought it in 1967 and gave it a play on his last name—and a friendly lion mascot, akin to something you'd see outside a preschool, which adds to the charm.

The Mozart Lounge in Denver traces its roots to the Mozart Hall, which catered to the area's German community in the 1800s. It moved here as Mozart Lounge in the 1950s, was rebranded for a time and then restored to its original name and glory.

R&R Lounge in Denver was founded in the 1950s under a different name and evolved into a historic gay bar, another neo-lit mainstay of the East Colfax area in Denver.

We stopped for pancakes at Pete's Kitchen (see page 250). Now, we raise a glass to Peter Contos at the **Satire Lounge** (FIG. 60), whose restaurant empire began here in Denver back in 1962. Contos, a Greek immigrant, owned some of Denver's most iconic restaurants, and this particular block is the crown jewel.

▶▶▶ Pull Over!

In Butte, Montana, a collection of bars teems with regional character. Be sure to stop at **Val's Alpine Bar** (scenic, but now closed), **The Scoop**, and **Cinz Bar** (FIG. 61). Don't miss **JFK Bar** (FIG. 62) in Anaconda or **Red's Bar** (FIG. 63) in Missoula.

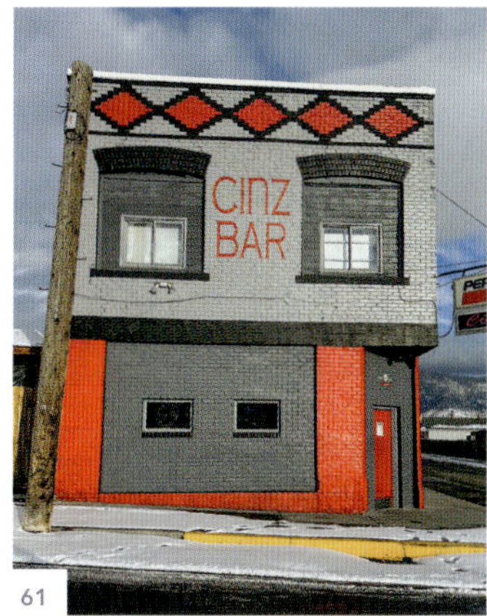

61

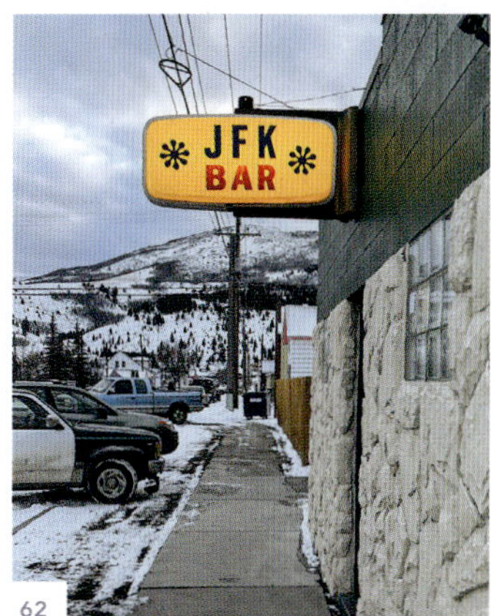

62

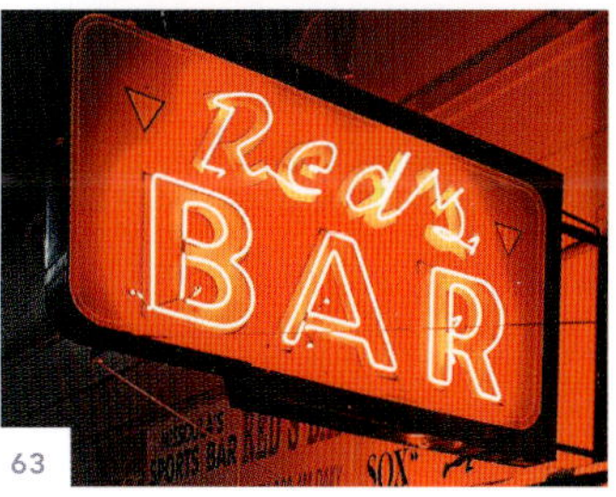

63

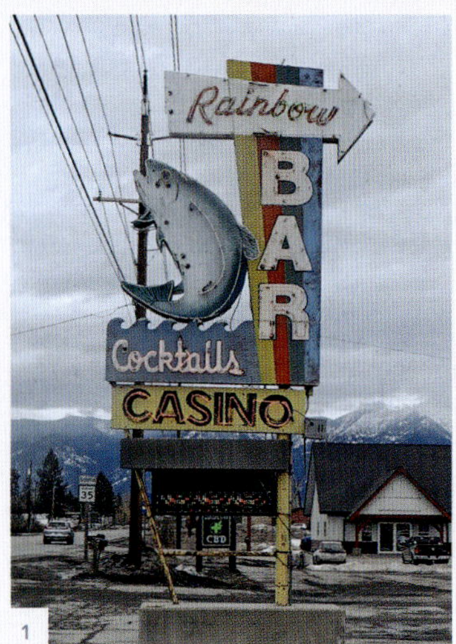

1

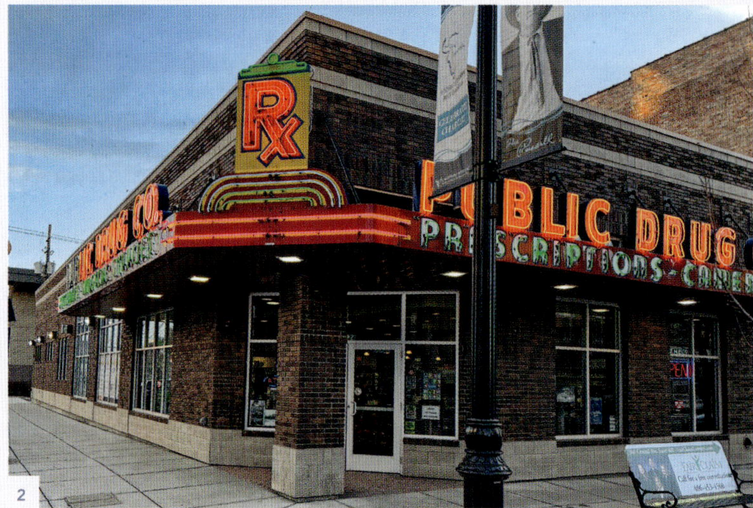

2

THERE'S MORE IN STORE!

Some spots I had to share before we leave this chapter!

1. Rainbow Bar, Kalispell, Montana
2. Public Drug Co., Great Falls, Montana
3. Joe's Liquor & Bar, Rock Springs, Wyoming
4. Temple City Motel, South Salt Lake, Utah
5. Brian's Top Notch Cafe, Great Falls, Montana
6. Neon Batman and Robin scaling a building in Neon Alley, Pueblo, Colorado
7. Stardust Motel, Wallace, Idaho
8. Antler Motel, Jackson Hole, Wyoming
9. Lariat Motel, Cheyenne, Wyoming

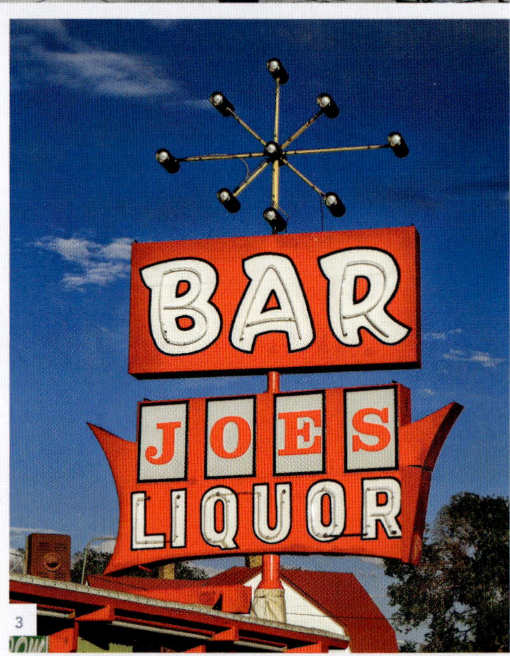

3

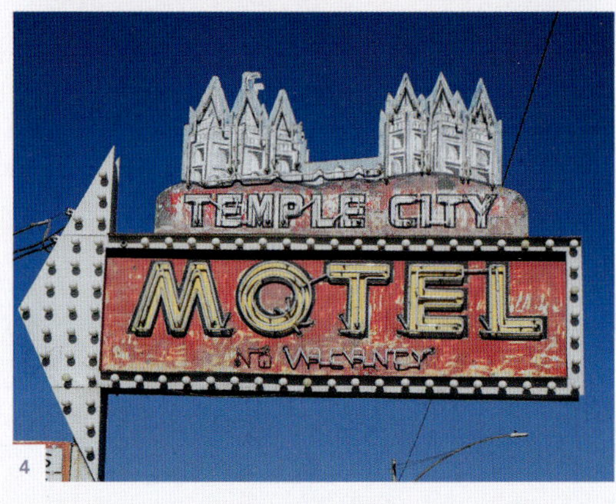

4

TOP
NOTCH
LUNCH
BREAKFAST - DINNER
CATERING
5

6

STARDUST
MOTEL
OPEN
7

ANTLER
MOTEL
8

Lariat
9

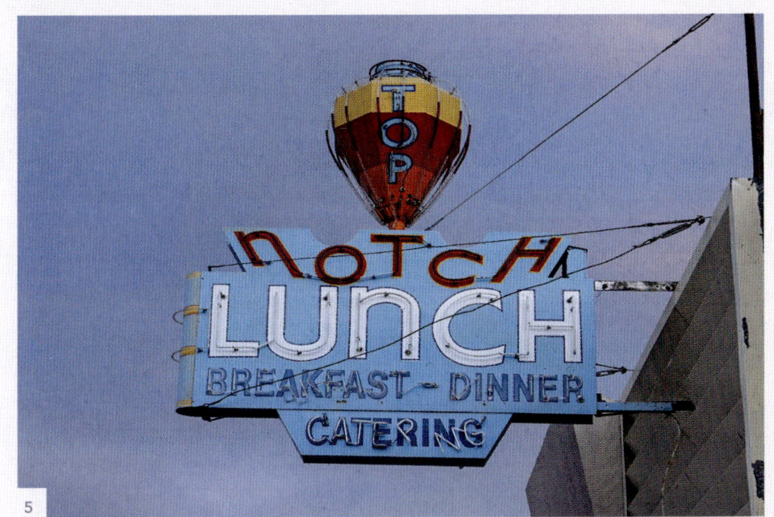

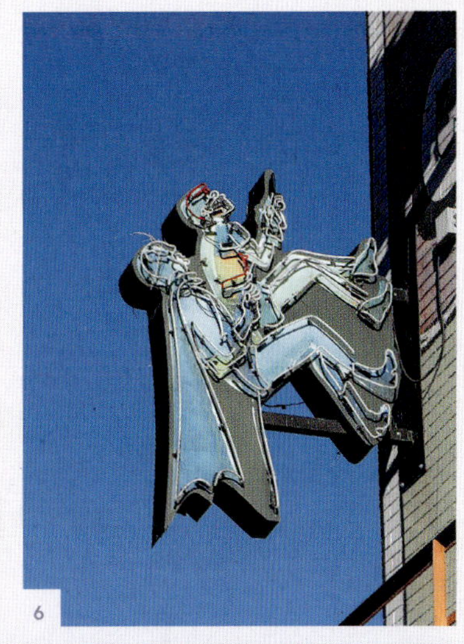

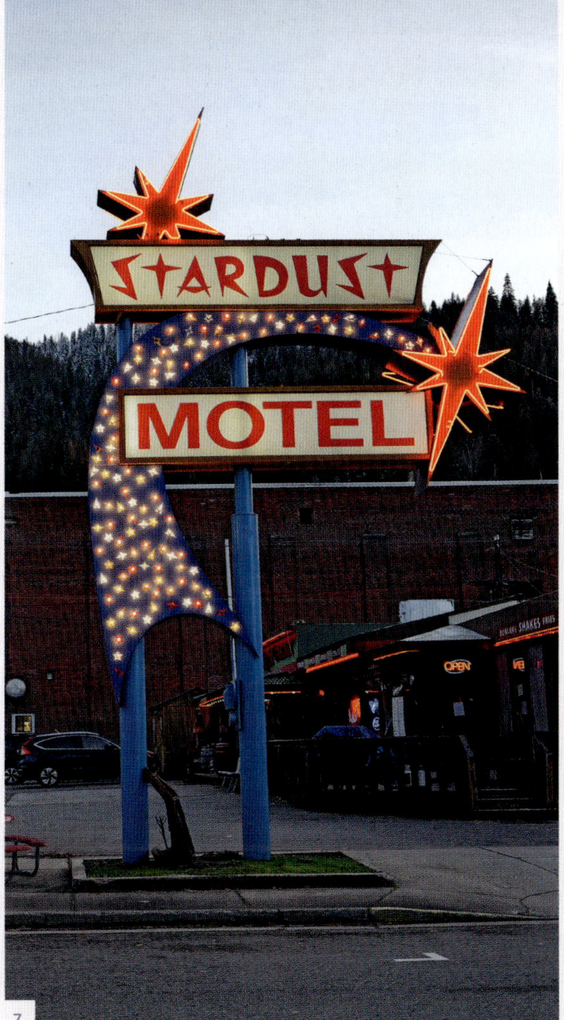

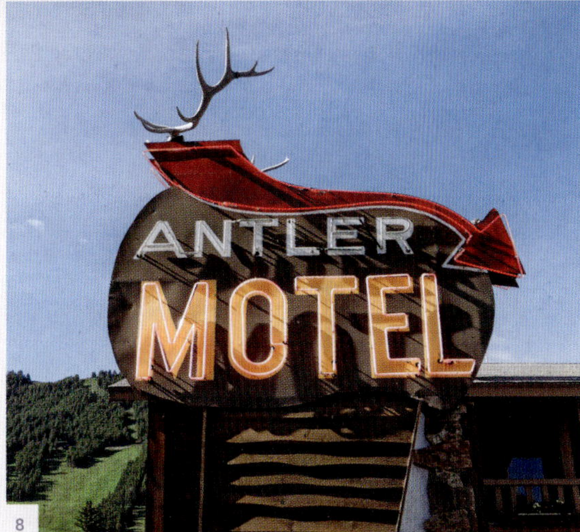

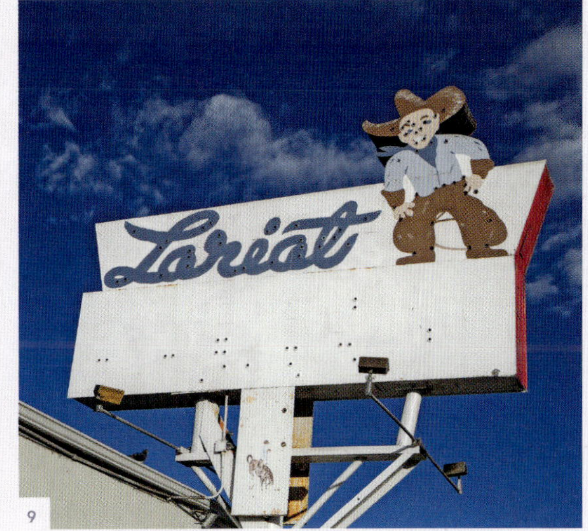

PACIFIC NORTHWEST

OREGON · WASHINGTON

Our adventure will take us across a dizzying array of terrain, from foggy coastal plains to plateaus, mountains, and dense forests! And oh, the stops we'll make, from The Last Blockbuster to a tiny country store so beautiful it should be in a movie.

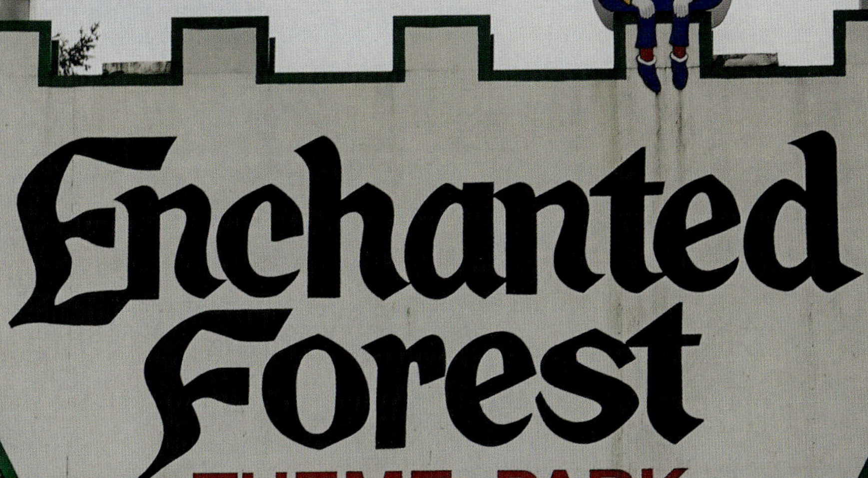

Exit into a fairy tale come to life at the Enchanted Forest in Turner, Oregon.

ROADSIDE QUIRKS

From ghosts to the Goonies and a lot in between, our trip through the Pacific Northwest will be an adventure!

Hello from Aloha, Oregon, and **Harvey Marine** (FIG. 1)! Harvey the rabbit began life as a different species. He was once a Texaco Big Friend statue that was reportedly damaged in the Columbus Day storm of 1962. The Big Friend was left with marine-equipment salesman Edgar Harvey for fiberglass repair, according to Roadside America, but the statue was never picked up. In the 1970s, the Big Friend was converted into a Big Rabbit named "Harvey," and not just because of the family name. Harvey was the name of Jimmy Stewart's invisible rabbit companion in the movie with that title, and Mr. Harvey was a fan of both that film and the luck rabbits are said to bring. Even though Harvey Marine closed after its namesake's death in 2017, Harvey still stands.

Astoria, Oregon's history and natural beauty are an easy sell for the drive here, but as a Gen Xer, I visited because *The Goonies*, the beloved 1985 movie, was filmed all around town. **Lower Columbia Bowl** (FIG. 2)—aka Chunk's bowling alley—is where he smears pizza and a strawberry milkshake on the plate-glass window, enthralled by the Fratelli police chase just outside.

The ***Goonies* House** (FIG. 3), where in the film the Walshes live and which is threatened with being turned into a golf course, sets the Goonies on a mission to save it with a little help from skeletal pirate One-Eyed Willy's long-hidden loot. The house recently changed hands and is now owned by a fan of the film. Data's house is right next door.

1

2

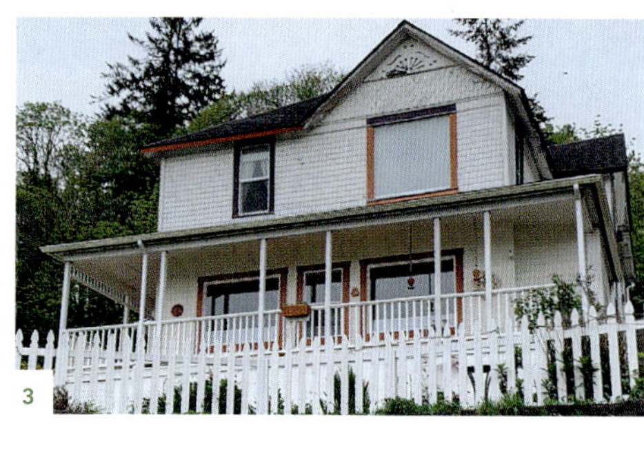

3

The centerpiece of any Astoria tour is the **Oregon Film Museum**, which is housed in the old Clatsop County Jail. *The Goonies* begins right here, with the Fratelli brothers escaping from the lockup, Mama Fratelli at the wheel of the black Jeep Cherokee. Appropriately enough, a Jeep marked with bullet holes can be found outside the prison, just like in the film. Inside, you'll find interactive exhibits and the old jail cells shown in the film, along with a gift shop that proves the *Goonies* phenomenon, just like the Goonies themselves, never says die.

Right across the street is the **Flavel House Museum**, which is briefly seen in the film. It's where Mikey Walsh's dad works as a curator. Farther down the coast, **Haystack Rock** (FIG. 4) in Cannon Beach is a must-visit for the *Goonies* completist—it appears during the Fratelli chase scene and later in the film.

This far down the coast, **The Original Pronto Pup** (FIG. 5) in Rockaway Beach features a massive depiction of a corn dog on the roof (and a tiny corn-dog mechanical ride for the little ones). Well, I should correct myself: As they say around here, "Every Pronto Pup is a corn dog, but not every corn dog is a Pronto Pup." The difference is the batter, which they say adds a savory twist to the flavor profile. Delicious inventions invariably have many fathers, but this restaurant claims to be the progenitor of the corn dog.

The Last Blockbuster (FIG. 6) has become the stuff of legend, the subject of a popular documentary, and one of the bucket-list stops for anyone born before 2005, let's say—and even younger ones curious about how our final-stage analog society was premised on renting physical media, being kind enough to rewind the VHS tapes, and returning them in a timely fashion to avoid opportunistic late fees. But in Bend, Oregon, it's all good memories—and an alarming reminder that what is routine can become a relic in no time. The store has become a media darling and a two-thumbs-up tourist destination since the Netflix documentary came out telling the story of Sandi Harding and her quixotic efforts to keep the shelves stocked, the lights on, and the creaky, original Blockbuster corporate computers running.

The night I was there, the place was busy with customers actually renting movies. They likely have the same streaming services we do; they can probably watch the movie they were renting on the phone in their pockets. But yet, here they were. There were once over nine thousand Blockbusters, but this is the last place on earth where you can make it a Blockbuster night.

On a trip through Oregon, you'd be wise to wind up in **Shaniko**, a proper ghost town set on a sagebrush-dotted landscape, with stirring vistas of purple mountain majesty on the horizon. The

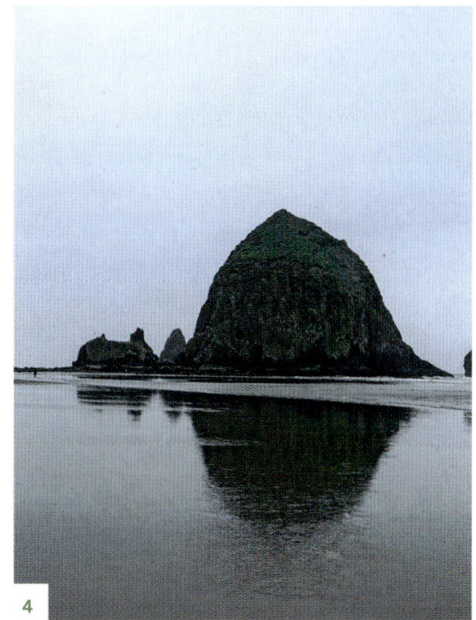

4

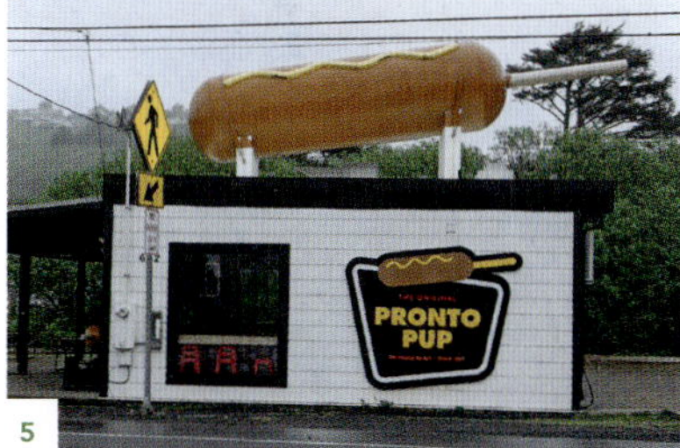

5

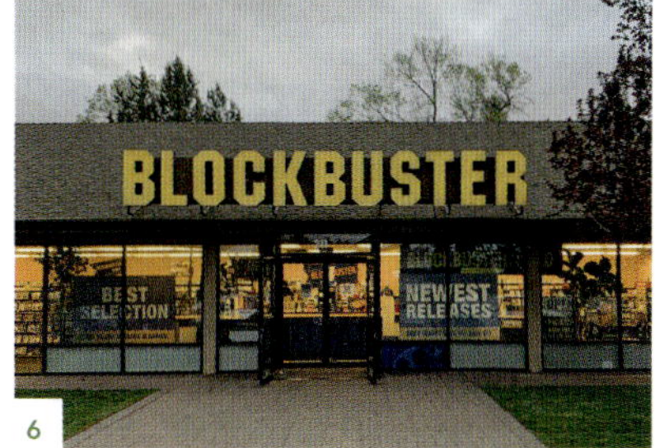

6

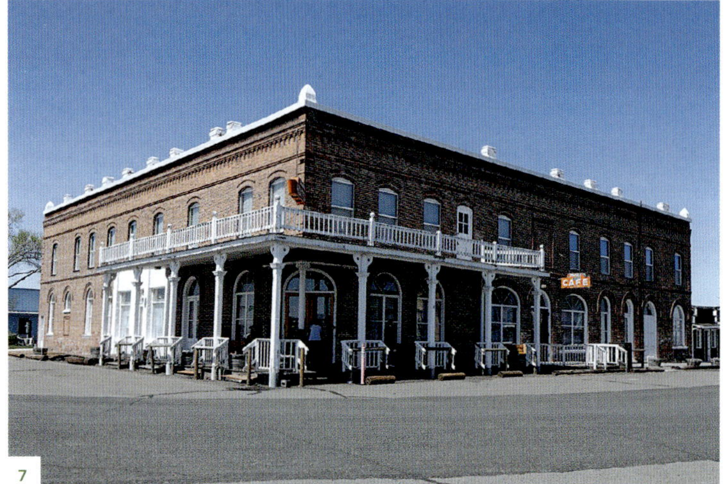

7

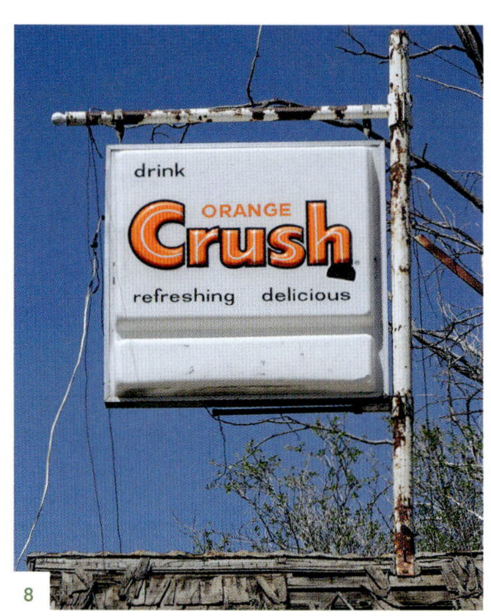

8

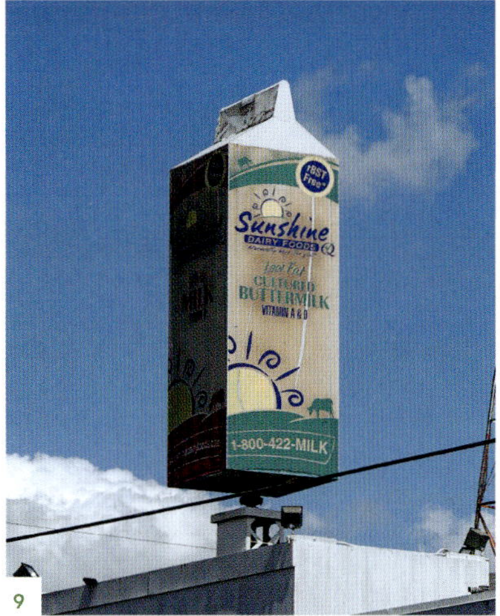

9

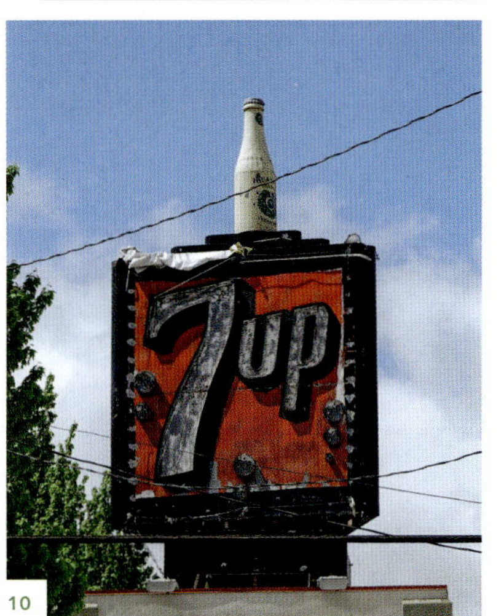

10

heart of the town is the **Shaniko Hotel** (FIG. 7). It recently reopened for overnight stays for the first time in decades.

Built by the Columbia Southern Railway, which had its terminus here, the hotel is replete with gilded-age grandeur, a reminder of when this town was thriving as a center of wool processing. Now it's populated by a few dozen hearty souls—and some ghosts, including a ball-playing child named Amelia. All are outnumbered by tourists visiting on occasions like Shaniko Days, which celebrated its fiftieth anniversary in 2024, a reminder that folks are determined to keep Shaniko from fading away.

In the blink-and-you'll-miss-it community of Kent is an old service station that I call the **Crush Barn** (FIG. 8). Yes, I have a crush on it, but of course I'm smitten especially by the old privilege sign for Crush orange soda. It's such a bright pop of Madison Avenue glamour in one of America's most remote places. Stickers on the old gas pumps indicate they were last inspected in the mid-1970s. Down the road there is also a shuttered building, featuring a Pepsi privilege sign, that once sold barbecue.

Big-food adventures continue with a giant quart of milk at the old **Sunshine Dairy** (FIG. 9) in Portland.

At the **Portland Bottling Company** (FIG. 10), a lovely, bubbly, art deco 7Up sign features a bottle on top, but in 2010, the brand was switched to the Guayaki Yerba Mate drink. Call it the un-Uncola. The sign reportedly rotated until the Columbus Day storm of 1962, which also damaged the statue that would become Harvey (see page 268).

Portland's most iconic sign—and the veritable symbol of the city—is the **Portland Oregon** scaffold sign (FIG. 11), capturing a white stag in frozen leap. Its majesty can be enjoyed from a number of vantage points, but the perspective from the Burnside Bridge is perhaps my favorite. The sign has seen a lot of change since its installation in 1940. It promoted a sugar company, White Satin, with an animation of sugar filling the outline of the state of Oregon. A later tenant, the White Stag apparel company, added the deer to the sign, and starting in 1959, the deer's nose was lit up, Rudolph-style, for the holidays. After another long stretch of saying "Made In Oregon," the latest change happened in 2010, when the city bought the sign from longtime owner Ramsay Signs, which had built it, and the sign was given its present verbiage—Portland Oregon. Despite the growing allure of LED, the sign is still lit by neon and incandescent bulbs, which generate a warmth you can feel—in your heart—while standing way down on the ground.

A good four hours or so to the south, in **Grants Pass, Oregon** (FIG. 12), a grand sign welcomes you, and sums up its longtime selling point. On July 20, 2020, the city threw a party for the sign (which is actually a replica of the original), which turned one hundred on that day. More than a century ago, John Hampshire was so taken by the fair weather that he came up with the slogan, had the sign made, and even paid for it. The city took its climate so seriously that the *Grants Pass Daily Courier* in 1919 declared daily above the masthead: "It's The Climate—We're Telling The World—Come and Enjoy It."

Around here, cavemen are serious business. The Caveman Club, founded in 1922, is a local booster group inspired by the famous Oregon Caves National Monument nearby, which became accessible by road that same year. Its members over the years have indulged in good-natured public shenanigans in caveman attire, all to promote the region.

The Caveman (FIG. 13)—capital *C* to show all due respect—is a local folk hero, and this big guy has been ready to go clubbing since 1971 in downtown Grants Pass. A brother of Muffler Men everywhere, the Caveman was manufactured by the same firm, International Fiberglass, and he's dealt with his share of challenges: He was set ablaze in 2004 and a decade later was the subject of a campaign to banish him for the offense of being a brutal blight on the community. A *Wall Street Journal* reporter pointed out that nearby Ashland has the Shakespeare Festival, and some here felt stuck with a knuckle-dragging Neanderthal as their official town greeter off Interstate 5.

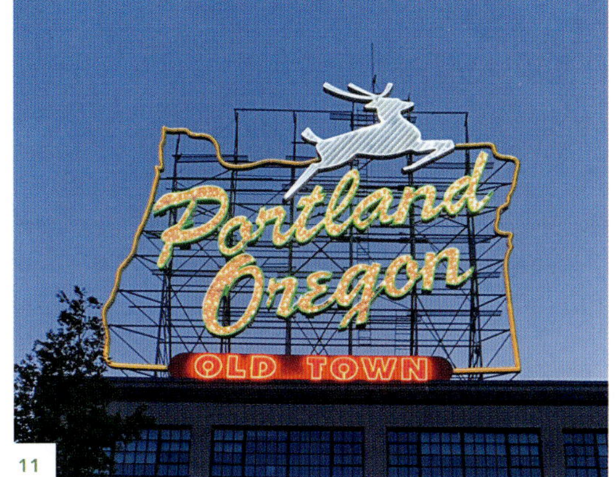

11

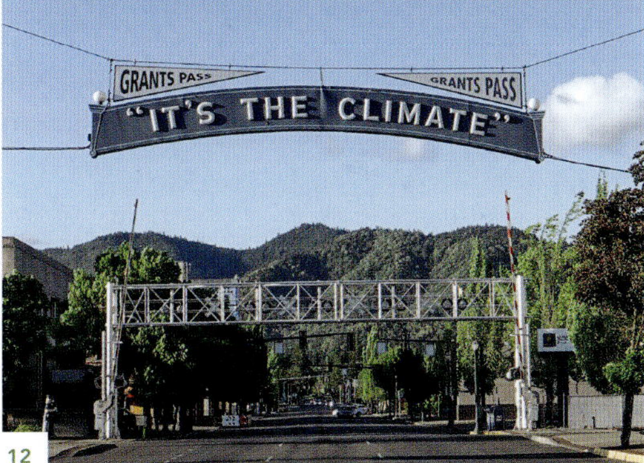

12

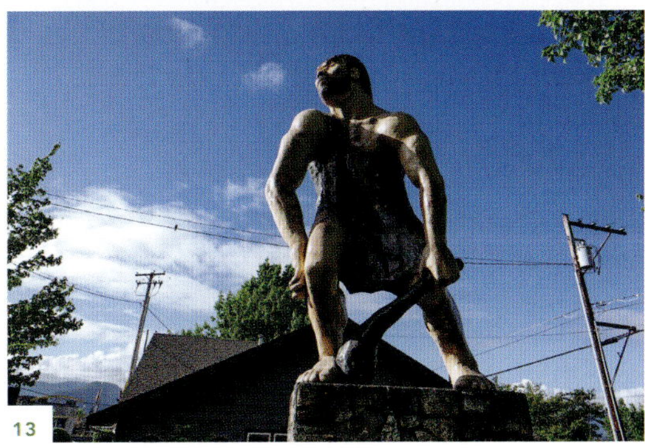
13

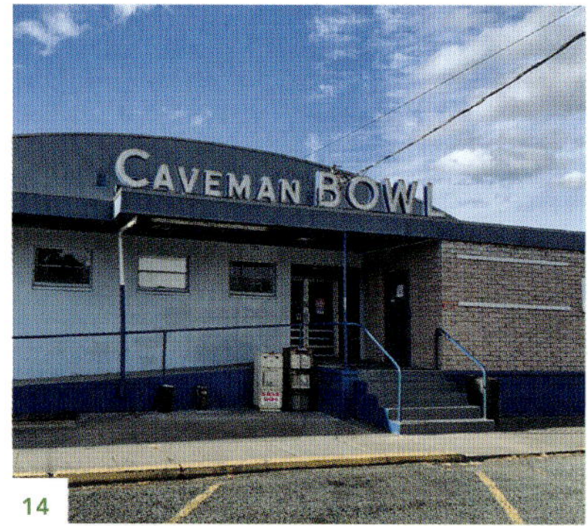

14

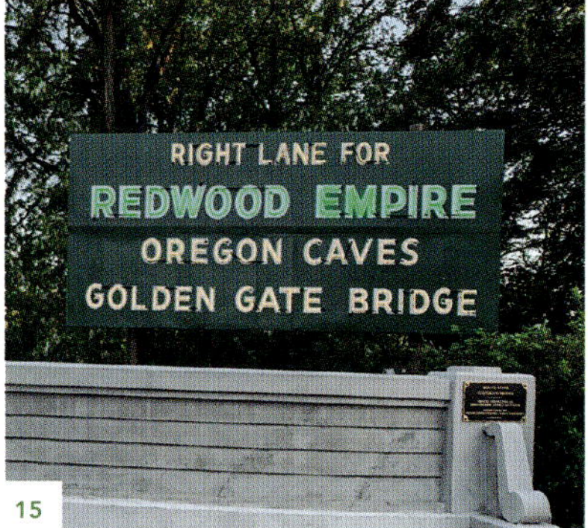

15

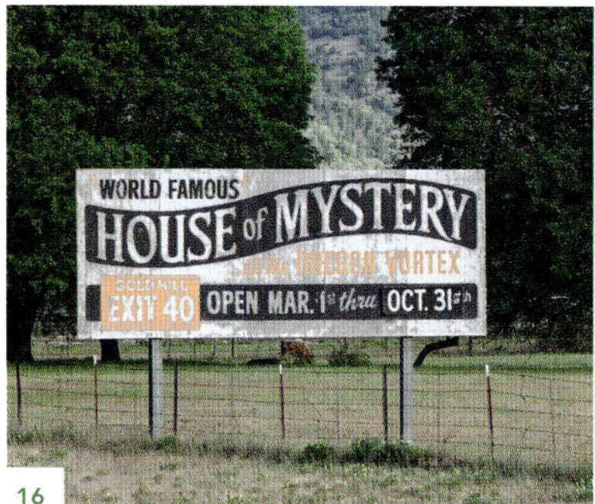

16

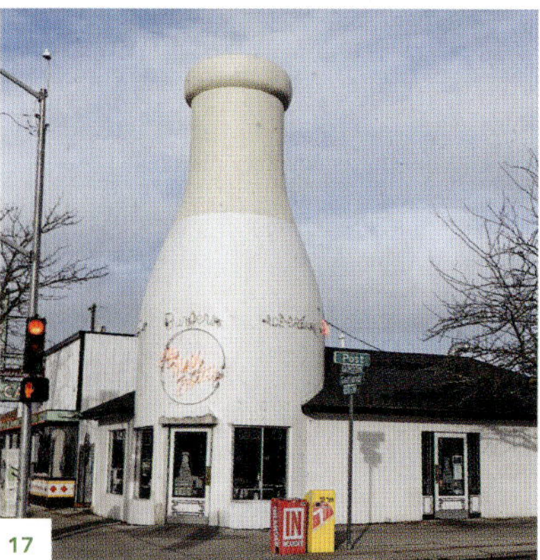
17

Even if they did succeed one day in banishing him, the Caveman's legacy would be hard to erase. Businesses in this town see him as a good hook, like **Caveman Bowl** (FIG. 14), around since the days when folks smoked Kent cigarettes inside, as the old stickers in the window remind us. (Those *were* prehistoric times!)

Another sign that hearkens to a simpler time says **Redwood Empire** (FIG. 15) in bright green neon and directs people from Grants Pass, Oregon, to the Oregon Caves and the Golden Gate Bridge, some 500 miles south. The sign's simple 1941 sincerity is redolent of early road trips to the newly accessible wonders along Northern California's fertile coastline, when travelers ambled down the hushed splendor of the Avenue of Giants, cradled by a canopy of redwoods millennia in the making, and ended at The Golden Gate Bridge, that modern marvel of 1937. The neon sign was refurbished in 2019 at great cost, after officials decided it had to be preserved just as it was.

Surely a number of tourists to the Oregon Caves have found themselves drawn into the **Oregon Vortex** and its **House of Mystery** (FIG. 16), which opened in 1930. Gravity-hill illusions are eternally fascinating, as are the lore and claims of supernatural intervention that prance around them (see Spook Hill on page 102 for another example).

We leave Oregon for a spot of milk in Spokane, Washington, at **Mary Lou's Milk Bottle** (FIG. 17). Long before it was called that, this building was an outpost of the Benewah Creamery. On December 6, 1934, Benewah and its headline-grabbing owner, Paul E. Newport, revealed an early Christmas gift for the people of Spokane: The popular dairy would be opening six stores shaped like gigantic milk bottles—38 feet tall and 15 feet in diameter, at a cost of $3,700 a pop. The bottles would purvey milk, cheese, butter, and other products. By most accounts, only two were constructed, including this one in Spokane's Garland District, which opened in February 1935, equipped with the "latest word in refrigeration." The 1930s were the zenith of roadside-architectural adventurism—big ducks, coffeepots, teakettles—and having a building reflect the product a business sold was a way to get the attention of newspaper editors and motorists alike. Newport also wanted to get kids to take note, telling the *Spokane Daily Chronicle* in March 1935 that he believed "the attention of children can be focussed upon milk by presenting it in a form that interests them."

The creamery closed by the 1970s, and rather than meet the bulldozer, the milk bottle served as a secondhand shop for a spell. It later became an ice-cream parlor and today houses Mary Lou's

Milk Bottle, noted for its comfort food and delicious milkshakes. This milk bottle has a twin in Spokane that is now home to the **Blue Door Theatre** (FIG. 18).

Next, hop on Interstate 90 and hightail it to Tacoma, Washington, to find **Bob's Java Jive** (FIG. 19). A form-follows-function cousin of the Coffee Pot and World's Largest Teapot along the Lincoln Highway (see pages 12 and 135), Bob's Java Jive took that name in 1955, when Bob and Lylabell Radonich bought the whimsical structure and turned it into a music venue. It may be heretical to say, but this coffeepot sure looks like a teapot.

According to most accounts, it opened in 1927 and was a drive-in restaurant—said to be the first of its kind in Puget Sound—and was called the Coffee Pot Restaurant for a spell, serving percolated coffee (of course) and "delicious hamburger sandwiches," according to newspaper ads from the 1930s. The Radoniches turned the building into an iconic part of the Pacific Northwest music scene. They also infused it with distinct character, giving it a jungle-tiki theme and, for a time, two caged chimpanzees that went by the names Java and Jive. Bob's Java Jive is now on the National Register of Historic Places.

The first **Perky's Espresso** opened in 1995, a late but welcome entrant in the mimetic architecture club. The buildings were shaped like coffeepots. This location, in Auburn, Washington (FIG. 20), remains as photogenic as ever. But for many, the attraction here is the baristas, who dress in bikinis, as it's now an outpost of the **Cowgirl Espresso** chain. When that chain was new, in the aughts, it got a flood of coverage for its "sexpresso" approach to reeling in customers.

Okay, can we finally see a big teapot? Yes! Behold the **Teapot Dome gasoline station** (FIG. 21) in Zillah, Washington. The station was built and opened in 1922 by Jack Ainsworth, who wanted to memorialize the biggest political scandal of his day in the form of a functioning gas station.

A little context is needed: The Teapot Dome scandal was the Watergate crisis of its day, consuming the nation in political intrigue. In this case, President Warren Harding's administration was in hot water. His secretary of the interior, Albert Fall, had leased government-owned petroleum reserve sites to two well-known oilmen, and one of the sites was at Teapot Dome in Wyoming. In exchange for his governmental largesse, Fall was showered with financial gifts and a no-interest loan that made him a rich man—and he didn't hide his windfall very well. (They never do.) The whole matter blew up like an overheated teapot, and Fall went to prison.

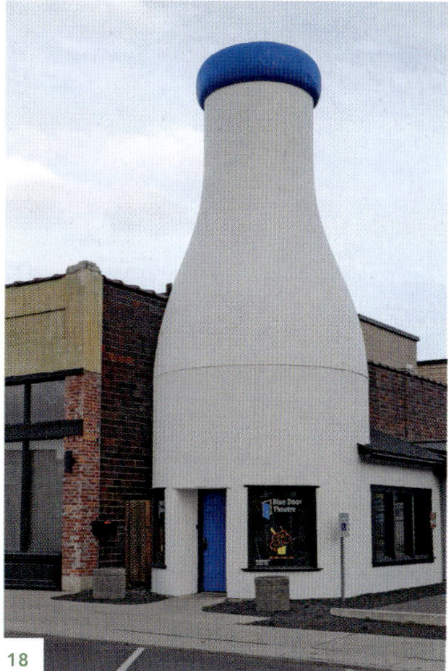

18

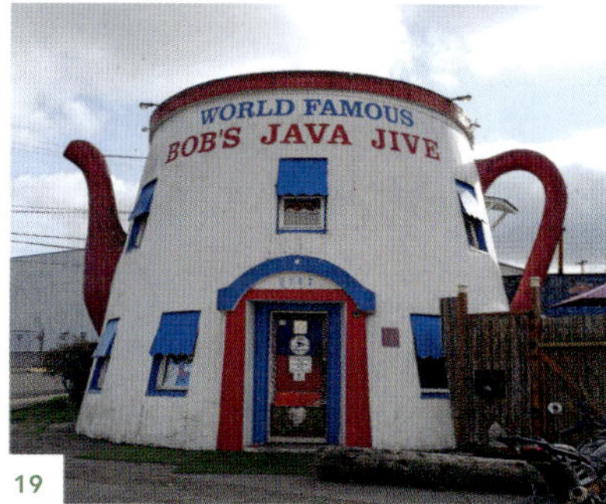

19

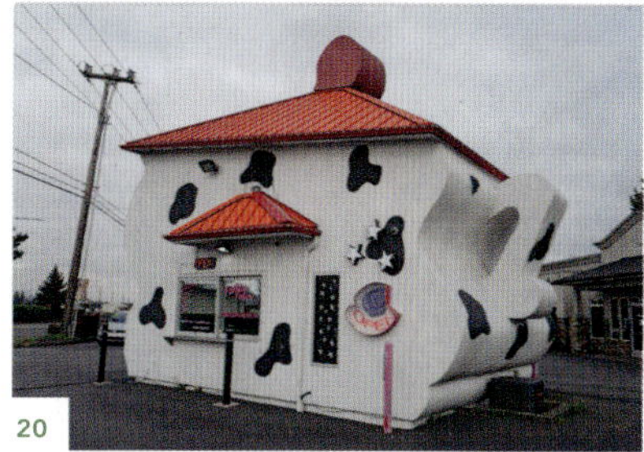

20

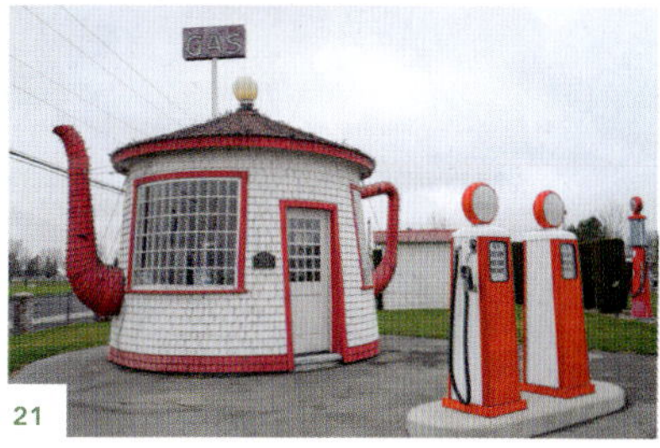

21

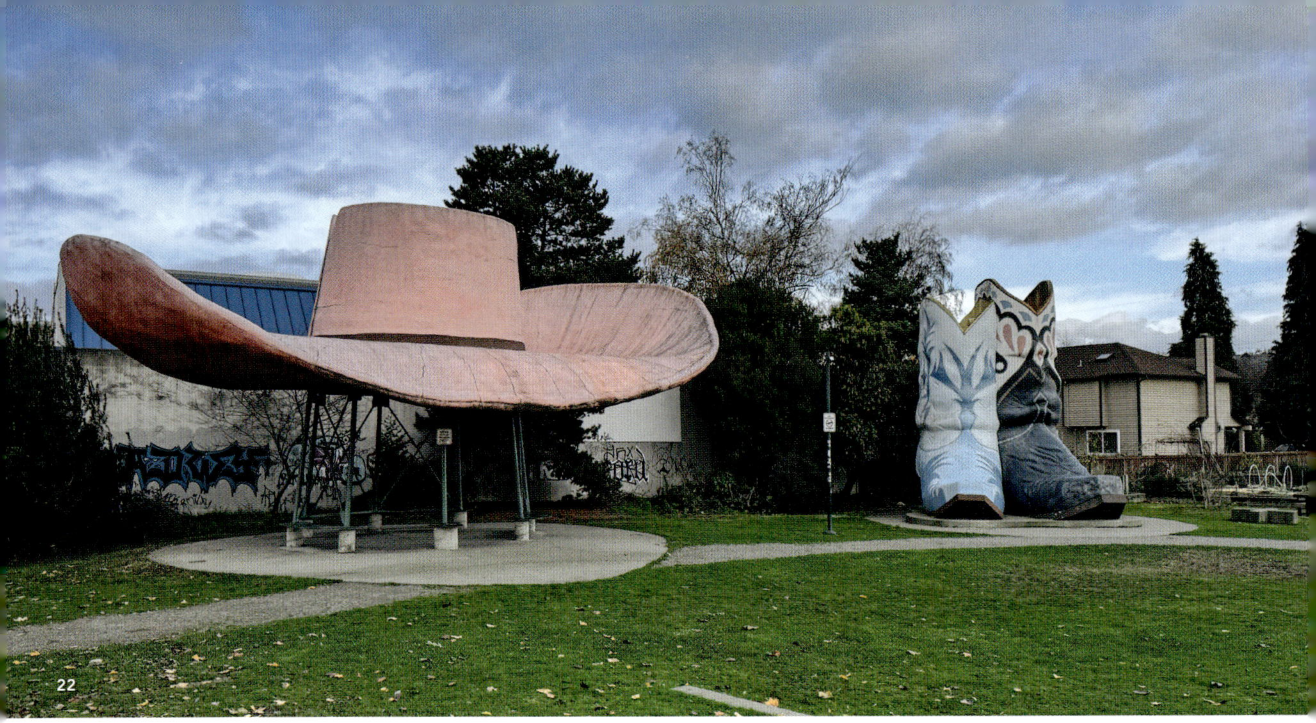

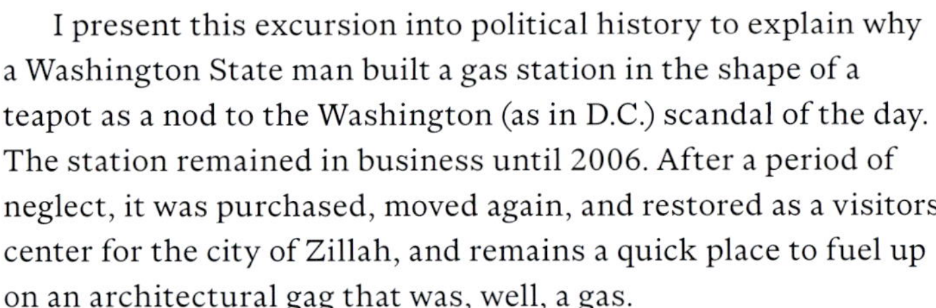

22

▸▸▸ Pull Over!

Archie McPhee, a Seattle curiosity shop founded in 1983, is full of wacky collectibles. It's also home to the World's Largest Rubber Chicken, on display at the Rubber Chicken Museum.

Smaller but no less quirky is **Ye Old Curiosity Shop**, opened in 1899 and still in the same family.

Ballyhoo Curiosity Shop describes itself as a cross "between a natural history museum and an antique store," and has a *Jumanji* feel.

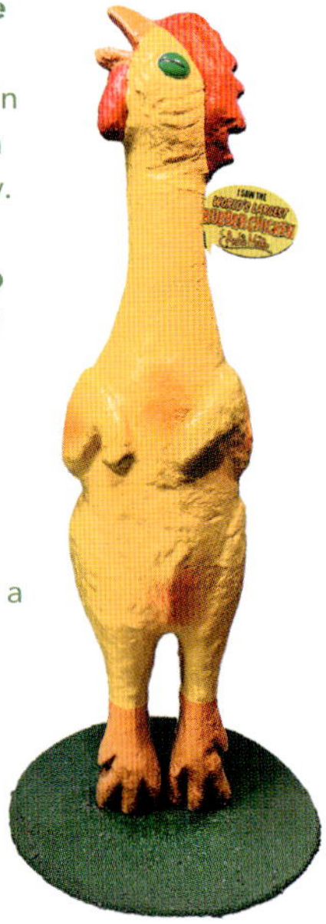

I present this excursion into political history to explain why a Washington State man built a gas station in the shape of a teapot as a nod to the Washington (as in D.C.) scandal of the day. The station remained in business until 2006. After a period of neglect, it was purchased, moved again, and restored as a visitors center for the city of Zillah, and remains a quick place to fuel up on an architectural gag that was, well, a gas.

From gasoline from a teapot to gasoline from a big Western hat, it must mean we're at **Hat 'n' Boots Park** (FIG. 22) in the Georgetown neighborhood of Seattle, which once did service as a gas station, and was famous enough to warrant a postcard, which was shown in the opening of 1983's film *National Lampoon's Vacation*. Built in 1954, Hat 'n' Boots was designed as the centerpiece of a planned Western-themed shopping center and was billed as the largest hat and boots in the world. The hat concealed the store, and the boots contained the restrooms. Popular though it was, the overall development never jelled; the station closed in 1988 and fell into disrepair until locals rallied to save the sculptures in the late 1990s when the site was threatened with development. Today, they are in **Oxbow Park**. You'll have to fuel up your car elsewhere.

And finally, a giant building shaped like a jug that once offered gasoline. The **Sandy Jug** has been a Portland fixture on Sandy Boulevard since 1929. It has housed a lunch counter and, for a long stretch, was home to an adult-entertainment club. Today, it's run by Warren Boothby and Marcus Archambeault, described

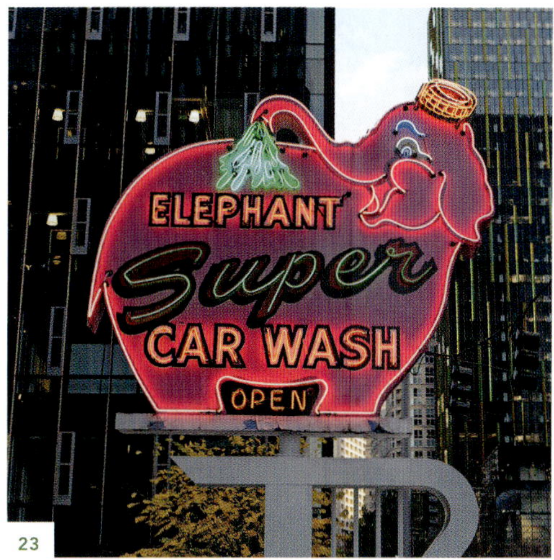

23

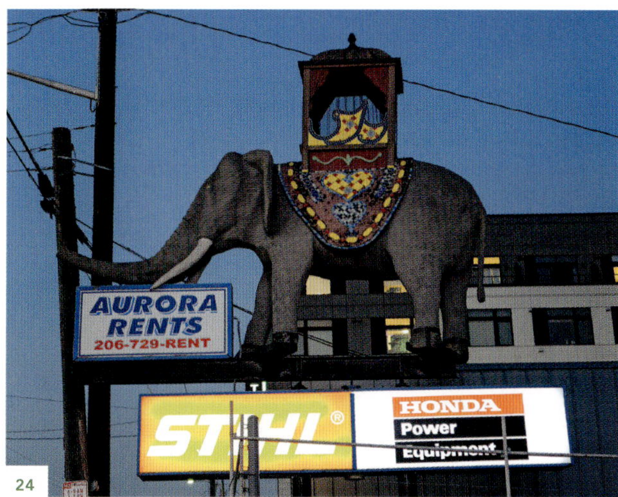

24

by the *Oregonian* as "bar revivalists" who've sensitively reinvigorated legacy taverns, preserving and highlighting historic character while updating what needs attention (see the Sandy Hut on page 279).

When a car needs a wash in the Seattle region, **Elephant Car Wash** (FIG. 23) and its many locations have been at your service since the 1950s. The neon sign/mascot is an icon in this town, designed by Beatrice Haverfield, who is known as Seattle's "Queen of Neon." Examples of the sign survive at locations in the Puget Sound area, but the iconic location in downtown Seattle closed in 2021. The larger of the two signs there, which rotated, was donated to the **Museum of History and Industry**, and the smaller one is just a few blocks from its original location, now on Amazon's campus. (See page 304 for a relative in Rancho Mirage, California.)

Long before the first Elephant Car Wash opened in the 1950s, Seattle already had a famous elephant. The rooftop-perched concrete pachyderm, today sitting atop a business called **Aurora Rents** (FIG. 24), an equipment-rental company, was constructed during the Great Depression for a tile store as a giant marketing tool, and you can still see evidence of the shop's handiwork on the statue—in particular the ornate howdah, or covered seat.

Midcentury icons don't come much bigger than the beloved **Space Needle**, constructed for the city's 1962 World's Fair. Out in Renton, Washington, however, is a Space Needle few see, the **U-Haul Space Needle** (FIG. 25) at the U-Haul store. (In Portland, Oregon, U-Haul's retail birthplace is marked with a sign.)

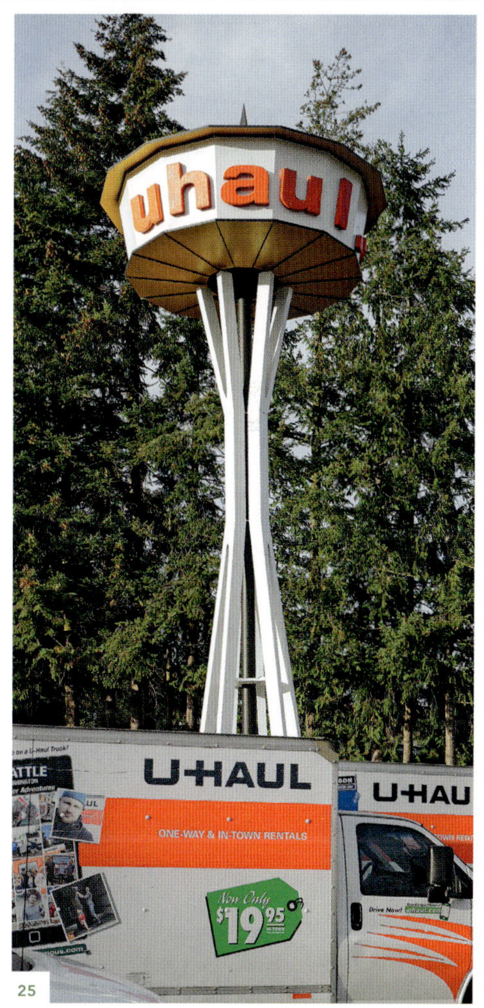

25

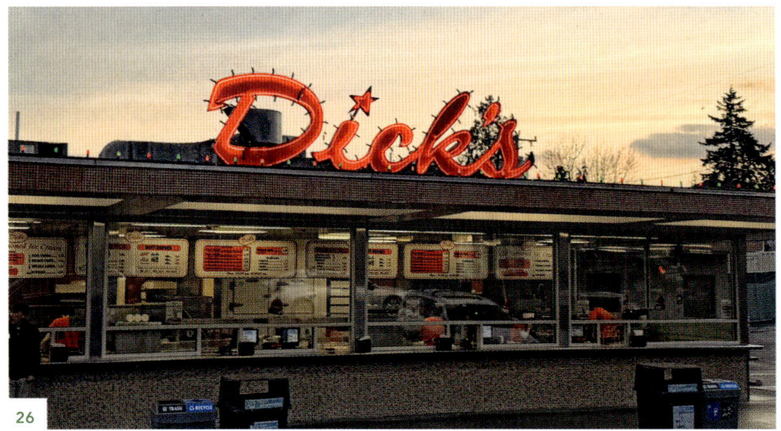

26

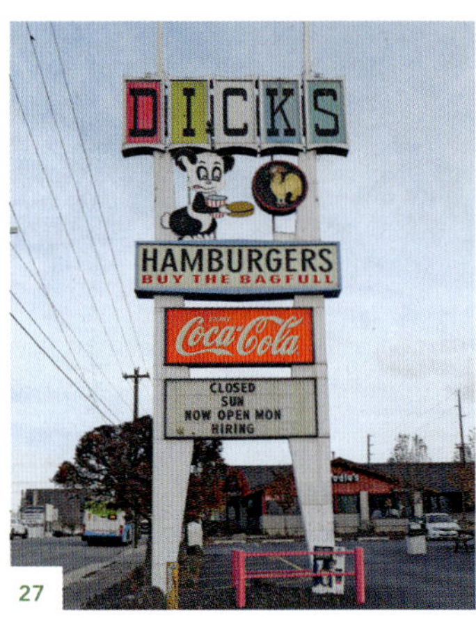

27

ROADSIDE EATS

With stops at countless drive-ins—as well as pizza and Chinese food thrown in—we just won't worry too much about calories. But hey, it's history that we're really after here, and there's no shortage of it.

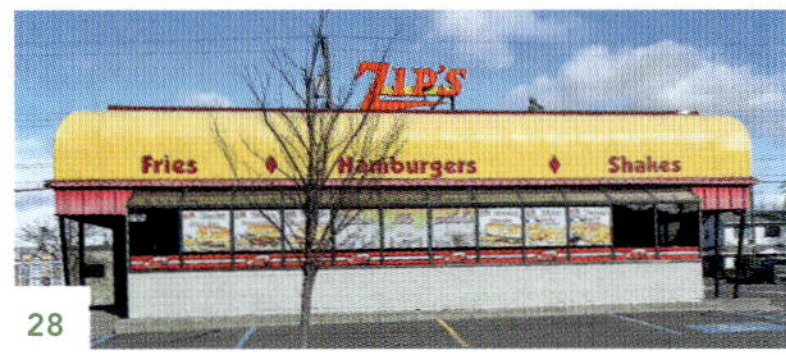

28

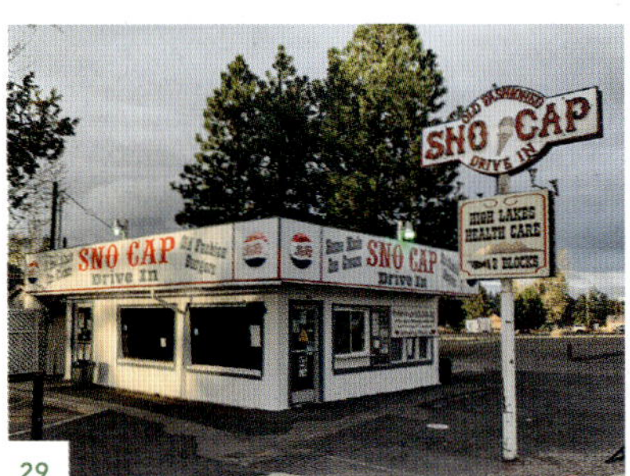

29

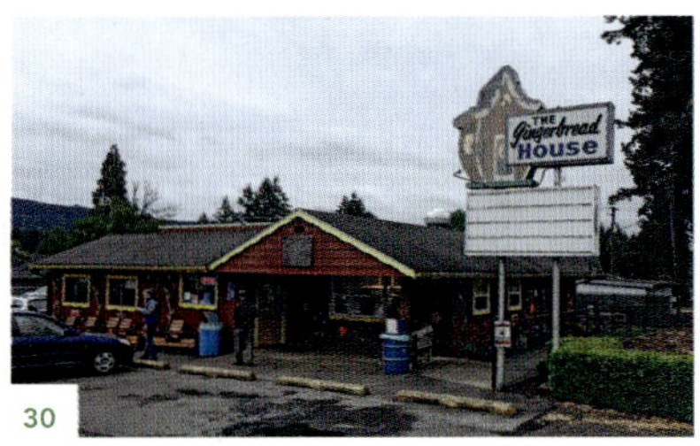

30

Welcome to the "Tale of Two Dick's." We begin in Seattle, where **Dick's Drive-In** (FIG. 26) opened in 1954, proved to be a hit, and spread throughout the region. Its slogan? "Eat a bag of Dick's." No carhops here. You'd walk up to the store, place your order, and munch while on the premises or take it home. Self-service, as they called the concept then.

Across the state, a drive-in named Kirk's Self Service in Spokane, selling 19-cent burgers, opened the same year with a very similar concept. By 1958, it rebranded as Panda Self-Service Drive-In (and developed into a tiny local chain) until switching its name to **Dick's Hamburgers** (FIG. 27) in the 1960s. It ditched the Panda name but not the mascot. Its slogan since day one? "Hamburgers by the bagful."

There is perpetual confusion in Washington State over the "two Dick's": Are they related? Was one inspired by the other? The answer appears to be no. At Dick's of Seattle, the menu is simpler, by design: hamburgers, fries, soda, milkshakes. At Dick's in Spokane, the menu is more extensive and has been since the 1950s. They are both roadside delights and visual feasts.

Zip's (FIG. 28) is a small chain in Spokane that dates to 1953 and serves hamburgers, fish, and other fried menu mainstays. The Zip in question was Robert "Zip" Zuber, and they've long prided themselves on their zippy service.

Sno Cap Drive In (FIG. 29) in Sisters, Oregon, is a family-owned road-food stand that has been here since 1952. Sno Cap is an icon, proven by the long lines you'll often find outside. Its name plays off the snowy caps of the volcanic Three Sisters mountains off in the distance.

In 2004, when McDonald's was coming to town, there was a revolt among the gentry. A newspaper reporter visited Sno Cap, and the co-owner gave a decidedly chill response, saying that McDonald's are everywhere, but a hometown spot with homemade ice cream like Sno Cap can't be found in every town.

That was then. The two have peacefully coexisted ever since. **McDonald's** in Sisters hides behind an Old West storefront like much of this charming community, which leans hard into the frontier theme for fun and profit.

The Gingerbread House (FIG. 30) in Mehama, Oregon, has been a chalet of comfort food since 1953. It's the perfect stop on the way along the Santiam Highway, and these days, it represents a miracle, having survived a devastating forest fire in 2020 that wiped out the nearby community of Detroit.

Pietro's (FIG. 31) in Milwaukie, Oregon, looks like an old-timey local pizza joint from the time they were called "parlors." The first location opened in Longview, Washington, in 1957, and it blossomed into a Pacific Northwest chain, scooped up by the Campbell Soup Company, a California restaurant consortium, and finally the owners of BJ's Brewhouse. The chain at one point had almost a hundred locations before returning to its roots—a local chain with games for the kids, beer for the adults, and yummy thin-crust pizza for all. Now there are only three locations.

When the sign at **Ming Wah** (FIG. 32), a Chinese restaurant in Spokane, Washington, collapsed in 2020, the owner was determined to restore it. And so were many in Spokane, especially artist Chris Bovey, who crowdsourced so much money for its restoration that the insurance was able to cover the balance, according to the *Spokesman-Review*. "I think there is a value in a sign being a landmark, instead of just a box sign, you know the Ming Wah sign and you've probably grown up with it," Bovey told the paper. Exactly.

The Republic Cafe and Ming Lounge (FIG. 33) is surely one of Portland's oldest restaurants, 1922 often cited as its birth year. For all those years, the Mui family have been owners of this institution in Portland's Old Town neighborhood. Its dining room and red-light cocktail lounge are legendary noirish getaways.

The Wishing Well (FIG. 34), which dates to the late 1940s, was once a swinging nightclub operated by Herman DeVault, where Willie Nelson, early in his career, is said to have performed.

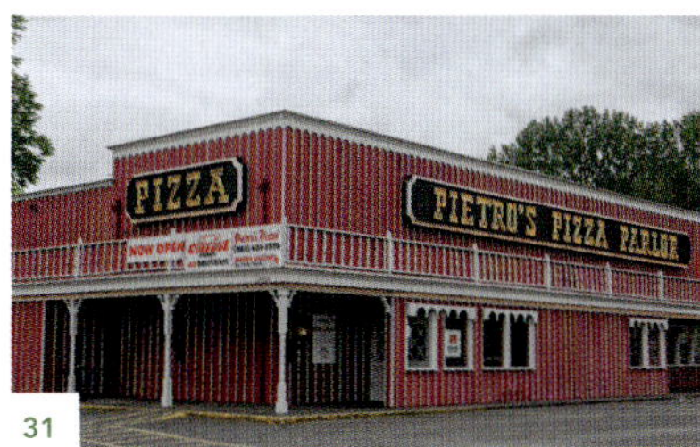

31

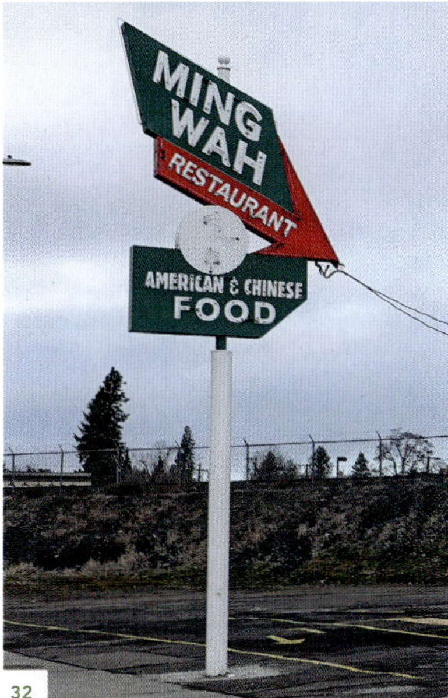

32

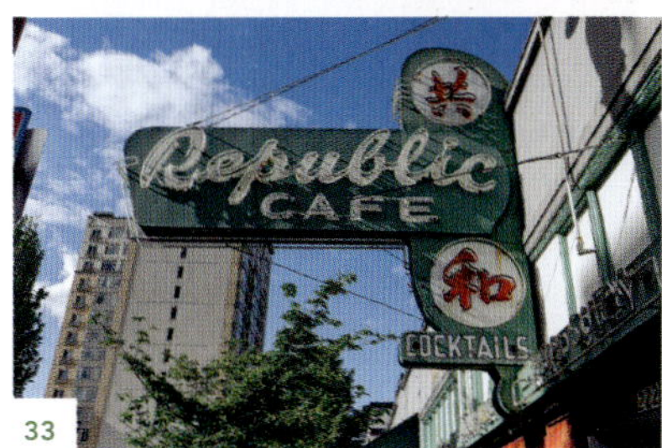

33

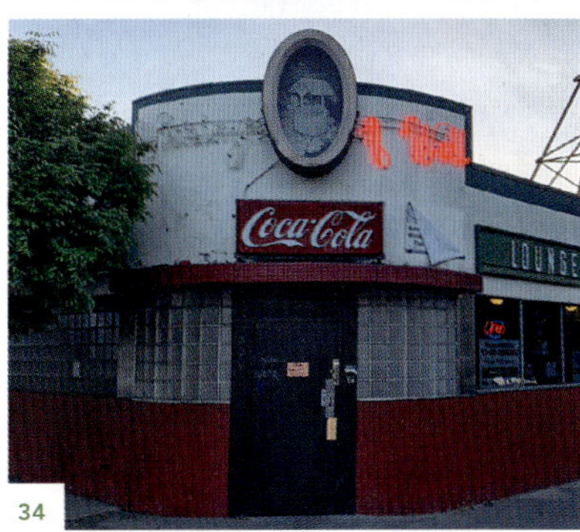

34

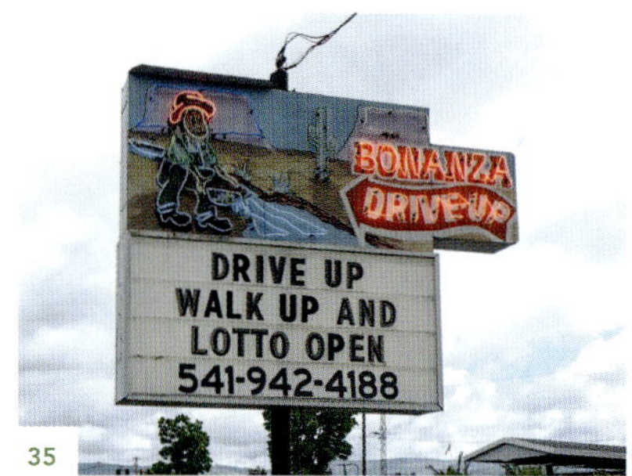

35

The Wishing Well has long been renowned for its Chinese food from the time DeVault hired Cedric Yen Lee, a well-regarded Chinatown chef, to run the kitchen, according to Lee's obit. By 1972, Lee owned the place, and it remains today a beloved part of classic Portland.

In Cottage Grove, Oregon, **Bonanza Drive-Up** (FIG. 35) has been open since 1949, and its burger made a *Wall Street Journal* roundup of America's best burger places. The article recommends "The Original."

Nick's Famous Coney Island in Portland has been a reliable spot for hot dogs since 1935, and you can chase down your chili-and-onion wiener with some brews at its historic counter.

With a name like **Pepp'rmint Stick Drive-In** (FIG. 36), you know you are in for a trip. From the striped mansard roof to the giant neon Pepsi privilege sign featuring the 1970s–80s logo, the Pepp'rmint Stick has been keeping tummies content in Union Gap, Washington, since 1948. Go big and have a half-pound burger and the colossal fries. If you overdo it, remind yourself that peppermint is said to help with indigestion.

The **Poodle Dog**'s (FIG. 37) origin story starts with two buddies, Rocco "Mac" Manza and E. J. "Jimmy" Zarelli, ambitious boys from Tacoma who got together in 1933 to open a roadside restaurant, a conduit to riches for many in those years of burgeoning automobile use. They called it the Poodle Dog, impressed by the Old Poodle Dog, a historic and high-end French restaurant in San Francisco.

Within five years, the restaurant had been greatly expanded and renovated, and a mere *year* after opening, they unveiled a swank ballroom next door, the Century Room. It attracted the biggest names of the Big Band era, including Tommy Dorsey and Duke Ellington. The ballroom is long gone, but touches of class like the Pup Room tavern remain.

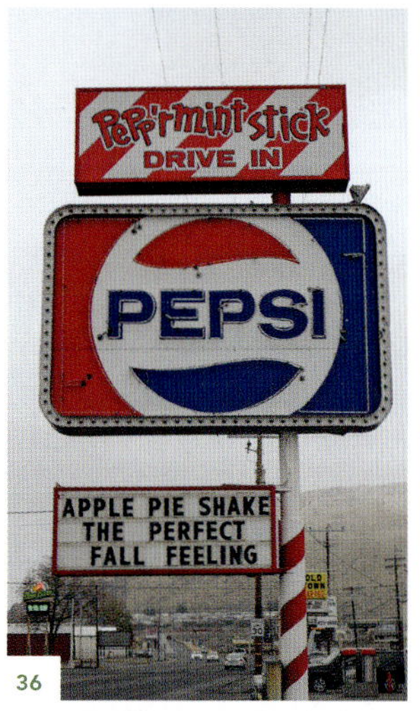

36

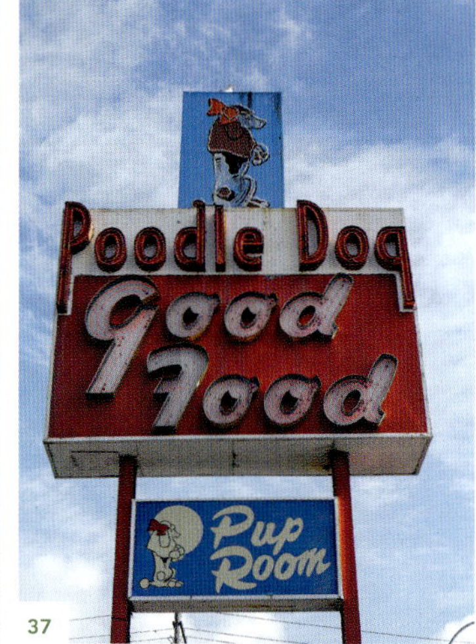

37

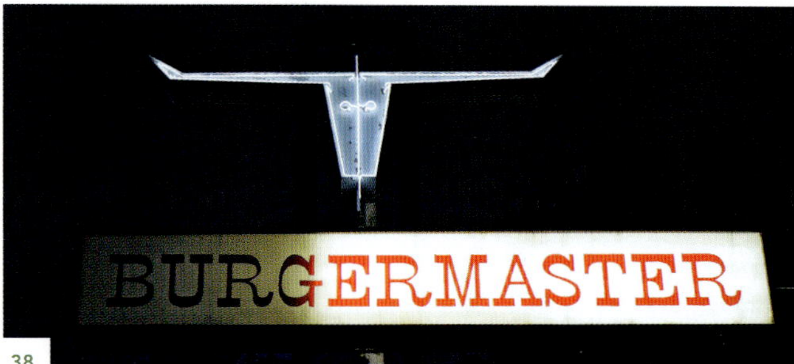

38

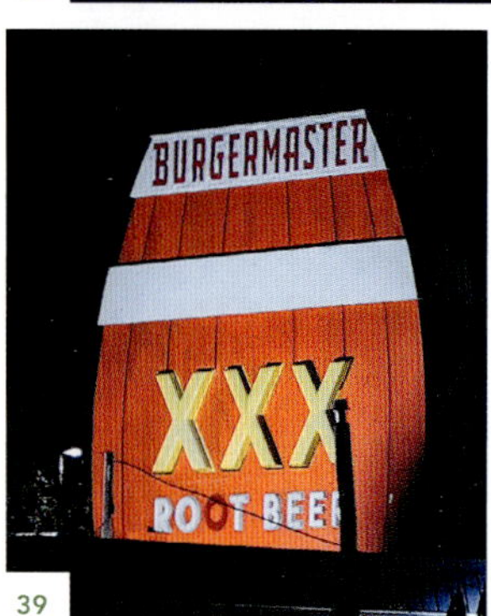

39

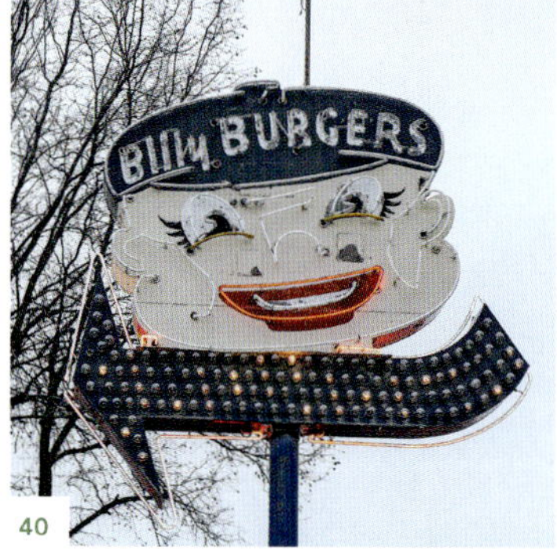

40

Burgermaster (FIG. 38) has been a Seattle road-food standard since 1952 and is still in the family of founder Phil Jensen. The burgers, of course, are revered, but other menu "masters" like the "Turkeymaster" have their devotees, too. The chain, which began serving grass-fed beef in 2004, was expanding to a fifth location at this writing, taking over the sadly shuttered Triple XXX Rootbeer Drive-In in Issaquah, keeping the iconic barrel-shaped facade (FIG. 39).

The **Billy Burgers** (FIG. 40) sign in Wilbur, Washington, is one of the most adorable you'll see in this book. The cherubic face was inspired by the infant son of the restaurant founders, Bill and Alice Bell. Billy Burgers, for which construction began in 1954, is so important in this small town that it's impossible to think of Wilbur, tucked along the wheat fields along rural Highway 2, without it.

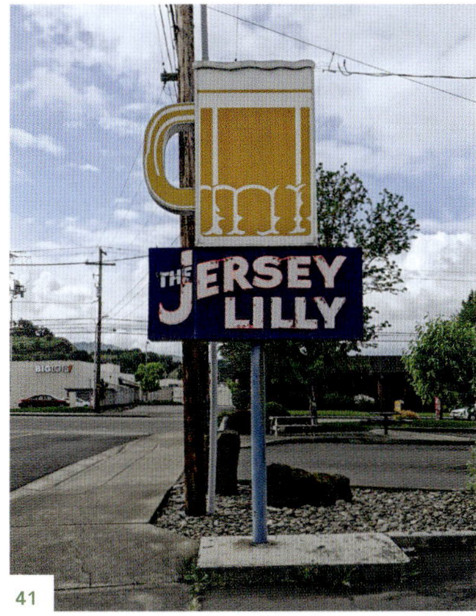

41

CHEERS!

What do Madonna, Bigfoot, and Judge Roy Bean have in common? Not much, except they ended up in this section. I'll drink to that!

The Jersey Lilly's sign (FIG. 41) promises beer—and the name promises a backstory. Texas Justice of the Peace Roy Bean ran his courtroom out of his saloon. That saloon was named after Lillie Langtry, the British actress who was the apple of Bean's eye and known as the Jersey Lilly. Saloons seeking to embrace Old West atmosphere have assumed the Jersey Lilly nickname, and a fine example is in Rosenburg, Oregon—an ode to the lasting power of unrequited love.

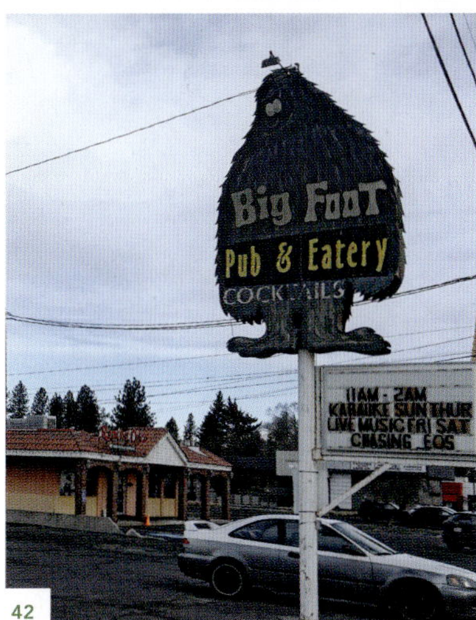

42

The Bigfoot Pub & Eatery (FIG. 42) in Spokane may be the closest you ever get to seeing old Sasquatch, at least if you stay out of the woods here. This bar has been here since 1972 and prides itself on its divey ways. Madonna fans might want to stop by to see a filming location for her 1985 flick, *Vision Quest*.

The Sandy Hut (FIG. 43) has stood the test of time for more than a century. It recently was purchased by Warren Boothby and Marcus Archambeault, the loving curators of historic Portland bars whom we met at the Sandy Jug (see page 274).

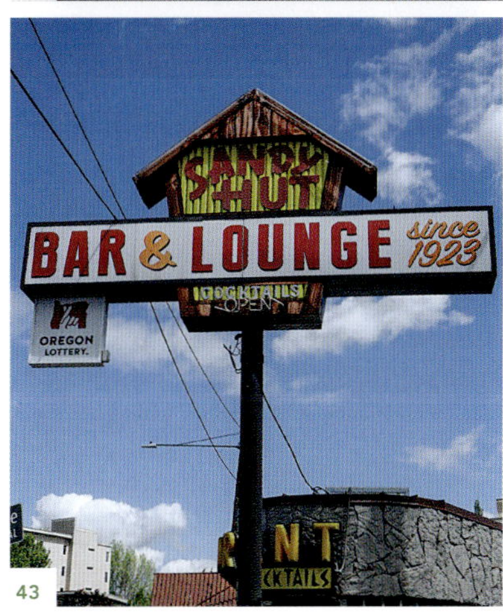

43

MAINSTAYS OF MAIN STREET

We're going to explore a lot of local life here, mostly mom-and-pops that left an impact on this region. And you may even begin to feel like a local as you learn about shops whose commercials have been airing for decades.

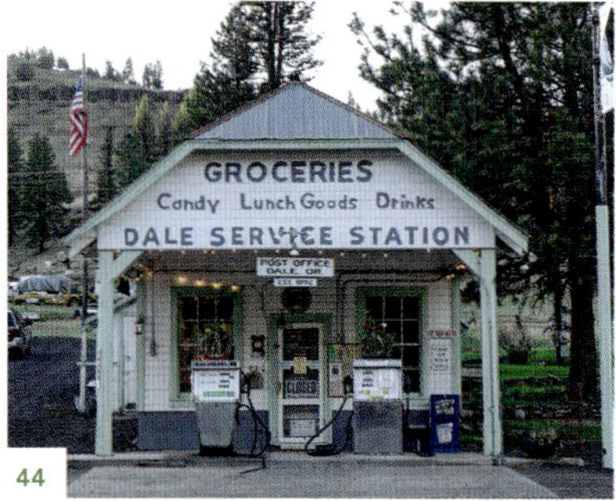

44

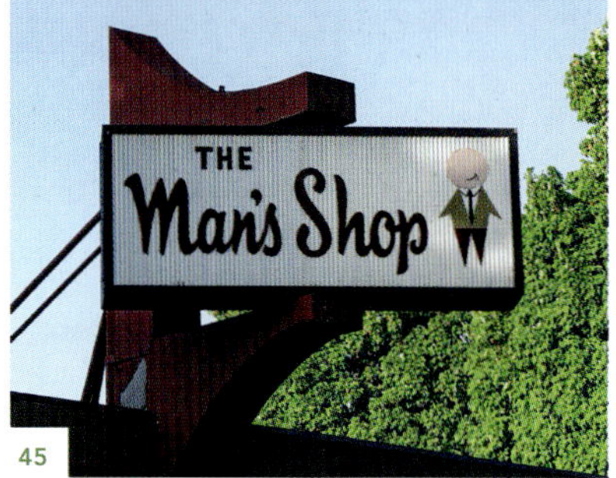

45

What brought me to the Beaver State was a charming country store I'd spotted in a *New York Times* essay about a cross-country road trip. That place is Dale, Oregon, and there's not much to it. That's not meant as a slight. It's a blip on a map and nestled in mountains—hushed and serene.

When I visited in May 2021, I met Butch and Charlene Phelps, the keepers of the **Dale Service Station** (FIG. 44). They are half the population of this Grant County wilderness community of Dale, population four. The Phelpses are also the postmasters, taking care of thirty-nine post office boxes serving surrounding communities. And they are the shopkeepers, stocking the basic necessities to spare you the long drive up U.S. 395 to the city of Pendleton. You can gas up your car here, too, and there's even part of an old rubber hose that used to go *ding ding* when you'd drive your wheels over it.

This place can be a lifesaver, literally, if you've run into trouble on the road, as there's scant cell service here in the middle of the Umatilla National Forest. This is the little country store that could, and it still does, thanks to Butch and Charlene, who moved out here a few decades back when they were ready for something new. They bought the place in a deal brokered at the counter inside. They left behind their lives in Beaverton, just outside Portland, and found more than a forested retreat here. As we said our goodbyes, Butch left me with two rules to live by: Be safe and have fun.

In its day, **The Man's Shop** (FIG. 45) in Portland's St. John's neighborhood was a destination for people who wanted custom tailoring in an old-school setting. The charming sign—featuring this adorable midcentury cartoon of a well-dressed, husky gentleman with a brown cardigan, skinny tie, tight slacks, and a knowing smile—watches over North Lombard Street, perhaps happy for the company on this now-desolate corner of a thriving little town. Let him be a reminder for us to treasure these places while we have them. (He's—alas—gone now. Enjoy him here.)

Here's another reminder of this. I drove by **Dan's Barber Shop** in Spokane, Washington, on an easy Sunday morning and was immediately smitten by its giant sign featuring scissors, just the sort of place I would have liked to get a trim. It was closed for the day, but now it's closed forever. Dan was Dionisios "Dan" Flambouras, who opened the salon in 1957 and died in 2007, but his shop outlived him by many years—and his legacy for far longer.

Another sentimental nod to a former business can be found in Portland on East Burnside Avenue. Welcome to Tip Top Cleaners. At least, that's what the sign says. The business is now called **Tip Top Vintage** (FIG. 46), which describes itself as a "collective of seasoned vintage goods dealers bringing their best for your perusal." I enjoyed perusing while grateful the owners were seasoned enough to know the best antique here was the priceless sign right outside.

If you grew up in Oregon and watched even a little television, you know about **Ron Tonkin** (FIG. 47). He appeared in many commercials for his namesake auto group over the years. His family was in the used-car business, but Tonkin revved it up, opening his own Chevy dealership while still in his twenties and becoming the youngest person ever to have done so, according to his obituary. He embraced electric bikes well before most people were concerned about the environmental need for battery-based transportation. His legacy is perhaps best captured in the bold 1960s sign at his first Chevy dealership in Portland.

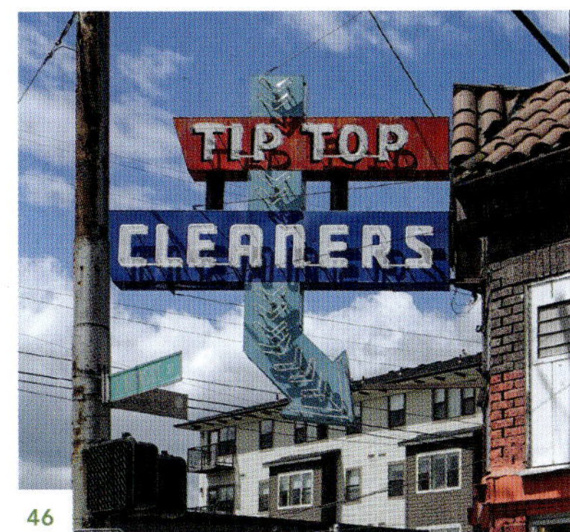

46

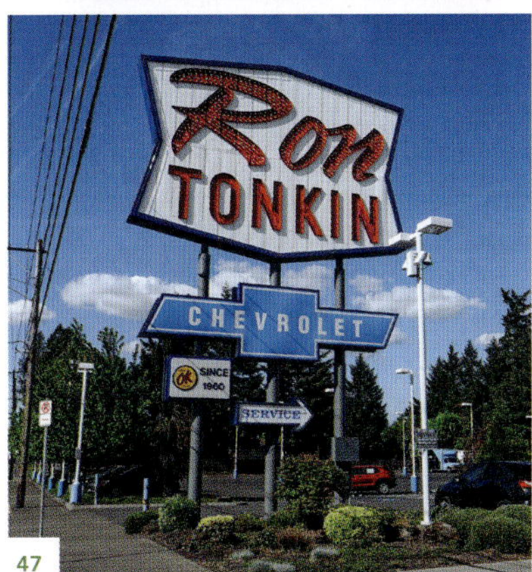

47

FROM LANES TO AISLES

Target opened in 1962, and so many of the discount chains from that era are long gone or on their deathbeds. Target thrives, and the spirit of innovation that has given it an edge is on display at the store you see here, one of my favorite examples of adaptive reuse.

This "small format" Target in southeast Portland was retro but not vintage. It opened in 2018, taking over the site of an AMF Pro 300 bowling alley. Many bemoaned the landlord's choice to hand over the keys to Target, but Target simply didn't move in and erase any trace of the former occupant. They embraced the history of the site, preserving the look of the original sign, which of course said "BOWL," and dressed up their entrance bollards with giant bowling balls.

What's more, Target kept the form of the canopy entrance, ensuring that a visit to this store was thrilling. The way Target handled this location is a vivid reminder of how a sixty-year-old business can remain so fresh and relevant today. Sadly, this experiment in adaptive reuse was not long for this world, and closed in 2023.

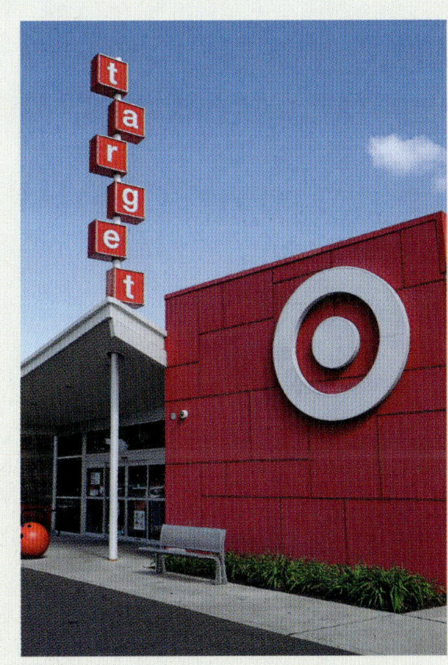

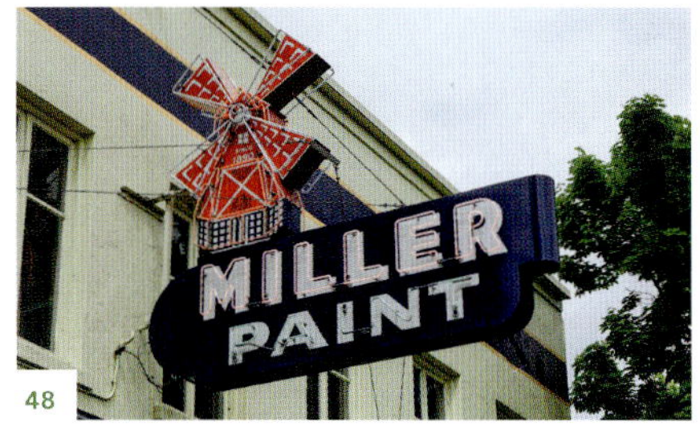

48

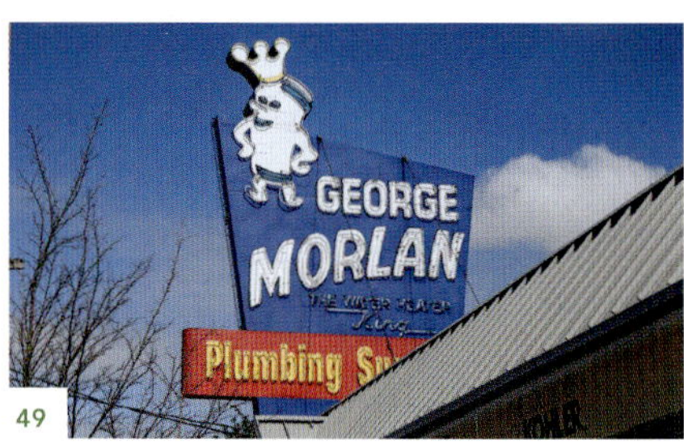

49

If the **Miller Paint** (FIG. 48) sign looks extra stunning here, it's because it had been recently renovated. The sign dates to 1938, the windmill a nod not to the family's origins (they were German, not Dutch, immigrants) but to a clever marketing slogan of the day: "Millers of Good Paint." (And of course the paint pigments were produced through stone milling.) The paint company was founded in 1890 by Ernest Miller, who saw an opening for making locally produced paints that stood up better to the soggy Northwestern climate. Today Miller Paint has dozens of locations across the Pacific Northwest, but this icon sits at the flagship store on SE Grand Avenue, where they've been since 1926.

Royalty and water heaters are two concepts I've kept separate for most of my life, though toilets have long been likened to the throne. Well, behold the **Water Heater King** (FIG. 49), the peppy mascot of Portland's George Morlan Plumbing. Morlan founded the shop in 1927 and would in time tap big business in electric water heaters. Profits heated up, too. A catchy advertising jingle—"George Morlan Plumbing—the Water Heater King!"—helped the business grow and today, there are eight locations in the area. But the location on Foster Road is the one to see, with the grand neon sign. The king is so proud, and his legs dance, so check him out at night.

Portland Outdoor Store has been an emporium of Western wear for more than a century. It's the sort of store one dreams of finding here on the edge of the Western Frontier. The Popick family, who founded it in 1919, have run the store for most of its history.

Western-themed retailers are a special treat, trading in Americana you can wear from head to toe. **Prineville Men's Wear** in Prineville, Oregon, has something the Portland store lacks—the rustic setting. The store has been in business since 1950.

Dutch Treats!

Who doesn't like a good windmill sign? The **Dutch Mill Cafe** in Tillamook, Oregon, has been renovated to lean into its vintage vibe with a 1950s-style decor. In Marysville, Washington, a windmill is MIA, but not so the old-school Dutch vibes at **Oosterwyk's Dutch Bakery**. Recent Dutch immigrant Gerard Willem Oosterwyk purchased the Marysville Home Bakery—then a Swedish bakery—in 1954 and turned it into a beloved business that's still in the family. In a 2014 interview, his daughter, who took over the shop after his death that year, told the *Everett Herald* that the royal crest seen on the sign was bestowed upon her dad by Queen Juliana of the Netherlands, who rewarded his masterful baking when the family still lived in Holland.

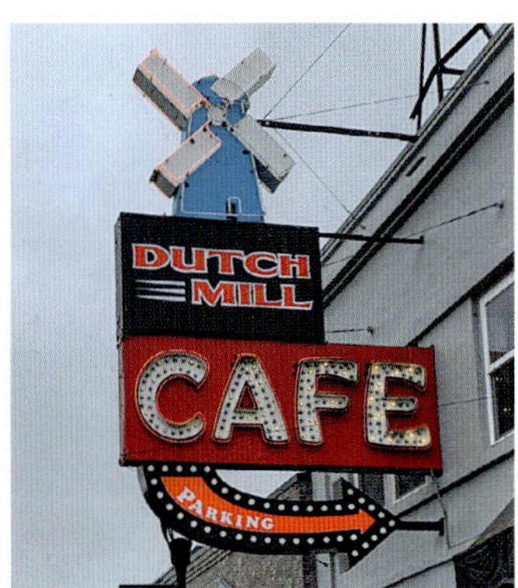

SWEET STOPS

The magic of soft serve under the glow of neon lights is one of the most divine experiences you can have on any road trip. Here are two options for you, and a family-run candy emporium for good measure!

Custard King (FIG. 50) in Astoria, Oregon, has escaped the inevitable brushes with death that come with being around since 1951. In 2015, new owners beautifully restored it, and the next set of owners briefly contemplated starting from scratch before realizing how much love there was for this place—and how hard it would be to get a new sign installed, according to an article in *The Astorian*. "It's really an iconic part of Astoria," one of those owners, Tara Gerlitz, told the news site. "Since we've been here working, people are always stopping by, not even from Astoria, that have heard about the Custard King."

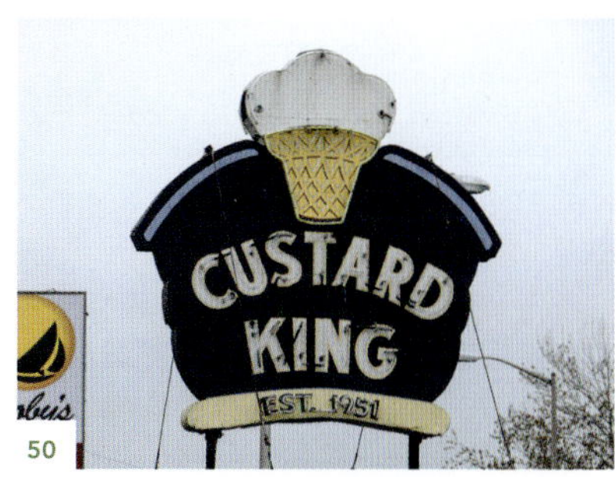

50

Whether you're a farmer, a lumberjack, a server technician, a retrologist, or a cowboy, **Tastee Treet** (FIG. 51) in Prineville, Oregon, has been an outpost of home—good burgers, good ice cream, good people—since 1957. And it hasn't changed very much since the 1950s. The current owners took over in 2020, saying that they felt obliged to continue a tradition that could always fall into the wrong hands—for instance, a chain, which would simply start over. "The sign is such an iconic piece of art," co-owner Brett Edgerly said in a 2020 newspaper interview.

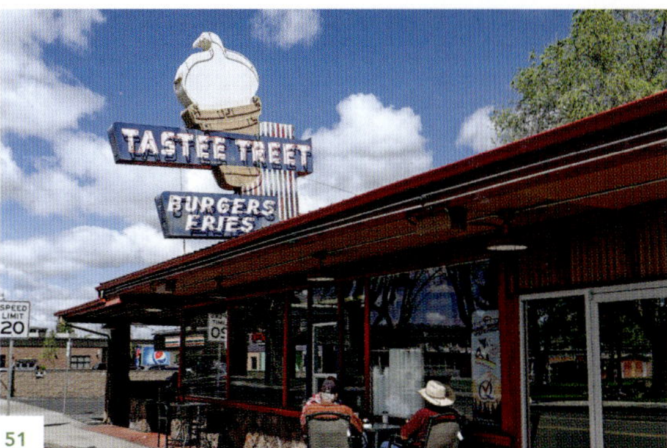

51

The sweetest candy shops are often the ones that stay in the family, and the **Johnson Candy Company** (FIG. 52) in Tacoma, Washington, is the dictionary definition of such. The candy-making has spanned three generations in the Hilltop neighborhood, and from this round building since 1948. It traces its foundation to 1925 when Russell Johnson began to mess around with some old chocolate molds at his parents' dairy shop. When he and his wife took control, they added a lunch counter and sold candies as well. In time, the candies won out, and the Johnson family never looked back.

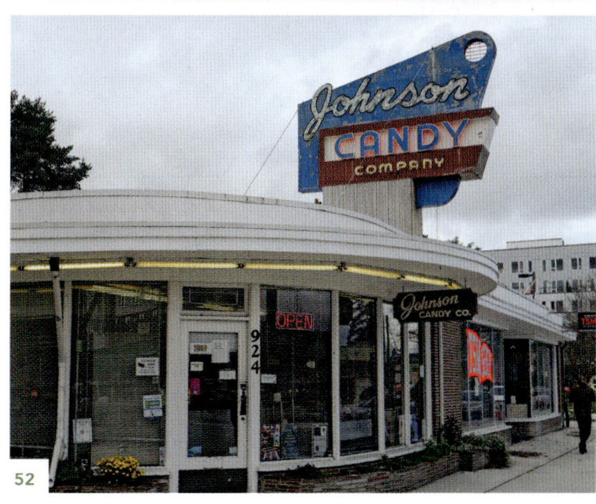

52

BLUE
MOON
1

THE
Palms
MOTOR
HOTEL
Welcome
Free
TV
2

FISH
BY'S
BURGERS
3

Bali-Hai
MOTEL
VACANCY
CLEAN SGL/DBL ROOMS
WI-FI·TV·MICRO·FRIDGE
SAVE·WEEKLY·MONTHLY
509-452-7178
MOTEL
4

O.K
TIRES
K
5

CHIN'S
KITCHEN
Portland's ORIGINAL
CHINESE FOOD to GO
6

SAFEWAY
SERVING
LAKEVIEW AND LAKE COUNTY
SINCE 1939
Outdoor Power
Plumbing
7

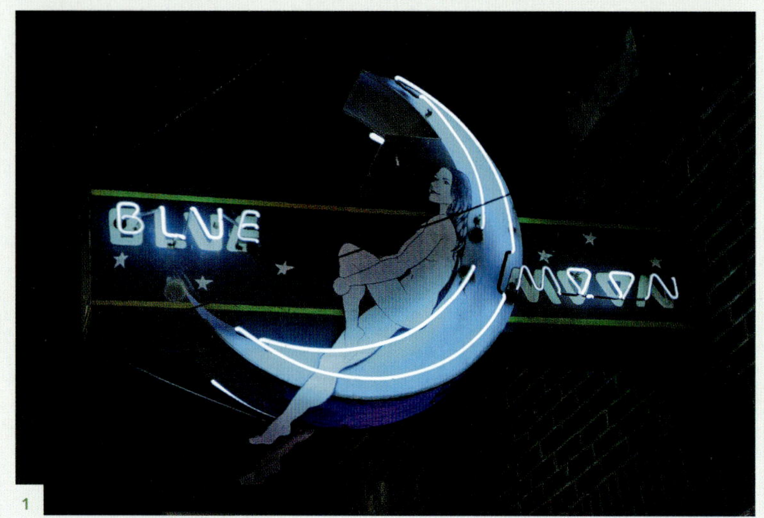

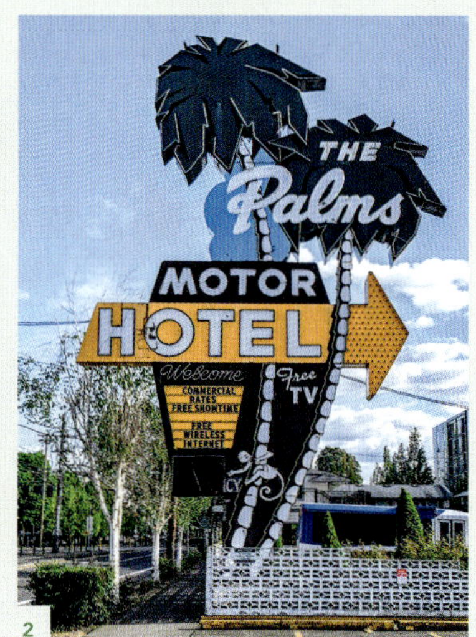

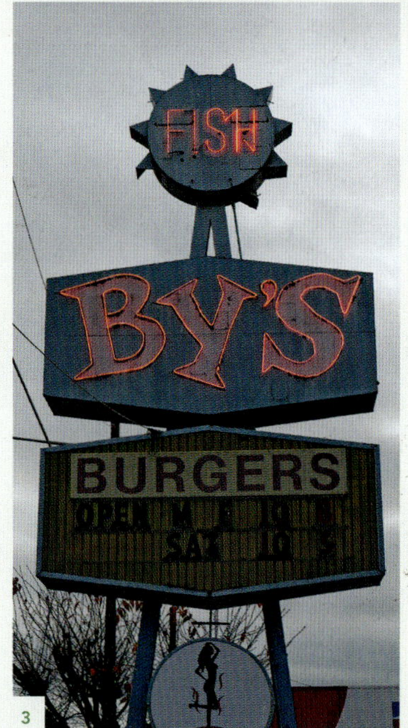

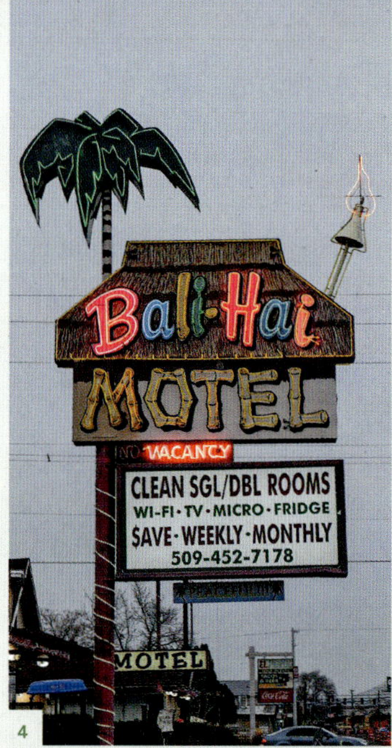

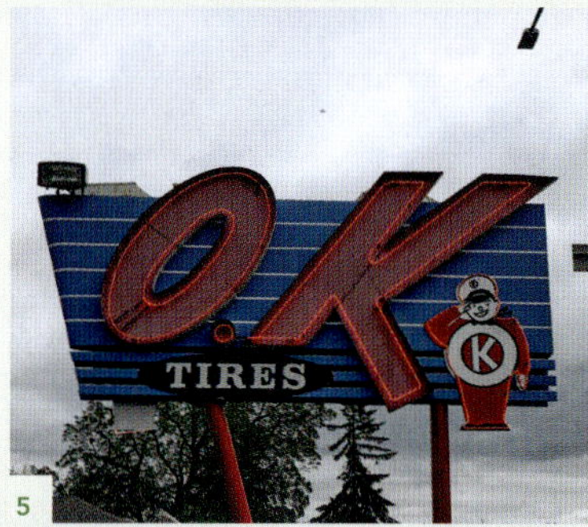

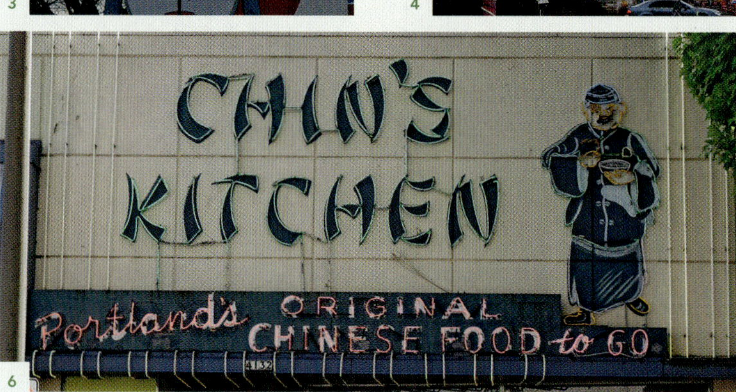

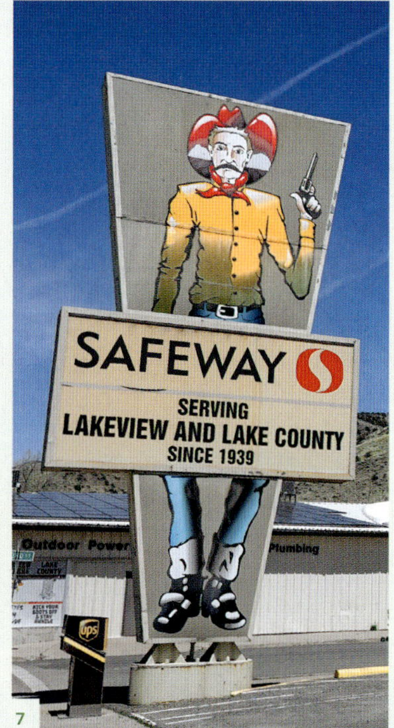

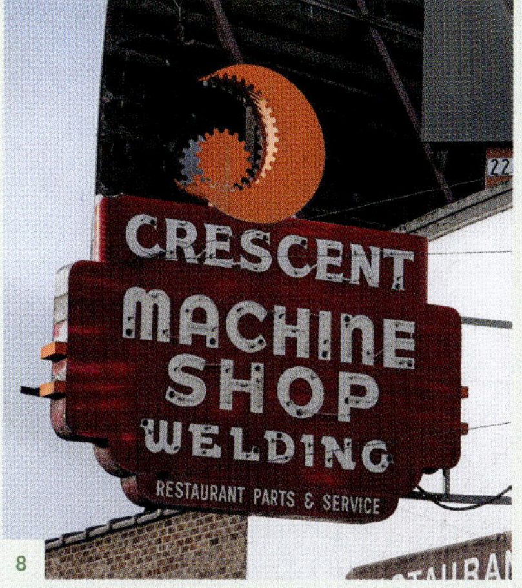

8

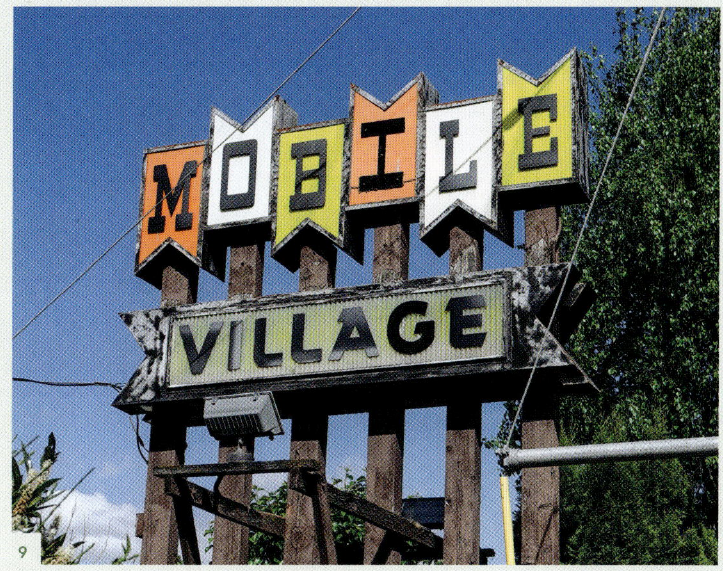

9

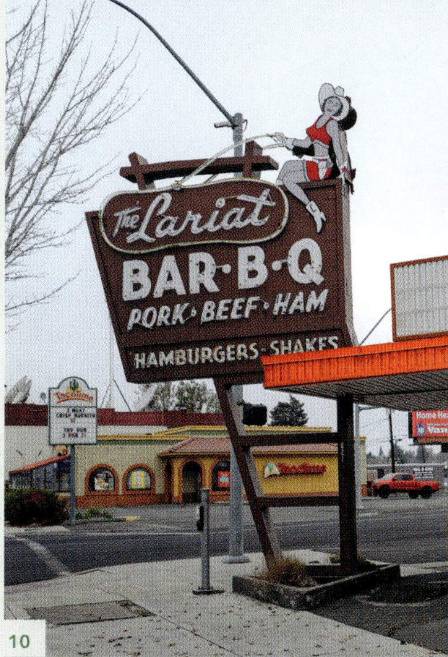

10

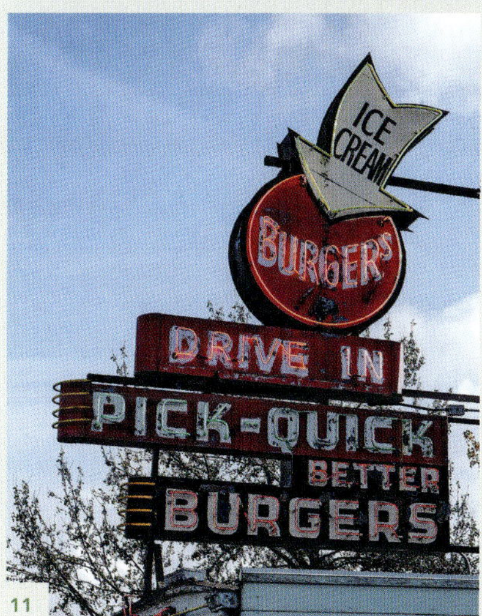

11

SIGNPOSTS UP AHEAD

Here are some gems you'll want to seek out on your own journey.

1. Blue Moon Tavern, Seattle, Washington
2. Palms Motel, Portland, Oregon
3. By's Fish and Chips, Seattle, Washington
4. Bali Hai Motel, Yakima, Washington
5. OK Tire of Salem, Salem, Oregon
6. Chin's Kitchen, Portland, Oregon
7. Safeway, Lakeview, Oregon
8. Crescent Machine Works, Spokane, Washington
9. Mobile Village, Portland, Oregon
10. Lariat Bar-B-Q, Yakima, Washington
11. Pick-Quick Drive-In, Fife, Oregon

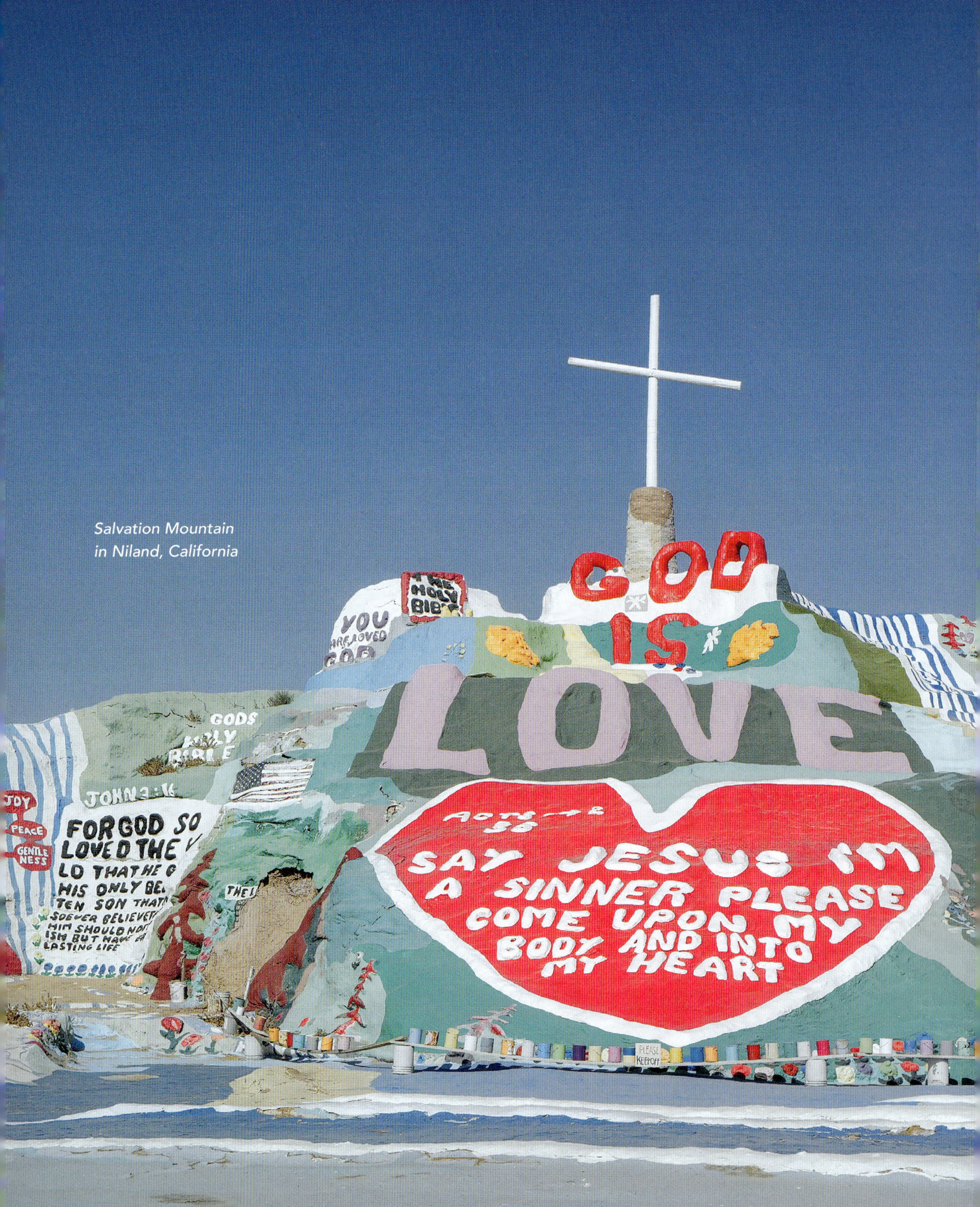

Salvation Mountain
in Niland, California

CALIFORNIA

My love for this state knows no bounds. When I first set eyes on it, from the air in 1996, I was smitten. Each time I return, it's like coming home, because, in a way, I grew up here, exposed to California in television shows and the movies. I decided that California deserves its own chapter, since in certain ways it's made of multiple "states." There's the coastal gold of the Southland, the beauty of the desert landscapes, the lush mountains brimming with alpine life, the hidden wonders of the Central Valley, the splendor of Northern California—all those and more, with so many variations within each of these areas. What to see? Everything! But here's a start.

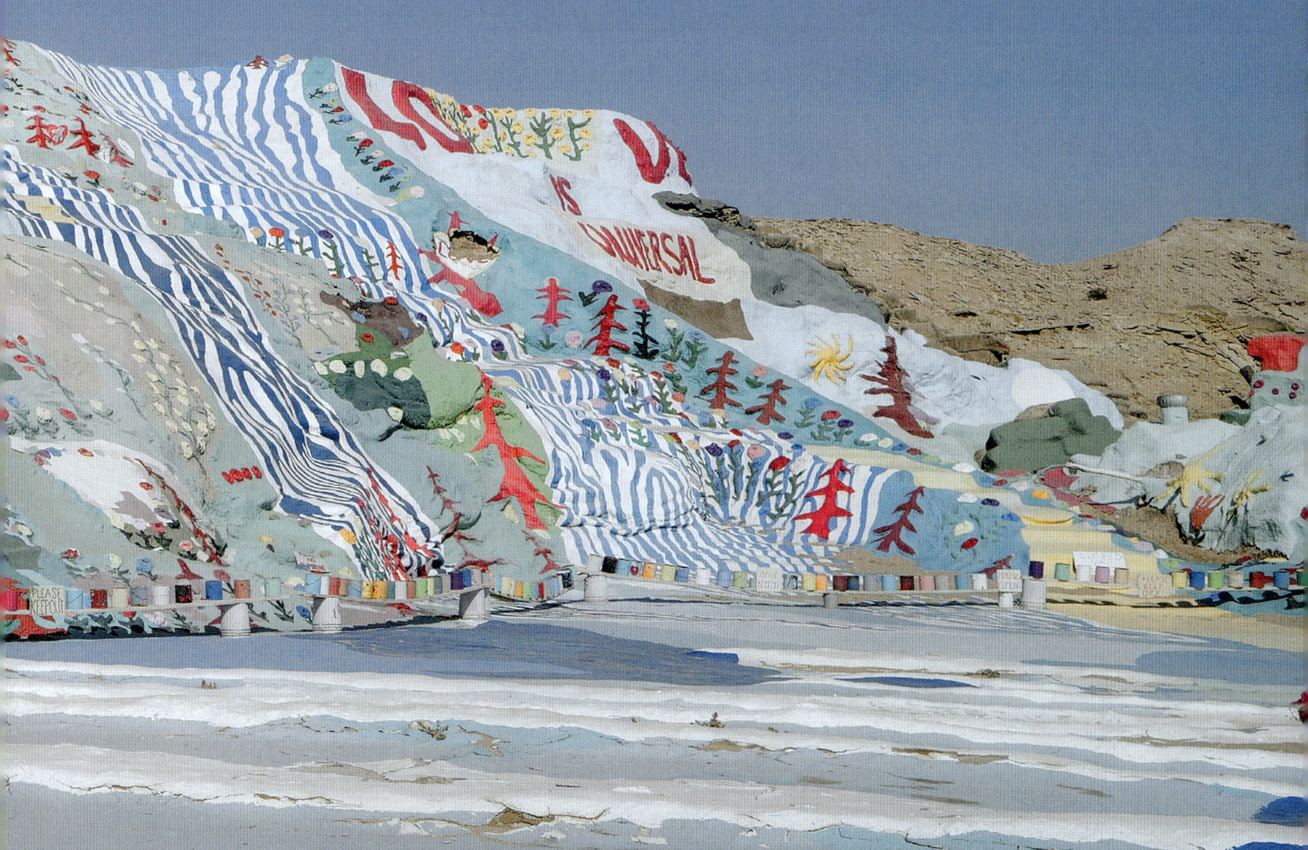

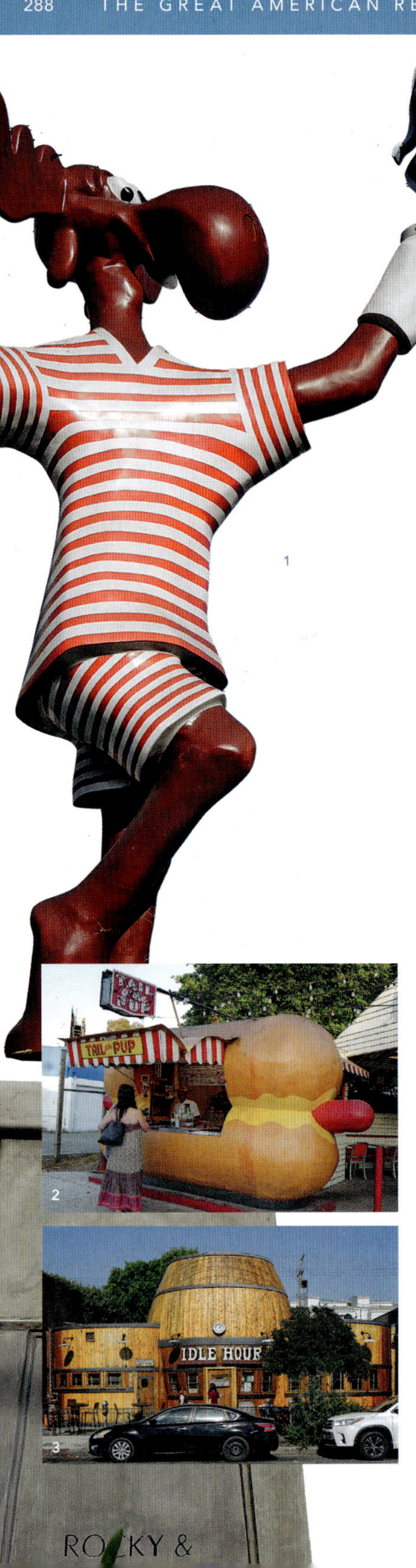

1

2

3

ROADSIDE QUIRKS

You could argue roadside quirks were invented in California. That's not entirely true or fair to the forty-nine other states, but California, the automobile, and the open road go together in a way that's so distinctly American.

It should not be a surprise that roadside architecture appeals to our belly, and what's not to love about the **Tail O' the Pup** (FIG. 2), in its new forever home of West Hollywood. The stand opened in 1946 and became an instant classic, appearing in movies and TV shows like *Columbo* and *The Rockford Files*. Beloved (and tiny) though it is, Tail O' the Pup has not been immune to the turmoil of L.A. real estate. The Pup went into storage in 2005 but, well over a decade later, was adopted by the history-minded 1933 Group, whose bars and restaurants have revived classic Los Angeles–area nightlife haunts like Formosa Cafe (see page 296).

The **Idle Hour** (FIG. 3), a jewel of Southern California's programmatic architecture crown, in North Hollywood, is another gem revived by the 1933 Group. Shaped like a gigantic whiskey barrel, it was built in 1941, a signal to motorists who were looking for some refreshment. The patio offers another surprise: a replica of the long-gone Bulldog Café, another vernacular masterpiece of Los Angeles architecture. The Idle Hour rescued the pipe-smoking pooch from a Los Angeles museum that was going to discard it.

The **Brolly Hut** of Inglewood, shaped like an umbrella, is the perfect mimetic building for taking cover from the rain. The umbrella theme carries throughout the place, from the sign to design details inside the fast-food restaurant.

In Los Angeles, it's inevitable that our search for quirkiness will take us to Sunset Strip. The statue of **Rocky and Bullwinkle** (FIG. 1), a vivid reminder of a cartoon TV series that was once a household name, is of Rocky, the flying squirrel, and Bullwinkle, the moose. It was installed outside the headquarters of the show's creator, Jay Ward Productions. The statue, which initially revolved, was a clever way of promoting the primetime cartoon series while also tweaking the spinning cowgirl statue atop a Las Vegas resort billboard across the street. Rocky and Bullwinkle long outlived the cowgirl, coming down from their original home in 2013 for a restoration and eventually landing here.

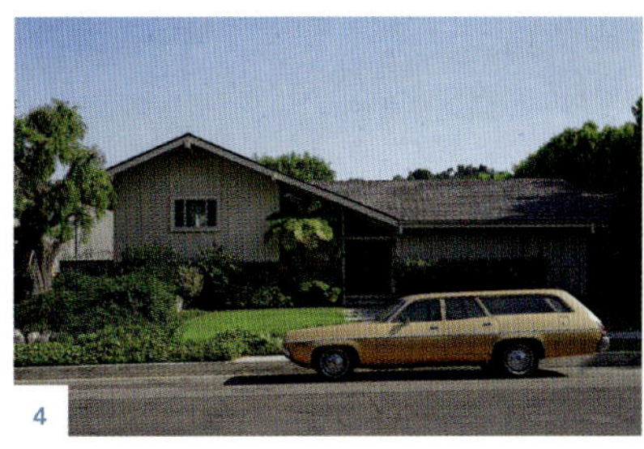
4

Now here's the story of **The Brady Bunch House** (FIG. 4) in Studio City, one of the first places I ever visited in California. The show was filmed on Stage 5 at Paramount, and the exterior was used only to film establishing shots, a mock window installed on the side to give the ranch a sense that it was a vast, two-story house. Over the years, the house was obscured by trees and a fence, but it was unmistakable as Casa Brady.

The "Brady-fication" of the house began in 2019 after HGTV bought it (famously outbidding Lance Bass) and teamed up with the Property Brothers, Drew and Jonathan Scott, along with Brady Bunch kids in the reality series *A Very Brady Renovation* and converted the house into the one we saw on TV, inside and out.

THE GIANT DONUTS OF LOS ANGELES

Behold the spot where the architecture is a hole in one. **The Donut Hole** (FIG. 5) is one of the sweetest examples of roadside Americana, an icon of La Puente since 1968. You drive into the tunnel and drive out with your very own delicious donut, or, if you're like me, maybe more than one. (The coffee is pretty good, too.)

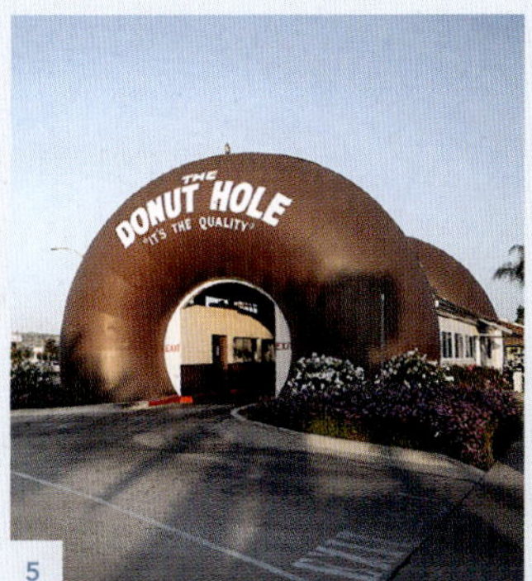

5

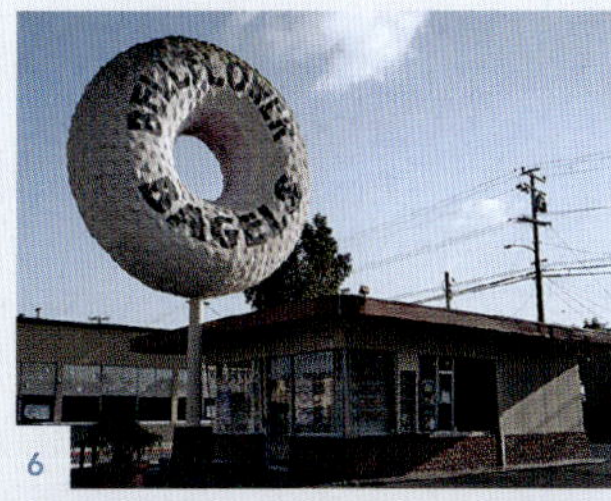

6

It's been said this is the L.A. area's most photographed donut shop, though that may well be **Randy's** (FIG. 7) by Los Angeles International Airport. Randy's is one of the places I hit when I arrive or just before I depart. It's been here since July 1953. It was once part of a chain called Big Do-Nut Drive-In, one of about ten locations and the second to open. A handful are still in existence, and each features gigantic donuts.

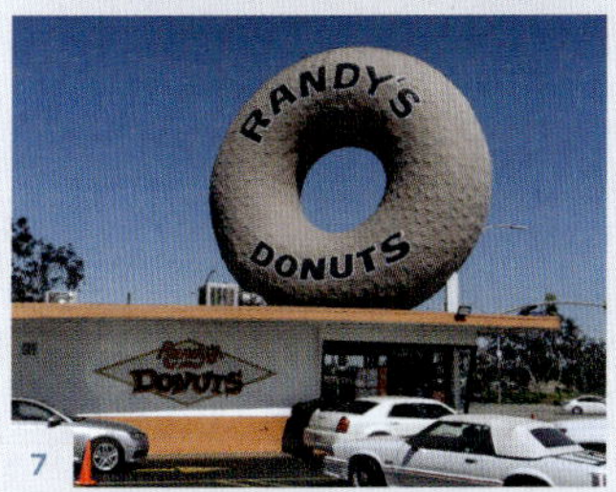

7

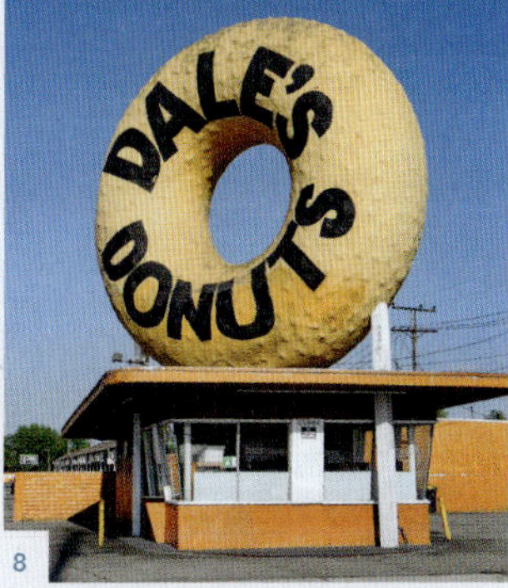

8

Behold some of the others, like **Dale's Donuts** (FIG. 8) in Compton and **Bellflower Bagels** (FIG. 6), a smaller donut (well, now bagel). The Big Do-Nut company was founded by Russell Wendell, and by 1955 had sold twenty-two million donuts, according to a press account of the time.

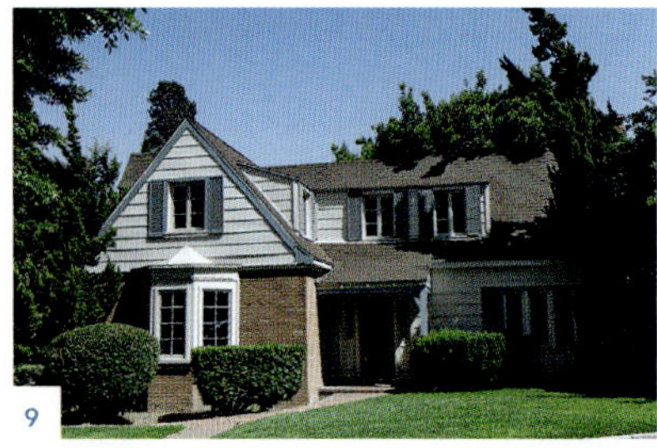
9

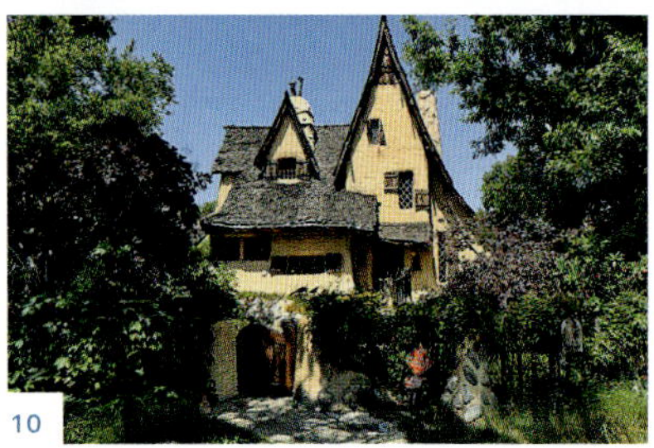
10

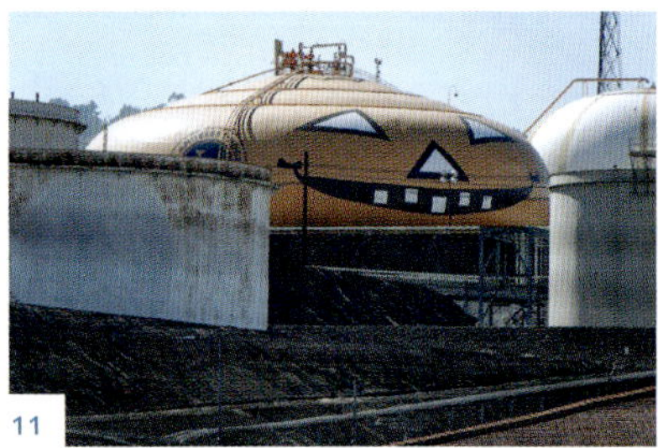
11

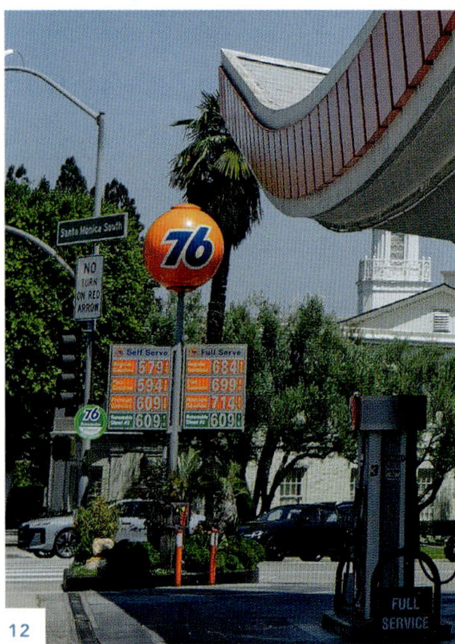

12

After the smash-hit series aired, the house sat for years until the cable network sold it to a superfan, Tina Trahan, for $3.2 million—at a loss—and she is showing her Bunch-ian bona fides with the cars parked outside—the same models used in the series.

Another fun TV house find is in Santa Monica: the ***Bewitched* House** (FIG. 9). It is said this house was the inspiration for the one on the TV sitcom, the replica (in reverse) built on the famous Columbia Ranch in Burbank. The real house remains, but sadly the one on the lot is no more, along with the rest of the property, including exteriors used to represent the homes in *I Dream of Jeannie*, *The Partridge Family,* and even the interior and exterior of the home in *National Lampoon's Christmas Vacation*. At least the *Friends* water fountain was saved!

The *Bewitched* House gives no indication a witch might live there, but Beverly Hills' **Spadena House** (FIG. 10) would suggest otherwise. The so-called Witch House was built as a set by an early film studio in 1920, a time when storybook architecture was the design darling. A renovation by its latest owner has only added to its sense of mystery and intrigue. It is *the* place to be for trick-or-treaters on Halloween, and how could it not?

Another big Halloween scene can be found down in Wilmington when, every autumn, a giant oil tank turns into a jack-o'-lantern called **Smilin' Jack** (FIG. 11), billed as the largest jack-o'-lantern on earth. Smilin' Jack—Horton Sphere Tank No. 304 if you want to use his birth name—first rose amid this patch of Union Oil gas tanks in 1952. In 1955, the *Los Angeles Times* wrote that someone exclaimed, "Why, it looks like a pumpkin," when the tank received a coat of red lead primer, and thus was born this cherished tradition.

The **76 Ball** is another roadside icon of California. The ball debuted at the 1962 Seattle World's Fair, where it was displayed at the Union 76 Skyride. Unocal, then-parent company, loved the design, planting the balls at thousands of gas stations and giving tiny foam ones away to serve as antenna toppers. After a corporate merger led to a mass culling of the balls in 2006, a public backlash validated their special role in the landscape and a brief dalliance with the color red was undone. The ultimate expression of the brand is found soaring at **Jack Colker's 76 Gas Station** (FIG. 12) in Beverly Hills, completed in 1965.

The **Cabazon Dinosaurs** (FIG. 13) are a sign that the drive from Los Angeles to Palm Springs is ending. But for some, the destination *is* the dinosaurs, which trace their parentage to sculptor and entrepreneur Claude Bell, who operated a roadside stop here that once included a restaurant, the Wheel Inn. Bell set two giant dinos to roaming here: One, Dinny the Brontosaurus,

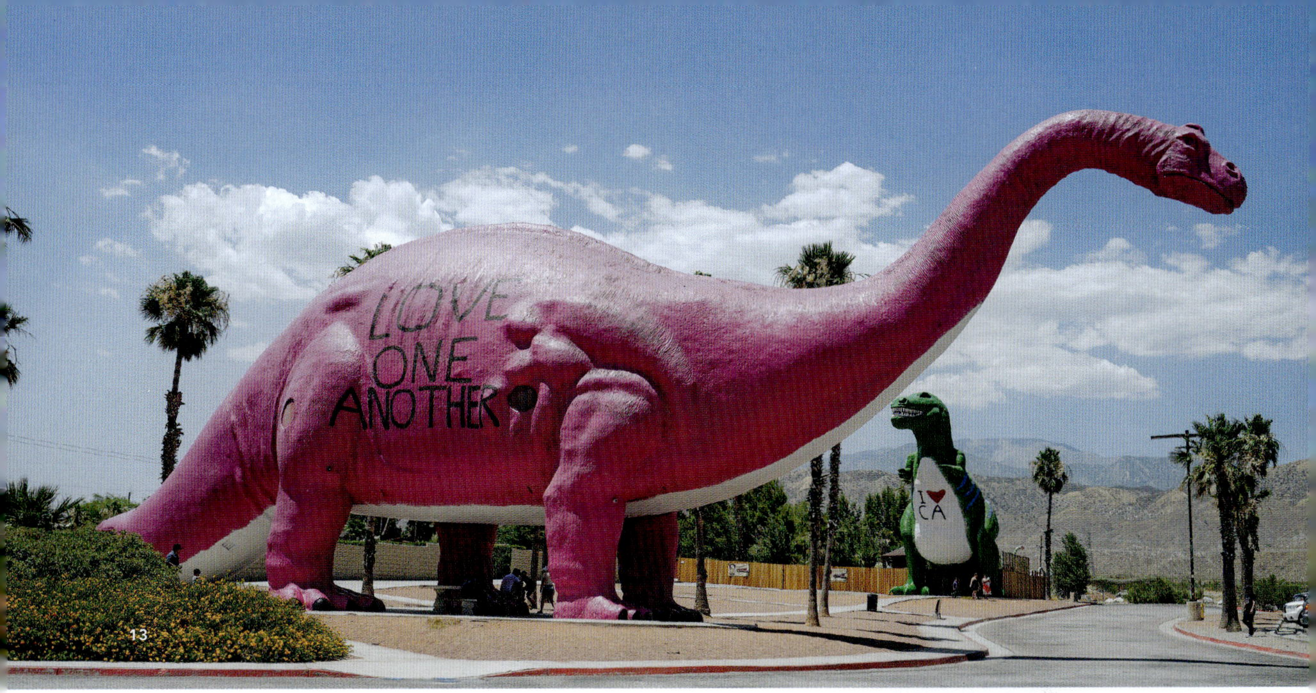

13

features a gift shop and small exhibit and was inspired by Lucy the Elephant (see page 10), reflecting Bell's New Jersey roots. The other dinosaur, Mr. Rex, stands in benign menace—a kids' slide on his tail was planned but, sadly, never built. The dinos were built between 1965 and the mid-1980s (around the time they appeared in *Pee-wee's Big Adventure*) and Bell envisioned a full park teeming with the beasts, but he died in 1988 at age ninety-one before his dream could be realized.

Out in the desert, the **World's Tallest Thermometer** (FIG. 14) in Baker records the extreme heat. The tower is 134 feet high and the maximum temperature it will read is also 134°F. That's a nod to the highest air temperature ever measured, and it happened in Death Valley's Furnace Creek, not far from Baker, in 1913. The roadside attraction was the idea of Willis Herron, who operated a restaurant, the Bun Boy, here in the Mojave Desert. His extension into building desert skyscrapers faced early engineering challenges. The first thermometer in 1991 snapped after it was buffeted by high winds. Today's version is far more robust. After a period where it seemed like the thermometer was doomed, it found salvation in the hands of the Herron family, who bought it back and spruced it up.

Before you leave Baker, admire the remnants of the **Royal Hawaiian Motel** (FIG. 15) and the towering **Bun Boy** sign, and get a photo at the big UFO at the far-out **Alien Beef Jerky.**

Our desert travels take us to Ghost Town Road, where a ghostly prospector advertises "**Calico Ghost Town** 3 Miles" ahead. It seems foreordained, then, that the past is indeed prologue, and

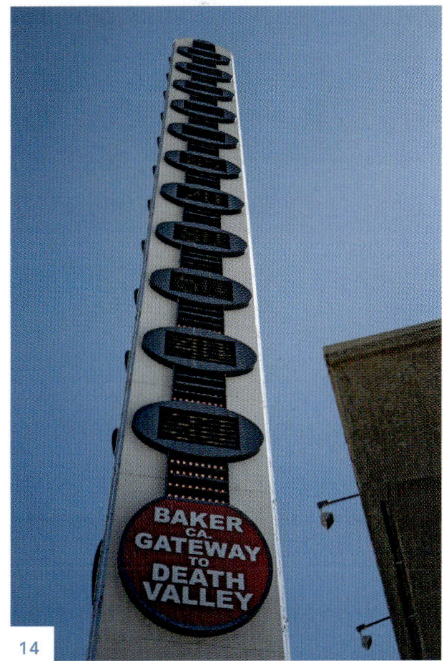

14

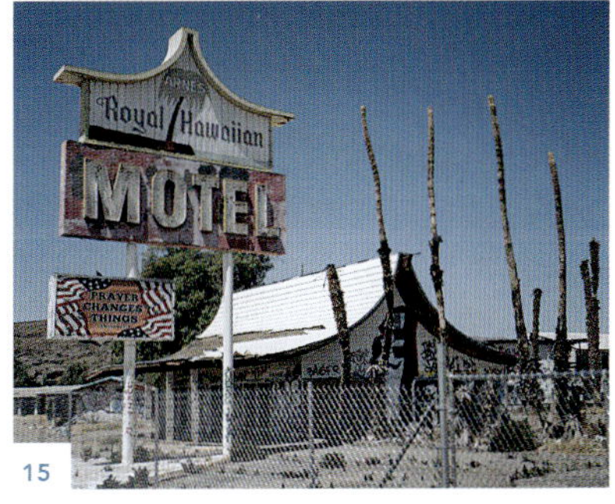

15

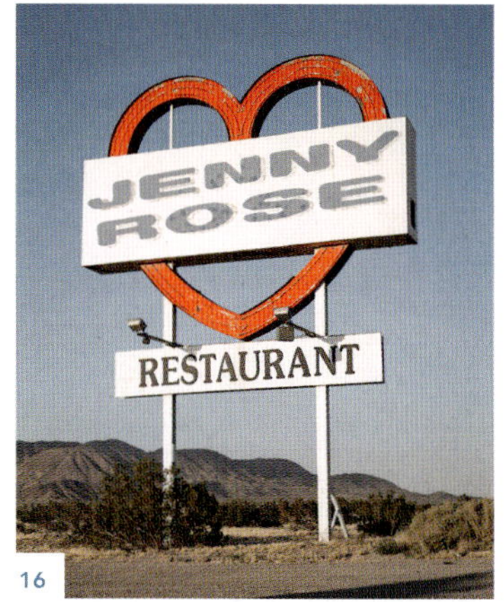

16

so it was for the **Jenny Rose** (FIG. 16) restaurant in Yermo. Its owners in 1988 took over a restaurant that was once called Hart's, as the sign would suggest. The sign and name ended up on the back of a 1993 Sheryl Crow album, *Tuesday Night Music Club*.

We must stop in **Needles**. This Route 66 town celebrates its pioneer-day heritage with a giant wooden **Borax Wagon** (FIG. 17). These mule-drawn wagons would transport borax—a mineral salt used in a range of products, including detergent—from Death Valley mines.

Needles is also the home turf of Spike, Snoopy's brother, in Charles M. Schulz's *Peanuts* comic strip, and the town salutes the bewhiskered beagle at the **Needles Regional Museum** (FIG. 18) downtown. (Spike turns fifty on August 13, 2025.)

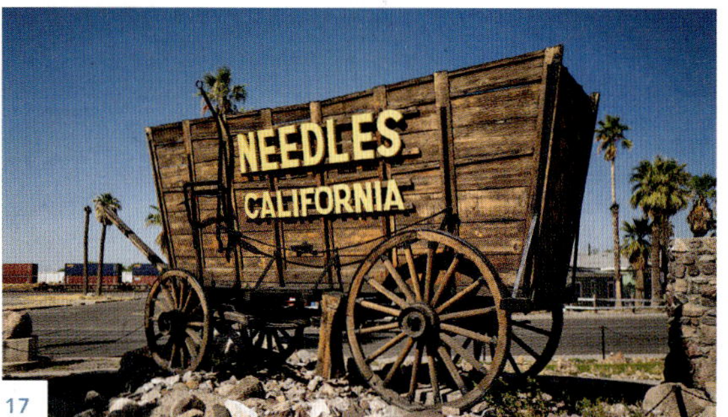

17

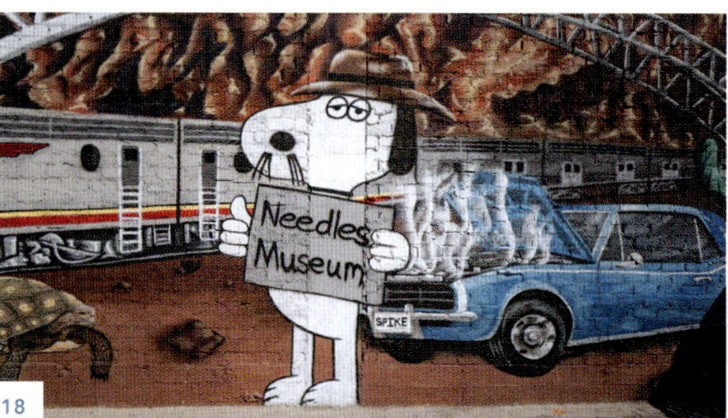

18

SPOTLIGHT:

VALLEY RELICS MUSEUM

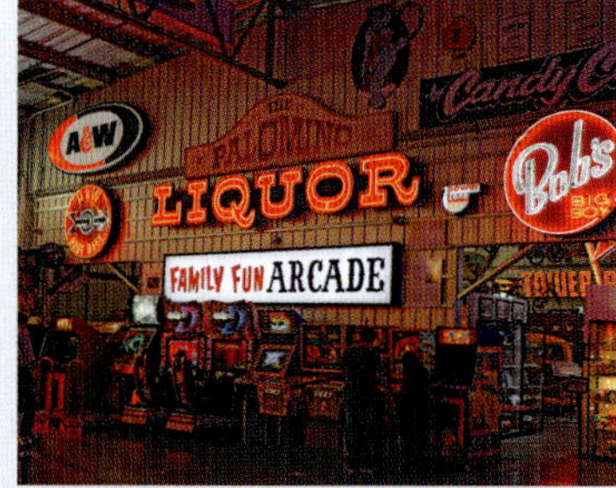

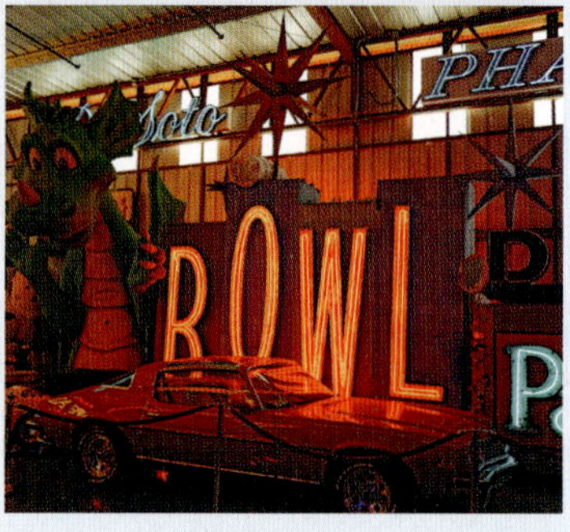

When I think of the classic postwar American suburb, the San Fernando Valley is front of mind. And the traces of those years are still evident for the commercial archaeologists exploring the region. But some of the best of that past was spared a visit to the landfill—or disappearance into a private collection—and ended up in the safe hands of the **Valley Relics Museum** in Van Nuys.

Much like the American Sign Museum in Cincinnati or the Neon Boneyard in Las Vegas, the Valley Relics Museum, founded by Tommy Gelinas in 2013, is a wonderland destination for the roadside Americana enthusiast—or even a fan of twentieth century pop culture. Beyond classic signs restored and on display, there are curiosities from Hollywood history, like Jack Webb's wood-paneled wall of Sony Trinitron 13-inch TV sets that allowed the *Dragnet* star and creator to monitor the major Los Angeles television stations. Or a sticker-covered door donated by Eve Plumb, Jan of *The Brady Bunch*. This was her bedroom door back in the days when she was starring as the middle sister on the ABC sitcom.

On the outskirts of Niland, an unforgiving stretch of earth in the Imperial Valley, is **Salvation Mountain** (see photo on pages 286–287). For some folks, this is the promised land, and they live here in **Slab City**, an off-the-grid, art-focused community of desert dwellers. Leonard Knight was drawn here from out East in the 1980s to create this remarkable testament to love. Knight made his mountain largely of local clay mixed with straw, with societal detritus like telephone poles and tires giving it ballast. Layers and layers of donated paint bring the mountain to colorful life. The edifice is emblazoned with paths, scripture passage, and most boldly, the words "God Is Love" topped by a white cross.

A nearby community is **Bombay Beach**, which sits on the briny Salton Sea. That increasing saltiness and subsequent ecological devastation that afflicted the Salton Sea starting in the 1970s drained life from Bombay Beach and environs, once a popular tourist destination. But Bombay Beach has turned into an unlikely seaside resort, a revival powered by hardy, artistic souls who have moved in and left their mark. Cool off at the **Ski Inn** bar and check out the **Bombay Beach Drive-In** (FIG. 19).

Roadside giants are a kind of unofficial greeter, and **Big Josh**, in Joshua Tree, now holds a muffler welcoming folks. He stands sentinel at The Station Joshua Tree, an old Richfield service station that has been converted into a shop brimming with curios. Make sure you explore the **Glass Outhouse**, an art installation set on a sandy field peppered with quirky items and, as the name would suggest, an outhouse covered in a one-way mirror.

Back toward the Los Angeles area, one of the most soaring relics of the glory days of air travel shines in neon in Long Beach. **Fly DC Jets** (FIG. 20) is so evocative—the look screams 1950s without saying so, and indeed, DC, short for Douglas Commercial, set up a manufacturing plant for its passenger aircraft here in 1957. Mercedes-Benz now runs the plant.

Also in SoCal is the legendary **Chicken Boy** (FIG. 21) in L.A.'s Highland Park neighborhood. He's a hybrid creature: a Muffler Man topped with an artist-created chicken head. The boy—really a muscular man—advertised a downtown L.A. fried chicken business, Chicken Boy, and was rescued from destruction by graphic artist Amy Inouye after the restaurant closed in 1984. Chicken Boy would reemerge on the rooftop of her studio in Highland Park in 2007, where he's ruled the roost ever since.

Perhaps more ominous is the mascot for **Western Exterminator**, Little Man (or Mr. Little), who holds a hammer behind his back while he scolds a truculent mouse. Western Exterminator opened in 1921, and the mascot came along in the 1930s. The giant neon sign is a dramatic sight from U.S. 101 in L.A.

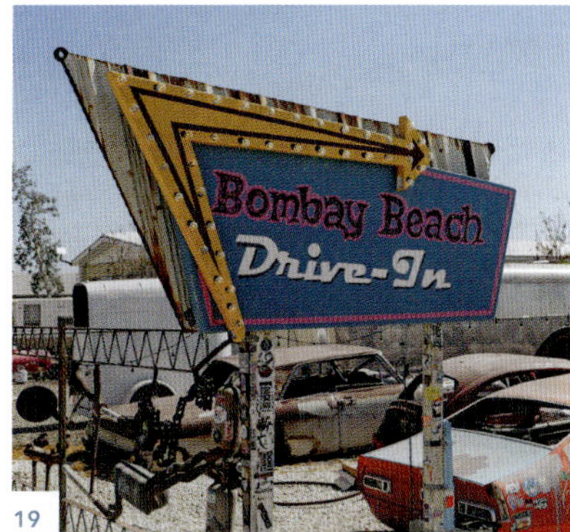

19

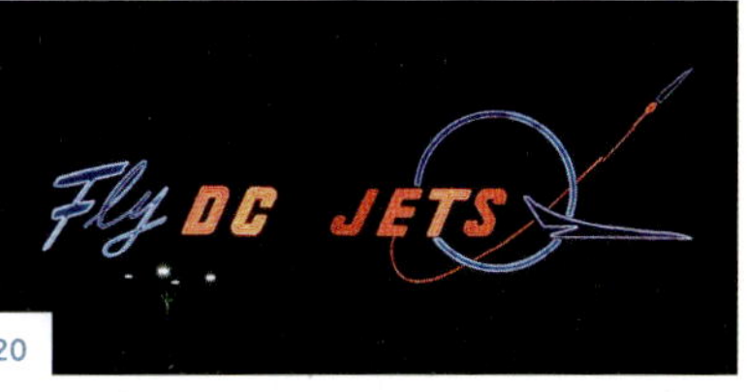

20

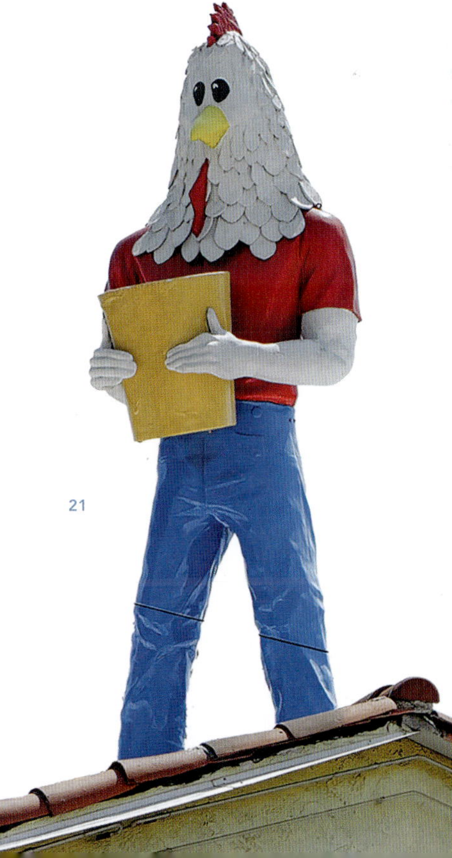
21

▶▶▶ Pull Over!

What is **Santa Claus** doing near the beach in Oxnard, sporting sunglasses while climbing down a chimney, in the company of toy soldiers, a reindeer, and a snowman holding a poinsettia-festooned surfboard? St. Nick ended up here after he was booted from his longtime home in Carpinteria, where he sat on Santa Claus Lane, a Christmas-themed strip mall that opened in 1950. He's on the job year-round.

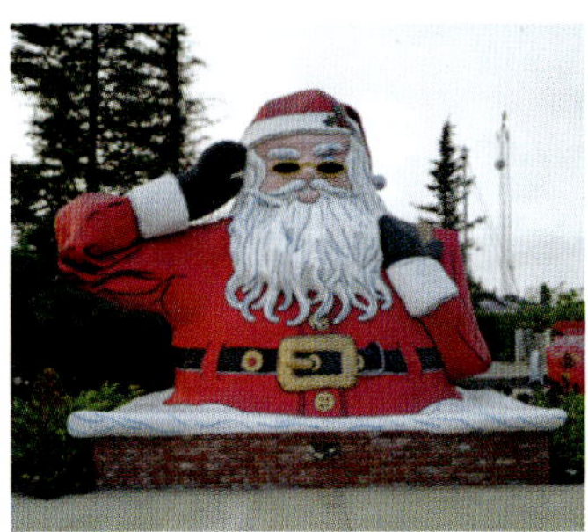

Rounding out California's quirky characters, I'd like to introduce you to a few gems that capture the state's agricultural heritage. Enjoy a photo op with a giant box of **Sun-Maid Raisins** in Kingsburg, billed as the world's largest. The box was built in 1992 by university students who filled it with 16,500 raisins, earning its Guinness Records status. The box depicts Lorraine Collett, who was picked to be the face of the brand in 1915.

Along I-99, watch for an 80-foot-high box of **Halo Oranges**, which captures motorists' attention in Delano. It is actually a storage warehouse for the sweet fruit.

This is not the first **Big Shoe** we've encountered on our journey. This one is in Bakersfield and was built by Chester Deschwanden in the late 1940s. His son, Donald, ran the shoe repair shop for many decades; Felipe Torres has been cobbling here since the early 2000s. The shoe is a size 768. The shoelace? A 50-foot-long rope.

As we power toward Northern California, I'm going to share a sign that's over the moon. For much of the twentieth century, the **Milk Farm** (FIG. 22) delighted weary travelers looking for comfort food

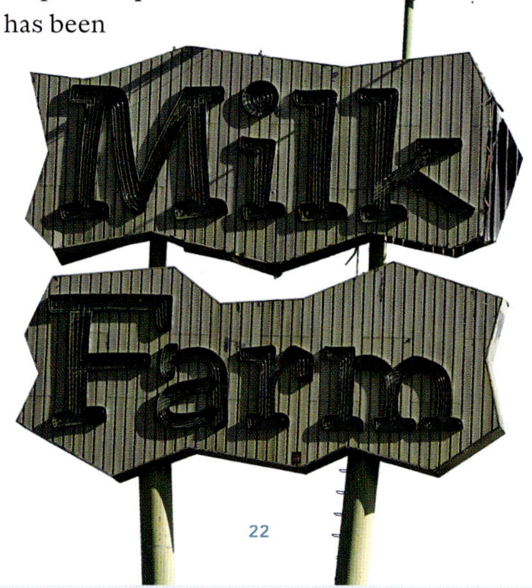

22

YOU'RE A ROADSIDE QUIRK, CHARLIE BROWN

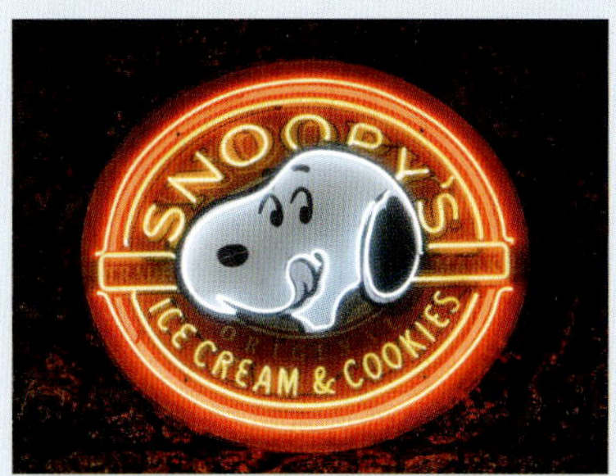

If you're even a casual fan of Peanuts, you owe it to yourself to visit the **Charles M. Schulz Museum and Research Center** in Santa Rosa, California, Schulz's home for much of his life. The museum has extraordinary exhibits, including a re-creation of Schulz's office. Across the street is the charming **Warm Puppy Café**, which always has a table set aside for Schulz, a special honor in the spot where he liked to have breakfast.

A separate building holds a gift shop and additional exhibits. And if you're like Schulz and like ice-skating, lace up and show off a little on **Snoopy's Home Ice**. If you're in L.A., there's a Peanuts "exhibit" worthy of the museum: The **Snoopy Bridge** in Tarzana is an overpass that leads to Tarzana Elementary School and features panels of Peanuts characters based on original artwork Schulz had donated to the school in the 1970s. A Reseda resident successfully pushed for their restoration in 2024.

and all-you-can-drink milk for a dime. You could even participate in milk-drinking contests. This place closed in 1986, and the Milk Farm building is long gone—but so beloved that a woman once placed her car between the building and the bulldozers and won the site a brief reprieve. At least the sign stayed.

The nearby **Nut Tree** (FIG. 23) was founded in 1921 in Vacaville, California. It started as a Lincoln Highway fruit stand that became a very big deal when the old road became I-80. In time, the Nut Tree became a thriving roadside complex with a carousel, a railroad attraction, an airport, an influential restaurant, and so much more. It closed in 1996. Today, the Nut Tree name is applied to a mixed-used development that retains traces of the original, including a revived play area and one of the old signs that had become a landmark on I-80.

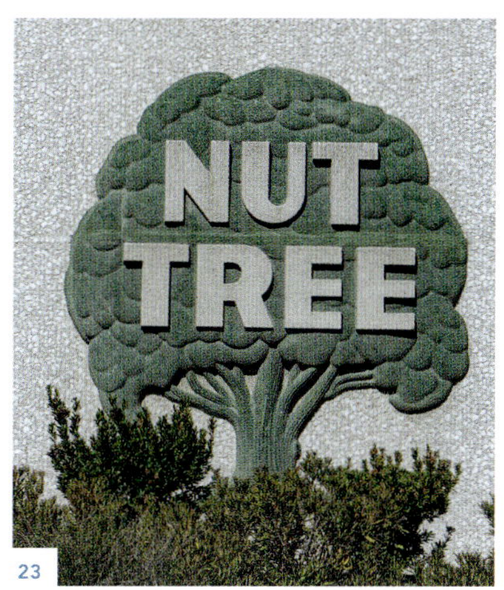

23

ROADSIDE EATS

Some of my favorite old-school restaurants and road-food stands are here in California. I'm sharing a selections of spots where you can't go wrong as you take your own Great American Retro Road Trip.

Green Bay, Wisconsin, and Burbank, California, aren't two cities you normally mention in the same sentence—unless the subject is chili. For it was at the turn of the last century that a Lithuanian immigrant named John Isaac got to selling a soupy style of chili in Green Bay. His son, Ernie, went west and gave us the roadside gift of **Chili John's** in 1946. Step inside and take a savory trip back in time at the counter.

Since opening in 1908, **Philippe the Original** (FIG. 24) has occupied a cherished spot in the hearts and bellies of Angelenos. French-dipped sandwiches arrived in 1918, and the business moved here in 1951, displaced by the 101 freeway. Phillippe is essential to L.A.'s soul, and it has competition in the form of **Cole's French Dip**, which also claims to have invented the French dip. But who am I to get in the middle of this? Let's just enjoy them for what they are.

Dan Tana's (FIG. 25) is a most pleasurable experience. Always bustling but comfy, the Italian restaurant has its regulars, but if you're like me and visit only once every few years, you feel like you're family, too, even if you're not a Hollywood macher. That warmth is likely the formula for Dan Tana's enduring success since opening in 1964 in a house on Santa Monica Boulevard.

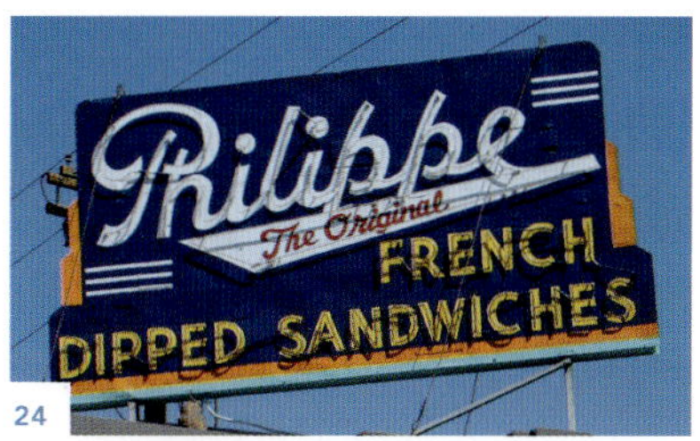

24

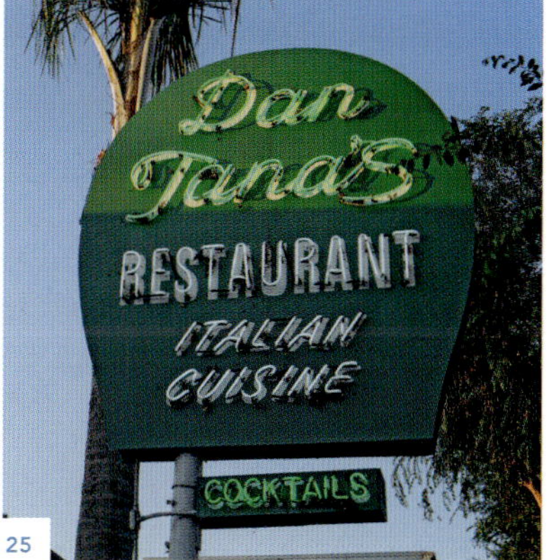

25

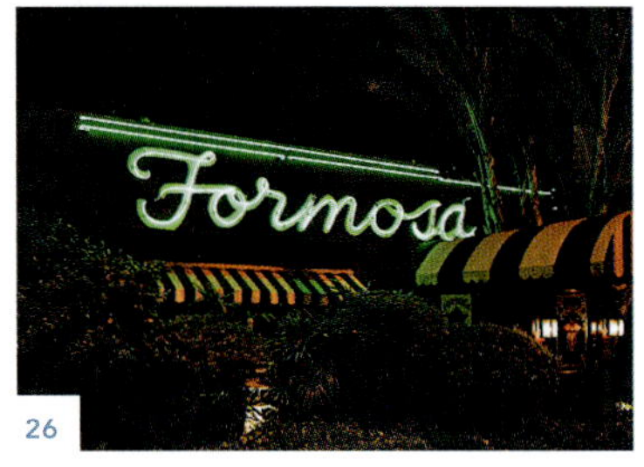

26

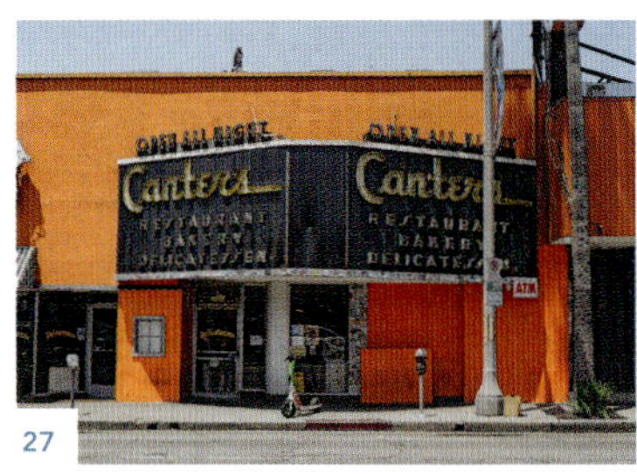

27

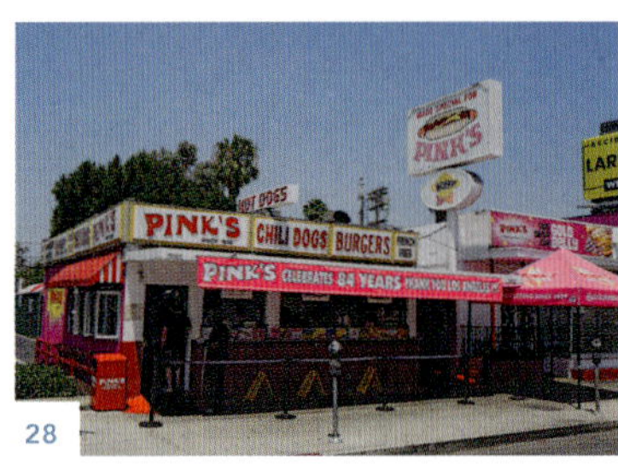

28

The **Formosa Cafe** (FIG. 26), a Santa Monica Boulevard classic with a rich history and the noirish vibe of 1940s L.A., faced an uncertain future in the last decade. Lucky for us, the 1933 Group stepped in and renovated it back to its glamorous heyday. The Pacific Electric Red Car trolley turned dining space that was attached to the restaurant has now been incorporated into it. The place is transcendent—you'll get lost in the haze of old L.A., now without the cigarette smoke.

Mentioning **Canter's** (FIG. 27) in L.A. is sort of like saying Katz's in New York—the very name sums up the experience you're going to have, a satisfying meal of Jewish delicatessen favorites all in a classic environment. If the space feels vast and the marquee cinematic, that's because it used to be a theater before Canter's moved here in 1953. Have a drink, bite, and even listen to live music at the Canter's Kibitz Room, part of a 1961 expansion next door.

On one of my first visits to Los Angeles I had dinner at **El Cholo**, a pioneering Mexican restaurant that's been open since 1923, and a pattern was set. Starting with its sign outside and the photos of celebrities whose faces you study in the lobby, the place is old school and inviting.

Vince's Spaghetti has been serving memorable meals in Ontario, California, since 1945, and they've since added two locations, all still in the Cuccia family. The menu is simple—the basics done right. Grandma Rose, originator of the recipes, would be proud.

Tony's Pizzaria in Ventura has the look of a New York storefront. Like many a good New York slice joint, Tony's has been here forever—in this case, since 1959, when John "Tony" Barrios set up shop. It is now run by his children who carry on Tony's saying—"Every pizza a master pizza!"

Pink's Hot Dogs (FIG. 28) is one of the great L.A. road-food stops, with origins as a pushcart in 1939 before this building came along in 1946. It took a lot of effort and faith on behalf of founders Paul and Betty Pink, but they'd built Pink's into an L.A. institution by the time they retired in 1985. Pink's is famous for its creative menu and Instagram-friendly environs.

▶▶▶ Pull Over!

The Apple Pan is a holy grail, famed for its quarter-pound hickory burgers, apple pie à la mode, and the communal ambience you can only have in a tiny restaurant tucked into a small house, its home since 1947. **Musso & Frank Grill** (FIG. 29), open since 1919, and **Miceli's**, open since 1949, are time machines to old Hollywood. And at **Casa Bianca Pizza Pie** (FIG. 30), on Colorado Boulevard in Eagle Rock, it's easy to imagine kids in the 1950s (and today, their great-grandkids) hanging out after school.

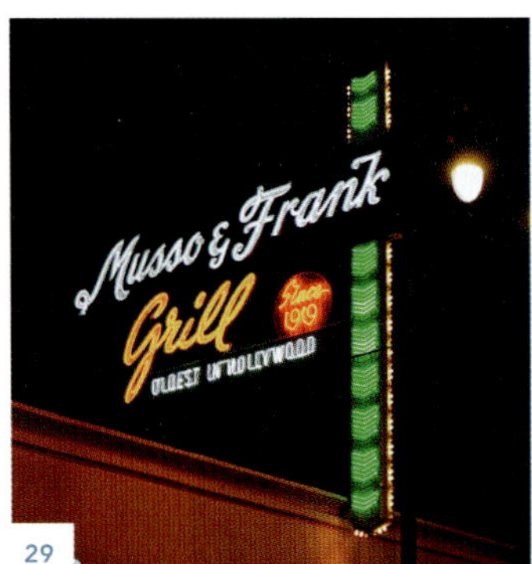

29

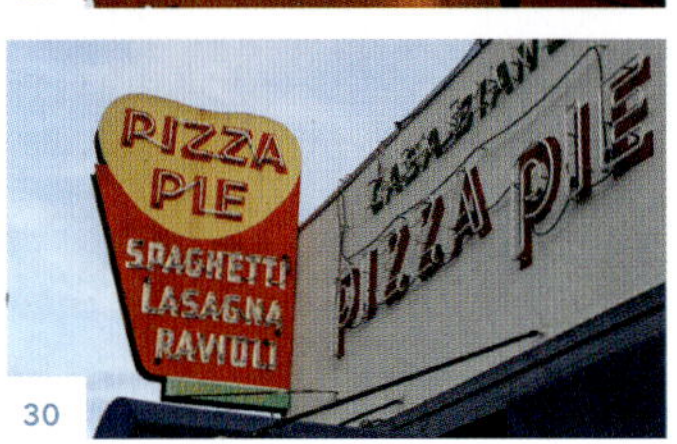

30

San Francisco is my favorite walking city, and I have a tradition of beginning my walks at **Sears Fine Food** (FIG. 31), which opened in 1938 and moved to this location in 1964. My preferred fuel? The eighteen Swedish pancakes with jam and butter.

I always like to check in on the sign for **John's Grill** (FIG. 32), a restaurant that is redolent with old San Francisco charm and was said to be a favorite of the writer Dashiell Hammett, author of *The Maltese Falcon*, whose iconic detective, Sam Spade, stops in for a bite at John's. Indeed, John's long touted itself as the home of the Maltese Falcon—a replica of the bird statue that figures in the story was donated to the restaurant decades ago. Somehow the bird and Hammett memorabilia were stolen in 2007, and were never recovered. Another replica, produced by art students, now sits in the restaurant and is much heavier than the original. Good luck stealing that.

Pea Soup Andersen's (FIG. 33) in Buellton, California, closed in 2024, just as it was about to celebrate its hundredth birthday. The restaurant, founded by Anton and Juliette Andersen, was a beloved part of the life and lore of the Central California coast. For now, another outlet of Andersen's survives, in Santa Nella.

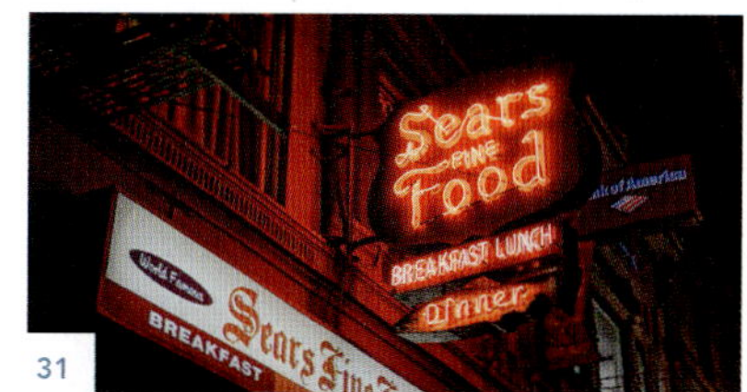

31

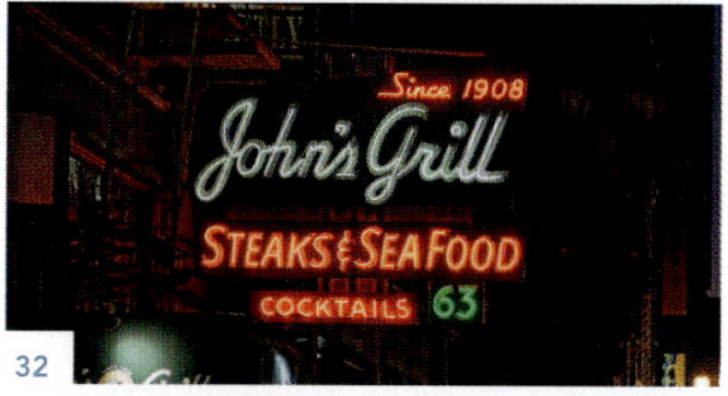

32

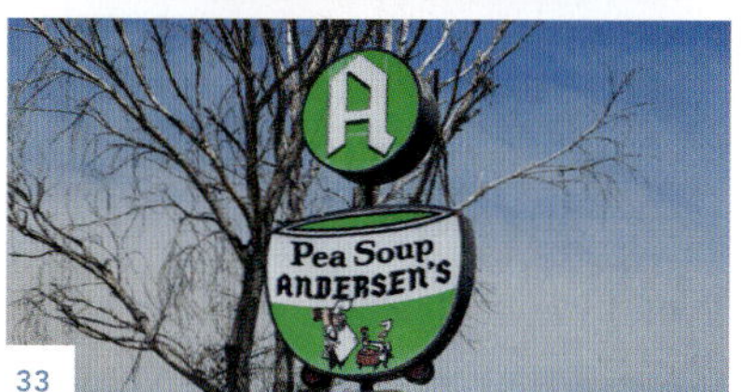

33

GOOGIE BEAUTIES

"Googie" is a term you'll hear a lot in Southern California—much like the "Doo Wop" style in Wildwood, New Jersey (see page 14). It refers to a vibrant architectural style that infused California commercial architecture in the 1950s and '60s. The features deployed included curving roofs, geometric shapes, vast plate-glass windows, references to space or jet travel, bold use of neon and incandescence in signage, and more. You know it when you see it.

Johnie's Coffee Shop, although shuttered, has found an afterlife as an intriguing historic artifact on Wilshire Boulevard.

Johnie's is work of Googie architectural masters Louis Armét and Eldon Davis, who are responsible for some of L.A.'s finest examples of the form. Their firm was also behind classics of the style such as **Pann's** (1958) and **Norms La Cienega** (1957; **FIG. 34**).

Another Googie beauty is **Chips Restaurant** (FIG. 35) in Hawthorne, with its dreamy typeface, the green offset tower, the zigzag roofline, the expansive windows, and more. Its composition is breathtaking.

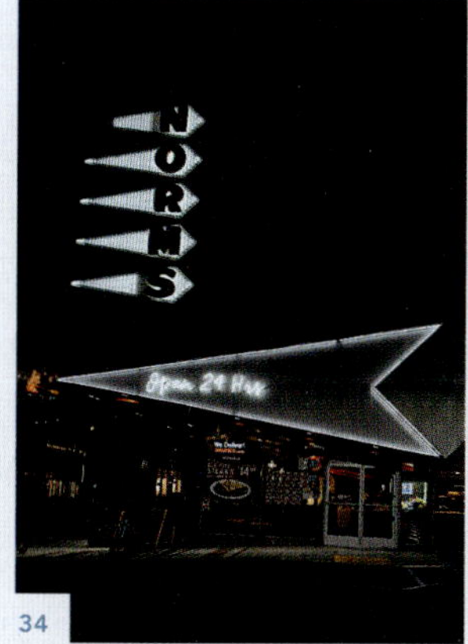

34

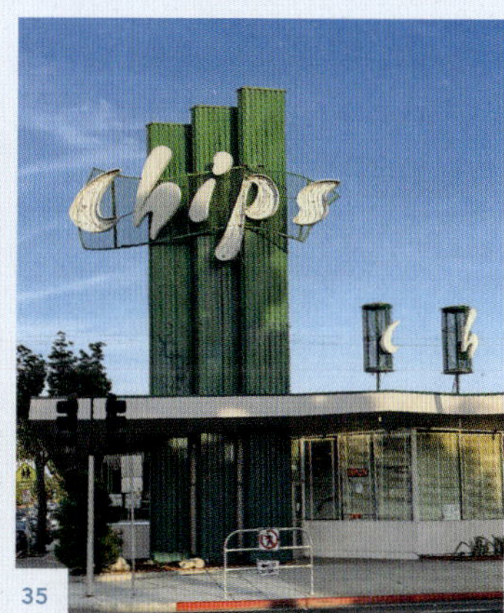

35

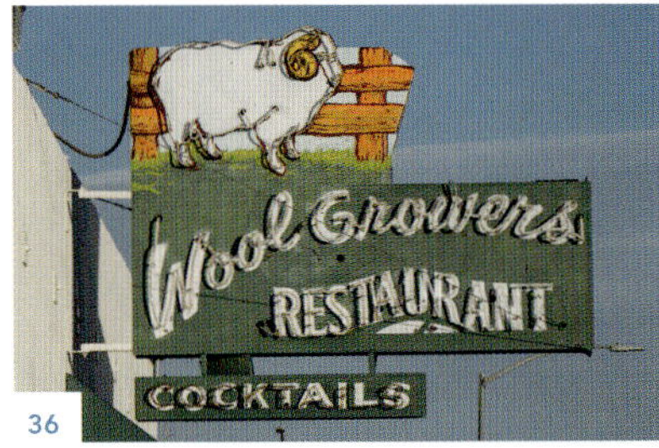

36

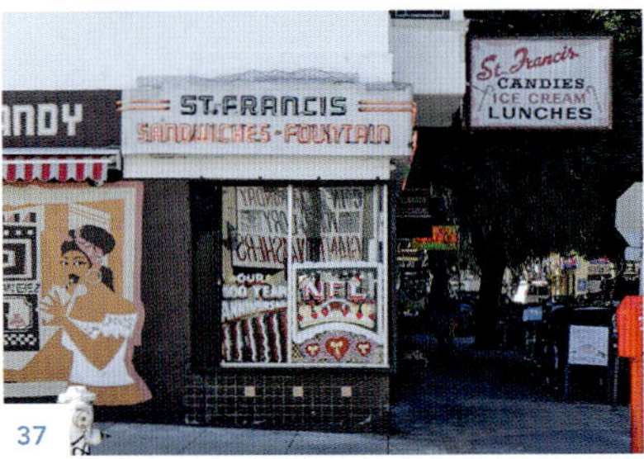

37

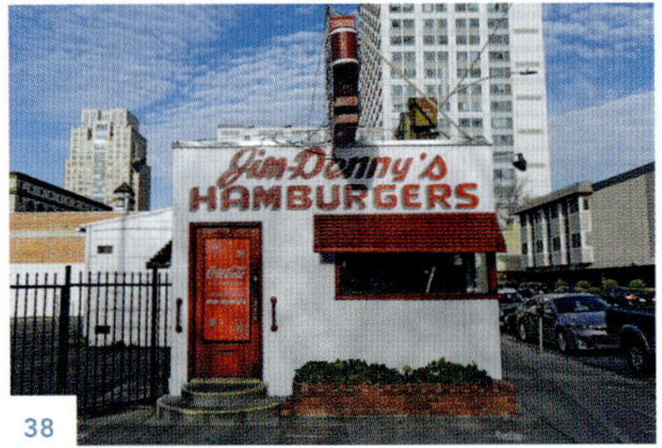

38

Wool Growers Restaurant and Cocktail Lounge (FIG. 36) has a curious sign that opens a window into Bakersfield history. In the nineteenth century an influx of people from the Basque region settled here, bringing sheepherding among their customs. Invariably the Basque culture reflected itself in restaurants, and Wool Growers came along in 1954. It's still run by the same family, offering hearty family-style fare while remaining a special link to Bakersfield's past.

St. Francis Fountain (FIG. 37) in San Francisco's Mission District is lovely, inside and out, and has been since 1918, though the soda counter arrived in the late 1940s. When new owners took over in 2002, they kept the soda fountain while refreshing the menu.

Jim-Denny's (FIG. 38), the wee white-stucco diner in downtown Sacramento, opened in 1934 and made it to the year 2020, shuttering right before the pandemic. But restaurateur N'Gina Guyton has revived the Bay Area classic and brought a refreshed menu (and patio seating) while hanging on to Jim Denny's patina.

Sacramento's **Pancake Circus** is overrun with clowns. The business once had nothing to do with the circus when it opened in 1961, but a later name change, first to Pancake Parade and then Pancake Circus, launched the carnival atmosphere. Customers have made a tradition of contributing clown-themed gifts to the ever-growing collection. The pancakes are really good, too—the lure of them might help coulrophobes get over their fears once and for all.

CHAINS OF FOOD

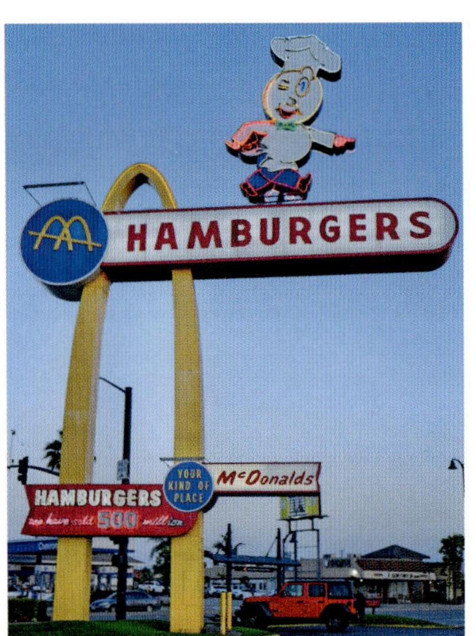

McDonald's Motherland

The McDonald's in Downey, California (left), opened on August 18, 1953. Nobody then appreciated that this location would become the oldest operating restaurant of what would be one of the most influential brands of the twentieth century. It was the third location of a slowly growing chain of burger places founded by two brothers from San Bernardino, Dick and Maurice McDonald. They had developed the Speedee Service System with a simple menu and an efficient, technology-enhanced assembly line that got customers their food fast. But burger huts in Southern California were a dime a dozen; the region was an incubator for fast-food chains.

It was Ray Kroc who realized how special McDonald's was. In 1954 he teamed up with the McDonald brothers, began to franchise aggressively, recast himself as the founder, and built his own store in Des Plaines, Illinois. By 1961, the brothers had been bought out for $1.8 million and the company was driven ever higher by Kroc's ambitions and the world's endless appetite for what his restaurants were cooking, with some help from clever, child-focused marketing.

The McDonald's chain grew quickly after that, but in Downey, at 10207 Lakewood Boulevard, the 1950s never quite went away. The red-and-white building and the unique single-arch sign featuring Chef Speedee remained, a relic from 1959. Multiple "retro" McDonald's pay homage to this Speedee sign, one in Lewiston, Idaho, and the other in Banning, California.

Corporate McDonald's embraced this sign in some of its throwback "Classic" locations. In 1990, the Downey McDonald's was absorbed into the McDonald's corporation, and it was rescued only by a preservationist and public outcry. If you visit, be sure to check out the little McDonald's museum right next door. The only other McDonald's of this architectural style still in operation is the 1960s "red and white" in San Jose, California.

McDonald's in the last decades has been eliminating the hip-roof brick buildings, known as the mansards for their distinct rooflines. These buildings were vital in the brand's penetration deeper into small towns, who'd resisted the earlier McDonald's buildings as garish and out of place. Even amid the uniformity, McDonald's franchisees were given freedom to have a little fun, especially if it meant making good with their communities.

Here are some other unique McDonald's that are worth seeking out:

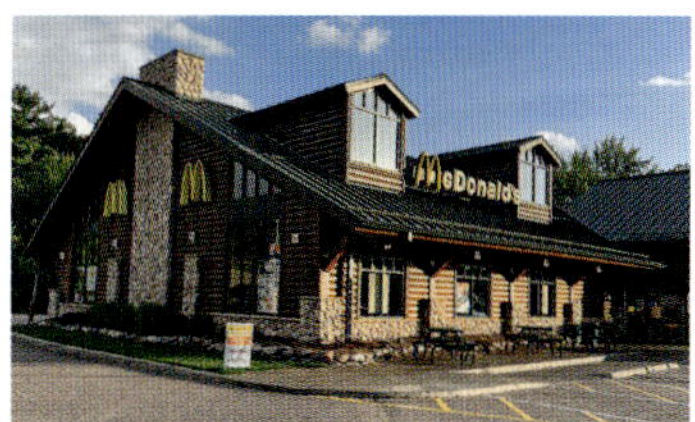

The McDonald's in Wisconsin Dells is housed in a giant log cabin.

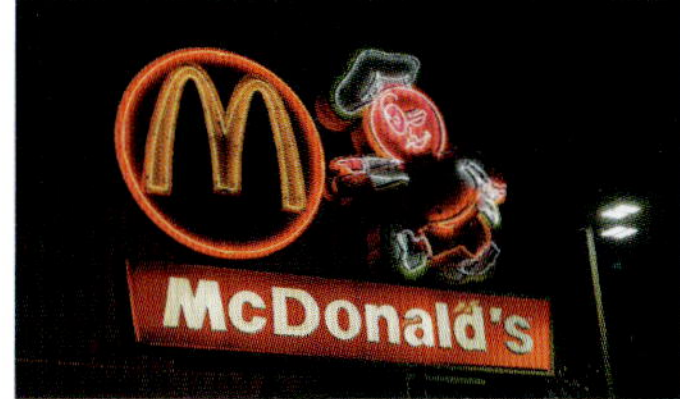

Speedee puts on a show at the McDonald's on North La Brea in West Hollywood.

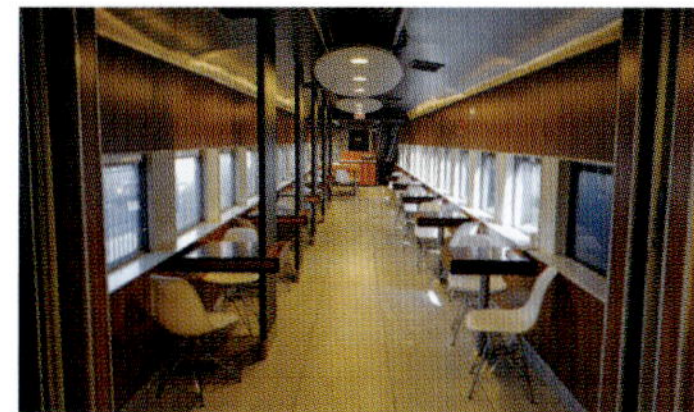

The Barstow McDonald's has a railroad theme.

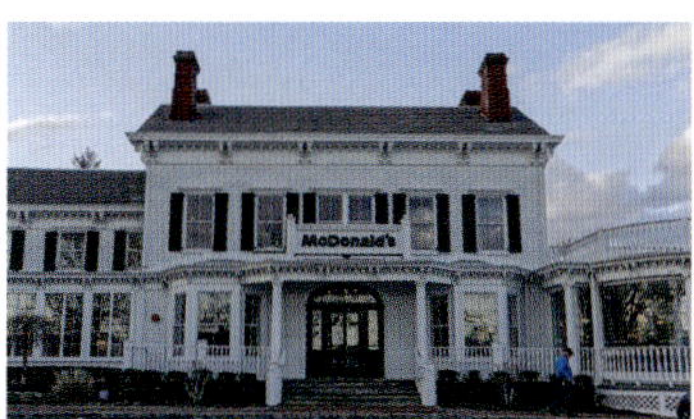

This McDonald's, in New Hyde Park, New York, was constructed in an old mansion—preservationists were lovin' it.

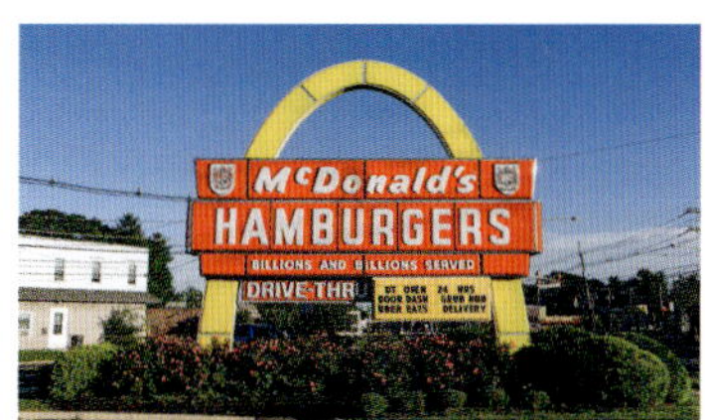

The McDonald's in Magnolia, New Jersey, is among a handful that still feature a single arch, a transitional style of sign.

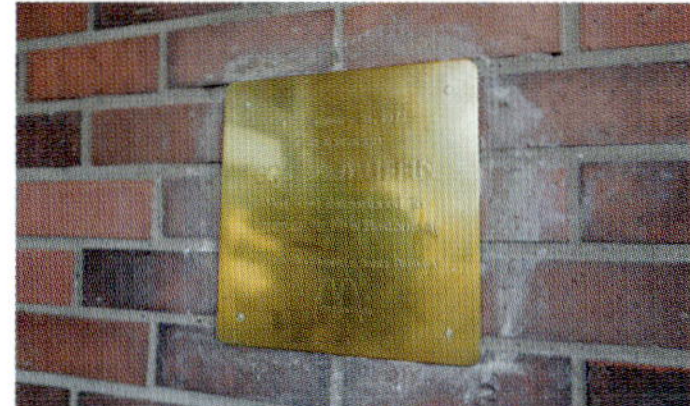

This McDonald's in Santa Barbara is where owner Herb Peterson invented the Egg McMuffin, a fact noted on a brass plaque.

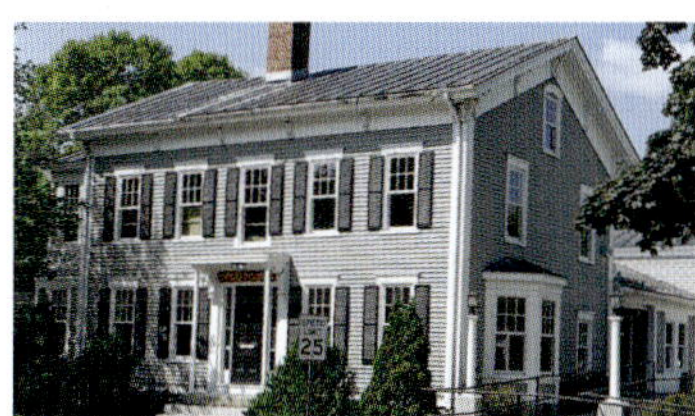

The McDonald's in Freeport, Maine, occupies a nineteenth-century home known as the Gore House, allowing the Golden Arches to get design approval.

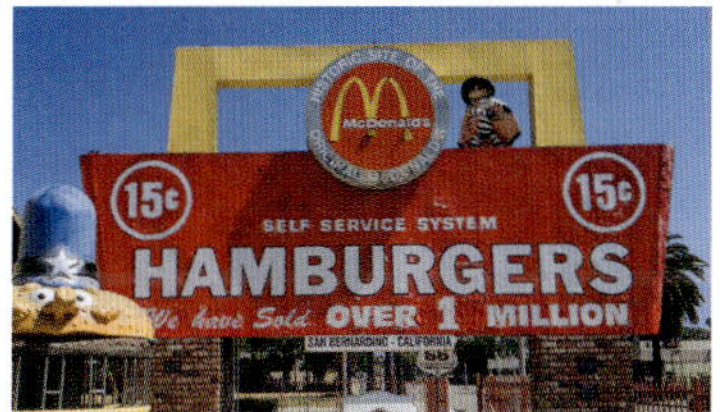

The unofficial McDonald's Museum in San Bernardino celebrates the chain's heritage at the site of the first McDonald's.

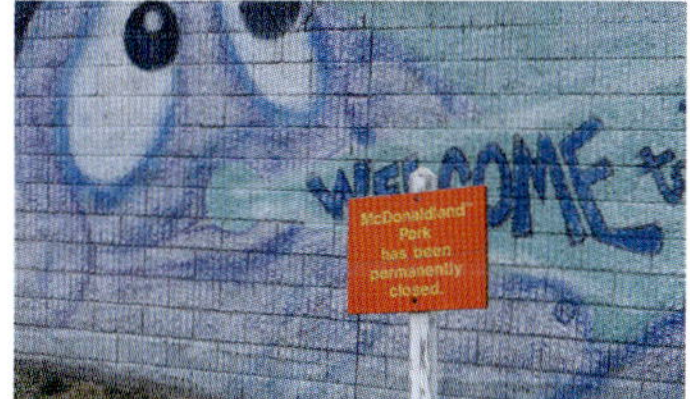

A fading mural is all that's left of a McDonaldland outdoor park in West St. Paul, Minnesota. These classic characters have been erased from stores.

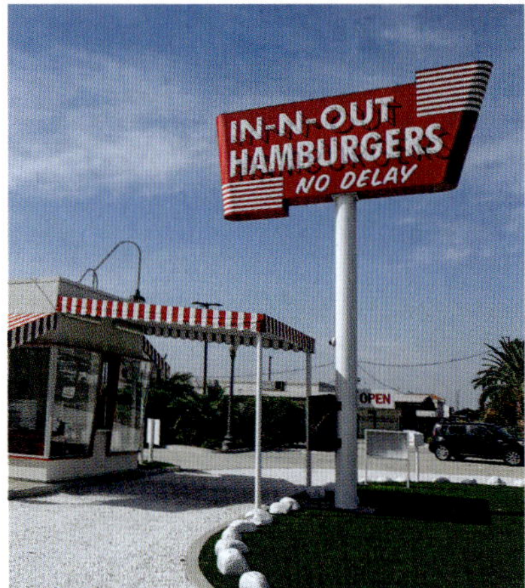

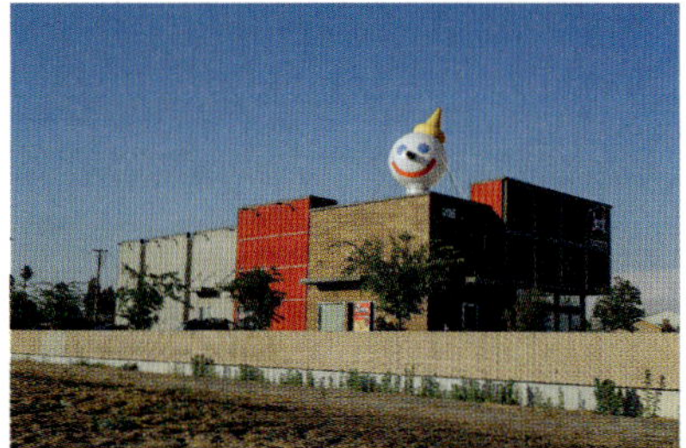

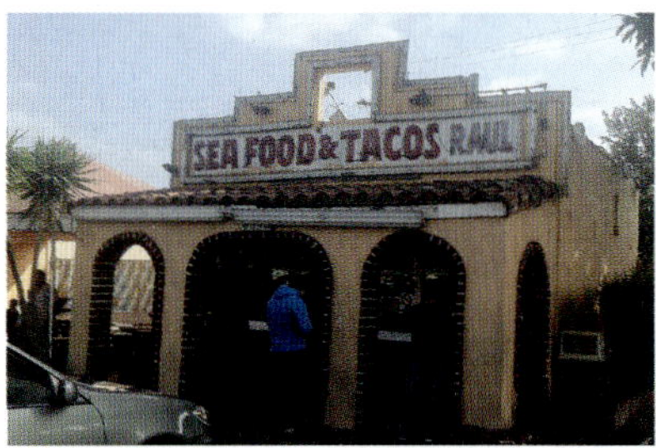

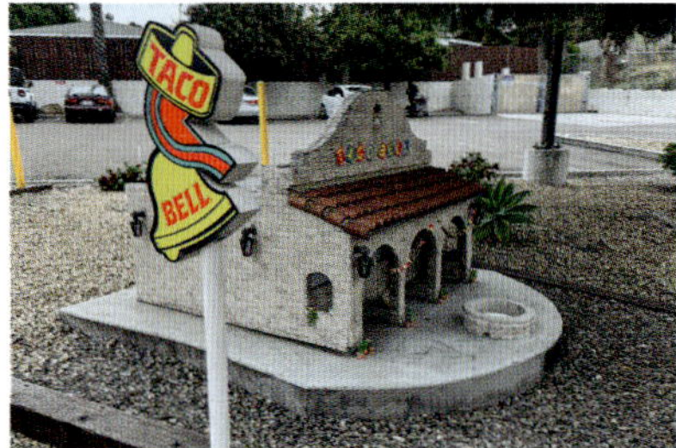

In-N-Out

Harry and Esther Snyder opened their first In-N-Out Burger in Baldwin Park in 1948, and this store is the closest you can get to that early In-N-Out experience, because the original was demolished for the construction of Interstate 10. So it's appropriate that it is the 10 that brings you there.

This store is a pristine exhibit that captures the look of the original, from the shack—measuring about 10 square feet—and red-and-white awning to the innovative two-way speaker to cater to hungry, in-a-hurry motorists. Even the sign at this In-N-Out is different: The distinctive In-N-Out arrow design was introduced in 1954, replacing the "No Delay" sign.

A modern-day In-N-Out restaurant is just one minute down Francisquito Avenue.

Jack in the Box

In Fowler, spot the giant Jack in the Box head perched on a restaurant there, the same head that in miniature once graced car antennas across California and took your order at drive-thru kiosks. Jack in the Box has fully embraced Jack the character, but in 1980, the Jack speaker boxes were blown up in a commercial as the brand sought to burnish its appeal among adults. (I shot one at the Valley Relics Museum; see sidebar on page 292.) Jack in the Box was founded in 1951 in San Diego and is among the big hamburger chains that also include Carl's Jr. and Fatburger.

Taco Bell

In 1962, Glen Bell opened the first Taco Bell in a little mission-style building in Downey, California (left, second from bottom). Taco Bell may never have come to be, and perhaps instead we'd all be talking about Taco Tia or El Taco, both chains that Bell operated and later moved on from because he wanted to work without partners. Taco Bell would be his true ring of opportunity, and he would sell to PepsiCo in 1978.

The chain's design evolved to today's sleek, purple-heavy scheme, yet the roadside still offers us examples of more festive designs. The original location in Downey has been rescued and sits on the campus of Taco Bell headquarters in Irvine. The oldest plastic sign, dating to the 1970s, survives at a location in Savannah, Georgia. Examples of 1980s and '90s Taco Bells are dwindling, and the ones most sought after feature the 1990s *Miami Vice* style, slathered with stripes and pastels. And perhaps my favorite Taco Bell is a miniature classic 1960s Taco Bell (left, bottom) that was built behind an existing Taco Bell in San Diego, a tribute to this location's early days as the first outlet of the chain in America's Finest City.

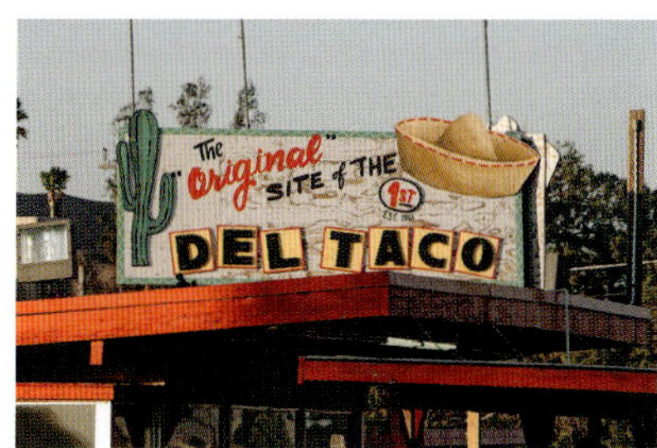

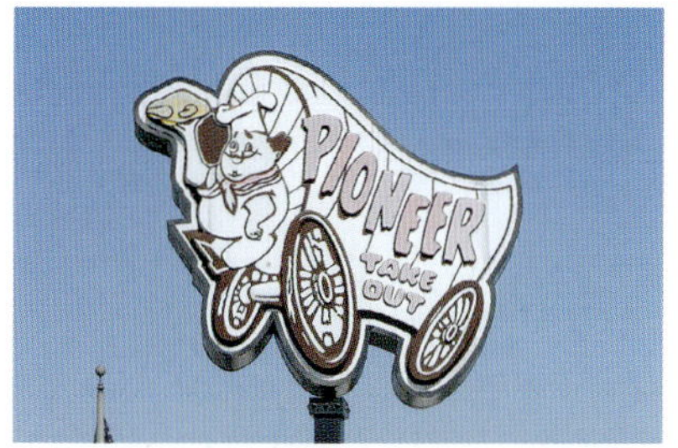

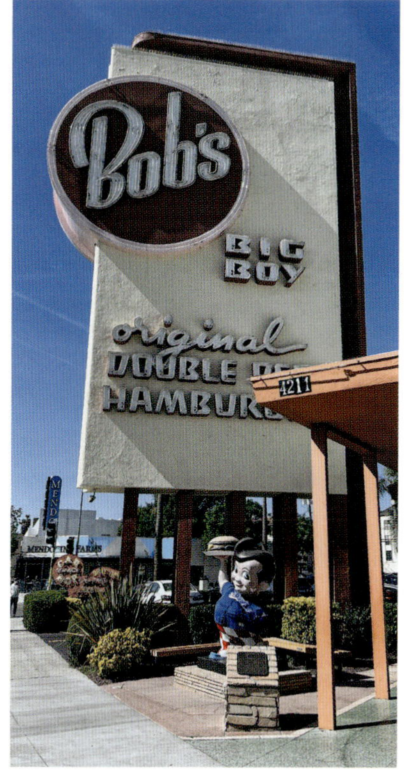

Del Taco

The first Del Taco opened far from Los Angeles, in the Mojave Desert town of Yermo, in 1964. The building still honors the history through signage pointing out its foundational role in the chain, even though it has long not been affiliated with it.

The mantle of numero uno has really passed to one of three original Del Tacos that are still in the family of chain cofounder Ed Hackbarth, in nearby Barstow. I visited in the summer of 2024 and picked up a bottle of Del Taco sauce featuring the old sun logo (which I had to toss at the TSA at LAX. *No!*) as well as a Christmas ornament with said logo. This location operates as the original through an agreement with Del Taco corporate.

Pioneer Chicken

Pioneer Chicken began in the early 1960s as a take-out chicken shack in the Echo Park neighborhood of Los Angeles. Founder H. R. Kaufman built up a business around the Pioneer name, featuring Pioneer Pete and his chuck wagon, immortalized in vacuum-formed plastic signage that revolved. Pioneer locations would number in the hundreds, mainly in Southern California. While the chain was an inescapable part of life in Southern California in the 1970s through 1990s, bankruptcy, managerial woes, and, well, Kentucky Fried Chicken were formidable foes. Eventually Popeye's swooped down and converted most Pioneer locations. Today, the two remaining Pioneer restaurants, in Bell Gardens and Boyle Heights, are time capsules.

Bob's Big Boy

The Bob's Big Boy story tests the flow-chart skills of even the most detail oriented, and the Big Boy name (and logo) has seen many permutations over the years and across the land (see page 143 for one notable branch in the Midwest). But the oldest in existence is the veritable flagship in Burbank, which opened in 1949 with the designs of architect Wayne McAllister—a little streamline moderne, a little 1950s Googie-style coffee shop, and a lot of gorgeous. It all began in 1936 when Bob Wien bought a hamburger stand in Glendale that become the first Bob's Big Boy. The concept was franchised under different Big Boy permutations, including Bob's, and the march of Double Decker burgers and kid-friendly statues was underway.

H. Salt Esq.

In California, H. Salt Esq., the fish-and-chips chain, carved out a space in the fast-food universe, and the old-timey British look and feel of the joints—filtered through 1960–70s sensibilities—make them so appealing. H. Salt was Haddon Salt, a British entrepreneur whose own dad ran a fish-and-chips joint in the mother country. He came to America intent on introducing us to fish-and-chips, knowing that GIs in World War II loved them. After a period of growth, and ill-fated ownership by Kentucky Fried Chicken, H. Salt sputtered and the chain muddled along, the remaining locations today operating independently.

A&W

On June 20, 1919, a humble little root beer stand opened in Lodi, California. Roy W. Allen's beverage sold for a nickel a frosty mug and would become the foundation of the A&W root beer chain of restaurants. The root beer recipe he bought from an Arizona pharmacist was a hit, and Allen soon recruited Frank Wright to help him run the business. Among their collaborations was teaming up the initials of their last names to create the A&W brand. Wright was eventually bought out, kindly leaving his initial behind. Allen kept franchising stores by the hundreds, pioneering the drive-in concept with "tray boys" hopping to customers in cars. One of the nicest survivors can be found in San Rafael, California.

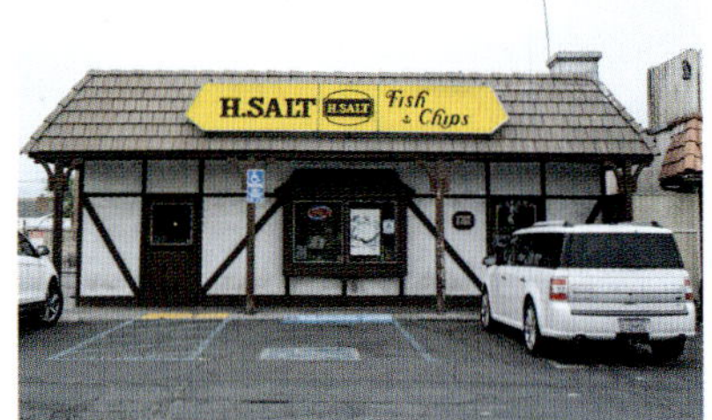

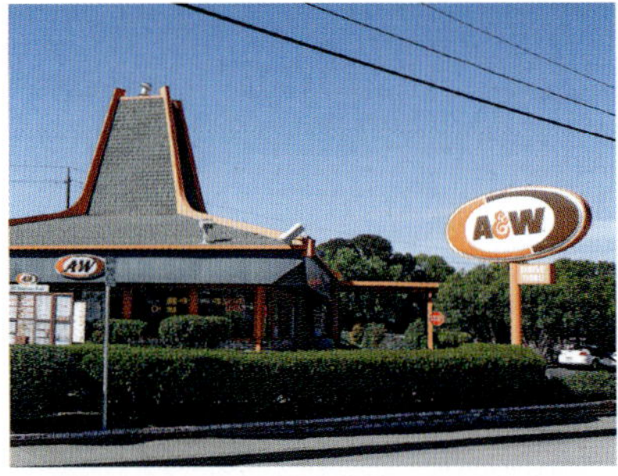

Shakey's Pizza

For many, Shakey's Pizza is a core happy memory: pizza parties to the tune of Dixieland jazz or barbershop quartets in an old-timey setting. Nostalgia has always been big, and in 1954, when the first Shakey's opened in Sacramento, the early decades of the twentieth century had a certain romantic allure. Shakey's grew into a large chain with a national presence, the first pizza chain to do so. The chain has dwindled in the United States, but if you want a taste of what once was, the Northridge Shakey's has vintage appeal to spare.

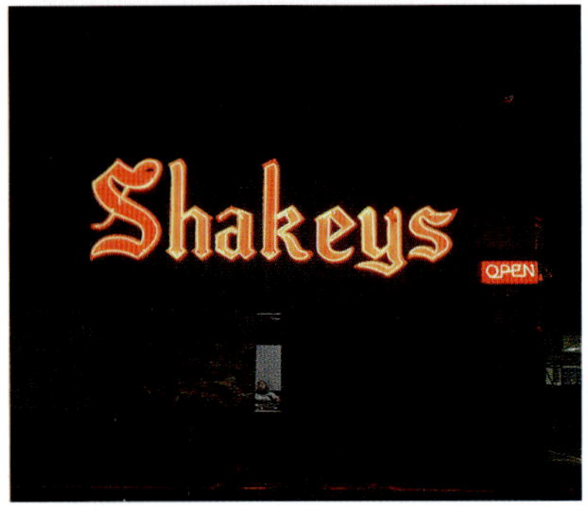

Taco Lita

Taco Lita was birthed during that great postwar eruption of taco stands, with some becoming chains, global in the case of Taco Bell, and others stalling, and often, retreating. Taco Lita, founded in 1956 as the "home of the glorified taco," had more than a dozen locations at its peak but is making its final stand here in Arcadia. And what a final stand it is, in this building from 1967.

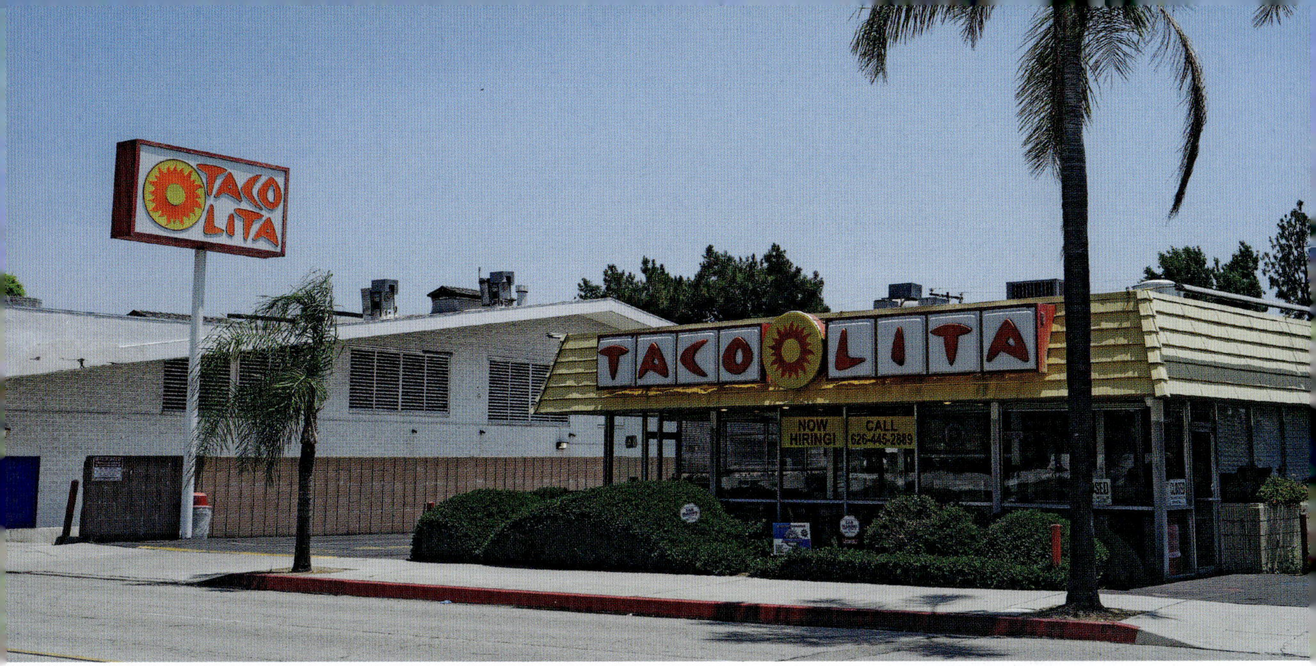

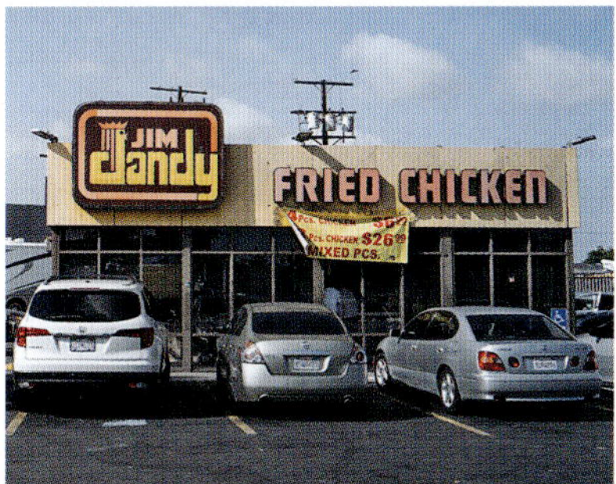

Jim Dandy Fried Chicken

Jim Dandy Fried Chicken restaurants were launched in 1969 in Los Angeles and grew quickly with locations around the country. The chain, though, has all but faded away. There is but one location, in Los Angeles, which was part of that initial burst of twenty-nine locations that were open by June 1970. Relics of Jim Dandy survive in Houston.

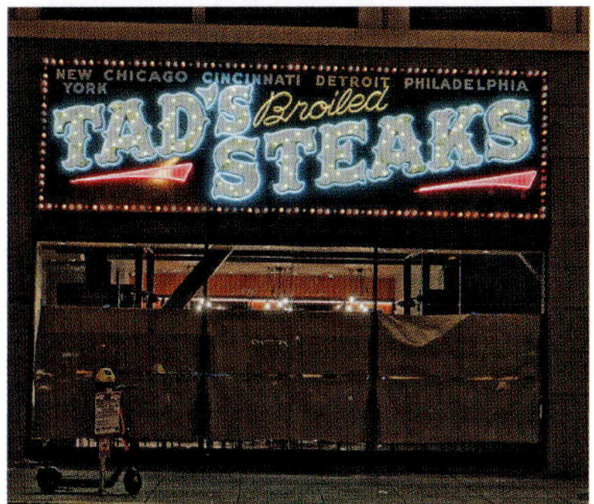

Tad's Steaks

Another entrant in the "last of its kind" category is Tad's Steaks. The budget T-bone steak chain, founded in 1955 on Powell Street in San Francisco, once extended to several cities, with a number in New York. Tad's was such a part of the old Times Square it was easy to think the chain was a native New Yorker. After the last in NYC location closed in 2020, the San Francisco store, the first, also became the last, a familiar theme.

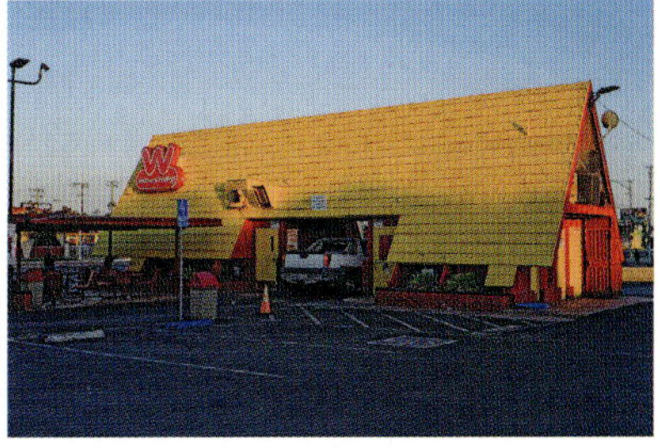

Wienerschnitzel

Wienerschnitzel is famous for its funny name and iconic yellow A-frame buildings, into which you would drive to pick up your hot dogs. The chain was founded in 1961 as Der Wienerschnitzel, and remains concentrated in California.

MAINSTAYS OF MAIN STREET

We'll see plenty of shops that are on traditional downtown streets, but, this being California, quite a number will be in that exquisite twentieth-century invention of practicality and convenience—strip malls—as well as a few off the beaten path.

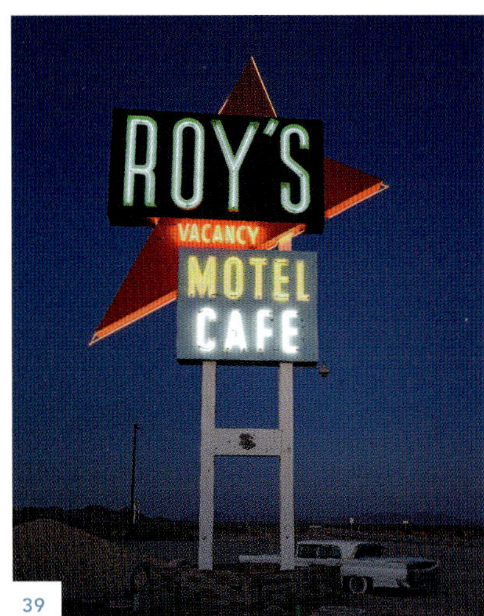

39

We're starting on America's Main Street, Route 66, which happens to be the main street here in the Mojave Desert ghost town of Amboy. But it hasn't given up the ghost thanks to **Roy's** (FIG. 39). Roy Crowl opened what was initially a garage in 1938 and later grew to include a motel. The sign came along in 1959, but when I-40 bypassed Amboy in 1973, it drained all the life from this stretch of Route 66. Well, almost. Four people were said to live here in the early 2000s, around the time the whole town was bought by restaurant entrepreneur and preservationist Albert Okura of Juan Pollo chicken fame. He reopened Roy's in 2008, and the sign was restored in 2019. (Note: A tiny version of the iconic Roy's sign can be found in Barstow at a restaurant that was owned by Mr. Okura.)

On a drive back from the desert, you'd be wise to wipe that dust off your car at **Rancho Super Car Wash** (FIG. 41) in Rancho Mirage. The freshly restored sign, designed by Beatrice Haverfield and installed around 1967, was added to the Rancho Mirage Register of Historic Places. Haverfield was Seattle's "Queen of Neon," and indeed this sign is descended from a pink pachyderm pack up that way (see page 275).

Let's get to shopping for a new car, and one of the swankiest places to do that has, since 1949, been **Casa de Cadillac** (FIG. 42) in Sherman Oaks, a pristine example of a postwar showroom. Think of all the car models—the 1950s tailfin affairs, the 1970s land boats—that have been displayed on that floor.

Car dealers in California go the extra mile, and **Felix Chevrolet** (FIG. 43) has been doing just that since 1921, when founder Winslow Felix opened a Chevrolet dealer here. At the same time, Felix the Cat was a popular cartoon character and Felix the Car Guy was pals with illustrator Pat Sullivan, who gave the dealership the paws-up to use his cute character. By 1958, the booming dealership erected the gigantic Felix neon sign to attract the notice of motorists on U.S. 101. Though LED lighting has replaced neon tubing, Felix is still the same adorable mascot.

Pull Over!

Googie-style car washes are a California signature. **Sun Day Carwash** in Highland Park, which recently restored its sign, and **Sparkle Car Wash** (FIG. 40) in San Bernardino, with a multicolored row of fins, command your attention.

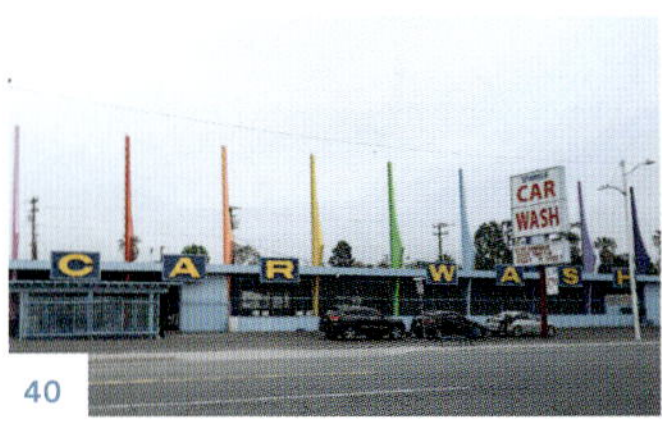

40

The **Ford** dealership in Woodland Hills, California, has an easy-to-miss throwback to the Ford of the 1970s and '80s, when the logo in signage was tucked inside a rectangle with the word "FORD" next to it. These are quite rare, and I know of only one other, at a dealership in Arroyo Grande, which is across the street from a Chevy dealer with a classic bow-tie neon sign.

Once we've put some miles on the car, we've got to worry about the tires, and **Clerou Tire Co.** (FIG. 44) in Bakersfield proudly shows off a little history, too. The pajama-wearing child, candle in his left hand and tire slung over his right shoulder, is a mascot known as the Fisk Boy, used in the punning campaign "Time to Re-tire."

Once you have your wheels, you have to keep them aligned and Bear Wheel Alignment turned that into a thriving business in the twentieth century. The **Happy Bear** imagery (FIG. 45) was used at auto shops that offered Bear-brand service and products, like this one in Long Beach. As a child, I would marvel at a Happy Bear sign in Hartsdale, New York, that suddenly vanished—an early lesson in roadside appreciation. Happy Bears are still on the prowl, and Southern California has an impressive pack.

For years, the place to get gas was a **Standard station**. The Standard Oil Company was broken up by the federal government in 1911, and the "baby Standards" developed their own unique brands, like Exxon, Mobil, and Chevron, though some kept using Standard branding for decades after. In San Francisco, more than 110 years after the Standard breakup, Chevron has designated one station, on Van Ness Avenue (FIG. 46), to serve as a Standard station, reportedly to protect the trademark. In every other respect, it looks like a Chevron station.

From tune-ups to tunes, our tour of California main streets continues with music shops and iconic discount stores. **Mr. C's Rare Records** opened in Old Towne Orange in 1977. Mr. C—Everett Caldwell—began collecting 45s to supply his daughters' jukebox in the family rumpus room. Enamored by the cover art and "out of sight" music, Mr. C took things to the point where his wife insisted "either you go or the records go," she told the *Orange County Register*. So he opened the record shop. Mr. C amassed an album archive that numbered more than a million at one point. The store was even immortalized in the film *That Thing You Do!* starring Tom Hanks.

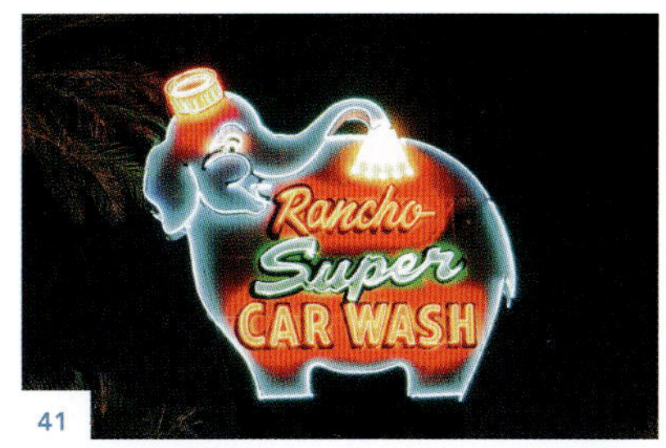

41

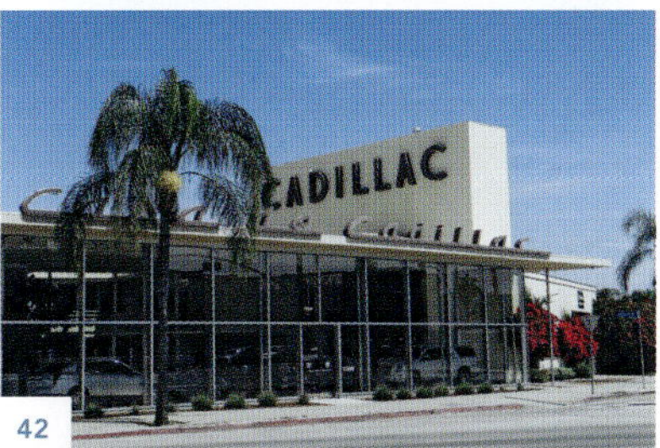

42

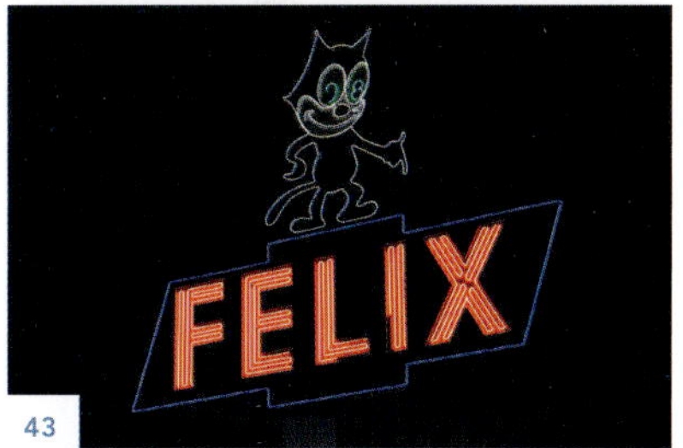

43

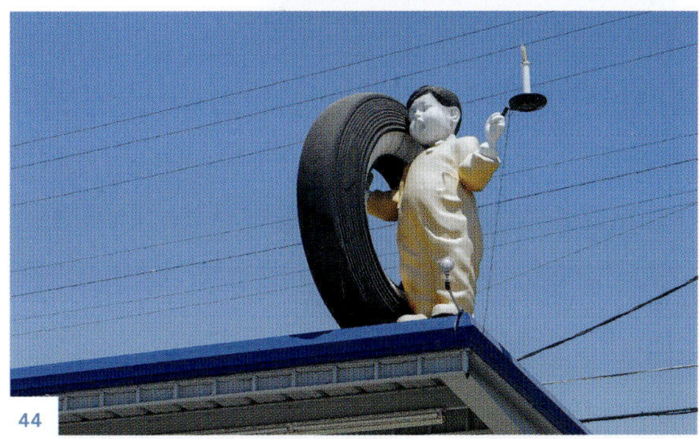
44

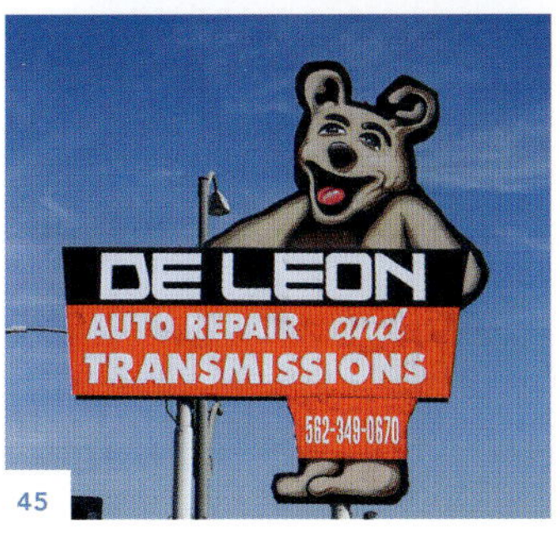

45

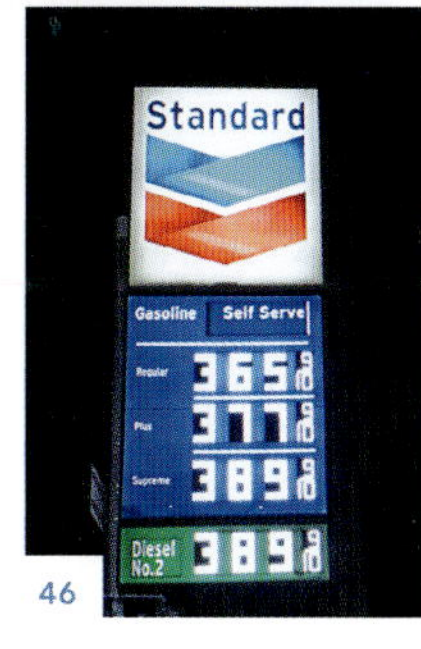

46

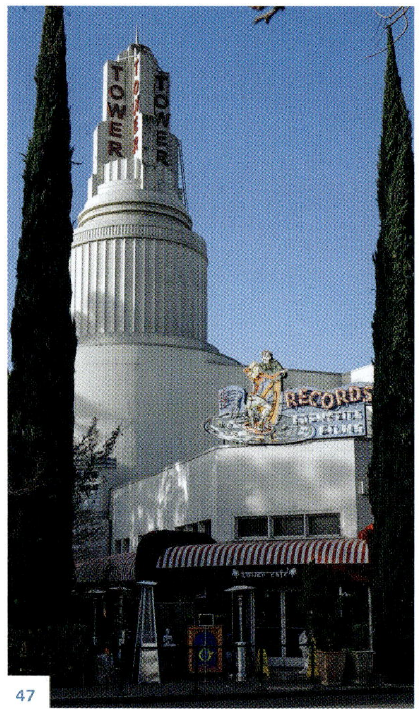

47

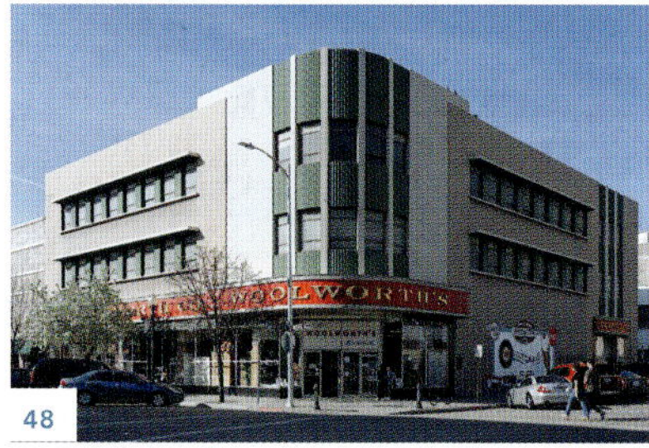

48

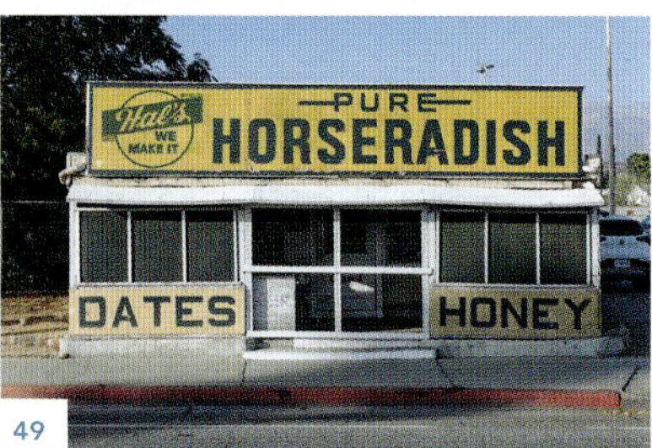

49

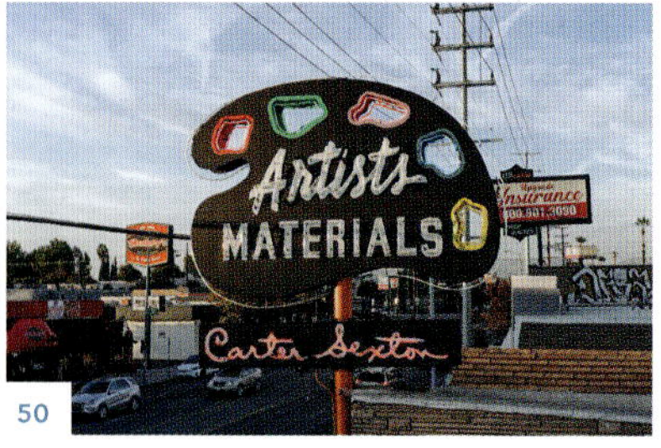

50

In Sacramento, we can explore the birthplace of the defunct but once influential **Tower Records** (FIG. 47) chain. It was once a colossus but went out of business in 2006, crippled by a host of problems, including digital music piracy. Well, if you can't beat 'em, join 'em—the brand now sells music online, and, irony of ironies, touts the sale of vinyl above everything else.

Woolworth's (FIG. 48), the five-and-dime chain that dominated American downtowns for more than a century, went bust in America in 1997. The chain was once so profitable that founder F. W. Woolworth built the world's tallest skyscraper for himself in lower Manhattan. He is depicted in the lobby counting the nickels that built his empire. The ghosts of Mr. Woolworth's chain still haunt many a street. The best-preserved Woolworth's—with old signage, luncheonette, and decorative and structural work largely intact—is in Bakersfield and opened in 1949. After this Woolworth's went bust in 1994, the space served as an antiques mall for a quarter century while the luncheonette still operated as the Woolworth Diner.

In 2021 the building was purchased by owners who are restoring the former Woolworth's as a multiuse property, giving great care to the site's history and relics. The luncheonette will be at the heart of what the owners do and will pay respect to the sit-ins at segregated Woolworth's luncheonettes during the civil rights movement.

I don't think I've ever craved a condiment as much as when I set eyes on **Hal's Horseradish** (FIG. 49) shop in the desert town of Banning. Sadly, Hal's has been closed since 2014, but its cheery, sun-blistered storefront still stands. It's as though proprietor Hal Embshoff has simply closed for the day, not forever.

When **Carter Sexton** (FIG. 50) began to sell drafting furniture for Hollywood studios, he was having trouble getting shipments delivered to his home in North Hollywood. So he found a storefront on Lauren Canyon Boulevard and set up shop under his name in 1944, using the space to sell art supplies. It remains a thriving business with a mixture of vintage signage.

Strike! That's the best word to describe the neon sign for Tarzana's **Corbin Bowl** (FIG. 51). Corbin opened in 1959 and survived a brush with death after the 1994 Northridge earthquake. Corbin's good looks have been immortalized in TV shows and movies—and in the memories of San Fernando Valley kids.

Covina Bowl (FIG. 52) was one of L.A.'s most magnificent specimens of Googie. The bowling alley's closure in 2017 may well have been the end of it, but Covina is enjoying an unexpected afterlife. A portion of the original structure, as well as the sign, restored to its original look, are now part of a housing

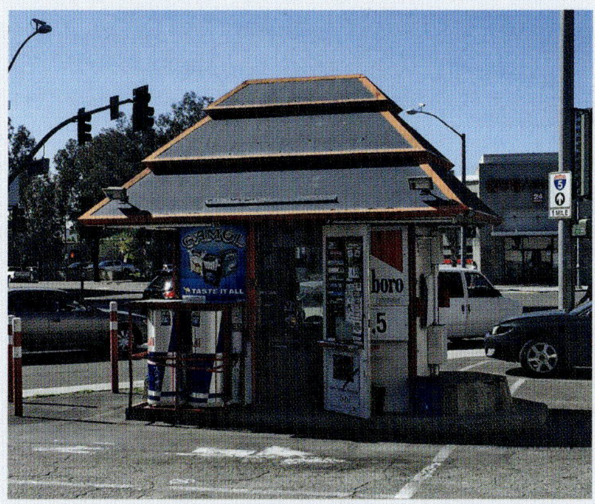

STRIP MALL SNAP SHACKS

Ah, Fotomat, the little hut in shopping plazas where you could drop off film and pick up your prints, a relic of a time when these buildings were the picture of progress. At the dawn of Fotomat in the mid-1960s, the huts were an innovative extension of drive-thru restaurant service. By 1971, there were more than a thousand huts. They kept growing until the usual mix of business saboteurs—e.g., changing consumer behavior and advances in technology—did them in. The old Fotomats have a way of hanging on and have curious afterlives, like this one in Glendale.

development, Covina Bowl by Trumark Housing, with design work inspired and deferential to the original bowling alley. This photo was taken in 2021 as the conversion was underway.

As we explore our figurative California Main Street, it's time to wash our clothes! **Coin-Op Laundry** (FIG. 53) in Bellflower is a quirky twist on mimetic architecture—yes, those are gigantic clothespins clipped on the roof as if to hold notes. It's a clever composition.

Bakersfield's **Sparkle** (FIG. 54) began as a laundry and cleaning service in November 1950, founded by Richard K. "Stubby" Newman Jr. A Sparkle truck would pick up your dirty duds and return them sparkling clean. Today the company is in the uniform and linen business. The sign for their factory is a vintage delight, the typeface established on day one.

Should we need the services of a pharmacist, **Elmore Pharmacy** (FIG. 55) in Red Bluff is here. The sight of this corner of Hopperesque beauty is like taking a swig of an old-fashioned reinvigorating tonic. Elmore is believed to be the oldest operating pharmacy in California, going back to the gold-rush era.

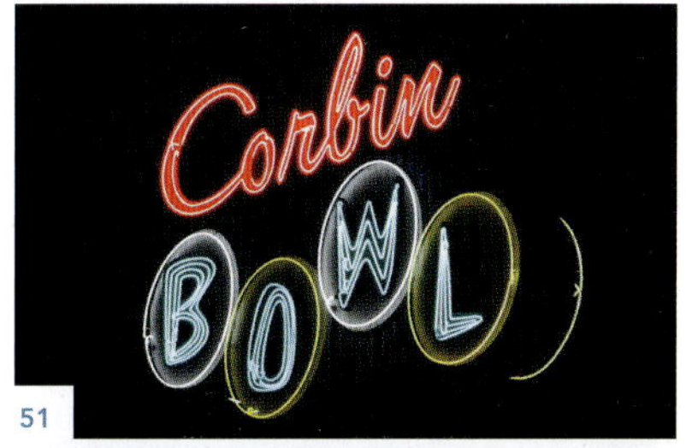

51

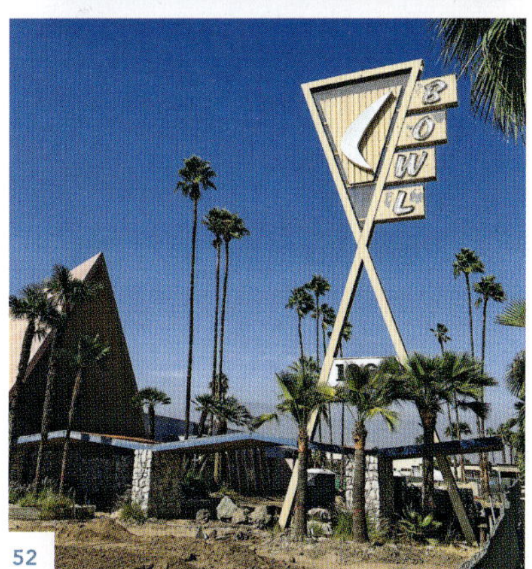

52

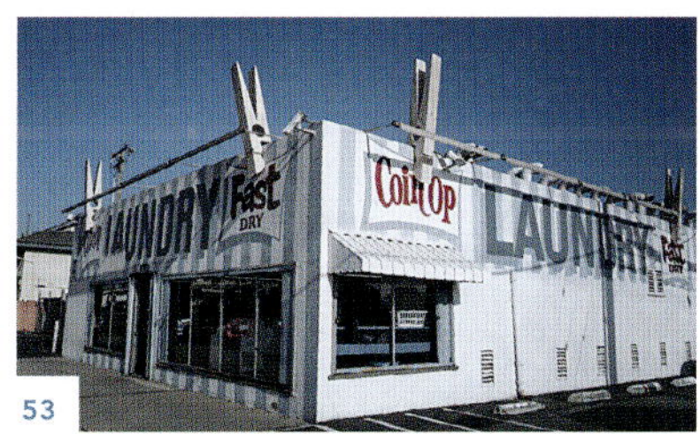

53

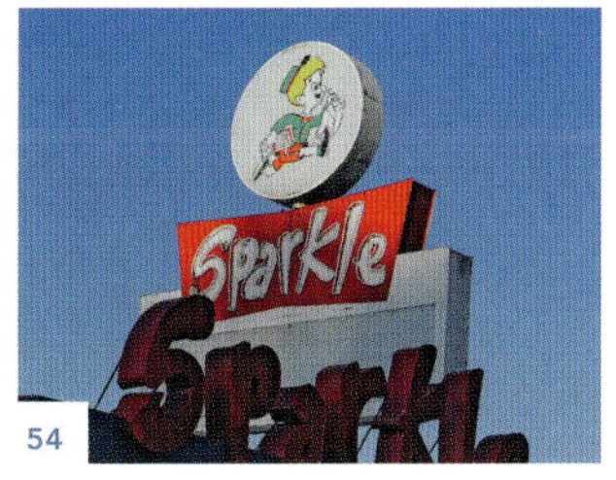

54

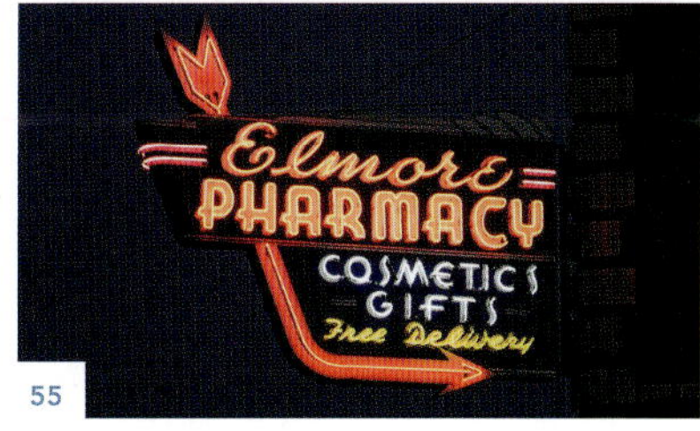

55

THE INN CROWD

California, ever so hospitable, offers us a range of nostalgic spots to spend the night—or at least snap some pics.

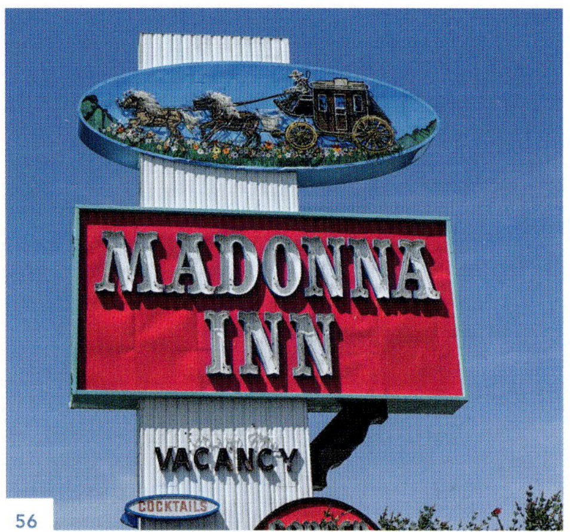

56

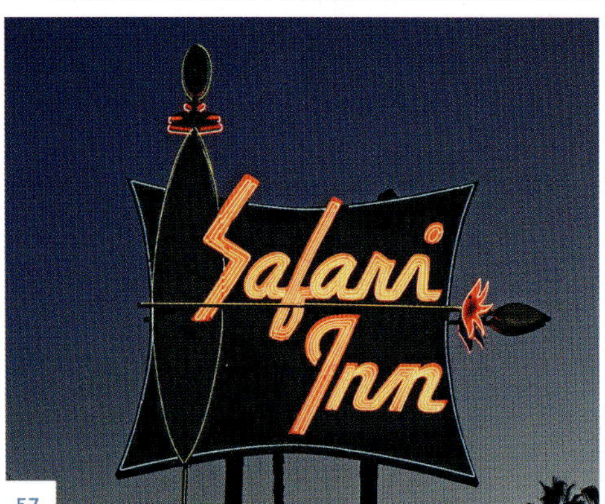

57

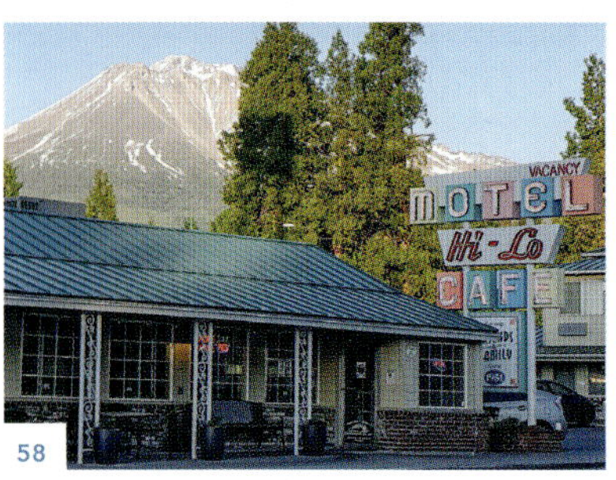

58

The **Madonna Inn** (FIG. 56) in San Luis Obispo is the most fabulous of all the motel stops in California—and perhaps the United States. Every single one of the 110 rooms has its own outlandish, fantastical design scheme, with the Caveman among the most sought after. The dining rooms are a vision in pink, and the bathrooms are over-the-top. The men's room has a waterfall urinal.

The inn was opened by Alex and Phyllis Madonna in 1958 and originally had twelve rooms. A fire wiped out the motel rooms in 1966, and they built back in the dramatic style you see today.

Johnny Carson used to joke about "Beautiful Downtown Burbank." For my money, the **Safari Inn** (FIG. 57) sign is one of the most beautiful sites in this city north of L.A. When Johnny's show moved to Burbank in 1972, the inn had already been around since 1958, and you've likely seen the Safari in many TV shows and movies.

Mount Shasta looms over the **Hi-Lo Motel & Cafe** (FIG. 58) in Weed, and they make for a striking pair. The name, you might think, could be a play on the presence of Shasta high above, and the motel and cafe down low. Or you might think it's a sly reference to the city's name, Weed. But it's neither. According to family lore, founders Frank and Gene Rizzo first spiffed up the rooms that were higher on the hilly property, and those fancier ones went for more than the ones down low. Economizing on letters in neon signage never hurt the bottom line. So the name Hi-Lo was born.

The **Wigwam Motel** in San Bernardino was part of a chain of teepee motels, welcoming Route 66 travelers since 1949.

SWEET STOPS

California has incubated a lot of famous fast-food joints, and that entrepreneurialism extends to ice cream—of the soft and hard varieties. Oh, and donuts. So many donut places. All good problems to have.

In its 1940s infancy, **Fosters Freeze** (FIG. 59) was California's answer to Dairy Queen and once numbered close to three hundred locations, but is now down to around sixty. Early signs were neon, before backlit plastic came along featuring that soft-serve mascot, Little Foster. Fosters was started by George Foster, initially as Foster's Old Fashion Freeze, in 1946 in Inglewood. He had a hunch that war-weary America was ready for the cold comforts of soft serve. His timing was impeccable, and Fosters Freeze grew up along with California during its fabled postwar boom years.

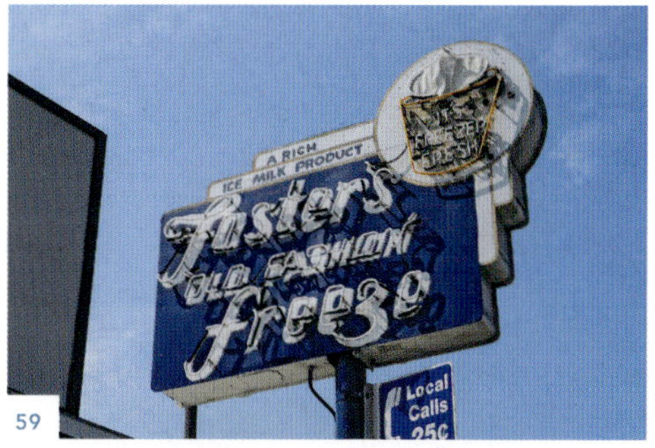

59

A mandatory stop on Route 66 is the **Donut Man** (FIG. 60) in Glendora. You haven't had a jelly donut until you've had their stuffed strawberry version. This shop opened in 1972, as part of a chain, but when owner Jim Nakano turned it into the Donut Man in 1985, a road-food legend was born.

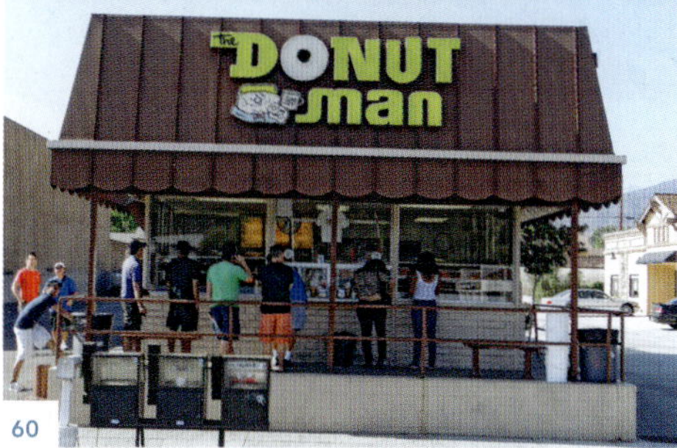

60

The gorgeous A-frame **Baskin-Robbins** (FIG. 61) in Gardena, California, retains the magic of the chain's early decades, when two brothers-in-law, who happened to be ice-cream men—Burt Baskin and Irv Robbins—combined their businesses to form Baskin-Robbins in 1948. The Gardena shop is one of a handful in Southern California that features an A-frame, and is the best-preserved of the lot.

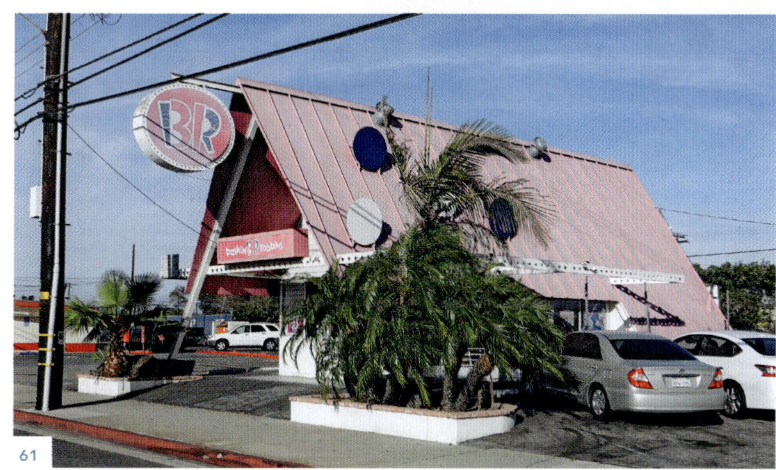

61

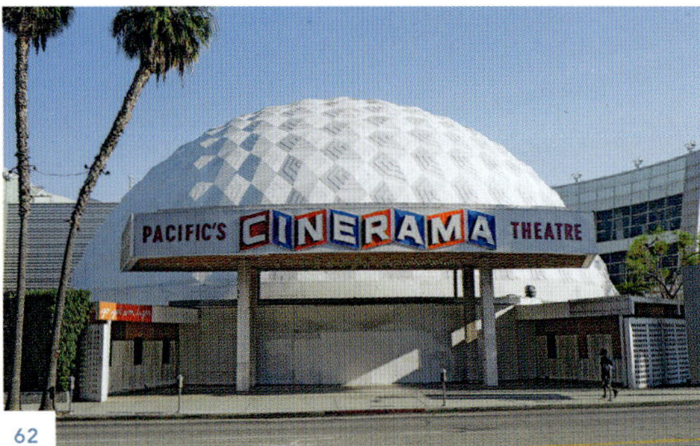

62

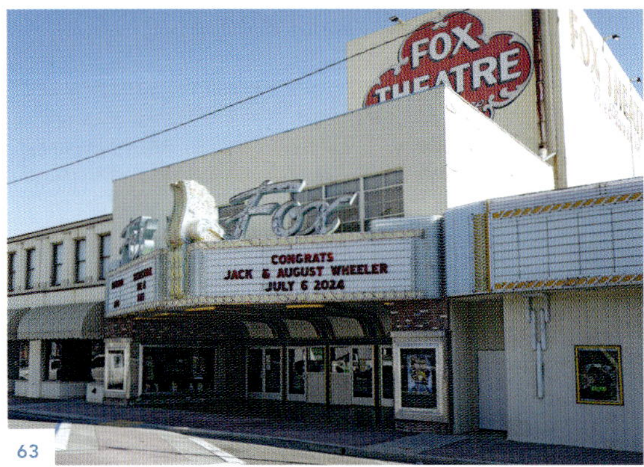

63

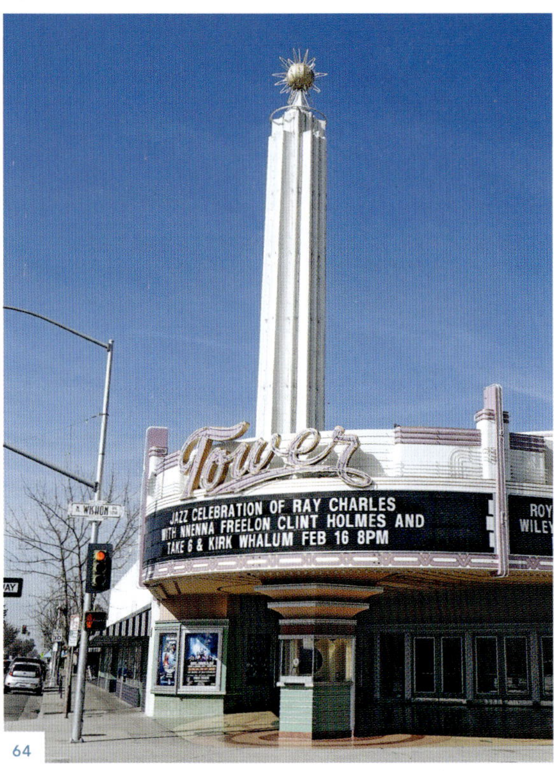

64

ON WITH THE SHOW

Theaters in California are an experience, as you would expect. Here are a handful that have their own interesting stories.

As Americans fell hard for television in the 1950s, movie studios had to think big to peel folks off their plastic-wrapped couches. The **Cinerama Dome** (FIG. 62), which opened in November 1963, the vanguard of a futuristic chain that never quite took hold, gave TV watchers a fantastical alternative. The theater was—and is—one of the most dramatic sights in the Southland. The massive geodesic dome is composed of 316 concrete panels assembled to offer structural support. An impressive engineering and aesthetic feat by the firm Welton Becket Associates, channeling the vision of Buckminster Fuller, the theater was home to the cutting-edge Cinerama movie-projection process that used a curved wide screen—and that screen is still there.

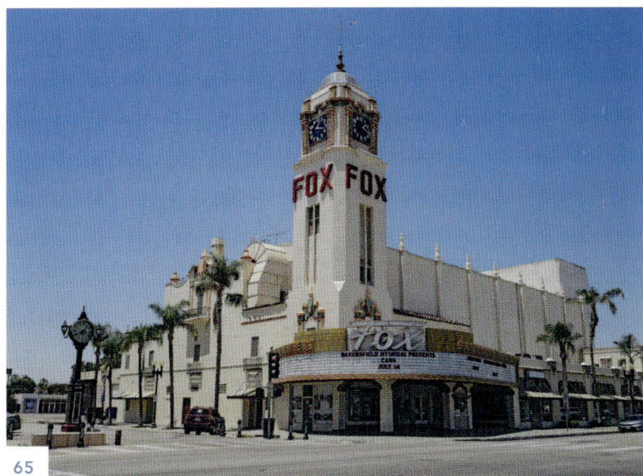

65

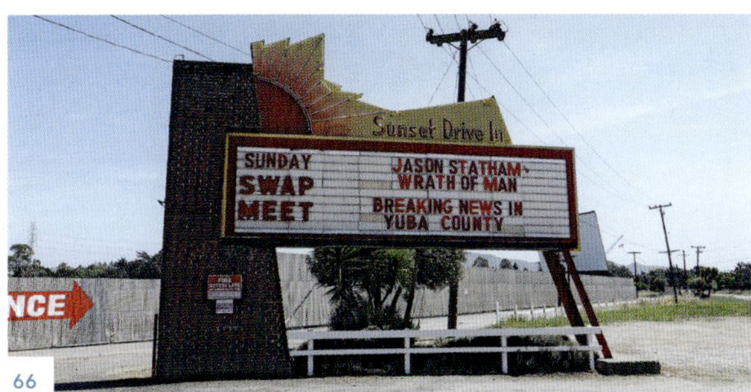

66

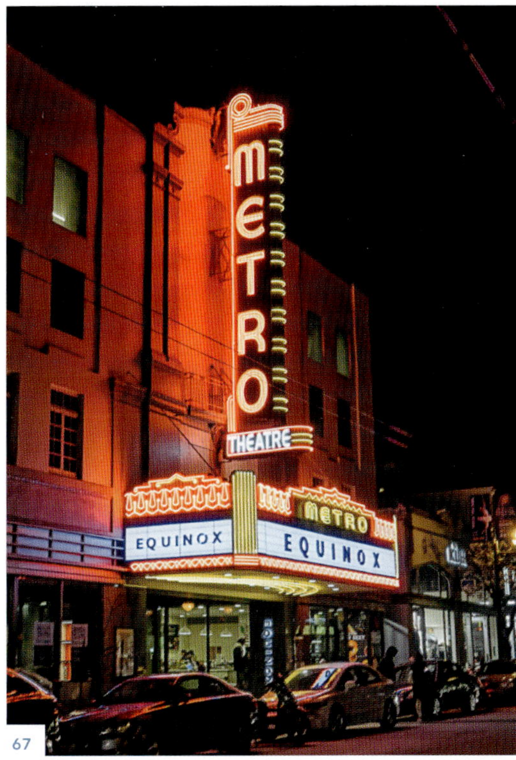

67

Fresno is a wonderful city to explore, and the Tower District, named after 1939's streamline moderne **Tower Theatre** (FIG. 64), is its heart and jewel. Admire the spire, a lovely touch in a theater with many others, and the terrazzo that compels you to make a dramatic entrance, Fred and Ginger style.

Small towns and cities had grand theaters, and the **Fox Theatre** (FIG. 63) in Taft, California, constructed in 1951, is proof of that. New management in 2023 implemented inclusive changes to reach wider audiences, from movies with captioning to films dubbed in Spanish.

The Historic Bakersfield Fox Theater (FIG. 65) dates to 1930 and scintillates with its Hollywood golden-age luster. It endured some difficult years, but with community support and fundraising, the theater was saved from destruction.

The **Metro Theatre** (FIG. 67) in San Francisco hasn't screened a film in two decades–it's now part of the Equinox chain–but the theater's original artwork and decorations have been preserved inside.

I certainly hope the sun never sets on the **Sunset Drive-In** (FIG. 66) and its beautiful sign in San Luis Obispo. It's been entertaining the people of SLO since 1950.

CHEERS!

California teems with amazing spots for a drink, with cinematic facades to draw you in. We'll begin with a trio of the classiest bar signs in America, and a visit to a terrifying 32-foot-tall clown.

▶▶▶ Pull Over!

In San Diego, we have a cluster of evocative bars: **Part Time Lover** (FIG. 68), a retro-inspired vinyl-listening bar with a cool facade; the **Turf Supper Club** (FIG. 69), with its remarkable vintage interior; and the **Aero Club Bar** (FIG. 70), with its sign ready for takeoff!

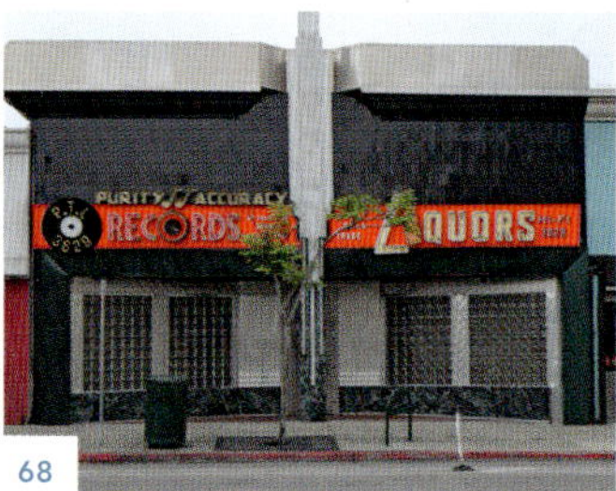

68

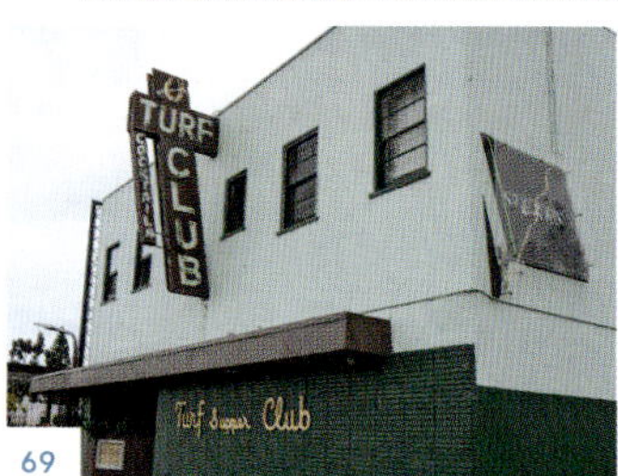

69

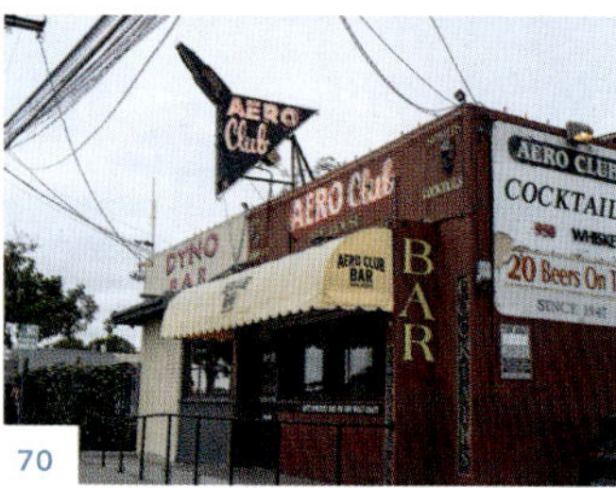

70

L.A.'s **Frolic Room** (FIG. 71) traces its roots back to Prohibition before becoming Bob's Frolic Room in 1934. The Frolic Room has been graced by many of the names immortalized on the stars outside. At one point, Howard Hughes owned the bar, along with the Pantages next door. Writer Charles Bukowski is said to have found liquid inspiration here. The list goes on!

In the century between its opening in 1905 and its renaming as the **Golden Gopher** (FIG. 72) in 2004, this Los Angeles bar has seen a lot of history. It was a derelict shell of itself when investors poured half a million into transforming it into a nightspot.

The third bar in our collection of Southland swank is **The Blue Room** (FIG. 73) in Burbank, which has on-brand turquoise leather seating and a sign that is one of the best over a watering hole since 1947.

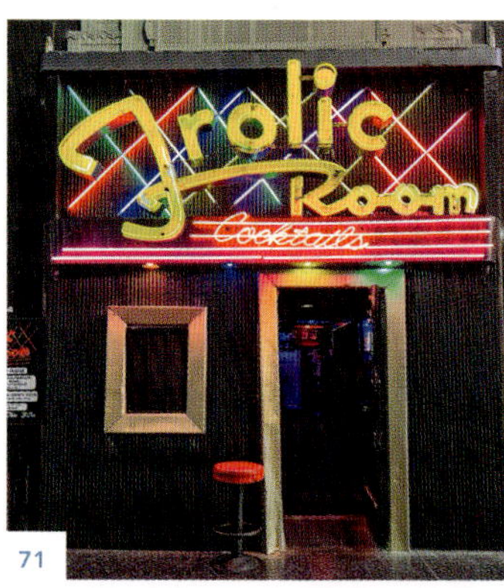

71

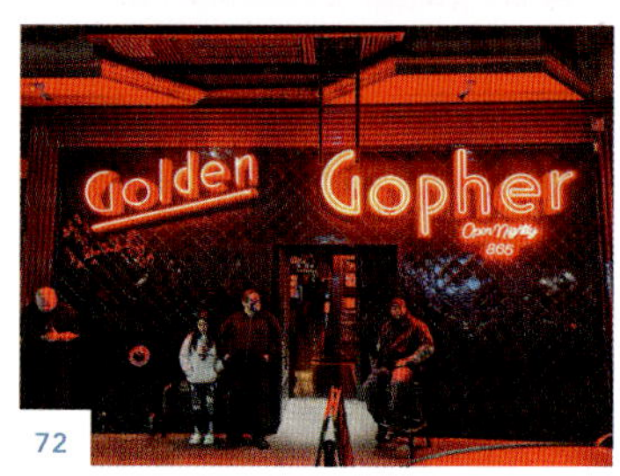

72

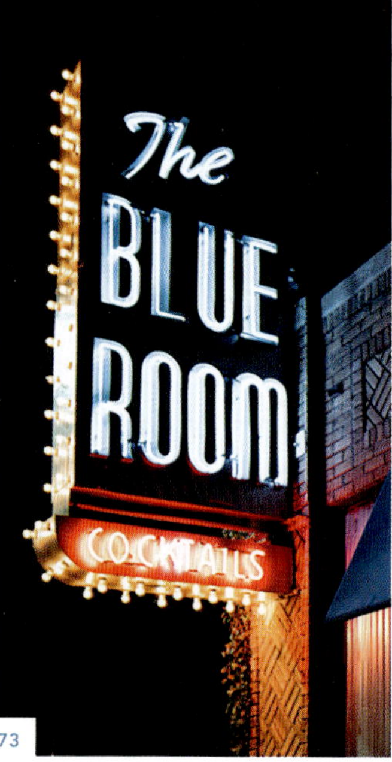

73

The quirkiest place to pick up booze in the Southland is **Circus Liquor** (FIG. 74) in North Hollywood, whose towering clown has been terrorizing since 1959. He has become a cultural touchstone—he has a cameo in the movie *Clueless*—and is an unofficial landmark of The Valley.

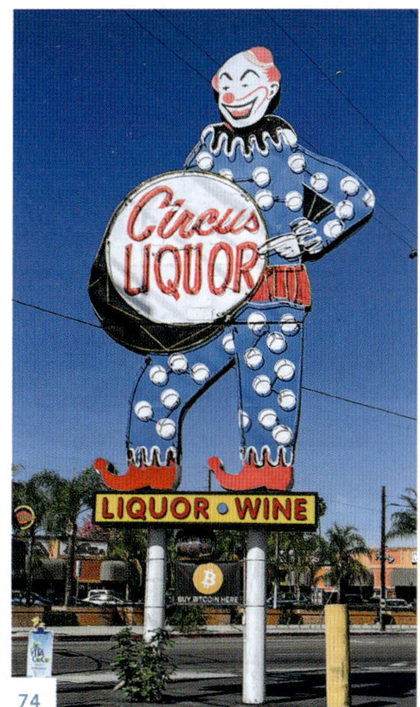

74

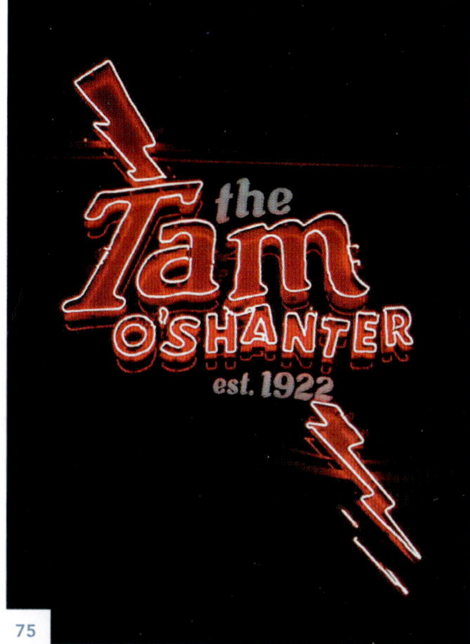

75

Billed as the closest watering hole to LAX, **Melody Bar & Grill** is a neat place for a cool shot. Landing planes dramatically pass the grungy old sign.

The Tam O'Shanter (FIG. 75) in Atwater Village is a taste of Los Angeles lore—it opened in 1922 and is still run by the same family. Disney fans will appreciate breaking bread in the same rooms that Walt Disney and his crew did countless times. See if you can check out Disney Table No. 31, with artwork etched into it by those long-ago Disney employees.

The **Hotsy Totsy Club** (FIG. 76) is the delightful dive bar of record on San Pablo Avenue in Albany, established in 1939—well, at least that's the first published mention of the place, in a crime article in the *Oakland Tribune*. The tavern owner chased a thief, who made off with some nickels from a pinball machine. The owner fired his rifle at him—and missed. Over the years it kept making headlines, mainly for delinquency of the tavern sort. In 1981, the barkeep won an ugliest bartender contest in Alameda County, all in good fun, part of a fundraiser.

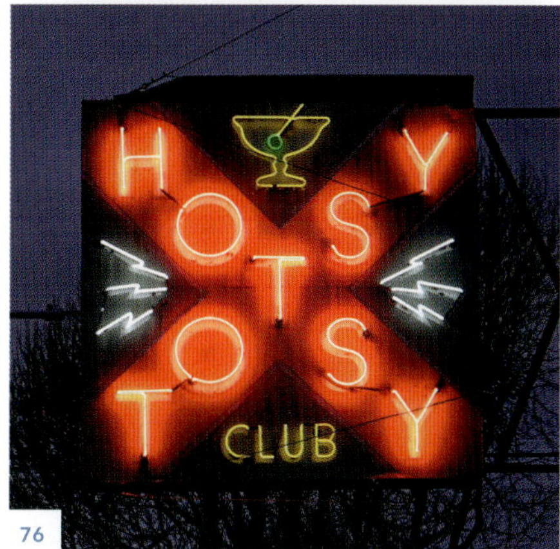

76

The **Tee-Off Restaurant and Lounge** has been a tradition on Santa Barbara's State Street since 1956. In 1992, a *Los Angeles Times* scribe observed: "If you're a child of the 1950s . . . probably the spot you'd identify with is the Tee-Off" in Santa Barbara.

In the desert, the **Bagdad Cafe** (FIG. 77) is fact following fiction. Before Hollywood, this was the Sidewinder Cafe, a desert dive in Newberry Springs. When it was turned into the Bagdad Cafe for the 1987 movie by that name, it suddenly got on the radar of tourists, and by 1995, it had taken on the movie's name.

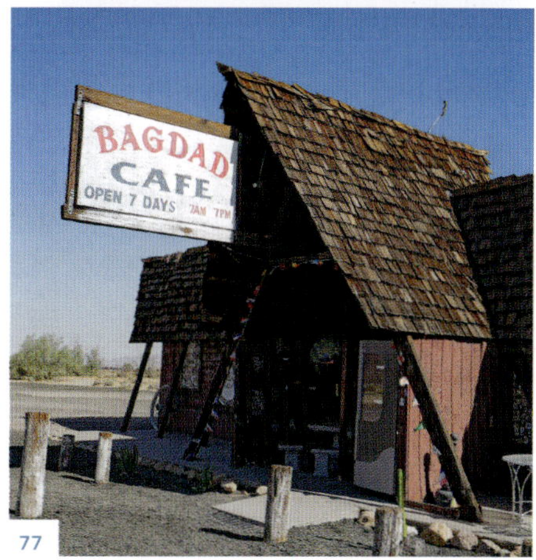

77

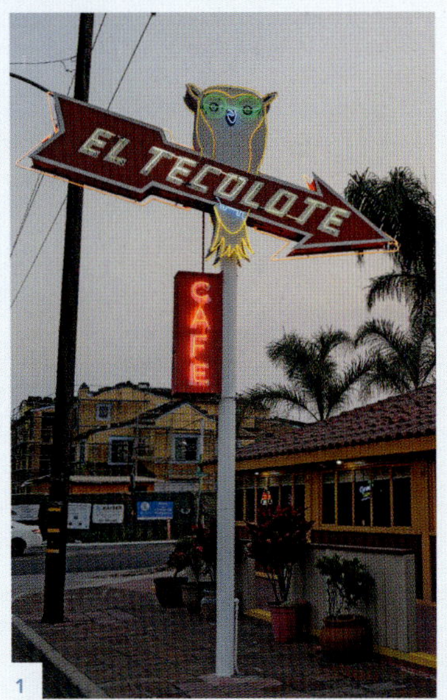

1

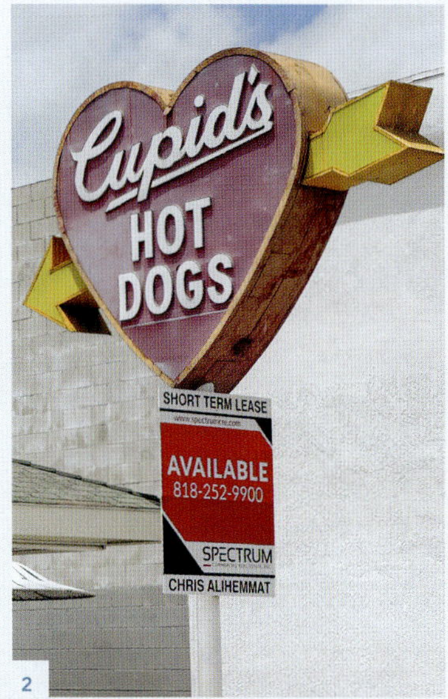

2

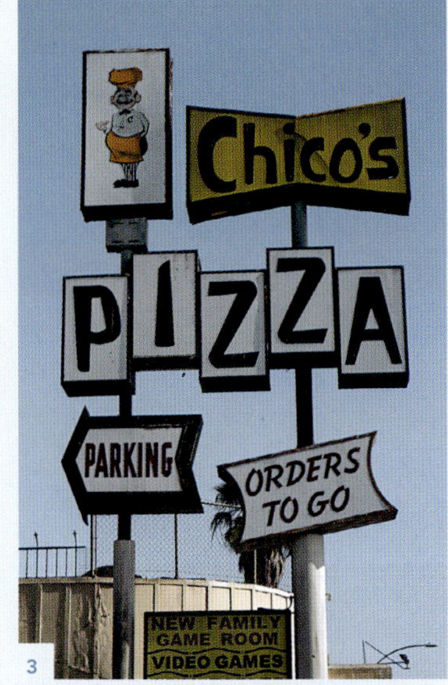

3

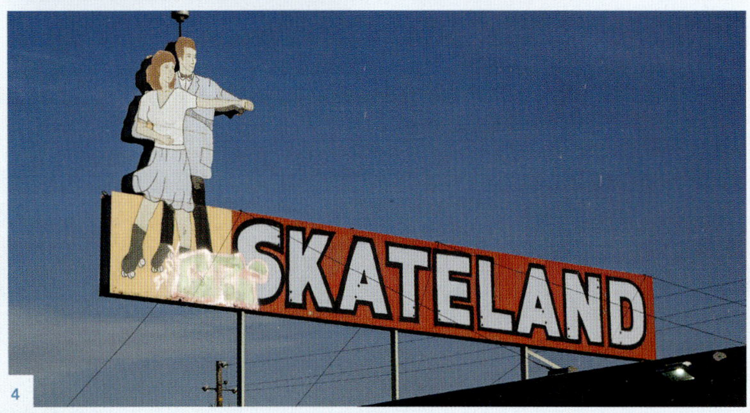

4

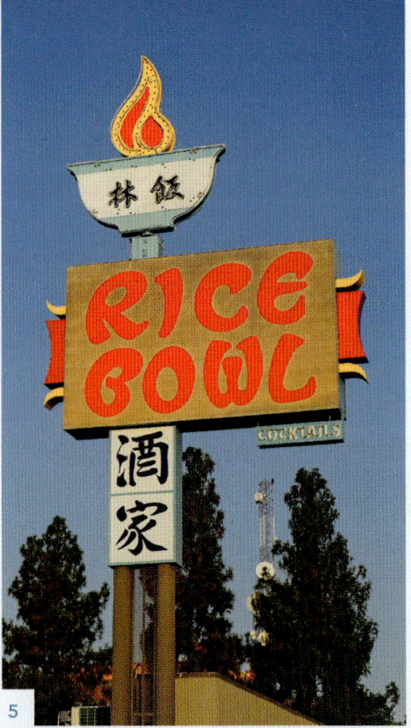

5

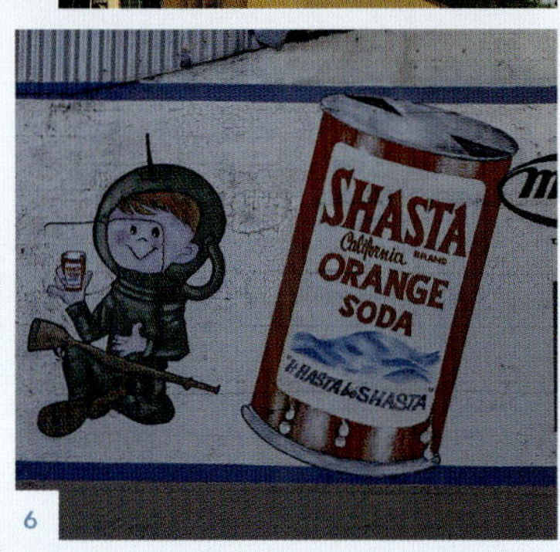

6

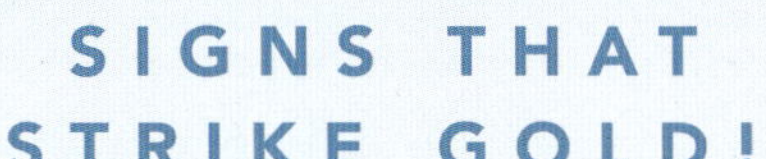

SIGNS THAT STRIKE GOLD!

1. El Tecolote, Camarillo
2. Cupid's Hot Dogs, Northridge
3. Chico's Pizza Parlor, Lynwood
4. Skateland, Bakersfield
5. Rice Bowl, Bakersfield
6. Shasta soda ghost sign, San Francisco
7. Magic Lamp Inn, Rancho Cucamonga
8. Donahoo's Golden Chicken, Pomona
9. Bill's Take Out, Santa Maria
10. Burger Spot, Tehachapi
11. Abandoned rest stop, Halloran Springs
12. Gunther's Ice Cream, Sacramento

MagicLamp
Inn
Cocktails
Dinners

7

Donahoo's
GOLDEN
CHICKEN
BOXED TO-GO

8

Bill's
takeout
HAMBURGERS
Patio IN REAR
523
SOFT SERVE

9

BURGER
SPOT

10

LO-GAS
EAT

11

GUNTHER'S
ICE CREAM

GUNTHER'S
ICE CREAM

GUNTHER'S
ICE CREAM

GUNTHER'S
ICE CREAM

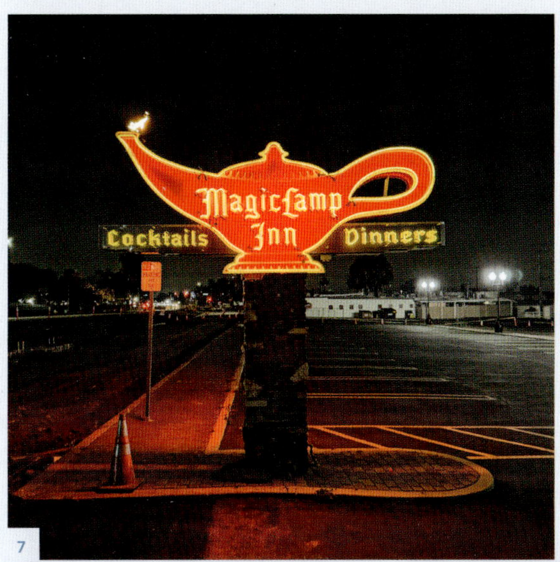

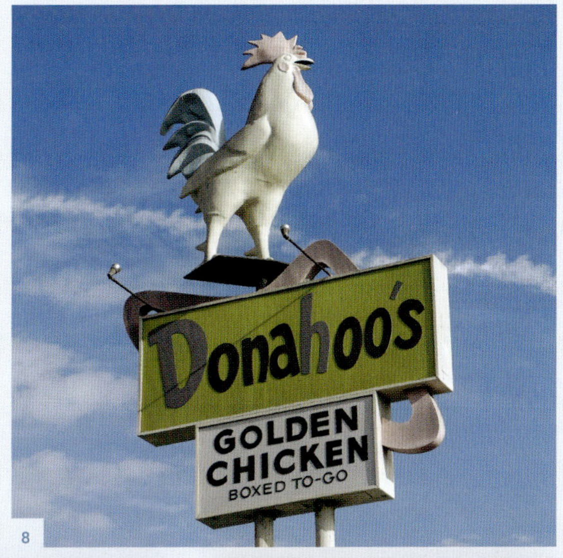

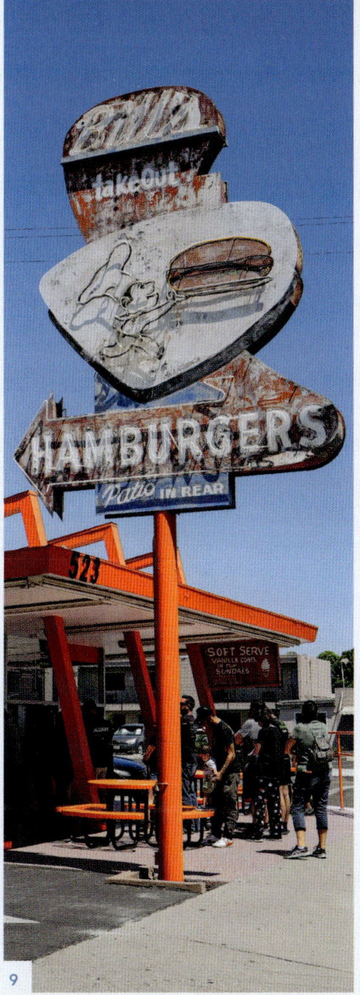

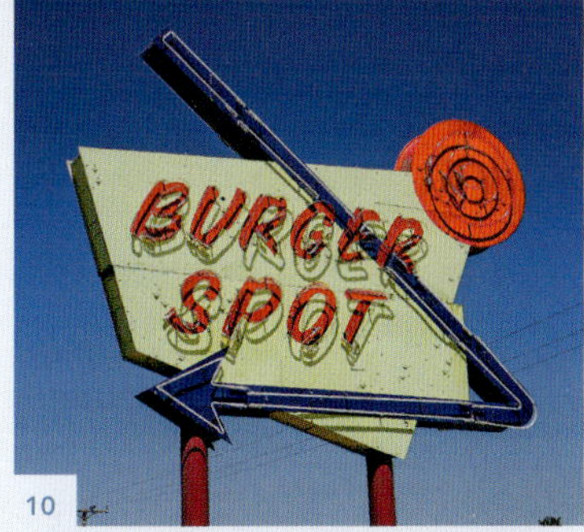

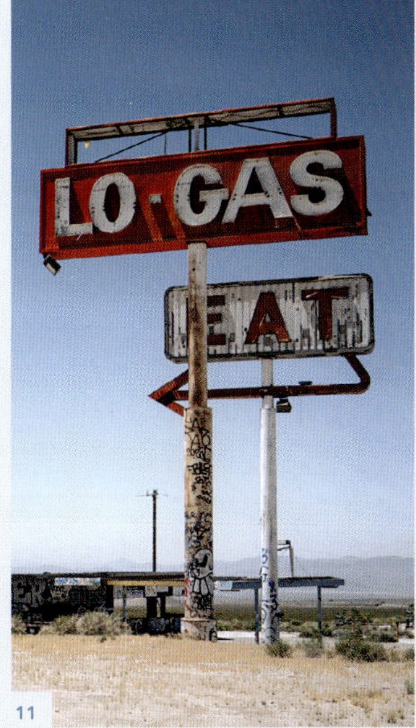

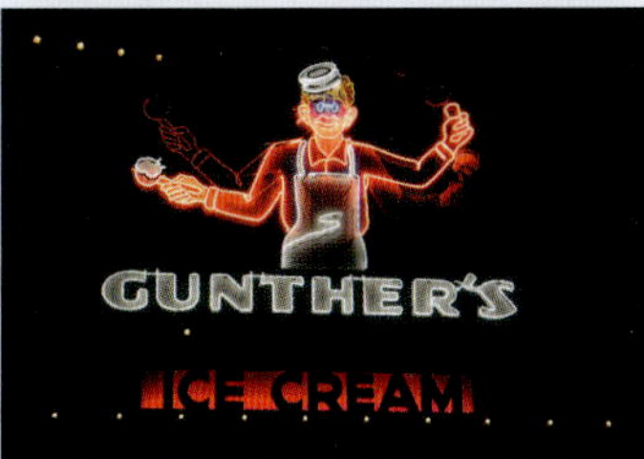

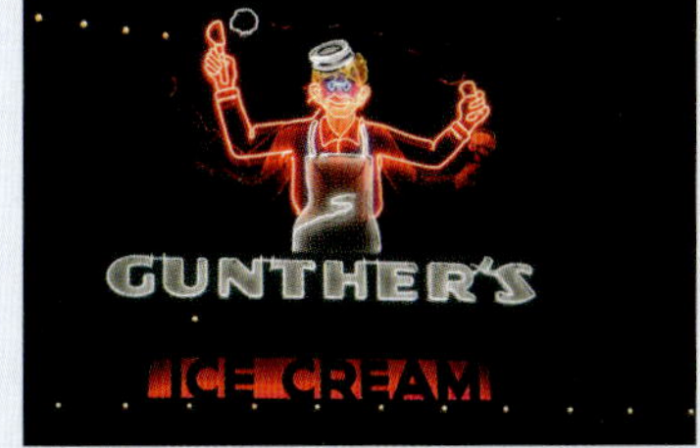

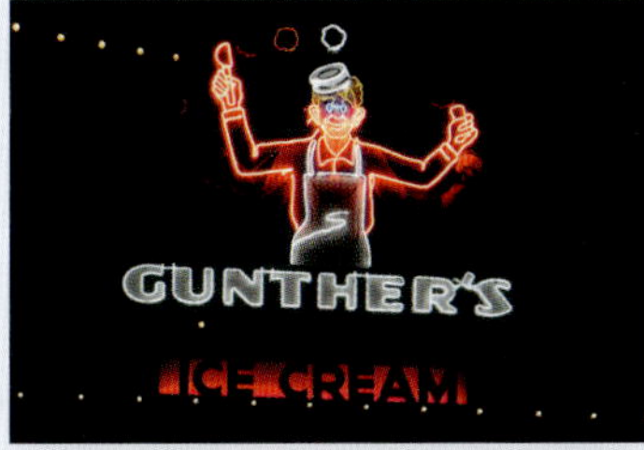

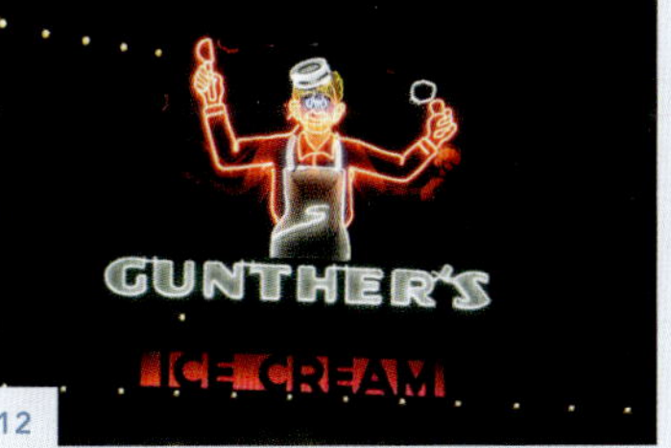

12

ACKNOWLEDGMENTS

As Cuban immigrants in the 1970s, my parents, Rolando and Pura Pujol, overcame considerable adversity to come to America and begin anew. They provided my sister, Isabel Santi, and me with a cradle of love and encouragement, even when the world around us did not make it easy.

Though I am a first-time book author in middle age, I will always consider the little books I wrote as an elementary-school student to have been my inaugural forays into publishing. I even secured a publisher: my dad. He typed my loose-leaf scribbles onto high-quality paper that he ingeniously bound inside homemade cardboard covers. I kept "editorial control" over the titles and scrawled them onto the covers in pen or marker. Our boutique publishing house put out four slim volumes, each a first and only edition, and to this day these books are among my most treasured possessions. There I was, an author at the age of eight, my first "book event" held before my second-grade parochial-school class. (Thank you, Sr. Chris, for hosting.) Encourage the children in your life—these gestures of support and love are never forgotten.

My journey in search of roadside Americana began early. Still, it wasn't until the Instagram era that I discovered so many other kindred spirits on similar quests of documentation and celebration. I've been lucky to make friends in this community whose talent and dedication inspire me.

I am indebted to so many fellow travelers, including Debra Jane Seltzer, roadside documentarian extraordinaire; the indispensable Society for Commercial Archaeology, which you should join if you enjoyed this book; the wondrous *Atlas Obscura*, whose podcasts are my companions on many long road trips; and the late CBS newsman Charles Kuralt, whose uplifting *On the Road* homilies about the American spirit still inspire me.

I always wanted to write a book, but I just never thought I would. I can't express enough my appreciation to those who knew this book could—and should—happen. People like my old *Daily News* boss, Scott Cohen, and my old *Morning Call* colleague, the late Mike Hirsch. And, of course, I wouldn't be here without the good people at Artisan, beginning with my editor, Shoshana Gutmajer, who knew this book was in me before I did and coaxed it out of me with an expert, caring hand, alongside Abby Knudsen, who led me to some Mountain West gems I would have otherwise missed. My deep appreciation also goes to Nancy Murray, the dedicated production director who ensured my photos looked their best; Laura Cherkas, the senior production editor who is a masterful wrangler of words and helped this all come together; and Jack Dunnington, the designer whose creative eye makes every page of this book shine like the brightest neon sign. (He even created one for the cover!)

Finally, I want to thank everyone who has followed me on social media or Substack. Without each and every one of you, this book would still be a dream, something for someday or maybe for never. But the day is here, and for that, I am forever grateful.

See you on the road!

INDEX